Teacher's Edition

by

Bonnie L. Walker

AGS Publishing
Circle Pines, Minnesota 55014-1796
1-800-328-2560
www.agsnet.com

About the Author

Bonnie L. Walker taught for 16 years in secondary schools and college. She holds a Ph.D. in curriculum theory and instructional design from the University of Maryland, an M.Ed. in secondary education, and a B.A. in English. She studied psycholinguistics at the University of Illinois Graduate School, and was a curriculum developer at the Model Secondary School for the Deaf at Gallaudet University. She is the author of *Basic English, Life Skills English, Basic English Composition,* and numerous curriculum materials in written expression, grammar, and usage. Since 1986, Dr. Walker has been president of a research and development company specializing in development of training and educational materials for special populations.

Photo credits for this textbook can be found on page 336.

The publisher wishes to thank the following educators for their helpful comments during the review process for *Basic English Grammar*. Their assistance has been invaluable.

Beverly C. Allen, Learning Disabilities Coordinator, L.D. Office, Norman Center, Kansas City, MO; **John DeTullio,** English Teacher, Tweedsmuir Middle School, Hamilton, ON, Canada; **Jacqueline DeWitt,** Teacher/Cooperative Consultation Consultant, Umatilla High School, Umatilla, FL; **Cathy Guzzo,** Transition/Special Education Coordinator, Penn Hills Senior High School, Pittsburgh, PA; **Susan Harrington,** Special Education Teacher–Option III, Salamanca Middle School, Salamanca, NY; **Alva Jones,** Special Education Consultant, Evans, GA; **Cecilia Lozano,** ESL Teacher, Douglas High School, Oklahoma City, OK; **Virginia Malling,** Special Education Teacher, Oak Ridge High School, Oak Ridge, TN; **Marie Ramey,** Department Chairperson, West Side High School, Newark, NJ; **Christine D. Russell,** Special Education Teacher, Stinson Middle School, San Antonio, TX; **Dr. William B. Whitaker,** Director of Adult High School and GED Programs, Rowan Cabarrus Community College, Salisbury, NC

Publisher's Project Staff

Director, Product Development: Karen Dahlen; Associate Director, Product Development: Teri Mathews; Senior Editor: Julie Maas; Development Assistant: Bev Johnson; Graphic Designer: Diane McCarty; Design Manager: Nancy Condon; Desktop Publishing Manager: Lisa Beller; Purchasing Agent: Mary Kaye Kuzma; Marketing Manager/Curriculum: Brian Holl

Editorial and production services provided by The Mazer Corporation.

Printed in the United States of America

ISBN 0-7854-2917-4

Product Number 93502

A 0 9 8 7 6 5 4 3 2

044005

Contents

Overview

Lesson Plans

Teacher's Resources

Basic English Grammar

Basic English Grammar is designed to meet the needs of secondary school students and adults who read well below grade level. Prior to the book being written, interviews were conducted with teachers, supervisors, and students across the United States. A need was identified for a textbook that would present grammatical rules and concepts one at a time and provide sufficient opportunities for appropriate practice.

All aspects of the text are carefully controlled, including instruction, examples, directions, and exercises. The sentence structure and vocabulary are clear and straightforward, which helps reluctant readers access the material more easily than they could with traditional grammar textbooks. In addition, the high-interest content of the activities appeals to older students.

Particular attention is given to subdividing the instruction so that only a single rule or a single concept is presented at one time, each accompanied by at least one practice exercise. The numerous practice exercises allow frequent review of students' understanding so that teachers can provide appropriate instructional intervention. Lessons are constructed so that succeeding activities incorporate previous instruction. Concepts introduced earlier are reinforced and assimilated in combination with new material.

Grammar and usage are integrated in each lesson to facilitate understanding of rules and their practical application to the patterns of written and spoken English. Students practice and apply each language skill in a variety of ways, taking the student from identification and classification through application and evaluation. These skills are essential if students are to apply grammar and usage to everyday writing.

The ability to communicate in clear, correct language is important in virtually every job and situation. *Basic English Grammar* provides the English grammar and usage skills students need to help them succeed when they make the transition from school to the workplace.

AGS Worktexts

Check Out AGS Worktexts! AGS offers additional language arts materials to help you tailor instruction to meet the diverse needs of your students. Each worktext contains 96 pages of information and motivating skill lessons with numerous opportunities for practice and reinforcement. These texts can be used with a basal program or as the core instructional tool.

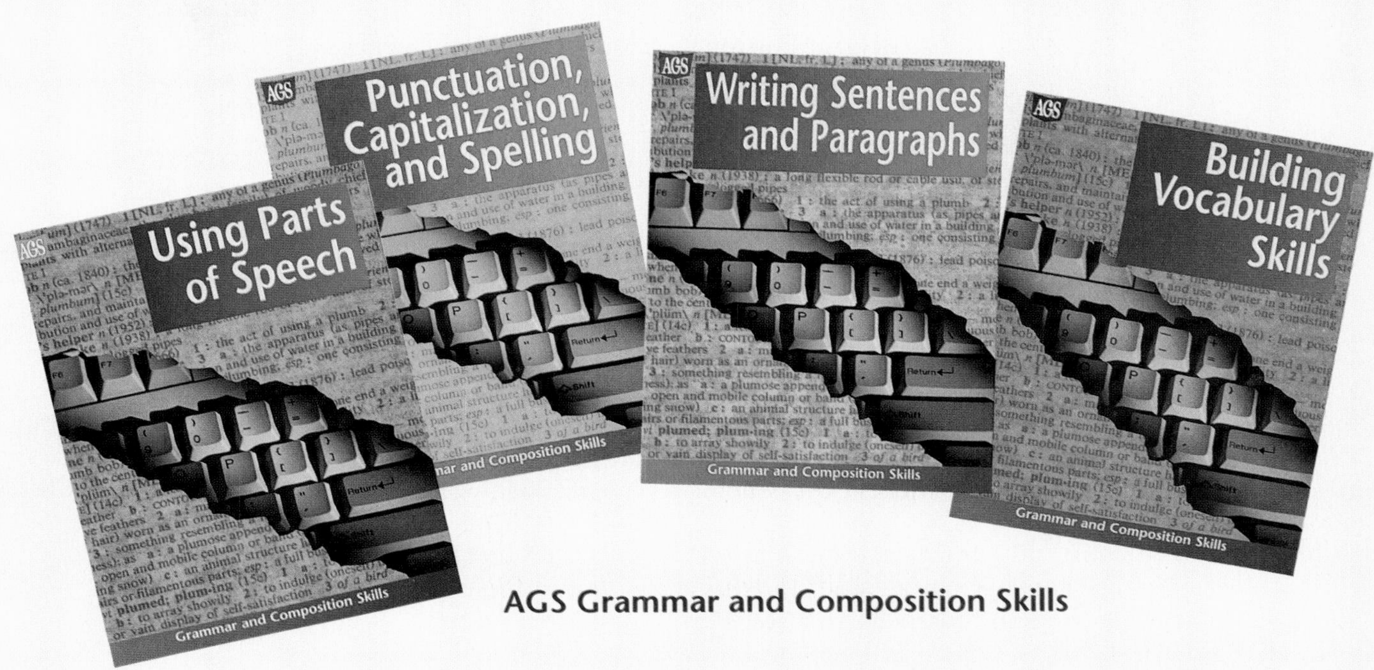

AGS Grammar and Composition Skills

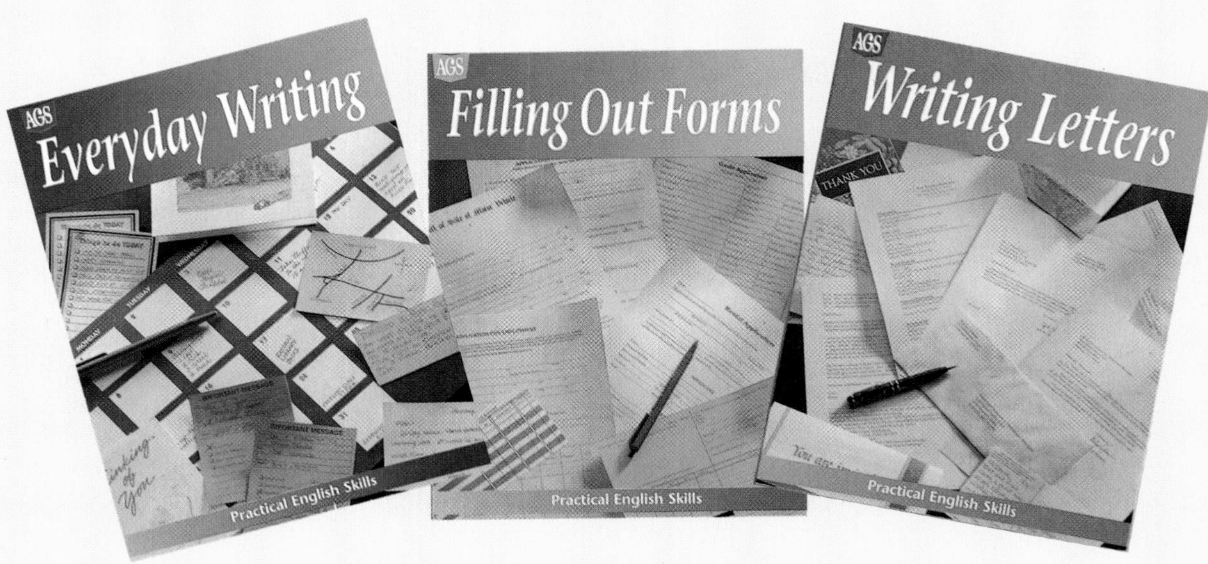

AGS Practical English Skills

AGS English Textbooks

Basic English is designed to build and reinforce basic language skills. Written at a lower reading level, the program is ideal for students and adults who need extra help with language concepts, or those who are learning English as a second language.

The program provides clear instruction of the basics of English usage. Lessons are constructed so that succeeding activities incorporate previous instruction. Concepts introduced earlier are reinforced and assimilated in combination with new material. Plenty of skills practice reinforces lessons on parts of speech, writing skills, and advanced skills such as developing themes and ideas. High-interest content and life-relevant examples and activities appeal to older students.

Reading Level: 3.9 Spache
Interest Level: Grades 6–12, ABE, ESL

Basic English Composition is designed to help secondary students and adults develop practical writing skills. Throughout the text, comprehension is enhanced through the use of simple sentence structure and low-level vocabulary. To add motivational interest, the instruction and activities revolve around a group of high school students experiencing a typical school year.

Prior to development of this text, the author conducted a series of interviews with teachers, curriculum supervisors, and students across the country. As a result, *Basic English Composition* reflects the needs by emphasizing writing sentences, then paragraphs, followed by reports and other projects. All were identified as important skills for students to have.

Reading Level: 3.8 Spache
Interest Level: Grades 6–12, ABE, ESL

The major goal of ***Life Skills English*** is to develop language skills that young people and adults need in their everyday life. The content in this textbook is based on feedback from interviews with teachers, supervisors, and students across the country.

Life Skills English teaches students how to seek and evaluate information. Students learn how to find information, how information is organized, and how to use reference tools to locate information. Students learn how to develop and use skills that they can apply to other subjects and everyday life.

Sentence structure and vocabulary are controlled throughout the text. This allows students to concentrate on content mastery. Chapter openers, examples, and exercises focus on relevant and practical applications. For example, students are taught how to read a food label, read the yellow pages, follow recipe directions, and read the want ads.

Reading Level: 3.7 Spache
Interest Level: Grades 6–12, ABE, ESL

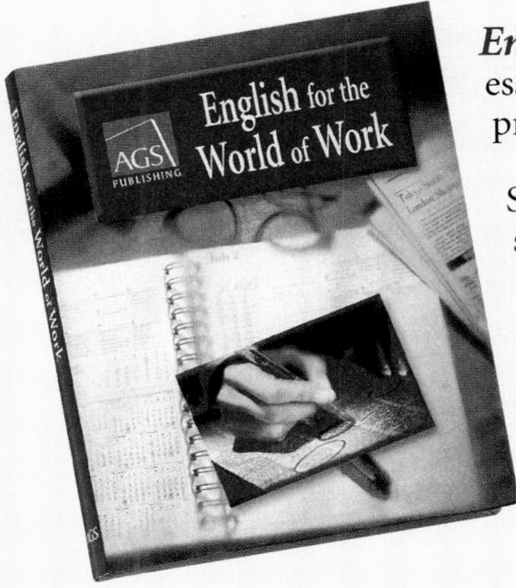

English for the World of Work develops communication skills that are essential for deciding on a career, obtaining a job, keeping a job, and being prepared for promotions.

Students prepare a career portfolio, which they can use later during their job searches. This textbook is intended for secondary students and adults who are planning to enter the working world soon after the course.

Content is practical and relevant. Activities and exercises are patterned after situations in the working world and are designed to develop better reading, writing, speaking, and listening skills. Effort has been made to keep the reading level below the fourth grade. Some concepts are dealt with at a slightly higher level than others. The Teacher's Edition provides suggestions for directing students' reading to help them achieve full comprehension.

Reading Level: 3.6 Spache
Interest Level: Grades 6–12, ABE, ESL

English to Use is designed to meet the communication needs of secondary students and adults who are reading below grade level or learning English as a second language. Each lesson integrates grammar and usage to facilitate an understanding of rules and their practical application to the patterns of written and spoken English. Students practice and apply each language skill in a variety of settings, from identification and classification to evaluative thinking and application.

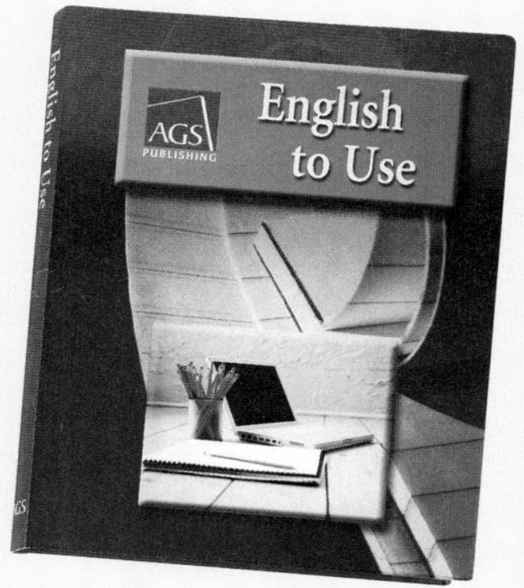

The instructions, examples, directions, and exercises are presented in a systematic, discrete manner. Particular attention is given to organizing the instruction so that only a single rule or a single concept is presented at a time. Lessons build upon each other throughout the book.

Sign language is featured throughout the text. By including illustrations, we hope to connect the spoken word with signing. It is not the intention of this text to provide a total program in signing—only an awareness.

Reading Level: 3.3 Spache
Interest Level: Grades 6–12, ABE, ESL

Student Text Highlights

- Each lesson is clearly labeled to help students focus on the skill or concept to be learned.
- Vocabulary terms are boldfaced and then defined in the margin at the top of the page and in the Glossary.
- Content is introduced and then followed by example boxes and activities.
- Focused activities give students opportunities to practice information they have just learned. Activities parallel the instruction and examples in each lesson.
- Reminder notes and tips help students recall and apply what they already know.
- Goals for Learning at the beginning of each chapter identify learner outcomes.

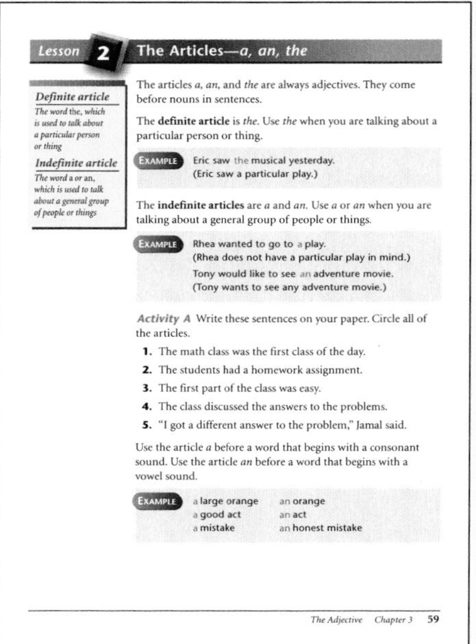

Lesson 2 The Articles—*a, an, the*

Definite article
The word the, *which is used to talk about a particular person or thing*

Indefinite article
The word a *or* an, *which is used to talk about a general group of people or things*

The articles *a, an,* and *the* are always adjectives. They come before nouns in sentences.

The **definite article** is *the*. Use *the* when you are talking about a particular person or thing.

EXAMPLE Eric saw the musical yesterday.
(Eric saw a particular play.)

The **indefinite articles** are *a* and *an*. Use *a* or *an* when you are talking about a general group of people or things.

EXAMPLE Rhea wanted to go to a play.
(Rhea does not have a particular play in mind.)
Tony would like to see an adventure movie.
(Tony wants to see any adventure movie.)

Activity A Write these sentences on your paper. Circle all of the articles.

1. The math class was the first class of the day.
2. The students had a homework assignment.
3. The first part of the class was easy.
4. The class discussed the answers to the problems.
5. "I got a different answer to the problem," Jamal said.

Use the article *a* before a word that begins with a consonant sound. Use the article *an* before a word that begins with a vowel sound.

EXAMPLE	a large orange	an orange
	a good act	an act
	a mistake	an honest mistake

The Adjective Chapter 3 59

Definite article
The word the, *which is used to talk about a particular person or thing*

Indefinite article
The word a *or* an, *which is used to talk about a general group of people or things*

Writing Tip

The possessive adjectives *its, their,* and *whose* are sometimes confused with the contractions *it's, they're,* and *who's*. When you write, be sure to choose the correct word.

Some languages have more than one word for the personal pronoun *you*. For example, the Spanish word *tu* means "you" in informal conversations.

Goals for Learning

- To recognize adjectives in sentences and identify the nouns or pronouns they describe
- To recognize articles
- To recognize and capitalize proper adjectives
- To recognize numbers as adjectives
- To recognize possessive pronouns and demonstrative pronouns as adjectives
- To use adjectives to make comparisons

- Chapter Reviews allow students and teachers to check for skill mastery. Multiple-choice items are provided for practice in taking standardized tests.
- Test-Taking Tips at the end of each Chapter Review help reduce text anxiety and improve test scores.

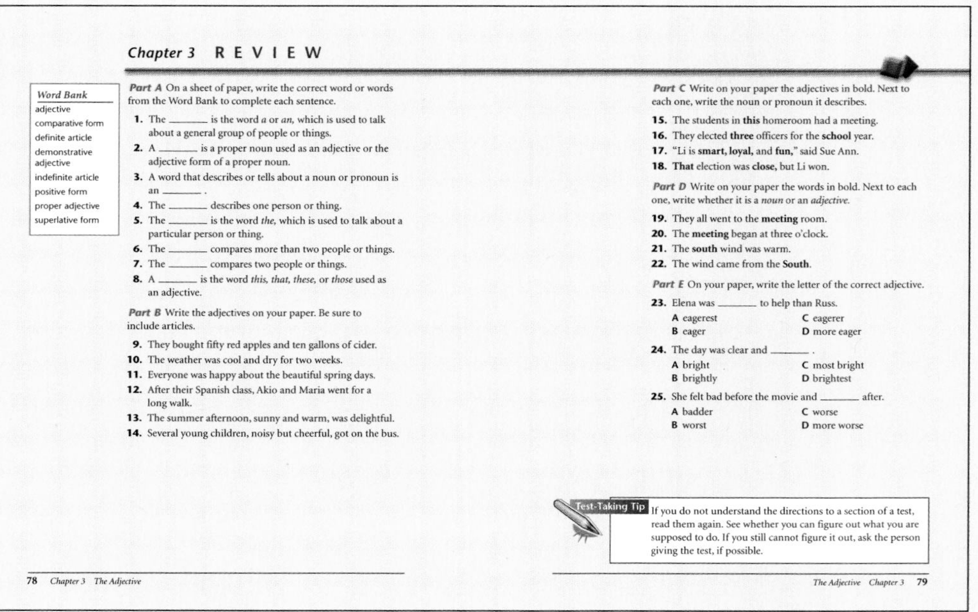

Chapter 3 REVIEW

Word Bank
adjective
comparative form
definite article
demonstrative adjective
indefinite article
positive form
proper adjective
superlative form

Part A On a sheet of paper, write the correct word or words from the Word Bank to complete each sentence.

1. The ______ is the word *a* or *an*, which is used to talk about a general group of people or things.
2. A ______ is a proper noun used as an adjective or the adjective form of a proper noun.
3. A word that describes or tells about a noun or pronoun is an ______.
4. The ______ describes one person or thing.
5. The ______ is the word *the*, which is used to talk about a particular person or thing.
6. The ______ compares more than two people or things.
7. The ______ compares two people or things.
8. A ______ is the word *this, that, these,* or *those* used as an adjective.

Part B Write the adjectives on your paper. Be sure to include articles.

9. They bought fifty red apples and ten gallons of cider.
10. The weather was cool and dry for two weeks.
11. Everyone was happy about the beautiful spring days.
12. After their Spanish class, Akio and Maria went for a long walk.
13. The summer afternoon, sunny and warm, was delightful.
14. Several young children, noisy but cheerful, got on the bus.

Part C Write on your paper the adjectives in bold. Next to each one, write the noun or pronoun it describes.

15. The students in **this** homeroom had a meeting.
16. They elected **three** officers for the **school** year.
17. "Li is **smart, loyal,** and **fun,**" said Sue Ann.
18. **That** election was **close,** but Li won.

Part D Write on your paper the words in bold. Next to each one, write whether it is a *noun* or an *adjective*.

19. They all went to the **meeting** room.
20. The **meeting** began at three o'clock.
21. The **south** wind was warm.
22. The wind came from the **South**.

Part E On your paper, write the letter of the correct adjective.

23. Elena was ______ to help than Russ.
A eagerest C eagerer
B eager D more eager
24. The day was clear and ______.
A bright C most bright
B brightly D brightest
25. She felt bad before the movie and ______ after.
A badder C worse
B worst D more worse

Test-Taking Tip If you do not understand the directions to a section of a test, read them again. See whether you can figure out what you are supposed to do. If you still cannot figure it out, ask the person giving the test, if possible.

78 *Chapter 3 The Adjective*

The Adjective Chapter 3 79

Spelling Builder

Plural Nouns

Some basic rules will help you spell plural nouns correctly.

- Add *-s* or *-es* to most nouns.
- For nouns that end with *-s, -z, -x, -sh,* and *-ch,* add *-es.*
- For nouns that end with a consonant before a *y,* change the *y* to *i* and add *-es.*
- For some nouns that end with *-f* or *-fe,* change the *f* or *fe* to *v* and add *-es.*

Write the plural form of each of these nouns on your paper.

1. half **2.** berry **3.** box **4.** spoon **5.** brush

Then, w
senten
Take t
pronu

◆ Information and hints can help students with frequently misspelled words, spelling demons, and more.

Vocabulary Builder

Less* or *Fewer

Use *less* when comparing things that have volume (like water). Also use *less* when comparing abstract nouns (like love). Use *fewer* when comparing things you can count (like pencils).

Jackie drank **less** milk than Jorge.
Tomas finished **fewer** of the math problems than Tara.

On your paper, complete each sentence with either *less* or *fewer.*

1. This pan holds _________ water than that one.
2. This book has _________ pages than that one.
3. Chin spent _________ hours studying than Pam.
4. Tino's face has _________ freckles than mine.
5. Kevin's party was _________ fun than Madri's.

◆ Information and activities on select words in the English language; designed to broaden students' vocabulary skills.

Technology Note

You can use your computer's grammar checker to see whether you've used *a* or *an* incorrectly. Some grammar programs also explain exceptions when using *a* and *an.* Remember, words beginning with a *y* sound use *a:* a unit. A word beginning with an unpronounced *h* uses *an:* an hour.

◆ Many features reinforce and extend student learning beyond the lesson content.

Writing Project

Using Pronouns When You Write

We often use pronouns to replace nouns. When you use pronouns, make sure the antecedent of each pronoun is clear.

On your paper, write 10 sentences that tell about someone you know well.

Include facts from this list:

- The person's age
- Where he or she lives
- A physical description
- His or her likes and dislikes
- His or her past achiever

Underline all the prono
the antecedent of each
unclear, revise your sen

◆ Writing activity gives students additional writing practice.

Where To Find It

Thesaurus

A thesaurus lists words with their synonyms. Synonyms are words that have the same or similar meanings. The words in a thesaurus are called entry words. They appear in alphabetical order. For example, if you look up the word *happy* in a thesaurus, you would find that some of its synonyms are *cheerful, cheery, glad, joyful, joyous,* and *merry.*

To locate an entry word quickly in a thesaurus, use the guide words at the top of each page. The guide words are the first and last entry words on the page.

Find the following words in a thesaurus. Write one synonym for each word. Then write a sentence for each synonym.

1. little **2.** big **3.** shy **4.** look **5.** wash

◆ Information and practice using well-known reference materials or resources.

Teacher's Edition Highlights

The comprehensive, wraparound Teacher's Edition provides instructional strategies at point of use. Everything from preparation guidelines to teaching tips and strategies is included in an easy-to-use format. Activities are featured at point of use for teacher convenience.

- Quick overviews of chapters and lessons save planning time.
- Lesson objectives are listed for easy reference.
- Page references are provided for convenience.
- Easy-to-follow lesson plans in three steps save time: Warm-Up Activity, Teaching the Lesson, and Reinforce and Extend.
- Relevant Web sites are listed in Online Connections.
- Career, Community, Home, and Global applications relate lessons to the world outside of the classroom.

Lesson at a Glance

Chapter 1 Lesson 2

Overview This lesson defines common and proper nouns and explains how they differ.

Objectives

- To distinguish between common and proper nouns.
- To capitalize proper nouns.
- To understand the use of abbreviations.

Student Pages 6–11

Teacher's Resource Library 

Workbook Activity 2

Activity 2

Alternative Activity 2

Vocabulary

abbreviation
common noun
proper noun

1 Warm-Up Activity

Write the following words in a column on the board: *country, team, title, name, street.* In a second column write the following words: *New York Yankees, Lord of the Rings, Canada, Main Street, Juanita.* Have students form pairs and ask them to match up a word from column 1 with a word from column 2. Invite volunteers to write their solutions on the board. Ask students to explain why they matched up the words as they did. (*Canada is the name of a country.*) Encourage them to point out how the paired words differ. (*Words from column 2 are capitalized and name something particular.*) Point out that this is the important distinction between common nouns and proper nouns as described in Lesson 2.

2 Teaching the Lesson

Have a volunteer read aloud the definitions of *common nouns* and *proper nouns* given on this page. Write the words *general* and *particular* on the board. Explain that the term *general* refers to the big picture; *particular* focuses on a particular person, place, thing, or idea. Point out that nouns naming particular items should be capitalized. Students should understand that they have compiled lists of common and proper nouns.

Write *Mister Smith* on the board. Ask students for another way to write *Mister Smith* (*Mr. Smith*). Point out that *Mr.* is a shortened form of a word, or an *abbreviation.* Lead students to understand that many abbreviations are parts of proper nouns and must be capitalized.

Invite a volunteer to write *Raiders of the Lost Ark* on the board. Explain that titles are considered proper nouns. Point out that short words, such as *of, to,* and *the,* remain lowercase.

Activity A

Before students complete Activity A on their own, have partners work together to write their own list of proper nouns to go with each common noun listed in the example box on this page.

Activity A Answers

Answers will vary. Possible answers follow. **1.** Mrs. Lee **2.** Fourth of July **3.** Cincinnati Bengals **4.** *The New York Times* **5.** Barry Manilow **6.** cartoon character **7.** football game **8.** country **9.** sea **10.** state

Lesson 2 Common and Proper Nouns

Common noun *The name of a general type of person, place, thing, or idea*

Proper noun *The name of a particular person, place, thing, or idea*

A **common noun** is the name of a general type of person, place, thing, or idea.

A **proper noun** is the name of a particular person, place, thing, or idea.

Capitalize a common noun only if it is the first word of a sentence or part of a title. Always capitalize a proper noun.

Writing Tip

President can be a common or a proper noun. Tino is *president* of the class. Today *President Juarez* will speak. Think about whether you are naming the job or a specific person. If you are naming a specific president, it is a proper noun.

EXAMPLE

Common Nouns	Proper Nouns
school	Springvale High School
museum	Museum of Modern Art
astronaut	John Glenn
president	Thomas Jefferson
state	Idaho
month	December
country	Canada
city	Atlanta
river	Mississippi River
writer	Edgar Allan Poe

Activity A Write these nouns on your paper. Write a proper noun next to each common noun. Write a common noun next to each proper noun.

Example university—Harvard University
Alaska—state

1. teacher
2. holiday
3. team
4. newspaper
5. singer
6. Bugs Bunny
7. Super Bowl
8. France
9. Atlantic Ocean
10. Ohio

Lesson 2 REVIEW

Write these nouns on your paper. Capitalize the proper nouns.

1. george washington
2. spain
3. recipe
4. labor day
5. river
6. *a separate peace*
7. french
8. city
9. albert einstein
10. president

Number your paper from 11 to 15. Read each of the following sentences. If the sentence is correct, write *correct* after the number. If the sentence has a capitalization mistake, write the sentence correctly.

11. Latisha took math 101, not math 201, this year.
12. Armando's favorite holiday is thanksgiving.
13. I'm going to take world history next year.
14. Kaitlin's grandmother lives in philadelphia.
15. Lisa and greg visited wicker park.

Writing Project

Using Nouns in Your Writing

A noun names a person, a place, a thing, or an idea. Using a variety of nouns in your writing makes it more interesting to readers.

On your paper, write 10 sentences that tell about your neighborhood. Include the names of as many buildings and items as possible. Here are some nouns you could use:

apartment	automobiles	bank	basketball hoops
birds	brick	driveway	fire hydrant
garage	grocery store	houses	lawn
neighbor	park	parking lot	road
school	street	street lights	telephone poles

Use nouns from the list, or choose others.

Underline all the nouns you used in your 10 sentences. Be sure to include proper and common nouns.

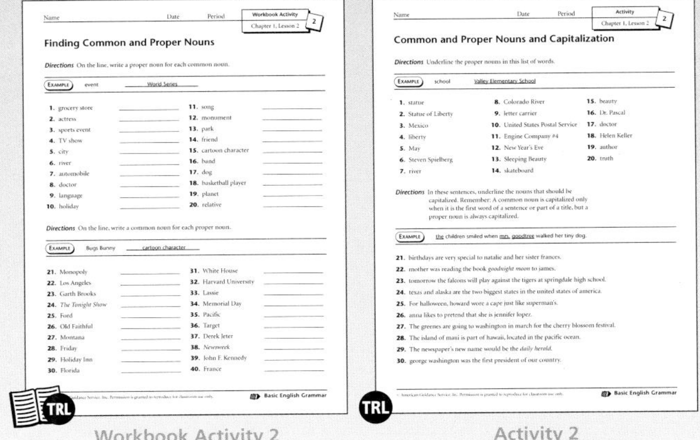

Name Date Period — Workbook Activity 2 — Chapter 1, Lesson 2

Finding Common and Proper Nouns

Directions On the line, write a proper noun for each common noun.

EXAMPLE event <u>World Series</u>

1. grocery store
2. actress
3. sports event
4. TV show
5. city
6. river
7. automobile
8. doctor
9. language
10. holiday
11. song
12. monument
13. park
14. friend
15. cartoon character
16. band
17. dog
18. basketball player
19. planet
20. relative

Directions On the line, write a common noun for each proper noun.

EXAMPLE Bugs Bunny <u>cartoon character</u>

21. Monopoly
22. Los Angeles
23. Garth Brooks
24. *The Tonight Show*
25. Ford
26. Old Faithful
27. Montana
28. Friday
29. Holiday Inn
30. Florida
31. White House
32. Harvard University
33. Lassie
34. Memorial Day
35. Pacific
36. Target
37. Derek Jeter
38. *Newsweek*
39. John F. Kennedy
40. France

 Basic English Grammar

TRL

Workbook Activity 2

Name Date Period — Activity 2 — Chapter 1, Lesson 2

Common and Proper Nouns and Capitalization

Directions Underline the proper nouns in this list of words.

EXAMPLE school <u>Valley Elementary School</u>

1. statue
2. Statue of Liberty
3. Mexico
4. liberty
5. May
6. Steven Spielberg
7. river
8. Colorado River
9. letter carrier
10. United States Postal Service
11. Engine Company #4
12. New Year's Eve
13. Sleeping Beauty
14. skateboard
15. beauty
16. Dr. Pascal
17. doctor
18. Helen Keller
19. author
20. truth

Directions In these sentences, underline the nouns that should be capitalized. Remember: A common noun is capitalized only when it is the first word of a sentence or part of a title, but a proper noun is always capitalized.

EXAMPLE <u>the</u> children smiled when <u>mrs.</u> <u>goodtree</u> walked her tiny dog.

21. birthdays are very special to natalie and her sister frances.
22. mother was reading the book *goodnight moon* to james.
23. tomorrow the falcons will play against the tigers at springdale high school.
24. texas and alaska are the two biggest states in the united states of america.
25. For halloween, howard wore a cape just like superman's.
26. anna likes to pretend that she is jennifer lopez.
27. The greenes are going to washington in march for the cherry blossom festival.
28. The island of maui is part of hawaii, located in the pacific ocean.
29. The newspaper's new name would be the *daily herald*.
30. george washington was the first president of our country.

 Basic English Grammar

TRL

Activity 2

Lesson 2 Review Answers

1. George Washington **2.** Spain **3.** recipe **4.** Labor Day **5.** river **6.** *A Separate Peace* **7.** French **8.** city **9.** Albert Einstein **10.** president **11.** Latisha took Math 101, not Math 201, this year. **12.** Armando's favorite holiday is Thanksgiving. **13.** Correct **14.** Kaitlin's grandmother lives in Philadelphia. **15.** Lisa and Greg visited Wicker Park.

Writing Project

Point out that writing is often more interesting when the nouns create a precise picture. *Sparrows twittered on the telephone pole,* for instance, gives a sharper image than *Some birds twittered on the telephone pole.* Remind students that using proper nouns is one way of bringing a sentence to life. In the writing exercise that follows, urge students to identify parks, schools, stores, streets, and neighbors by their proper names.

Answers to Writing Project: Students' sentences will vary. Check to be sure that students have underlined all of the nouns in their sentences.

LEARNING STYLES

Body/Kinesthetic

Divide the class into small groups and ask students to choose five nouns that they could describe by means of mime or physical gestures. These should include at least two proper nouns (places, titles, and famous people). Collect their lists and distribute suitable words to a designated performer from each group. Performers should attempt to convey the meaning of their words silently to their group within a designated time limit. Keep score on the board.

The Noun Chapter 1 11

- Spelling, Speaking, and Writing Practice activities provide additional reinforcement of content covered in the Student Text.
- Learning Styles provide teaching strategies to help meet the needs of students with diverse ways of learning. Modalities include Auditory/Verbal, Body/Kinesthetic, Interpersonal/Group Learning, Logical/Mathematical, and Visual/Spatial. Additional teaching activities are provided for LEP/ESL students.
- Answers for all activities in the Student Text appear in the Teacher's Edition. Answers to the Teacher's Resource Library and Student Workbook appear at the back of this Teacher's Edition and on the TRL CD-ROM.
- Activity, Workbook, and Test pages from the Teacher's Resource Library are shown at reduced size at point of use.

Teacher's Edition Highlights

- The Planning Guide saves valuable preparation time by organizing all materials for each chapter.
- A complete listing of lessons allows you to preview each chapter quickly.
- Assessment options are highlighted for easy reference. The options include Lesson Reviews, Chapter Reviews, Chapter Mastery Tests A and B, and Midterm and Final Tests.

Chapter 1

Planning Guide

The Noun

	Student Text Lesson				Language Skills		
	Student Pages	Vocabulary	Practice Exercises	Lesson Review	Identification Skills	Writing Skills	Punctuation Skills
Lesson 1 What Is a Noun?	2–5	✔	✔	✔	✔	✔	✔
Lesson 2 Common and Proper Nouns	6–11	✔	✔	✔	✔	✔	✔
Lesson 3 Concrete and Abstract Nouns	12–14	✔	✔	✔	✔	✔	✔
Lesson 4 Singular and Plural Nouns	15–19	✔	✔	✔	✔	✔	✔
Lesson 5 Possessive Nouns	20–23	✔	✔	✔	✔	✔	✔

Chapter Activities

Teacher's Resource Library
Community Connection 1: Nouns in Newspaper Headlines
Media and Literature Connection 1: Nouns Tell Stories

Assessment Options

Student Text
Chapter 1 Review

Teacher's Resource Library
Chapter 1 Mastery Tests A and B

1A

	Student Text Features						Teaching Strategies						Learning Styles						Teacher's Resource Library			
	Spelling Builder	Vocabulary Builder	Where To Find It	Writing Project	Using What You've Learned	Writing Tips/Notes/ Technology Notes	Teacher Alert	Online Connection	Applications (Home, Career, Community, Global)	Speaking Practice	Spelling Practice	Writing Practice	Auditory/Verbal	Body/Kinesthetic	Interpersonal/Group Learning	Logical/Mathematical	Visual/Spatial	LEP/ESL	Workbook Activities	Activities	Alternative Activities	Self-Study Guide
			5			✔	4		4			4			3	5			1	1	1	✔
				11		✔	8		8, 9				7	11			9	10	2	2	2	✔
		14														13	14		3	3	3	✔
	19					✔	17		17, 18		19				16			17	4	4	4	✔
					23	✔	21	22	23	22							21		5	5	5	✔

Pronunciation Key

a	hat	e	let	ī	ice	ô	order	u̇	put	sh	she	ə { a	in about
ā	age	ē	equal	o	hot	oi	oil	ü	rule	th	thin	e	in taken
ä	far	ėr	term	ō	open	ou	out	ch	child	ŦH	then	i	in pencil
â	care	i	it	ȯ	saw	u	cup	ng	long	zh	measure	o	in lemon
												u	in circus

- Page numbers of Student Text and Teacher's Edition features help teachers customize lesson plans.
- Many teaching strategies and learning styles are listed to help include students with diverse needs.
- All activities for the Teacher's Resource Library are listed.
- A Pronunciation Guide is provided to help teachers work with students to pronounce difficult words correctly.

Alternative Activities

The Teacher's Resource Library (TRL) contains a set of lower-level worksheets called Alternative Activities. These worksheets cover the same content as the regular Activities but are written at a second-grade reading level.

Skill Track Software

Use the Skill Track Software for Basic English Grammar for additional reinforcement of this chapter. The software program allows students using AGS textbooks to be assessed for mastery of each chapter and lesson of the textbook. Students access the software on an individual basis and are assessed with multiple-choice items.

1B

Teacher's Resource Library Highlights

TRL All of the activities you will need to reinforce and extend the text are conveniently located in the Teacher's Resource Library (TRL) CD-ROM. All of the reproducible activities pictured in the Teacher's Edition are ready to select, view, and print. Additionally, you can preview other materials by linking directly to the AGS Web site.

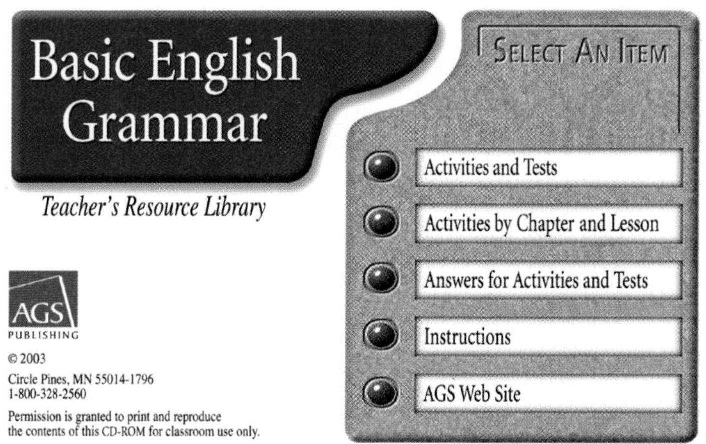

Workbook

Workbook Activities are available to reinforce and extend skills from each lesson of the textbook. A bound workbook format is also available.

Activities

Activities for each lesson of the textbook give students additional skill practice.

Alternative Activities

These activities cover the same content as the Activities but are written at a second-grade reading level.

Community Connection/Media and Literature Connection

Relevant activities help students apply their knowledge in the community and reinforce concepts covered in class. Media and Literature Connection activities reinforce learning by having students identify concepts covered in class in print media and literature pieces. Both kinds of activities promote critical thinking.

Self-Study Guide

An assignment guide provides the student with an outline for working through the text independently. The guide provides teachers with the flexibility for individualized instruction or independent study.

Mastery Tests

Chapter, Midterm, and Final Mastery Tests are convenient assessment options.

Answer Key

All answers to reproducible activities are included in the TRL and in the Teacher's Edition.

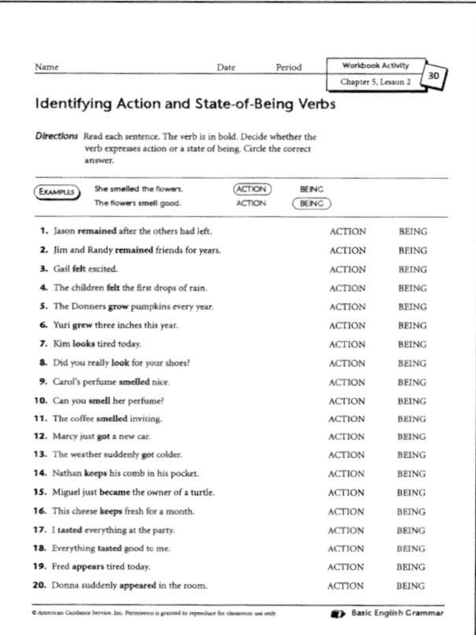

Name Date Period — Workbook Activity 30, Chapter 5, Lesson 2

Identifying Action and State-of-Being Verbs

Directions Read each sentence. The verb is in bold. Decide whether the verb expresses action or a state of being. Circle the correct answer.

EXAMPLES She **smelled** the flowers. (ACTION) BEING
The flowers **smell** good. ACTION (BEING)

1. Jason **remained** after the others had left. ACTION BEING
2. Jim and Randy **remained** friends for years. ACTION BEING
3. Gail **felt** excited. ACTION BEING
4. The children **felt** the first drops of rain. ACTION BEING
5. The Donners **grow** pumpkins every year. ACTION BEING
6. Yuri **grew** three inches this year. ACTION BEING
7. Kim **looks** tired today. ACTION BEING
8. Did you really **look** for your shoes? ACTION BEING
9. Carol's perfume **smelled** nice. ACTION BEING
10. Can you **smell** her perfume? ACTION BEING
11. The coffee **smelled** inviting. ACTION BEING
12. Marcy just **got** a new car. ACTION BEING
13. The weather suddenly **got** colder. ACTION BEING
14. Nathan **keeps** his comb in his pocket. ACTION BEING
15. Miguel just **became** the owner of a turtle. ACTION BEING
16. This cheese **keeps** fresh for a month. ACTION BEING
17. I **tasted** everything at the party. ACTION BEING
18. Everything **tasted** good to me. ACTION BEING
19. Fred **appears** tired today. ACTION BEING
20. Donna suddenly **appeared** in the room. ACTION BEING

© American Guidance Service, Inc. Permission is granted to reproduce for classroom use only. Basic English Grammar

Workbook Activities

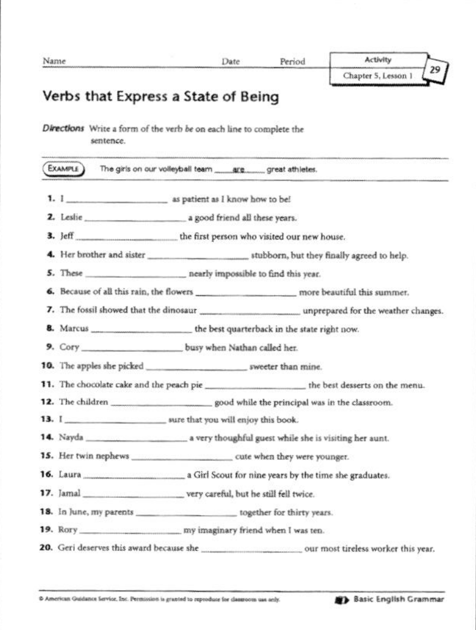

Name Date Period — Activity 29, Chapter 5, Lesson 1

Verbs that Express a State of Being

Directions Write a form of the verb *be* on each line to complete the sentence.

EXAMPLE The girls on our volleyball team __are__ great athletes.

1. I ________ as patient as I know how to be!
2. Leslie ________ a good friend all these years.
3. Jeff ________ the first person who visited our new house.
4. Her brother and sister ________ stubborn, but they finally agreed to help.
5. These ________ nearly impossible to find this year.
6. Because of all this rain, the flowers ________ more beautiful this summer.
7. The fossil showed that the dinosaur ________ unprepared for the weather changes.
8. Marcus ________ the best quarterback in the state right now.
9. Cory ________ busy when Nathan called her.
10. The apples she picked ________ sweeter than mine.
11. The chocolate cake and the peach pie ________ the best desserts on the menu.
12. The children ________ good while the principal was in the classroom.
13. I ________ sure that you will enjoy this book.
14. Nayda ________ a very thoughful guest while she is visiting her aunt.
15. Her twin nephews ________ cute when they were younger.
16. Laura ________ a Girl Scout for nine years by the time she graduates.
17. Jamal ________ very careful, but he still fell twice.
18. In June, my parents ________ together for thirty years.
19. Rory ________ my imaginary friend when I was ten.
20. Geri deserves this award because she ________ our most tireless worker this year.

© American Guidance Service, Inc. Permission is granted to reproduce for classroom use only. Basic English Grammar

Activities

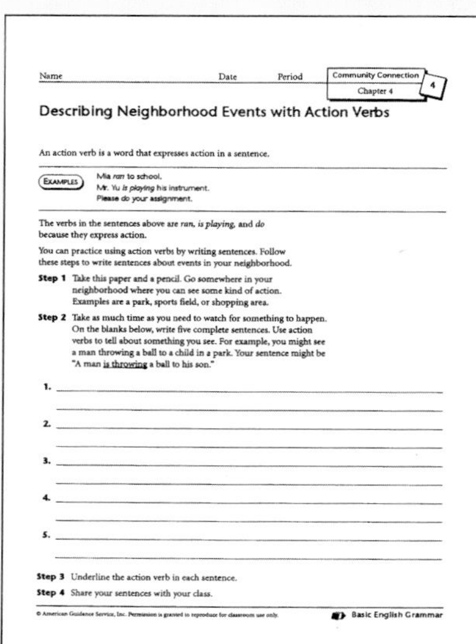

Name Date Period — Community Connection 4, Chapter 4

Describing Neighborhood Events with Action Verbs

An action verb is a word that expresses action in a sentence.

EXAMPLES Mia *ran* to school.
Mr. Yu *is playing* his instrument.
Please *do* your assignment.

The verbs in the sentences above are *ran, is playing,* and *do* because they express action.

You can practice using action verbs by writing sentences. Follow these steps to write sentences about events in your neighborhood.

Step 1 Take this paper and a pencil. Go somewhere in your neighborhood where you can see some kind of action. Examples are a park, sports field, or shopping area.

Step 2 Take as much time as you need to watch for something to happen. On the blanks below, write five complete sentences. Use action verbs to tell about something you see. For example, you might see a man throwing a ball to a child in a park. Your sentence might be "A man is throwing a ball to his son."

1. ________
2. ________
3. ________
4. ________
5. ________

Step 3 Underline the action verb in each sentence.

Step 4 Share your sentences with your class.

© American Guidance Service, Inc. Permission is granted to reproduce for classroom use only. Basic English Grammar

Community Connection

Name Date Period — Mastery Test A, Page 1, Chapter 3

Chapter 3 Mastery Test A

Part A Circle each of the adjectives in these sentences. Underline the nouns that the adjectives describe.

1. Clare planned a large, hot breakfast for a cold morning.
2. Clare's mother enjoys a hearty breakfast.
3. Clare served her mother a tall glass of fresh orange juice.
4. She made six fluffy waffles and four pieces of French toast.
5. Those waffles and that French toast looked very tasty.

Part B Rewrite these sentences. Capitalize the proper adjectives.

6. My french class comes before my english class.
7. I enjoy eating spicy indian curry.
8. My friend An has a vietnamese passport.
9. We went to New York City to hear latin music.
10. Is Nigeria an african country?

Part C Identify the kind of adjective each word is. Write *Article, Number, Proper, Demonstrative,* or *Possessive.*

11. American ________	16. an ________
12. their ________	17. eighty ________
13. those ________	18. Mexican ________
14. the ________	19. this ________
15. several ________	20. player's ________

© American Guidance Service, Inc. Permission is granted to reproduce for classroom use only. Basic English Grammar

Mastery Tests

Skill Track Software

Skill Track Software

The Skill Track software program allows students using AGS textbooks to be assessed for mastery of each chapter and lesson of the textbook. Students access the software on an individual basis and are assessed with multiple-choice items.

Students can enter the program through two paths:

Lesson
Six items assess mastery of each lesson.

Chapter
Two parallel chapter assessment forms are provided to determine chapter mastery. The two forms are equal in length and cover the same concepts with different items. The number of items in each chapter assessment varies by chapter, as the items are drawn from content in each lesson of the textbook.

The program includes high-interest graphics that accompany the items. Students are allowed to retake the chapter or lesson assessments over again at the instructor's discretion. The instructor has the ability to run and print out a variety of reports to track students' progress.

Skills Chart

Basic English Grammar

Identification Skills	CHAPTER											
Parts of Speech												
Nouns	1	2	3	4	5	6	7	8	9	10	11	12
Pronouns		2	3	4	5	6	7	8	9	10	11	12
Adjectives			3	4	5	6	7	8	9	10	11	12
Verbs		2		4	5	6	7	8	9	10	11	12
Adverbs						6	7	8	9	10	11	12
Prepositions							7	8	9	10	11	12
Conjunctions								8	9	10	11	12
Interjections								8	9	10	11	12
Phrases												
Noun											11	12
Adjective							7	8	9	10	11	12
Verb				4	5	6	7	8	9	10	11	12
Adverb							7	8	9	10	11	12
Prepositional							7	8	9	10	11	12
Infinitive							7	8	9	10	11	12
Gerund												12
Participle				4								12
Clauses												
Noun											11	12
Adjective											11	12
Adverb								8	9	10	11	12
Dependent								8	9	10	11	12
Independent								8	9	10	11	12
Sentences												
Subject									9	10	11	12
Predicate		2	3	4	5	6	7	8	9	10	11	12
Complete	1	2	3	4	5	6	7	8	9	10	11	12
Incomplete/Fragments										10	11	12
Compound									9	10	11	12
Complex											11	12
Compound-Complex											11	12
Object Complement										10	11	12
Patterns										10	11	
Purposes									9	10	11	12
Antecedents		2	3	4	5	6	7	8	9	10	11	12
Appositives											11	12
Articles			3	4	5	6	7	8	9	10	11	12
Degrees of Comparison			3			6						
Direct/Indirect Quotations											11	
Direct Object										10	11	12
Gender		2	3									
Indirect Object										10	11	12

	CHAPTER											
Intransitive Verbs										10	11	12
Person		2	3	4	5	6	7	8	9	10	11	12
Transitive Verbs										10	11	12
Verb Forms				4	5	6	7	8	9	10	11	12
Verb Tenses				4	5	6	7	8	9	10	11	12
Diagramming Skills												
Sentence Diagramming										10		
Writing Skills												
Punctuation Skills	1	2	3	4	5	6	7	8	9	10	11	12
Sentences	1	2	3	4	5	6	7	8	9	10	11	12
Paragraphs				4	5	6	7		9	10	11	12
Writing Addresses								8				
Writing Directions	1					6						
Writing Letters/Notes			3					8	9		11	
Drawing Illustrations/Diagrams				4	5		7			10		
Spelling/Vocabulary Skills												
Abbreviations	1									10	11	12
Contractions		2	3			6			9		11	
Definitions	1	2	3	4	5	6	7	8	9	10	11	12
Dictionary Use	1			4	5							
Homonyms		2			5		7				11	
Idioms												12
Irregular Spellings							7	8		10		
Suffixes								8		10		
Parts of Speech	1	2	3	4	5	6	7	8				12
Prefixes				4								
Pronunciation	1		3	4		6	7		9		11	12
Spelling and Pronunciation Demons				4	5	6	7	8	9			
Syllabication	1		3			6						
Synonyms		2		4	5	6						
Research and Study Skills												
Finding Relevant Information	1	2	3	4	5	6	7	8	9	10	11	12
Using Reference Materials	1	2	3	4	5	6	7	8	9	10	11	12
Understanding Instructions	1	2	3	4	5	6	7	8	9	10	11	12
Following Written Instructions	1	2	3	4	5	6	7	8	9	10	11	12
Using Technology	1	2	3	4	5	6	7	8	9	10	11	12
Speaking Skills												
Hearing Differences in Pronunciation			3	4		6			9			
Reading Aloud	1	2	3	4	5	6	7	8	9		11	12
Critical Thinking Skills												
Applying Information	1	2	3	4	5	6	7	8	9	10	11	12
Classifying and Categorizing	1	2	3	4	5	6	7	8	9	10	11	12
Organizing Information	1	2	3	4	5	6	7	8	9	10	11	12
Drawing Conclusions	1	2	3	4	5	6	7	8	9	10	11	12

Learning Styles

The learning style activities in the *Basic English Grammar* Teacher's Edition provide activities to help students with special needs understand the lesson. These activities focus on the following learning styles: Visual/Spatial, Auditory/Verbal, Body/Kinesthetic, Logical/Mathematical, Interpersonal/Group Learning, LEP/ESL. These styles reflect Howard Gardner's theory of multiple intelligences. The writing activities suggested in this student text are appropriate for students who fit Gardner's description of Verbal/Linguistic Intelligence.

The activities are designed to help teachers capitalize on students' individual strengths and dominant learning styles. The activities reinforce the lesson by teaching or expanding upon the content in a different way.

Following are examples of activities featured in the *Basic English Grammar* Teacher's Edition.

Visual/Spatial

Students benefit from seeing illustrations or demonstrations beyond what is in the text.

Learning Styles

Visual/Spatial

Select a variety of pictures to which students are likely to respond—images of war, beauty, tranquility, and ugliness. These might be photographs from magazines, reproductions of fine art, or even cartoons. Hold them up one by one for the students to look at. For each picture, ask students to write an abstract noun. Help them find nouns by asking "What mood or feeling does this picture give you?" After they have seen the pictures, invite volunteers to share their lists of nouns with the class.

Logical/Mathematical

Students learn by using logical/mathematical thinking in relation to the lesson content.

Learning Styles

Logical/Mathematical

Invite students to devise a series of simple symbols to identify concrete nouns. For example, a square might indicate that the noun represents an object that takes up space; an eye might indicate that the object described is visible. Have students test their symbols on the nouns in this lesson. Write a list of words on the board, and invite students to mark concrete nouns with the appropriate symbols.

Interpersonal/Group Learning

Learners benefit from working with at least one other person on activities that involve a process and an end product.

Learning Styles

Interpersonal/Group Learning

Tell students that collective nouns are used in reference to sports, animals, and the arts. Provide examples, such as *team* for sports, *herd* for animals, and *orchestra* for the arts. Divide the class into groups. Have the groups choose a category and brainstorm a list of collective nouns related to the category. Have the groups share their lists.

Body/Kinesthetic

Learners benefit from activities that include physical movement or tactile experiences.

Learning Styles

Body/Kinesthetic

Divide the class into small groups and ask students to choose five nouns that they could describe by means of mime or physical gestures. These should include at least two proper nouns (places, titles, and famous people). Collect their lists and distribute suitable words to a designated performer from each group. Performers should attempt to convey the meaning of their words silently to their group within a designated time limit. Keep score on the board.

Auditory/Verbal

Students benefit from having someone read the text aloud or listening to the text on audiocassette. Musical activities appropriate for the lesson may help auditory learners.

Learning Styles

Auditory/Verbal

Have students form pairs to write sentences that include proper nouns. Then divide the class into two equal teams. Ask the first student in Team 1 to read a sentence. Have the first student in Team 2 name the proper noun in that sentence. If he or she fails to answer correctly, the next student in line should try. Continue until all the students on both teams have had a turn reading and answering.

LEP/ESL

Students benefit from activities that promote English language acquisition and interaction with English-speaking peers.

Learning Styles

LEP/ESL

Invite students with limited English proficiency to explain to the class how they form plurals in their primary language. Encourage them to print examples on the board. With partners, students can compare the way the plurals are formed in their first language and in English.

by
Bonnie L. Walker

AGS Publishing
Circle Pines, Minnesota 55014-1796
1-800-328-2560

About the Author

Bonnie L. Walker taught for 16 years in secondary schools and college. She holds a Ph.D. in curriculum theory and instructional design from the University of Maryland, an M.Ed. in secondary education, and a B.A. in English. She studied psycholinguistics at the University of Illinois Graduate School, and was a curriculum developer at the Model Secondary School for the Deaf at Gallaudet University. She is the author of *Basic English, Life Skills English, Basic English Composition,* and numerous curriculum materials in written expression, grammar, and usage. Since 1986, Dr. Walker has been president of a research and development company specializing in development of training and educational materials for special populations.

Photo credits for this textbook can be found on page 336.

The publisher wishes to thank the following educators for their helpful comments during the review process for *Basic English Grammar*. Their assistance has been invaluable.

Beverly C. Allen, Learning Disabilities Coordinator, L.D. Office, Norman Center, Kansas City, MO; **John DeTullio,** English Teacher, Tweedsmuir Middle School, Hamilton, ON, Canada; **Jacqueline DeWitt,** Teacher/Cooperative Consultation Consultant, Umatilla High School, Umatilla, FL; **Cathy Guzzo,** Transition/Special Education Coordinator, Penn Hills Senior High School, Pittsburgh, PA; **Susan Harrington,** Special Education Teacher–Option III, Salamanca Middle School, Salamanca, NY; **Alva Jones,** Special Education Consultant, Evans, GA; **Cecilia Lozano,** ESL Teacher, Douglas High School, Oklahoma City, OK; **Virginia Malling,** Special Education Teacher, Oak Ridge High School, Oak Ridge, TN; **Marie Ramey,** Department Chairperson, West Side High School, Newark, NJ; **Christine D. Russell,** Special Education Teacher, Stinson Middle School, San Antonio, TX; **Dr. William B. Whitaker,** Director of Adult High School and GED Programs, Rowan Cabarrus Community College, Salisbury, NC

Publisher's Project Staff

Director, Product Development: Karen Dahlen; Associate Director, Product Development: Teri Mathews; Senior Editor: Julie Maas; Development Assistant: Bev Johnson; Graphic Designer: Diane McCarty; Design Manager: Nancy Condon; Desktop Publishing Manager: Lisa Beller; Purchasing Agent: Mary Kaye Kuzma; Marketing Manager/Curriculum: Brian Holl

Editorial and production services provided by The Mazer Corporation.

Printed in the United States of America

ISBN 0-7854-2916-6

Product Number 93500

A 0 9 8 7 6 5 4 3 2 1

Contents

Basic English Grammar *Contents* **iii**

Chapter 3 The Adjective . . . 54

Chapter 4 The Action Verb . . . 80

iv *Contents* *Basic English Grammar*

Basic English Grammar Contents **v**

vi *Contents Basic English Grammar*

Basic English Grammar Contents **vii**

Using This Section

How to Use This Book: A Study Guide

Overview This section may be used to introduce the study of English grammar, to preview the book's features, and to review effective study skills.

Objectives

- To introduce the study of English grammar.
- To preview the student textbook.
- To review study skills.

Student Pages viii–xiii

Teacher's Resource Library 

How to Use This Book 1–7

Introduction to the Book

Have volunteers read aloud the three paragraphs of the introduction. Discuss with students why studying English grammar is important and what people can learn from studying English grammar.

How to Study

Read aloud each bulleted statement, pausing to discuss with students why the suggestion is a part of good study habits. Distribute copies of the How to Use This Book 1, "Study Habits Survey," to students. Read the directions together and then have students complete the survey. After they have scored their surveys, ask them to make a list of the study habits they plan to work on improving. After three or four weeks, have students complete the survey again to see if they have improved their study habits. Encourage them to keep and review the survey every month or so to see whether they are maintaining and improving their study habits.

To help students organize their time and work in an easy-to-read format, have them fill out How to Use This Book 2, "Weekly Schedule." Encourage them to keep the schedule in a notebook or folder where they can refer to it easily. Suggest that they review the schedule periodically and update it as necessary.

How to Use This Book: A Study Guide

Welcome to *Basic English Grammar*. This book includes many of the grammar skills you will need now and later in life. You may be wondering why you should study English grammar. Think about the world around you. When you write, read, or speak, you draw on your knowledge of grammar. Knowing how to write sentences correctly will help you communicate more effectively, both in writing and speaking. Knowing how words fit together in sentences will help you understand what you read. We use language every day when we write, read, and speak. In this book, you will learn about the different parts of speech. You will learn about word placement and punctuation. You will put words together to create sentences and paragraphs. You will also practice your vocabulary and spelling skills.

As you read this book, notice how each lesson is organized. Information is presented and then followed by examples and activities. Read the information. Then practice what you have read. If you have trouble with a lesson, try reading it again.

It is important that you understand how to use this book before you start to read it. It is also important to know how to be successful in this course. The first section of the book can help you to achieve these things.

How to Study

These tips can help you study more effectively:

- Plan a regular time to study.
- Choose a quiet desk or table where you will not be distracted. Find a spot that has good lighting.
- Gather all the books, pencils, paper, and other equipment you will need to complete your assignments.
- Decide on a goal. For example: "I will finish reading and taking notes on Chapter 1, Lesson 1, by 8:00."
- Take a five- to ten-minute break every hour to keep alert.
- If you start to feel sleepy, take a break and get some fresh air.

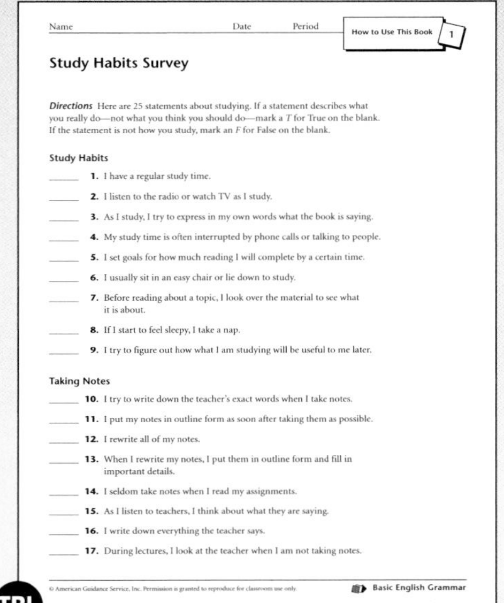

Name ______ Date ______ Period ______ How to Use This Book 1

Study Habits Survey

Directions Here are 25 statements about studying. If a statement describes what you really do—not what you think you should do—mark a *T* for True on the blank. If the statement is not how you study, mark an *F* for False on the blank.

Study Habits

______ **1.** I have a regular study time.

______ **2.** I listen to the radio or watch TV as I study.

______ **3.** As I study, I try to express in my own words what the book is saying.

______ **4.** My study time is often interrupted by phone calls or talking to people.

______ **5.** I set goals for how much reading I will complete by a certain time.

______ **6.** I usually sit in an easy chair or lie down to study.

______ **7.** Before reading about a topic, I look over the material to see what it is about.

______ **8.** If I start to feel sleepy, I take a nap.

______ **9.** I try to figure out how what I am studying will be useful to me later.

Taking Notes

______ **10.** I try to write down the teacher's exact words when I take notes.

______ **11.** I put my notes in outline form as soon after taking them as possible.

______ **12.** I rewrite all of my notes.

______ **13.** When I rewrite my notes, I put them in outline form and fill in important details.

______ **14.** I seldom take notes when I read my assignments.

______ **15.** As I listen to teachers, I think about what they are saying.

______ **16.** I write down everything the teacher says.

______ **17.** During lectures, I look at the teacher when I am not taking notes.

 Basic English Grammar

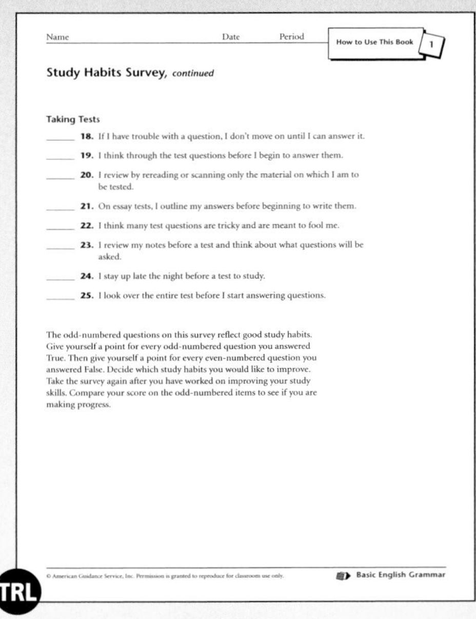

Name ______ Date ______ Period ______ How to Use This Book 1

Study Habits Survey, *continued*

Taking Tests

______ **18.** If I have trouble with a question, I don't move on until I can answer it.

______ **19.** I think through the test questions before I begin to answer them.

______ **20.** I review by rereading or scanning only the material on which I am to be tested.

______ **21.** On essay tests, I outline my answers before beginning to write them.

______ **22.** I think many test questions are tricky and are meant to fool me.

______ **23.** I review my notes before a test and think about what questions will be asked.

______ **24.** I stay up late the night before a test to study.

______ **25.** I look over the entire test before I start answering questions.

The odd-numbered questions on this survey reflect good study habits. Give yourself a point for every odd-numbered question you answered True. Then give yourself a point for every even-numbered question you answered False. Decide which study habits you would like to improve. Take the survey again after you have worked on improving your study skills. Compare your score on the odd-numbered items to see if you are making progress.

 Basic English Grammar

How to Use This Book 1, Pages 1 and 2

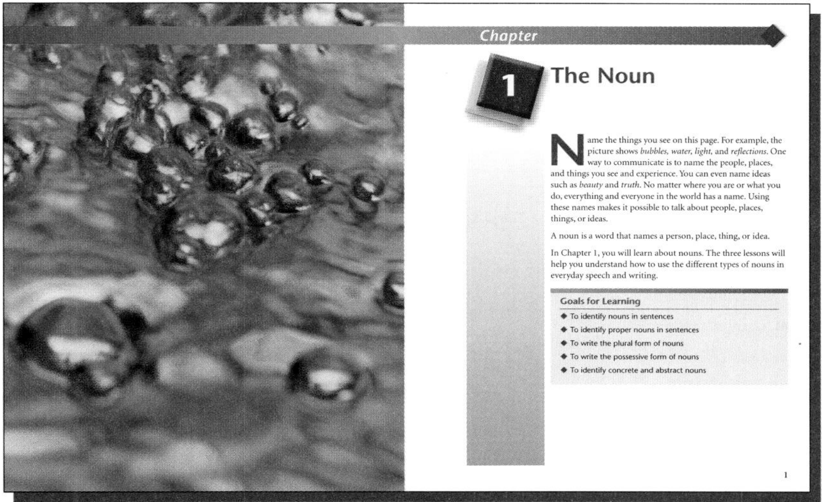

Chapter

1 The Noun

Name the things you see on this page. For example, the picture shows *bubbles, water, light,* and *reflections.* One way to communicate is to name the people, places, and things you see and experience. You can even name ideas such as *beauty* and *truth.* No matter where you are or what you do, everything and everyone in the world has a name. Using these names makes it possible to talk about people, places, things, or ideas.

A noun is a word that names a person, place, thing, or idea.

In Chapter 1, you will learn about nouns. The three lessons will help you understand how to use the different types of nouns in everyday speech and writing.

Goals for Learning

- To identify nouns in sentences
- To identify proper nouns in sentences
- To write the plural form of nouns
- To write the possessive form of nouns
- To identify concrete and abstract nouns

1

Before Beginning Each Chapter

- Read the chapter title and study the photograph. What does the photo tell you about the chapter title?
- Read the opening paragraphs.
- Study the Goals for Learning. The Chapter Review and tests will ask questions related to these goals.
- Look at the Chapter Review. The questions cover the most important information in the chapter.

Look for these Features

Writing Tip
Quick tips to help improve writing skills

Writing Tip
The antecedent of each pronoun that you use must be clear to readers. Unclear antecedents confuse readers.

Note
Hints or reminders that point out important information

Look for this box for helpful tips!

Give students an opportunity to become familiar with the textbook features and the chapter and lesson organization and structure of *Basic English Grammar.* List the following text features on the board: Table of Contents, Part Opener, Chapter Opener, Lesson, Lesson Review, Chapter Review, Appendix A: The Writing Process, Glossary, Index.

Have students skim their textbooks to find these features. You may wish to remind students that they can use the Table of Contents to help identify and locate major features in the text. They can also use the Index to identify specific topics and the text pages on which they are discussed. Ask volunteers to call out a feature or topic and its page reference from the Table of Contents or Index. Have other students check to see that the specific features or topics do appear on the pages cited.

Before Beginning Each Chapter

When students begin their study of Chapter 1, you may wish to have them read aloud and follow each of the bulleted suggestions on page ix. Actually trying the suggestions will help students understand what they are supposed to do and recognize how useful the suggestions are when previewing a chapter. At the beginning of other chapters, refer students to page ix and encourage them to follow the suggestions. You may wish to continue to do this as a class each time or allow students to work independently.

In addition to the suggestions on page ix, the text in the Teacher's Edition that accompanies each Chapter Opener offers teaching suggestions for introducing the chapter. The text also includes a list of Teacher's Resource Library materials for the chapter.

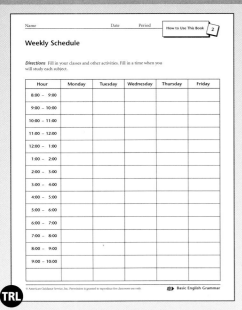

Chapter Openers organize information in easy-to-read formats. Have a volunteer find and read the Chapter 1 title on page 1. Read aloud the second bulleted statement on page ix and have a volunteer read aloud the opening paragraphs of the chapter. Discuss the topics that students will study in the chapter. Then have volunteers take turns reading aloud the Goals for Learning for Chapter 1. Discuss with students why knowing these goals can help them when they are studying the chapter. Finally, have students skim the Chapter Review to identify important information presented in the chapter. After the brief preview of the chapter, have students turn to the first lesson.

Look for these Features

Use the information on pages ix and x to identify features included in each chapter. As a class locate examples of these features in Chapter 1. Read the examples and discuss their purpose.

Name Date Period — How to Use This Book 2

Weekly Schedule

Directions Fill in your classes and other activities. Fill in a time when you will study each subject.

Hour	Monday	Tuesday	Wednesday	Thursday	Friday
8:00 – 9:00					
9:00 – 10:00					
10:00 – 11:00					
11:00 – 12:00					
12:00 – 1:00					
1:00 – 2:00					
2:00 – 3:00					
3:00 – 4:00					
4:00 – 5:00					
5:00 – 6:00					
6:00 – 7:00					
7:00 – 8:00					
8:00 – 9:00					
9:00 – 10:00					

 Basic English Grammar

TRL

How to Use This Book 2

Before Beginning Each Lesson

With students, read through the information in "Before Beginning Each Lesson" on page x. Then assign each of the five lessons in Chapter 1 to a small group of students. Have them restate the lesson title in the form of a statement or a question and make a list of features in their lesson. After their survey of the lesson, they should be prepared to report to the class on their findings.

Technology Note
Technology tips that relate to language

Using What You've Learned
An exercise that practices something taught in the chapter

Vocabulary Builder
Vocabulary practice

Spelling Builder
Spelling practice

Where To Find It
Information about various reference materials such as dictionaries, encyclopedias, and more

Writing Project
Writing practice

Before Beginning Each Lesson

Read the lesson title and restate it in the form of a question.

For example, write:
What are common and proper nouns?

Look over the entire lesson, noting the following:

- bold words
- text organization
- exercises
- notes in the margins
- photos
- lesson review

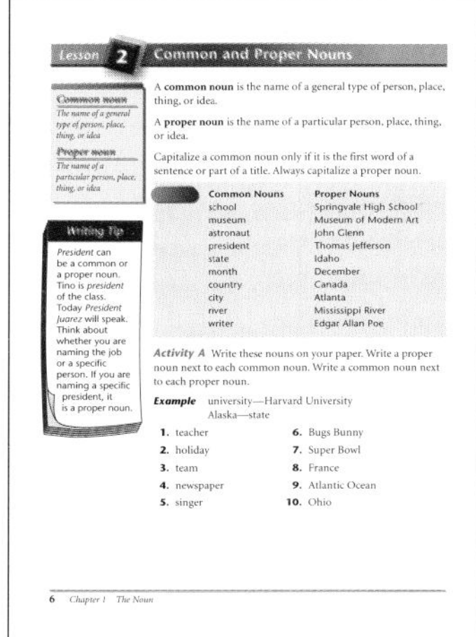

Lesson 2 Common and Proper Nouns

Common noun
The name of a general type of person, place, thing, or idea

Proper noun
The name of a particular person, place, thing, or idea

A **common noun** is the name of a general type of person, place, thing, or idea.

A **proper noun** is the name of a particular person, place, thing, or idea.

Capitalize a common noun only if it is the first word of a sentence or part of a title. Always capitalize a proper noun.

Common Nouns	Proper Nouns
school	Springvale High School
museum	Museum of Modern Art
astronaut	John Glenn
president	Thomas Jefferson
state	Idaho
month	December
country	Canada
city	Atlanta
river	Mississippi River
writer	Edgar Allan Poe

Writing Tip
President can be a common or a proper noun. Tino is *president* of the class. Today *President Juarez* will speak. Think about whether you are naming the job or a specific person. If you are naming a specific president, it is a proper noun.

Activity A Write these nouns on your paper. Write a proper noun next to each common noun. Write a common noun next to each proper noun.

Example university—Harvard University
Alaska—state

1. teacher
2. holiday
3. team
4. newspaper
5. singer
6. Bugs Bunny
7. Super Bowl
8. France
9. Atlantic Ocean
10. Ohio

6 Chapter 1 The Noun

As You Read the Lesson

- Read the major headings.
- Read the subheads and paragraphs that follow.
- Read the content in the Example boxes.
- Before moving on to the next lesson, see if you understand the concepts you read. If you do not, reread the lesson. If you are still unsure, ask for help.
- Practice what you have learned by doing the activities in each lesson.

> ***Bold type***
> *Words seen for the first time will appear in bold type*
>
> ***Glossary***
> *Words listed in this column are also found in the glossary*

Using the Bold Words

Knowing the meaning of all the boxed words in the left column will help you understand what you read.

These words appear in **bold type** the first time they appear in the text and are often defined in the paragraph.

A **common noun** is the name of a general type of person, place, thing, or idea.

All of the words in the left column are also defined in the **glossary.**

Common noun—(kom′ ən noun) The name of a general type of person, place, thing, or idea. (p. 6)

Word Study Tips

- Start a vocabulary file with index cards to use for review.
- Write one term on the front of each card. Write the chapter number, lesson number, and definition on the back.
- You can use these cards as flash cards by yourself or with a study partner to test your knowledge.

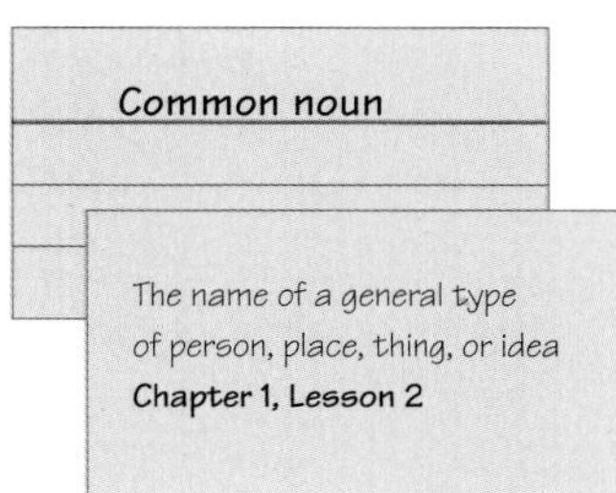

How to Use This Book: A Study Guide **xi**

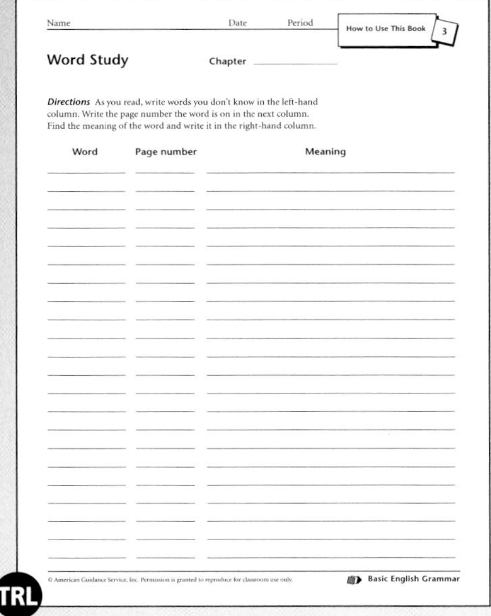

Name Date Period **How to Use This Book 3**

Word Study Chapter ______

Directions As you read, write words you don't know in the left-hand column. Write the page number the word is on in the next column. Find the meaning of the word and write it in the right-hand column.

Word	Page number	Meaning

 Basic English Grammar

TRL

How to Use This Book 3

As You Read the Lesson

Read aloud the statements in the section "As You Read the Lesson" on page xi. Have students preview lessons in Chapter 1 and note lesson titles, example boxes, and activities. Remind students as they study each lesson to follow this study approach.

Using the Bold Words

Read aloud the information on page xi. Make sure students understand what the term *bold* means. Explain to students that the words in bold are important vocabulary terms. Then ask them to look at the boxed words on page 82. Have a volunteer read the boxed word *subject* and then find and read the sentence in the text in which that word appears in bold type. Have another volunteer read the definition of the word in the box.

Point out that boxed words may appear on other pages in a lesson besides the first page. Have students turn to page 84 and look at the boxed words on that page. Explain that these words appear in a box here because they are used in the text on this page. Have volunteers find and read the sentences in the text in which the vocabulary words are used. Have students turn to the Glossary at the back of the book and read the definition of the words on page 84.

Word Study Tips

Have a volunteer read aloud the word study tips on page xi. You may wish to demonstrate how to make a vocabulary card by filling out an index card for the word *subject* and its definition (page 82).

Distribute copies of How to Use This Book 3, "Word Study," to students. Suggest that as they read, students write unfamiliar words, their page numbers, and their definitions on the sheet. Point out that having such a list will be very useful for reviewing vocabulary before taking a test. Point out that students can use words they listed on How to Use This Book 3 to make their vocabulary card file.

Using the Reviews

Have students turn to page 85 and examine the Lesson 1 Review. Emphasize that Lesson Reviews provide opportunities for students to focus on important skills introduced in the lesson. Then have students turn to pages 116 and 117. Point out that a Chapter Review is intended to help them focus on and review the key terms and skills presented in a chapter before they are tested on the material. Suggest that they complete the review after they have studied their notes, vocabulary lists, and worksheets.

Preparing for Tests

Encourage students to offer their opinions about tests and their ideas on test-taking strategies. What do they do to study for a test? List their comments on the board. Then read the set of bulleted statements on page xii. Add these suggestions to the list on the board if they are not already there.

Discuss why each suggestion can help students when they are taking a test. Lead students to recognize that these suggestions, along with the Test-Taking Tips in their textbooks, can help them improve their test-taking skills.

Have students turn to the Chapter Review at the end of any chapter in the textbook and find the Test-Taking Tip. Ask several volunteers to read aloud the tips they find in the Chapter Reviews. Discuss how using the tips can help students study and take tests more effectively.

Writing Practice

Read aloud the statements in the section "Writing Practice" on page xii. Have students preview Appendix A beginning on page 318. Explain to them that every chapter includes a Writing Project. Have them review the Writing Project on page 115. Explain that they can use the steps of the writing process as outlined in the Appendix to complete this and other writing projects and assignments.

Using the Reviews

- Answer the questions in the Lesson Reviews.
- In the Chapter Reviews, answer the questions about vocabulary under Part A. Study the words and definitions. Say them aloud to help you remember them.
- Answer the questions under the other parts of the Chapter Reviews.
- Review the Test-Taking Tips.

Preparing for Tests

- Complete the activities in each lesson. Make up similar activity questions to practice what you have learned. You may want to do this with a classmate and share your questions.
- Review your answers to lesson activities, Lesson Reviews, and Chapter Reviews.
- Test yourself on vocabulary words and key ideas.
- Use graphic organizers as study tools.

Writing Practice

- Read and review Appendix A: The Writing Process at the back of this book.
- Follow the directions outlined in each step of the process. For example, read the information under Prewriting. Choose a topic you feel strongly about. Gather information to develop a paper about that topic.
- Write a first draft on your topic. Then revise and proofread your draft.
- Share your draft with others and ask for their opinions. Using your comments and your readers' comments, rewrite your draft.
- Read and revise your second draft. Proofread it and revise it again as needed.
- When your paper is final, share it with others. Also, take the time to evaluate what you have written. Ask yourself, "What would I do differently next time?"

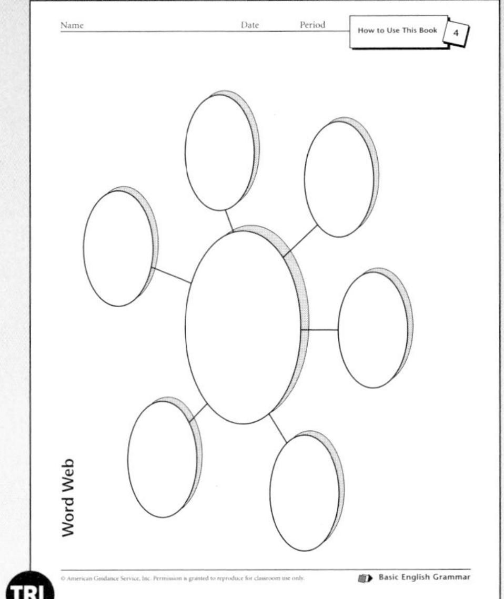

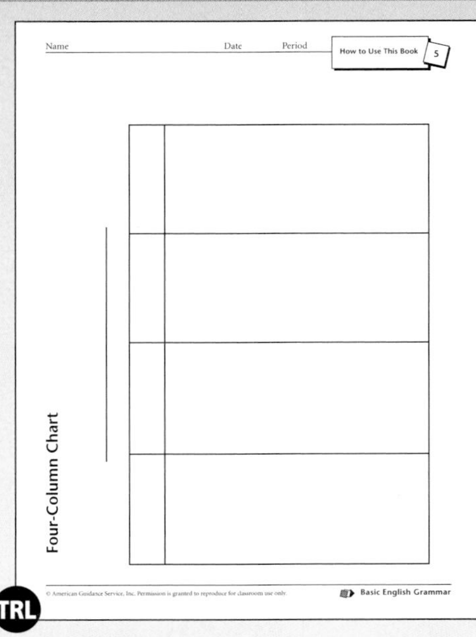

How to Use This Book 4 and 5

xii *How to Use This Book: A Study Guide*

Using Graphic Organizers

A graphic organizer is a visual representation of information. It can help you see how ideas are related to each other. A graphic organizer can help you study for a test or organize information before you write. Here are some examples.

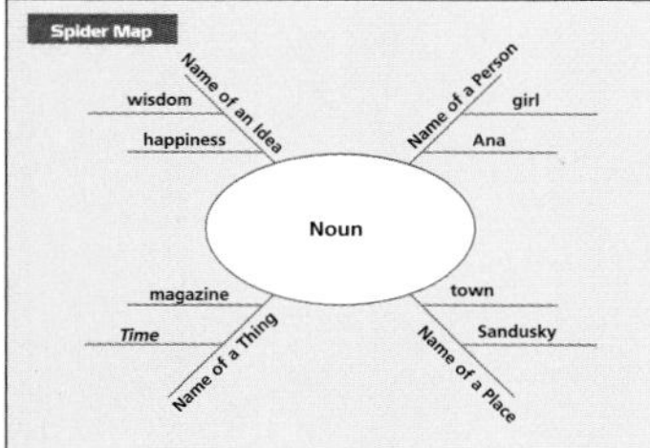

Spider Map

The Spider Map shown here can be used to connect related ideas to a central idea or concept. Write the main or central idea or concept in the circle in the center. Identify related ideas and write them on the lines that angle out from the circle. Write examples that support the ideas on the horizontal lines that are attached to the angled lines.

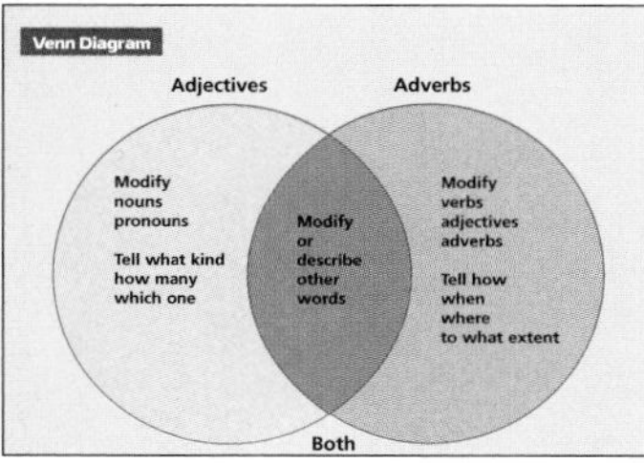

Venn Diagram

The Venn diagram shown here can be used to compare and contrast two things. For example, this diagram compares and contrasts adjectives and adverbs. List the characteristics for adjectives in the left circle. List the characteristics for adverbs in the right circle. In the intersection of the two circles, list the characteristics that both have.

Using Graphic Organizers

Explain to students that graphic organizers provide ways of organizing information visually to make it easier to understand and remember. Emphasize that there are many different kinds of graphic organizers including word webs, spider maps, Venn diagrams, and charts.

Tell students that they can use a variety of organizers to record information for a variety of purposes. For example, a Venn diagram is useful for comparing and contrasting information. Draw a Venn diagram on the board. Show students how to use the diagram to compare and contrast two items, such as a ball and a globe. Discuss how the diagram clearly shows the similarities and differences between the two items.

Display other organizers, such as a spider map, word web, and chart. Ask volunteers to suggest ways that these organizers can be used to record information. Then encourage students to record information on graphic organizers and use them as study tools.

Have students refer back to the pages in this section, "How to Use This Book," as often as they wish while using this textbook.

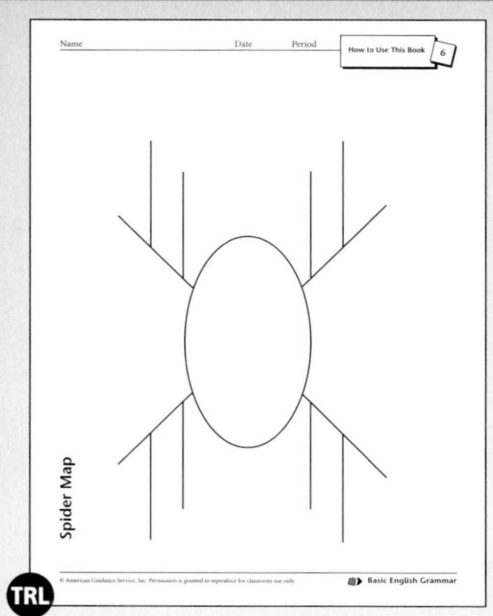

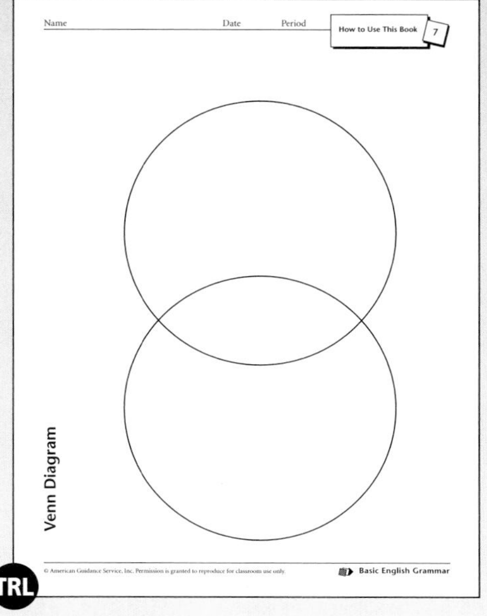

How to Use This Book 6 and 7

Part

Parts of Speech

It takes many flavors to create the foods we enjoy. From pepper to nutmeg, ginger to cinnamon, each contributes its own flavor. Some add sweetness, some add tartness, and others provide texture. Parts of speech work similarly to help us create good writing. Each part of speech plays its role. We need to understand these roles to write successfully. The study of grammar helps us learn rules for putting the right words in the right places.

Each word in the English language can be put into at least one of eight main groups. These groups are called parts of speech.

Parts of Speech

Nouns	Words that name people, places, things, and ideas
Pronouns	Words that replace nouns
Adjectives	Words that describe nouns or pronouns
Verbs	Words that express action or a state of being
Adverbs	Words that answer questions about verbs, adjectives, and other adverbs by telling *how, when, where,* or *how much*
Prepositions	Words that show a relationship between a noun or pronoun and the rest of the sentence
Conjunctions	Words that connect sentences or parts of a sentence
Interjections	Words that express feelings

In Part 1 of this book, you will learn about these parts of speech.

Introducing Part 1

Ask students if they have ever watched or helped someone cook a meal. After discussing their experiences, have students examine the picture on page xiv. Explain that the photograph shows a variety of spices and herbs and invite students to identify any that they can. Ask why cooks use these ingredients in their cooking and help students conclude that cooks use them to enhance the flavor of foods. Direct the discussion so that students consider how cooks use recipes, or directions, and their own experience to know exactly which spices to use in which dishes to make a delicious meal.

Ask if anyone can see a similarity between cooks using spices and herbs and recipes to create meals and writers using words and grammar rules to create written work. If necessary, explain that the parts of speech—*nouns, pronouns, adjectives, verbs, adverbs, prepositions, conjunctions,* and *interjections*—are like spices and herbs. They enhance the language and can be used precisely to make writing interesting and enjoyable to read. Grammar rules identify how to use these parts of speech in sentences much as recipes identify how to use spices or herbs in cooking.

Explain to students that by the end of Part 1 of this book, they will have identified the rules for using words in writing. With this mastery, they can focus on their ideas and the whole experience of writing.

1

Planning Guide

The Noun

	Student Text Lesson				Language Skills		
	Student Pages	Vocabulary	Practice Exercises	Lesson Review	Identification Skills	Writing Skills	Punctuation Skills
Lesson 1 What Is a Noun?	2–5	✔	✔	✔	✔	✔	✔
Lesson 2 Common and Proper Nouns	6–11	✔	✔	✔	✔	✔	✔
Lesson 3 Concrete and Abstract Nouns	12–14	✔	✔	✔	✔	✔	✔
Lesson 4 Singular and Plural Nouns	15–19	✔	✔	✔	✔	✔	✔
Lesson 5 Possessive Nouns	20–23	✔	✔	✔	✔	✔	✔

Chapter Activities

Teacher's Resource Library

Community Connection 1: Nouns in Newspaper Headlines

Media and Literature Connection 1: Nouns Tell Stories

Assessment Options

Student Text

Chapter 1 Review

Teacher's Resource Library

Chapter 1 Mastery Tests A and B

Student Text Features						Teaching Strategies						Learning Styles						Teacher's Resource Library			
Spelling Builder	Vocabulary Builder	Where To Find It	Writing Project	Using What You've Learned	Writing Tips/Notes/ Technology Notes	Teacher Alert	Online Connection	Applications (Home, Career, Community, Global)	Speaking Practice	Spelling Practice	Writing Practice	Auditory/Verbal	Body/Kinesthetic	Interpersonal/Group Learning	Logical/Mathematical	Visual/Spatial	LEP/ESL	Workbook Activities	Activities	Alternative Activities	Self-Study Guide
		5			✔	4		4			4			3	5			1	1	1	✔
			11		✔	8		8, 9				7	11			9	10	2	2	2	✔
	14														13	14		3	3	3	✔
19					✔	17		17, 18		19				16			17	4	4	4	✔
				23	✔	21	22	23	22							21		5	5	5	✔

Pronunciation Key

a	hat	e	let	ī	ice	ô	order	u̇	put	sh	she	ə { a	in about
ā	age	ē	equal	o	hot	oi	oil	ü	rule	th	thin	e	in taken
ä	far	ėr	term	ō	open	ou	out	ch	child	ᴛʜ	then	i	in pencil
â	care	i	it	ȯ	saw	u	cup	ng	long	zh	measure	o	in lemon
												u	in circus

Alternative Activities

The Teacher's Resource Library (TRL) contains a set of lower-level worksheets called Alternative Activities. These worksheets cover the same content as the regular Activities but are written at a second-grade reading level.

Skill Track Software

Use the Skill Track Software for Basic English Grammar for additional reinforcement of this chapter. The software program allows students using AGS textbooks to be assessed for mastery of each chapter and lesson of the textbook. Students access the software on an individual basis and are assessed with multiple-choice items.

Chapter at a Glance

Chapter 1: The Noun

pages 1–25

Lessons

1. **What Is a Noun?**
   pages 2–5
2. **Common and Proper Nouns**
   pages 6–11
3. **Concrete and Abstract Nouns**
   pages 12–14
4. **Singular and Plural Nouns**
   pages 15–19
5. **Possessive Nouns**
   pages 20–23

Chapter 1 Review

pages 24–25

Skill Track Software for Basic English Grammar

Teacher's Resource Library

Workbook Activities 1–5

Activities 1–5

Alternative Activities 1–5

Community Connection 1

Media and Literature Connection 1

Chapter 1 Self-Study Guide

Chapter 1 Mastery Tests A and B

(Answer Keys for the Teacher's Resource Library begin on page 340 of this Teacher's Edition.)

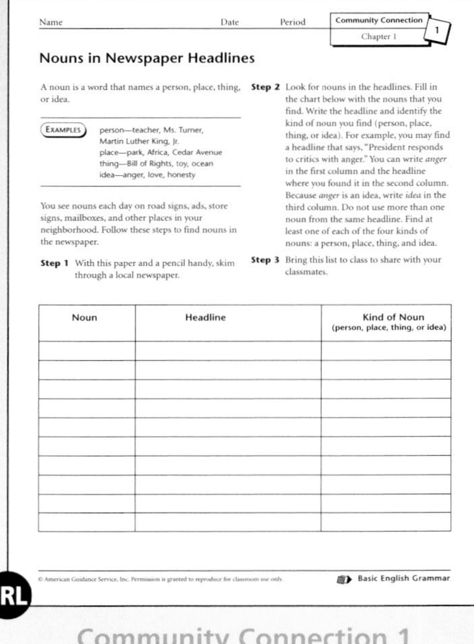

Name Date Period

Community Connection 1 — Chapter 1

Nouns in Newspaper Headlines

A noun is a word that names a person, place, thing, or idea.

EXAMPLES
person—teacher, Ms. Turner, Martin Luther King, Jr.
place—park, Africa, Cedar Avenue
thing—Bill of Rights, toy, ocean
idea—anger, love, honesty

You see nouns each day on road signs, ads, store signs, mailboxes, and other places in your neighborhood. Follow these steps to find nouns in the newspaper.

Step 1 With this paper and a pencil handy, skim through a local newspaper.

Step 2 Look for nouns in the headlines. Fill in the chart below with the nouns that you find. Write the headline and identify the kind of noun you find (person, place, thing, or idea). For example, you may find a headline that says, "President responds to critics with anger." You can write *anger* in the first column and the headline where you found it in the second column. Because *anger* is an idea, write *idea* in the third column. Do not use more than one noun from the same headline. Find at least one of each of the four kinds of nouns: a person, place, thing, and idea.

Step 3 Bring this list to class to share with your classmates.

Noun	Headline	Kind of Noun (person, place, thing, or idea)

 Basic English Grammar

TRL

Community Connection 1

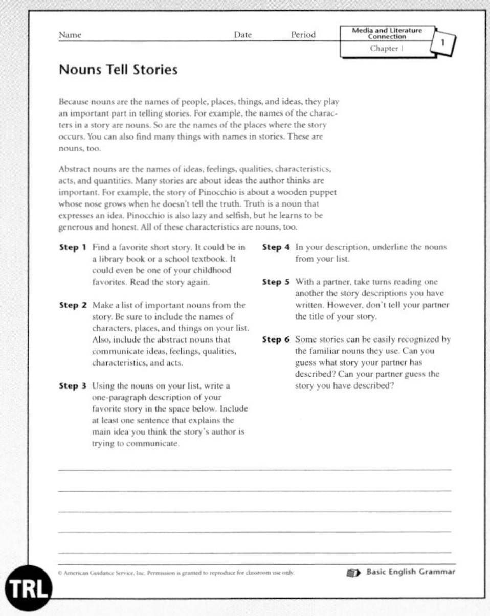

Name Date Period

Media and Literature Connection 1 — Chapter 1

Nouns Tell Stories

Because nouns are the names of people, places, things, and ideas, they play an important part in telling stories. For example, the names of the characters in a story are nouns. So are the names of the places where the story occurs. You can also find many things with names in stories. These are nouns, too.

Abstract nouns are the names of ideas, feelings, qualities, characteristics, acts, and quantities. Many stories are about ideas the author thinks are important. For example, the story of Pinocchio is about a wooden puppet whose nose grows when he doesn't tell the truth. Truth is a noun that expresses an idea. Pinocchio is also lazy and selfish, but he learns to be generous and honest. All of these characteristics are nouns, too.

Step 1 Find a favorite short story. It could be in a library book or a school textbook. It could even be one of your childhood favorites. Read the story again.

Step 2 Make a list of important nouns from the story. Be sure to include the names of characters, places, and things on your list. Also, include the abstract nouns that communicate ideas, feelings, qualities, characteristics, and acts.

Step 3 Using the nouns on your list, write a one-paragraph description of your favorite story in the space below. Include at least one sentence that explains the main idea you think the story's author is trying to communicate.

Step 4 In your description, underline the nouns from your list.

Step 5 With a partner, take turns reading one another the story descriptions you have written. However, don't tell your partner the title of your story.

Step 6 Some stories can be easily recognized by the familiar nouns they use. Can you guess what story your partner has described? Can your partner guess the story you have described?

 Basic English Grammar

TRL

Media and Literature Connection 1

Chapter

The Noun

Name the things you see on this page. For example, the picture shows *bubbles, water, light,* and *reflections.* One way to communicate is to name the people, places, and things you see and experience. You can even name ideas such as *beauty* and *truth*. No matter where you are or what you do, everything and everyone in the world has a name. Using these names makes it possible to talk about people, places, things, or ideas.

A noun is a word that names a person, place, thing, or idea.

In Chapter 1, you will learn about nouns. The three lessons will help you understand how to use the different types of nouns in everyday speech and writing.

Goals for Learning

- To identify nouns in sentences
- To identify proper nouns in sentences
- To write the plural form of nouns
- To write the possessive form of nouns
- To identify concrete and abstract nouns

Name Date Period *SELF-STUDY GUIDE*

Chapter 1: The Noun

Goal 1.1 *To identify nouns in sentences*

Date	Assignment	Score
______	**1.** Read pages 1–2. Complete Activities A–B on page 2.	______
______	**2.** Read page 3. Complete Activities C–D on page 3.	______
______	**3.** Read page 4. Complete Activities E–F on page 4.	______
______	**4.** Complete Workbook Activity 1.	______
______	**5.** Complete the Lesson 1 Review on page 5.	______

Comments:

Goal 1.2 *To identify proper nouns in sentences*

Date	Assignment	Score
______	**6.** Read pages 6–7. Complete Activities A–C on pages 6–7.	______
______	**7.** Read page 8. Complete Activity D on page 8.	______
______	**8.** Read page 9. Complete Activities E–F on page 9.	______
______	**9.** Read page 10. Complete Activities G–H on page 10.	______
______	**10.** Complete Workbook Activity 2.	______
______	**11.** Complete the Lesson 2 Review on page 11.	______

Comments:

 Basic English Grammar

TRL

Name Date Period *SELF-STUDY GUIDE*

Chapter 1: The Noun, continued

Goal 1.3 *To identify concrete and abstract nouns*

Date	Assignment	Score
______	**12.** Read pages 12–13. Complete Activities A–B on pages 12–13.	______
______	**13.** Complete Workbook Activity 3.	______
______	**14.** Complete the Lesson 3 Review on page 14.	______

Comments:

Goal 1.4 *To write the plural form of nouns*

Date	Assignment	Score
______	**15.** Read page 15. Complete Activities A–B on page 15.	______
______	**16.** Read page 16. Complete Activities C–D on page 16.	______
______	**17.** Read pages 17–18. Complete Activities E–F on page 18.	______
______	**18.** Complete Workbook Activity 4.	______
______	**19.** Complete the Lesson 4 Review on page 19.	______

Comments:

Goal 1.5 *To write the possessive form of nouns*

Date	Assignment	Score
______	**20.** Read page 20. Complete Activity A on page 20.	______
______	**21.** Read pages 21–22. Complete Activities B–D on pages 21–22.	______
______	**22.** Complete Workbook Activity 5.	______
______	**23.** Complete the Lesson 5 Review on page 23.	______
______	**24.** Complete the Chapter 1 Review on pages 24–25.	______

Comments:

Student's Signature ____________________ Date ________

Instructor's Signature ____________________ Date ________

 Basic English Grammar

TRL

Chapter 1 Self-Study Guide, Pages 1–2

Introducing the Chapter

Use the photograph to introduce the idea that everything has a name. Ask students to identify everything they see in the photograph by name. Then ask them to identify people and things in the classroom. Encourage them to use both common nouns and proper nouns and list their suggestions on the board. Ask students to make up sentences about the classroom by using the words listed on the board. Ask students if they could discuss the classroom without using such words. Then point out that all the words on the board are nouns, or words that name people, places, things, and ideas. Tell students that in Chapter 1 they will learn about different kinds of nouns.

Writing Tips, Notes, and Technology Notes

Ask volunteers to read the tips and notes that appear in the margins throughout the chapter. Then discuss them with the class.

Teacher's Resource

The AGS Teaching Strategies in English Transparencies may be used with this chapter. The transparencies add an interactive dimension to expand and enhance the *Basic English Grammar* program content.

Career Interest Inventory

The AGS Harrington-O'Shea Career Decision-Making System–Revised (CDM) may be used with this chapter. Students can use the CDM to explore their interests and identify careers. The CDM defines career areas that are indicated by students' responses on the inventory.

Lesson at a Glance

Chapter 1 Lesson 1

Overview This lesson defines a noun, a collective noun, and a compound noun and gives examples of each.

Objectives

- To define noun, collective noun, and compound noun.
- To provide examples of nouns that name a person, place, thing, and idea, collective nouns, and compound nouns.

Student Pages 1–5

Teacher's Resource Library 

Workbook Activity 1

Activity 1

Alternative Activity 1

Vocabulary

collective noun
compound noun
hyphen
noun

Warm-Up Activity

Point to people and objects in the classroom and have students name them. Write the names on the board. Tell students that the names for people and objects are nouns. Explain to them that the names of places and ideas are also nouns. Explain that this lesson will help students identify different kinds of nouns.

Give small student groups two minutes to brainstorm a list of nouns. Encourage them to list nouns that describe people, things, places, and ideas. If necessary facilitate the brainstorm session by providing examples, such as *firefighter, helmet, fire station,* and *bravery.* Ask each group to share nouns from their list with the class. Write the nouns on the board or chart paper.

Lesson  What Is a Noun?

Noun
A word that names a person, a place, a thing, or an idea

A **noun** is a word that names a person, a place, a thing, or an idea.

EXAMPLE

Persons	hero, Maria, nurse, carpenter
Places	city, park, country, Nevada
Things	parachute, song, the Constitution
Ideas	problem, friendship, freedom, beauty

Activity A Write five nouns that belong in each group. Use the examples in parentheses as a guide.

1. time (day, second)
2. places (garage, city)
3. things (book, coat)
4. amounts (size, liter)
5. events (concert, party)
6. persons (student, man)
7. actions (race, trip)
8. qualities (honesty, trust)
9. idea (freedom, victory)
10. characteristic (size, height)

A noun can name a part of something.

A wheel is part of a car.
A tail is part of a dog.

Activity B Here is a list of nouns. Write words that name four parts of each thing. Use the example as a guide.

Example car—wheels, engine, gears, seats

1. school
2. forest
3. newspaper
4. library
5. garden

2 Teaching the Lesson

With the class, read the definition of the word *noun.* Ask a volunteer to identify the four noun categories. Have the volunteer make a chart on the board with the columns labeled with the categories *persons, places, things,* and *ideas.* Refer to the list of nouns that students brainstormed in the Warm-Up Activity. Provide an opportunity for every student to choose one word from the list and write it in the appropriate column on the chart.

Explain to students that some nouns have special features. Have students read the definitions of *collective noun* and *compound noun.* Have them read the examples of these nouns and give additional examples. Finally, read aloud the definition of *hyphen.* Explain that one use of a hyphen is to join the parts of a compound noun, as in *father-in-law* and *self-confidence.*

Activity A

Ask students to read the examples in parentheses and consider how the words fit in the group by making up a sentence such as "A garage is a place where people keep their cars."

Collective noun
The name of a group of people, places, or things

Compound noun
Two words joined together to form one new noun

Collective nouns get their name from the word *collect,* which means "to gather together." Collective nouns include names that gather people, places, things, or ideas into groups.

A **collective noun** is the name of a group of people or things.

EXAMPLE	
Groups of People	crew, chorus, U.S. Navy
Groups of Things	litter, bunch, swarm

Activity C Find nouns that name groups of things or people in these sentences. Write the nouns on your paper.

1. The baseball team practiced every day.
2. Alex's club had a meeting every Thursday.
3. The whole neighborhood went to the picnic.
4. Carla decided to join the Peace Corps.
5. The jury found the man innocent.

A **compound noun** is two words joined together to form one new noun.

EXAMPLE

news + paper = newspaper
flash + light = flashlight
basket + ball = basketball

Activity D Write a sentence using each of these compound nouns. Be sure to capitalize the first word and use end punctuation. Underline the nouns in your sentences.

1. sunflower
2. highway
3. suitcase
4. toothpick
5. classroom
6. treetop
7. sunlight
8. moonbeam
9. blueberry
10. waterfall

3 Reinforce and Extend

LEARNING STYLES

Interpersonal/Group Learning

Tell students that collective nouns are used in reference to sports, animals, and the arts. Provide examples, such as *team* for sports, *herd* for animals, and *orchestra* for the arts. Divide the class into groups. Have the groups choose a category and brainstorm a list of collective nouns related to the category. Have the groups share their lists.

Activity A Answers

Answers will vary. Possible answers follow. **1.** hour, week, year, month, minute **2.** library, country, store, school, office **3.** sweater, desk, dog, jacket, shirt **4.** dollar, cent, pint, quart, acre **5.** play, game, parade, holiday, feast **6.** woman, child, baby, infant, teacher **7.** decision, stroll, vacation, jog, sprint **8.** beauty, truth, sincerity, fairness, kindness **9.** loyalty, charity, evil, hate, success **10.** width, length, depth, weight, color

Activity B

Have a volunteer read the examples of nouns that name a part of something. Ask students to name other parts of a car and a dog. List the words and point out that they are all nouns. Read the directions together.

Activity B Answers

Answers will vary. Possible answers follow. **1.** teacher, desk, classroom, library **2.** trees, leaves, flowers, stream **3.** comics, articles, sports, news **4.** books, shelves, librarian, magazines **5.** soil, flowers, vegetables, insects

Activity C

Encourage students to review the examples in the lesson, if necessary, as they do the exercise.

Activity C Answers

1. team **2.** club **3.** neighborhood **4.** Peace Corps **5.** jury

Activity D

Remind students that a complete sentence must have a subject, which may be a compound noun, and a predicate. Have volunteers use the example compound words in sentences.

Activity D Answers

Answers will vary. Sample sentences follow. **1.** Sarah picked the sunflower from the garden. **2.** We drove down the highway to the mall. **3.** Mr. Estevez packed his suitcase for the trip. **4.** Is that a toothpick by the cash register? **5.** The students filed into the classroom.

Writing Practice

List these general nouns on the board.

appliances	games
music	art

Ask students to brainstorm specific nouns related to one of the general nouns. Have students write a short paragraph using the general noun. Then have students rewrite the paragraph using the specific nouns. Discuss with students which paragraph is more interesting and why.

Activity E

Remind students that some nouns may be compound, hyphenated, and two or more separate but related words. Ask students to use a dictionary to find examples of compound nouns, hyphenated nouns, and nouns that are two words.

Activity E Answers

brother, sister-in-law, weekend, Jamal, sleeping bag, midnight, earthquake, house, rumble, lightning, thunderstorm, raindrops, roof, window, bedroom

Activity F

Read the directions together. Repeat the reminders given for Activity E. Have students share the nouns they list.

Activity F Answers

1. Amanda, team **2.** Nicole, Ramon, committee, Jamison Park **3.** Kaitlin, bicycle, library, school **4.** author, Stephen King **5.** Mrs. Wong, White House, mid-August

Hyphen
A short dash between parts of a word

A noun can be a group of related words. Sometimes the noun has a **hyphen.**

A hyphen is a short dash between parts of a word. We use a hyphen to join parts of words such as *mid-November* or *father-in-law.*

Writing Tip

Choose specific nouns to make your writing more interesting. Start with a general noun such as *dog* and ask yourself, "What breed of dog?" The answer might be *collie, beagle,* or *spaniel.*

Other groups of related words without hyphens are also nouns.

Example

swimming pool	Abraham Lincoln
United States	bus stop

Activity E Find 15 nouns in this paragraph and write them on your paper.

> Because his brother and sister-in-law were visiting for the weekend, Jamal had to sleep in a sleeping bag. He woke suddenly at midnight. "It's an earthquake," he thought. He felt the house shake, and he heard a loud rumble. When he saw the lightning, however, he knew it was just a thunderstorm. Soon he heard the raindrops pounding on the roof. He ran to close the window in his bedroom.

Activity F Find the nouns in these sentences and write them on your paper.

1. Amanda swims on a team.
2. Nicole and Ramon formed a committee to clean up Jamison Park.
3. Kaitlin rides her bicycle to the library after school.
4. Her favorite author is Stephen King.
5. Mrs. Wong visited the White House in mid-August.

At Home

Have students identify items in their home that are compound nouns. Provide suggestions, such as can opener, tabletop, backyard, and hair dryer. They may wish to include in their list items they see in the yard and garage as well as in the house or apartment. Ask students to bring the lists of compound nouns to the class and compare their lists with those of their classmates.

Teacher Alert

Sometimes hyphenated nouns such as *pass-through* are called hyphenated compounds, and two-word nouns such as *magnetic pole* are called open compounds. Compound words such as *butterfly* are then called closed compounds. Some students may find the use of the terms *hyphenated compound, open compound,* and *closed compound* helpful when they are identifying nouns made up of two or more words.

Career Connection

Point out that many compound nouns name businesses, work locations, and careers, for example, *insurance company, newsroom,* and *pastry chef.* Have students choose and identify as many compound nouns as they can think of related to a business, work location, or career of their choice. Ask students to tell whether each word is a closed compound, an open compound, or a hyphenated compound.

1. Write the nouns in this paragraph on your paper.

 On Saturday, Tamika put on her running shoes. She was going to jog along the river. She wanted to see the new statue of Harriet Tubman near the waterfall. However, she noticed a crowd on the path near the bridge, and she saw the mayor. Tamika decided to return another day when fewer people would be along her route.

2. Write five sentences about your favorite activity. Be sure that each sentence begins with a capital letter and has correct end punctuation. Underline all the nouns.

Where To Find It

Dictionary

A dictionary contains lists of words, arranged in alphabetical order. It can help you understand unfamiliar words and can tell you how to spell words correctly.

Each word defined in a dictionary is an entry.

> **hor·net** \'hȯr-nət\ *n* [ME *hernet,* fr. OE *hyrnet;* akin to OHG *hornaz* hornet, L *crabro*] (bef. 12c): any of the larger social wasps (family Vespidæ)—compare YELLOW JACKET

An entry word appears in bold and is divided into syllables. The phonetic spelling appears in brackets after the word to help you pronounce it. The abbreviations following the phonetic spelling tell you the part of speech for the entry word. The definition of the word follows the part of speech.

Look carefully at the entry word. Sometimes it has more than one pronunciation and more than one definition. The word may also be more than one part of speech. Most dictionaries also include the history of some words.

To find entry words, use the guide words at the top of each page. The guide words are the first and last words on the page. All the words listed on that page will come alphabetically between the two guide words.

1. Would you find the noun *horse* on a page with the guide words *horn* and *hose?* Explain why or why not.
2. Look up the word *recipe.* Write its meanings.
3. Choose a word you spelled incorrectly on a test. Look it up in the dictionary, and write its correct spelling.

Lesson 1 Review Answers

1. Saturday, Tamika, running shoes, river, statue, Harriet Tubman, waterfall, crowd, path, bridge, mayor, Tamika, day, people, route **2.** Students' sentences will vary. Check for capital letters, correct end punctuation, and underlined nouns.

Where To Find It

Write a dictionary entry on the board or on a transparency. Label each part of the entry with a number. After students have read the feature, have them record the numbers on a sheet of paper and name each feature. Provide dictionaries for students to use as they write responses to questions 2 and 3.

Answers to Where To Find It: 1. Yes, because *horse* falls between *horn* and *hose* alphabetically. **2.** Answers should match the definitions for *recipe* in your classroom dictionary. **3.** Answers will vary. Check that students have spelled their words correctly.

Learning Styles

Logical/Mathematical

Have students use magazine or advertisement pictures to depict compound nouns. For example, they might use pictures of a stick of butter and a housefly to represent the compound word *butterfly.* Ask students to tape five sets of pictures to a sheet of paper. They can challenge partners to use the picture clues to identify the compound nouns represented.

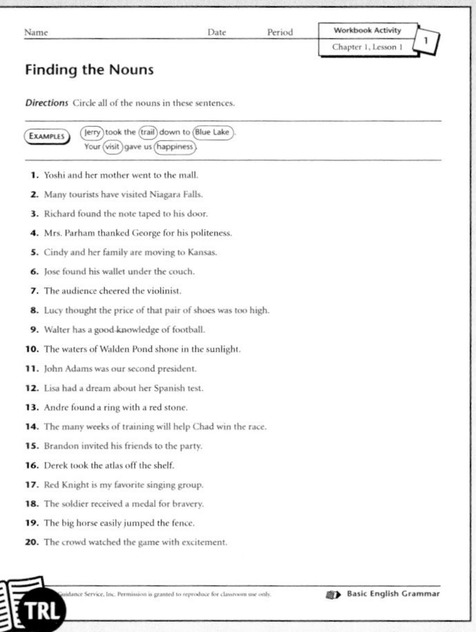

Name Date Period Workbook Activity 1 Chapter 1, Lesson 1

Finding the Nouns

Directions Circle all of the nouns in these sentences.

EXAMPLES (Jerry) took the (trail) down to (Blue Lake). Your (visit) gave us (happiness).

1. Yoshi and her mother went to the mall.
2. Many tourists have visited Niagara Falls.
3. Richard found the note taped to his door.
4. Mrs. Parham thanked George for his politeness.
5. Cindy and her family are moving to Kansas.
6. Jose found his wallet under the couch.
7. The audience cheered the violinist.
8. Lucy thought the price of that pair of shoes was too high.
9. Walter has a good knowledge of football.
10. The waters of Walden Pond shone in the sunlight.
11. John Adams was our second president.
12. Lisa had a dream about her Spanish test.
13. Andre found a ring with a red stone.
14. The many weeks of training will help Chad win the race.
15. Brandon invited his friends to the party.
16. Derek took the atlas off the shelf.
17. Red Knight is my favorite singing group.
18. The soldier received a medal for bravery.
19. The big horse easily jumped the fence.
20. The crowd watched the game with excitement.

 Basic English Grammar

TRL

Workbook Activity 1

Name Date Period Activity 1 Chapter 1, Lesson 1

Identifying Nouns

Directions Write one noun that belongs in each group. Study the examples in parentheses.

EXAMPLE family (sister, brother) mother

1. idea (peace, friendship) ____
2. place (backyard, street) ____
3. action (war, contest) ____
4. characteristic (size, height) ____
5. amount (inch, ton) ____
6. thing (ball, computer) ____
7. time (day, year) ____
8. quality (dignity, strength) ____
9. person (father, helper) ____
10. event (concert, program) ____

Directions Circle the collective nouns in the list.

EXAMPLES rock (group) (class)

11. trunk
12. team
13. flock
14. apple
15. herd
16. bunch
17. telephone
18. collection
19. assortment
20. carton

 Basic English Grammar

TRL

Activity 1

Lesson at a Glance

Chapter 1 Lesson 2

Overview This lesson defines common and proper nouns and explains how they differ.

Objectives

- To distinguish between common and proper nouns.
- To capitalize proper nouns.
- To understand the use of abbreviations.

Student Pages 6–11

Teacher's Resource Library 

Workbook Activity 2

Activity 2

Alternative Activity 2

Vocabulary

abbreviation
common noun
proper noun

1 Warm-Up Activity

Write the following words in a column on the board: *country, team, title, name, street.* In a second column write the following words: *New York Yankees, Lord of the Rings, Canada, Main Street, Juanita.* Have students form pairs and ask them to match up a word from column 1 with a word from column 2. Invite volunteers to write their solutions on the board. Ask students to explain why they matched up the words as they did. (*Canada is the name of a country.*) Encourage them to point out how the paired words differ. (*Words from column 2 are capitalized and name something particular.*) Point out that this is the important distinction between common nouns and proper nouns as described in Lesson 2.

Lesson 2 Common and Proper Nouns

Common noun
The name of a general type of person, place, thing, or idea

Proper noun
The name of a particular person, place, thing, or idea

A **common noun** is the name of a general type of person, place, thing, or idea.

A **proper noun** is the name of a particular person, place, thing, or idea.

Capitalize a common noun only if it is the first word of a sentence or part of a title. Always capitalize a proper noun.

EXAMPLE

Common Nouns	Proper Nouns
school	Springvale High School
museum	Museum of Modern Art
astronaut	John Glenn
president	Thomas Jefferson
state	Idaho
month	December
country	Canada
city	Atlanta
river	Mississippi River
writer	Edgar Allan Poe

Writing Tip

President can be a common or a proper noun. Tino is *president* of the class. Today *President Juarez* will speak. Think about whether you are naming the job or a specific person. If you are naming a specific president, it is a proper noun.

Activity A Write these nouns on your paper. Write a proper noun next to each common noun. Write a common noun next to each proper noun.

Example university—Harvard University
Alaska—state

1. teacher
2. holiday
3. team
4. newspaper
5. singer
6. Bugs Bunny
7. Super Bowl
8. France
9. Atlantic Ocean
10. Ohio

2 Teaching the Lesson

Have a volunteer read aloud the definitions of *common nouns* and *proper nouns* given on this page. Write the words *general* and *particular* on the board. Explain that the term *general* refers to the big picture; *particular* focuses on a particular person, place, thing, or idea. Point out that nouns naming particular items should be capitalized. Students should understand that they have compiled lists of common and proper nouns.

Write *Mister Smith* on the board. Ask students for another way to write *Mister Smith* (*Mr. Smith*). Point out that *Mr.* is a shortened form of a word, or an *abbreviation.* Lead students to understand that many abbreviations are parts of proper nouns and must be capitalized.

Invite a volunteer to write *Raiders of the Lost Ark* on the board. Explain that titles are considered proper nouns. Point out that short words, such as *of, to,* and *the,* remain lowercase.

Activity A

Before students complete Activity A on their own, have partners work together to write their own list of proper nouns to go with each common noun listed in the example box on this page.

Activity A Answers

Answers will vary. Possible answers follow. **1.** Mrs. Lee **2.** Fourth of July **3.** Cincinnati Bengals **4.** *The New York Times* **5.** Barry Manilow **6.** cartoon character **7.** football game **8.** country **9.** sea **10.** state

Activity B Write these nouns on your paper. Capitalize the proper nouns. A proper noun names a particular person, place, thing, or idea.

1. actor
2. brazil
3. lake
4. jupiter
5. nathan
6. road
7. memorial day
8. mr. wong
9. colorado river
10. miami

The name of a particular place is a proper noun. The name of a country, state, city, street, or building is a proper noun.

EXAMPLE

Common Nouns	Proper Nouns
city	San Francisco
river	the Nile River
street	Lee Street
apartment	Apartment 406
route	Route 50
high school	Montgomery High School
park	Central Park

Activity C Write these sentences on your paper. Capitalize the proper nouns. Every sentence will have at least one proper noun.

1. Roberto mailed a package to houston, texas.
2. His friend lives at 602 river drive, apartment 119.
3. Last year roberto went to a new high school.
4. He liked northview senior high very much.
5. I met josie at the corner of schoolhouse road and high street.

Activity B

Ask students to write the answers to the following questions. *Who is someone you admire? What is the name of your city or town and state? Where do you go to school? What sport or leisure activity do you enjoy?* Reread each question. Have students share their answers and tell whether they capitalized an answer. Have students complete Activity B and discuss answers.

Activity B Answers

1. actor **2.** Brazil **3.** lake **4.** Jupiter **5.** Nathan **6.** road **7.** Memorial Day **8.** Mr. Wong **9.** Colorado River **10.** Miami

Activity C

Before students complete Activity C, have them write their own list of proper nouns to go with each common noun listed in the example box on this page. Then have students take turns reading their answers. As students do Activity C, emphasize that some sentences may have more than one proper noun and that each part of a proper noun made up of more than one word should be capitalized.

Activity C Answers

1. Roberto mailed a package to Houston, Texas. **2.** His friend lives at 602 River Drive, Apartment 119. **3.** Last year Roberto went to a new high school. **4.** He liked Northview Senior High very much. **5.** I met Josie at the corner of Schoolhouse Road and High Street.

3 Reinforce and Extend

LEARNING STYLES

Auditory/Verbal

Have students form pairs to write sentences that include proper nouns. Then divide the class into two equal teams. Ask the first student in Team 1 to read a sentence. Have the first student in Team 2 name the proper noun in that sentence. If he or she fails to answer correctly, the next student in line should try. Continue until all the students on both teams have had a turn reading and answering.

Teacher Alert

Point out that abbreviations of the names of organizations and agencies often consist of the first letters of the words making up their complete titles.

These abbreviations are capitalized and generally do not include periods. Write the following abbreviations on the board, and ask students if they know what the letters stand for: IRS, NBC, YMCA, INS, UN. (*Internal Revenue Service, National Broadcasting Company, Young Men's Christian Association, Immigration and Naturalization Service, United Nations*) Invite students to think of other familiar abbreviations formed from initial letters.

Activity D

Draw the outline of an envelope on the board. Invite students to write their name and address in the top left corner of the envelope and the name and address of a friend or relative in the middle of the envelope. Have the class check to see that the volunteers have capitalized the address properly and used abbreviations where appropriate.

Activity D Answers

1. Mr. Joe Keller
   Route 2, Box 206
   Marshall, IA 50152
2. Mrs. Karen Blackhorse
   99 Norris Ave.
   Waterloo, NY 13165
3. Mr. C. J. Diaz
   1580 Eaton Way
   Burke, VA 22015
4. Dr. Dionne Williams
   41 Maple Lane
   Lyon, CA 94104
5. Ms. Holli Rezek
   3189 Regent St.
   Ocean Springs, MS 39564

Abbreviation
A short form of a word

An **abbreviation** is a short form of a word. Capitalize the abbreviation if the whole word is a proper noun.

Example

Proper Noun	**Abbreviation**
New York	NY
Doctor Martinez	Dr. Martinez
Dearborn Avenue	Dearborn Ave.

Activity D Most of the words in an address are proper nouns. Write these addresses on your paper. Capitalize all of the proper nouns. Use abbreviations when you can. Use the U.S. Postal Service abbreviations for states.

1. mr. joe keller
   route 2, box 206
   marshall, iowa 50152
2. mrs. karen blackhorse
   99 norris avenue
   waterloo, new york 13165
3. mr. c. j. diaz
   1580 eaton way
   burke, virginia 22015
4. doctor dionne williams
   41 maple lane
   lyon, california 94104
5. ms. holli rezek
   3189 regent street
   ocean springs, mississippi 39564

Names of parts of the country are proper nouns. However, directions are common nouns.

Example

Part of the Country	I visited the West last winter.
Direction	Susan will drive north next summer.

Global Connection

Encourage students with relatives and friends in various parts of the world to write the addresses of these people when presenting Activity D. Have students note the differences in the way foreign addresses are written.

Activity E Write these sentences on your paper. Capitalize the proper nouns. Not every sentence will have a proper noun.

1. When alex graduated from high school, he took a trip to the south.
2. On the first day, he drove 300 miles southwest.
3. He started in baltimore and spent the first night in north carolina.
4. On the second day, alex drove west to visit some friends in tennessee.
5. The next day alex headed southeast to florida.

The name of a language and a particular school course are proper nouns. The name of a school subject is a common noun.

Proper Nouns	Common Nouns
German	language
Photography II	art
Introduction to Algebra	mathematics

Activity F Write the word or words that should appear in each sentence to make it correct.

1. Karl got an A in (English, english).
2. Next year Alex is taking (math and history, Math and History).
3. Jennifer signed up for (math I, Math I).
4. Who teaches your (science, Science) class this year?
5. Miguel decided to take (introduction to music, Introduction to Music) for extra credit.
6. Dana signed up for (French, french).
7. Do you enjoy your (art, Art) class?
8. It is usually warm in (hawaii, Hawaii).
9. I hope to visit the (South, south) soon.
10. In college Judy took (art 101, Art 101).

Activity E

Point out that directional nouns can be either common or proper, according to how they are used. Invite students to use the following words in sentences, first as a part of the country and then as a direction: *northeast, south, southwest.* Write the sentences on the board as students say them, having them identify when to capitalize the directional words.

Activity E Answers

1. When Alex graduated from high school, he took a trip to the South. **2.** On the first day, he drove 300 miles southwest. **3.** He started in Baltimore and spent the first night in North Carolina. **4.** On the second day, Alex drove west to visit some friends in Tennessee. **5.** The next day Alex headed southeast to Florida.

Activity F

Ask students to think of subjects that they would like to study in school. Then ask them to invent particular course names for these subjects. Have them write their ideas on the board under the headings *Proper Nouns* and *Common Nouns.*

Activity F Answers

1. English **2.** math and history **3.** Math I **4.** science **5.** Introduction to Music **6.** French **7.** art **8.** Hawaii **9.** South **10.** Art 101

Learning Styles

Visual/Spatial

Invite students to create a chart on the board of subjects and courses that all the members of the class are taking. Have them write subject names across the top of the chart and student names down the left side of the chart. Under the subject names, have students fill in the specific courses and languages they are taking.

Career Connection

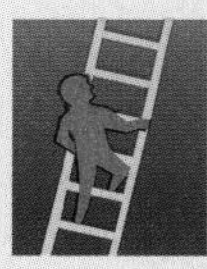

Have students find a few company names in the yellow pages of the telephone directory and write each company address as they would for the address on an envelope. Have them make up names and titles of people at the companies to use in the addresses. Remind them that when writing job application letters, they should find out the correct spelling of the full name and title of the person to whom the letter will be sent.

Activity G

Point out that words such as *a, an, the,* and *of* are usually not capitalized in titles unless they are the first word. Then ask for volunteers to write titles for the following on the board: favorite book; favorite movie; favorite TV show; favorite song. (Point out the rule for the use of underlining and quotation marks given on this page.) Help students find and correct any mistakes in capitalization in the titles. Then have them complete Activity G independently.

Activity G Answers

1. *The Red Badge of Courage* **2.** *The Sound of Music* **3.** "The Star-Spangled Banner" **4.** *The World Almanac* **5.** Dr. Martin Luther King, Jr.

Activity H

You may wish to review what students have learned about proper nouns and capitalization before having them complete this activity. Some students may also benefit from working with a partner or in a small group.

Activity H Answers

1. Wednesday, Alex, Florida **2.** Alex, Jennifer, South **3.** Mr. Wilson, Jennifer **4.** Millstream Drive **5.** Alex, French

Learning Styles

LEP/ESL

Point out that not all titles are originally written in English. Ask students learning English to contribute the names of songs, stories, movies, books, or TV shows from their own culture. Have them pair up with English-speaking students to create suitable English titles for these works. These need not be literal translations. Invite volunteers to write the titles on the board, both in the original and English versions. Check the English titles for correct capitalization.

A noun can be a title. Books, songs, movies, and people are some of the things that can have titles. A title is a proper noun. Capitalize the first word and all main words in a title.

President John Adams	*Star Wars*
A Tale of Two Cities	"America the Beautiful"

Italicize or underline the title of a movie, book, magazine, opera, or play. Put quotation marks around the title of a song, poem, or short story.

Activity G Write these titles on your paper. Capitalize the first word and all main words.

1. *the red badge of courage*
2. *the sound of music*
3. "the star-spangled banner"
4. *the world almanac*
5. dr. martin luther king, jr.

Activity H Write these sentences on your paper. Capitalize the proper nouns.

1. On wednesday, alex came home from florida.
2. "Hello, alex," jennifer said. "Welcome home from the south."
3. "Your boss, mr. wilson, called you yesterday," Jennifer told him.
4. "He wants you to report to the office on millstream drive tomorrow."
5. "Thanks," alex said. "Why are you home? I thought you were taking a french class."

Lesson 2 REVIEW

Write these nouns on your paper. Capitalize the proper nouns.

1. george washington
2. spain
3. recipe
4. labor day
5. river
6. *a separate peace*
7. french
8. city
9. albert einstein
10. president

Number your paper from 11 to 15. Read each of the following sentences. If the sentence is correct, write *correct* after the number. If the sentence has a capitalization mistake, write the sentence correctly.

11. Latisha took math 101, not math 201, this year.
12. Armando's favorite holiday is thanksgiving.
13. I'm going to take world history next year.
14. Kaitlin's grandmother lives in philadelphia.
15. Lisa and greg visited wicker park.

Writing Project

Using Nouns in Your Writing

A noun names a person, a place, a thing, or an idea. Using a variety of nouns in your writing makes it more interesting to readers.

On your paper, write 10 sentences that tell about your neighborhood. Include the names of as many buildings and items as possible. Here are some nouns you could use:

apartment	automobiles	bank	basketball hoops
birds	brick	driveway	fire hydrant
garage	grocery store	houses	lawn
neighbor	park	parking lot	road
school	street	street lights	telephone poles

Use nouns from the list, or choose others.

Underline all the nouns you used in your 10 sentences. Be sure to include proper and common nouns.

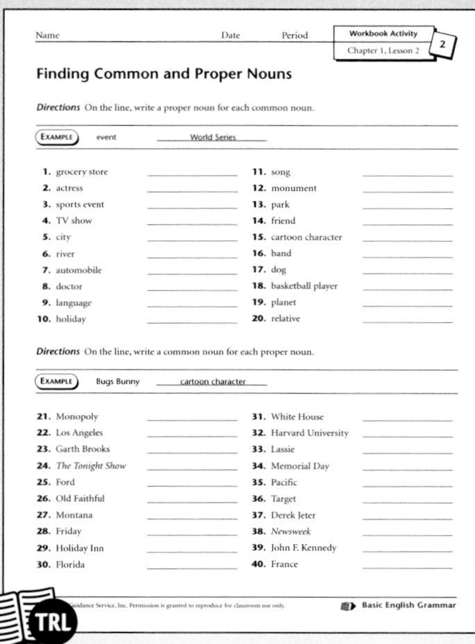

Name Date Period | Workbook Activity 2 | Chapter 1, Lesson 2

Finding Common and Proper Nouns

Directions On the line, write a proper noun for each common noun.

EXAMPLE event World Series

1. grocery store	______	**11.** song	______
2. actress	______	**12.** monument	______
3. sports event	______	**13.** park	______
4. TV show	______	**14.** friend	______
5. city	______	**15.** cartoon character	______
6. river	______	**16.** band	______
7. automobile	______	**17.** dog	______
8. doctor	______	**18.** basketball player	______
9. language	______	**19.** planet	______
10. holiday	______	**20.** relative	______

Directions On the line, write a common noun for each proper noun.

EXAMPLE Bugs Bunny cartoon character

21. Monopoly	______	**31.** White House	______
22. Los Angeles	______	**32.** Harvard University	______
23. Garth Brooks	______	**33.** Lassie	______
24. *The Tonight Show*	______	**34.** Memorial Day	______
25. Ford	______	**35.** Pacific	______
26. Old Faithful	______	**36.** Target	______
27. Montana	______	**37.** Derek Jeter	______
28. Friday	______	**38.** *Newsweek*	______
29. Holiday Inn	______	**39.** John F. Kennedy	______
30. Florida	______	**40.** France	______

 Basic English Grammar

TRL

Workbook Activity 2

Name Date Period | Activity 2 | Chapter 1, Lesson 2

Common and Proper Nouns and Capitalization

Directions Underline the proper nouns in this list of words.

EXAMPLE school Valley Elementary School

1. statue	**8.** Colorado River	**15.** beauty
2. Statue of Liberty	**9.** letter carrier	**16.** Dr. Pascal
3. Mexico	**10.** United States Postal Service	**17.** doctor
4. liberty	**11.** Engine Company #4	**18.** Helen Keller
5. May	**12.** New Year's Eve	**19.** author
6. Steven Spielberg	**13.** Sleeping Beauty	**20.** truth
7. river	**14.** skateboard	

Directions In these sentences, underline the nouns that should be capitalized. Remember: A common noun is capitalized only when it is the first word of a sentence or part of a title, but a proper noun is always capitalized.

EXAMPLE the children smiled when mrs. goodtree walked her tiny dog.

21. birthdays are very special to natalie and her sister frances.
22. mother was reading the book *goodnight moon* to james.
23. tomorrow the falcons will play against the tigers at springdale high school.
24. texas and alaska are the two biggest states in the united states of america.
25. For halloween, howard wore a cape just like superman's.
26. anna likes to pretend that she is jennifer lopez.
27. The greenes are going to washington in march for the cherry blossom festival.
28. The island of maui is part of hawaii, located in the pacific ocean.
29. The newspaper's new name would be the *daily herald*.
30. george washington was the first president of our country.

 Basic English Grammar

TRL

Activity 2

Lesson 2 Review Answers

1. George Washington 2. Spain 3. recipe 4. Labor Day 5. river 6. *A Separate Peace* 7. French 8. city 9. Albert Einstein 10. president 11. Latisha took Math 101, not Math 201, this year. 12. Armando's favorite holiday is Thanksgiving. 13. Correct 14. Kaitlin's grandmother lives in Philadelphia. 15. Lisa and Greg visited Wicker Park.

Writing Project

Point out that writing is often more interesting when the nouns create a precise picture. *Sparrows twittered on the telephone pole,* for instance, gives a sharper image than *Some birds twittered on the telephone pole.* Remind students that using proper nouns is one way of bringing a sentence to life. In the writing exercise that follows, urge students to identify parks, schools, stores, streets, and neighbors by their proper names.

Answers to Writing Project: Students' sentences will vary. Check to be sure that students have underlined all of the nouns in their sentences.

Learning Styles

Body/Kinesthetic

Divide the class into small groups and ask students to choose five nouns that they could describe by means of mime or physical gestures. These should include at least two proper nouns (places, titles, and famous people). Collect their lists and distribute suitable words to a designated performer from each group. Performers should attempt to convey the meaning of their words silently to their group within a designated time limit. Keep score on the board.

Lesson at a Glance

Chapter 1 Lesson 3

Overview This lesson explains the difference between concrete and abstract nouns.

Objective

- To distinguish between concrete and abstract nouns.

Student Pages 12–14

Teacher's Resource Library 

Workbook Activity 3

Activity 3

Alternative Activity 3

Vocabulary

abstract noun
concrete noun

Warm-Up Activity

Write the following words on the board: *peace, radiator, Emily, wonder, sadness, island.* Remind students that these are all nouns: each word names a person, place, thing, or idea. Then ask them how they would divide these six words into two groups of three words each. Lead students to understand that *peace, wonder,* and *sadness* are abstract nouns, representing ideas that cannot be seen or touched.

Teaching the Lesson

Invite a volunteer to read the definitions of concrete nouns and abstract nouns. Point out that one way to test whether a noun is concrete or abstract is to ask the following questions: *Does it name an object that takes up space? Can I see, hear, smell, taste, or feel it?* If the answer to either one of these questions is yes, the noun is concrete. Have students ask these questions about nouns in this section as they complete the activities.

Lesson 3 Concrete and Abstract Nouns

Concrete noun
A word that names something you can see or touch

Abstract noun
A word that names an idea that you cannot see or touch

A noun may be abstract or concrete.

A **concrete noun** is a word that names something you can see or touch. The name of a person, place, or thing is a concrete noun.

An **abstract noun** is a word that names something you can think about or talk about. You cannot see it or touch it. An abstract noun is an idea.

EXAMPLE

Concrete Nouns	Abstract Nouns
money	expense
clock	time
college	education
painting	art

Activity A Read each pair of nouns. On your paper, write the abstract noun in each pair.

Example apple appetite appetite

1. teacher learning
2. bravery soldier
3. steel strength
4. value dollar
5. spirit cheerleader
6. doctor health
7. humor smile
8. flag freedom
9. pain bruise
10. family love

Activity A

To be sure students grasp the concepts of abstract nouns and concrete nouns, you may wish to do the first two or three items orally as a class. After students complete the activity, encourage them to make up their own related pairs of abstract and concrete nouns. Invite students to read their word pairs aloud and have the class identify the abstract noun in each pair.

Activity A Answers

1. learning **2.** bravery **3.** strength **4.** value **5.** spirit **6.** health **7.** humor **8.** freedom **9.** pain **10.** love

Activity B Find the nouns in these sentences. Write them on your paper. Identify each one as *concrete* or *abstract*.

1. Alex valued his friendship with Adam.
2. Tonya had too much energy in class.
3. You could see the happiness on his face as he crossed the finish line.
4. Hard work and a little luck got him the contract.
5. The car wash was a success.
6. Kim earned the respect of her teachers.
7. The students clapped with pride as the team marched onto the field.
8. The witness promised to tell the truth.
9. Tears of joy ran down her face.
10. Julio stared at his brother with admiration.

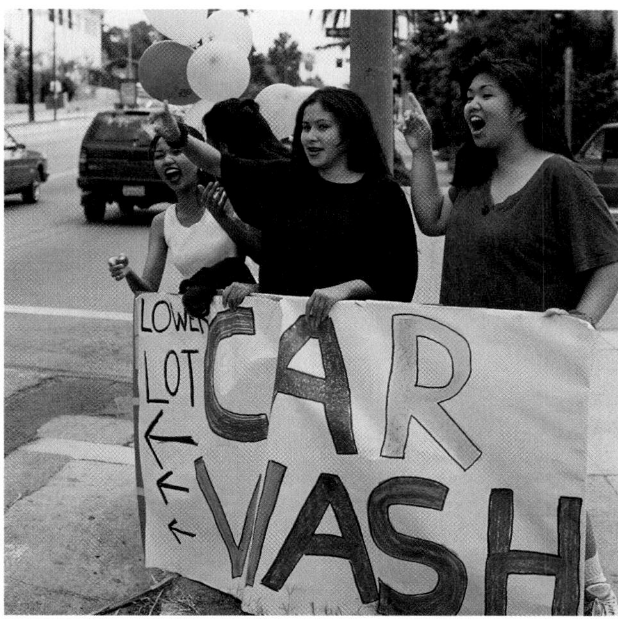

The girls' hard work made the event successful.

Activity B

Encourage students to tell why they have identified a noun as concrete or abstract. In sentence 1, for example, students should be able to say that *Alex* and *Adam* are concrete nouns because you can see and touch people. *Friendship* is abstract because it represents a quality. After students have completed the activity, invite them to explain their answers.

Activity B Answers

1. Alex (concrete), friendship (abstract), Adam (concrete) 2. Tonya (concrete), energy (abstract), class (concrete) 3. happiness (abstract), face (concrete), finish line (concrete) 4. work (abstract), luck (abstract), contract (concrete) 5. car wash (concrete), success (abstract) 6. Kim (concrete), respect (abstract), teachers (concrete) 7. students (concrete), pride (abstract), team (concrete), field (concrete) 8. witness (concrete), truth (abstract) 9. Tears (concrete), joy (abstract), face (concrete) 10. Julio (concrete), brother (concrete), admiration (abstract)

3 Reinforce and Extend

Learning Styles

Logical/Mathematical

Invite students to devise a series of simple symbols to identify concrete nouns. For example, a square might indicate that the noun represents an object that takes up space; an eye might indicate that the object described is visible. Have students test their symbols on the nouns in this lesson. Write a list of words on the board, and invite students to mark concrete nouns with the appropriate symbols.

Lesson 3 Review Answers

1. Alex Jones (concrete), car (concrete) 2. week (abstract), amount (abstract), money (concrete) 3. money (concrete), bank (concrete), interest (concrete) 4. decision (abstract), car (concrete) 5. car (concrete), mileage (abstract) 6. Alex (concrete), ad (concrete), newspaper (concrete) 7. phone number (concrete), appointment (abstract) 8. Alex (concrete), automobiles (concrete), weeks (abstract) 9. car (concrete), price (abstract) 10. Alex (concrete), feeling (abstract), seller (concrete)

Have students exchange their paragraphs with a partner for peer editing.

Students' paragraphs will vary. Check to be sure that students have underlined the nouns and identified them correctly.

Vocabulary Builder

Point out that the word *sight,* which involves vision, is spelled like *light.* Suggest to students that since light is necessary for vision, they may find the following rhyme useful to help them distinguish between *site* and *sight:*

You'll need a light
To get a good sight!

Answers to Vocabulary Builder: 1. site 2. sight 3. site 4. sight 5. site

Learning Styles

Visual/Spatial

Select a variety of pictures to which students are likely to respond—images of war, beauty, tranquility, and ugliness. These might be photographs from magazines, reproductions of fine art, or even cartoons. Hold them up one by one for the students to look at. For each picture, ask students to write an abstract noun. Help them find nouns by asking "What mood or feeling does this picture give you?" After they have seen the pictures, invite volunteers to share their lists of nouns with the class.

Lesson 3 REVIEW

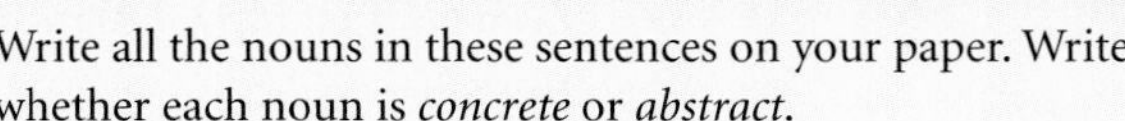

Write all the nouns in these sentences on your paper. Write whether each noun is *concrete* or *abstract.*

1. Alex Jones wanted a car very much.
2. Every week he saved a certain amount of money.
3. He put his money in a bank and received interest.
4. A decision about a car would not be easy.
5. He wanted a small car that would get good gas mileage.
6. Alex saw an ad in the newspaper.
7. He called the phone number and made an appointment.
8. Alex looked at automobiles for weeks.
9. Then he found the perfect car. The price was right.
10. Alex had a good feeling. He trusted the seller.

On another sheet of paper, write a paragraph about a pet you own or would like to own. Be sure to describe the animal's characteristics and why you like or would like the animal. When you have finished, underline the nouns. Identify each one as *concrete* or *abstract.*

Vocabulary Builder

Site* and *Sight

The words *site* and *sight* are both nouns. They have different meanings.

Site is a place. *We will build our house on that site.*
Sight refers to vision. *The sunset was a beautiful sight.*

On your paper, write the word that correctly completes each sentence.

1. We wanted a (site, sight) with a view of the ocean.
2. Jean was a lovely (site, sight) in her new dress.
3. What is the (site, sight) for the 2008 Olympics?
4. The eye doctor will check your (site, sight).
5. The old parking lot was a perfect (site, sight) for a skateboard park.

Name Date Period — Workbook Activity 3, Chapter 1, Lesson 3

Identifying Concrete and Abstract Nouns

Directions On the lines, write three abstract nouns that belong in each group. Look at the examples in parentheses.

EXAMPLE virtues honesty generosity truth

1. action (pace, process) ______ ______ ______
2. quality (heroism, confidence) ______ ______ ______
3. quantity (ounce, weight) ______ ______ ______
4. time (hour, Thursday) ______ ______ ______
5. feeling (joy, sorrow) ______ ______ ______

Directions On the lines, write three concrete nouns that belong in each group. Look at the examples in parentheses.

EXAMPLE food bread green beans pasta

6. drink (lemonade, milk) ______ ______ ______
7. tree (oak, pine) ______ ______ ______
8. fabric (linen, polyester) ______ ______ ______
9. animal (moose, panda) ______ ______ ______
10. tool (hammer, ax) ______ ______ ______

 Basic English Grammar

TRL

Workbook Activity 3

Name Date Period — Activity 3, Chapter 1, Lesson 3

Concrete and Abstract Nouns

Directions Underline the nouns in each sentence. Above each noun, write an *A* if it is an abstract noun or a *C* if it is a concrete noun. Remember: Concrete nouns are words that name things you can see or touch. Abstract nouns are words that name ideas that you cannot see or touch.

EXAMPLE C C A — Julie read a book about education.

1. Stacy experienced loneliness at her new school.
2. The mayor disagreed about the large expense.
3. The blister on my foot caused much pain.
4. Her new job took too much time.
5. Jesse had confidence when he shared his idea with the class.
6. Regular exercise can improve your health.
7. The talent show was a huge success.
8. Freedom of speech is an important civil right.
9. Annie's role in the play required lots of energy.
10. Friendship can be the best source of happiness.
11. We will celebrate our independence in July.
12. In his excitement to leave, Frank left his coat at Gerald's house.
13. Maya's grandfather will tell you about the courage of the pioneers.
14. Louis loves the emotions expressed in this poem.
15. The campaign increased my interest in politics.

 Basic English Grammar

TRL

Activity 3

Lesson 4 Singular and Plural Nouns

> ***Singular noun***
> *The name of one person, place, thing, or idea*
>
> ***Plural noun***
> *The name of more than one person, place, thing, or idea*

A **singular noun** is the name of one person, place, thing, or idea.

A **plural noun** is the name of more than one person, place, thing, or idea.

Most plural nouns end in *-s* or *-es*. When the plural noun ends in *-es*, the plural has an extra syllable. Say aloud the words below to hear the difference between them.

EXAMPLE

Singular Nouns	Plural Nouns
committee	committees
peach	peaches
leash	leashes

Activity A Write the plural of each singular noun on your paper. Add either *-s* or *-es*. Say the plural aloud. You will hear the extra syllable when the plural noun ends in *-es*.

Example town—towns guess—guesses

1. address
2. car
3. school
4. ladder
5. mountain
6. wish
7. idea
8. tax
9. patch
10. icicle

Activity B Number your paper from 1 to 10. Next to each number, write whether the word is *singular* or *plural*.

1. bosses
2. nations
3. fuss
4. majority
5. agents
6. crowds
7. doctor
8. Alex
9. circus
10. Elm Street

Activity A

Have students say the singular and plural form of each word. Point out that the end sounds will give them a clue to the word's spelling.

Activity A Answers

1. addresses 2. cars 3. schools
4. ladders 5. mountains 6. wishes
7. ideas 8. taxes 9. patches 10. icicles

Activity B

Suggest that students put the words *a* or *an* before each noun. If it sounds correct, the word is probably singular.

Activity B Answers

1. plural 2. plural 3. singular
4. singular 5. plural 6. plural
7. singular 8. singular 9. singular
10. singular

Lesson at a Glance

Chapter 1 Lesson 4

Overview This lesson presents singular and plural nouns and explains how they are formed

Objectives

- To write the plural form of regular and irregular nouns.
- To distinguish between singular and plural nouns.
- To locate and correct misspelled plural nouns in sentences.

Student Pages 15–19

Teacher's Resource Library 

Workbook Activity 4
Activity 4
Alternative Activity 4

Vocabulary

plural noun
singular noun

1 Warm-Up Activity

Before starting the lesson, write the words *singular* and *plural* on the board. Elicit from students that *singular* means "one" and *plural* "more than one." Ask them why it might be important to have both singular and plural forms. Suggest that early people would have found the distinction useful. (The difference between "man with club coming this way" and "men with clubs" might have been a matter of life and death!)

2 Teaching the Lesson

Write some of the words from this page on the board—*car, idea, boss,* and *address.* Ask students to make a rule about creating the plural form of these nouns. (*Create the plural by adding* -s *or* -es.) Now write the following words on the board: *sky, knife, man, sheep.* Ask students to apply the same rule. Lead them to understand that there are several ways of creating plurals in English. Some of these involve rules; some require memory. This lesson will help students understand how to form several types of plural nouns.

Activity C

Have students complete Activity C as a group activity. Draw a chart on the board, similar to the example shown on the page, with the main headings *Nouns That Change* and *Nouns That Do Not Change.* Under each main heading, make two columns with the subheads *Singular* and *Plural.* Write the two activity examples (*boy* and *penny*) in the appropriate spaces in the chart and discuss their plural spellings. Then discuss the plural spelling of each activity item and invite students to write the singular and plural forms of each noun given in the chart.

Activity C Answers

1. monkey, monkeys **2.** chimney, chimneys **3.** country, countries **4.** body, bodies **5.** journey, journeys **6.** injury, injuries **7.** army, armies **8.** navy, navies **9.** bay, bays **10.** day, days

Activity D

Write this sentence on the board: *The boys and their familys went on many journies together.* Help students apply the spelling rules on the page to find and correct the spelling mistakes in the sentence. Then have them complete Activity D independently.

Activity D Answers

1. countries, spies, armies **2.** cities **3.** injuries **4.** parties **5.** days, keys

3 Reinforce and Extend

Learning Styles

Interpersonal/Group Learning

Have students form small groups, and give them the following sentence: *The ________ came to our school open house.* Ask them to fill in the blank using their own last names in plural form. Write a master list on the board. Then have students form a rule that applies to creating plural proper names. (*Normally add an* -s; *add* -es *when the name ends in* -s, -ch, -sh, -x, *or* -z.)

Nouns that end in *-y* and have a consonant before the *y* become plural by changing the *y* to *i* and adding *-es*.

Nouns that end in *-y* and have a vowel before the *y* become plural by simply adding *-s*.

Example

Nouns That Change		Nouns That Do Not Change	
country	countries	turkey	turkeys
party	parties	valley	valleys
sky	skies	toy	toys

Activity C Write these nouns on your paper. Next to each noun, write its plural.

Example boy—boys penny—pennies

1. monkey
2. chimney
3. country
4. body
5. journey
6. injury
7. army
8. navy
9. bay
10. day

Activity D Find the spelling mistakes in these sentences. Write the sentences correctly on your paper. Sentences may have more than one error.

1. Both countrys had spys in their armys.
2. He received keys to two of the citys he visited on his journey.
3. The doctor said their injurys were not serious.
4. The boys attended two birthday partys last month.
5. How many dayes will it take to make the new keyes?

We make the plural of most nouns that end in *-f* or *-fe* by adding *-s.*

EXAMPLE roof—roofs chief—chiefs

Pay attention to the pronunciation of the plural form. It will help you remember whether to change the *f* to *ve.* For example, notice the difference between *leaf* and *leaves.* Do you hear the *v* sound in *leaves?* Now say *roof* and *roofs* aloud. Do you hear the *f* sound in *roofs?*

Some nouns that end in *-f* or *-fe* change the *f* to *v* and add *-s* or *-es.*

EXAMPLE leaf—leaves calf—calves
knife—knives wolf—wolves

To form the plural of some nouns ending with a consonant and *-o,* we add *-es.* We add only *-s* to others.

EXAMPLE hero—heroes photo—photos
tomato—tomatoes hairdo—hairdos

To form the plural of nouns ending with a vowel and *-o,* we add *-s.*

EXAMPLE radio—radios rodeo—rodeos

A few nouns become plural by changing letters within the word.

EXAMPLE man—men foot—feet
mouse—mice woman—women
tooth—teeth goose—geese

Sometimes the singular and plural nouns are the same.

EXAMPLE one deer a herd of deer
one sheep a flock of sheep
one trout a school of trout
one series two series

AT HOME

Encourage students to create their own personal dictionaries of irregular spellings. They can copy each rule presented on page 17, along with the examples, onto a separate notebook page. Whenever they come across another noun that fits one of those rules, they can add it to the page. Students can use their personal dictionaries to check spelling when completing homework assignments or when writing personal or business letters.

LEARNING STYLES

LEP/ESL

Invite students with limited English proficiency to explain to the class how they form plurals in their primary language. Encourage them to print examples on the board. With partners, students can compare the way the plurals are formed in their first language and in English.

TEACHER ALERT

Hyphenated compound nouns have plural rules of their own: Usually add *-s* or *-es* to the most important word in the compound. Share this rule with the class. Then write the following words on the board and discuss with students how to form the plurals: *son-in-law, attorney-at-law, right-of-way, court-martial, head-of-state, e-mail.* (Answers: *sons-in-law, attorneys-at-law, rights-of-way, courts-martial, heads-of-state, e-mails*)

Remind students that pronunciation can help them form plurals correctly. For example, they are unlikely to say *attorney-at-laws* or *es-mail.* Then refer students to the note on page 17, which discusses the pronunciation of plurals.

Activity E

Do the first activity item orally with the class. Encourage students to refer back to page 17 as they complete the remaining items in Activity E on their own.

Activity E Answers

1. deer, men 2. sheep 3. trout 4. World Series 5. loaves, potatoes

Activity F

Suggest that students use a dictionary as they complete Activity F. If necessary, put a sample dictionary entry for both a regular and irregular noun on the board to show students how plural spellings are indicated in a dictionary entry. After students complete Activity F, invite them to share their sentences with the class.

Activity F Answers

Sentences will vary. Plurals are given.
1. calves 2. men 3. geese 4. children 5. ladies 6. monkeys 7. tomatoes 8. mice 9. chiefs 10. women

IN THE COMMUNITY

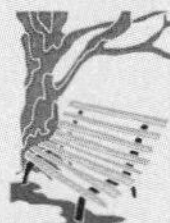

Have students copy or collect printed material from local businesses. Material may include menus, brochures, advertisements, business cards, prospectuses, or signs. Have students identify examples of plural nouns in the material. Encourage students to copy the original sentences on poster board, identifying the sources and underlining the nouns.

Activity E Find the spelling mistakes in these sentences. Write the sentences correctly on your paper.

1. Two deers surprised the mans in the woods.
2. The rancher bought 80 sheeps.
3. We went fishing and caught seven trouts.
4. The Reds won two World Serieses in a row.
5. They ate two loafs of bread and 10 potatos.

Activity F Write the plural of each singular noun on your paper. Then write a sentence using each plural noun.

Example tooth—teeth The dentist examined my teeth.

1. calf
2. man
3. goose
4. child
5. lady
6. monkey
7. tomato
8. mouse
9. chief
10. woman

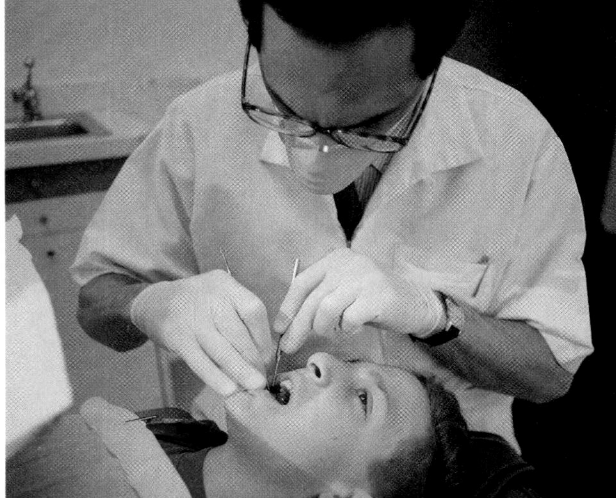

Dr. Cho checked Daniel's teeth.

Lesson 4 REVIEW

Write the plural of each noun on your paper.

1. radio
2. tomato
3. key
4. spy
5. child
6. tax
7. dish
8. potato
9. deer
10. foot

Find six plural nouns in this paragraph. Write them in order on your paper.

The 15 party guests arrived early and stayed for several hours. Everyone liked the snacks. People stood in small groups around the punch bowl. They talked about the games that the football team had won that season.

Spelling Builder

Plural Nouns

Some basic rules will help you spell plural nouns correctly.

- Add *-s* or *-es* to most nouns.
- For nouns that end with *-s, -z, -x, -sh,* and *-ch,* add *-es.*
- For nouns that end with a consonant before a *y,* change the *y* to *i* and add *-es.*
- For some nouns that end with *-f* or *-fe,* change the *f* or *fe* to *v* and add *-es.*

Write the plural form of each of these nouns on your paper.

1. half 2. berry 3. box 4. spoon 5. brush

Then, write a sentence for each singular noun. Write a different sentence for each plural noun. Exchange papers with a classmate. Take turns reading your sentences aloud. Listen to the differences in pronunciation between the singular and plural noun pairs.

Lesson 4 Review Answers

1. radios 2. tomatoes 3. keys 4. spies 5. children 6. taxes 7. dishes 8. potatoes 9. deer 10. feet

Plural nouns from the paragraph: *guests, hours, snacks, people, groups, games*

Spelling Builder

Point out that the rules included in this Spelling Builder will help students form many plural nouns. Some nouns, however, follow no set rules. These nouns have what are known as irregular plurals. They include words such as *child* (*children*), *man* (*men*), and *ox* (*oxen*). Lead students to understand that they must simply memorize irregular plurals. Many of them are in such frequent use, however, that they are rarely misused. Few people say *childs* or *mouses.*

Answers to Spelling Builder: 1. halves 2. berries 3. boxes 4. spoons 5. brushes

Sentences will vary. Encourage the classmate who is listening to identify whether the nouns are singular or plural.

Spelling Practice

Point out to students that they will hear and read many thousands of words in English that they will never have to spell. Perfect spelling is necessary only in the written language. Suggest that they look through old compositions or journals, taking note of words that they have misspelled in the past. They should also refer to lists of frequently misspelled words, copying down those that they find difficult and are likely to use in writing. Lead students to understand that it is important for them to spell the words they write correctly so that written communication will not be misunderstood.

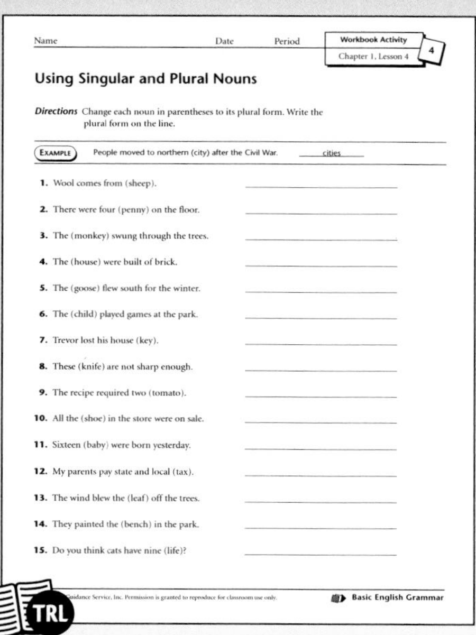

Name Date Period **Workbook Activity 4** Chapter 1, Lesson 4

Using Singular and Plural Nouns

Directions Change each noun in parentheses to its plural form. Write the plural form on the line.

EXAMPLE People moved to northern (city) after the Civil War. cities

1. Wool comes from (sheep).
2. There were four (penny) on the floor.
3. The (monkey) swung through the trees.
4. The (house) were built of brick.
5. The (goose) flew south for the winter.
6. The (child) played games at the park.
7. Trevor lost his house (key).
8. These (knife) are not sharp enough.
9. The recipe required two (tomato).
10. All the (shoe) in the store were on sale.
11. Sixteen (baby) were born yesterday.
12. My parents pay state and local (tax).
13. The wind blew the (leaf) off the trees.
14. They painted the (bench) in the park.
15. Do you think cats have nine (life)?

 Basic English Grammar

TRL

Workbook Activity 4

Name Date Period **Activity 4** Chapter 1, Lesson 4

Spelling Singular and Plural Nouns

Directions If the noun is singular, write its plural form on the line. If the noun is plural, write its singular form on the line.

EXAMPLES car cars; watches watch

1. museums
2. spy
3. goose
4. churches
5. knife
6. navies
7. sky
8. plates
9. bus
10. leaf
11. woman
12. puppy
13. libraries
14. pear
15. kitties
16. deer
17. roof
18. injury
19. coin
20. uncles

Directions Circle the correct plural noun.

EXAMPLE Beth made three (loaves, loafs) of sourdough bread.

21. Sam jumped down and landed on both (feet, foots).
22. The birthday card sent Pim good (wishs, wishes).
23. (Mice, Mouses) scurried through the pantry.
24. The ripe (peachs, peaches) were ready for picking.
25. Many (children, childs) like to play games on (computeres, computers).
26. The school was at the corner of two (streets, streetes).
27. Both Kevin and his brother are going to (parties, partys) this weekend.
28. The store sells many (turkies, turkeys) before Thanksgiving.
29. Ali asked the (womans, women) for directions to the library.
30. The lifeguards patrolled the (beaches, beachs).

 Basic English Grammar

TRL

Activity 4

Lesson at a Glance

Chapter 1 Lesson 5

Overview This lesson explains possessive nouns and how they are formed.

Objectives

- To distinguish between plurals and possessives.
- To identify possessive nouns in sentences.
- To write the singular and plural possessive forms of nouns.

Student Pages 20–23

Teacher's Resource Library 

Workbook Activity 5

Activity 5

Alternative Activity 5

Lesson 5 Possessive Nouns

Possessive noun
A word that shows ownership or a relationship between two words

Apostrophe
A punctuation mark that indicates a noun is possessive

A **possessive noun** is one that shows ownership or a relationship. A possessive noun ends in *-s* and has an **apostrophe** ('). An apostrophe is a punctuation mark that indicates that a noun is possessive.

EXAMPLE

Ownership	That jacket belongs to Jennifer. That is Jennifer's jacket.
Relationship	Nicole is the sister of Devon. Nicole is Devon's sister.

Remember that most plural nouns end in *-s* or *-es.* A noun that is possessive also ends in *-s.* Plural and possessive nouns sound the same when we say them aloud. Many people mix up plurals and possessives when they write them. A written possessive noun looks different from a plural noun. The possessive noun uses an apostrophe. Look at the examples. Notice the difference in the meaning.

EXAMPLE

Plural Noun	**Possessive Noun**
I read three books.	The book's cover is torn.
The cars had engine trouble.	The car's engine failed.

Activity A Write the word in bold in each sentence on your paper. Next to each word, write whether it is *plural* or *possessive.*

Example Alaska has some of the **country's** highest mountains.
country's—possessive

1. **Alex's** insurance policy came in the mail.
2. The policy had several **pages.**
3. A few of Alex's **friends** stopped by the house.
4. They came to see their **friend's** new car.
5. They went out to inspect the **car's** tires.

Vocabulary

apostrophe
possessive noun

Warm-Up Activity

Draw a question mark, an exclamation mark, a period, and a comma on the board. As you do so, ask students to identify what you are drawing. Then write an apostrophe in the same sequence of marks. Ask students what this mark is called. Invite volunteers to write examples of the use of apostrophes on the board. (Some may show its use in contractions.) Explain that the apostrophe is a versatile and powerful symbol. This lesson will show how it is used to indicate ownership, or possession, in nouns.

2 Teaching the Lesson

Point to an object in the classroom and say aloud, "This is the student's desk" or "book" or "computer monitor." Then ask the class to explain to whom the object belongs. Some may suggest that it belongs to a student; others may realize that it could belong to several students. (If they do not arrive at the second possibility, suggest it to them.) Now write the sentence on the board without using an apostrophe, and ask the same question. Lead students to understand not only that an apostrophe is missing but that its placement makes an important distinction. Show how an *'s* or *s'* changes the meaning of this simple statement.

Activity A

Before having students complete the activity on their own, ask them to find the words in bold that have an apostrophe. Remind students that possessives are formed with an apostrophe; plurals are not.

Activity A Answers

1. Alex's—possessive 2. pages—plural 3. friends— plural 4. friend's—possessive 5. car's—possessive

Technology Note

Suppose you are not sure whether the word should be *cars* or *car's*. The Spell Check feature on your computer may tell you whether a possessive noun or a plural noun fits the sentence. However, remember to check the spelling on your own for errors that the computer program does not recognize (such as *there* and *their*).

A possessive noun can be singular or plural.

Rule 1 Make a singular noun possessive by adding an apostrophe and *-s* ('s).

EXAMPLE		
	Wes	Wes's laptop
	principal	principal's office

Rule 2 Make a plural noun possessive by adding only an apostrophe (').

EXAMPLE		
	ladies	ladies' purses
	magazines	magazines' covers

Rule 3 When a plural noun does not end in *-s*, make it possessive by adding an apostrophe and *-s ('s)*.

EXAMPLE		
	women	women's shoes
	geese	geese's feathers

Activity B Write the possessive nouns in these sentences on your paper. Next to each possessive noun, write whether it is *singular* or *plural*.

Example Kim's bicycle has a flat tire.
Kim's—singular

1. The teachers' meeting was canceled.
2. The cat slept on the sofa's cushion.
3. Alex had to replace the camera's batteries.
4. The mice's tracks led under the baseboard.
5. Last week the children's room was painted.

Teacher Alert

Refer students to the Technology Note on this page. Point out that the spelling and grammar checks on their computer software can be very helpful, especially at picking up careless mistakes. Urge students not to accept everything that the computer advises, however. Remind them that computers often misinterpret a writer's intentions. Encourage students to understand fully why the computer is suggesting an alteration before clicking on *change*.

Activity B

Draw four columns on the board with the heads *Singular, Singular Possessive, Plural,* and *Plural Possessive.* Under *Singular,* write *girl, boat, spy, woman;* under *Plural* write *girls, boats, spies, women.* Then have students suggest phrases that show possession to go with each singular noun and each plural noun. Give oral examples, such as girl's pen, spies' secrets. Write these examples and students' suggestions on the board. Elicit from students the correct spelling and where to place the apostrophe for each phrase.

Activity B Answers

1. teachers'—plural 2. sofa's—singular 3. camera's—singular 4. mice's—plural 5. children's—plural

3 Reinforce and Extend

Learning Styles

Visual/Spatial

Divide the class into pairs. Give each pair a colorful magazine picture. On the board, print the following categories: (1) sentence with a singular noun; (2) sentence with a plural noun; (3) sentence with a singular possessive; (4) sentence with a plural possessive. Encourage the partners to use their magazine picture to create a sentence for each of the four categories. Afterward, ask each pair to read one sentence aloud. Have the class name the sentence category.

Activity C

Before students complete Activity C, ask volunteers to say and spell the singular and plural form of each activity item.

Activity C Answers

1. chapter's, chapters' 2. agent's, agents' 3. person's, persons' 4. state's, states' 5. fox's, foxes' 6. president's, presidents' 7. child's, children's 8. church's, churches' 9. crowd's, crowds' 10. navy's, navies' 11. job's, jobs' 12. thing's, things' 13. noun's, nouns' 14. goose's, geese's 15. wife's, wives' 16. audience's, audiences' 17. man's, men's 18. foot's, feet's 19. sunflower's, sunflowers' 20. county's, counties'

Speaking Practice

After the class reviews and corrects answers for Activity C, have students form pairs and ask the pairs to compose sentences using any five of the 20 nouns listed, in both singular and plural possessive forms. Have them take turns reading their sentences aloud to the class. For each sentence, designate another pair to identify the possessive noun and say whether it is singular or plural. Encourage every student to read to the class.

Activity D

Before students do the activity on their own, read through each item with them and help them determine which answer choice in each item is singular possessive and which is plural possessive.

Activity D Answers

1. cents' 2. weeks' 3. minute's 4. dollars' 5. week's

Activity C Write the singular possessive form and the plural possessive form for these words on your paper.

Example book book's books'

1.	chapter	**11.**	job
2.	agent	**12.**	thing
3.	person	**13.**	noun
4.	state	**14.**	goose
5.	fox	**15.**	wife
6.	president	**16.**	audience
7.	child	**17.**	man
8.	church	**18.**	foot
9.	crowd	**19.**	sunflower
10.	navy	**20.**	county

Use apostrophes in phrases such as *one cent's worth* or *a week's vacation*. If the word is plural and ends in *-s*, add only an apostrophe.

EXAMPLE	**Singular**	**Plural**
	one dollar's worth	twenty dollars' worth
	a week's vacation	two weeks' vacation

Activity D Write the correct word on your paper.

1. Mark likes to put in his two (cents', cent's) worth.
2. Alex gets two (weeks', week's) vacation every year.
3. You will have only a (minutes', minute's) wait.
4. I'd like four (dollar's, dollars') worth of stamps.
5. We hoped for a rest at the (week's, weeks') end.

ONLINE CONNECTION

Suggest that students log on to a Web site maintained by Capital Community College in Hartford, Connecticut: **ccc.commnet.edu/grammar** Have them click on *nouns* in the *Word and Sentence Level* selection box. Students will be able to review the material contained in this chapter as well as learn more information on all aspects of noun usage. Encourage them to try one of this Web site's quizzes after reading the material.

Lesson 5 REVIEW

Write the possessive nouns in these sentences on your paper. Add apostrophes where they are needed.

1. Alexs job is very important to him.
2. He has worked in the Wilsons store for one year.
3. Mr. Wilson sells mens sports clothes.
4. Every week at the salespersons meeting, they talk about their work.
5. Mr. Wilsons plan is to make Alex a manager some day.

Some nouns in these sentences are in bold. Write them on your paper. Next to each noun, write whether it is a *plural noun* or a *possessive noun*. Add an apostrophe if it is needed.

6. Jennifer and Alex went to New York City with their **parents.**
7. **Jennifers** favorite place was the Statue of Liberty.
8. One of the **familys** favorite places was Lincoln Center.
9. On their way to lunch, they saw a **womens** street band.
10. The **crowds** of people and the subways were exciting.

Write the correct word on your paper.

11. He got five (dollars, dollars') worth of gas.
12. My (sisters, sister's) boyfriend is coming for dinner.
13. The (monkeys, monkey's) chattering made everyone laugh.
14. We drove to work in (Alexs, Alex's) new car.
15. The (cars, car's) engine roared to life.

Using What You've Learned

Ask five friends or family members to name their favorite snacks. Write a sentence about each person and the snack he or she chose. Circle the nouns in your sentences.

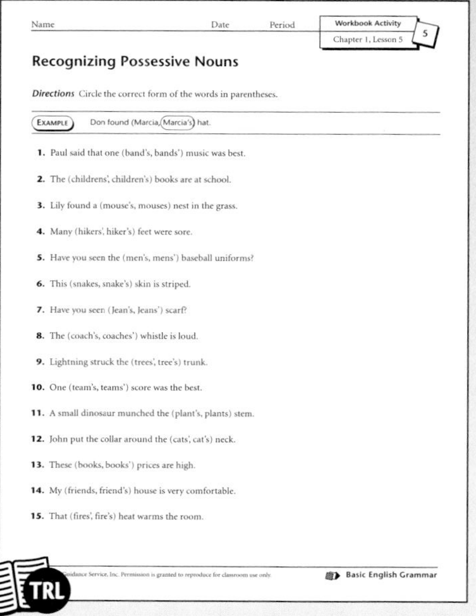

Name Date Period | Workbook Activity 5 | Chapter 1, Lesson 5

Recognizing Possessive Nouns

Directions Circle the correct form of the words in parentheses.

EXAMPLE Don found (Marcia, Marcia's) hat.

1. Paul said that one (band's, bands') music was best.
2. The (childrens', children's) books are at school.
3. Lily found a (mouse's, mouses) nest in the grass.
4. Many (hikers', hiker's) feet were sore.
5. Have you seen the (men's, mens') baseball uniforms?
6. This (snakes, snake's) skin is striped.
7. Have you seen (Jean's, Jeans') scarf?
8. The (coach's, coaches') whistle is loud.
9. Lightning struck the (trees', tree's) trunk.
10. One (team's, teams') score was the best.
11. A small dinosaur munched the (plant's, plants) stem.
12. John put the collar around the (cats', cat's) neck.
13. These (books, books') prices are high.
14. My (friends, friend's) house is very comfortable.
15. That (fires', fire's) heat warms the room.

 Basic English Grammar

TRL

Workbook Activity 5

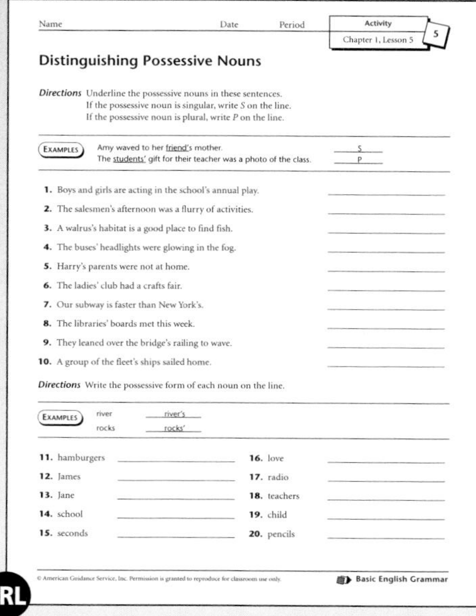

Name Date Period | Activity 5 | Chapter 1, Lesson 5

Distinguishing Possessive Nouns

Directions Underline the possessive nouns in these sentences. If the possessive noun is singular, write *S* on the line. If the possessive noun is plural, write *P* on the line.

EXAMPLES Amy waved to her friend's mother. S
The students' gift for their teacher was a photo of the class. P

1. Boys and girls are acting in the school's annual play. ______
2. The salesmen's afternoon was a flurry of activities. ______
3. A walrus's habitat is a good place to find fish. ______
4. The buses' headlights were glowing in the fog. ______
5. Harry's parents were not at home. ______
6. The ladies' club had a crafts fair. ______
7. Our subway is faster than New York's. ______
8. The libraries' boards met this week. ______
9. They leaned over the bridge's railing to wave. ______
10. A group of the fleet's ships sailed home. ______

Directions Write the possessive form of each noun on the line.

EXAMPLES river river's
rocks rocks'

11. hamburgers	______	16. love	______
12. James	______	17. radio	______
13. Jane	______	18. teachers	______
14. school	______	19. child	______
15. seconds	______	20. pencils	______

 Basic English Grammar

TRL

Activity 5

Lesson 5 Review Answers

1. Alex's 2. Wilsons' 3. men's 4. salespersons' 5. Mr. Wilson's 6. parents—plural 7. Jennifer's—possessive 8. family's— possessive 9. women's—plural, possessive 10. crowds—plural 11. dollars' 12. sister's 13. monkey's 14. Alex's 15. car's

Using What You've Learned

Invite volunteers to write their favorite sentences on the board, circling the nouns. Then make a chart on the board with columns headed *Common, Proper, Singular, Plural,* and *Possessive.* Write the circled nouns down the left side of the chart, and discuss with the class to determine which columns to check for each noun. For example, the word *Alex's* would receive checks under *proper, singular,* and *possessive.*

AT HOME

Students who have trouble mastering the concepts of forming plurals and possessives can make flash cards to use at home. Suggest that students write the singular form of a noun on one side of the card. On the other side, they can write the plural, singular possessive, and plural possessive form of the noun. Students can use the cards themselves or they can work with a family member.

Chapter 1 Review

Use the Chapter Review to prepare students for tests and to reteach content from the chapter.

Chapter 1 Mastery Test 

The Teacher's Resource Library includes two parallel forms of the Chapter 1 Mastery Test. The difficulty level of the two forms is equivalent. You may wish to use one form as a pretest and the other form as a posttest.

Review Answers

Part A

1. abstract noun **2.** proper noun **3.** apostrophe **4.** abbreviation **5.** noun **6.** singular noun **7.** collective noun **8.** possessive noun **9.** compound noun **10.** concrete noun **11.** plural noun **12.** common noun **13.** hyphen

Part B

14. party—concrete **15.** surprise—abstract, teacher—concrete **16.** group—concrete, students—concrete, classroom—concrete, circled **17.** Raf—concrete; Jennifer's—concrete; guitar—concrete; Ottawa—concrete **18.** Alex—concrete, Jennifer—concrete, friends'—concrete, mess—abstract

Chapter 1 REVIEW

Word Bank
abbreviation
abstract noun
apostrophe
collective noun
common noun
compound noun
concrete noun
hyphen
noun
plural noun
possessive noun
proper noun
singular noun

Part A On a sheet of paper, write the correct word or words from the Word Bank to complete each sentence.

1. A word that names an idea that you cannot see or touch is an ________ .
2. The name of a particular person, place, thing, or idea is a ________ .
3. An ________ is a punctuation mark that indicates a noun is possessive.
4. A short form of a word is an ________ .
5. A ________ names a person, a place, a thing, or an idea.
6. The name of one person, place, thing, or idea is a ________ .
7. A ________ is a group of people, places, or things.
8. A word that shows ownership or a relationship between two things is a ________ .
9. Two words joined together to form one new noun is a ________ .
10. A word that names something you can see or touch is a ________ .
11. The name of more than one person, place, thing, or idea is a ________ .
12. A ________ is the name of a general type of person, place, thing, or idea.
13. A ________ is a short dash between parts of a word.

Part B Write the nouns in these sentences on your paper. Identify each noun as *concrete* or *abstract*. Circle any that are compound.

14. The party was over.
15. It had been a big surprise for their teacher.
16. A group of students gathered in the classroom.
17. Raf played Jennifer's guitar that she bought in Ottawa.
18. Alex and Jennifer cleaned up their friends' mess.

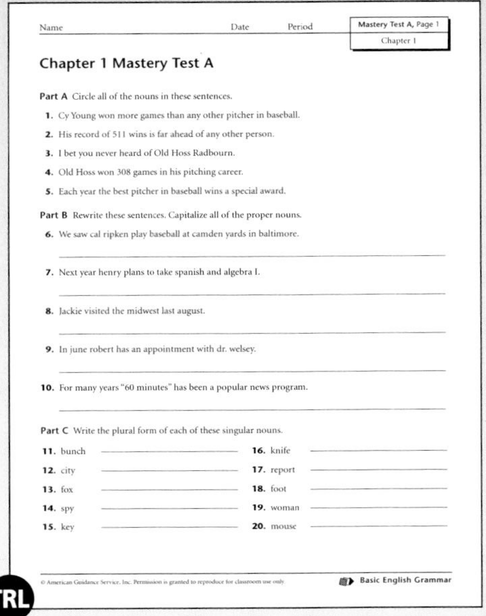

Name Date Period | Mastery Test A, Page 1 | Chapter 1

Chapter 1 Mastery Test A

Part A Circle all of the nouns in these sentences.

1. Cy Young won more games than any other pitcher in baseball.
2. His record of 511 wins is far ahead of any other person.
3. I bet you never heard of Old Hoss Radbourn.
4. Old Hoss won 308 games in his pitching career.
5. Each year the best pitcher in baseball wins a special award.

Part B Rewrite these sentences. Capitalize all of the proper nouns.

6. We saw cal ripken play baseball at camden yards in baltimore.
7. Next year henry plans to take spanish and algebra I.
8. Jackie visited the midwest last august.
9. In june robert has an appointment with dr. welsey.
10. For many years "60 minutes" has been a popular news program.

Part C Write the plural form of each of these singular nouns.

11. bunch ________	**16.** knife ________
12. city ________	**17.** report ________
13. fox ________	**18.** foot ________
14. spy ________	**19.** woman ________
15. key ________	**20.** mouse ________

 Basic English Grammar

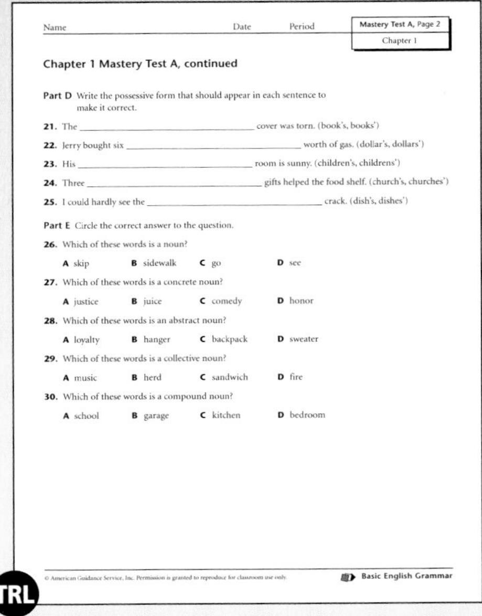

Name Date Period | Mastery Test A, Page 2 | Chapter 1

Chapter 1 Mastery Test A, continued

Part D Write the possessive form that should appear in each sentence to make it correct.

21. The ________ cover was torn. (book's, books')
22. Jerry bought six ________ worth of gas. (dollar's, dollars')
23. His ________ room is sunny. (children's, childrens')
24. Three ________ gifts helped the food shelf. (church's, churches')
25. I could hardly see the ________ crack. (dish's, dishes')

Part E Circle the correct answer to the question.

26. Which of these words is a noun?
    A skip **B** sidewalk **C** go **D** see
27. Which of these words is a concrete noun?
    A justice **B** juice **C** comedy **D** honor
28. Which of these words is an abstract noun?
    A loyalty **B** hanger **C** backpack **D** sweater
29. Which of these words is a collective noun?
    A music **B** herd **C** sandwich **D** fire
30. Which of these words is a compound noun?
    A school **B** garage **C** kitchen **D** bedroom

 Basic English Grammar

Chapter 1 Mastery Test A

Part C Write all of the proper nouns in these sentences on your paper. Capitalize each one.

19. In august, jennifer and alex will return to school.
20. Next year jennifer will be a senior at jackson high school.
21. Her brother also works part-time at mr. wilson's store.
22. This year jennifer is taking french, math, and science.

Part D Write the plural form of each of these singular nouns. Circle any compound noun.

23. wolf **24.** quiz **25.** grandchild

Part E On your paper, write the letter of the word or group of words that correctly completes each sentence.

26. Miguel went to ______ .
A Wade high school **C** wade high school
B Wade High school **D** Wade High School

27. "Did you get your ______ worth?" she asked.
A moneys **C** monies
B money's **D** moneys'

28. We baked four ______ of bread.
A loafs **C** loaves'
B loaves **D** loaf's

29. I like to read ______ stories.
A Charles Dickens' **C** Charles Dickens's
B Charles Dickens **D** Charles Dickenses

30. The ______ live four miles west of town.
A Johnsons **C** Johnsones
B Johnsons's **D** Johnson's

Test-Taking Tip When a teacher announces a test, listen carefully. Write down the topics that will be included. Write down the names of any specific readings the teacher says to review.

Review Answers

Part C

19. August, Jennifer, Alex
20. Jennifer, Jackson High School
21. Mr. Wilson's 22. Jennifer, French

Part D

23. wolves 24. quizzes
25. grandchildren—compound

Part E

26. D 27. B 28. B 29. C 30. A

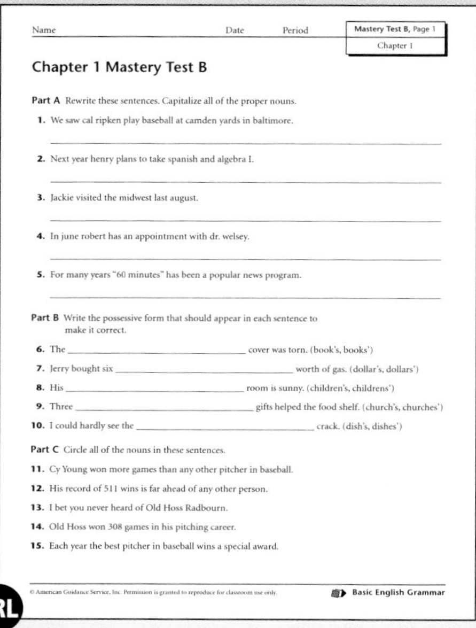

Name Date Period | Mastery Test B, Page 1 | Chapter 1

Chapter 1 Mastery Test B

Part A Rewrite these sentences. Capitalize all of the proper nouns.

1. We saw cal ripken play baseball at camden yards in baltimore.
______
2. Next year henry plans to take spanish and algebra I.
______
3. Jackie visited the midwest last august.
______
4. In june robert has an appointment with dr. welsey.
______
5. For many years "60 minutes" has been a popular news program.
______

Part B Write the possessive form that should appear in each sentence to make it correct.

6. The ______ cover was torn. (book's, books')
7. Jerry bought six ______ worth of gas. (dollar's, dollars')
8. His ______ room is sunny. (children's, childrens')
9. Three ______ gifts helped the food shelf. (church's, churches')
10. I could hardly see the ______ crack. (dish's, dishes')

Part C Circle all of the nouns in these sentences.

11. Cy Young won more games than any other pitcher in baseball.
12. His record of 511 wins is far ahead of any other person.
13. I bet you never heard of Old Hoss Radbourn.
14. Old Hoss won 308 games in his pitching career.
15. Each year the best pitcher in baseball wins a special award.

 Basic English Grammar

TRL

Name Date Period | Mastery Test B, Page 2 | Chapter 1

Chapter 1 Mastery Test B, continued

Part D Circle the correct answer to the question.

16. Which of these words is a noun?
A skip **B** sidewalk **C** go **D** see

17. Which of these words is a concrete noun?
A justice **B** juice **C** comedy **D** honor

18. Which of these words is an abstract noun?
A loyalty **B** hanger **C** backpack **D** sweater

19. Which of these words is a collective noun?
A music **B** herd **C** sandwich **D** fire

20. Which of these words is a compound noun?
A school **B** garage **C** kitchen **D** bedroom

Part E Write the plural form of each of these singular nouns.

21. bunch ______ **26.** knife ______
22. city ______ **27.** report ______
23. fox ______ **28.** foot ______
24. spy ______ **29.** woman ______
25. key ______ **30.** mouse ______

 Basic English Grammar

TRL

Chapter 1 Mastery Test B

Chapter

Planning Guide

The Pronoun

	Student Text Lesson				Language Skills		
	Student Pages	Vocabulary	Practice Exercises	Lesson Review	Identification Skills	Writing Skills	Punctuation Skills
Lesson 1 What Is a Pronoun?	28–29	✔	✔	✔	✔	✔	✔
Lesson 2 Personal Pronouns	30–34	✔	✔	✔	✔	✔	✔
Lesson 3 Relative Pronouns	35–38	✔	✔	✔	✔	✔	✔
Lesson 4 Pronouns That Ask Questions	39–42	✔	✔	✔	✔	✔	✔
Lesson 5 Demonstrative Pronouns	43–45	✔	✔	✔	✔	✔	✔
Lesson 6 Indefinite Pronouns	46–49	✔	✔	✔	✔	✔	✔
Lesson 7 Contractions	50–51	✔	✔	✔	✔	✔	✔

Chapter Activities

Teacher's Resource Library

Community Connection 2: Listening for Pronouns

Media and Literature Connection 2: Hunting for Formal and Informal Writing

Assessment Options

Student Text

Chapter 2 Review

Teacher's Resource Library

Chapter 2 Mastery Tests A and B

Student Text Features						Teaching Strategies						Learning Styles						Teacher's Resource Library			
Spelling Builder	Vocabulary Builder	Where To Find It	Writing Project	Using What You've Learned	Writing Tips/Notes/ Technology Notes	Teacher Alert	Online Connection	Applications (Home, Career, Community, Global)	Speaking Practice	Spelling Practice	Writing Practice	Auditory/Verbal	Body/Kinesthetic	Interpersonal/Group Learning	Logical/Mathematical	Visual/Spatial	LEP/ESL	Workbook Activities	Activities	Alternative Activities	Self-Study Guide
29					✔	28				29								6	6	6	✔
					✔	31, 33		30, 31	32			33				31	31	7	7	7	✔
	36					36		38						37	38			8	8	8	✔
				41	✔	41	40				41		40, 42					9	9	9	✔
					✔			45						44			43	10	10	10	✔
		49				46, 48		47, 49						48		47		11	11	11	✔
			51		✔	50												12	12	12	✔

Pronunciation Key

a	hat	e	let	ī	ice	ô	order	ů	put	sh	she	ə { a	in about
ā	age	ē	equal	o	hot	oi	oil	ü	rule	th	thin	e	in taken
ä	far	ėr	term	ō	open	ou	out	ch	child	ŦH	then	i	in pencil
â	care	i	it	ȯ	saw	u	cup	ng	long	zh	measure	o	in lemon
												u	in circus

Alternative Activities

The Teacher's Resource Library (TRL) contains a set of lower-level worksheets called Alternative Activities. These worksheets cover the same content as the regular Activities but are written at a second-grade reading level.

Skill Track Software

Use the Skill Track Software for Basic English Grammar for additional reinforcement of this chapter. The software program allows students using AGS textbooks to be assessed for mastery of each chapter and lesson of the textbook. Students access the software on an individual basis and are assessed with multiple-choice items.

Chapter at a Glance

Chapter 2: The Pronoun

pages 26–53

Lessons

Skill Track Software for Basic English Grammar

Teacher's Resource Library TRL

Workbook Activities 6–12

Activities 6–12

Alternative Activities 6–12

Community Connection 2

Media and Literature Connection 2

Chapter 2 Self-Study Guide

Chapter 2 Mastery Tests A and B

(Answer Keys for the Teacher's Resource Library begin on page 340 of this Teacher's Edition.)

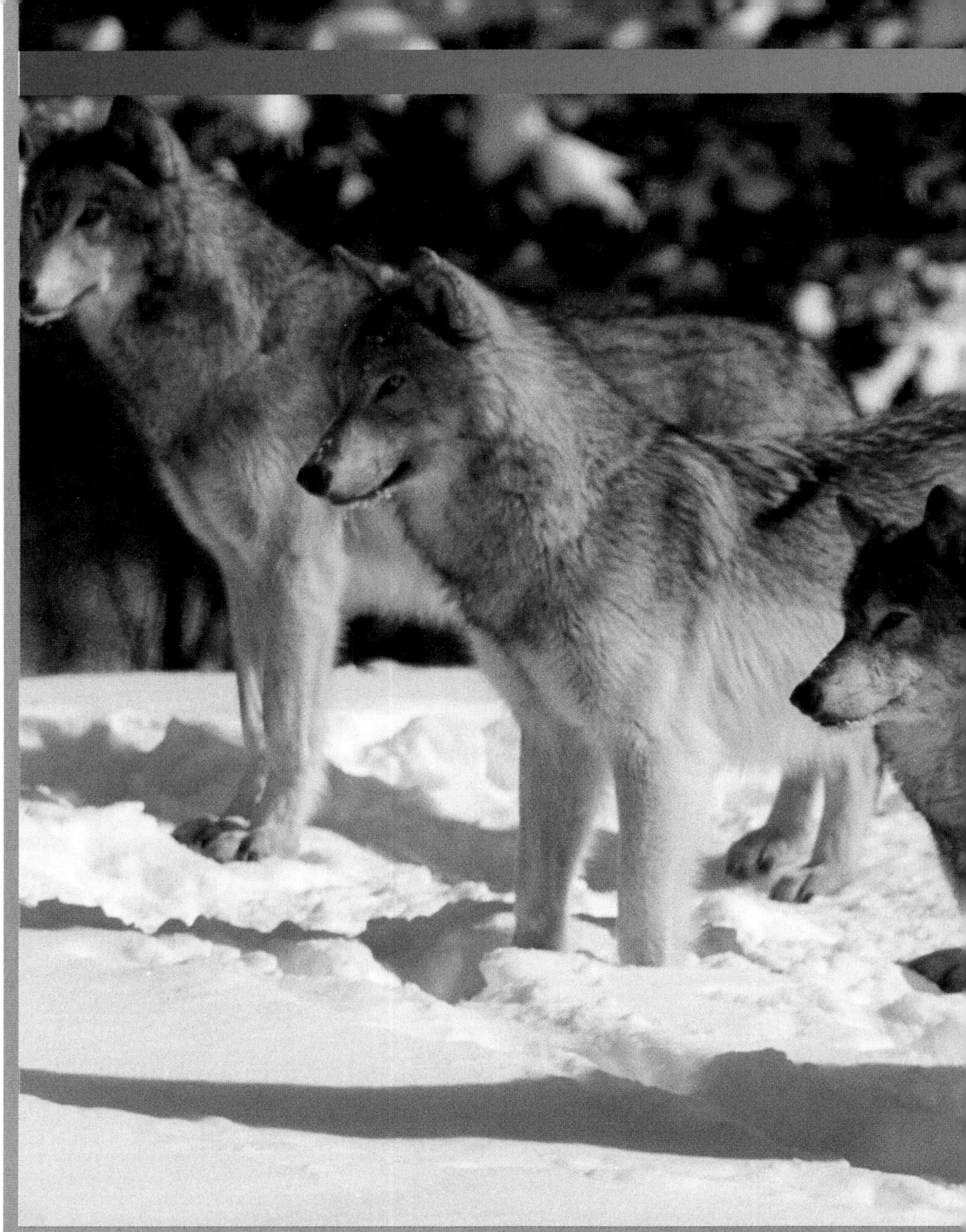

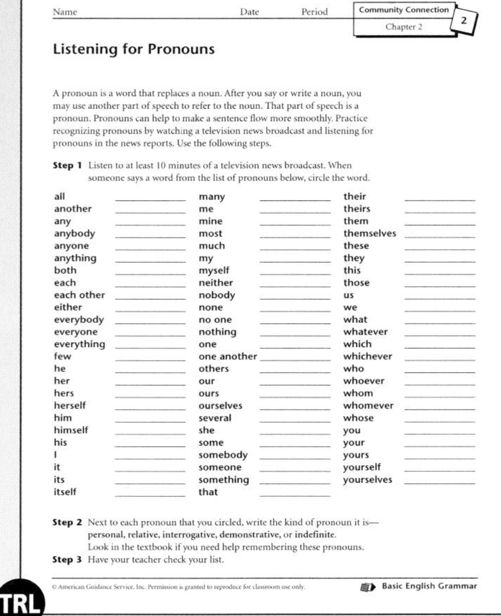

Name ______ Date ______ Period ______ Community Connection 2 Chapter 2

Listening for Pronouns

A pronoun is a word that replaces a noun. After you say or write a noun, you may use another part of speech to refer to the noun. That part of speech is a pronoun. Pronouns can help to make a sentence flow more smoothly. Practice recognizing pronouns by watching a television news broadcast and listening for pronouns in the news reports. Use the following steps.

Step 1 Listen to at least 10 minutes of a television news broadcast. When someone says a word from the list of pronouns below, circle the word.

all ______	many ______	their ______
another ______	me ______	theirs ______
any ______	mine ______	them ______
anybody ______	most ______	themselves ______
anyone ______	much ______	these ______
anything ______	my ______	they ______
both ______	myself ______	this ______
each ______	neither ______	those ______
each other ______	nobody ______	us ______
either ______	none ______	we ______
everybody ______	no one ______	what ______
everyone ______	nothing ______	whatever ______
everything ______	one ______	which ______
few ______	one another ______	whichever ______
he ______	others ______	who ______
her ______	our ______	whoever ______
hers ______	ours ______	whom ______
herself ______	ourselves ______	whomever ______
him ______	several ______	whose ______
himself ______	she ______	you ______
his ______	some ______	your ______
I ______	somebody ______	yours ______
it ______	someone ______	yourself ______
its ______	something ______	yourselves ______
itself ______	that ______	

Step 2 Next to each pronoun that you circled, write the kind of pronoun it is—**personal, relative, interrogative, demonstrative,** or **indefinite.** Look in the textbook if you need help remembering these pronouns.

Step 3 Have your teacher check your list.

 Basic English Grammar

TRL

Community Connection 2

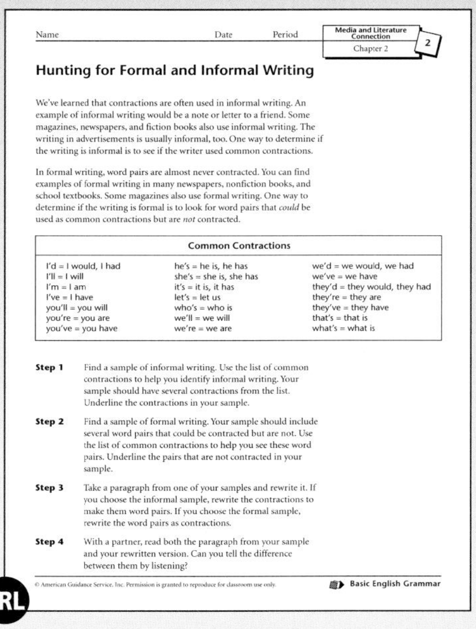

Name ______ Date ______ Period ______ Media and Literature Connection 2 Chapter 2

Hunting for Formal and Informal Writing

We've learned that contractions are often used in informal writing. An example of informal writing would be a note or letter to a friend. Some magazines, newspapers, and fiction books also use informal writing. The writing in advertisements is usually informal, too. One way to determine if the writing is informal is to see if the writer used common contractions.

In formal writing, word pairs are almost never contracted. You can find examples of formal writing in many newspapers, nonfiction books, and school textbooks. Some magazines also use formal writing. One way to determine if the writing is formal is to look for word pairs that *could* be used as common contractions but are *not* contracted.

Common Contractions		
I'd = I would, I had	he's = he is, he has	we'd = we would, we had
I'll = I will	she's = she is, she has	we've = we have
I'm = I am	it's = it is, it has	they'd = they would, they had
I've = I have	let's = let us	they're = they are
you'll = you will	who's = who is	they've = they have
you're = you are	we'll = we will	that's = that is
you've = you have	we're = we are	what's = what is

Step 1 Find a sample of informal writing. Use the list of common contractions to help you identify informal writing. Your sample should have several contractions from the list. Underline the contractions in your sample.

Step 2 Find a sample of formal writing. Your sample should include several word pairs that could be contracted but are not. Use the list of common contractions to help you see these word pairs. Underline the pairs that are not contracted in your sample.

Step 3 Take a paragraph from one of your samples and rewrite it. If you choose the informal sample, rewrite the contractions to make them word pairs. If you choose the formal sample, rewrite the word pairs as contractions.

Step 4 With a partner, read both the paragraph from your sample and your rewritten version. Can you tell the difference between them by listening?

 Basic English Grammar

TRL

Media and Literature Connection 2

Chapter

The Pronoun

Imagine that someone asks you, "What are these wolves doing?" You might answer, "*They* are watching something." You might add, "*They* are standing together. *One* is standing farther back than the *others*. *Those* in front may be older or wiser. *What* are *they* looking at?"

Each word in italic type refers to the word *wolves*. These words are pronouns, or words we use in place of nouns.

In Chapter 2, you will learn how to recognize and use pronouns. Each lesson in the chapter focuses on different types of pronouns and their correct use in writing and speaking.

Goals for Learning

- To identify pronouns in sentences
- To identify the antecedents of pronouns
- To identify the type of pronoun such as personal, indefinite, relative, and demonstrative
- To identify correct usage of pronouns in sentences
- To write contractions with pronouns

Introducing the Chapter

Draw students' attention to the photograph and ask questions about it. Encourage students to answer in complete sentences. Write their responses on the board and underline the pronouns. Have students tell you to what each pronoun refers. Tell students that pronouns take the place of nouns and in Chapter 2 they will learn about different kinds of pronouns.

Writing Tips, Notes, and Technology Notes

Ask volunteers to read the tips and notes that appear in the margins throughout the chapter. Then discuss them with the class.

Teacher's Resource

The AGS Teaching Strategies in English Transparencies may be used with this chapter. The transparencies add an interactive dimension to expand and enhance the *Basic English Grammar* program content.

Career Interest Inventory

The AGS Harrington-O'Shea Career Decision-Making System–Revised (CDM) may be used with this chapter. Students can use the CDM to explore their interests and identify careers. The CDM defines career areas that are indicated by students' responses on the inventory.

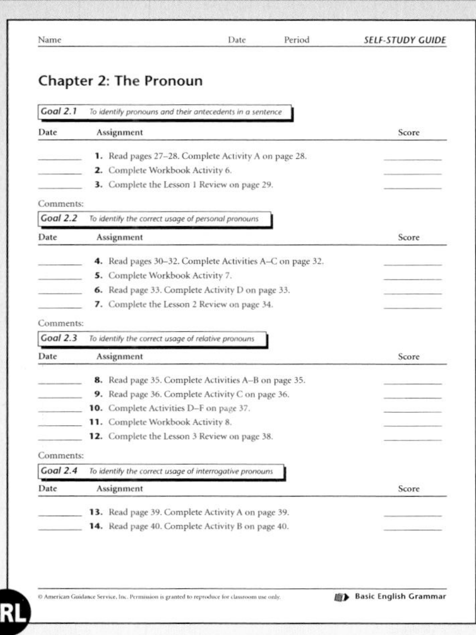

Name ______ Date ______ Period ______ *SELF-STUDY GUIDE*

Chapter 2: The Pronoun

Goal 2.1 *To identify pronouns and their antecedents in a sentence*

Date	Assignment	Score
______	**1.** Read pages 27–28. Complete Activity A on page 28.	______
______	**2.** Complete Workbook Activity 6.	______
______	**3.** Complete the Lesson 1 Review on page 29.	______

Comments:

Goal 2.2 *To identify the correct usage of personal pronouns*

Date	Assignment	Score
______	**4.** Read pages 30–32. Complete Activities A–C on page 32.	______
______	**5.** Complete Workbook Activity 7.	______
______	**6.** Read page 33. Complete Activity D on page 33.	______
______	**7.** Complete the Lesson 2 Review on page 34.	______

Comments:

Goal 2.3 *To identify the correct usage of relative pronouns*

Date	Assignment	Score
______	**8.** Read page 35. Complete Activities A–B on page 35.	______
______	**9.** Read page 36. Complete Activity C on page 36.	______
______	**10.** Complete Activities D–F on page 37.	______
______	**11.** Complete Workbook Activity 8.	______
______	**12.** Complete the Lesson 3 Review on page 38.	______

Comments:

Goal 2.4 *To identify the correct usage of interrogative pronouns*

Date	Assignment	Score
______	**13.** Read page 39. Complete Activity A on page 39.	______
______	**14.** Read page 40. Complete Activity B on page 40.	______

Basic English Grammar

TRL

Name ______ Date ______ Period ______ *SELF-STUDY GUIDE*

Chapter 2: The Pronoun, continued

Date	Assignment	Score
______	**15.** Complete Workbook Activity 9.	______
______	**16.** Complete Activities C–D on page 41.	______
______	**17.** Complete the Lesson 4 Review on page 42.	______

Comments:

Goal 2.5 *To identify the correct usage of demonstrative pronouns*

Date	Assignment	Score
______	**18.** Read page 43. Complete Activity A on page 43.	______
______	**19.** Complete Activities B–D on page 44.	______
______	**20.** Complete Workbook Activity 10.	______
______	**21.** Complete the Lesson 5 Review on page 45.	______

Comments:

Goal 2.6 *To identify the correct usage of indefinite pronouns*

Date	Assignment	Score
______	**22.** Read pages 46–47. Complete Activity A on page 47.	______
______	**23.** Read page 48. Complete Activity B on page 48.	______
______	**24.** Complete Workbook Activity 11.	______
______	**25.** Complete the Lesson 6 Review on page 49.	______

Comments:

Goal 2.7 *To write contractions from pronouns*

Date	Assignment	Score
______	**26.** Read page 50. Complete Activity A on page 50.	______
______	**27.** Complete Workbook Activity 12.	______
______	**28.** Complete the Lesson 7 Review on page 51.	______
______	**29.** Complete the Chapter 2 Review on pages 52–53.	______

Comments:

Student's Signature ______ Date ______

Instructor's Signature ______ Date ______

Basic English Grammar

TRL

Chapter 2 Self-Study Guide, Pages 1–2

Lesson at a Glance

Chapter 2 Lesson 1

Overview This lesson introduces pronouns and explains antecedents.

Objectives

- To recognize pronouns.
- To identify the antecedents of pronouns.

Student Pages 28–29

Teacher's Resource Library 

Workbook Activity 6

Activity 6

Alternative Activity 6

Vocabulary

antecedent
pronoun

Warm-Up Activity

Ask students to listen very carefully as you pretend to leave the following message on a telephone answering machine:

> Hello, Mr. Suarez, this is Anita Chu. Anita Chu is phoning Mr. Suarez to find out if there are any weekend jobs available at Mr. Suarez's store. Anita Chu hopes to hear from Mr. Suarez soon.

Ask students what was odd about the message. Elicit that the speech was unnatural; that in natural speech we use pronouns to refer to people and things mentioned earlier. Invite students to supply pronouns.

Teaching the Lesson

Have students read the definition and example for antecedent. Suggest that an easy way to identify an antecedent is to ask a *who* or *what* question about the pronoun. Write on the board: *Jean bought a new computer game. She is using it now.* Point to the pronoun *she* and ask, "Who is *she*?" (*Jean*) What is it? (*computer game*) Lead students to understand that the answers are the antecedents of the pronouns.

Lesson 1 What Is a Pronoun?

Pronoun
A word that replaces a noun

Antecedent
The noun that the pronoun replaces

A **pronoun** is a word that replaces a noun. Without pronouns, you would have to repeat the same nouns over and over again.

EXAMPLE Chang said that Chang was going to call Chang's brother.
Chang said that he was going to call his brother.

Every pronoun has an **antecedent.** The antecedent is the noun that the pronoun replaces. The pronoun must agree with the antecedent in number and gender.

EXAMPLE Maria is a junior.
She is on the student council.
(*Maria* is the antecedent for the pronoun *she.*)

Writing Tip

The antecedent of each pronoun that you use must be clear to readers. Unclear antecedents confuse readers.

Activity A On a sheet of paper, write the pronouns in bold from the following paragraph. Then write the antecedent that the pronoun has replaced.

Example Erica is a writer. **She** lives in Chicago.
pronoun—she antecedent—Erica

David and Amanda joined the gym last week. **They** received a special student discount. The gym is easy to get to. **It** is on the corner of Elm Street and Park Avenue. Mr. Cruz teaches a class in weight lifting. **He** won a bronze medal in last year's state contest. Amanda plans to go to the gym before school because **she** has a part-time job after school. David says **he** wants to go to Mr. Cruz's afternoon class.

Activity A

Have a volunteer read the first two sentences aloud. Ask the class, "Who are *they*?" Point out that the answer to this question is the antecedent.

Activity A Answers

pronoun	antecedent
They	David and Amanda
It	the gym
He	Mr. Cruz
she	Amanda
he	David

3 Reinforce and Extend

TEACHER ALERT

Draw students' attention to the Writing Tip on page 28. Then read the following sentences aloud: *I want my sisters to meet John and Wendy. They will be in town next weekend.* Ask students *who* will be in town. Point out that because the pronoun *they* can refer to either sisters or John and Wendy, the reader is confused.

Lesson 1 REVIEW

List the words in bold on your paper. Next to each noun, write a pronoun that could replace it.

1. Brittany searched the halls of the school. **Brittany** couldn't find **Brittany's** art class. **Brittany** saw **Brittany's** friend Alex. Alex pointed out the room, and **Brittany and Alex** agreed to meet after class.

Write each pronoun in bold on your paper. Then write the antecedent next to each pronoun.

2. Jack and I went to the game, and then **we** went to the dance.
3. Jack drove **his** father's van.
4. Alicia's history book is in **her** locker.
5. Mr. and Mrs. Martinez drove **their** daughter to school.

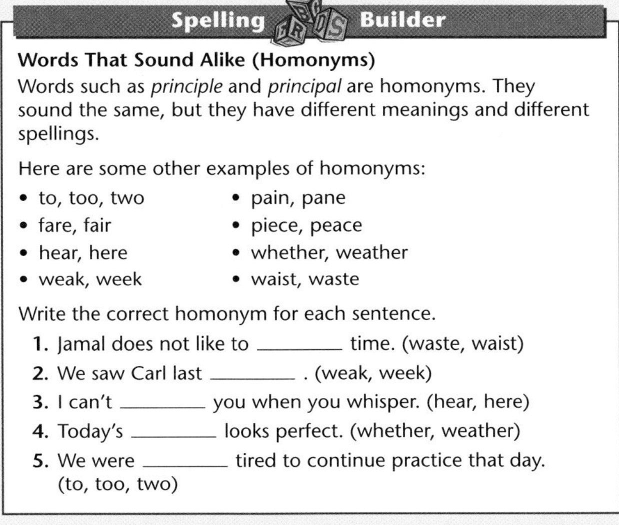

Spelling Builder

Words That Sound Alike (Homonyms)

Words such as *principle* and *principal* are homonyms. They sound the same, but they have different meanings and different spellings.

Here are some other examples of homonyms:

- to, too, two
- fare, fair
- hear, here
- weak, week
- pain, pane
- piece, peace
- whether, weather
- waist, waste

Write the correct homonym for each sentence.

1. Jamal does not like to ________ time. (waste, waist)
2. We saw Carl last ________ . (weak, week)
3. I can't ________ you when you whisper. (hear, here)
4. Today's ________ looks perfect. (whether, weather)
5. We were ________ tired to continue practice that day. (to, too, two)

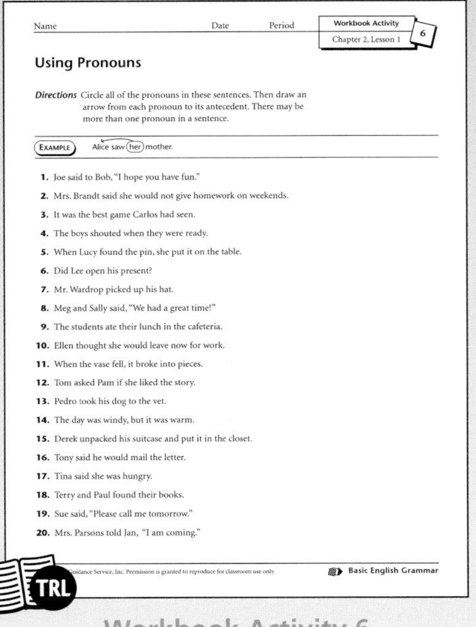

Name Date Period

Workbook Activity 6 Chapter 2, Lesson 1

Using Pronouns

Directions Circle all of the pronouns in these sentences. Then draw an arrow from each pronoun to its antecedent. There may be more than one pronoun in a sentence.

EXAMPLE Alice saw (her) mother.

1. Joe said to Bob, "I hope you have fun."
2. Mrs. Brandt said she would not give homework on weekends.
3. It was the best game Carlos had seen.
4. The boys shouted when they were ready.
5. When Lucy found the pin, she put it on the table.
6. Did Lee open his present?
7. Mr. Wardrop picked up his hat.
8. Meg and Sally said, "We had a great time!"
9. The students ate their lunch in the cafeteria.
10. Ellen thought she would leave now for work.
11. When the vase fell, it broke into pieces.
12. Tom asked Pam if she liked the story.
13. Pedro took his dog to the vet.
14. The day was windy, but it was warm.
15. Derek unpacked his suitcase and put it in the closet.
16. Tony said he would mail the letter.
17. Tina said she was hungry.
18. Terry and Paul found their books.
19. Sue said, "Please call me tomorrow."
20. Mrs. Parsons told Jan, "I am coming."

 Basic English Grammar

TRL

Workbook Activity 6

Name Date Period

Activity 6 Chapter 2, Lesson 1

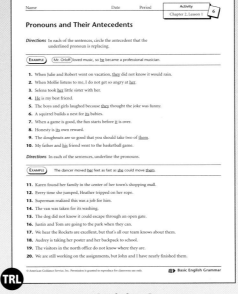

Pronouns and Their Antecedents

Directions In each of the sentences, circle the antecedent that the underlined pronoun is replacing.

EXAMPLE (Mr. Orloff) loved music, so he became a professional musician.

1. When Julie and Robert went on vacation, they did not know it would rain.
2. When Mollie listens to me, I do not get so angry at her.
3. Selena took her little sister with her.
4. He is my best friend.
5. The boys and girls laughed because they thought the joke was funny.
6. A squirrel builds a nest for its babies.
7. When a game is good, the fun starts before it is over.
8. Honesty is its own reward.
9. The doughnuts are so good that you should take two of them.
10. My father and his friend went to the basketball game.

Directions In each of the sentences, underline the pronouns.

EXAMPLE The dancer moved her feet as fast as she could move them.

11. Karen found her family in the center of her town's shopping mall.
12. Every time she jumped, Heather tripped on her rope.
13. Superman realized this was a job for him.
14. The van was taken for its washing.
15. The dog did not know it could escape through an open gate.
16. Justin and Tom are going to the park when they can.
17. We hear the Rockets are excellent, but that's all our team knows about them.
18. Audrey is taking her poster and her backpack to school.
19. The visitors in the north office do not know where they are.
20. We are still working on the assignments, but John and I have nearly finished them.

 Basic English Grammar

TRL

Activity 6

Lesson 1 Review Answers

1. Brittany—she, Brittany's—her, Brittany—She, Brittany's—her, Brittany and Alex—they 2. we—Jack and I 3. his—Jack's 4. her—Alicia's 5. their—Mr. and Mrs. Martinez's

Spelling Builder

Write the following sentence on the board. *The bear ate so many berries that the bush was bare.* Ask a volunteer to read the sentence aloud and to underline the two words that sound alike. Ask why the two words are spelled differently. (*They are different words with different meanings.*) Point out that these words are homonyms, or words that sound alike but have different spellings and different meanings. Explain to students that such words are sometimes called *homophones.*

Answers to Spelling Builder: 1. waste 2. week 3. hear 4. weather 5. too

Spelling Practice

Give students more practice with homonyms by asking them to write the following sentences as you read them:

Did you see the sea?

That's a deer, dear.

They're over there, buying their tickets.

Invite volunteers to write their solutions on the board, underlining the homonyms.

Lesson at a Glance

Chapter 2 Lesson 2

Overview This lesson presents personal pronouns, including compound personal pronouns.

Objectives

- To identify types of personal pronouns.
- To recognize the use of personal pronouns in sentences.
- To define compound personal pronouns.

Student Pages 30–34

Teacher's Resource Library 

Workbook Activity 7

Activity 7

Alternative Activity 7

Vocabulary

compound personal pronoun
first-person pronoun
personal pronoun
second-person pronoun
third-person pronoun

1 Warm-Up Activity

Catch students' attention by announcing, "Me want you to give I your attention. Please take out your books and put they on your desks."

Ask students what was strange about this announcement. Elicit from them that several of the words were used incorrectly. Write the same sentences on the board and invite volunteers to find the correct form of words. Lead students to understand that all of the misused words are personal pronouns. Explain that this lesson will help them identify the role of personal pronouns in sentences.

2 Teaching the Lesson

Point out that pronouns adapt their behavior to different circumstances, and they can often be identified as male or female.

Ask students the difference between the words *he* and *she.* They will point out that one refers to a male and the other to a female. Explain that this is known as the *gender* of a pronoun. Point out that pronouns must have the same gender as their antecedents. The antecedent will also determine a pronoun's number—that is, whether it is singular or plural.

3 Reinforce and Extend

Career Connection

Point out to students that in the past some English words that named people in the workforce were masculine even when they referred to women; for example, *fireman* and *mailman.* Today these words have been replaced by genderless terms, such as *firefighter* and *letter carrier.*

Lesson 2 Personal Pronouns

Personal pronoun
A pronoun that refers to a person or a thing

First-person pronoun
A pronoun that refers to the person who is speaking

Second-person pronoun
A pronoun that refers to the person who is being spoken to

Third-person pronoun
A pronoun that refers to the person or thing that is being talked about

Personal pronouns refer to people or things. They distinguish among the speaker, the person spoken to, and the person or thing spoken about.

A **first-person pronoun** refers to the speaker.

EXAMPLE I am late.

A **second-person pronoun** refers to the person spoken to.

EXAMPLE You are late.

A **third-person pronoun** refers to the person or thing spoken about.

EXAMPLE He is late.

Personal pronouns express number. They can be singular or plural. A singular pronoun refers to one person or thing. A plural pronoun refers to more than one person or thing.

EXAMPLE

Singular	I am late.	She is leaving.
Plural	We are late.	They are leaving.

Personal pronouns express gender. The three genders are masculine (male), feminine (female), and neuter (things that are neither masculine nor feminine). A pronoun must agree with its antecedent. For example, you must replace a feminine noun with a feminine pronoun.

EXAMPLE

Masculine	John is tall.	He is tall.
Feminine	Mary is my friend.	She is my friend.
Neuter	The notebook is lost.	It is lost.

We use personal pronouns in different ways in a sentence.

- As the subject of a sentence
- As the object of a sentence
- As a possessive that shows ownership

Personal pronouns change in form depending on how we use them in sentences.

He is on the basketball team.
(*He* is the subject of the sentence.)

Julie gave him the book.
(*Him* is the object of the verb.)

That backpack is hers.
(*Hers* is possessive.)

Here is a chart that shows all of the personal pronouns.

Personal Pronouns			
	Subject	**Object**	**Possessive**
Singular			
First Person	I	me	my, mine
Second Person	you	you	your, yours
Third Person	he, she, it	him, her, it	his, her, hers, its
Plural			
First Person	we	us	our, ours
Second Person	you	you	your, yours
Third Person	they	them	their, theirs

Global Connection

In some languages, nouns are either masculine or feminine. The gender of the word is often indicated by the word's ending or by the form of the article or adjective that describes it. Pronouns used to replace these nouns are either masculine or feminine. Invite students who speak a second language to share pronouns in that language and give examples of their use in sentences.

Teacher Alert

Be sure students understand the meaning of subject, object, and possessive before moving on in the lesson.

Learning Styles

Visual/Spatial

Remind students how to find information from a chart by pointing to an item in the first column and tracing your finger across the row. Then invite a volunteer to quiz the class by asking for information from the chart. He or she should point to an item and challenge classmates to identify the word according to its position.

Learning Styles

LEP/ESL

Ask English language learners to duplicate on the board the the pronouns in the chart on this page. Ask them to print the personal pronouns from their primary language next to the English ones. One by one, have the students say aloud a simple sentence using an English personal pronoun. Then have them repeat the sentence using the non-English personal pronoun.

Activity A

After reading the directions together, invite volunteers to demonstrate how to find the activity example answer in the chart.

Activity A Answers

1. they 2. it 3. me 4. you 5. his

Activity B

Ask a volunteer to explain why *her* was used to replace *Yoko* in the activity example. Then do the first two items orally with the class before having students complete the activity independently.

Activity B Answers

1. I have them. 2. They are lost. 3. It is flying overhead. 4. Her house is in the country. 5. "That is their room," Amanda said.

Activity C

Help students recall the definition of antecedent. Have them refer to page 28 if necessary. Read the first two sentences of the paragraph aloud to the class. Elicit from students that *them* is the first pronoun. Then invite a volunteer to identify the antecedent. Ask students why *them* was used to refer back to Jan and Lu instead of *him* or *her.*

Activity C Answers

1. them—Jay and Lu 2. He—Max
3. He—Max, I—Lu, him—Max, she—Lu
4. I—Jay, it—dance

Speaking Practice

After students have completed Activity C and checked their answers, invite a volunteer to read the original paragraph aloud. Then ask for a second volunteer to replace the pronouns with the antecedents and to read the paragraph again. Discuss with students which sentences in the second version sound most unusual. Create with the class other versions, including selected antecedents. Encourage students to practice reading these alternative versions aloud.

Some languages have more than one word for the personal pronoun *you.* For example, the Spanish word *tu* means "you" in informal conversations. You use it when talking with friends and family. The word *usted* also means "you." Using *usted* in more formal situations indicates respect. In English, we have only one way to say *you.*

Activity A Identify these pronouns. Write them on your paper. Refer to the chart on page 31.

Example first person, singular, subject—I
second person, plural, possessive—your, yours

1. third person, plural, subject
2. third person, singular, object, neuter
3. first person, singular, object
4. second person, plural, subject
5. third person, singular, masculine, possessive

Activity B Rewrite each of these sentences on your paper. Replace the words in bold with a pronoun.

Example I saw **Yoko** yesterday. I saw **her** yesterday.

1. I have **a hammer and a saw.**
2. **The gloves** are lost.
3. **An airplane** is flying overhead.
4. **Anita's** house is in the country.
5. "That is **Laura and Jennifer's** room," Amanda said.

Activity C Find the pronouns in the following paragraph. Write them on your paper. Then write the antecedents of those pronouns.

> Jay and Lu walked out of school with Max. Jay and Lu were laughing at a joke Max had told them.
>
> "He tells great stories," Jay said.
>
> "He is the funniest person I know!" Lu agreed. "Has Mrs. Estevez asked him to tell jokes at the school dance?" she asked.
>
> "I don't know, but it is next week!" Jay said.

Compound personal pronoun

A pronoun formed by combining a singular personal pronoun and -self or a plural personal pronoun and -selves

We form **compound personal pronouns** by adding *-self* to singular personal pronouns and *-selves* to plural personal pronouns. We refer to them as the "*-self*" pronouns.

EXAMPLE

I hurt myself.
(*Myself* indicates action done to the pronoun *I*.)

The baby played by herself.
(*Herself* indicates action done by the noun *baby*.)

Vince ate the whole salad himself.
(*Himself* shows emphasis.)

-Self Pronouns		
	Singular	**Plural**
First person	myself	ourselves
Second Person	yourself	yourselves
Third Person	himself, herself, itself	themselves

Activity D Write the *-self* pronouns in these sentences on your paper. Next to each *-self* pronoun, write *singular* or *plural.*

Example Mikala studied her English by herself.
herself—singular

1. The glass fell off the shelf by itself.
2. Samantha and Janet cleaned the kitchen themselves.
3. We cooked dinner by ourselves.
4. The baby sat up by himself.
5. Can you do your homework by yourself?

Activity D

Before students begin this activity, have them study the *-self* pronouns in the chart. Then have partners test each other by asking questions such as, "What are the third person singular *-self* pronouns?"

Activity D Answers

1. itself—singular **2.** themselves—plural **3.** ourselves—plural **4.** himself—singular **5.** yourself—singular

Teacher Alert

Point out that *-self* pronouns always come after the noun or pronoun to which they refer. They should not be used to replace subject or object pronouns in a sentence. Examples:

- Ali and I took the train. (not *Ali and myself*)
- He handed it to Jen and me. (not *Jen and myself*)

You may wish to explain to students that compound personal pronouns are also called *reflexive pronouns* when they refer to the subject of the sentence. For example, *himself* in the sentence "Jackson bought himself two new CDs." is a reflexive pronoun.

Learning Styles

Auditory/Verbal

Have students review the chart on this page. Then read to them the following sentences and ask them to substitute the correct *-self* pronoun for the word *blank:*

- I did it *blank.*
- You can read this *blank.*
- The land *blank* is very valuable.
- She told the story *blank.*
- We went there by *blank.*

Invite volunteers to make up similar examples and quiz their classmates orally.

Lesson 2 Review Answers

1. They—Laura and Jennifer **2.** She—Ms. Turner **3.** him—James Melcher **4.** it—book **5.** their/theirs **6.** I **7.** you **8.** me **9.** it **10.** her **11.** she **12.** It—day **13.** their—students **14.** They—Lilly and Pete **15.** herself—Rosa

Lesson 2 REVIEW

Write the pronouns in bold in these sentences on your paper. Next to each pronoun, write the noun or nouns that the pronoun has replaced.

1. Laura and Jennifer are both seniors. **They** are old friends.

2. Ms. Turner is the math teacher. **She** also teaches science.

3. James Melcher is in the class. Jennifer knows **him** well.

4. "Can I borrow your book?" James asked Jennifer. "Here **it** is," Jennifer said.

Identify these pronouns. Write them on your paper.

5. third person, plural, possessive

6. first person, singular, subject

7. second person, plural, object

Rewrite each sentence. Replace the words in bold with a pronoun.

8. "The teacher gave **Gina** homework," Gina said.

9. Gina decided to do **her homework** early.

10. The teacher told **Gina** to write a paragraph in Spanish.

11. "What is the paragraph about?" **Karen** asked.

Write the personal pronouns in these sentences on your paper. Next to each personal pronoun, write its antecedent.

12. The first day of school was over. It had been very pleasant.

13. The students enjoyed seeing their old friends.

14. Lilly and Pete are in the same math class. They plan to study together.

15. Rosa walked home by herself after school.

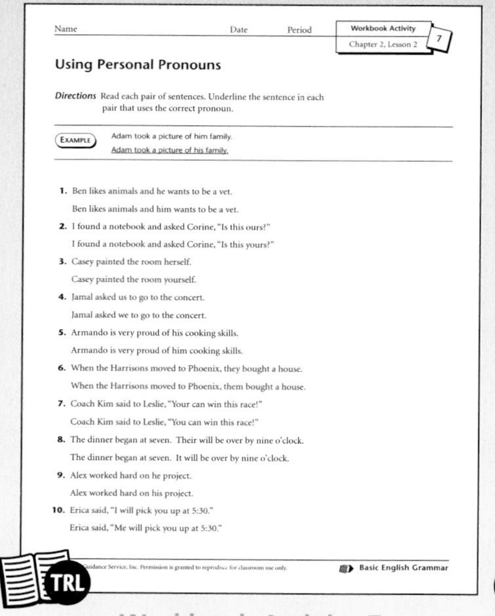

Name Date Period | Workbook Activity 7 | Chapter 2, Lesson 2

Using Personal Pronouns

Directions Read each pair of sentences. Underline the sentence in each pair that uses the correct pronoun.

EXAMPLE Adam took a picture of him family.
Adam took a picture of his family.

1. Ben likes animals and he wants to be a vet.
   Ben likes animals and him wants to be a vet.
2. I found a notebook and asked Corine, "Is this ours?"
   I found a notebook and asked Corine, "Is this yours?"
3. Casey painted the room herself.
   Casey painted the room yourself.
4. Jamal asked us to go to the concert.
   Jamal asked we to go to the concert.
5. Armando is very proud of his cooking skills.
   Armando is very proud of him cooking skills.
6. When the Harrisons moved to Phoenix, they bought a house.
   When the Harrisons moved to Phoenix, them bought a house.
7. Coach Kim said to Leslie, "Your can win this race!"
   Coach Kim said to Leslie, "You can win this race!"
8. The dinner began at seven. Their will be over by nine o'clock.
   The dinner began at seven. It will be over by nine o'clock.
9. Alex worked hard on he project.
   Alex worked hard on his project.
10. Erica said, "I will pick you up at 5:30."
    Erica said, "Me will pick you up at 5:30."

 Basic English Grammar

TRL

Workbook Activity 7

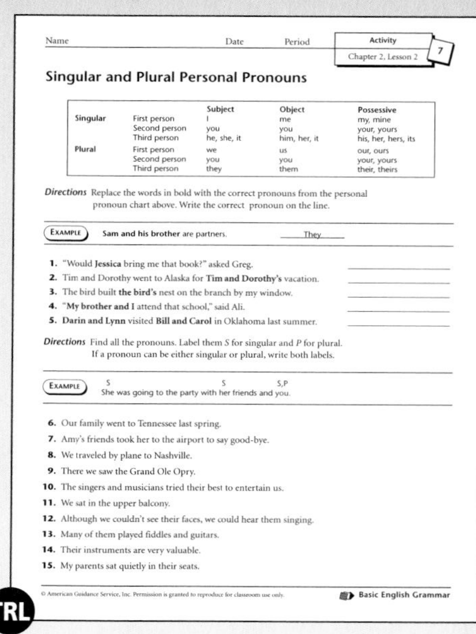

Name Date Period | Activity 7 | Chapter 2, Lesson 2

Singular and Plural Personal Pronouns

		Subject	Object	Possessive
Singular	First person	I	me	my, mine
	Second person	you	you	your, yours
	Third person	he, she, it	him, her, it	his, her, hers, its
Plural	First person	we	us	our, ours
	Second person	you	you	your, yours
	Third person	they	them	their, theirs

Directions Replace the words in bold with the correct pronouns from the personal pronoun chart above. Write the correct pronoun on the line.

EXAMPLE **Sam and his brother** are partners. They

1. "Would **Jessica** bring me that book?" asked Greg. ______
2. Tim and Dorothy went to Alaska for **Tim and Dorothy's** vacation. ______
3. The bird built **the bird's** nest on the branch by my window. ______
4. "**My brother and I** attend that school," said Ali. ______
5. **Darin and Lynn** visited **Bill and Carol** in Oklahoma last summer. ______

Directions Find all the pronouns. Label them *S* for singular and *P* for plural. If a pronoun can be either singular or plural, write both labels.

EXAMPLE She (S) was going to the party with her (S) friends and you (S,P).

6. Our family went to Tennessee last spring.
7. Amy's friends took her to the airport to say good-bye.
8. We traveled by plane to Nashville.
9. There we saw the Grand Ole Opry.
10. The singers and musicians tried their best to entertain us.
11. We sat in the upper balcony.
12. Although we couldn't see their faces, we could hear them singing.
13. Many of them played fiddles and guitars.
14. Their instruments are very valuable.
15. My parents sat quietly in their seats.

 Basic English Grammar

TRL

Activity 7

Lesson 3 Relative Pronouns

> **Relative pronoun**
> *A pronoun such as* who, whom, whose, which, that, *and* what

The **relative pronouns** are *who, whom, whose, which, that,* and *what.* Like personal pronouns, relative pronouns must agree with their antecedents.

Who, whom, and *whose* refer to people.

EXAMPLE Who is fixing lunch?
(*Who* is a subject.)
The person whom I met yesterday is late.
(*Whom* is an object.)
Whose house is that?
(*Whose* is possessive.)

Which and *what* refer to things. *That* refers to people or things.

Activity A Write these sentences on your paper. Circle the relative pronouns.

1. The car that Alex bought is blue and white.
2. Alex wanted a car that had four doors.
3. Alex has a friend who is a mechanic.
4. The mechanic works in the garage that is on Maple Street.
5. Alex also had a friend whose father owned a garage.

Activity B The relative pronouns in these sentences are in bold. Write each relative pronoun on your paper. Next to each relative pronoun, write its antecedent.

Example Dina has a ring **that** belonged to her grandmother.
that—relative pronoun ring—antecedent

1. The man **who** owned the garage sold Alex new tires.
2. He is the man **whom** I met last week.
3. Andy likes cars **that** have four-wheel drive.
4. The mechanic has a car **that** is an antique.
5. Did you see the screwdriver **that** I was using?

Lesson at a Glance

Chapter 2 Lesson 3

Overview This lesson presents relative pronouns, including compound relative pronouns.

Objective

- To identify relative pronouns and their antecedents in sentences.

Student Pages 35–38

Teacher's Resource Library 

Workbook Activity 8

Activity 8

Alternative Activity 8

Vocabulary

compound relative pronoun
relative pronoun

1 Warm-Up Activity

Write the following incomplete sentences on the board:

- The car ____ passed us was going 100 m.p.h.
- You can have ____ you want.
- That's the woman ____ daughter you met.

Underneath these sentences write the words *that, whose,* and *whichever.* Invite students to fill in the blanks. Inform them that these words are known as relative pronouns. Explain that this lesson will help them understand the use of relative pronouns.

2 Teaching the Lesson

Discuss the definition of relative pronouns. Be sure that students understand the distinction between relative pronouns that refer to people and those that refer to things. Emphasize that the word *that* can refer to people or things.

Activity A

Before students begin this activity, have a volunteer read the definitions and examples aloud. Complete the first item orally with the class.

Activity A Answers

1. that 2. that 3. who 4. that 5. whose

Activity B

Before having students complete the activity independently, review the definition of antecedent (p. 28). Then have a volunteer read the activity example and explain the answers given.

Activity B Answers

1. who—man 2. whom—man 3. that—cars 4. that—car 5. that—screwdriver

Activity C

Before students begin this activity, ask them what they notice about compound relative pronouns. Elicit from them that these pronouns are all formed of two words, the second word, in each case, being *-ever.* Explain that *compound* means made up of more than one part.

Activity C Answers

1. whatever 2. whatever 3. Whoever
4. whatever 5. whomever

Vocabulary Builder

Ask students to imagine that the young child of someone they like very much is clearly overweight. Which word would they use to describe the child: *fat* or *chubby?* Lead students to understand that fat has a negative connotation, while *chubby* is a much more positive way of viewing someone who is overweight (the neutral term). Before students complete the Vocabulary Builder questions, write the following pairs of words on the board: *thrifty/stingy* and *cautiously/cowardly.* Discuss with students what these words have in common and how their connotations differ.

Answers to Vocabulary Builder:
1. negative 2. positive 3. positive
4. negative 5. neutral

3 Reinforce and Extend

Teacher Alert

The compound relative pronoun *whatever* has gained a meaning of its own in recent years, particularly among young people. Point out that when used on its own, *whatever* has come to mean "it's not important" or "I don't care." Suggest to students that this is typical of the way languages evolve.

Compound relative pronoun
A pronoun such as whoever, whomever, whichever, *and* whatever

The **compound relative pronouns** are *whoever, whomever, whichever,* and *whatever.* The antecedent of a compound relative pronoun may not be stated but may be understood by the listener or reader.

EXAMPLE Jackets and coats are in the stores now.
I'll choose whichever is the best value.
(The antecedents of *whichever* are *jackets* and *coats.*)
Whoever wants to go hiking should come now.
(The antecedent of *whoever* is not stated but is understood.)

Activity C Find the compound relative pronouns in these sentences. Write them on your paper.

1. Do whatever you think should be done.
2. You may have whatever you want for dinner.
3. Whoever wants to go first should come upstairs now.
4. You can find whatever you need at the store.
5. You can invite whomever you want.

Vocabulary Builder

Connotation* and *Denotation
Denotation is the dictionary definition of a word. *Connotation* is an idea suggested by or associated with a word or phrase. A word can have a positive or negative connotation. For example, *cheap* and *inexpensive* both mean that something does not cost very much, but *cheap* usually has a negative connotation. A word that is neither positive nor negative is neutral and therefore has no connotation.

Write on your paper whether the connotation of the word in bold is *positive, negative,* or *neutral.*

1. The boy in the blue sweater is **scrawny.**
2. The boy in the blue sweater is **slender.**
3. Why are you **chuckling?**
4. Why are you **snickering?**
5. Why are you **laughing?**

Activity D Write the pronouns in the list below on your paper.

1. himself	**6.** he	**11.** car
2. whoever	**7.** Ms. Woo	**12.** you
3. Andy	**8.** I	**13.** bus
4. which	**9.** what	**14.** its
5. that	**10.** whom	**15.** friend

Activity E Make two columns on your paper. Write *Personal Pronouns* at the top of the first column. Write *Relative Pronouns* at the top of the second column. Then write the pronouns below in the correct column.

1. we	**6.** whose	**11.** you
2. that	**7.** whichever	**12.** which
3. mine	**8.** what	**13.** ours
4. I	**9.** themselves	**14.** whom
5. who	**10.** whoever	**15.** us

Activity F Write the correct pronoun in each sentence on your paper.

1. There are the shoes (who, that) I want.
2. The puppy (who, that) I found at the shelter is so lovable.
3. There is the girl (whom, what) I met at the library.
4. I like a house (who, that) has a big yard.
5. Did you see the lady (which, who) was wearing the red hat?

Kim is studying by herself.

Activity D

Ask students to name the types of pronouns they have learned and to give two examples of each type.

Activity D Answers

Only pronouns are listed. **1.** himself **2.** whoever **4.** which **5.** that **6.** he **8.** I **9.** what **10.** whom **12.** you **14.** its

Activity E

Remind students of the difference between personal and possessive pronouns. Before students begin Activity E, be sure they understand that they are to create two columns on their paper. Suggest that students work with a partner to complete the activity.

Activity E Answers

Personal Pronouns	Relative Pronouns
1. we	2. that
3. mine	5. who
4. I	6. whose
9. themselves	7. whichever
11. you	8. what
13. ours	10. whoever
15. us	12. which
	14. whom

Activity F

Suggest that students try each pronoun in parentheses in the sentence to see which one sounds most correct before they write their answers.

Activity F Answers

1. that **2.** that **3.** whom **4.** that **5.** who

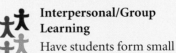

Learning Styles

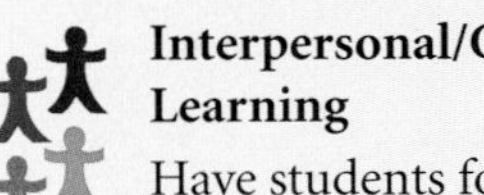

Interpersonal/Group Learning

Have students form small groups and work together to make charts of relative pronouns similar to the charts on pages 31 and 33. Help students create appropriate heads for their charts. Invite volunteers to write their charts on the board.

Lesson 3 Review Answers

1. who—mechanic **2.** Whoever—Andy and Frank **3.** whatever—video **4.** whom—man **5.** whose—friend **6.** itself—personal pronoun **7.** whatever—relative pronoun **8.** its—personal pronoun **9.** he—personal pronoun **10.** them—personal pronoun **11.** whoever—relative pronoun **12.** Who **13.** that **14.** who **15.** that

AT HOME

Ask students to choose a passage containing relative pronouns from a book, magazine, or newspaper when they are at home. Have them write several of the sentences, omitting the relative pronouns and keeping a note of the words on a separate sheet. In class, have students form pairs and exchange their sentences. Each pair should write the appropriate relative pronouns and then check their answers with the answer key.

LEARNING STYLES

Logical/Mathematical

Challenge the class to create a set of icons for the six relative pronouns *who, whom, whose, which, what,* and *that.* First, invite a student to print them in alphabetical order on the board. Then divide the class into six groups. Assign a relative pronoun to each group. Encourage each group to create an icon or symbol that will help the class remember the pronoun. Afterward, have a volunteer make a poster of the six icons and post it in the classroom for ready reference.

Lesson 3 REVIEW

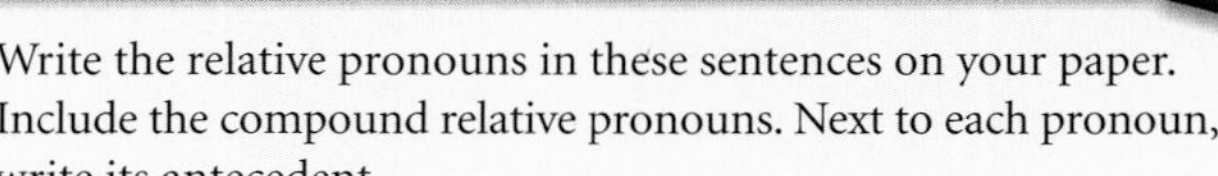

Write the relative pronouns in these sentences on your paper. Include the compound relative pronouns. Next to each pronoun, write its antecedent.

1. The mechanic who checked Alex's car did a good job.

2. Alex said to Andy and Frank, "Whoever wants to go for a ride should come now."

3. When you rent a video, choose whatever you would like to see.

4. There is the man whom I met in Florida.

5. Will had a friend whose sister was in the play.

Write these pronouns on your paper. Next to each one, write *personal pronoun* or *relative pronoun.*

6. itself

7. whatever

8. its

9. he

10. them

11. whoever

Write the correct pronoun in each sentence.

12. (Who, What) is that man?

13. The skateboard (who, that) Tara bought was expensive.

14. She is the teacher (who, which) won an award.

15. Did you see the pen (who, that) I was using?

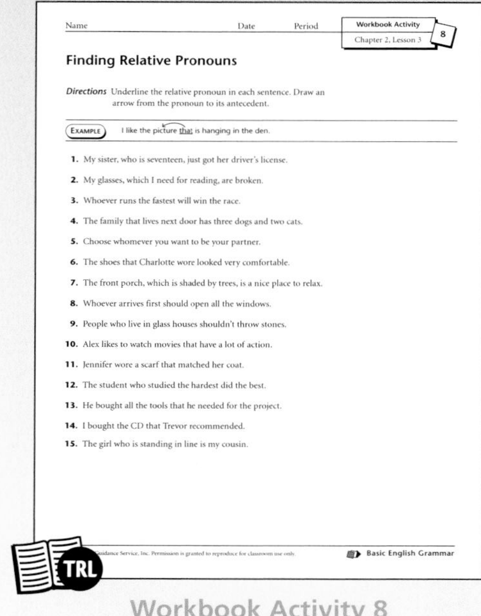

Name Date Period | Workbook Activity 8 | Chapter 2, Lesson 3

Finding Relative Pronouns

Directions Underline the relative pronoun in each sentence. Draw an arrow from the pronoun to its antecedent.

EXAMPLE I like the picture that is hanging in the den.

1. My sister, who is seventeen, just got her driver's license.
2. My glasses, which I need for reading, are broken.
3. Whoever runs the fastest will win the race.
4. The family that lives next door has three dogs and two cats.
5. Choose whomever you want to be your partner.
6. The shoes that Charlotte wore looked very comfortable.
7. The front porch, which is shaded by trees, is a nice place to relax.
8. Whoever arrives first should open all the windows.
9. People who live in glass houses shouldn't throw stones.
10. Alex likes to watch movies that have a lot of action.
11. Jennifer wore a scarf that matched her coat.
12. The student who studied the hardest did the best.
13. He bought all the tools that he needed for the project.
14. I bought the CD that Trevor recommended.
15. The girl who is standing in line is my cousin.

 Basic English Grammar

TRL

Workbook Activity 8

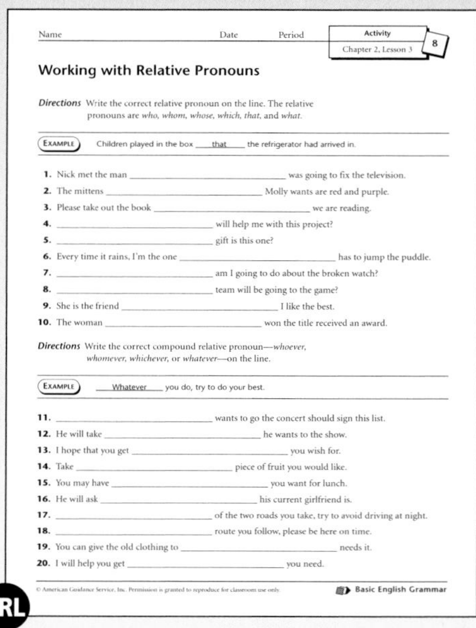

Name Date Period | Activity 8 | Chapter 2, Lesson 3

Working with Relative Pronouns

Directions Write the correct relative pronoun on the line. The relative pronouns are *who, whom, whose, which, that,* and *what.*

EXAMPLE Children played in the box that the refrigerator had arrived in.

1. Nick met the man ______ was going to fix the television.
2. The mittens ______ Molly wants are red and purple.
3. Please take out the book ______ we are reading.
4. ______ will help me with this project?
5. ______ gift is this one?
6. Every time it rains, I'm the one ______ has to jump the puddle.
7. ______ am I going to do about the broken watch?
8. ______ team will be going to the game?
9. She is the friend ______ I like the best.
10. The woman ______ won the title received an award.

Directions Write the correct compound relative pronoun—*whoever, whomever, whichever,* or *whatever*—on the line.

EXAMPLE Whatever you do, try to do your best.

11. ______ wants to go the concert should sign this list.
12. He will take ______ he wants to the show.
13. I hope that you get ______ you wish for.
14. Take ______ piece of fruit you would like.
15. You may have ______ you want for lunch.
16. He will ask ______ his current girlfriend is.
17. ______ of the two roads you take, try to avoid driving at night.
18. ______ route you follow, please be here on time.
19. You can give the old clothing to ______ needs it.
20. I will help you get ______ you need.

 Basic English Grammar

TRL

Activity 8

Lesson 4 Pronouns That Ask Questions

Interrogative pronoun

A pronoun that asks a question: who, whom, which, what, *and* whose

The **interrogative pronouns** are *who, whom, which, what,* and *whose.* They are called interrogative pronouns because they ask questions.

EXAMPLE

Who is planning the party?
Whom did you ask to the party?
Which purse did Jennifer buy?
What books are we to read for homework?
Whose backpack is on the floor?

Who, whom, which, what, and *whose* are interrogative pronouns only when they ask a question. Otherwise, they are relative pronouns.

EXAMPLE

Interrogative	Who is going to the party?
Relative	Ramon asked a girl who lives on his street.

Activity A Some pronouns in these sentences are in bold. Write them on your paper. Next to each one, write *interrogative* or *relative.*

1. **Which** season of the year do you like best?
2. **What** is the name of your book?
3. Tell me the people **who** are going to the dance.
4. **Whom** do you like the most?
5. He is the man **whose** wallet I found.

Lesson at a Glance

Chapter 2 Lesson 4

Overview This lesson presents interrogative pronouns, defines indirect questions, and explains the difference between the use of interrogative and relative pronouns.

Objectives

- To identify interrogative pronouns in sentences.
- To distinguish between direct and indirect questions.

Student Pages 39–42

Teacher's Resource Library 

Workbook Activity 9
Activity 9
Alternative Activity 9

Vocabulary

interrogative pronoun

1 Warm-Up Activity

Choose a student and begin asking rapid-fire questions. (Examples: What were you doing last night? Who were you with? What did you do after that?) Ask the class what you were doing. Elicit from them the verb *interrogate* (or introduce the word, explaining that it is frequently used to describe official questioning). Point out that there is a family of pronouns known as interrogative pronouns, which are used in asking questions. These include the words *who, whom, whose, which,* and *what.* This lesson will explain their use.

2 Teaching the Lesson

Invite a volunteer to read the interrogative pronouns listed at the top of this page. Ask students what they notice about this list. Elicit from them that these words include most of the relative pronouns discussed in Lesson 3. Point out that whether the word is a relative pronoun or an interrogative pronoun depends upon its use in a sentence.

Activity A

Before students begin the activity, have them point out the sentences that ask questions.

Activity A Answers

1. Which—interrogative 2. What—interrogative 3. who—relative 4. Whom—interrogative 5. whose—relative

Activity B

Invite a volunteer to read the examples for direct and indirect questions. Ask the class to identify an important way these examples differ. Lead students to understand that an indirect question is in statement form and therefore lacks a question mark at the end.

Activity B Answers

1. direct 2. indirect 3. direct 4. indirect 5. direct

3 Reinforce and Extend

ONLINE CONNECTION

Draw students' attention to the Technology Note on this page. Point out that because anyone can publish material on the World Wide Web, some sites are more reliable than others. Explain that Web sites ending in *.edu* such as **umich.edu,** the University of Michigan Web site, are associated with educational institutions and may provide more accurate information than some *.com* sites. Invite students to search the Web using key phrases such as *English grammar or English language.* Have them find a *.edu* site and print out a page to share with the class.

LEARNING STYLES

Body/Kinesthetic

Have students spend a few moments jotting down simple questions that they might ask a classmate. (Examples: *Where do you live? What time is it?*) Then have small groups of students sit in circles. One student should turn to the student on his or her right and ask a question. The next student should repeat the question in indirect form. (*Bob asked me where I live. Kalisha asked me what time it is.*) Have students practice repeating direct and indirect questions around their circles, helping each other with the wording when problems arise. Invite groups to "perform" their questions for the class.

Technology Note

When you use the wrong pronoun, people don't know whom or what you mean. Similarly, when you type the wrong ending on an Internet address, you won't reach the Web site that you're looking for. Four common endings in Internet addresses are *.com, .gov, .org,* and *.edu.*

- businesses usually use *.com*
- local, state, and federal governments use *.gov*
- organizations usually use *.org*
- educational institutions use *.edu*

You can use an interrogative pronoun to ask a question directly or indirectly.

EXAMPLE		
	Direct Question	What are you doing?
	Indirect Questions	She asked what you are doing.
		Tell me what you are doing.

Activity B Decide whether each sentence is a direct question or an indirect question. Write *direct* or *indirect* on your paper.

1. Who is going?
2. Ben asked Alex where he went.
3. Which kind of sandwich would you like?
4. Show me what book you have.
5. How do you feel today?

Interrogative pronouns must agree with their antecedents. Unlike personal and relative pronouns, interrogative pronouns do not have antecedents that can be stated. The antecedents are the answers to the questions that the interrogative pronouns ask.

Use *who, whom,* or *whose* when the answer to the question is a person or people.

EXAMPLE	
Subject	Who is your neighbor?
Object	Whom did you see at the mall?
Possessive	Whose decision was that?

Use *what* when the answer to the question is a thing, place, or idea.

EXAMPLE What are your assignments for the next week?

Use *which* when the answer to the question is a choice between two or more definite people or things.

EXAMPLE Which magazines do you read?

Activity C Write the correct pronoun on your paper.

1. (Which, What) of these fish is larger?
2. (Whom, Whose) did Kevin ask to the dance?
3. (Who, What) will win the World Series?
4. (Who, Whose) mother teaches at our school?
5. (Which, What) do you want for dinner?

Activity D Make two columns on your paper. Write *Interrogative Pronouns* at the top of the first column. Write *Relative Pronouns* at the top of the second column. Then find the interrogative and relative pronouns in the sentences below. Write them in the correct column.

Example Which of the tests that you took was the hardest?

Interrogative Pronouns	Relative Pronouns
Which	that

1. Alex has a friend whose uncle lives in Canada.
2. Name all of the cities that you have visited.
3. What is the name of your book?
4. Choose the book that you want.
5. Tell me which book you like best.
6. Who is the coach of your baseball team?
7. Which tree is taller?
8. What is your favorite subject in school?
9. Do whatever you think is right.
10. Which of the books is the one that the author signed?

Using What You've Learned

Write five questions to ask a classmate. Ask about activities your classmate did during the past week. Use an interrogative pronoun at the beginning of each question. Underline the interrogative pronouns you used in your questions. Then pair up with a classmate. Each of you can take turns asking and answering questions. Write your classmate's answers on your paper.

Activity C

Read aloud the first item and discuss the answer choices. Ask students which pronoun belongs in the sentence and why. Students can then complete the activity on their own.

Activity C Answers

1. Which 2. Whom 3. Who 4. Whose 5. What

Activity D

You may wish to have students do this activity as a group. Ask for a volunteer to make the columns and write the answers on the board.

Activity D Answers

Interrogative Pronouns	Relative Pronouns
3. What	1. whose
5. which	2. that
6. Who	4. that
7. Which	9. whatever
8. What	10. that
10. Which	

Using What You've Learned

Model this exercise by inviting volunteers to ask you questions orally about your week. Write sample questions on the board and identify the interrogative pronouns.

Writing Practice

Ask students to imagine that they have the opportunity to interview a celebrity of their choice—an actor, athlete, rock star, etc. Have them write the questions that they would like to ask their guest, and encourage them to make up the answers he or she might give. Ask them to circle the interrogative pronouns. Invite students to pair up and perform their interviews for the class.

Teacher Alert

People often confuse the use of *who* and *whom*. You may wish to point out that if students are unsure of whether to use *who* or *whom*, they can change the question to a statement. If the sentence already has a subject, *whom* should be used. For example, the question "(*Who, Whom*) did you see on the bus?" already has a subject in the word *you*. It could be changed to "You did see whom on the bus." Therefore *whom* is the correct choice for the question form as well.

Lesson 4 Review Answers

1. Which—direct 2. who—indirect 3. What—direct 4. whose—indirect 5. Whom—direct 6. It—personal, what—relative, they—personal 7. What—interrogative 8. Whatever—relative, me—personal 9. Which—interrogative, we—personal 10. Whichever—relative 11. Who—interrogative, us—personal 12. I—personal, that—relative, I—personal 13. which—relative, he—personal 14. What—interrogative, it—personal; I—personal, that—relative, I—personal, her—personal 15. Whomever—relative, you—personal, it—personal

Learning Styles

Body/Kinesthetic

Invite partners to present a "snapshot" of something by posing in silence. (For example, two students might pose silently in front of the room as if they are riding a bike together. Or they might stand silently as if one is singing into a microphone and the other is playing a guitar.) After each set of partners "poses," have the class use the five interrogative pronouns—*who, whom, which, what,* and *whose*—to ask the partners questions about their snapshot. Challenge the class to use all five pronouns to ask questions of each set of partners.

Lesson 4 REVIEW

Write the interrogative pronoun in each question on your paper. Then identify the question as *direct* or *indirect.*

1. Which ocean do you live closest to—the Atlantic or the Pacific?
2. He asked who wrote that book.
3. What country did Queen Elizabeth I rule?
4. Tell me whose jacket is on the chair.
5. Whom did you see at the mall?

Write the pronouns in these sentences on your paper. Next to each pronoun, write whether it is *personal, relative,* or *interrogative.*

6. It was Friday night. Alex and Andy talked about what they would like to do.
7. "What is playing at the movies?" Alex asked.
8. "Whatever is playing is okay with me," Andy said.
9. "Which theater should we go to?" Alex asked.
10. "Whichever has the best prices," Andy joked.
11. "Who else might like to go with us?" Alex asked.
12. "I think that I will ask Susan," Andy answered.
13. Alex thought for a moment about which girl he could ask.
14. "What is the name of Susan's friend? Is it Laura? I think that I will ask her," Alex decided.
15. "Whomever you decide to ask, make it quick. The movie starts soon," Andy said.

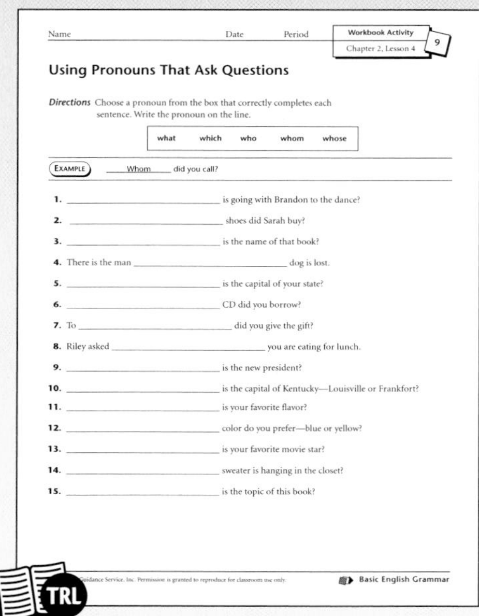

Name Date Period

Workbook Activity 9
Chapter 2, Lesson 4

Using Pronouns That Ask Questions

Directions Choose a pronoun from the box that correctly completes each sentence. Write the pronoun on the line.

what	which	who	whom	whose

EXAMPLE ___Whom___ did you call?

1. ______________ is going with Brandon to the dance?
2. ______________ shoes did Sarah buy?
3. ______________ is the name of that book?
4. There is the man ______________ dog is lost.
5. ______________ is the capital of your state?
6. ______________ CD did you borrow?
7. To ______________ did you give the gift?
8. Riley asked ______________ you are eating for lunch.
9. ______________ is the new president?
10. ______________ is the capital of Kentucky—Louisville or Frankfort?
11. ______________ is your favorite flavor?
12. ______________ color do you prefer—blue or yellow?
13. ______________ is your favorite movie star?
14. ______________ sweater is hanging in the closet?
15. ______________ is the topic of this book?

Basic English Grammar

TRL

Workbook Activity 9

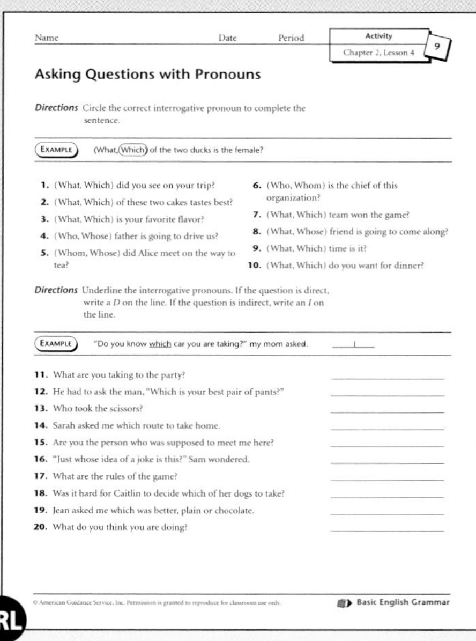

Name Date Period

Activity 9
Chapter 2, Lesson 4

Asking Questions with Pronouns

Directions Circle the correct interrogative pronoun to complete the sentence.

EXAMPLE (What, Which) of the two ducks is the female?

1. (What, Which) did you see on your trip?
2. (What, Which) of these two cakes tastes best?
3. (What, Which) is your favorite flavor?
4. (Who, Whose) father is going to drive us?
5. (Whom, Whose) did Alice meet on the way to tea?
6. (Who, Whom) is the chief of this organization?
7. (What, Which) team won the game?
8. (What, Whose) friend is going to come along?
9. (What, Which) time is it?
10. (What, Which) do you want for dinner?

Directions Underline the interrogative pronouns. If the question is direct, write a *D* on the line. If the question is indirect, write an *I* on the line.

EXAMPLE "Do you know which car you are taking?" my mom asked. ___I___

11. What are you taking to the party? ______
12. He had to ask the man, "Which is your best pair of pants?" ______
13. Who took the scissors? ______
14. Sarah asked me which route to take home. ______
15. Are you the person who was supposed to meet me here? ______
16. "Just whose idea of a joke is this?" Sam wondered. ______
17. What are the rules of the game? ______
18. Was it hard for Caitlin to decide which of her dogs to take? ______
19. Jean asked me which was better, plain or chocolate. ______
20. What do you think you are doing? ______

Basic English Grammar

TRL

Activity 9

Lesson 5 Demonstrative Pronouns

Demonstrative pronoun
A pronoun that points out a particular person or thing: this, these, that, *and* those

Demonstrative pronouns point out particular persons or things. The demonstrative pronouns are *this, these, that,* and *those.* We use *this* and *that* with singular nouns. We use *these* and *those* with plural nouns.

EXAMPLE

Singular	This is my pencil.
Plural	These are my pencils.
Singular	That is an expensive car.
Plural	Those are expensive cars.

This and *these* point out persons and things that are close.

EXAMPLE
This is my house.
These are the tickets to tonight's concert.

That and *those* point out persons and things that are far away.

EXAMPLE
That is my house on the corner.
Those are my boots near the front door.

Activity A Write these sentences on your paper. Circle the demonstrative pronouns.

1. Is that the movie you saw?
2. Those are new socks.
3. These are the pictures from my vacation.
4. Are these your favorite colors?
5. Is this the book you wanted?
6. Did Darleen buy that?
7. Put those away.
8. This is my favorite CD.
9. That is so bright.
10. These would make a nice bouquet.

Lesson at a Glance

Chapter 2 Lesson 5

Overview This lesson presents demonstrative pronouns.

Objectives

- To have students identify demonstrative pronouns in sentences.
- To distinguish between personal, relative, interrogative, and demonstrative pronouns.

Student Pages 43–45

Teacher's Resource Library 

Workbook Activity 10
Activity 10
Alternative Activity 10

Vocabulary

demonstrative pronoun

1 Warm-Up Activity

Demonstrate pencil sharpening by holding up two pencils, point to the pencil sharpener and say, "I want to sharpen these, so I am going to use that." Then walk over to the sharpener and say, "I put this into this; then I turn this." Afterwards explain that the words *this, that,* and *these* are examples of demonstrative pronouns. They get their name from the word *demonstrate,* which means "to explain" or "to make clear." Point out that demonstrative pronouns make ideas clear by identifying exactly which person or object is being discussed.

2 Teaching the Lesson

Hand a book or other object to a student and say "Put this on my desk." Then point to an object on another student's desk and say "Please hand me that." Write the words *this* and *that* on the board and ask students how they are used differently. Elicit that *this* refers to things near at hand and *that* to things farther away.

3 Reinforce and Extend

LEARNING STYLES

LEP/ESL

Point out that the concept of demonstrative pronouns is important in many languages. Invite students learning English to demonstrate how they refer to things near at hand and farther away in their first languages. Use simple examples such as *this is a pencil* and *that is a desk,* encouraging students to repeat the phrase both in English and in their own language.

Activity A

Write the first item on the board. Ask students to read the sentence aloud and identify the demonstrative pronoun. Invite a volunteer to come to the board and circle the demonstrative pronoun. After students complete the activity, ask them to tell which nouns the demonstrative pronouns are explaining or pointing out.

Activity A Answers

1. that 2. Those 3. These 4. these 5. this 6. that 7. those 8. This 9. That 10. These

Activity B

Suggest that students try each pronoun in parentheses in the sentence to see which one sounds most correct before they write their answers. After the activity, invite students to read the sentences with the answers in place. Have them explain how they made their choice.

Activity B Answers

1. This 2. those 3. This 4. These 5. that

Activity C

Before they do the activity on their own, have students form pairs and look for an example of a singular and a plural demonstrative pronoun. Invite pairs to share their findings with the class.

Activity C Answers

1. this—singular 2. That—singular
3. These—plural 4. Those—plural
5. These—plural 6. This—singular
7. that—singular 8. these—plural
9. This—singular 10. Those—plural

Activity D

Before having students complete the activity independently, invite volunteers to give an oral example sentence for each pronoun.

Activity D Answers

Sentences will vary. Check that *that* is used as a demonstrative pronoun, not as a relative pronoun.

LEARNING STYLES

Interpersonal/Group Learning

Divide the class into groups of four. Invite each group to create a short story using the four demonstrative pronouns—*this, that, these,* and *those.* Then ask each group to read its story to the class.

Writing Tip

A demonstrative pronoun must agree in number with the noun it identifies. Ask yourself: How many of this noun do I mean? If the answer is one, use *this* or *that.* If the answer is more than one, use *these* or *those.*

Activity B Write the correct pronoun on your paper.

1. (This, These) is my house.
2. Are (that, those) the people who just moved in?
3. "(This, Those) just came for you," Mrs. Thomas said as she handed Jennifer a big package.
4. Tom bought two new CDs. "(These, That) are really great!" he said to Jamal.
5. A car went speeding down the street. "Did you see (this, that)?" asked Amanda.

Activity C Write the demonstrative pronouns in these sentences on your paper. Next to each one, write whether it is *singular* or *plural.*

Example Are these Alex's gloves?
these—plural

1. Is this the recipe you told me about?
2. That is my backpack on the bench.
3. These are the books for Mrs. Johannsen's class.
4. Those are the flowers Jasmine took to her grandmother.
5. These are the toys Mya wants to give to the shelter.
6. This is the package that arrived today.
7. "Who sent that?" asked Jennifer.
8. Which of these do you want to try?
9. This is my e-mail address.
10. Those were the only choices.

Activity D Write a sentence using each of the demonstrative pronouns—*this, that, these,* and *those.* Make some of the sentences statements and some questions.

44 *Chapter 2 The Pronoun*

Lesson 5 REVIEW

Write the demonstrative pronouns in these sentences on your paper. Next to each one, write whether it is *singular* or *plural.*

1. Do you think Nicole would like these?
2. Those are exactly alike.
3. Pick that up, please.
4. These are very beautiful poems.
5. Is this yours?
6. Did you see that?
7. Tim gave me this.
8. Does that belong to Anna?
9. This is Sal's house.
10. Those are friends of Tyrone.

Write the pronouns in these sentences on your paper. Next to each pronoun, write whether it is *personal, relative, interrogative,* or *demonstrative.*

11. Alex works at a store that sells men's clothes.
12. "What department am I in tonight?" Alex asked.
13. "Go to the stockroom and help them with inventory."
14. Alex asked the people who were in the stockroom what he should do first.
15. "You can start by counting those," said the woman who was in charge.

Lesson 5 Review Answers

1. these—plural **2.** Those—plural **3.** that—singular **4.** These—plural **5.** this—singular **6.** that—singular **7.** this—singular **8.** that—singular **9.** This—singular **10.** Those—plural **11.** that—relative **12.** What—interrogative, I—personal **13.** them—personal **14.** who—relative, what—relative, he—personal **15.** You—personal, those—demonstrative, who—relative

In the Community

Ask students to visualize a place in their community that they know well—a ballpark, Main Street, the school, or a restaurant. Have them spend a few minutes jotting down things that they would see if they visited that location. Then ask them to imagine that they are showing a newcomer around the place. Have them write down what they would point out to their guest, using demonstrative pronouns. Example: *These are the bleachers. That's the dugout. Those are the umpires.* Choose a student to act as a newcomer and model a dialogue with him or her, pointing out objects in the classroom. Then invite pairs of students to perform their own guided tours of the community with the help of demonstrative pronouns.

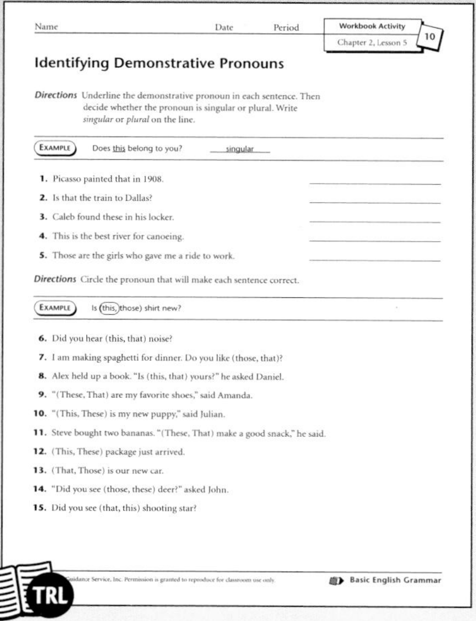

Name Date Period

Workbook Activity 10 — Chapter 2, Lesson 5

Identifying Demonstrative Pronouns

Directions Underline the demonstrative pronoun in each sentence. Then decide whether the pronoun is singular or plural. Write *singular* or *plural* on the line.

EXAMPLE Does this belong to you? singular

1. Picasso painted that in 1908. ______
2. Is that the train to Dallas? ______
3. Caleb found these in his locker. ______
4. This is the best river for canoeing. ______
5. Those are the girls who gave me a ride to work. ______

Directions Circle the pronoun that will make each sentence correct.

EXAMPLE Is (this, those) shirt new?

6. Did you hear (this, that) noise?
7. I am making spaghetti for dinner. Do you like (those, that)?
8. Alex held up a book. "Is (this, that) yours?" he asked Daniel.
9. "(These, That) are my favorite shoes," said Amanda.
10. "(This, These) is my new puppy," said Julian.
11. Steve bought two bananas. "(These, That) make a good snack," he said.
12. (This, These) package just arrived.
13. (That, Those) is our new car.
14. "Did you see (those, these) deer?" asked John.
15. Did you see (that, this) shooting star?

 Basic English Grammar

TRL

Workbook Activity 10

Name Date Period

Activity 10 — Chapter 2, Lesson 5

Using Demonstrative Pronouns

Directions Underline the antecedents for the demonstrative pronouns in these sentences. If the antecedent is singular, write *S* above it. If the antecedent is plural, write *P* above it.

EXAMPLE These are the new sweaters (P) my sister bought.

1. Those are the boys who helped me.
2. This is the proof we found.
3. These are extra stamps.
4. Is this your homework?
5. That is going to fall down someday.
6. What are we going to do with those?
7. The students are having these for lunch.
8. This belongs to these people.
9. Have you ever seen a park like this before?
10. Those are very dangerous train tracks.
11. He was trying to write a story, but he only wrote this.
12. Albert is here to fix this.
13. Have you seen any of those?
14. If I could have these, I'd love to have more cookies.
15. Are those the keys I lost?

Directions Complete each sentence by filling in a correct demonstrative pronoun. If the antecedent is near, write *N* on the line. If the antecedent is far, write *F* on the line.

EXAMPLE This coat I am wearing is nearly worn out. N

16. ______ are the mountains where I like to hike. ______
17. Whoever was sitting on ______ will be sorry. ______
18. Were you looking for ______ at Meagan's house? ______
19. When there are piles of mail like ______, I can't open it all. ______
20. ______ was the third time the doorbell had rung. ______

 Basic English Grammar

TRL

Activity 10

Lesson at a Glance

Chapter 2 Lesson 6

Overview This lesson presents indefinite pronouns and explains agreement of verbs and indefinite pronouns in sentences.

Objective

- To identify and use indefinite pronouns correctly in sentences.

Student Pages 46–49

Teacher's Resource Library 

Workbook Activity 11

Activity 11

Alternative Activity 11

Vocabulary

indefinite pronoun

1 Warm-Up Activity

Ask students to imagine that a friend is going to meet them at 7:00 precisely. Add that a second friend might join them later but isn't sure. Now write the words *definite* and *indefinite* on the board. Elicit from students that the first appointment is definite. Lead them to understand that the second is indefinite, meaning unclear or vague.

Point out that pronouns can also be definite or indefinite. While *he* or *she* are pronouns that refer to definite people, *anyone* or *everybody* is vague, or indefinite. Have students read aloud the lists of singular and plural indefinite pronouns and those that can be both. Point out that none of these words refers to particular people.

2 Teaching the Lesson

Write on the board "I loves popcorn." Invite a student to read the sentence and ask for a response from the class. Elicit that the correct form of words is "I love popcorn." Point out to students that they have corrected the sentence by making the verb agree with the subject. Lead them to understand that a singular subject takes a singular form of the verb; a plural subject takes a plural form of the verb. Point out that most of the time we make subjects and verbs agree automatically. With indefinite pronouns, however, we sometimes have to stop and think. Make your point by writing "Everybody love/loves popcorn" on the board. Discuss with students which form of the verb agrees with the indefinite pronoun. Have them review the list of singular and plural indefinite pronouns, and invite them to create sentences of their own.

Lesson 6 Indefinite Pronouns

Indefinite pronoun

A pronoun that does not refer to a specific person or thing

Indefinite pronouns replace nouns that are understood by the listener or reader. Some indefinite pronouns are singular. Some indefinite pronouns are plural.

Singular Indefinite Pronouns			
another	each other	much	one
anybody	either	neither	one another
anyone	everybody	nobody	somebody
anything	everyone	no one	someone
each	everything	nothing	something

Use the singular form of the verb with a singular indefinite pronoun. Do not get confused by words that come between the subject and verb.

EXAMPLE **Singular** Everyone has a sweatshirt.
Neither of us wants to miss the play.

Plural Indefinite Pronouns				
both	few	many	others	several

Use the plural form of the verb with a plural indefinite pronoun.

EXAMPLE **Plural** Several of the athletes have arrived.
The others are on their way.

3 Reinforce and Extend

TEACHER ALERT

Subject-verb agreement and pronoun-pronoun agreement with indefinite pronouns may be a difficult concept for students to grasp. If necessary, provide additional examples of correct and incorrect usage.

Activity A Write the indefinite pronouns in these sentences on your paper.

1. Everyone brought food to the picnic.
2. Jack did not know anyone at the party.
3. Several of the boys were late.
4. Try to be nice to one another.
5. Everything is ready for the party.

Some indefinite pronouns may be singular or plural, depending on their use. These indefinite pronouns may be singular or plural:

all	any	half	most	none	some

When an indefinite pronoun refers to a singular noun, the indefinite pronoun is singular.

EXAMPLE None of the exam was hard.
(*None* refers to *exam,* a singular noun.)
All of the garden looks beautiful.
(*All* refers to *garden,* a singular noun.)

When an indefinite pronoun refers to a plural noun, the indefinite pronoun is plural.

EXAMPLE None of the assignments were hard.
(*None* refers to *assignments,* a plural noun.)
All of the roses look beautiful.
(*All* refers to *roses,* a plural noun.)

When an indefinite pronoun is the antecedent of another pronoun, be sure that both pronouns agree in number.

EXAMPLE All of the girls took their jackets.
(*All* is plural and is the antecedent of *their.*)
Each of the boys has his wallet.
(*One* is singular and is the antecedent of *his.*)

Activity A

Have students work with a partner to complete this activity. Afterward, have pairs share their answers with the class. Invite volunteers to identify the sentences in which the indefinite pronoun is the subject of the sentence (items 1, 3, and 5) and to explain the subject-verb agreement.

Activity A Answers

1. Everyone 2. anyone 3. Several 4. one another 5. Everything

IN THE COMMUNITY

Remind students that whenever they have an opportunity to speak before their peers, coworkers, or any group of people, they should write down what they will say and then review it to be sure that they have used pronouns correctly. They should check that the antecedents are obvious and that subject-verb agreement is correct. Point out that a clear presentation makes ideas easier to follow and understand.

LEARNING STYLES

Visual/Spatial

Divide the class into pairs. Give each pair a colorful magazine picture. Challenge each pair to use its picture to create five sentences that contain an indefinite pronoun. Afterward, have pairs read their sentences. Ask a student to print each indefinite pronoun on the board. Challenge the class to provide examples for all the indefinite pronouns contained in the boxes on pages 46 and 47. Note: Keep these pictures for use in the Learning Styles activity on page 82.

Activity B

Have students complete this activity as a group. Invite volunteers to read each sentence and the answer choices aloud. Then have students discuss and choose the correct answer. Be sure students understand why an answer is correct before going on to the next item.

Activity B Answers

1. his or her **2.** their **3.** their **4.** has **5.** is **6.** her **7.** its **8.** are **9.** is **10.** is

Teacher Alert

Point out that many of the indefinite pronouns have built-in clues to indicate that they are singular. Have students review the list of singular indefinite pronouns on page 46. Ask them what they notice about the endings of the words. Elicit from students that several have the common endings *body, one,* or *thing.* Explain that when used as the subject, these singular words will always take the singular form of the verb.

Learning Styles

Interpersonal/Group Learning

Have students look at the list of indefinite pronouns that may be singular or plural. Point out that the key to understanding which form of the verb to use with these pronouns lies in the little phrase that follows. Write on the board:

- Some of the cake is/are
- Some of the cakes is/are

Invite volunteers to choose the correct verb and to complete the sentences. Lead students to understand that the verb will agree with the noun after the words *of the.* Ask students to form small groups to create sentences of their own beginning with *all, half, none,* and *some* and using the verbs *is* or *are.* Invite each group to write one of its sentences on the board and to explain why it chose the verb form.

Sometimes the gender of the indefinite pronoun is not clear. You may use both the masculine and feminine pronouns *his or her.* You can also rewrite the sentence using plural pronouns.

Everyone **brought** his or her **ticket.**
All of the students brought their **tickets.**

Activity B Write the correct answer on your paper.

1. Everyone carried (his or her, their) lunch on the field trip.
2. Many of the parents went with (his or her, their) children.
3. Few could drive (his or her, their) cars to the museum.
4. Each of the students (has, have) the combination to his or her locker.
5. Neither of the boys (is, are) wearing a coat.
6. Each girl brought (her, their) own supplies.
7. Neither of the coats is missing (its, their) buttons.
8. All of the employees (is, are) on time.
9. Nobody (am, is) as smart as Alex.
10. No one (are, is) wearing a watch.

All of the students enjoyed the field trip.

Lesson 6 REVIEW

Write a sentence for each of these indefinite pronouns.

1. someone
2. everyone
3. no one
4. anybody
5. nothing
6. none
7. everything
8. something
9. all
10. nobody

Write the correct word on your paper.

11. Everyone in Mr. Wilson's store (prepare, prepares) for the fall sale.
12. All of the salespeople (arrives, arrive) at work early that day.
13. Everybody is quiet as (they, he or she) works.
14. "Why (is, are) everyone so quiet?" one of the women asked.
15. "Some of us (remembers, remember) last year's sale," Alex said.

Where To Find It

Thesaurus

A thesaurus lists words with their synonyms. Synonyms are words that have the same or similar meanings. The words in a thesaurus are called entry words. They appear in alphabetical order. For example, if you look up the word *happy* in a thesaurus, you would find that some of its synonyms are *cheerful, cheery, glad, joyful, joyous,* and *merry.*

To locate an entry word quickly in a thesaurus, use the guide words at the top of each page. The guide words are the first and last entry words on the page.

Find the following words in a thesaurus. Write one synonym for each word. Then write a sentence for each synonym.

1. little 2. big 3. shy 4. look 5. wash

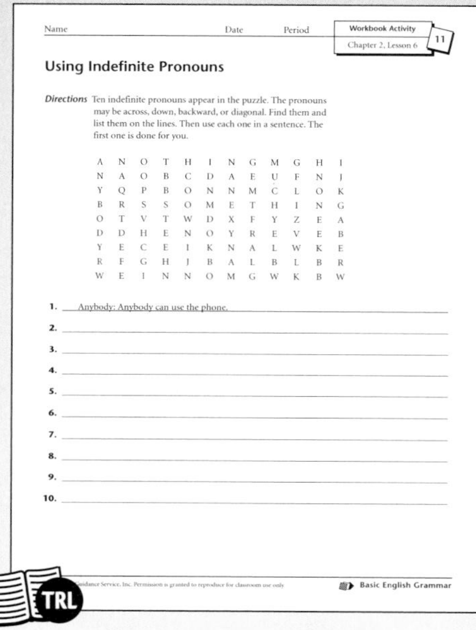

Name Date Period **Workbook Activity 11** Chapter 2, Lesson 6

Using Indefinite Pronouns

Directions Ten indefinite pronouns appear in the puzzle. The pronouns may be across, down, backward, or diagonal. Find them and list them on the lines. Then use each one in a sentence. The first one is done for you.

A	N	O	T	H	I	N	G	M	G	H	I
N	A	O	B	C	D	A	E	U	F	N	J
Y	Q	P	B	O	N	N	M	C	L	O	K
B	R	S	S	O	M	E	T	H	I	N	G
O	T	V	T	W	D	X	F	Y	Z	E	A
D	D	H	E	N	O	Y	R	E	V	E	B
Y	E	C	E	I	K	N	A	L	W	K	E
R	F	G	H	J	B	A	L	B	L	B	R
W	E	I	N	N	O	M	G	W	K	B	W

1. Anybody: Anybody can use the phone.
2. ___
3. ___
4. ___
5. ___
6. ___
7. ___
8. ___
9. ___
10. ___

Basic English Grammar

TRL

Workbook Activity 11

Name Date Period **Activity 11** Chapter 2, Lesson 6

Indefinite Pronouns with Verbs

Directions Underline the indefinite pronouns in these sentences.

EXAMPLE The others took the path to the beach.

1. Could I have another glass of milk?
2. Nothing could have stopped me from getting here.
3. Is there something I could do for you?
4. Write down each word as I say it.
5. Samuel said he would like to have another.
6. No one said anything.
7. Does everyone have a ticket?
8. There were too few to give one to everyone.
9. Both of the girls bought new shoes.
10. I know several good hiding places.
11. Either of the women could have been her sister.
12. Anything you want you can have, if you will work for it.
13. How much do you want?
14. What is the length of each piece?
15. The story is about everything that happens at school.

Directions Underline the indefinite pronoun and circle the correct form of the verb in each sentence.

EXAMPLE Both Jim and his brother (need, needs) new uniforms.

16. Some of them (was, were) colorful.
17. Everyone (is, are) going to be there.
18. Neither of us (want, wants) to have a piece of cake.
19. The others (have, has) already left.
20. (Is, Are) anyone flying to Los Angeles?

Basic English Grammar

TRL

Activity 11

Lesson 6 Review Answers

1–10. Sentences will vary. Look for correct subject-verb and pronoun-pronoun agreement. 11. prepares 12. arrive 13. he or she 14. is 15. remember

Where To Find It

Point out that a thesaurus is a very useful tool if you are looking for a new way of saying something or want to be reminded of a word that has slipped your mind. Students should realize, however, that many of the synonyms listed in a thesaurus will be unfamiliar to them and perhaps inappropriate for their purposes. Suggest that students avoid using a word that they do not know.

Have students respond to items 1–5 in small groups. Provide each group with a thesaurus and have students take turns looking up the assigned words. After students have completed their responses, invite them to find unfamiliar synonyms for familiar words such as *friendly, angry,* or *walk.*

Answers to Where To Find It:
Answers will vary. Possible answers follow. 1. little—small, limited, short 2. big—great, large, sizable 3. shy—backward, modest, timid 4. look—hunt, search, seek 5. wash—bathe, dampen, moisten, wet

At Home

Encourage students to make a list of the different types of pronouns to keep at home. They might also like to jot down any ideas in the chapter that they had difficulty with, for example, subject-verb agreement with indefinite pronouns. Suggest that students use the list and notes when writing personal letters and for completing writing assignments in other classes.

Lesson at a Glance

Chapter 2 Lesson 7

Overview This lesson defines contractions and explains their use.

Objective

- To identify contractions.

Student Pages 50–51

Teacher's Resource Library 

Workbook Activity 12

Activity 12

Alternative Activity 12

Vocabulary

contraction

Warm-Up Activity

Draw a smiley face on the board and say, "He's happy." Draw a face with a scowl and say, "She's sad." Invite volunteers to write these descriptions beside the appropriate faces. (Have the class suggest corrections if necessary.) Ask students why they used apostrophes in these sentences. Lead students to understand that the apostrophe represents a missing letter or letters. Point out that *he's* and *she's* are both known as contractions. Explain that this lesson introduces a variety of contractions formed with pronouns.

Teaching the Lesson

Have students read the list of common contractions on this page. Point out that the letter *s* can stand for *is, has,* or *us,* and that the letter *d* can stand for *would* or *had.* Suggest that the best way to understand what words a contraction represents is to try saying it both ways in full. Model this by writing *We'd like to go* on the board. Invite a volunteer to say this sentence using the two possible versions of *we'd* (*we had* and *we would*). Elicit from the class that the letter *d* stands for *would* in this instance.

Lesson 7 Contractions

Contraction
Two words made into one by replacing one or more letters with an apostrophe

In Chapter 1, you learned how to use an apostrophe (') to show possession in nouns.

EXAMPLE Annie's cat the fans' cheers

We also use an apostrophe in a **contraction.** A contraction is a word made from two words by leaving out one or more letters. An apostrophe takes the place of the missing letter(s). Contractions can come from a pronoun and a verb.

To *contract* means to "make shorter or smaller." We form *contractions* by taking out letters and combining two words.

Common Contractions	
I'd = I would, I had	who's = who is
I'll = I will	we'll = we will
I'm = I am	we're = we are
I've = I have	we'd = we would, we had
you'll = you will	we've = we have
you're = you are	they'd = they would, they had
you've = you have	they're = they are
he's = he is, he has	they've = they have
she's = she is, she has	that's = that is
it's = it is, it has	what's = what is
let's = let us	

Writing Tip

We use contractions in informal writing, such as a friendly letter or a note to a friend. We also use contractions in everyday speaking, not in formal writing.

Activity A Write each contraction in these paragraphs as two words on your paper.

We're studying the solar system in our science class. It's held fifth period. Mr. Vargas is an interesting teacher who knows a lot about the planets and stars.

I'd like to know more about Mars. It's the fourth closest planet to the sun. The diameter of Mars is 4,223 miles. That's a little more than half the diameter of Earth. The only planets smaller than Mars are Pluto and Mercury.

We'll study other galaxies next semester. I'm hoping Mr. Vargas teaches that class, too.

Activity A

Invite a student to read this passage aloud. Have the other students listen with their books shut, jotting down any contractions they hear. List their ideas on the board. Then have students open their books and complete the activity individually.

Activity A Answers

1. We are **2.** It is **3.** I would **4.** It is **5.** That is **6.** We will **7.** I am

3 Reinforce and Extend

TEACHER ALERT

Two of the words most commonly confused by students of English are *its* and *it's.* Write on the board the following sentences:

- It's a bear.
- The bear wants its dinner.

Ask students which is the contraction and which is the possessive. Lead them to understand that only the contraction uses the apostrophe.

Lesson 7 REVIEW

Remember that a contraction has an apostrophe to stand for missing letters. Find the contractions in this paragraph, and write them on your paper. Then rewrite each contraction as two words.

By the time Maya Angelou was 25, she'd been a cook, a dancer, and a streetcar conductor. Since then she's become a director, an actor, and a playwright. However, that's not what has made her famous. She's one of America's most popular writers. If you've read her first book, *I Know Why the Caged Bird Sings*, you know why she's so well liked. It's an autobiography that tells of her life up to age 16. I'm sure you'd like her poetry, too.

Writing Project

Using Pronouns When You Write

We often use pronouns to replace nouns. When you use pronouns, make sure the antecedent of each pronoun is clear.

On your paper, write 10 sentences that tell about someone you know well.

Include facts from this list:

- The person's age
- Where he or she lives
- A physical description
- His or her likes and dislikes
- His or her past achievements, hopes, and dreams

Underline all the pronouns in your sentences. Circle the noun that is the antecedent of each pronoun. If any of the antecedents seem unclear, revise your sentences to make them clear.

Lesson 7 Review Answers

she'd—she had, she's—she has, that's—that is, She's—She is, you've—you have, she's—she is, It's—It is, I'm—I am; you'd—you would

Writing Project

Model this activity by writing a few sample sentences on the board about someone you know well. Invite students to identify the pronouns and their antecedents. Before students start their own work, point out that they will probably identify their subject by name in the first sentence. Suggest that every so often they restate the name, so that the sentences do not become too full of monotonous pronouns.

After students have completed their sentences, have them exchange papers with a partner and check carefully to make sure that pronouns and antecedents are correctly identified.

Answers for Writing Project: Answers will vary. Check to be sure students underlined the pronouns and that the antecedents are clear.

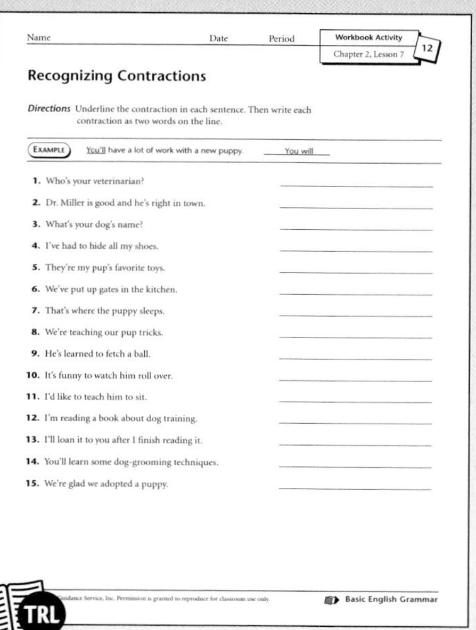

Name Date Period

Workbook Activity 12
Chapter 2, Lesson 7

Recognizing Contractions

Directions Underline the contraction in each sentence. Then write each contraction as two words on the line.

EXAMPLE You'll have a lot of work with a new puppy. You will

1. Who's your veterinarian? ______
2. Dr. Miller is good and he's right in town. ______
3. What's your dog's name? ______
4. I've had to hide all my shoes. ______
5. They're my pup's favorite toys. ______
6. We've put up gates in the kitchen. ______
7. That's where the puppy sleeps. ______
8. We're teaching our pup tricks. ______
9. He's learned to fetch a ball. ______
10. It's funny to watch him roll over. ______
11. I'd like to teach him to sit. ______
12. I'm reading a book about dog training. ______
13. I'll loan it to you after I finish reading it. ______
14. You'll learn some dog-grooming techniques. ______
15. We're glad we adopted a puppy. ______

Basic English Grammar

TRL

Workbook Activity 12

Name Date Period

Activity 12
Chapter 2, Lesson 7

Creating Contractions

Directions The underlined pronouns and verbs can be changed to contractions. Write the contraction for each pair on the line.

EXAMPLE She is the best athlete on the team. She's

1. What is the distance between Las Vegas and San Diego? ______
2. I asked them what they have been doing. ______
3. Let us be the first people on Mars. ______
4. This is the funniest letter that she has received. ______
5. Who is responsible for the equipment? ______
6. We have traveled a long way to get here. ______
7. It is not far from Jim's house to mine. ______
8. The hike was dangerous and we are very tired. ______
9. We would like to learn how to snowboard next winter. ______
10. When the race is over, I am going to be the winner. ______
11. Rolondo says you will have to finish the project for him. ______
12. If you don't take this to her, then I will have to. ______
13. That is the coat with the broken zipper. ______
14. Emily wants to know when we will leave. ______
15. I would like to walk around the park with Jared. ______
16. This garden is beautiful because it has been tended well. ______
17. He is the best dancer at the party. ______
18. If there was an opportunity to go, they would take it. ______
19. You must be joking if you think they are ready. ______
20. You are my sunshine. ______

Basic English Grammar

TRL

Activity 12

Chapter 2 Review

Use the Chapter Review to prepare students for tests and to reteach content from the chapter.

Chapter 2 Mastery Test 

The Teacher's Resource Library includes two parallel forms of the Chapter 2 Mastery Test. The difficulty level of the two forms is equivalent. You may wish to use one form as a pretest and the other form as a posttest.

Review Answers

Part A

1. pronoun **2.** interrogative pronoun **3.** antecedent **4.** first-person pronoun **5.** contraction **6.** second-person pronoun **7.** third-person pronoun **8.** relative pronoun **9.** compound relative pronoun **10.** personal pronoun **11.** demonstrative pronoun **12.** indefinite pronoun **13.** compound personal pronoun

Part B

14. It—day **15.** her—Jennifer **16.** She—Jennifer **17.** They—Jennifer and friend **18.** This—place **19.** us—Laura and Jennifer

Chapter 2 REVIEW

Word Bank
antecedent
compound personal pronoun
compound relative pronoun
contraction
demonstrative pronoun
first-person pronoun
indefinite pronoun
interrogative pronoun
personal pronoun
pronoun
relative pronoun
second-person pronoun
third-person pronoun

Part A On a sheet of paper, write the correct word or words from the Word Bank to complete each sentence.

1. A word that replaces a noun is a ________ .

2. An ________ asks a question.

3. The ________ is the noun that the pronoun replaces.

4. A ________ refers to the person who is speaking.

5. A ________ is a word made from two words by replacing one or more letters with an apostrophe.

6. A ________ refers to the person you are speaking to.

7. A ________ refers to the person or thing you are talking about.

8. A ________ is a pronoun such as *who, whom, whose, which, that,* and *what.*

9. A ________ is a pronoun such as *whoever, whomever, whichever,* and *whatever.*

10. A ________ is a pronoun that refers to a person or a thing.

11. A ________ points out a particular person or thing.

12. An ________ does not refer to a specific person or thing.

13. A ________ a "-self" pronoun.

Part B Write the pronouns in these sentences on your paper. Write the antecedent next to each pronoun.

14. It was Jennifer's first day at the new high school.

15. Jennifer looked for her new homeroom.

16. She walked up the stairs to the third floor.

17. Jennifer found an old friend. They were in the same homeroom.

18. "This must be the place," said Jennifer.

19. "Lucky us!" laughed Laura and Jennifer.

Name ________ Date ________ Period ________ **Mastery Test A, Page 1** Chapter 2

Chapter 2 Mastery Test A

Part A Write the pronoun that correctly completes each sentence.

1. Each girl invited ________ own family to attend. (their, her)

2. Jeremy and ________ are trying out for the volleyball team. (me, I)

3. All of the boys are going to see ________ favorite singing group. (his, their)

4. Ian was late for ________ class. (his, him)

5. These are the cookies ________ Nayda is taking home. (what, that)

6. Damon bought ________ a new bike. (hisself, himself)

7. ________ prefer to play tennis. (We, Us)

8. ________ of these books should I give to Debbie? (Which, What)

9. Everyone served ________ at dinner. (themselves, theirselves)

10. Everybody knows ________ painted that picture. (who, whom)

Part B Identify the kind of pronoun that is in bold in each sentence. Write *demonstrative, relative, indefinite, personal,* or *interrogative.*

11. **It** was spring at last. ________

12. **Everyone** was tired of bad weather. ________

13. Look at **that** sky! ________

14. Have **you** ever seen anything so blue? ________

15. They wanted a car **that** had four doors. ________

Part C Write the antecedent for each pronoun in bold in these sentences.

16. Cory has a friend **whose** car is for sale. ________

17. "Where is **my** backpack?" asked Marie. ________

18. Kimberly ate **her** lunch outside. ________

19. The man **who** plays saxophone is on stage. ________

20. Jason and Todd waited for **their** ride. ________

 Basic English Grammar

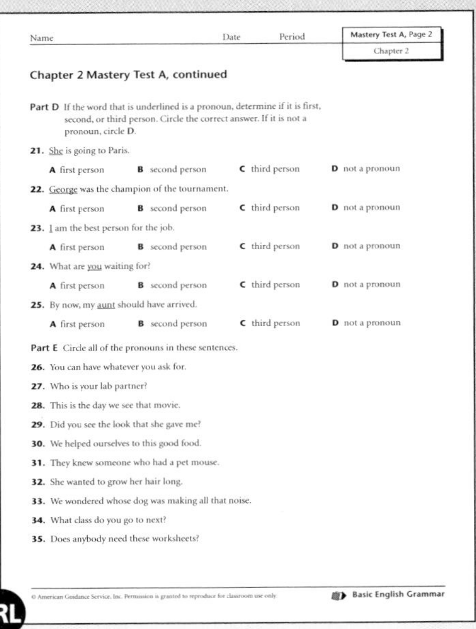

Name ________ Date ________ Period ________ **Mastery Test A, Page 2** Chapter 2

Chapter 2 Mastery Test A, continued

Part D If the word that is underlined is a pronoun, determine if it is first, second, or third person. Circle the correct answer. If it is not a pronoun, circle D.

21. <u>She</u> is going to Paris.

A first person **B** second person **C** third person **D** not a pronoun

22. <u>George</u> was the champion of the tournament.

A first person **B** second person **C** third person **D** not a pronoun

23. <u>I</u> am the best person for the job.

A first person **B** second person **C** third person **D** not a pronoun

24. What are <u>you</u> waiting for?

A first person **B** second person **C** third person **D** not a pronoun

25. By now, my <u>aunt</u> should have arrived.

A first person **B** second person **C** third person **D** not a pronoun

Part E Circle all of the pronouns in these sentences.

26. You can have whatever you ask for.

27. Who is your lab partner?

28. This is the day we see that movie.

29. Did you see the look that she gave me?

30. We helped ourselves to this good food.

31. They knew someone who had a pet mouse.

32. She wanted to grow her hair long.

33. We wondered whose dog was making all that noise.

34. What class do you go to next?

35. Does anybody need these worksheets?

 Basic English Grammar

Chapter 2 Mastery Test A

Part C Write the pronouns in bold on your paper. Next to each pronoun, write whether it is *personal, relative, interrogative, demonstrative,* or *indefinite.*

20. **It** was the dry season of the year.

21. **Everyone** was watering **his** or **her** yard.

22. "**Everybody** must try to save water," Mr. Jones announced.

23. "**What** should **we** do?" **one** of the neighbors asked.

24. "I suggest **that each** of **us** waters only once a week," Mrs. Mendez said.

Part D On your paper, write the letter of the pronoun that correctly completes each sentence.

25. Chris is a person ________ likes to be active.
A whom **B** which **C** who **D** whose

26. Biking is an exercise ________ he enjoys.
A that **B** whom **C** who **D** whatever

27. He wears a helmet to protect ________ .
A hisself **B** ourselves **C** oneself **D** himself

Part E On your paper, write each contraction as two words.

28. Alex decided he'd take the puppy for a walk.

29. Jennifer said she'd go to the mall, and we'd meet her there.

30. I'll let you know when I'm ready to leave.

Test-Taking Tip When you have vocabulary to learn, make flash cards. Write a word on the front of each card. Write the definition on the back. Use the flash cards in a game to test your vocabulary skills.

Review Answers

Part C

20. It—personal **21.** Everyone—indefinite, his—personal, her—personal **22.** Everybody—indefinite **23.** What—interrogative, we—personal, one—indefinite **24.** that—relative, each—indefinite, us—personal

Part D

25. C **26.** A **27.** D

Part E

28. he would **29.** she would; we would **30.** I will; I am

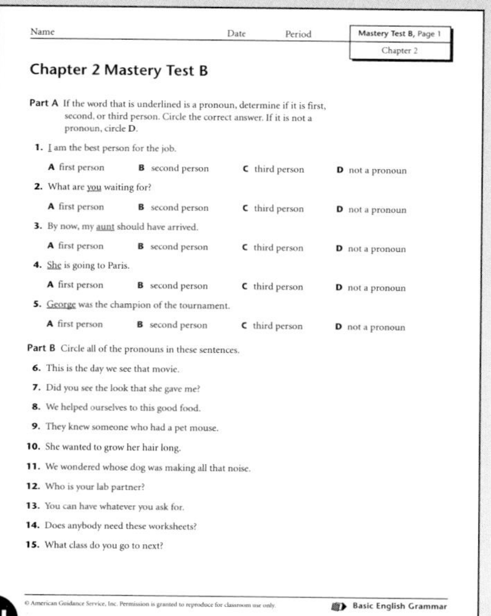

Name Date Period | Mastery Test B, Page 1 | Chapter 2

Chapter 2 Mastery Test B

Part A If the word that is underlined is a pronoun, determine if it is first, second, or third person. Circle the correct answer. If it is not a pronoun, circle D.

1. I am the best person for the job.
A first person **B** second person **C** third person **D** not a pronoun

2. What are you waiting for?
A first person **B** second person **C** third person **D** not a pronoun

3. By now, my aunt should have arrived.
A first person **B** second person **C** third person **D** not a pronoun

4. She is going to Paris.
A first person **B** second person **C** third person **D** not a pronoun

5. George was the champion of the tournament.
A first person **B** second person **C** third person **D** not a pronoun

Part B Circle all of the pronouns in these sentences.

6. This is the day we see that movie.

7. Did you see the look that she gave me?

8. We helped ourselves to this good food.

9. They knew someone who had a pet mouse.

10. She wanted to grow her hair long.

11. We wondered whose dog was making all that noise.

12. Who is your lab partner?

13. You can have whatever you ask for.

14. Does anybody need these worksheets?

15. What class do you go to next?

 Basic English Grammar

TRL

Name Date Period | Mastery Test B, Page 2 | Chapter 2

Chapter 2 Mastery Test B, continued

Part C Identify the kind of pronoun that is in bold in each sentence. Write *demonstrative, relative, indefinite, personal,* or *interrogative.*

16. **It** was spring at last. ________

17. **Everyone** was tired of bad weather. ________

18. Look at **that** sky! ________

19. Have **you** ever seen anything so blue? ________

20. They wanted a car **that** had four doors. ________

Part D Write the antecedent for each pronoun in bold in these sentences.

21. Kimberly ate **her** lunch outside. ________

22. "Where is **my** backpack?" asked Marie. ________

23. Cory has a friend **whose** car is for sale. ________

24. Jason and Todd waited for **their** ride. ________

25. The man **who** plays saxophone is on stage. ________

Part E Write the pronoun that correctly completes each sentence.

26. Everyone served ________ at dinner. (themselves, theirselves)

27. Everybody knows ________ painted that picture. (who, whom)

28. Each girl invited ________ own family to attend. (their, her)

29. Jeremy and ________ are trying out for the volleyball team. (me, I)

30. Damon bought ________ a new bike. (hisself, himself)

31. ________ prefer to play tennis. (We, Us)

32. ________ of these books should I give to Debbie? (Which, What)

33. All of the boys are going to see ________ favorite singing group. (his, their)

34. Ian was late for ________ class. (his, him)

35. These are the cookies ________ Nayda is taking home. (what, that)

 Basic English Grammar

TRL

Chapter 2 Mastery Test B

Chapter

Planning Guide

The Adjective

	Student Text Lesson				Language Skills		
	Student Pages	Vocabulary	Practice Exercises	Lesson Review	Identification Skills	Writing Skills	Punctuation Skills
Lesson 1 What Is an Adjective?	56–58	✔	✔	✔	✔	✔	✔
Lesson 2 The Articles—*a, an, the*	59–61	✔	✔	✔	✔	✔	✔
Lesson 3 Proper Adjectives	62–64	✔	✔	✔	✔	✔	✔
Lesson 4 Nouns as Adjectives	65–66		✔	✔	✔	✔	✔
Lesson 5 Possessive Pronouns as Adjectives	67–68		✔	✔	✔	✔	✔
Lesson 6 Numbers as Adjectives	69–71		✔	✔	✔	✔	✔
Lesson 7 Demonstrative Adjectives	72–73	✔	✔	✔	✔	✔	✔
Lesson 8 Using Adjectives to Make Comparisons	74–77	✔	✔	✔	✔	✔	✔

Chapter Activities

Teacher's Resource Library

Community Connection 3: Adjectives in Literature

Media and Literature Connection 3: The Search for the Greatest Superlative in the Universe

Assessment Options

Student Text

Chapter 3 Review

Teacher's Resource Library

Chapter 3 Mastery Tests A and B

Student Text Features						Teaching Strategies						Learning Styles						Teacher's Resource Library			
Spelling Builder	Vocabulary Builder	Where To Find It	Writing Project	Using What You've Learned	Writing Tips/Notes/Technology Notes	Teacher Alert	Online Connection	Applications (Home, Career, Community, Global)	Speaking Practice	Spelling Practice	Writing Practice	Auditory/Verbal	Body/Kinesthetic	Interpersonal/Group Learning	Logical/Mathematical	Visual/Spatial	LEP/ESL	Workbook Activities	Activities	Alternative Activities	Self-Study Guide
					✔	57		57				58		57	58			13	13	13	✔
61					✔			59, 60, 61		61				60				14	14	14	✔
				64	✔	63, 64										63		15	15	15	✔
								66			66	65						16	16	16	✔
		68			✔	67	68		68									17	17	17	✔
	71													71		70	70	18	18	18	✔
			73										73					19	19	19	✔
						75		76, 77				75				76		20	20	20	✔

Pronunciation Key

a	hat	e	let	ī	ice	ô	order	ù	put	sh	she	ə { a	in about
ā	age	ē	equal	o	hot	oi	oil	ü	rule	th	thin	e	in taken
ä	far	ėr	term	ō	open	ou	out	ch	child	ŦH	then	i	in pencil
â	care	i	it	ȯ	saw	u	cup	ng	long	zh	measure	o	in lemon
												u	in circus

Alternative Activities

The Teacher's Resource Library (TRL) contains a set of lower-level worksheets called Alternative Activities. These worksheets cover the same content as the regular Activities but are written at a second-grade reading level.

Skill Track Software

Use the Skill Track Software for Basic English Grammar for additional reinforcement of this chapter. The software program allows students using AGS textbooks to be assessed for mastery of each chapter and lesson of the textbook. Students access the software on an individual basis and are assessed with multiple-choice items.

Chapter at a Glance

Chapter 3: The Adjective
pages 54–79

Lessons

Skill Track Software for Basic English Grammar 

Teacher's Resource Library TRL

- Workbook Activities 13–20
- Activities 13–20
- Alternative Activities 13–20
- Community Connection 3
- Media and Literature Connection 3
- Chapter 3 Self-Study Guide
- Chapter 3 Mastery Tests A and B

(Answer Keys for the Teacher's Resource Library begin on page 340 of this Teacher's Edition.)

Name Date Period — Community Connection 3, Chapter 3

Adjectives in Literature

An adjective is a word that describes a noun or pronoun. Adjectives tell *what kind, which one, how many,* or *how much. Happy, dry, purple, five, the,* and *that* are examples of adjectives.

Adjectives are often used in literature such as short stories, books, and poems. Adjectives make language come alive for the reader. Authors use these words to tell more about characters, places, and things. Use these steps to find adjectives in literature.

Step 1 Go to the library or your bookshelf at home. Find a poem, novel, or short story that interests you.

Step 2 Read the poem or a page from the novel or short story.

Step 3 In the first blank below, write the author's name and the title of the work you chose. Use the next blanks to write each adjective you find on the page.

Step 4 Next to each adjective, write the kind of adjective it is: *article, proper, common noun, number, possessive, demonstrative, positive, comparative,* or *superlative.*

Step 5 Have your teacher check your work.

Author/Title: ____________________

 Basic English Grammar

TRL

Community Connection 3

Name Date Period — Media and Literature Connection 3, Chapter 3

The Search for the Greatest Superlative in the Universe

A *superlative* is a fancy word for the best-of-the-best. It means that something surpasses all others. If you start paying attention, you'll hear and see superlatives used all the time, particularly in advertising. Here's how you can find superlatives. Look for words that describe things or people as totally supreme!

As you know, adjectives can be used to compare people and things. The three forms are the *positive, comparative,* and *superlative*: good, better, best.

In advertising, writers almost always use the superlative form of adjectives. They don't want you to think that their product is just as good as or better than any other product. They want you to think that their product is the MOST FABULOUS, MOST POWERFUL, and LEAST EXPENSIVE product in the WORLD. Now we are going to find out how they did. We are going to search for the greatest superlative in the universe!

Step 1 Find seven or more ads that give examples of superlatives. Your ads can come from newspapers, magazines, the Internet, or other printed material.

Step 2 Decide which three of the superlatives you find in the ads are the most interesting, most outrageous, or least believable. Write these superlatives on the lines below. Make sure that you include the superlative adjectives used and the subjects they describe. (The subject is usually the name of the product.)

Step 3 Meet with a partner and read each other your three best superlatives. With your partner, decide which of your examples is the greatest, most wonderful, and most totally fantastic superlative.

Step 4 You and your partner will join with another pair of students. Each student will read his or her greatest superlative to this new team. By show of hands, have your group elect a delegate to represent your team in the final round.

Step 5 Your team's delegate will read his or her greatest superlative to the whole class. Your teacher, using his or her arms, will be the "human applause-o-meter" to help determine which example is the greatest superlative in the universe. Cheer your team on to victory!

Superlative 1: ____________________

Superlative 2: ____________________

Superlative 3: ____________________

 Basic English Grammar

TRL

Media and Literature Connection 3

Chapter

The Adjective

Look at the *plump, shiny* blueberries in this photograph. Study the *delicate, bumpy red* raspberries. When you use words such as these, readers can imagine what the berries look like without seeing a picture. These descriptive words are adjectives.

An adjective is a word that describes or tells about a noun or pronoun. One way that you can make your writing clearer and more interesting is by using adjectives.

In Chapter 3, you will learn about adjectives. Each lesson in the chapter focuses on a different type of adjective and its use in writing and speaking.

Goals for Learning

- To recognize adjectives in sentences and identify the nouns or pronouns they describe
- To recognize articles
- To recognize and capitalize proper adjectives
- To recognize numbers as adjectives
- To recognize possessive pronouns and demonstrative pronouns as adjectives
- To use adjectives to make comparisons

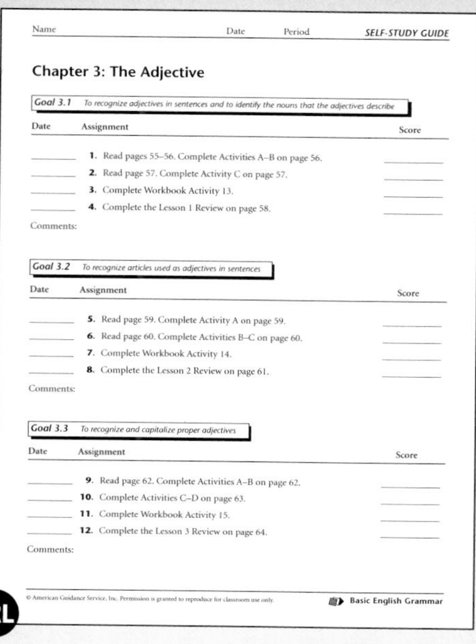

Name ______ Date ______ Period ______ *SELF-STUDY GUIDE*

Chapter 3: The Adjective

Goal 3.1 *To recognize adjectives in sentences and to identify the nouns that the adjectives describe*

Date	Assignment	Score
______	**1.** Read pages 55–56. Complete Activities A–B on page 56.	______
______	**2.** Read page 57. Complete Activity C on page 57.	______
______	**3.** Complete Workbook Activity 13.	______
______	**4.** Complete the Lesson 1 Review on page 58.	______

Comments:

Goal 3.2 *To recognize articles used as adjectives in sentences*

Date	Assignment	Score
______	**5.** Read page 59. Complete Activity A on page 59.	______
______	**6.** Read page 60. Complete Activities B–C on page 60.	______
______	**7.** Complete Workbook Activity 14.	______
______	**8.** Complete the Lesson 2 Review on page 61.	______

Comments:

Goal 3.3 *To recognize and capitalize proper adjectives*

Date	Assignment	Score
______	**9.** Read page 62. Complete Activities A–B on page 62.	______
______	**10.** Complete Activities C–D on page 63.	______
______	**11.** Complete Workbook Activity 15.	______
______	**12.** Complete the Lesson 3 Review on page 64.	______

Comments:

 Basic English Grammar

TRL

Name ______ Date ______ Period ______ *SELF-STUDY GUIDE*

Chapter 3: The Adjective, continued

Goal 3.4 *To recognize nouns used as adjectives*

Date	Assignment	Score
______	**13.** Read page 65. Complete Activity A on page 65.	______
______	**14.** Complete Workbook Activity 16.	______
______	**15.** Complete the Lesson 4 Review on page 66.	______

Comments:

Goal 3.5 *To recognize possessive pronouns used as adjectives in sentences*

Date	Assignment	Score
______	**16.** Read page 67. Complete Activities A–B on page 67.	______
______	**17.** Complete Workbook Activity 17.	______
______	**18.** Complete the Lesson 5 Review on page 68.	______

Comments:

Goal 3.6 *To recognize numbers as adjectives*

Date	Assignment	Score
______	**19.** Read page 69. Complete Activity A on page 69.	______
______	**20.** Read page 70. Complete Activities B–C on page 70.	______
______	**21.** Complete Workbook Activity 18.	______
______	**22.** Complete the Lesson 6 Review on page 71.	______

Comments:

© American Guidance Service, Inc. Permission is granted to reproduce for classroom use only. Basic English Grammar

TRL

Chapter 3 Self-Study Guide, Pages 1–3

Introducing the Chapter

Draw students' attention to the photograph of berries on the page and identify them as blueberries and raspberries. Encourage students to use words to describe the berries. Suggest that they use words telling how the berries look and how they think the berries might taste. Record their responses on the board. Tell students that these are adjectives and adjectives tell about nouns and pronouns. Explain that in Chapter 3 they will learn about different kinds of adjectives.

Writing Tips, Notes, and Technology Notes

Ask volunteers to read the tips and notes that appear in the margins throughout the chapter. Then discuss them with the class.

Teacher's Resource

The AGS Teaching Strategies in English Transparencies may be used with this chapter. The transparencies add an interactive dimension to expand and enhance the *Basic English Grammar* program content.

Career Interest Inventory

The AGS Harrington-O'Shea Career Decision-Making System–Revised (CDM) may be used with this chapter. Students can use the CDM to explore their interests and identify careers. The CDM defines career areas that are indicated by students' responses on the inventory.

Lesson at a Glance

Chapter 3 Lesson 1

Overview This lesson explains what an adjective is and the ways adjectives can be used to describe nouns and pronouns.

Objectives

- To identify adjectives and the words they describe.
- To add adjectives to sentences.

Student Pages 56–58

Teacher's Resource Library 

Workbook Activity 13

Activity 13

Alternative Activity 13

Vocabulary

adjective

Warm-Up Activity

Write *She is a good teacher* on the board and circle the word *teacher.* Then ask students to think for a moment of single words that might replace the word *good.* Write their ideas on the board in a cluster diagram around the circled word. Ask students what these words add to the sentence. Discuss how they make the sentence clearer and more interesting. Point out to students that these words are adjectives. Explain that adjectives are among the most valuable tools we have in expressing ourselves verbally.

2 Teaching the Lesson

Write *car* on the board and ask students to think of an adjective that might describe a car. Ask where you should write the words. Help students conclude that adjectives normally go before the nouns they describe. Now write *car fast* on the board, and ask students if an adjective can ever go after a noun. As a hint, explain that they will have to add a few extra words. Lead students to understand that in the sentence *That car is fast,* the adjective *fast* is describing the noun *car* although it appears after it in the sentence.

Lesson 1 What Is an Adjective?

Adjective
A word that describes a noun or pronoun

An **adjective** is a word that describes a noun or pronoun. An adjective may tell *what kind, which one, how many,* or *how much.* You can use more than one adjective to describe a noun or pronoun.

EXAMPLE

What Kind? We stayed in a small mountain cabin.
Which One? I live in the blue house.
How Many? We have lived in five cities.
How Much? They had some time.

Writing Tip

Replace general adjectives like *happy* and *good* with more specific adjectives like *excited* and *tasty.* These specific adjectives will help readers understand exactly what you mean and will make your writing more interesting.

Activity A Write on your paper the adjectives in bold. Next to each adjective, write the noun that the adjective describes.

Example Carlos bought an **expensive new** reel.
expensive new—reel

1. What a **fantastic summer** vacation they had at the lake!
2. We did not have **enough** time to do everything.
3. On the **first** day we were there, Vince caught a **huge** fish.
4. The **next** day, Carlos hooked **three** trout.
5. At night, a **large black** bear came into **our** camp.

Activity B Write these sentences on your paper. Add one or more adjectives to describe each noun in bold.

1. Students brought **books** to class.
2. **People** brought **food.**
3. **School** started early.
4. I saw **mountains** and **rivers.**
5. Janaya planted **tomatoes** and **cucumbers.**

Activity A

If students are comfortable with the definition of adjectives, have them do this activity orally.

Activity A Answers

1. fantastic, summer—vacation 2. enough—time 3. first—day, huge—fish 4. next—day, three—trout 5. large, black—bear, our—camp

Activity B

Do the first item with students before having them complete the activity independently.

Activity B Answers

Answers will vary. Possible answers follow. 1. Students brought new books to class. 2. Several people brought hot food. 3. This school started early. 4. I saw large mountains and clear rivers. 5. Janaya planted plum tomatoes and seedless cucumbers.

Most adjectives come before the noun that they describe. Adjectives may, however, follow the noun for emphasis. When an adjective follows the noun, the adjective is set off from the rest of the sentence with commas.

EXAMPLE The sleepy boy was crying.
The boy, sleepy and hungry, was crying.

Sometimes an adjective comes after the verb.

EXAMPLE He was sleepy and hungry.
They seem happy.

Activity C Write the adjectives in these sentences on your paper. Next to each adjective, write the noun or pronoun that the adjective describes.

1. The lake was beautiful on that morning.
2. The water was clear and cool.
3. Rajeev saw a large fish jump out of the sparkling water.
4. Vince used a trusty old rod.
5. By late afternoon, they had caught many fish.

The mountain air was cool and fresh.

Activity C

Help students understand that adjectives describing a noun may follow the noun. If necessary, write several more examples on the board before beginning this exercise.

Activity C Answers

1. beautiful—lake, that—morning 2. clear, cool—water 3. large—fish, sparkling—water 4. trusty, old—rod 5. late—afternoon, many—fish

3 Reinforce and Extend

TEACHER ALERT

Be sure students understand that an adjective sometimes follows a linking, or state-of-being, verb. You may wish to provide students with a list of linking verbs. Common examples include *be, become, seem, look, feel, appear, turn, grow, sound, smell,* and *taste.*

AT HOME

Have students choose a favorite room in their homes and spend a few minutes making a list of adjectives that describe that room and the things in it. Urge them to choose specific, vivid adjectives that help bring the room to life for outsiders. Invite volunteers to present their favorite descriptive adjectives to the class, explaining why they are appropriate.

LEARNING STYLES

Interpersonal/Group Learning

Have students look carefully at the example of adjectives that come after a noun, set off by commas. Write similar examples on the board. (Examples: *Jackson, quick and agile, easily won the race. The floorboards, old and rotten, needed replacing.*) Now have students form small groups and give them each a selection of familiar nouns. (Examples: *elephant, lake, waiter, rock star, mountain*) Ask the groups to write five sentences in the same form as those on the board: the noun, followed by two adjectives set off by commas. Invite groups to share their sentences with the class.

Lesson 1 Review Answers

1. chilly—weather **2.** heavy—coat **3.** several—classes **4.** favorite—class **5.** easy—Math **6.** the—boys, eight—hours **7.** a, long—time **8.** hopeful—They **9.** tired, cold—They **10.** their, next—trip, better—luck

Answers will vary. Possible answers follow. **11.** Diana has (a) (big) dog. **12.** David bought (a) (winter) coat. **13.** The fisher cast (a) line into (the) (calm) lake. **14.** It was (late) morning. **15.** (The) (department) store had a (huge) sale. **16.** I have (a) (good) job. **17.** Ramon plays (classical) piano. **18.** Annie's (gray) jacket has (a) (small) hole in it. **19.** My (older) sister bought (new) shoes. **20.** Andy is (a) (good) friend.

Learning Styles

Logical/Mathematical

On the board, write *Adjective, Noun.* Ask the students to call out persons, places, and things they see in the classroom. Write their suggestions in a vertical list under the word *Noun* on the board. Then challenge them to describe each noun by calling out an adjective. Write these under the word *Adjective.* Continue the activity by challenging the class to come up with two adjectives to describe each noun. Print responses on the board next to the first adjective given for each noun.

Learning Styles

Auditory/Verbal

Invite students who are enthusiastic storytellers to present a short narration for the class. They might tell a familiar fairy tale, the plot of a book or movie, or a personal narrative. Urge the storyteller to speak clearly and slowly. As he or she narrates the story, have students jot down any adjectives they hear. After the presentation, invite students to read their lists of adjectives. Challenge students to remember what these words described in the presentation.

Lesson 1 REVIEW

Write the adjectives in bold on your paper. Next to each one, write the noun or pronoun that the adjective describes.

1. In October, the weather can be **chilly.**
2. David decided to wear a **heavy** coat.
3. He had **several** classes on Wednesdays.
4. David's **favorite** class was math.
5. Math was **easy** for him.

Write the adjectives in these sentences on your paper. Next to each adjective, write the noun or pronoun that the adjective describes.

6. The boys fished for eight hours.
7. For a long time, nothing happened.
8. They remained hopeful.
9. They were tired and cold.
10. Perhaps their next trip will bring better luck.

Rewrite these sentences on your paper. Add at least one adjective to each sentence. Then circle all the adjectives in your sentences.

11. Diana has a dog.
12. David bought a coat.
13. The fisher cast a line into the lake.
14. It was morning.
15. The store had a sale.
16. I have a job.
17. Ramon plays piano.
18. Annie's jacket has a hole in it.
19. My sister bought shoes.
20. Andy is a friend.

58 *Chapter 3 The Adjective*

Name Date Period

Workbook Activity 13
Chapter 3, Lesson 1

Identifying Adjectives

Directions Find the adjectives in each sentence and circle them. Then draw an arrow from the adjective to the word it describes. *The, a,* and *an* are always adjectives. Do not circle them for this exercise.

EXAMPLE The (bright) (red) flowers cheered up the patient.

1. Cardinals like to live in thick woods.
2. Young children love to feed wild birds during the cold weather months.
3. I like my pumpkin pie hot and spicy.
4. The cat's soft fur invited petting.
5. The cold water was refreshing.
6. Laura, lovely and sweet-tempered as always, is a popular girl at school.
7. "Where is that large, heavy box that they delivered?" asked Gary.
8. After the swim in the lake, Dina felt cool and relaxed.
9. "Where did you buy this delicious cake?" Natasha asked.
10. It was a bushy, brown squirrel that was scampering in the tall oak tree.
11. Alex is funny, polite, and cheerful.
12. Brandon is tired and grumpy.
13. Cammy adores her sweet puppy named Winston.
14. Because the weather was freezing, everyone came inside for hot cocoa.
15. The ice cream, tasty and cold, hit the spot after the long walk.

 Basic English Grammar

TRL

Workbook Activity 13

Name Date Period

Activity 13
Chapter 3, Lesson 1

Locating Adjectives in Sentences

Directions Find the noun in bold in each sentence. On the line, write two adjectives that can describe that noun.

EXAMPLE Candace drove a **car**. fast, red

1. Daniel saw a family of **raccoons**. ______
2. I will take a **trip** to Chicago next spring. ______
3. Have you seen a **backpack** here? ______
4. Dana has **hair**. ______
5. Kelly and Tim rode the **roller coaster**. ______
6. Maureen bought a **puppy**. ______
7. Few students passed the **exam**. ______
8. Sarah has a **job** as a firefighter. ______
9. The **smells** coming from the kitchen made us hungry. ______
10. The **day** was perfect for a picnic. ______

Directions Each word in the box at the right is an adjective. Choose one adjective from the box that fits the meaning of each sentence. Then write that word on the line.

11. Raymond has an ______ disposition.
12. In the winter, the weather in Brownsville can be ______.
13. The ______ lake glistened in the early morning light.
14. Katie's tomatoes grew ______ and red in her garden.
15. Jonathon's ______ class is math.

Word Box
chilly
shining
round
favorite
energetic

 Basic English Grammar

TRL

Activity 13

Lesson 2 The Articles—*a, an, the*

Definite article
The word the, *which is used to talk about a particular person or thing*

Indefinite article
The word a *or* an, *which is used to talk about a general group of people or things*

The articles *a, an,* and *the* are always adjectives. They come before nouns in sentences.

The **definite article** is *the*. Use *the* when you are talking about a particular person or thing.

EXAMPLE Eric saw the musical yesterday.
(Eric saw a particular play.)

The **indefinite articles** are *a* and *an*. Use *a* or *an* when you are talking about a general group of people or things.

EXAMPLE Rhea wanted to go to a play.
(Rhea does not have a particular play in mind.)
Tony would like to see an adventure movie.
(Tony wants to see any adventure movie.)

Activity A Write these sentences on your paper. Circle all of the articles.

1. The math class was the first class of the day.
2. The students had a homework assignment.
3. The first part of the class was easy.
4. The class discussed the answers to the problems.
5. "I got a different answer to the problem," Jamal said.

Use the article *a* before a word that begins with a consonant sound. Use the article *an* before a word that begins with a vowel sound.

EXAMPLE

a large orange	an orange
a good act	an act
a mistake	an honest mistake

Lesson at a Glance

Chapter 3 Lesson 2

Overview This lesson presents the articles *a, an,* and *the* and explains their use as adjectives.

Objectives

- To identify articles in sentences.
- To determine when to use *the, a,* or *an.*

Student Pages 59–61

Teacher's Resource Library 

Workbook Activity 14
Activity 14
Alternative Activity 14

Vocabulary

definite article
indefinite article

1 Warm-Up Activity

Ask a student to hand you a book from a bookshelf. (If the student asks "Which book?" reply "Just a book.") Then ask another student to bring you *the* book from the same shelf, emphasizing the article *the.* When the student asks which book, specify one. Ask the class why the second student needed to know which book you wanted. Help the class conclude that the word *the* signifies a specific, or particular, object; the word *a* indicates a general group. Write the words *the* and *a* on the board. Under *the,* write *definite article* and *particular.* Under *a,* write *indefinite article* and *general.*

2 Teaching the Lesson

Write the words *ant, egg, icicle, oak, umbrella,* and *hour* on the board. Before each word, write the article *a.* Invite students to read what is on the board. Ask them what the problem is. Help students note that to simplify pronunciation, these words require the use of the indefinite article *an.* Challenge students to come up with a rule regarding the use of *an.* (*Nouns beginning with vowel sounds take the indefinite article* an.)

3 Reinforce and Extend

GLOBAL CONNECTION

Invite students who speak another language to explain the masculine and feminine forms of articles and the masculine and feminine endings of adjectives in their primary language. Encourage students who are comfortable writing in their primary language to write sample sentences on the board. Ask them to point out the articles and other adjectives and the noun or pronoun each adjective describes.

Activity A

Read the first sentence aloud to the class. Ask students how many articles they heard. Then have them look at the sentence. Identify the articles with the class before students continue individually.

Activity A Answers

1. (The) math class was (the) first class of (the) day. **2.** (The) students had (a) homework assignment. **3.** (The) first part of (the) class was easy. **4.** (The) class discussed (the) answers to (the) problems. **5.** "I got (a) different answer to (the) problem," Jamal said.

Activity B

Invite a volunteer to read sentence 1 aloud twice—first with *a* and then with *an*. Ask students which article belongs in the sentence and why. Ask students to explain how they knew when to use *a* or *an*.

Activity B Answers

1. an 2. an 3. a 4. an 5. a

Activity C

Have students complete this exercise in pairs. Afterward, ask pairs for their solutions. Urge them to explain their choice of articles.

Activity C Answers

1. a 2. an 3. the 4. the 5. an 6. a 7. the 8. a 9. the 10. an

Learning Styles

Interpersonal/Group Learning

Have partners work together to write six sentences that use *a, an,* or *the.* Suggest that they try to use at least two different articles in each sentence. Invite each pair to read their sentences aloud and explain why they used *a, an,* or *the* in each sentence.

In the Community

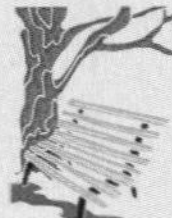

Have students hunt for the articles *a, an,* and *the* on Main Street. Ask them to copy down store window signs and slogans that are prominently displayed by local businesses and professionals. Have students bring their copy to class with the words *a, an,* and *the* underlined. Invite students to present their findings and to explain whether the articles have been used correctly.

You can use your computer's grammar checker to see whether you've used *a* or *an* incorrectly. Some grammar programs also explain exceptions when using *a* and *an.* Remember, words beginning with a *y* sound use *a:* a unit. A word beginning with an unpronounced *h* uses *an:* an hour.

Activity B Write the correct article for each sentence on your paper.

1. Suki packed (a, an) apple for her lunch.
2. They waited for (a, an) hour.
3. The teacher spoke in (a, an) soft voice.
4. They had (a, an) English lesson.
5. I read (a, an) book about elephants.

Use the articles *a* and *an* with singular nouns. You can use the article *the* with both singular and plural nouns.

Example

I bought a magazine.
(*Magazine* is singular.)

David bought the magazine.
(*Magazine* is singular.)

He bought the magazines.
(*Magazines* is plural.)

Activity C Write on your paper the correct article for each sentence.

1. Calvin is (a, an) talented writer.
2. He has written (a, an) article.
3. The article is about (a, the) Rocky Mountains.
4. He enjoys studying (a, the) land.
5. He thinks rocks make (an, the) interesting topic.
6. She had (a, an) message for her boss.
7. Look up the topic in (a, the) index.
8. They saw (a, an) horror movie.
9. Susan likes (an, the) blue coat in the window.
10. Jack is (an, a) honest man.

Lesson 2 REVIEW

Write on your paper the correct article for each sentence.

1. Look at all (a, the) traffic.
2. Did you enjoy eating (a, the) peaches?
3. Mrs. Jones put (a, the) groceries on the table.
4. We went to Toronto to see (a, an) play.
5. Chicago is (a, an) American city.
6. They did (a, the) activity in class.
7. A hammer is (a, an) useful tool.
8. Did you see (a, the) pencils I left here?
9. Being invited was (a, an) honor.
10. I was in (a, an) earthquake in California.

Spelling Builder

Words That Are Almost Alike

In the English language, many words look and sound almost alike. Examples include: *loose, lose; personal, personnel; quite, quiet; than, then; formally, formerly; were, where; affect, effect; advice, advise; choose, chose;* and *accept, except.*

Say the words *loose* and *lose* aloud. Pronounce each one carefully. Here are their different meanings and uses.

Loose Free; not tight
Used as an adjective

Lose To misplace; to fail to win
Used as a verb

Write on your paper the correct word for each sentence.

1. The team will (loose, lose) without its best player.
2. Be careful not to (loose, lose) your homework.
3. Ned's pants are too (loose, lose) without a belt.
4. The gate keeps the dog from getting (loose, lose).
5. Josie hates to (loose, lose) at checkers.

Name Date Period — Workbook Activity 14, Chapter 3, Lesson 2

Identifying and Using Articles

Directions Circle the definite and indefinite articles in these sentences.

EXAMPLE (A) thesaurus and (an) almanac were on (the) library shelf.

1. An unusual silence came over the crowd.
2. The president and a senator will attend the ceremony.
3. Evita will bring a punch bowl for the party.
4. The forest fire destroyed a hundred acres of trees.
5. George put a radio, a compass, and an orange in the backpack.

Directions Decide whether *a, an,* or *the* correctly completes each sentence. Write the correct article on the line.

EXAMPLE Stacy did not know ___the___ best route.

6. Do you have ________ envelope that I can use?
7. Did you see ________ books I left here?
8. Look at ________ bluebird outside the window.
9. I would like to have ________ drink of water.
10. What happened to ________ house while we were away?
11. The recipe calls for ________ egg and some flour.
12. Sandy's trip to Japan was ________ exciting adventure.
13. Today my brother drove for ________ first time.
14. ________ hundred years ago, only a few people had telephones.
15. For the holiday, Justin's family had ________ elegant party.

 Basic English Grammar

TRL

Workbook Activity 14

Name Date Period — Activity 14, Chapter 3, Lesson 2

Definite and Indefinite Articles

Directions Write the correct article on the line to complete each sentence.

EXAMPLE Sarah was so hungry that she ate ___the___ apple from her lunch.

1. George wanted to go on ________ vacation.
2. Have you seen ________ new shopping mall yet?
3. Will you take ________ old car to ________ hardware store downtown?
4. I'm shopping for ________ used car.
5. I am afraid of ________ dark.
6. Cathy is going to buy ________ apple and ________ pear.
7. Wake me up in ________ hour.
8. Jean awoke at ________ hour of sunrise.
9. ________ green coat is Bob's favorite.
10. You will need to bring ________ lunch.

Directions Circle the correct article. Then write *S* for singular or *P* for plural above the underlined noun.

EXAMPLE (An, (The)) many colors [P] of (a, (the)) sunset [S] were growing darker.

11. (An, The) prizes sat on (a, an) table next to the door.
12. She had waited for (an, the) hour before he showed up.
13. (An, The) hours seemed to go so slowly.
14. (A, The) boys wondered where (a, the) girl had gone.
15. If you want (a, an) honest opinion, ask Mollie.

 Basic English Grammar

TRL

Activity 14

Lesson 2 Review Answers

1. the 2. the 3. the 4. a 5. an 6. the 7. a 8. the 9. an 10. an

Spelling Builder

Have students read the pairs of easily confused words. Invite volunteers to say each pair, correcting their pronunciation if necessary. Point out that the key to knowing which word to use lies in understanding its meaning. Have partners look up paired words in a dictionary and use them in sentences. Discuss how the words are used differently.

Answers to Spelling Builder: 1. lose 2. lose 3. loose 4. loose 5. lose

Spelling Practice

Point out that most people (even authors and English teachers!) have difficulty spelling certain words. Suggest to students that one way of remembering spelling is to create a memory device known as a "mnemonic." A mnemonic can be a trick or a rhyme that will jog your memory when you encounter a confusing word. For instance, in spelling *ceiling,* you might repeat *i before e except after c.* In trying to remember whether *lose* has one *o* or two, you might say "*lose,* which means to misplace, has misplaced one of its *o*s." Have students review the list of easily confused words in the Spelling Builder, and challenge them to think of mnemonics for other spellings.

CAREER CONNECTION

Job applicants are often asked to explain orally or in writing why they would like a certain job. Discuss with students how using articles correctly with job titles (for example, *a* secretary, *an* assistant manager) demonstrates a command of the English language that can help their chances of being hired. Incorrect usage, on the other hand, could have a negative effect.

Lesson at a Glance

Chapter 3 Lesson 3

Overview This lesson presents proper adjectives and explains how they are formed.

Objectives

- To identify and use proper adjectives in sentences.
- To distinguish proper adjectives from proper nouns.

Student Pages 62–64

Teacher's Resource Library 

Workbook Activity 15

Activity 15

Alternative Activity 15

Vocabulary

proper adjective

1 Warm-Up Activity

Point out that the United States is a country with a multicultural society, made up of people whose ancestors came from all parts of the world. Write on the board *We have ____ ancestors.* Then ask students to point out on a map or globe the names of countries or continents from which their own or a friend's ancestors came. Have them use the adjective that describes this place of origin (*Irish, African, Native American*) and write that word in the blank space on the board, making sure that they use capital letters. Point out that these words are all types of proper adjectives.

2 Teaching the Lesson

Have students read the definition of *proper adjectives* at the top of page 62. Then write *American* on the board, and invite volunteers to use this word as an adjective in sentences. Ask students to give their sentences orally. If they use the article *an* or *the* in front of *American,* have them write their sentences on the left of the board. If they use *American* without an article, have them write their sentences on the right. When there are examples for each side, ask students why you have separated the two uses of *American.* Elicit that one set of sentences is missing the article. Lead students to understand that these sentences use the word *American* as a proper adjective, even if it occurs after the noun it describes. Write *adjective* over the right-hand side and noun over the left.

Activity A

Have a volunteer read the instructions for Activity A aloud. Before they begin writing the sentences, ask students what words besides proper adjectives they might find capitalized.

Activity A Answers

1. Bess had Spanish → class during first period. 2. She almost forgot her Spanish → book. 3. In her English → class, Bess was studying Shakespearean → literature. 4. This year in social studies, we learned about Native American → cultures. 5. Bess had never tasted Thai → food.

Activity B

Invite volunteers to provide sample sentences orally before having students write their sentences in Activity B.

Lesson 3 Proper Adjectives

Proper adjective

A proper noun used as an adjective, or the adjective form of a proper noun

Proper adjectives are proper nouns that we use as adjectives. Proper adjectives can also be adjective forms of proper nouns. A proper adjective always begins with a capital letter.

EXAMPLE

Proper Noun	He is a Canadian.
Proper Adjective	He is a Canadian citizen.
Proper Noun	I visited Italy.
Proper Adjective	I love Italian food.

Activity A Write these sentences on your paper. Find the proper adjectives. Then draw an arrow from the proper adjective to the noun or pronoun it describes. Read carefully. Not all of the capitalized words are proper adjectives.

Example Helen likes Irish stories.

1. Bess had Spanish class during first period.
2. She almost forgot her Spanish book.
3. In her English class, Bess was studying Shakespearean literature.
4. This year in social studies, we learned about American Indian cultures.
5. Bess had never tasted Thai food.

Some people use the proper adjective *American Indian* instead of *Native American.* Both describe people whose ancestors lived in the Americas before settlers arrived from Europe.

Activity B Use these proper adjectives in sentences. Write the sentences on your paper. Draw an arrow from the proper adjective to the word it describes.

1. Spanish
2. German
3. Chinese
4. Democratic
5. African
6. Brazilian
7. American
8. Olympic
9. Swiss
10. Republican

Activity C Complete each sentence with a proper adjective. Write the sentences on your paper.

1. We ordered ________ dressing for our salad.
2. Mr. Cruz likes ________ cheese.
3. Latasha studied the ________ language last year.
4. They live in Germany, but they are ________ citizens.
5. He belongs to the ________ Party.
6. Is ________ cooking easier than it looks?
7. We saw examples of ________ art.
8. Both his grandparents are ________.
9. Ashley enjoys ________ cooking.
10. We studied ________ history last year.

Activity D Write the words in bold on your paper. Next to each word, write whether it is used as a *proper noun* or a *proper adjective*. If it is an adjective, write the noun or pronoun it describes next to it.

Example Leigh learned about **Japanese** poetry yesterday.
Japanese, proper adjective—poetry

1. I like **French** onion soup.
2. Chang lives in **Philadelphia.**
3. He is a **Philadelphia** boy.
4. Kareem watched the **Russian** jugglers.
5. The high school band will march in the **Thanksgiving Day** parade.

3 Reinforce and Extend

TEACHER ALERT

Because a word may be spelled the same whether it is a proper adjective or a proper noun, emphasize how important it is for students to read all the words in a sentence before they write an answer for each item.

LEARNING STYLES

Visual/Spatial

Point out that proper adjectives created from the names of countries can end with *-an* (*American*), *-ian* (*Canadian*), *-ish* (*Irish*), and *-ese* (*Chinese*). Others have their own unique word (*French*). Ask groups of students to make a chart with columns labeled *-an, -ian, -ish, -ese,* and *other.* Have the groups look up countries, regions, or continents and find the proper adjective formed from that place name. Students should write their adjectives in the appropriate column of their charts.

Activity B Answers

Sentences will vary. Possible answers follow. **1.** Juana enjoys Spanish → dancing. **2.** Many German → tourists visit Florida. **3.** The Chinese → language is very difficult to learn. **4.** My parents belonged to the Democratic → Party. **5.** Lions live on the African → plains. **6.** I enjoy listening to Brazilian → music. **7.** The American → athletes did well in the competition. **8.** The Olympic → games were very exciting. **9.** I like Swiss → cheese on my sandwiches. **10.** The Republican → candidates held a rally.

Activity C

Write three sentences on the board with blanks in place of proper adjectives. Invite students to fill in each blank with a proper adjective. To stress that there is no one correct answer for the activity items, accept several responses for each of the sample sentences.

Activity C Answers

Answers will vary. Possible proper adjectives are listed. **1.** Russian **2.** Swiss **3.** French **4.** British **5.** Republican **6.** Chinese **7.** African **8.** Indian **9.** Italian **10.** European

Activity D

Write *Labor Day* on the board. Ask students whether this is a proper noun or a proper adjective. Lead them to understand that it can be either. Invite students to create sentences in which it is used as a noun or an adjective.

Activity D Answers

1. French, proper adjective—onion soup **2.** Philadelphia, proper noun **3.** Philadelphia, proper adjective—boy **4.** Russian, proper adjective—jugglers **5.** Thanksgiving Day, proper adjective—parade.

Lesson 3 Review Answers

1. Jack likes to drive that old German → car. **2.** We read several Spanish and Italian → folktales. **3.** They spent the summer camping along the Maine → coast. **4.** Melina's father is American, and her mother is Canadian. **5.** You are invited to our Memorial Day → picnic.

Answers will vary. Possible answers follow. **6.** Margaret's brother is studying Asian → art. **7.** Our town has a Fourth of July → celebration. **8.** Haritha wore an Indian → sari. **9.** She is studying United States → history. **10.** The candidate was a member of the Democratic → Party. **11.** The South American → musicians were entertaining. **12.** We read several Chinese → folktales in class. **13.** The Mexican → food was delicious. **14.** Have you ever seen a French → film? **15.** The Irish → countryside is beautiful! **16.** Russian—proper noun **17.** Danish—proper adjective **18.** New Year's Eve—proper adjective **19.** Boston—proper adjective **20.** Japanese—proper noun

Using What You've Learned

Before they start writing their notes, remind students that proper adjectives are formed from more than the names of countries. The names of holidays can become adjectives (*Veterans Day service*), so can the names of months (*beautiful April weather*). Write some sample sentences on the board. Encourage students to use more than one type of proper adjective in their notes.

Teacher Alert

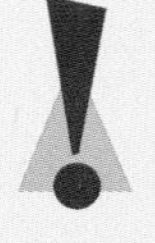

Students should be reminded that *Democratic* is a proper adjective only when used to describe one of the political parties of the United States (*the Democratic Party*). When used to describe other nouns (for example, a *democratic idea* or a *democratic policy*), it is considered a common adjective and is not capitalized.

Lesson 3 REVIEW

Write these sentences on your paper. Capitalize all of the proper adjectives. Then draw an arrow from each proper adjective to the noun it describes.

1. Jack likes to drive that old german car.
2. We read several spanish and italian folktales.
3. They spent the summer camping along the maine coast.
4. Melina's father is american, and her mother is canadian.
5. You are invited to our memorial day picnic.

Use each proper noun as a proper adjective in a sentence. You may need to change the form of the word. Write the sentences on your paper. Draw an arrow from each proper adjective to the noun or pronoun it describes.

6. Asia
7. Fourth of July
8. India
9. United States
10. Democrat
11. South America
12. China
13. Mexico
14. France
15. Ireland

Write the words in bold on your paper. Next to each one, write whether it is used as a *proper noun* or a *proper adjective.*

16. Nina speaks **Russian.**
17. Anna is a **Danish** citizen.
18. Did you go to the **New Year's Eve** party?
19. Roy has a **Boston** accent.
20. The instructions are in **Japanese.**

Using What You've Learned

On your paper, write a short note to a friend. Describe an imaginary trip to a place you have never been. Use at least three proper adjectives in your description. When you have finished, underline the proper adjectives. Then share your note with a classmate.

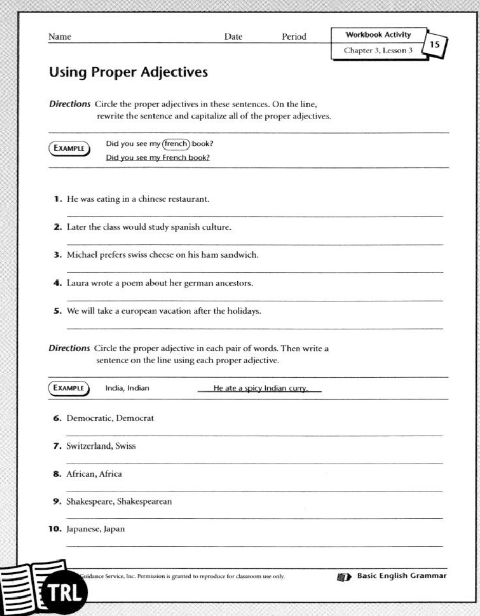

Name Date Period | Workbook Activity 15 | Chapter 3, Lesson 3

Using Proper Adjectives

Directions Circle the proper adjectives in these sentences. On the line, rewrite the sentence and capitalize all of the proper adjectives.

EXAMPLE Did you see my french book?
Did you see my French book?

1. He was eating in a chinese restaurant.
2. Later the class would study spanish culture.
3. Michael prefers swiss cheese on his ham sandwich.
4. Laura wrote a poem about her german ancestors.
5. We will take a european vacation after the holidays.

Directions Circle the proper adjective in each pair of words. Then write a sentence on the line using each proper adjective.

EXAMPLE India, Indian He ate a spicy Indian curry.

6. Democratic, Democrat
7. Switzerland, Swiss
8. African, Africa
9. Shakespeare, Shakespearean
10. Japanese, Japan

 Basic English Grammar

TRL

Workbook Activity 15

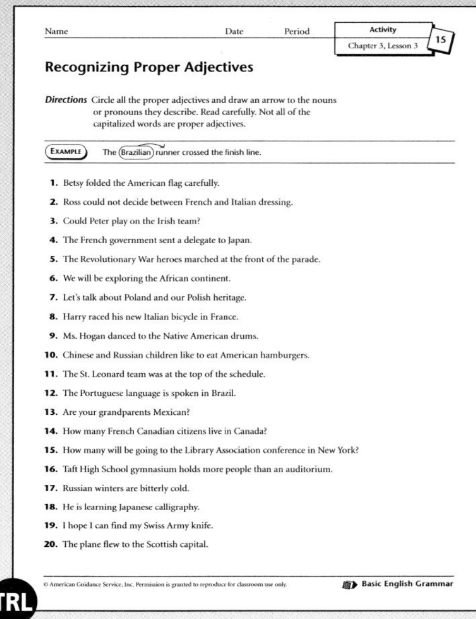

Name Date Period | Activity 15 | Chapter 3, Lesson 3

Recognizing Proper Adjectives

Directions Circle all the proper adjectives and draw an arrow to the nouns or pronouns they describe. Read carefully. Not all of the capitalized words are proper adjectives.

EXAMPLE The Brazilian runner crossed the finish line.

1. Betsy folded the American flag carefully.
2. Ross could not decide between French and Italian dressing.
3. Could Peter play on the Irish team?
4. The French government sent a delegate to Japan.
5. The Revolutionary War heroes marched at the front of the parade.
6. We will be exploring the African continent.
7. Let's talk about Poland and our Polish heritage.
8. Harry raced his new Italian bicycle in France.
9. Ms. Hogan danced to the Native American drums.
10. Chinese and Russian children like to eat American hamburgers.
11. The St. Leonard team was at the top of the schedule.
12. The Portuguese language is spoken in Brazil.
13. Are your grandparents Mexican?
14. How many French Canadian citizens live in Canada?
15. How many will be going to the Library Association conference in New York?
16. Taft High School gymnasium holds more people than an auditorium.
17. Russian winters are bitterly cold.
18. He is learning Japanese calligraphy.
19. I hope I can find my Swiss Army knife.
20. The plane flew to the Scottish capital.

 Basic English Grammar

TRL

Activity 15

Lesson 4 Nouns as Adjectives

We often use common nouns as adjectives. To decide whether a word is a noun or an adjective, look at how the writer used it in the sentence.

EXAMPLE

Noun	Luke plays the piano.
Adjective	Luke enjoys his piano lessons. (*Piano* describes the noun *lessons.*)
Noun	Keri plays baseball.
Adjective	Keri plays on the baseball team. (*Baseball* describes the noun *team.*)

Activity A Write the words in bold on your paper. Next to each word, write whether it is a *noun* or an *adjective*. If it is an adjective, write the noun it describes.

Example She works for the **city.**
city—noun
She likes **city** life.
city—adjective, life

1. I'm looking for a **summer** job.
2. My sister found a great job for the **summer.**
3. Vera will be working as a **park** leader.
4. She will probably work at the **park** near our house.
5. She gets to be outside all day playing **basketball** with little kids.
6. Wasn't Vera one of the best **basketball** players on the girls' team?
7. In fact, three different **college** coaches have called her.
8. Vera has not decided which **college** she will go to yet.
9. They have offered her **scholarships** to play at their schools.
10. The **scholarship** application was very long.

Lesson at a Glance

Chapter 3 Lesson 4

Overview This lesson presents common nouns used as adjectives.

Objectives

- To identify common nouns used as adjectives in sentences.
- To use common nouns as adjectives in sentences.

Student Pages 65–66

Teacher's Resource Library 

Workbook Activity 16
Activity 16
Alternative Activity 16

1 Warm-Up Activity

Write the following incomplete phrases on the board: ___ *training;* ___ *store;* ___ *shredder.* Then read the following clues to the class, asking them to fill in the blanks on the board: *a time when baseball players practice for the season; a place to buy footwear; a machine for destroying documents.* Lead students to understand that these words can be either adjectives or nouns, depending on how they are used in a sentence.

2 Teaching the Lesson

Help students determine whether a word is serving as a noun or an adjective by suggesting that they remove the word in question and read the sentence without it. Point out that an adjective can often be removed without doing much damage to the sense of a sentence. The noun it modifies, however, is usually crucial to the reader's understanding.

Activity A

Write the first item in the activity on the board and ask students to find a noun and an adjective that is not an article in the sentence. Then have students work with a partner to complete the activity.

3 Reinforce and Extend

LEARNING STYLES

Auditory/Verbal
Ask a volunteer to begin naming aloud the nouns—persons, places, things—in the classroom. Encourage the other students to listen carefully to the volunteer and to raise their hands when they hear a noun that they can turn into an adjective. Ask a member of the class to compose a sentence that uses the noun as an adjective.

Activity A Answers

1. summer—adjective, job **2.** summer—noun **3.** park—adjective, leader **4.** park—noun **5.** basketball—noun **6.** basketball—adjective, players **7.** college—adjective, coaches **8.** college—noun **9.** scholarships—noun **10.** scholarship—adjective, application

Lesson 4 Review Answers

1. lunch—bag **2.** newspaper—meeting **3.** school—paper **4.** sports—reporter **5.** team—members **6.** track—event **7.** spaghetti—dinner **8.** bus—ride **9.** interview—notes **10.** computer—room

Answers will vary. Possible answers follow. **11.** The baseball → game was too long. **12.** This fruit → spread is wonderful on toast. **13.** Where are our winter → coats? **14.** My dad added tomato → paste to the sauce. **15.** Jason performed in the school → play. **16.** I am excited for the holiday → season to begin. **17.** farm—adjective **18.** farm—noun **19.** country—noun **20.** country—adjective

Writing Practice

Brainstorm with the class for a list of nouns that can be used as adjectives. From this list, randomly assign each student five of the words. Ask students to write an imaginative narrative using their five words as adjectives. Have them underline their adjectives. Invite volunteers to read their narratives to the class.

At Home

Encourage students to look for nouns used as adjectives in newspaper and magazine advertisements or reviews. Have them list the adjectives with the nouns described. Then invite students to share their lists with the class.

Lesson 4 REVIEW

Write on your paper the common nouns used as adjectives. Next to each adjective, write the noun it describes.

1. Jovan grabbed his lunch bag and ran out the door.
2. He was going to be late for the newspaper meeting.
3. Jovan enjoyed working on the school paper.
4. As the sports reporter, he went to all the games.
5. Talking to team members before and after the games was fun.
6. Last week, he covered a big track event.
7. The night before, he joined the team for a spaghetti dinner.
8. On the bus ride the next day, he spoke to the coaches and athletes.
9. He jotted down his interview notes in a notebook.
10. After the game, he went to the computer room at school to write his article.

Write a sentence on your paper using each common noun as an adjective. Draw an arrow from each adjective to the noun it describes.

11. baseball
12. fruit
13. winter
14. tomato
15. school
16. holiday

Write the words in bold on your paper. Next to each word, write whether it is a *noun* or an *adjective.*

17. Jamie likes **farm** life.
18. Her parents live on a **farm.**
19. It is in the **country,** far from the city.
20. She enjoys fresh, **country** air.

Name Date Period

Workbook Activity 16
Chapter 3, Lesson 4

Using Nouns as Adjectives

Directions Each word in bold is a common noun used as an adjective. On the line, write the word the adjective describes.

EXAMPLE May I borrow a sheet of **notebook** paper? paper

1. Katrina teaches an **exercise** class every day. ______
2. The **world** map shows all the continents. ______
3. Dennis always has milk with his **breakfast** cereal. ______
4. The **mountain** road was steep and narrow. ______
5. I need to buy **office** supplies. ______

Directions Decide if the word in bold is a noun or an adjective. Write *noun* or *adjective* on the line.

EXAMPLE Jason bought a **class** ring. adjective

6. The **basketball** court was covered in snow. ______
7. George enjoyed playing **basketball**. ______
8. We enjoy walking in the **park**. ______
9. Let's rest on the **park** bench. ______
10. The family enjoys a **salad** for lunch. ______
11. Marge bought a new **salad** bowl. ______
12. The **computer** room is crowded today. ______
13. The students were waiting to use a **computer**. ______
14. The temperature is below average this **winter**. ______
15. School closed early due to the **winter** storm. ______

Basic English Grammar

TRL

Workbook Activity 16

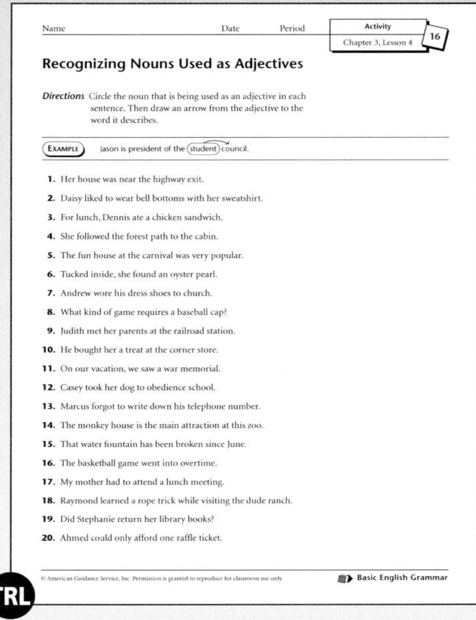

Name Date Period

Activity 16
Chapter 3, Lesson 4

Recognizing Nouns Used as Adjectives

Directions Circle the noun that is being used as an adjective in each sentence. Then draw an arrow from the adjective to the word it describes.

EXAMPLE Jason is president of the (student) council.

1. Her house was near the highway exit.
2. Daisy liked to wear bell bottoms with her sweatshirt.
3. For lunch, Dennis ate a chicken sandwich.
4. She followed the forest path to the cabin.
5. The fun house at the carnival was very popular.
6. Tucked inside, she found an oyster pearl.
7. Andrew wore his dress shoes to church.
8. What kind of game requires a baseball cap?
9. Judith met her parents at the railroad station.
10. He bought her a treat at the corner store.
11. On our vacation, we saw a war memorial.
12. Casey took her dog to obedience school.
13. Marcus forgot to write down his telephone number.
14. The monkey house is the main attraction at this zoo.
15. That water fountain has been broken since June.
16. The basketball game went into overtime.
17. My mother had to attend a lunch meeting.
18. Raymond learned a rope trick while visiting the dude ranch.
19. Did Stephanie return her library books?
20. Ahmed could only afford one raffle ticket.

Basic English Grammar

TRL

Activity 16

Lesson 5 Possessive Pronouns as Adjectives

Possessive pronouns can also be possessive adjectives. They describe nouns.

His house is next door. (Which house is next door? *His* house is next door.)
Is that their yard? (Whose yard is that? It is *their* yard.)

Writing Tip

The possessive adjectives *its, their,* and *whose* are sometimes confused with the contractions *it's, they're,* and *who's.* When you write, be sure to choose the correct word.

We can use a possessive adjective to describe a possessive noun.

That is my sister's bike.
(The possessive adjective *my* describes *sister.* The possessive noun *sister's* shows ownership.)

Activity A The possessive adjectives are in bold. Write them on your paper. Next to each one, write the noun it describes.

Example He left **his** hat on the bus. his—hat

1. I always like to get **my** money's worth.
2. **Our** family has always shopped in **their** store.
3. **Your** dog has a guilty look on **its** face.
4. We are having **her** birthday party next Saturday.
5. **His** picture was in the newspaper yesterday.

Activity B Find the possessive adjectives in these sentences. Write them on your paper. Next to each one, write the noun it describes.

1. His bike is missing.
2. Your coat was in the living room.
3. I helped my mother's friend look for her ring.
4. There was a rabbit in my garden.
5. Their dog likes to hide its bones under our porch.

Lesson at a Glance

Chapter 3 Lesson 5

Overview This lesson presents possessive adjectives.

Objective

- To identify possessive pronouns as adjectives and the nouns they describe in sentences.

Student Pages 67–68

Teacher's Resource Library 

Workbook Activity 17
Activity 17
Alternative Activity 17

1 Warm-Up Activity

Invite a volunteer to read aloud the first two sentences of this lesson. Ask students to name possessive pronouns. List the pronouns on the board; then have students turn back to the chart on page 31. Ask them to look under the column headed *Possessive.* Point out that not all of these words can be used to describe a noun. Select with the class those possessive pronouns that double as possessive adjectives. (They are *my, your, his, her, its, our, your,* and *their.*) Invite volunteers to try some of these out.

2 Teaching the Lesson

Draw students' attention to the Writing Tip box on this page. Point out that nouns take an apostrophe to show possession, but that possessive adjectives do not. Ensure that students understand the difference between *its* and *it's, their* and *they're,* and *whose* and *who's* by using these words in sentences on the board.

Activity A

Do the example and the first item orally. After students have completed the activity, have them share their answers with the class.

Activity A Answers

1. my—money's 2. Our—family, their—store 3. Your—dog, its—face 4. her—party 5. His—picture

3 Reinforce and Extend

Teacher Alert

Be sure students understand that the words *my, your, his, her, its, our, your,* and *their* can be called either possessive pronouns or possessive adjectives when they are used before a noun. Emphasize that neither term is more or less correct than the other.

Activity B

Before students complete the activity on their own, have pairs of students create original sentences, underlining the possessive adjectives and the nouns they modify.

Activity B Answers

1. His—bike 2. Your—coat 3. my—mother's, her—ring 4. my—garden 5. Their—dog, its—bones, our—porch

Lesson 5 Review Answers

1. their—homework 2. Your—answer 3. my—answer 4. his—answer 5. our—answers 6. their—problems 7. our—math 8. my—calculator 9. its—battery 10. his—brother's

Where To Find It

Explain to students that encyclopedias will not have a separate article on every topic. Sometimes they will have to use the index, often located in a separate volume. The index will refer students to articles that include information about the subject. When a computer encyclopedia does not have a separate article on a subject, it will often offer to perform a word search, looking for all articles containing a requested word or phrase.

Answers to Where To Find It: Give students access to a variety of encyclopedia resources to complete this activity. Their answers will vary. Encourage students to find facts that interest them.

Speaking Practice

Point out that the effectiveness of information presented orally greatly depends upon the ability of the presenter to speak with expression and clarity. Invite volunteers to read the text of the Where To Find It box aloud to the class. Ask them to imagine that they are presenting this information to a group for the first time. Encourage readers to speak slowly, clearly, and with expression.

Online Connection

Many online encyclopedias are available by subscription only. Some commercial sites, however, offer open access to standard reference works. *The Britannica Concise,* an abridged version of the multivolume classic, is available online for no fee at **education.yahoo.com.**

Lesson 5 REVIEW

Find the possessive adjectives in these sentences. Write them on your paper. Next to each one, write the noun it describes.

1. Dave and Vince did their math homework together.
2. "Your second answer is wrong," Dave said.
3. "Here is my answer."
4. Dave tried to explain his answer.
5. "I think both of our answers are wrong," Vince said.
6. They compared their problems.
7. "We should check our math," Vince suggested.
8. "Use my calculator to check."
9. The calculator did not work because its battery was dead.
10. Vince found some new batteries in his brother's desk.

Where To Find It

Encyclopedia

Suppose you wanted to find information about your state. One place to find information is in an encyclopedia. An encyclopedia contains articles on many topics. The articles are alphabetized by topic. You can find a variety of print encyclopedias in the library. You can also find some on CD-ROM or the Internet.

Start your search by choosing a specific topic. To find a topic in a print encyclopedia, use the guide words or letters on the outside of the books and on the inside pages. To find a topic in a computer encyclopedia, type your topic in the topic or article search window. Select "enter."

1. Use a print or computer encyclopedia to find an article about your state.
2. Write the name of your state on your paper, and list five facts from the article.

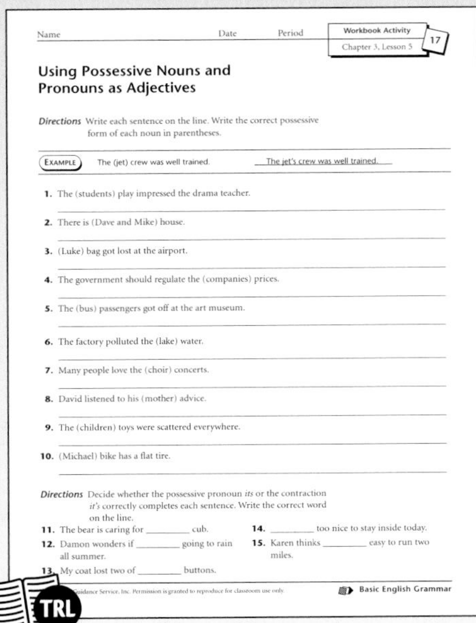

Name Date Period | Workbook Activity 17 | Chapter 3, Lesson 5

Using Possessive Nouns and Pronouns as Adjectives

Directions Write each sentence on the line. Write the correct possessive form of each noun in parentheses.

EXAMPLE The (jet) crew was well trained. The jet's crew was well trained.

1. The (students) play impressed the drama teacher.
2. There is (Dave and Mike) house.
3. (Luke) bag got lost at the airport.
4. The government should regulate the (companies) prices.
5. The (bus) passengers got off at the art museum.
6. The factory polluted the (lake) water.
7. Many people love the (choir) concerts.
8. David listened to his (mother) advice.
9. The (children) toys were scattered everywhere.
10. (Michael) bike has a flat tire.

Directions Decide whether the possessive pronoun *its* or the contraction *it's* correctly completes each sentence. Write the correct word on the line.

11. The bear is caring for ________ cub.
12. Damon wonders if ________ going to rain all summer.
13. My coat lost two of ________ buttons.
14. ________ too nice to stay inside today.
15. Karen thinks ________ easy to run two miles.

 Basic English Grammar

TRL

Workbook Activity 17

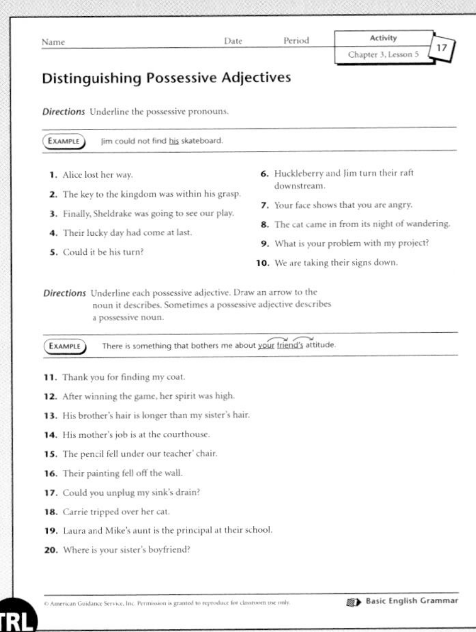

Name Date Period | Activity 17 | Chapter 3, Lesson 5

Distinguishing Possessive Adjectives

Directions Underline the possessive pronouns.

EXAMPLE Jim could not find his skateboard.

1. Alice lost her way.
2. The key to the kingdom was within his grasp.
3. Finally, Sheldrake was going to see our play.
4. Their lucky day had come at last.
5. Could it be his turn?
6. Huckleberry and Jim turn their raft downstream.
7. Your face shows that you are angry.
8. The cat came in from its night of wandering.
9. What is your problem with my project?
10. We are taking their signs down.

Directions Underline each possessive adjective. Draw an arrow to the noun it describes. Sometimes a possessive adjective describes a possessive noun.

EXAMPLE There is something that bothers me about your friend's attitude.

11. Thank you for finding my coat.
12. After winning the game, her spirit was high.
13. His brother's hair is longer than my sister's hair.
14. His mother's job is at the courthouse.
15. The pencil fell under our teacher' chair.
16. Their painting fell off the wall.
17. Could you unplug my sink's drain?
18. Carrie tripped over her cat.
19. Laura and Mike's aunt is the principal at their school.
20. Where is your sister's boyfriend?

 Basic English Grammar

TRL

Activity 17

Lesson  Numbers as Adjectives

A number can be an adjective. We use numbers as adjectives to describe nouns. Numbers describe by telling how many.

EXAMPLE Mrs. Baca brought twenty baskets of apples. (She brought how many baskets? She brought *twenty.*)
Twelve people came to the meeting.
(How many people came? *Twelve* came.)

An indefinite pronoun can be an adjective. Indefinite pronouns used as adjectives describe by telling how many, but the amounts they describe are not exact. Remember, an indefinite pronoun refers to a noun that is not named.

EXAMPLE Several people tried out for the play.
Few students got roles in the play.

Activity A Find the number words or indefinite pronouns that are used as adjectives in these sentences. Write them on your paper. Next to each adjective, write the noun it describes.

Example Many students read that article.
Many—students

1. Twenty-five people signed up for the class.
2. One student dropped out.
3. After a few weeks, the teacher gave a test.
4. Several members of the class got a perfect grade.
5. Most students enjoyed the class.

Activity A

Invite a volunteer to explain the directions and the example. Then have students do the activity.

Activity A Answers

1. Twenty-five—people 2. One—student 3. few—weeks
4. Several—members 5. Most—students

Lesson at a Glance

Chapter 3 Lesson 6

Overview This lesson presents numbers and indefinite pronouns as adjectives. It also explains how to distinguish between an indefinite pronoun and an indefinite adjective.

Objectives

- To identify and use numbers and indefinite pronouns as adjectives in sentences.
- To distinguish between numbers and indefinite pronouns used as pronouns and as adjectives.

Student Pages 69–71

Teacher's Resource Library 

Workbook Activity 18

Activity 18

Alternative Activity 18

1 Warm-Up Activity

Write the following phrases on the board: *ten apples; many houses; seven children; both puppies.* Underline the first word of each phrase and ask students what part of speech it is. Elicit from the class that the underlined words are all used as adjectives. Then have students turn to page 46, and invite a volunteer to read the chart of plural indefinite pronouns. Ask students what they notice about this list. Lead them to understand that several of the words introduced as indefinite pronouns can also be used as adjectives.

2 Teaching the Lesson

Write on the board the following examples: *Few soldiers returned* and *Few returned.* Draw students' attention to the word *Few.* Point out that in one sentence it is used as an adjective describing a noun; in the other it is used as a pronoun in place of a noun. Challenge students to identify the sentence in which *few* is an adjective and to explain why (*sentence one; it describes the noun soldiers*). Point out that in example two *Few* is an indefinite pronoun, replacing *soldiers* as the subject of the sentence.

Activity B

Have students give sample sentences aloud for each item listed before doing the activity on their own.

Activity B Answers

1–10. Answers will vary. Example sentences for 1–5 are given. Check to see that students used adjectives correctly. **1.** Few people came to the concert. **2.** Thirty-three students play in the orchestra. **3.** One kitten is grey. **4.** I'll have some soup. **5.** Janis likes most types of music.

Activity C

Read with students the example sentences on page 70. Point out that the key to recognizing an adjective is to identify whether it describes a noun or pronoun.

Activity C Answers

1. eighty—adjective **2.** several—adjective **3.** Everyone—pronoun **4.** Many—adjective **5.** No one—pronoun

Reinforce and Extend

Learning Styles

LEP/ESL

Encourage students to work with partners to reinforce their understanding of number words and their corresponding numerals. Ask them to relate the number words in Activities A–C to the numerals that the words name. Extend the activity by having students make a two-column chart listing number words in one column and numerals in the other column.

Activity B Use each of these words as an adjective in a sentence. Write the sentences on your paper. Circle the noun or pronoun that each adjective describes.

1. few
2. thirty-three
3. one
4. some
5. most
6. eighty
7. four
8. several
9. all
10. each

A word is an adjective if it describes a noun or pronoun. A word is a pronoun if it replaces a noun in a sentence.

Example
Pronoun Several of the athletes arrived late.
Adjective Several months went by before I saw her again. (How many months? *several*)

Activity C Write the words in bold on your paper. Next to each word, write *pronoun* or *adjective.*

1. The hurricane winds were **eighty** miles an hour.
2. The storm lasted for **several** hours.
3. **Everyone** on the block watched the storm.
4. **Many** trees blew down in the neighborhood.
5. **No one** could cook dinner or watch TV.

The storm damaged some of the houses.

Learning Styles

Visual/Spatial

Write on slips of paper descriptive phrases or sentences using indefinite pronouns as adjectives. Make sure that these descriptions are easy to visualize. (Examples: *many dogs chasing a cat; both houses are red; some people wearing hats; few people are driving cars.*) Have students form pairs and give each pair a descriptive phrase. Ask them to draw what is written quickly and then to exchange their picture with another pair. Students should try to guess the original phrase by looking at the picture. Remind them that their guess must include an indefinite pronoun used as an adjective.

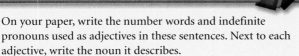

Lesson 6 REVIEW

On your paper, write the number words and indefinite pronouns used as adjectives in these sentences. Next to each adjective, write the noun it describes.

1. One Sunday, several friends visited the San Diego Zoo.
2. Each animal was in a natural setting.
3. We watched three chimpanzees swing from trees.
4. Eight lions and six tigers climbed over a rocky ledge.
5. There were many birds flying around the park.

Complete each sentence by adding a number word or an indefinite pronoun used as an adjective. Write the sentences on your paper.

6. Winds blew at ________ miles an hour.
7. ________ friends on our block are going on a picnic today.
8. Nathan is taking ________ classes this year.
9. The movie lasted for ________ minutes.
10. ________ people were unhappy about the decision.

Vocabulary Builder

Less* or *Fewer

Use *less* when comparing things that have volume (like water). Also use *less* when comparing abstract nouns (like love). Use *fewer* when comparing things you can count (like pencils).

Jackie drank **less** milk than Jorge.
Tomas finished **fewer** of the math problems than Tara.

On your paper, complete each sentence with either *less* or *fewer.*

1. This pan holds ________ water than that one.
2. This book has ________ pages than that one.
3. Chin spent ________ hours studying than Pam.
4. Tino's face has ________ freckles than mine.
5. Kevin's party was ________ fun than Madri's.

Lesson 6 Review Answers

1. One—Sunday, several—friends **2.** Each—animal **3.** three—chimpanzees **4.** Eight—lions, six—tigers **5.** many—birds **6–10.** Answers will vary. Answers should be complete sentences.

Vocabulary Builder

Help students with the concept of countable and uncountable quantities by writing a mixed list on the board: *kittens, wood, clouds, dreams, jars, water, concrete, video games,* and so on. Ask students to help you rearrange these words into two columns, *countable* and *uncountable.* If students are unsure about where to put a word, suggest that they ask "Can I count _____?" filling the blank with the item in question.

Answers to Vocabulary Builder: 1. less **2.** fewer **3.** fewer **4.** fewer **5.** less

LEARNING STYLES

Interpersonal/Group Learning

Recall the song "She'll Be Coming Round the Mountain" and the nursery rhyme "Pease Porridge Hot." Encourage volunteers to find the number used as an adjective—"She'll be driving six white horses" and "pease porridge in the pot—nine days old." Divide the class into groups of three. Challenge each group to think of a song or nursery rhyme that uses a number as an adjective. Make a list of the songs and rhymes and post it. Encourage students to add to the list as they think of more songs and rhymes in the upcoming days.

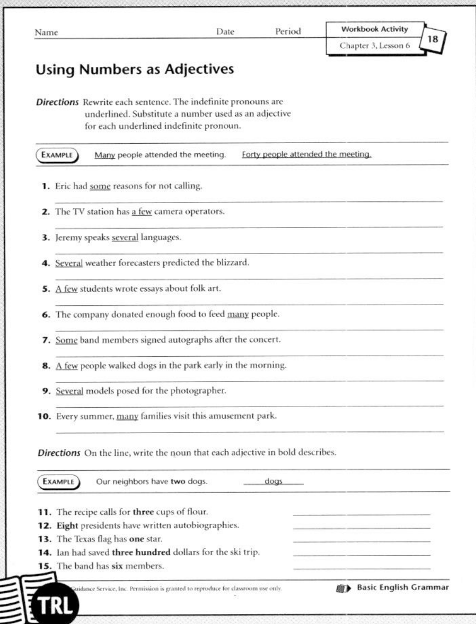

Name Date Period

Workbook Activity 18
Chapter 3, Lesson 6

Using Numbers as Adjectives

Directions Rewrite each sentence. The indefinite pronouns are underlined. Substitute a number used as an adjective for each underlined indefinite pronoun.

EXAMPLE Many people attended the meeting. Forty people attended the meeting.

1. Eric had some reasons for not calling.
2. The TV station has a few camera operators.
3. Jeremy speaks several languages.
4. Several weather forecasters predicted the blizzard.
5. A few students wrote essays about folk art.
6. The company donated enough food to feed many people.
7. Some band members signed autographs after the concert.
8. A few people walked dogs in the park early in the morning.
9. Several models posed for the photographer.
10. Every summer, many families visit this amusement park.

Directions On the line, write the noun that each adjective in bold describes.

EXAMPLE Our neighbors have **two** dogs. dogs

11. The recipe calls for **three** cups of flour. ________
12. **Eight** presidents have written autobiographies. ________
13. The Texas flag has **one** star. ________
14. Ian had saved **three hundred** dollars for the ski trip. ________
15. The band has **six** members. ________

 Basic English Grammar

TRL

Workbook Activity 18

Name Date Period

Activity 18
Chapter 3, Lesson 6

Using Indefinite Pronouns and Numbers as Adjectives

Directions In the following paragraph, underline the numbers and indefinite pronouns that are used as adjectives.

EXAMPLE Even with many rain showers, a thousand voters went to the polls.

I reminded myself several times, but I still forgot to bring the two dollars I needed for the bus. After some time passed, I decided to walk to the ballpark. It was three miles, but I knew my team needed all the players. A team needs nine players to start the game, and several members had been sick recently. Each person counted. No one wanted to lose the game, because our team had a one-game lead. Could I make it in twenty minutes? Before long there were only a few blocks to go. I ran most of the way. Everyone cheered when I showed up.

Directions If an underlined word is an adjective, write an *A* above it. If it is a pronoun, write a *P* above it. Remember: A word is an adjective if it describes a noun or pronoun. A word is a pronoun if it replaces a noun in a sentence.

EXAMPLE P A
Someone took all the food.

1. Everyone in the club donated twenty dollars.
2. After several days, many people returned home.
3. No one could find the three beads I dropped.
4. All students must watch a video that is thirty minutes long.
5. Did you find anyone?
6. Some thought ten dogs might be too many pets.
7. Several insects flew in through the four open windows.
8. I knew someone in one photograph.
9. A few children met the two famous clowns.
10. Lily did not have any helpers.

 Basic English Grammar

TRL

Activity 18

The Adjective *Chapter 3* 71

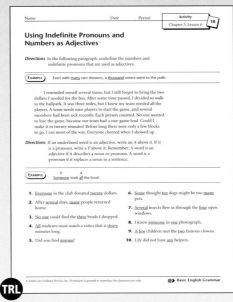

Lesson at a Glance

Chapter 3 Lesson 7

Overview This lesson explains how demonstrative pronouns can be used as adjectives.

Objectives

- To distinguish between demonstrative pronouns and adjectives.
- To identify demonstrative adjectives and the nouns they describe.

Student Pages 72–73

Teacher's Resource Library TRL

Workbook Activity 19

Activity 19

Alternative Activity 19

Lesson 7 Demonstrative Adjectives

Demonstrative adjective

The word this, that, these, *or* those *used as an adjective*

We can use demonstrative pronouns as adjectives. The **demonstrative adjectives** are *this, that, these,* and *those.* They answer the question *which one or ones?*

EXAMPLE **Pronoun** That is an error.

Adjective That error was Todd's. (Which error was Todd's? *That* error was Todd's.)

Activity A Write on your paper the words in bold. Next to each one, write *adjective* or *pronoun.*

Example **That** computer is broken.
That—adjective

1. "**This** Sunday, let's go to the football game together," Alex said.
2. "My sister gave me **these** tickets."
3. "Do you think **that** team will win a game **this** year?" Andy asked.
4. "Some of **those** new players are great," Alex answered.
5. "**This** should be a good season," Andy said.

Activity B Write these sentences on your paper. Underline each demonstrative adjective. Then draw an arrow from each demonstrative adjective to the noun that it describes.

Example Those → players are on our team.

1. The football game that day was exciting.
2. Where are those snacks you promised?
3. Look in that cabinet over the refrigerator.
4. That is where my mother keeps those things.
5. These sandwiches look good enough to eat.

Vocabulary

demonstrative adjective

Warm-Up Activity

Ask students to review the definition of an adjective—a word used to describe a noun or pronoun. (Have them look back at page 56 if necessary.) Then challenge students to prove that the demonstrative pronouns *this* and *that* can act as adjectives.

Teaching the Lesson

Have students read the definition and example at the top of this page. Create other pairs of simple sentences to demonstrate the distinction between pronouns and adjectives. (Examples: *This is wonderful/This movie is wonderful; Those aren't mine/Those shoes aren't mine.*) Point out that the demonstrative adjective will almost always be followed by the noun it describes.

Activity A

Write *this, that, these,* and *those* on four cards. Have students take a card and use the word in sentences as a pronoun and as an adjective. Repeat this activity so that every student has a chance to participate.

Activity A Answers

1. This—adjective 2. these—adjective 3. that—adjective, this—adjective 4. those—adjective 5. This—pronoun

Activity B

Have students explain the directions in their own words before they begin this activity.

Activity B Answers

1. The football game that → day was exciting. 2. Where are those → snacks you promised? 3. Look in that → cabinet over the refrigerator. 4. That is where my mother keeps those → things. 5. These → sandwiches look good enough to eat.

Lesson 7 REVIEW

Find the demonstrative adjectives in these sentences. Write them on your paper. Next to each one, write the noun it describes.

1. On that day, we went to a baseball game.
2. Those people behind us yelled through the whole game.
3. I would have liked to see that last play again.
4. We could have watched this game on TV at home.
5. That would have been less fun than this game has been.
6. I felt bad for those umpires when the fans booed them.
7. Would you like to keep these ticket stubs?
8. Do you think that friend of yours could get us tickets again?
9. I want to keep these plastic cups from our drinks.
10. My sister has a set of those cups.

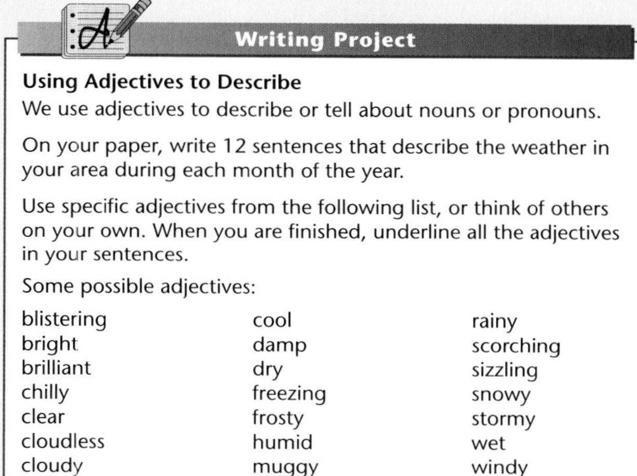

Writing Project

Using Adjectives to Describe

We use adjectives to describe or tell about nouns or pronouns.

On your paper, write 12 sentences that describe the weather in your area during each month of the year.

Use specific adjectives from the following list, or think of others on your own. When you are finished, underline all the adjectives in your sentences.

Some possible adjectives:

blistering	cool	rainy
bright	damp	scorching
brilliant	dry	sizzling
chilly	freezing	snowy
clear	frosty	stormy
cloudless	humid	wet
cloudy	muggy	windy

Lesson 7 Review Answers

1. that—day **2.** Those—people **3.** that—play **4.** this—game **5.** this—game **6.** those—umpires **7.** these—stubs **8.** that—friend **9.** these—cups **10.** those—cups

Writing Project

Before students write their sentences, encourage them to list adjectives they associate with the seasons of the year. Write the headings *Fall, Winter, Spring,* and *Summer* on the board. Have students take turns writing an adjective describing something about each season. Invite students to compare their words with those listed in their text.

Answers to Writing Project: Students should have written 12 sentences about the weather. There should be at least one adjective in each sentence. Check to be sure that students underlined the adjectives in their sentences.

3 Reinforce and Extend

Learning Styles

Body/Kinesthetic

Ask students to work in pairs to make up sentences that distinguish the meanings of the demonstrative adjectives *that, this, these,* and *those.* Students should demonstrate the meanings through role-play as they say their sentences. For example, a partner could hold up a book and say, "This book is mine," and could point to another book and say, "That book is yours."

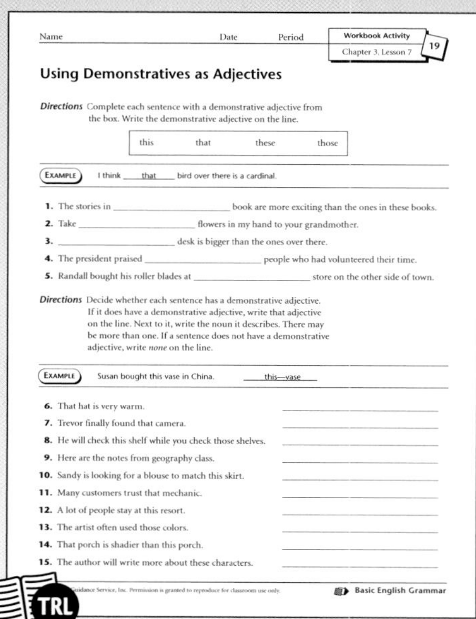

Name Date Period — Workbook Activity 19 — Chapter 3, Lesson 7

Using Demonstratives as Adjectives

Directions Complete each sentence with a demonstrative adjective from the box. Write the demonstrative adjective on the line.

this that these those

EXAMPLE I think __that__ bird over there is a cardinal.

1. The stories in ______ book are more exciting than the ones in these books.
2. Take ______ flowers in my hand to your grandmother.
3. ______ desk is bigger than the ones over there.
4. The president praised ______ people who had volunteered their time.
5. Randall bought his roller blades at ______ store on the other side of town.

Directions Decide whether each sentence has a demonstrative adjective. If it does have a demonstrative adjective, write that adjective on the line. Next to it, write the noun it describes. There may be more than one. If a sentence does not have a demonstrative adjective, write *none* on the line.

EXAMPLE Susan bought this vase in China. __this—vase__

6. That hat is very warm. ______
7. Trevor finally found that camera. ______
8. He will check this shelf while you check those shelves. ______
9. Here are the notes from geography class. ______
10. Sandy is looking for a blouse to match this skirt. ______
11. Many customers trust that mechanic. ______
12. A lot of people stay at this resort. ______
13. The artist often used those colors. ______
14. That porch is shadier than this porch. ______
15. The author will write more about these characters. ______

 Basic English Grammar

TRL

Workbook Activity 19

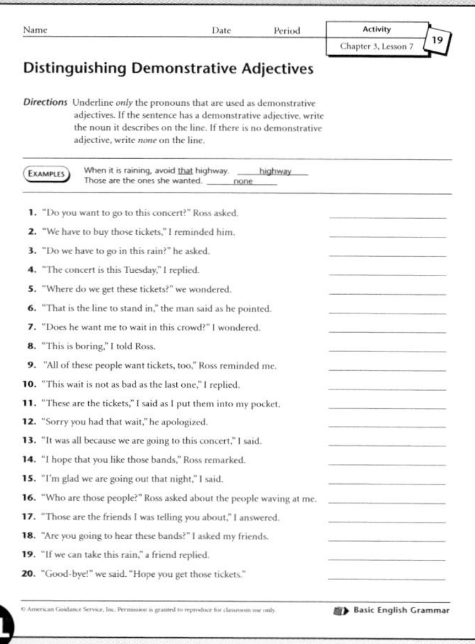

Name Date Period — Activity 19 — Chapter 3, Lesson 7

Distinguishing Demonstrative Adjectives

Directions Underline *only* the pronouns that are used as demonstrative adjectives. If the sentence has a demonstrative adjective, write the noun it describes on the line. If there is no demonstrative adjective, write *none* on the line.

EXAMPLES When it is raining, avoid that highway. __highway__
Those are the ones she wanted. __none__

1. "Do you want to go to this concert?" Ross asked. ______
2. "We have to buy those tickets," I reminded him. ______
3. "Do we have to go in this rain?" he asked. ______
4. "The concert is this Tuesday," I replied. ______
5. "Where do we get these tickets?" we wondered. ______
6. "That is the line to stand in," the man said as he pointed. ______
7. "Does he want me to wait in this crowd?" I wondered. ______
8. "This is boring," I told Ross. ______
9. "All of these people want tickets, too," Ross reminded me. ______
10. "This wait is not as bad as the last one," I replied. ______
11. "These are the tickets," I said as I put them into my pocket. ______
12. "Sorry you had that wait," he apologized. ______
13. "It was all because we are going to this concert," I said. ______
14. "I hope that you like those bands," Ross remarked. ______
15. "I'm glad we are going out that night," I said. ______
16. "Who are those people?" Ross asked about the people waving at me. ______
17. "Those are the friends I was telling you about," I answered. ______
18. "Are you going to hear these bands?" I asked my friends. ______
19. "If we can take this rain," a friend replied. ______
20. "Good-bye!" we said. "Hope you get those tickets." ______

 Basic English Grammar

TRL

Activity 19

The Adjective *Chapter 3* 73

Lesson at a Glance

Chapter 3 Lesson 8

Overview This lesson presents the degrees of comparison.

Objectives

- To compare with adjectives.
- To identify and use different degrees of comparison with adjectives in sentences.

Student Pages 74–77

Teacher's Resource Library 

Workbook Activity 20

Activity 20

Alternative Activity 20

Lesson 8 Using Adjectives to Make Comparisons

Positive form
The form of an adjective used to describe one person or thing

Comparative form
The form of an adjective used to compare two people or things

Superlative form
The form of an adjective used to compare more than two people or things

Adjectives describe people or things. We also use adjectives to compare two or more people or things. Adjectives have three forms—the **positive form,** the **comparative form,** and the **superlative form.**

EXAMPLE

Positive	Comparative	Superlative
strong	stronger	strongest
careful	more careful	most careful
good	better	best

Use these rules to form comparisons.

Rule 1 Use the positive form to describe one person or thing.
That scooter is *fast.*

Rule 2 Use the comparative form to compare two people or things.
That scooter is *faster* than this scooter.

Rule 3 Use the superlative form to compare more than two people or things.
Of all the scooters I have seen, this one is the *fastest.*

EXAMPLE

Positive	Alice wears large shoes.
Comparative	Alice's shoes are larger than mine.
Superlative	Alice has the largest shoes of all.

Activity A On your paper, write the form of the adjective that correctly completes each sentence.

1. Who is (taller, tallest)—Jennie or Olivia?
2. Mrs. Kim knits the (softer, softest) blankets.
3. Miko is the (funnier, funniest) of all my friends.
4. Orange juice is (tasty, tastiest).
5. I think apples are (sweeter, sweetest) than oranges.

Vocabulary

comparative form
positive form
superlative form

1 Warm-Up Activity

On the board, make a chart with the labels *Comparative* and *Superlative.* Hold up two pencils, identical except in length, and invite students to compare them. Elicit that one is longer (or shorter) than the other. Congratulate students for correctly using the comparative form of the adjective *long.* Write *longer* under the heading *Comparative* on the board. Then hold up a third pencil, longer than the first two, and ask students to compare it to the others. When students have defined it as the longest, write *longest* under *Superlative.* Add the comparative and superlative forms of other common adjectives to the chart.

2 Teaching the Lesson

Draw three stick figures on the board and label them *tall, taller,* and *tallest.* Then write the word *intelligent* under the figure labeled *tall.* Ask students to create the comparative and superlative forms of *intelligent* for the two other figures (*more intelligent, most intelligent*). Continue the lesson by writing a variety of short and long words under the figures and inviting students to name the comparative and superlative forms. Lead students to understand that longer adjectives use the words *more* and *most* to make their comparative and superlative forms.

Using the same three figures, start with the tallest and work down with comparatives and superlatives using the words *less* and *least* (*tall, less tall, least tall,* etc.).

Activity A

Invite a volunteer to read aloud the rules of comparison on this page. Make sure that students understand the examples before they begin the activity.

Activity A Answers

1. taller 2. softest 3. funniest 4. tasty 5. sweeter

Most one-syllable adjectives make their comparative form by adding *-er.* They form their superlative forms by adding *-est.*

Activity B Write each adjective on your paper. Write the comparative and superlative forms next to each one.

Example tall—taller, tallest

1. young
2. old
3. kind
4. short
5. green
6. slow
7. high
8. strict
9. bright
10. late

Other adjectives make their comparative and superlative forms by using *more* and *most.*

EXAMPLE

Positive	Comparative	Superlative
easy	easier	easiest
popular	more popular	most popular

Longer adjectives use the words *more* or *less* to make their comparative form. They make the superlative form by using *most* or *least.*

EXAMPLE

Positive	Comparative	Superlative
powerful	more powerful	most powerful
	less powerful	least powerful
healthful	more healthful	most healthful
	less healthful	least healthful
relaxed	more relaxed	most relaxed
	less relaxed	least relaxed
fortunate	more fortunate	most fortunate
	less fortunate	least fortunate

Activity B

Suggest that students make a chart on their papers with the headings *Positive, Comparative,* and *Superlative.* Then have students write the activity answers in their charts.

Activity B Answers

1. young—younger, youngest **2.** old—older, oldest **3.** kind—kinder, kindest **4.** short—shorter, shortest **5.** green—greener, greenest **6.** slow—slower, slowest **7.** high—higher, highest **8.** strict—stricter, strictest **9.** bright—brighter, brightest **10.** late—later, latest

3 Reinforce and Extend

TEACHER ALERT

This may be a good opportunity to remind students of some common spelling rules, such as changing *y* to *i* before adding *-er* and *-est* to two-syllable words that end in consonant *-y*, and doubling the final consonant of one-syllable words that end in a consonant following a vowel (CVC words). Use the words *happy* and *sad* as examples.

LEARNING STYLES

Auditory/Verbal

Prepare a list of adjectives used in this lesson. Divide the class into two teams. Read the positive, comparative, or superlative form of one of the adjectives on your list. The team whose turn it is has to identify the degree of comparison and supply the two missing forms. Award points for correct answers and keep score on the board.

Activity C

Create a chart on the board with the headings *Positive, Comparative,* and *Superlative.* List the following adjectives in the Positive column: *silly, hopeful, frightened, horrible, courageous.* Then help students fill in the chart by comparing each of these adjectives. Elicit from students when to use *-er* and *-est, more* and *most,* and *less* and *least.* After students complete Activity C, ask a volunteer to add the adjectives in bold to the appropriate columns in the chart. Then help students compare these adjectives to fill in the chart.

Activity C Answers

1. least comfortable—superlative **2.** terrible—positive **3.** most talented—superlative **4.** sadder—comparative **5.** less expensive—comparative

Activity D

Have students take turns using *good, better, best* and *bad, worse, worst* in oral sentences.

Activity D Answers

Answers will vary. Check to see that students used adjectives correctly. Possible answers for the first five sentences follow. **1.** This information is the least useful in the book. **2.** My house is smaller than Maria's. **3.** This was the most successful trip of all. **4.** These drawings are even more wonderful than his earlier ones. **5.** Greg is a less careful driver than Adam.

Activity E

Divide the class into small groups. Have group members take turns being the "group reader." Explain that the reader will read an activity item aloud two times with a different answer in place each time. Other members of the group should write down the correct answer. Students can then compare and explain their answers.

Activity E Answers

1. reddest **2.** taller **3.** oldest **4.** best **5.** more graceful

Activity C Write the adjectives in bold on your paper. Next to each one, write whether it is *positive, comparative,* or *superlative.*

Example David is the **most helpful** person I know.
most helpful—superlative

1. That is the **least comfortable** chair.
2. Taylor thought the movie was **terrible.**
3. The young girl was the **most talented** actress in the play.
4. I have never seen a **sadder** face.
5. This coat is **less expensive** than the other one.

A few adjectives make their comparative and superlative forms in an irregular way.

EXAMPLE	Positive	Comparative	Superlative
	good	better	best
	bad	worse	worst

Activity D Write each adjective in a sentence on your paper.

1. least useful
2. smaller
3. most successful
4. more wonderful
5. less careful
6. better
7. worst
8. heaviest
9. lighter
10. best

Activity E Write the adjective that correctly completes each sentence on your paper.

1. That is the (redder, reddest) sunset I have ever seen.
2. Which of those two buildings is (taller, tallest)?
3. St. Augustine is the (oldest, older) city in Florida.
4. That movie was the (goodest, best) I have ever seen.
5. Sita is (gracefuller, more graceful) than I could ever be.

LEARNING STYLES

Visual/Spatial

Have students choose an adjective and draw a picture illustrating its positive, comparative, and superlative forms. (Make sure that some illustrations depict the less/least comparisons.) Students should label their drawings and post them around the room.

IN THE COMMUNITY

Ask students to write opinion letters to newspapers, letters of complaint to businesses, or letters to request information from groups and associations. Point out that their readers are likely to pay closer attention to the letters if the ideas are presented in grammatically correct language. Suggest that students take the time to read their letters aloud before sending them. Hearing what they have written can help them catch mistakes. Students should pay special attention to the use of comparative and superlative forms of adjectives.

Lesson 8 REVIEW

Make three columns on your paper. Label them *positive*, *comparative*, and *superlative*. Write on your paper the adjectives in the correct column.

1. bad
2. prettier
3. less difficult
4. worse
5. more careful
6. less comfortable
7. most generous
8. least horrible
9. worst
10. popular

Write the adjectives in bold on your paper. Next to each one, write whether it is *positive, comparative,* or *superlative.*

11. This fabric feels **nice,** but that one feels **nicer.**
12. Of the two athletes, Brandon is the **faster** runner.
13. That story was **funny.**
14. Hector plays tennis **better** than his twin brother Paco.
15. Of all the photographs, this one is the **best.**

Write these adjectives on your paper. Next to each one, write the comparative and superlative forms.

16. bad
17. useful
18. fast
19. famous
20. stern
21. soft
22. comfortable
23. smart
24. angry
25. good

On your paper, write the adjective that correctly completes each sentence.

26. His headache is (worse, worst) than it was yesterday.
27. That is the (most big, biggest) cat I've ever seen.
28. Tanya is (younger, youngest) than Jake.
29. This food at this restaurant is (better, best) than that one.
30. This is the (dangerousest, most dangerous) corner in town.

Lesson 8 Review Answers

1. bad—positive **2.** prettier—comparative **3.** less difficult—comparative **4.** worse—comparative **5.** more careful—comparative **6.** less comfortable—comparative **7.** most generous—superlative **8.** least horrible—superlative **9.** worst—superlative **10.** popular—positive **11.** nice—positive, nicer—comparative **12.** faster—comparative **13.** funny—positive **14.** better—comparative **15.** best—superlative **16.** bad—worse, worst **17.** useful—more useful, most useful **18.** fast—faster, fastest **19.** famous—more famous, most famous **20.** stern—sterner, sternest **21.** soft—softer, softest **22.** comfortable—more comfortable, most comfortable **23.** smart—smarter, smartest **24.** angry—angrier, angriest **25.** good—better, best **26.** worse **27.** biggest **28.** younger **29.** better **30.** most dangerous

GLOBAL CONNECTION

Have students use an encyclopedia or the Internet to find information about two foreign countries. Ask them to write sentences comparing these countries with the United States. Encourage students to use the comparative and superlative forms of adjectives in their sentences. Invite volunteers to report their findings to the class.

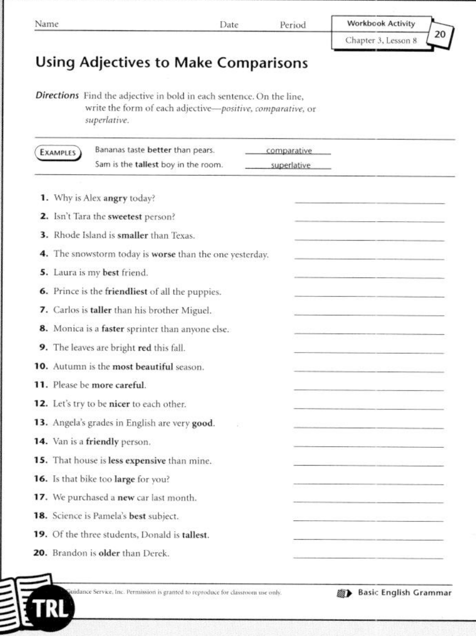

Name Date Period | **Workbook Activity** 20 | Chapter 3, Lesson 8

Using Adjectives to Make Comparisons

Directions Find the adjective in bold in each sentence. On the line, write the form of each adjective—*positive, comparative,* or *superlative.*

EXAMPLES
Bananas taste **better** than pears. comparative
Sam is the **tallest** boy in the room. superlative

1. Why is Alex **angry** today? ______
2. Isn't Tara the **sweetest** person? ______
3. Rhode Island is **smaller** than Texas. ______
4. The snowstorm today is **worse** than the one yesterday. ______
5. Laura is my **best** friend. ______
6. Prince is the **friendliest** of all the puppies. ______
7. Carlos is **taller** than his brother Miguel. ______
8. Monica is a **faster** sprinter than anyone else. ______
9. The leaves are bright **red** this fall. ______
10. Autumn is the **most beautiful** season. ______
11. Please be **more careful**. ______
12. Let's try to be **nicer** to each other. ______
13. Angela's grades in English are very **good**. ______
14. Van is a **friendly** person. ______
15. That house is **less expensive** than mine. ______
16. Is that bike too **large** for you? ______
17. We purchased a **new** car last month. ______
18. Science is Pamela's **best** subject. ______
19. Of the three students, Donald is **tallest**. ______
20. Brandon is **older** than Derek. ______

 Basic English Grammar

TRL

Workbook Activity 20

Name Date Period | **Activity** 20 | Chapter 3, Lesson 8

Creating Comparative Adjectives

Directions Fill in the blanks with the missing comparative adjectives. Show the *positive, comparative,* and *superlative* degrees for each adjective.

EXAMPLES

Positive	Comparative	Superlative
tasty	tastier	tastiest
red	redder	reddest

	Positive	Comparative	Superlative
1.	______	sweeter	______
2.	good	______	______
3.	______	______	heaviest
4.	______	______	most colorful
5.	______	older	______
6.	graceful	______	______
7.	______	less careful	______
8.	smart	______	______
9.	______	______	most amazing
10.	______	worse	______
11.	pink	______	______
12.	______	______	saddest
13.	______	more terrible	______
14.	happy	______	______
15.	______	______	funniest
16.	______	less awkward	______
17.	______	______	most loveable
18.	______	sharper	______
19.	tiny	______	______
20.	______	______	least tiring

 Basic English Grammar

TRL

Activity 20

Chapter 3 Review

Use the Chapter Review to prepare students for tests and to reteach content from the chapter.

Chapter 3 Mastery Test 

The Teacher's Resource Library includes two parallel forms of the Chapter 3 Mastery Test. The difficulty level of the two forms is equivalent. You may wish to use one form as a pretest and the other form as a posttest.

Review Answers

Part A

1. indefinite article 2. proper adjective 3. adjective 4. positive form 5. definite article 6. superlative form 7. comparative form 8. demonstrative adjective

Part B

9. fifty, red, ten 10. The, cool, dry, two 11. happy, the, beautiful, spring 12. their, Spanish, a, long 13. The summer, sunny, warm, delightful 14. Several, young, noisy, cheerful, the

Chapter 3 REVIEW

Word Bank
adjective
comparative form
definite article
demonstrative adjective
indefinite article
positive form
proper adjective
superlative form

Part A On a sheet of paper, write the correct word or words from the Word Bank to complete each sentence.

1. The ______ is the word *a* or *an,* which is used to talk about a general group of people or things.
2. A ______ is a proper noun used as an adjective or the adjective form of a proper noun.
3. A word that describes or tells about a noun or pronoun is an ______ .
4. The ______ describes one person or thing.
5. The ______ is the word *the,* which is used to talk about a particular person or thing.
6. The ______ compares more than two people or things.
7. The ______ compares two people or things.
8. A ______ is the word *this, that, these,* or *those* used as an adjective.

Part B Write the adjectives on your paper. Be sure to include articles.

9. They bought fifty red apples and ten gallons of cider.
10. The weather was cool and dry for two weeks.
11. Everyone was happy about the beautiful spring days.
12. After their Spanish class, Akio and Maria went for a long walk.
13. The summer afternoon, sunny and warm, was delightful.
14. Several young children, noisy but cheerful, got on the bus.

Name ______ Date ______ Period ______ | Mastery Test A, Page 1 | Chapter 3

Chapter 3 Mastery Test A

Part A Circle each of the adjectives in these sentences. Underline the nouns that the adjectives describe.

1. Clare planned a large, hot breakfast for a cold morning.
2. Clare's mother enjoys a hearty breakfast.
3. Clare served her mother a tall glass of fresh orange juice.
4. She made six fluffy waffles and four pieces of French toast.
5. Those waffles and that French toast looked very tasty.

Part B Rewrite these sentences. Capitalize the proper adjectives.

6. My french class comes before my english class.
7. I enjoy eating spicy indian curry.
8. My friend An has a vietnamese passport.
9. We went to New York City to hear latin music.
10. Is Nigeria an african country?

Part C Identify the kind of adjective each word is. Write *article, number, proper, demonstrative,* or *possessive.*

11. American ______ 16. an ______
12. their ______ 17. eighty ______
13. those ______ 18. Mexican ______
14. the ______ 19. this ______
15. several ______ 20. player's ______

 Basic English Grammar

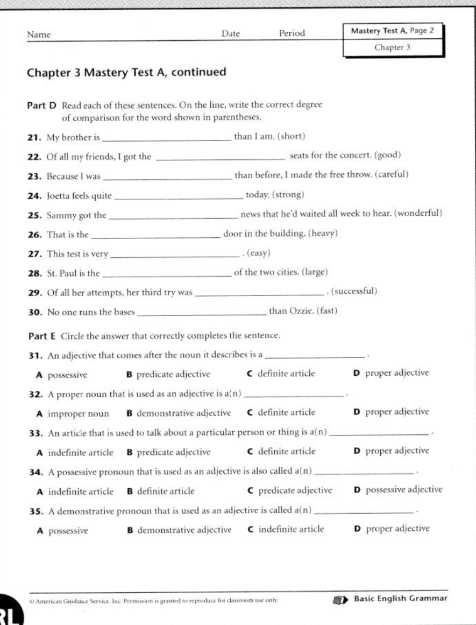
Name ______ Date ______ Period ______ | Mastery Test A, Page 2 | Chapter 3

Chapter 3 Mastery Test A, continued

Part D Read each of these sentences. On the line, write the correct degree of comparison for the word shown in parentheses.

21. My brother is ______ than I am. (short)
22. Of all my friends, I got the ______ seats for the concert. (good)
23. Because I was ______ than before, I made the free throw. (careful)
24. Joetta feels quite ______ today. (strong)
25. Sammy got the ______ news that he'd waited all week to hear. (wonderful)
26. That is the ______ door in the building. (heavy)
27. This test is very ______ . (easy)
28. St. Paul is the ______ of the two cities. (large)
29. Of all her attempts, her third try was ______ . (successful)
30. No one runs the bases ______ than Ozzie. (fast)

Part E Circle the answer that correctly completes the sentence.

31. An adjective that comes after the noun it describes is a ______ .
A possessive **B** predicate adjective **C** definite article **D** proper adjective
32. A proper noun that is used as an adjective is a(n) ______ .
A improper noun **B** demonstrative adjective **C** definite article **D** proper adjective
33. An article that is used to talk about a particular person or thing is a(n) ______ .
A indefinite article **B** predicate adjective **C** definite article **D** proper adjective
34. A possessive pronoun that is used as an adjective is also called a(n) ______ .
A indefinite article **B** definite article **C** predicate adjective **D** possessive adjective
35. A demonstrative pronoun that is used as an adjective is called a(n) ______ .
A possessive **B** demonstrative adjective **C** indefinite article **D** proper adjective

 Basic English Grammar

Chapter 3 Mastery Test A

Part C Write on your paper the adjectives in bold. Next to each one, write the noun or pronoun it describes.

15. The students in **this** homeroom had a meeting.

16. They elected **three** officers for the **school** year.

17. "Li is **smart, loyal,** and **fun,**" said Sue Ann.

18. **That** election was **close,** but Li won.

Part D Write on your paper the words in bold. Next to each one, write whether it is a *noun* or an *adjective.*

19. They all went to the **meeting** room.

20. The **meeting** began at three o'clock.

21. The **south** wind was warm.

22. The wind came from the **South.**

Part E On your paper, write the letter of the correct adjective.

23. Elena was ________ to help than Russ.

A eagerest
B eager
C eagerer
D more eager

24. The day was clear and ________ .

A bright
B brightly
C most bright
D brightest

25. She felt bad before the movie and ________ after.

A badder
B worst
C worse
D more worse

Test-Taking Tip

If you do not understand the directions to a section of a test, read them again. See whether you can figure out what you are supposed to do. If you still cannot figure it out, ask the person giving the test, if possible.

Review Answers

Part C

15. this—homeroom **16.** three—officers, school—year **17.** smart—Li, loyal—Li, fun—Li **18.** That—election, close—election

Part D

19. meeting—adjective **20.** meeting—noun **21.** south—adjective **22.** south—noun

Part E

23. D **24.** A **25.** C

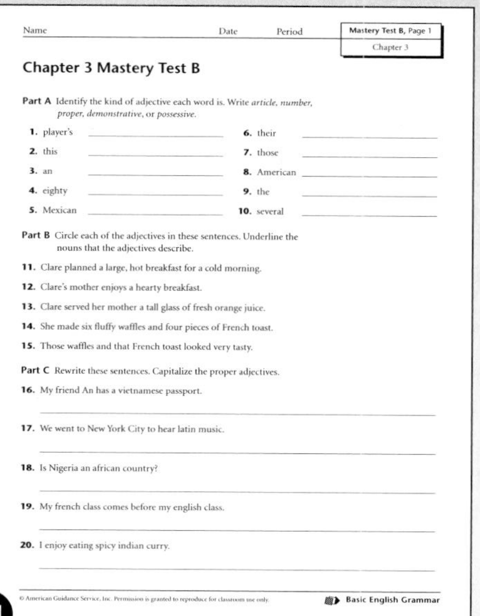

Name ________ Date ________ Period ________ **Mastery Test B, Page 1** Chapter 3

Chapter 3 Mastery Test B

Part A Identify the kind of adjective each word is. Write *article, number, proper, demonstrative,* or *possessive.*

1. player's ________
2. this ________
3. an ________
4. eighty ________
5. Mexican ________
6. their ________
7. those ________
8. American ________
9. the ________
10. several ________

Part B Circle each of the adjectives in these sentences. Underline the nouns that the adjectives describe.

11. Clare planned a large, hot breakfast for a cold morning.

12. Clare's mother enjoys a hearty breakfast.

13. Clare served her mother a tall glass of fresh orange juice.

14. She made six fluffy waffles and four pieces of French toast.

15. Those waffles and that French toast looked very tasty.

Part C Rewrite these sentences. Capitalize the proper adjectives.

16. My friend An has a vietnamese passport.

17. We went to New York City to hear latin music.

18. Is Nigeria an african country?

19. My french class comes before my english class.

20. I enjoy eating spicy indian curry.

 Basic English Grammar

TRL

Name ________ Date ________ Period ________ **Mastery Test B, Page 2** Chapter 3

Chapter 3 Mastery Test B, continued

Part D Circle the answer that correctly completes the sentence.

21. A proper noun that is used as an adjective is a(n) ________ .

A improper noun **B** demonstrative adjective **C** definite article **D** proper adjective

22. A possessive pronoun that is used as an adjective is also called a(n) ________ .

A indefinite article **B** definite article **C** predicate adjective **D** possessive adjective

23. An adjective that comes after the noun it describes is a ________ .

A possessive **B** predicate adjective **C** definite article **D** proper adjective

24. A demonstrative pronoun that is used as an adjective is called a(n) ________ .

A possessive **B** demonstrative adjective **C** indefinite article **D** proper adjective

25. An article that is used to talk about a particular person or thing is a(n) ________ .

A indefinite article **B** predicate adjective **C** definite article **D** proper adjective

Part E Read each of these sentences. On the line, write the correct degree of comparison for the word shown in parentheses.

26. No one runs the bases ________ than Ozzie. (fast)

27. Of all her attempts, her third try was ________ . (successful)

28. St. Paul is the ________ of the two cities. (large)

29. My brother is ________ than I am. (short)

30. Of all my friends, I got the ________ seats for the concert. (good)

31. Because I was ________ than before, I made the free throw. (careful)

32. This test is very ________ . (easy)

33. That is the ________ door in the building. (heavy)

34. Sammy got the ________ news that he'd waited all week to hear. (wonderful)

35. Joetta feels quite ________ today. (strong)

 Basic English Grammar

TRL

Chapter 3 Mastery Test B

Chapter

Planning Guide

The Action Verb

	Student Text Lesson				Language Skills		
	Student Pages	Vocabulary	Practice Exercises	Lesson Review	Identification Skills	Writing Skills	Punctuation Skills
Lesson 1 What Is an Action Verb?	82–85	✔	✔	✔	✔	✔	✔
Lesson 2 Verbs Express Tense	86–90	✔	✔	✔	✔	✔	✔
Lesson 3 Regular and Irregular Verbs	91–95	✔	✔	✔	✔	✔	✔
Lesson 4 The Progressive Forms	96–100	✔	✔	✔	✔	✔	✔
Lesson 5 Subject-Verb Agreement	101–105		✔	✔	✔	✔	✔
Lesson 6 Using the Verb *Do*	106–108		✔	✔	✔	✔	✔
Lesson 7 The Conditional Verb	109–112	✔	✔	✔	✔	✔	✔
Lesson 8 Active and Passive Verbs	113–115	✔	✔	✔	✔	✔	✔

Chapter Activities

Teacher's Resource Library

Community Connection 4: Describing Neighborhood Events with Action Verbs

Media and Literature Connection 4: Watch Out for the Action Verbs!

Assessment Options

Student Text

Chapter 4 Review

Teacher's Resource Library

Chapter 4 Mastery Tests A and B

Student Text Features						Teaching Strategies						Learning Styles						Teacher's Resource Library			
Spelling Builder	Vocabulary Builder	Where To Find It	Writing Project	Using What You've Learned	Writing Tips/Notes/ Technology Notes	Teacher Alert	Online Connection	Applications (Home, Career, Community, Global)	Speaking Practice	Spelling Practice	Writing Practice	Auditory/Verbal	Body/Kinesthetic	Interpersonal/Group Learning	Logical/Mathematical	Visual/Spatial	LEP/ESL	Workbook Activities	Activities	Alternative Activities	Self-Study Guide
					✔	83		84, 85					83			84		21	21	21	✔
				88		87		87			90	87		88	89	90		22	22	22	✔
					✔	92		94				93	95	95			92	23	23	23	✔
					✔		98	97	100			97		99		99		24	24	24	✔
	104				✔	101		102				103	103		104		105	25	25	25	✔
		108				107						108				107		26	26	26	✔
					✔	109, 110		111					112	110		112		27	27	27	✔
114			115			114				114								28	28	28	✔

Pronunciation Key

a	hat	e	let	ī	ice	ô	order	ů	put	sh	she	ə { a	in about
ā	age	ē	equal	o	hot	oi	oil	ü	rule	th	thin	e	in taken
ä	far	ėr	term	ō	open	ou	out	ch	child	ᴛʜ	then	i	in pencil
â	care	i	it	ȯ	saw	u	cup	ng	long	zh	measure	o	in lemon
												u	in circus

Alternative Activities

The Teacher's Resource Library (TRL) contains a set of lower-level worksheets called Alternative Activities. These worksheets cover the same content as the regular Activities but are written at a second-grade reading level.

Skill Track Software

Use the Skill Track Software for Basic English Grammar for additional reinforcement of this chapter. The software program allows students using AGS textbooks to be assessed for mastery of each chapter and lesson of the textbook. Students access the software on an individual basis and are assessed with multiple-choice items.

Chapter at a Glance

Chapter 4: The Action Verb

pages 80–117

Lessons

Skill Track Software for Basic English Grammar

Teacher's Resource Library

- Workbook Activities 21–28
- Activities 21–28
- Alternative Activities 21–28
- Community Connection 4
- Media and Literature Connection 4
- Chapter 4 Self-Study Guide
- Chapter 4 Mastery Tests A and B

(Answer Keys for the Teacher's Resource Library begin on page 340 of this Teacher's Edition.)

Name Date Period | Community Connection 4 | Chapter 4

Describing Neighborhood Events with Action Verbs

An action verb is a word that expresses action in a sentence.

EXAMPLES
Mia *ran* to school.
Mr. Yu *is playing* his instrument.
Please *do* your assignment.

The verbs in the example sentences are *ran, is playing,* and *do.* They are all called action verbs because they express action.

You can practice using action verbs by writing sentences. Follow these steps to write sentences about events in your neighborhood.

Step 1 Take this paper and a pencil. Go somewhere in your neighborhood where you can see some kind of action. Examples are a park, sports field, or shopping area.

Step 2 Take as much time as you need to watch for something to happen. On the lines below, write five complete sentences. Use action verbs to tell about something you see. For example, you might see a man throwing a ball to a child in a park. Your sentence might be "A father is throwing a ball to his son."

1. ______________________
2. ______________________
3. ______________________
4. ______________________
5. ______________________

Step 3 Underline the action verbs in your sentences.

Step 4 Share your sentences with your class.

 Basic English Grammar

TRL

Community Connection 4

Name Date Period | Media and Literature Connection 4 | Chapter 4

Watch Out for the Action Verbs!

The red-hot Rosedale Raccoons burned the timid Ragdale Rabbits in overtime action today. After blasting through the Rabbit defense, Raccoon great Randy Young slammed the ball through the hoop 42 times, shattering the backboard and eliminating the Rabbits from this year's championship play.

Whoa! If you are looking for energetic action verbs, sports are a good place to find them. We can all learn how to make our verbs more exciting by listening to, watching, reading about, and playing sports.

Step 1 Hunt for some really vivid sports action verbs. You can find them by listening to games on the radio, watching sports news on television, reading the sports pages in the newspaper, or searching on the Internet.

Step 2 Perhaps you skateboard, snowboard, ski, surf, or blade. What kind of terms do you use in the sports activities you enjoy? If you play a team sport, listen to how your coach and the other players talk about the sport.

Step 3 Keep a list of the action verbs you use and hear. Here are a few to start. Write your action verbs on the lines.

dunk
slam
hit
crush
blast
burn
snap
eliminate
grind
wipe out

Step 4 On a separate sheet of paper, write a one-paragraph story about something that happened to you recently. In this story, you will use strong action verbs from your list. For example, you didn't just eat breakfast this morning. You slammed the cereal into your mouth and began to grind it with your teeth.

Step 5 Read your story to the class.

 Basic English Grammar

TRL

Media and Literature Connection 4

Chapter

The Action Verb

You could describe the cheetah in this photograph as *running, bounding, chasing, racing, flashing,* or *dashing.* These strong action words help bring the cheetah's movement to life. You can also use action words to describe quieter actions like *eating, planning,* or *thinking.* All these action words are called verbs.

Verbs express action or state of being. An action verb is a word that tells what someone or something does, did, or will do.

In Chapter 4, you will learn about action verbs. Each lesson in the chapter focuses on the form and correct use of action verbs in sentences.

Goals for Learning

- To identify verbs and verb phrases in sentences
- To understand verb tense and use tense consistently in sentences
- To recognize regular and irregular verbs
- To understand subject-verb agreement
- To identify the correct form of verbs in sentences
- To understand conditional verbs
- To recognize active and passive verbs

81

Introducing the Chapter

Have students examine the picture. If necessary, identify the animal as a cheetah and explain that cheetahs are the world's fastest land animals. Ask students to identify what the cheetah is doing. (*running*) You might also have them think of synonyms for *running,* such as *sprinting.* Encourage students to name other animals and to use words that tell what they do to move. You could begin by saying, "A turtle lumbers. A mouse skitters." Explain to students that in Chapter 4 they will learn about action words, or verbs.

Writing Tips, Notes, and Technology Notes

Ask volunteers to read the tips and notes that appear in the margins throughout the chapter. Then discuss them with the class.

Teacher's Resource

The AGS Teaching Strategies in English Transparencies may be used with this chapter. The transparencies add an interactive dimension to expand and enhance the *Basic English Grammar* program content.

Career Interest Inventory

The AGS Harrington-O'Shea Career Decision-Making System–Revised (CDM) may be used with this chapter. Students can use the CDM to explore their interests and identify careers. The CDM defines career areas that are indicated by students' responses on the inventory.

Name Date Period *SELF-STUDY GUIDE*

Chapter 4: The Action Verb

Goal 4.1 *To identify verbs in sentences*

Date	Assignment	Score
______	**1.** Read pages 81–82. Complete Activity A on page 82.	______
______	**2.** Complete Activities B–C on page 83.	______
______	**3.** Read page 84. Complete Activities D–E on page 84.	______
______	**4.** Complete Workbook Activity 21.	______
______	**5.** Complete the Lesson 1 Review on page 85.	______

Comments:

Goal 4.2 *To understand and use verb tense*

Date	Assignment	Score
______	**6.** Read page 86. Complete Activity A on page 86.	______
______	**7.** Read pages 87–88. Complete Activities B–C on page 88.	______
______	**8.** Complete Activities D–E on page 89.	______
______	**9.** Complete Workbook Activity 22.	______
______	**10.** Complete the Lesson 2 Review on page 90.	______

Comments:

Goal 4.3 *To recognize regular and irregular verbs*

Date	Assignment	Score
______	**11.** Read page 91. Complete Activity A on page 91.	______
______	**12.** Read pages 92–93. Complete Activities B–C on pages 92–93.	______

 Basic English Grammar

TRL

Name Date Period *SELF-STUDY GUIDE*

Chapter 4: The Action Verb, continued

Date	Assignment	Score
______	**13.** Read page 94. Complete Activities D–E on page 94.	______
______	**14.** Complete Workbook Activity 23.	______
______	**15.** Complete the Lesson 3 Review on page 95.	______

Comments:

Goal 4.4 *To recognize progressive verbs*

Date	Assignment	Score
______	**16.** Read page 96. Complete Activity A on page 96.	______
______	**17.** Read page 97. Complete Activity B on page 97.	______
______	**18.** Complete Activities C–F on pages 98–99.	______
______	**19.** Complete Workbook Activity 24.	______
______	**20.** Complete the Lesson 4 Review on page 100.	______

Comments:

Goal 4.5 *To understand subject-verb agreement*

Date	Assignment	Score
______	**21.** Read pages 101–102. Complete Activities A–B on pages 101–102.	______
______	**22.** Read pages 103–104. Complete Activities C–E on pages 103–104.	______
______	**23.** Complete Workbook Activity 25.	______
______	**24.** Complete the Lesson 5 Review on page 105.	______

Comments:

 Basic English Grammar

TRL

Chapter 4 Self-Study Guide, Pages 1–3

Lesson at a Glance

Chapter 4 Lesson 1

Overview This lesson presents the concept of verbs as words that express action; it also shows the relationship of the subject and verb in a sentence and introduces verb phrases.

Objective

- To identify verbs, verb phrases, and subjects in sentences.

Student Pages 82–85

Teacher's Resource Library 

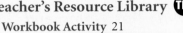

Workbook Activity 21

Activity 21

Alternative Activity 21

Vocabulary

action verb
helping verb
main verb
subject
verb
verb phrase

Lesson 1 What Is an Action Verb?

Verb
A word that expresses action or state of being

Action verb
A word that tells what someone or something (subject) does, did, or will do

Subject
The part of a sentence that tells who or what the sentence is about

A **verb** is a word that expresses action or state of being. An **action verb** is a word that expresses the action in a sentence. The verb tells what the **subject** does, did, or will do. The subject is the part of the sentence that tells who or what the sentence is about. Find the verb in a sentence by asking yourself two questions:

1. Who or what is doing something? (subject)
2. What are they doing? (verb)

EXAMPLE
Every evening Jiro reads the mail.
Who is doing something? *Jiro* (subject)
What does he do? *reads* (verb)

A sentence can have more than one verb.

EXAMPLE
Antonia washed and dried the glasses after dinner.
She opened her notebook and began her assignment.

Some verbs express mental action, which cannot be seen.

EXAMPLE
Pedro likes his car.
Tanesha thinks about her test.

Activity A Write on your paper the verbs in these sentences.

1. Mr. Okada parked his car.
2. Several of his friends shouted and waved to him.
3. He likes all the people at the office.
4. Yoshimi called her boss.
5. Yoshimi reminded her about the meeting.

1 Warm-Up Activity

Write the following words on the board: *applaud, desk, cheer, quietly, strong, fast, walk, animals.* Encourage a volunteer to circle the words that express action. Help students conclude that verbs express action.

2 Teaching the Lesson

After students read page 82, write the following words on the board: *drive, run, wonder, love, want, play.* Ask students to divide these verbs into two groups, based on the information they have just read. Lead them to understand that three of the verbs (*drive, run,* and *play*) describe physical action; the other three (*wonder, love,* and *want*) express mental action. Rearrange the words in two columns, labeled *Physical* and *Mental.* Encourage students to add other verbs to these lists. Leave them on the board for future reference.

Help students understand that every sentence is based around the simple framework of a subject and verb. Say the following words: *Kira drives.* Ask students if this is a sentence. Elicit from them that it has a subject *Kira* and a verb *drives* and expresses a complete idea. Therefore it is a sentence. Now add the phrase *her car to work* to the end of the sentence. Help them conclude that the subject and verb have remained the same. Point out that the simple core of the sentence continues to provide the subject and verb.

Activity A

Write sentences on the board with these verbs: *work, believe, dance, laugh, hope.* Ask students to read each sentence aloud and identify the verb. Help students determine which verbs express physical action and which express mental action.

Activity A Answers

1. parked 2. shouted, waved 3. likes 4. called 5. reminded

Activity B Write on your paper the subjects and verbs in these sentences. Write *S* next to the subject and *V* next to the verb.

Example The assistant opens the mail.
assistant—S opens—V

1. In the office everyone works hard.
2. Some people sort mail.
3. Mrs. Davis prepares the payroll.
4. Her assistant enters the information into a computer.
5. The computer prints the checks.

Activity C Write on your paper the verb or verbs in each sentence.

Example The athletes went to the field and played.
went, played

1. Mr. Ochoa rode his bike to work on Tuesday.
2. He drank some juice and ate a bagel.
3. Mr. Ochoa called the new client, Ms. Peters.
4. He sat in the meeting room and prepared a report.
5. Ms. Peters and her assistant arrived on time.

Ms. Peters meets with Mr. Ochoa and his staff.

Activity B

Ask students to use the verbs that were listed on the board in the Warm-Up Activity in oral sentences. Have students identify the subject and the verb in each sentence.

Activity B Answers

1. everyone—S, works—V **2.** people—S, sort—V **3.** Mrs. Davis—S, prepares—V **4.** assistant—S, enters—V **5.** computer—S, prints—V

Activity C

Write these pairs of verbs on the board: *eat/drink, skipped/hopped, ran/hid, sing/dance.* Invite volunteers to create a sentence for each pair of verbs. Students can use the example sentence as a model.

Activity C Answers

1. rode **2.** drank, ate **3.** called **4.** sat, prepared **5.** arrived

3 Reinforce and Extend

Teacher Alert

You may wish to provide additional instruction on simple subjects. Emphasize that for the activities in this lesson, the subject refers to the noun or pronoun that answers the question *Who or what is doing something?* Point out that students are not to include any words or phrases that describe the subject or tell more about the verb.

Learning Styles

Body/Kinesthetic

Write a few short sentences containing action verbs on the board and number each one—for example, **1.** *Sharisse rides a bicycle.* **2.** *I love pizza.* Give students a number representing a sentence. Each student silently identifies the verb for his or her sentence and mimes its action for the class. Other students should guess which sentence is being acted out.

The Action Verb *Chapter 4* 83

Activity D

Work with students to make a list of helping verbs on poster board. Suggest that students look at Activities D and E for ideas. The list should include *have, has, had, should, could, will,* and *may.* Students can refer to the list as they complete the activity.

Activity D Answers

1. had spoken 2. had remembered 3. recognized 4. will help 5. has announced

Activity E

Encourage students to create their own list of five verbs, including at least two verb phrases. Have partners exchange lists and practice making up sentences for each verb or verb phrase.

Activity E Answers

Sentences will vary.

In the Community

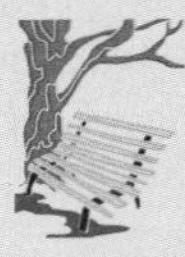

To help raise public awareness of an organization's needs, volunteers or employees may be asked to write copy for radio and television announcements, newspaper articles, posters, and flyers. The use of strong action verbs in any public service announcement can help grab people's attention and will, therefore, be more effective in getting the message to the community at large. Have students listen for public service announcements on the radio and television. Ask them to note the strong action verbs. Then have them recall some examples of public service announcements for the class.

Verb phrase
A main verb and one or more helping verbs

Main verb
The last verb in a verb phrase

Helping verb
A verb that combines with a main verb to form a verb phrase

A **verb phrase** contains a **main verb** and one or more **helping verbs.** A main verb is the last verb in a verb phrase. A helping verb combines with a main verb to form a verb phrase.

EXAMPLE

Mr. Lopez has poured his water.
poured—main verb *has*—helping verb
Pat will come with us.
come—main verb *will*—helping verb

Activity D Write on your paper the verb or verb phrase in each of these sentences. Underline the main verb in each verb phrase once. Underline the helping verb in each verb phrase twice.

1. Mrs. Stamos had spoken to Mr. Franklin.
2. Later, he had remembered their talk.
3. He recognized the problem immediately.
4. They will help each other.
5. Mr. Franklin has announced a new policy.

Writing Tip

Many verbs can also be nouns. For example: Keep your *balance* (noun) as you *balance* (verb) your packages.

Activity E Write a sentence for each verb or verb phrase. Underline each subject once and each verb or verb phrase twice.

1. accept
2. balance
3. will comfort
4. contain
5. had lifted
6. have been
7. examine
8. write
9. has remembered
10. will think

Learning Styles

Visual/Spatial

Divide the class into pairs. Give each pair a magazine picture. Challenge the pairs to find five nouns in their picture. Then ask them to write five verbs to show the action of the nouns. Have students combine the nouns and verbs to make sentences. For example, students might write subject/verb combinations such as *The curtains blow in the breeze. People are driving a car. Fruit grows on trees. Athletes are playing soccer.* Afterward, invite pairs to share their pictures and sentences with the class.

Lesson 1 REVIEW

On your paper, write the verbs in these sentences.

1. Many different people work at the post office.
2. The public appreciates their efforts.
3. Letters and packages stream into the post office all day and night.
4. Letter carriers load the mail into sacks and deliver it.
5. Millions of pieces of mail travel from place to place.

On your paper, write the subject and verb in each sentence. Write *S* next to the subject and *V* next to the verb.

6. Ms. Ando enjoys her work.
7. She writes for a magazine.
8. Mr. Sweeney helps her.
9. A photographer takes pictures for the articles.
10. Many people read the magazine.

On your paper, write the verb or verb phrase in each sentence. Some sentences have more than one verb on verb phrase. Underline the main verb in each verb phrase once. Underline the helping verb in each verb phrase twice.

11. Mr. Turner scrambled the eggs and put bread into the toaster.
12. He smiled at his wife.
13. She had set the table and had poured their juice.
14. They sat and read the paper.
15. Mr. and Mrs. Turner will start every day the same way.

Write each verb or verb phrase in a sentence on your paper.

16. call
17. will believe
18. has answered
19. start
20. have made

Lesson 1 Review Answers

1. work **2.** appreciates **3.** stream **4.** load, deliver **5.** travel **6.** Ms. Ando—S, enjoys—V **7.** She—S, writes—V **8.** Mr. Sweeney—S, helps—V **9.** photographer—S, takes—V **10.** people—S, read—V **11.** scrambled, put **12.** smiled **13.** had set, had poured **14.** sat, read **15.** will start **16–20.** Sentences will vary.

CAREER CONNECTION

Every job requires different skills and responsibilities. Have students research a career of their choice. Then have them create a poster about the career that describes those skills and responsibilities through a combination of action verbs and pictures. Include some of the following in the poster:

- picture of people working at the job
- some requirements of the job
- some benefits and rewards of the job
- a short history of the job

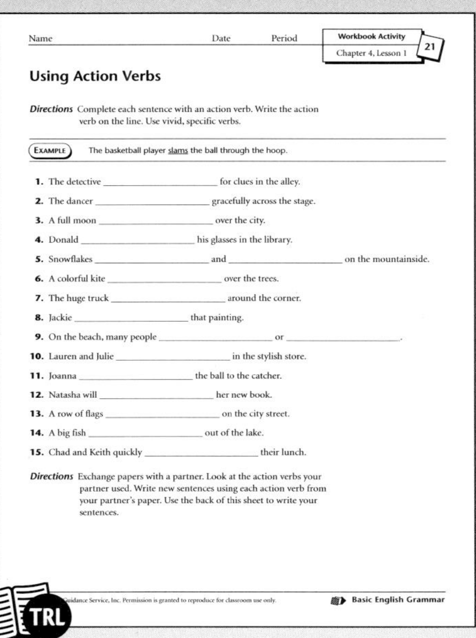

Name Date Period **Workbook Activity 21** Chapter 4, Lesson 1

Using Action Verbs

Directions Complete each sentence with an action verb. Write the action verb on the line. Use vivid, specific verbs.

EXAMPLE The basketball player slams the ball through the hoop.

1. The detective ______ for clues in the alley.
2. The dancer ______ gracefully across the stage.
3. A full moon ______ over the city.
4. Donald ______ his glasses in the library.
5. Snowflakes ______ and ______ on the mountainside.
6. A colorful kite ______ over the trees.
7. The huge truck ______ around the corner.
8. Jackie ______ that painting.
9. On the beach, many people ______ or ______.
10. Lauren and Julie ______ in the stylish store.
11. Joanna ______ the ball to the catcher.
12. Natasha will ______ her new book.
13. A row of flags ______ on the city street.
14. A big fish ______ out of the lake.
15. Chad and Keith quickly ______ their lunch.

Directions Exchange papers with a partner. Look at the action verbs your partner used. Write new sentences using each action verb from your partner's paper. Use the back of this sheet to write your sentences.

Basic English Grammar

TRL

Workbook Activity 21

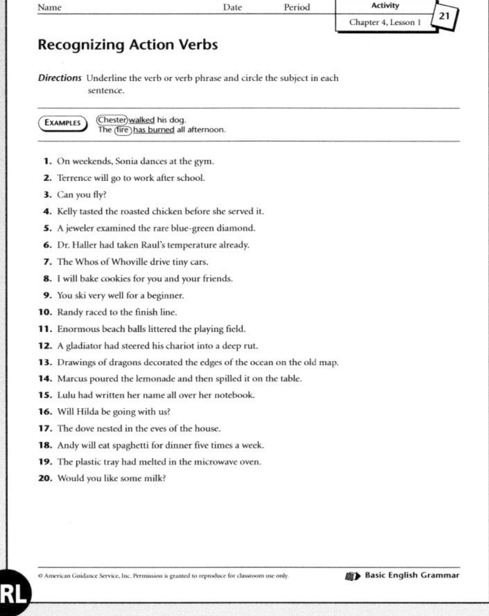

Name Date Period **Activity 21** Chapter 4, Lesson 1

Recognizing Action Verbs

Directions Underline the verb or verb phrase and circle the subject in each sentence.

EXAMPLES Chester walked his dog.
The fire has burned all afternoon.

1. On weekends, Sonia dances at the gym.
2. Terrence will go to work after school.
3. Can you fly?
4. Kelly tasted the roasted chicken before she served it.
5. A jeweler examined the rare blue-green diamond.
6. Dr. Haller had taken Raul's temperature already.
7. The Whos of Whoville drive tiny cars.
8. I will bake cookies for you and your friends.
9. You ski very well for a beginner.
10. Randy raced to the finish line.
11. Enormous beach balls littered the playing field.
12. A gladiator had steered his chariot into a deep rut.
13. Drawings of dragons decorated the edges of the ocean on the old map.
14. Marcus poured the lemonade and then spilled it on the table.
15. Lulu had written her name all over her notebook.
16. Will Hilda be going with us?
17. The dove nested in the eves of the house.
18. Andy will eat spaghetti for dinner five times a week.
19. The plastic tray had melted in the microwave oven.
20. Would you like some milk?

Basic English Grammar

TRL

Activity 21

The Action Verb Chapter 4 85

Lesson 2 Verbs Express Tense

Tense
The time when an action takes place

Infinitive
To plus the present tense of a verb

Simple tenses
Present, past, and future

The verb in a sentence expresses **tense.** A verb tense tells the time when an action takes place. Verbs use endings, helping verbs, or both to express tense.

Every verb has an **infinitive** form which is *to* plus the present tense of the verb. Verbs can express three **simple tenses**—present, past, and future. Use the present tense when the action is happening now or if it usually happens. Use the past tense when the action has already happened. Use the future tense when the action will happen in the future.

Example

Infinitive	to fish
Present Tense	I fish in that river all summer. (shows an action done in the present time)
Past Tense	I fished in that river last summer. (shows an action done in the past)
Future Tense	I will fish in that river next summer. (shows an action that will be done in the future)

Activity A Write the verbs in bold on your paper. Next to each verb, write its tense—*present, past,* or *future.*

1. The team **will play** their first football game on Saturday.
2. The team **practices** every day.
3. Team members **wondered** about their opponents.
4. The coach **called** the team together.
5. He **talked** to them about the game plan.

Lesson at a Glance

Chapter 4 Lesson 2

Overview This lesson presents the three simple tenses (present, past, future) and three perfect tenses (present perfect, past perfect, future perfect). It explains how regular verbs form their different tenses.

Objectives

- To find verbs and verb phrases in sentences.
- To identify the tense of verbs and verb phrases in sentences.

Student Pages 86–90

Teacher's Resource Library 

Workbook Activity 22

Activity 22

Alternative Activity 22

Vocabulary

future perfect
infinitive
past perfect
present perfect
simple tenses
tense

Warm-Up Activity

Write these three sentence starters on the board: *Usually they . . . Yesterday, they . . . Tomorrow, they . . .* Beside them write the following action verbs: *want, play, paint.* Invite students to choose one of these verbs and to use them in three sentences beginning with each sentence starter. Have other volunteers choose other verbs. As students say their sentences, have them note how the form of verb changes in each one. Point out that they have been using the three simple tenses: present, past, and future.

Teaching the Lesson

The following exercises will help reassure students that they are already familiar with the use of the perfect tenses.

Instruct a volunteer to write on the board as many *x*s as possible when you say go. After a few seconds, say *stop*, and ask the class, "How many *x*s had ________ written before I said stop?" Elicit their answers in the past perfect tense. "______ had written 10 *x*s before you said *stop.*" Now draw students' attention to the definition and example of the past perfect tense on page 87. Point out that one action was completed (*writing 10 x*s) before another began (*saying* stop).

Help students understand the future perfect tense by giving them a word problem: *A school bus travels at a rate of one mile every five minutes. How many miles will it have traveled at the end of ten minutes? Fifteen minutes? Twenty minutes?* Students should respond in the future perfect tense (*It will have traveled two miles. Three miles. Four miles.*)

Read the definition of future perfect with the class, and point out that an action will be completed (*driving two miles*) before a certain time in the future (*ten minutes*).

Activity A

Write the first activity item on the board but replace the verb with a blank. Invite students to fill in the blank with a verb in the present, past, or future tense.

Activity A Answers

1. will play—future 2. practices—present 3. wondered—past 4. called—past 5. talked—past

Present perfect
Shows an action started in the past and continuing to the present

Past perfect
Shows one action completed before another action began

Future perfect
Shows an action that will be completed before a certain time in the future

The three perfect tenses are **present perfect, past perfect,** and **future perfect.** The perfect tenses use the helping verb *have* with the past tense of a verb.

EXAMPLE

Present Perfect
Denbe has tackled his opponent many times. (shows an action that started in the past and continues to the present)
Past Perfect
Denbe had tackled him before the whistle blew. (shows that one action was completed before another action began)
Future Perfect
In a few seconds, Denbe will have tackled his opponent. (shows an action that will be completed before a certain time in the future)

Regular verbs form their past tense by adding *-ed* or *-d* to the present tense. Irregular verbs form their past tense and past participles in different ways. *Have* is an irregular verb.

We use the different forms of *have* to form the perfect tenses.

(To) Have		
Present	(singular) (plural)	Denbe **has** the ball now. They **have** six points.
Past		The team **had** the lead.
Future		The team **will have** the ball.
Present Perfect	(singular) (plural)	He **has had** the ball four times. They **have had** the ball most of the quarter.
Past Perfect		When the game ended, they **had had** enough.
Future Perfect		In one week, they **will have had** a winning season.

3 Reinforce and Extend

Teacher Alert

Students should understand that the future tense is not the only way that English speakers refer to events to come. Point out that in casual speech people often use a form of the verb *be* plus the phrase *going to* in place of *will.* (Example: *We are going to win tomorrow.*) Sometimes people will simply use a form of the verb *be* and a verb ending in *-ing* to express future action. (Example: *I'm staying with my grandparents next summer.*) Write examples on the board, and explain that these are perfectly acceptable in speech and informal writing. Lead students to understand, however, that the official future tense is the one using the helping verb *will.*

Global Connection

Tell students that speakers of all languages have ways to express relationships in time. Write the following sentences on the board:

I have a book.
I had a book.
I will have a book.

Have students who speak languages other than English translate each sentence into their own language. Discuss the varied ways in which distinctions in tense can be made—not always with a change in verb form.

Learning Styles

Auditory/Verbal

Students may have difficulty understanding the concept of the present perfect tense as it is defined. Lead them to understand that this is a form of speech that they frequently use in everyday speech. Without explaining your purpose, ask students a number of questions using the present perfect tense. (Example: *What have you done since you got up this morning?*) Insist on answers in complete sentences. (*I've brushed my teeth.*) After a few questions and answers, write some of the appropriate responses on the board. Explain that many of the language rules students are learning involve concepts they already use correctly.

Activity B

Remind students that a phrase must consist of more than one word. Point out that if there is only one verb in a sentence it cannot be part of a verb phrase.

Activity B Answers

1. have had 2. has scored 3. has planned 4. have earned 5. has ordered

Activity C

Point out that the helping verb often comes immediately before the main verb. Suggest to students that first they locate the verb *have* in the activity items and then look at the word immediately following it. If this is another verb, then *have* is a helping verb.

Activity C Answers

1. helping verb 2. helping verb 3. main verb 4. main verb 5. helping verb

Using What You've Learned

Students may think only in terms of the verbs *be* and *have* for their captions. (Example: *My hair was short/Now my hair is long.*) Encourage them to use action verbs. Brainstorm with the class for past/present ideas using action verbs. (Example: *When I was little, I wanted to be a wrestler. Now I want to be a doctor.*)

Learning Styles

Interpersonal/Group Learning

Have pairs of students compose three sentences in which *have* is a helping verb or a main verb. Ask pairs to exchange their sentences and to identify how the verb *have* is used in each. Have students read aloud their sentences and identifications. Write any problem sentences on the board.

The verb *have* can be a main verb or a helping verb. When it is a helping verb, it is part of a verb phrase.

I have good friends. (main verb)
(*have* used alone)

I have made good friends. (helping verb)
(*have* used to form the present perfect tense of the verb *made*)

Activity B Write the verb phrase in each sentence on your paper.

1. The Wilson Wildcats have had a great season.
2. The team has scored many touchdowns.
3. Coach Shaw has planned a team party.
4. The Wildcats have earned the celebration.
5. The coach has ordered trophies for the players.

Activity C Decide whether *have* is the main verb or the helping verb in each sentence. Write *main verb* or *helping verb* on your paper.

1. The quarterback has worked hard today.
2. He has thrown several good passes.
3. The team has a good record so far.
4. They have one win and no losses.
5. The coach has expressed high hopes for the rest of the season.

Using What You've Learned

On your paper, draw a before-and-after cartoon showing a way you have changed. You might show how a haircut, trip, or growth spurt changed you. Under the *before* picture, write a caption using a past tense verb. Under the *after* picture, write a caption using a present tense verb.

Activity D On your paper, write the present perfect, past perfect, and future perfect tenses of the following verbs in sentences. Then underline the verb or verb phrase in each sentence.

Example jump — He has jumped. He had jumped. He will have jumped.

1. act
2. discuss
3. improve
4. lock
5. move
6. offer
7. open
8. pass
9. yell
10. listen

Activity E On your paper, write all six tenses of the following verbs in sentences. Use the third person singular (he, she, or it). Then underline the verb or verb phrase in each sentence.

Example whisper

present	She whispers.
past	She whispered.
future	She will whisper.
present perfect	She has whispered.
past perfect	She had whispered.
future perfect	She will have whispered.

1. walk
2. work
3. fish
4. listen
5. roar
6. call
7. talk
8. clean
9. shout
10. watch

Learning Styles

Logical/Mathematical

Invite a student to describe a typical day in his or her life in chronological order. Have other students use this information to draw a time line on the board. Make sure that each event uses an action verb. (Example: *7 A.M. catch school bus; 3 P.M. go to volleyball practice.*) Use this time line to practice the past and future perfect tenses. For the past perfect, point to any event in the day except the first and ask, "What had Corey done by the time he went to volleyball practice?" For the future perfect, use the same technique but rephrase the question: "What will Hannah have done by the time she eats supper?" Elicit answers in the appropriate tense.

Activity D

Review with students the definitions of the perfect tenses given on page 87. Invite students to give examples of each tense.

Activity D Answers

Pronouns will vary. **1.** He has acted. He had acted. He will have acted. **2.** He has discussed. He had discussed. He will have discussed. **3.** He has improved. He had improved. He will have improved. **4.** He has locked. He had locked. He will have locked. **5.** He has moved. He had moved. He will have moved. **6.** He has offered. He had offered. He will have offered. **7.** He has opened. He had opened. He will have opened. **8.** He has passed. He had passed. He will have passed. **9.** He has yelled. He had yelled. He will have yelled. **10.** He has listened. He had listened. He will have listened.

Activity E

Suggest that student partners write out each verb in all six tenses before using them in sentences. Partners should compose their sentences together and take turns acting as scribe.

Activity E Answers

Pronouns will vary. **1.** She walks. She walked. She will walk. She has walked. She had walked. She will have walked. **2.** She works. She worked. She will work. She has worked. She had worked. She will have worked. **3.** She fishes. She fished. She will fish. She has fished. She had fished. She will have fished. **4.** She listens. She listened. She will listen. She has listened. She had listened. She will have listened. **5.** She roars. She roared. She will roar. She has roared. She had roared. She will have roared. **6.** She calls. She called. She will call. She has called. She had called. She will have called. **7.** She talks. She talked. She will talk. She has talked. She had talked. She will have talked. **8.** She cleans. She cleaned. She will clean. She has cleaned. She had cleaned. She will have cleaned. **9.** She shouts. She shouted. She will shout. She has shouted. She had shouted. She will have shouted. **10.** She watches. She watched. She will watch. She has watched. She had watched. She will have watched.

Lesson 2 Review Answers

1. had planned—past perfect 2. will keep—future 3. make—present 4. decorated—past 5. purchased—past 6. Arrive—present 7. will love—future 8. enjoyed—past 9. have had—present perfect 10. will have told—future perfect 11. He asks. He asked. He will ask. He has asked. He had asked. He will have asked. 12. He sews. He sewed. He will sew. He has sewed. He had sewed. He will have sewed. 13. He cooks. He cooked. He will cook. He has cooked. He had cooked. He will have cooked. 14. He packs. He packed. He will pack. He has packed. He had packed. He will have packed. 15. He spells. He spelled. He will spell. He has spelled. He had spelled. He will have spelled. 16. He offers. He offered. He will offer. He has offered. He had offered. He will have offered. 17. He paints. He painted. He will paint. He has painted. He had painted. He will have painted. 18. He calls. He called. He will call. He has called. He had called. He will have called. 19. He shouts. He shouted. He will shout. He has shouted. He had shouted. He will have shouted. 20. He types. He typed. He will type. He has typed. He had typed. He will have typed. 21. helping verb 22. helping verb 23. main verb 24. helping verb 25. main verb

Writing Practice

Have students write a series of sentences about members of their family including the pets if they wish. Their sentences should use all six of the tenses identified in this lesson. Help students who are having difficulty with finding examples of the perfect tenses. Have students exchange their sentences with partners to peer edit.

Learning Styles

Visual/Spatial

Have students create a chart on the board with the headings *present, past, future, present perfect, past perfect, and future perfect.* Down the sides of the chart list some of the verbs used in this chapter. Invite students to fill out the correct form of each verb.

Lesson 2 REVIEW

Write the verb or verb phrase in bold on your paper. Identify the tense of each verb or verb phrase as *present, past, future, present perfect, past perfect,* or *future perfect.*

1. Amy and her brother **had planned** a surprise party.
2. They **will keep** it a secret from their sister, Julia.
3. They **make** a piñata for the party.
4. They **decorated** it with ribbon.
5. Amy **purchased** snacks and toys to fill it.
6. "**Arrive** on time," Amy told everyone.
7. "Julia **will love** this surprise!" said her brother.
8. Everyone **enjoyed** the party, especially the piñata.
9. "I **have had** a wonderful time!" said Julia.
10. By Monday, Julia **will have told** everyone about the piñata.

On your paper, write all six tenses of the following verbs in sentences. Use the third person singular (he, she, or it). Then underline the verb or verb phrase in each sentence.

11. ask
12. sew
13. cook
14. pack
15. spell
16. offer
17. paint
18. call
19. shout
20. enjoy

Decide whether *have* is the main verb or the helping verb in each sentence. Write *main verb* or *helping verb* on your paper.

21. The circus has arrived in town.
22. The trainers have practiced with their animals.
23. We had tickets for the afternoon show.
24. The clowns had thrown confetti into the crowd.
25. The acrobats have many stunts to do.

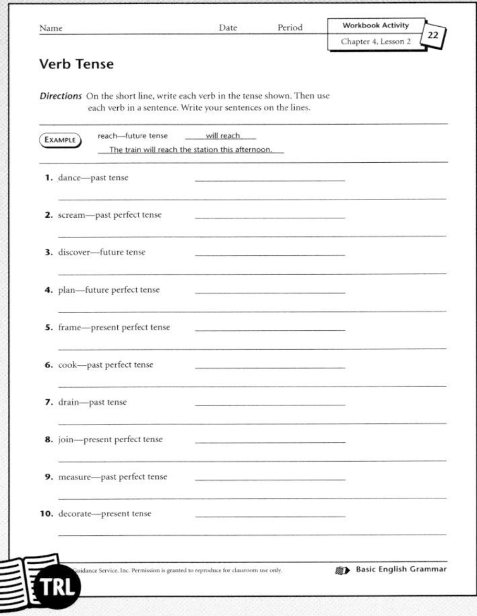

Name Date Period Workbook Activity 22 Chapter 4, Lesson 2

Verb Tense

Directions On the short line, write each verb in the tense shown. Then use each verb in a sentence. Write your sentences on the lines.

EXAMPLE reach—future tense will reach
The train will reach the station this afternoon.

1. dance—past tense
2. scream—past perfect tense
3. discover—future tense
4. plan—future perfect tense
5. frame—present perfect tense
6. cook—past perfect tense
7. drain—past tense
8. join—present perfect tense
9. measure—past perfect tense
10. decorate—present tense

 Basic English Grammar

Workbook Activity 22

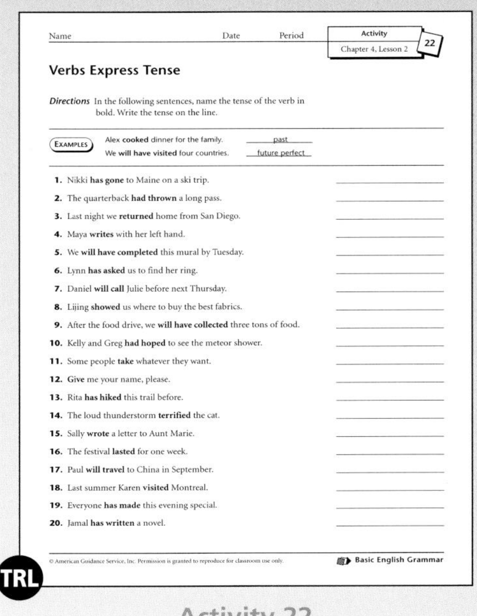

Name Date Period Activity 22 Chapter 4, Lesson 2

Verbs Express Tense

Directions In the following sentences, name the tense of the verb in bold. Write the tense on the line.

EXAMPLES Alex **cooked** dinner for the family. past
We **will have visited** four countries. future perfect

1. Nikki **has gone** to Maine on a ski trip.
2. The quarterback **had thrown** a long pass.
3. Last night we **returned** home from San Diego.
4. Maya **writes** with her left hand.
5. We **will have completed** this mural by Tuesday.
6. Lynn **has asked** us to find her ring.
7. Daniel **will call** Julie before next Thursday.
8. Lijing **showed** us where to buy the best fabrics.
9. After the food drive, we **will have collected** three tons of food.
10. Kelly and Greg **had hoped** to see the meteor shower.
11. Some people **take** whatever they want.
12. **Give** me your name, please.
13. Rita **has hiked** this trail before.
14. The loud thunderstorm **terrified** the cat.
15. Sally **wrote** a letter to Aunt Marie.
16. The festival **lasted** for one week.
17. Paul **will travel** to China in September.
18. Last summer Karen **visited** Montreal.
19. Everyone **has made** this evening special.
20. Jamal **has written** a novel.

 Basic English Grammar

Activity 22

Lesson 3 Regular and Irregular Verbs

Past participle
The verb form used to form the perfect tenses

Regular verb
A verb that forms its past tense and past participle by adding -ed or -d

Irregular verb
A verb that does not form its past tense and past participle by adding -ed or -d

Verbs have three main forms—infinitive (present), past, and **past participle.** The past participle is the verb form we use to form the perfect tenses. **Regular verbs** form their past and past participles by adding *-ed* or *-d.*

EXAMPLE	Infinitive	Present	Past	Past Participle
	to act	act, acts	acted	(have, has) acted
	to call	call, calls	called	(have, has) called

Irregular verbs do not follow the usual rules. An irregular verb does not form its past tense and past participle by adding *-ed* or *-d.* Sometimes the past and past participles are different. In a few cases, even the present tense has different forms. The verbs *be, have,* and *do* are examples of irregular verbs. We use them as helping verbs and main verbs. Two other common verbs that have unusual forms are *eat* and *go.*

Some Irregular Verbs			
Infinitive	**Present**	**Past**	**Past Participle**
to be	am, is, are	was, were	(have, has) been
to have	have, has	had	(have, has) had
to do	do, does	did	(have, has) done
to eat	eat, eats	ate	(have, has) eaten
to go	go, goes	went	(have, has) gone

Activity A On your paper, write the correct form of the verb in parentheses to complete each sentence.

1. Mrs. Kim (be) the coach two years ago.
2. The children have already (eat) their lunch.
3. Amir has (have) his job for nearly a year.
4. They (do) their chores every night.
5. Carlos has (go) to band practice.

Lesson at a Glance

Chapter 4 Lesson 3

Overview This lesson defines the past participle and introduces irregular verbs. It describes how the past tense and past participle of irregular verbs differ from those of regular verbs.

Objectives

- To identify the three main forms of irregular verbs.
- To distinguish between the use of past and perfect forms of irregular verbs in sentences.

Student Pages 91–95

Teacher's Resource Library 

Workbook Activity 23
Activity 23
Alternative Activity 23

Vocabulary

irregular verb
past participle
regular verb

1 Warm-Up Activity

Write on the board the following sentences: *I work at Mel's garage* and *She paints the house.* Then write the word *Yesterday* in front of these sentences and ask students to make the necessary changes to the verbs. Ask students what the rule is for creating the past tense of most verbs based on this model. Elicit that the past tense is formed by adding *-ed.* Now write *I am at Mel's garage* and *She eats at the house* on the board. Again write *Yesterday* in front of these sentences, and have students make the necessary changes to the verbs. Ask them what they notice about the second examples. Point out that not all verbs follow the same regular pattern. Those that don't are known as irregular verbs.

2 Teaching the Lesson

Have students read the text and study the chart on this page. Review with them the definition of past participle and write on the board some examples of regular and irregular verbs in their three forms. Explain to students that irregular verbs follow no pattern. An English speaker must memorize these forms. Reassure students, however, that for native English speakers, much of this learning takes place in early childhood. Make this point by asking pairs of questions that use irregular verbs and require answers in the past tense and present perfect tense. Examples: *What did you eat yesterday?* and *What have you eaten today?* Write examples of their answers on the board. Lead students to understand that a successful command of English requires a knowledge of all the common irregular verbs.

Activity A

Remind students to look for clues in the activity sentences. The helping verb *have* will take the past participle of the main verb. Point out that all the verbs in Activity A are included in the chart above.

Activity A Answers

1. was 2. eaten 3. had 4. do 5. gone

Activity B

Give students an opportunity to practice using the past and past participle forms of the irregular verbs given in the chart on page 92. Begin by writing sample sentences on the board: have students identify the past and past participle tenses of each verb. Then encourage volunteers to say sentences using the past and past participle forms of the other verbs in the chart.

Activity B Answers

1. found 2. kept 3. cut 4. heard 5. fed 6. lost 7. made 8. cost 9. sent 10. bent

3 Reinforce and Extend

Learning Styles

LEP/ESL

Draw students' attention to the box on this page defining the word *irregular*. Point out that the prefix *ir-* reverses the meaning of the root word that follows. The prefixes *un-* and *il-* can have the same function in English. Give familiar examples: *irresponsible, illegal, unhappy*. Then have students form mixed groups of English speakers and English language learners. Ask groups to find one common word for each prefix in the dictionary. Students should look up the root word and the word with the prefix and write the definitions for both. Have them read the definitions carefully: *ir-*, *un-*, and *il-* are not always negative prefixes. Urge students to make sure that all group members can pronounce and understand the word. Invite students to share their findings with the class.

Irregular means "not regular or not usual." The word is formed by adding the prefix *ir-* to the word *regular*. This prefix means "not."

We use the past participle with *have, has,* or *had* to form the perfect tenses of irregular verbs. For some irregular verbs, the past tense and past participle are the same.

Irregular Verbs with Same Past Tense and Past Participle

Present	Past	Past Participle
bend(s)	bent	(has) bent
cut(s)	cut	(has) cut
cost(s)	cost	(has) cost
feed(s)	fed	(has) fed
find(s)	found	(has) found
hear(s)	heard	(has) heard
keep(s)	kept	(has) kept
lose(s)	lost	(has) lost
make(s)	made	(has) made
send(s)	sent	(has) sent

Activity B On your paper, write the past or past participle form of the verb.

1. Ms. Lee has (find) the answer.
2. Carol (keep) her old clothes.
3. Leon has (cut) his finger on the glass.
4. They have (hear) that joke before.
5. Phillip had (feed) the dogs already.
6. Raquel (lose) the science book.
7. The player has (make) the touchdown.
8. The shirt (cost) way too much!
9. He has (send) the letter by overnight mail.
10. I have (bend) my bicycle wheel on the curb.

Teacher Alert

Some irregular verbs, such as *see* and *go*, are misused by many English-speaking people. In colloquial speech, the past participle is often used in place of the past tense. (Examples: *I seen him in the hall. She gone home.*) Hearing these words used incorrectly on a regular basis can create a problem for students, especially those students acquiring English. Suggest that all students practice saying and writing sentences with these verbs used correctly.

For some irregular verbs, the past tense and past participle are different.

Irregular Verbs with Different Past Tense and Past Participle		
Present	**Past**	**Past Participle**
begin(s)	began	(has) begun
break(s)	broke	(has) broken
choose(s)	chose	(has) chosen
drive(s)	drove	(has) driven
fall(s)	fell	(has) fallen
fly (flies)	flew	(has) flown
forget(s)	forgot	(has) forgotten
give(s)	gave	(has) given
grow(s)	grew	(has) grown
hide(s)	hid	(has) hidden
know(s)	knew	(has) known
ride(s)	rode	(has) ridden
see(s)	saw	(has) seen
swim(s)	swam	(has) swum
take(s)	took	(has) taken
write(s)	wrote	(has) written

Activity C On your paper, write the correct form of the verb in parentheses to complete each sentence.

1. Mitsu has (know) Brad for many years.
2. Kiara (ride) in the holiday parade last year.
3. Hasan has (write) his cousin in Africa.
4. The vase (break) when it fell off the counter.
5. Calvin has (saw) that musical twice.

Activity C

Write two or three sample sentences on the board before students begin this activity. (Examples: *I see him last Sunday. They have ride into the sunset.*) Discuss with students strategies for understanding whether to use the past tense or the past participle.

Activity C Answers

1. known **2.** rode **3.** written **4.** broke **5.** seen

Learning Styles

Auditory/Verbal

Ask students to review the lists of irregular verbs on pages 92 and 93. Then have them form small groups, and assign each group five verbs. Students should write two simple questions for each verb: one requiring an answer in the past tense, the other requiring an answer in a perfect tense. Write model questions on the board. (Examples: *Where did you take the exam? How many branches have fallen?*) Invite groups to stand in teams around the room, and have them ask each other questions orally. Students should take turns answering.

Activity D

Have students identify the words that separate the verb phrase in each of the examples. Point out that the second sentence is a question. Explain that the first word of a question is often the first part of a verb phrase. Provide two or three more examples of questions that demonstrate this fact.

Activity D Answers

1. has given **2.** Have heard **3.** has seen **4.** had known **5.** Have ridden

Activity E

Before having students complete the activity on their own, review the six tenses of verbs and ask students for example sentences using each tense.

Activity E Answers

1. future **2.** past **3.** present **4.** past **5.** past perfect **6.** present perfect **7.** future **8.** future perfect **9.** past perfect **10.** present

At Home

Ask students to imagine that they are reporters assigned to interview a member of their own family. Before they plan their interviews, have students help you develop model questions, using verbs from the charts on pages 91, 92, and 93. Encourage students to use irregular verbs and to create questions that prompt answers in the past or perfect tenses. (Examples: *Why did you choose music as a career? How long had you known Dad before you married him?*) Have them ask at least 10 questions. Suggest that they tape or video record the interviews. Invite students to share their questions and answers with the class.

The words in a verb phrase are usually written together. However, they may be separated by another word or words in the sentence.

Example

She has finally written the report.
Has Rica really gone to the store?
Leroy will probably finish his assignment after the show.

Activity D Write the verb phrase in each sentence on your paper. Ignore any words that come between the helping verb and the main verb.

1. James has always given his best.
2. Have you ever heard that song before?
3. Victor has often seen him at the field.
4. I had not known the answer until today.
5. Have you ever ridden a scooter?

Activity E Write the tense of each verb or verb phrase in bold on your paper.

1. She **will drive** me to the store tomorrow.
2. Yesterday Beth **lost** her gloves.
3. Ms. Potter **feeds** the rabbits.
4. The coach finally **chose** all of the players.
5. Melissa **had known** most of the players for years.
6. A reporter **has written** about many of the games.
7. She **will send** the e-mail after school.
8. By noon Renee **will have made** the team.
9. Connie **had** seldom **found** such a bargain.
10. Carl **forgets** his glasses sometimes.

Lesson 3 REVIEW

On your paper, write the correct form of the verb in parentheses to complete each sentence. Then write the tense next to each verb or verb phrase.

1. We have (eat) dinner at that cafe before.
2. Jeff has (be) at practice all afternoon.
3. Alice has (do) the assignment correctly.
4. The members (swim) every week.
5. Have the girls (go) to the movies?
6. I will (keep) my thoughts to myself.
7. Alex (hear) the band practicing last week.
8. Who has (bend) this fork?
9. She has (forget) to whom to send the letter.
10. They had (know) each other for years.

On your paper, write the verb phrase in each sentence.

11. Helen has written a poem for English class.
12. Did you ever do your report?
13. Ramon has often fed the chickens.
14. She had not broken her promise.
15. Have you chosen your topic?

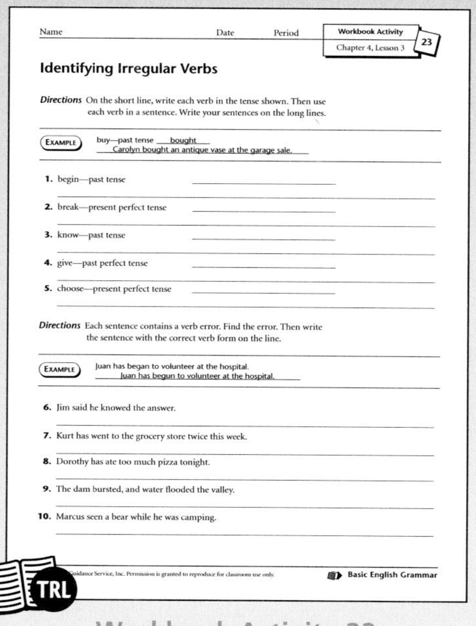

Name Date Period **Workbook Activity** Chapter 4, Lesson 3 **23**

Identifying Irregular Verbs

Directions On the short line, write each verb in the tense shown. Then use each verb in a sentence. Write your sentences on the long lines.

EXAMPLE buy—past tense bought
Carolyn bought an antique vase at the garage sale.

1. begin—past tense
2. break—present perfect tense
3. know—past tense
4. give—past perfect tense
5. choose—present perfect tense

Directions Each sentence contains a verb error. Find the error. Then write the sentence with the correct verb form on the line.

EXAMPLE Juan has began to volunteer at the hospital.
Juan has begun to volunteer at the hospital.

6. Jim said he knowed the answer.
7. Kurt has went to the grocery store twice this week.
8. Dorothy has ate too much pizza tonight.
9. The dam bursted, and water flooded the valley.
10. Marcus seen a bear while he was camping.

 Basic English Grammar

TRL

Workbook Activity 23

Name Date Period **Activity** Chapter 4, Lesson 3 **23**

Irregular Verb Forms

Directions Write the correct form of the verb in parentheses on the line.

EXAMPLE Jack bought his sweater at the department store. (buy)

1. Barak has ______ the show already. (see)
2. Heather is ______ her old bike away. (give)
3. Mark ______ Julia to go to the dance with him. (choose)
4. Will you ______ to the skating rink with me? (go)
5. Jamie has ______ a lot of ice cream today! (eat)
6. Which band have you ______ for the prom? (choose)
7. Tanya ______ her mother's antique vase. (break)
8. Matt is ______ his homework. (do)
9. Mr. Tran has ______ French for years. (teach)
10. Yesterday, Shira ______ a new book. (begin)
11. What have you ______ with my pen? (do)
12. We ______ our old television to friends. (give)
13. Ahmed had ______ his father's favorite song. (sing)
14. Are you ______ Muffin how to sit? (teach)
15. She is one of the funniest people I have ______. (know)
16. Few people have ______ across the English Channel. (swim)
17. Stephanie ______ that dress to the choir concert last week. (wear)
18. Has Mrs. Dean ______ other books like this one? (write)
19. This hot weather is ______ all the temperature records. (break)
20. Cory ______ to close the windows. (forget)

 Basic English Grammar

TRL

Activity 23

Lesson 3 Review Answers

1. eaten—present perfect **2.** been—present perfect **3.** done—present perfect **4.** swim—present **5.** gone—present perfect **6.** keep—future **7.** heard—past **8.** bent—present perfect **9.** forgotten—present perfect **10.** known—past perfect **11.** has written **12.** Did do **13.** has fed **14.** had broken **15.** Have chosen

LEARNING STYLES

Interpersonal/Group Learning

Write the following words in no particular order on the board: *alien invaders, eat, grow, spaceships, find, choose, be, terror, fly.* Have students form pairs and ask them to use these words in a short story. Explain that the verbs must be in the past tense or in one of the perfect tenses. Encourage students to use vivid adjectives and imaginative details. Ask them to underline their verbs and to exchange their stories with another pair to check. Invite pairs to read their stories to the class.

LEARNING STYLES

Body/Kinesthetic

Invite students who enjoy mime to choose one of the irregular verbs listed in this lesson and to devise an action to answer the questions "What have I done?" or "What did I do?" For example, a student might pretend to be feeding chickens or driving a car. After miming the action, he or she should ask the class, "What have I done?"—eliciting the answer, "You have fed the chickens." The question "What did I do?" should prompt a response in the past tense.

Lesson at a Glance

Chapter 4 Lesson 4

Overview This lesson presents the progressive forms of verbs and the different forms of the verb *be.*

Objectives

- To locate verbs in sentences.
- To use the verb *be* correctly in sentences.
- To identify and use the 12 forms of regular verbs in sentences.

Student Pages 96–100

Teacher's Resource Library 

Workbook Activity 24

Activity 24

Alternative Activity 24

Lesson 4 The Progressive Forms

> ***Progressive form***
> *The form of a verb that ends in -ing and shows continuing action*
>
> ***Present participle***
> *A verb form that shows continuing action*

The **progressive form** of a verb ends in *-ing* and shows continuing action. Compare these two sentences.

EXAMPLE
Present
Kim practices the guitar twice a week.
(shows an action that is done frequently)
Present Progressive
Kim is practicing the guitar.
(shows an action that is being done now)

The **present participle** shows continuing action.

EXAMPLE

Present	Present Participle
work	working
see	seeing

A progressive form is a verb phrase. It is made from a form of the verb *be* plus the present participle.

EXAMPLE

Present Progressive	He is working.
Past Progressive	He was working.
Future Progressive	He will be working.
Present Perfect Progressive	He has been working.
Past Perfect Progressive	He had been working.
Future Perfect Progressive	He will have been working.

Activity A Write the verb phrase in each sentence on your paper.

1. Hai Sin was practicing her flute when the phone rang.
2. Soon Tom will be practicing the drums.
3. Sam has been practicing for 30 minutes.
4. Cathy had been practicing when I called her.
5. Soon the band will have been practicing for an hour.

Vocabulary

present participle
progressive form

Warm-Up Activity

Introduce the progressive forms by performing a simple action and asking students "What am I doing?" Their answers should take the present progressive form: "You are looking out the window." "You are standing on one foot." Then ask students what they were doing at eight o'clock last night. They will answer in the past progressive form. After a few questions and answers, ask students what they noticed about the verbs they were using. Elicit that the main verbs ended in *-ing.* Challenge students to make a connection between the present and the past questions. Lead them to understand that in each case they were describing an action that was in the process of happening or continuing.

Teaching the Lesson

Have students read the six progressive forms of the verb *work* on this page. Ask them to compare and contrast these forms with the simple and perfect tenses they read about in Lesson 2. Elicit that the main verb of the progressive form always ends in *-ing* and that the helping verb *be* determines whether the action takes place in the past, present, or future. Help students understand the difference between the simple and progressive forms of verbs. Write the following sentences on the board: *They will watch a movie* and *They will be watching a movie.* Ask students how these statements differ. Lead them to understand that the progressive form describes an action that is in the process of taking place at a precise moment. *They will be watching a movie at eight o'clock tomorrow night.*

Activity A

Before students begin the activity, have them use the six progressive forms of these verbs in sentences: *paint, sing, play, think,* and *speak.* First help students form the present participle of each verb. Then have them say sentences like those shown in the example box for the verb *work.*

Activity A Answers

1. was practicing 2. will be practicing 3. has been practicing 4. had been practicing 5. will have been practicing

Be is an irregular verb. Here are the different forms of *be*.

(To) Be		
Simple Tenses		
Present	**Past**	**Future**
I am	I was	I shall be
you are	you were	you will be
he is	he was	he will be
we are	we were	we shall be
you are	you were	you will be
they are	they were	they will be
Perfect Tenses		
Present Perfect	**Past Perfect**	**Future Perfect**
I have been	I had been	I shall have been
you have been	you had been	you will have been
he has been	he had been	he will have been
we have been	we had been	we shall have been
you have been	you had been	you will have been
they have been	they had been	they will have been

Activity B On your paper, write the correct form of the verb *be* to complete each sentence.

1. I have _______ on an airplane six times.
2. Jack will _______ going to Seattle next week.
3. Doris has _______ in my class every year.
4. By noon, Mac will have _______ working for four hours.
5. Sara _______ leaving for Florida on Friday.

Activity B

Have students complete these sentences with a form of the verb *be:*

He has _____ very sick.
Sarah _____ visiting last week.
I will _____ leaving soon.

Activity B Answers

1. been 2. be 3. been 4. been 5. is *or* will be

3 Reinforce and Extend

Global Connection

Students might be interested to learn the pronunciation and spelling of the verb *be* in several languages. Write *be* in the center of a web diagram and ask students for other English forms of the verb *be.* Add these to the outside of the web. Then invite students who speak other languages to say forms of the verb *be* in the other language. Have them write these forms of *be* in the web. Encourage students to explain when each of the forms shown in the web is used.

Learning Styles

Auditory/Verbal

Divide the class into groups of three. Assign each group one line of the "to be" list in the box on page 97. Note that the box contains 12 lines showing the simple and perfect forms of the verb *to be.* Ask each group to create three sentences using its three tenses. Then invite students to take turns reading their sentences to the class. Challenge other groups to identify the form of the verb *to be*—stating whether it is simple or perfect and past, present, or future.

Activity C

Invite volunteers to use each verb phrase listed in an oral sentence before having students write sentences on their own.

Activity C Answers

Sentences will vary.

Activity D

Have partners work together to write examples of verbs in the three perfect and six progressive tenses. Then invite them to share their verbs with the class. Suggest that students refer to the examples on page 96 as they do Activity D.

Activity D Answers

1. past perfect 2. present progressive 3. future progressive 4. present perfect progressive 5. present progressive

Activity E

Suggest that as students do the activity, they read the sentences to themselves twice, with a different answer in place each time. They should choose the answer that sounds correct.

Activity E Answers

1. playing 2. played 3. going 4. raising 5. raised

ONLINE CONNECTION

Have students read the Technology Note box on this page. Point out that there are many effective search engines. Some of the best known can be found at **www.altavista.com, www.askjeeves.com, www.google.com,** and **www.yahoo.com.** There is even a Web site specializing in information about search engines at **www.searchenginewatch.com.** Ask students to choose one of the four Web sites listed above and to type in the phrase *progressive verbs.* Have them visit a few sites and print out information that strikes them as useful or interesting. Ask them to share their findings with the class.

One way to learn more about a topic is to look it up using an Internet search engine. A search engine looks through Internet Web sites to find those that contain information about a specific topic. You can type in a topic to get the search engine started.

Activity C Write each verb phrase in a sentence on your paper.

1. will have been going
2. has been working
3. had been eating
4. is beginning
5. were whispering

Activity D Write the tense of each verb phrase in bold on your paper.

1. Mario **had** never **gone** to Texas before this year.
2. He **is flying** there for a vacation.
3. He **will be leaving** at noon.
4. Mario **has been packing** all morning.
5. They **are going** to the airport now.

Activity E On your paper, write the correct verb in parentheses to complete each sentence.

1. Rosa has been (playing, played) the trumpet for several years.
2. She has (playing, played) in the Wilson band for two years.
3. This year the band is (going, gone) to Florida for a national contest.
4. The band members have been (raising, raised) money all year.
5. So far they have (raising, raised) more than one thousand dollars.

Activity F Write a sentence for each verb, using the tense given in parentheses. Then underline the verb or verb phrase in each sentence.

Example play (present progressive)
Dylan <u>is playing</u> the trombone.

1. drive (future progressive)
2. have (past progressive)
3. fish (present progressive)
4. see (future perfect progressive)
5. pour (past perfect progressive)
6. go (simple past)
7. wonder (present perfect progressive)
8. jump (present perfect)
9. pack (simple present)
10. work (future)

The Wilson High band members listen carefully to their band director.

Activity F

Before starting the exercise, have students review the examples of the progressive form on page 96 and the table of tenses for the verb *be* on page 97. Have pairs of students complete the sentences. Remind them that whenever the word *progressive* appears, the main verb will end in *-ing*.

Activity F Answers

Sentences will vary.

Learning Styles

Interpersonal/Group Learning

Make two sets of six cards. On one set of cards, write each of the six progressive forms. On the other set, write each of these verbs: *go, fly, leave, pack, whisper, jump.* Place the cards facedown in separate piles. Have pairs of students take turns selecting a card from each pile. They should announce their selections and then return the cards. Mix up the cards after two or three turns. When all students have selected cards, give them a few moments to write a sentence using the tense and verb they selected.

Learning Styles

Visual/Spatial

Write the names of the six simple and six progressive verb forms in rows on one side of the board. Then invite students to go to the board and draw a small cartoon or sketch illustrating an action. Ask them to explain to the class what their drawing depicts, using the present progressive form. (Example: *She is playing field hockey.*) When the board is full of student artwork, call for two student "teachers" to conduct the class. One should point to a verb form. The other should point to one of the drawings. They should then invite volunteers to describe the action in the verb form indicated. Example: *She will have been playing field hockey.* Allow students to consult the tables on pages 96 and 97 before they give their answers.

Lesson 4 Review Answers

Sentences will vary. Verb forms are given. **1.** sharpens **2.** sharpened **3.** will sharpen **4.** has (have) sharpened **5.** had sharpened **6.** will have sharpened **7.** is (am, are) sharpening **8.** was (were) sharpening **9.** will be sharpening **10.** have (has) been sharpening **11.** had been sharpening **12.** will have been sharpening

Verbs are given in the order they appear in the paragraph. played—past, earned—past, lived—past, studied—past, played—past, joined—past, moved—past, was playing—past progressive, invented—past, was recording—past progressive, formed—past, loved—past, performed—past, continued—past, sold—past, died—past, will remember—future

Speaking Practice

Invite groups of three or four students to practice reading the paragraph about Louis Armstrong aloud as a team. Students should first take turns reading the paragraph individually to each other. Have them listen for pronunciation, pacing, and expression. Then ask group members to practice reading alternate sentences. Encourage them to listen carefully to the previous reader and to pick up where he or she left off without breaking the narrative flow. Invite groups to perform their team readings for the class.

Lesson 4 REVIEW

On your paper, write sentences using the verb *sharpen* in each of the six regular tenses and the six progressive forms. *Sharpen* is a regular verb. The first sentence has been done for you.

1. present—Phillip **sharpens** his pencil before class.
2. past
3. future
4. present perfect
5. past perfect
6. future perfect
7. present progressive
8. past progressive
9. future progressive
10. present perfect progressive
11. past perfect progressive
12. future perfect progressive

On your paper, write the verbs or verb phrases in this paragraph. Next to each verb or verb phrase, write its tense.

Louis Armstrong played the trumpet. He earned a special place in American history. As a child, he lived in an orphanage in New Orleans. There he first studied the cornet. In 1922, he played on a Mississippi riverboat. He joined a band in Chicago. Then in 1924, Armstrong moved to New York City. Soon he was playing the trumpet. He invented a completely new style. By 1925, he was recording his music. Later he formed his own band. People also loved his husky voice. In the 1930s, Armstrong performed in movies. His popularity continued for the rest of his life. One of his records, "Hello, Dolly!" sold two million copies in 1964. Armstrong died in 1971. People will remember this man and his music for a long time.

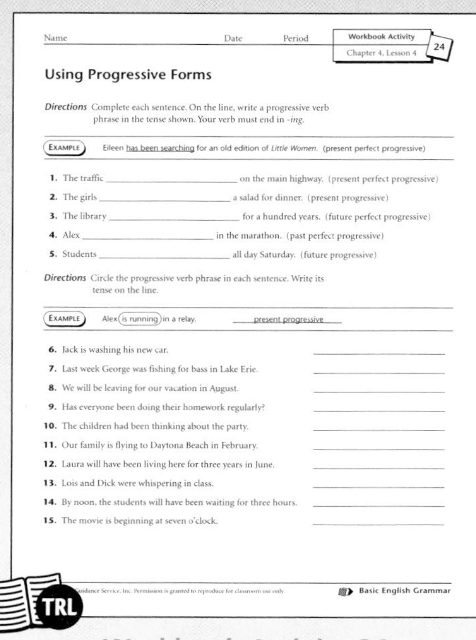

Name ____ Date ____ Period ____

Workbook Activity 24
Chapter 4, Lesson 4

Using Progressive Forms

Directions Complete each sentence. On the line, write a progressive verb phrase in the tense shown. Your verb must end in *-ing*.

EXAMPLE Eileen has been searching for an old edition of *Little Women*. (present perfect progressive)

1. The traffic ______________ on the main highway. (present perfect progressive)
2. The girls ______________ a salad for dinner. (present progressive)
3. The library ______________ for a hundred years. (future perfect progressive)
4. Alex ______________ in the marathon. (past perfect progressive)
5. Students ______________ all day Saturday. (future progressive)

Directions Circle the progressive verb phrase in each sentence. Write its tense on the line.

EXAMPLE Alex (is running) in a relay. present progressive

6. Jack is washing his new car. ______________
7. Last week George was fishing for bass in Lake Erie. ______________
8. We will be leaving for our vacation in August. ______________
9. Has everyone been doing their homework regularly? ______________
10. The children had been thinking about the party. ______________
11. Our family is flying to Daytona Beach in February. ______________
12. Laura will have been living here for three years in June. ______________
13. Lois and Dick were whispering in class. ______________
14. By noon, the students will have been waiting for three hours. ______________
15. The movie is beginning at seven o'clock. ______________

Basic English Grammar

TRL

Workbook Activity 24

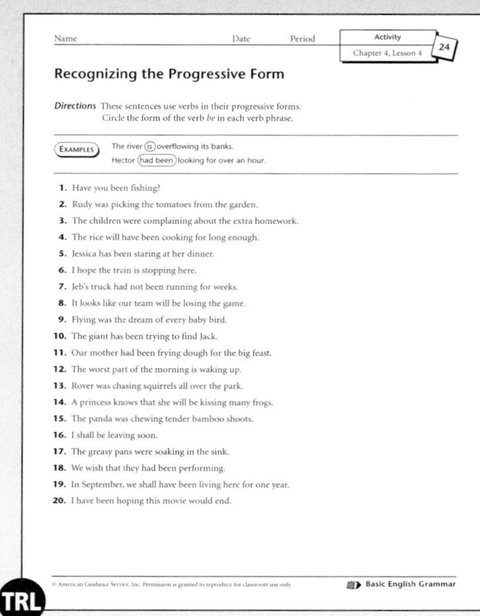

Name ____ Date ____ Period ____

Activity 24
Chapter 4, Lesson 4

Recognizing the Progressive Form

Directions These sentences use verbs in their progressive forms. Circle the form of the verb *be* in each verb phrase.

EXAMPLES The river (is) overflowing its banks.
Hector (had been) looking for over an hour.

1. Have you been fishing?
2. Rudy was picking the tomatoes from the garden.
3. The children were complaining about the extra homework.
4. The rice will have been cooking for long enough.
5. Jessica has been staring at her dinner.
6. I hope the train is stopping here.
7. Jeb's truck had not been running for weeks.
8. It looks like our team will be losing the game.
9. Flying was the dream of every baby bird.
10. The giant has been trying to find Jack.
11. Our mother had been frying dough for the big feast.
12. The worst part of the morning is waking up.
13. Rover was chasing squirrels all over the park.
14. A princess knows that she will be kissing many frogs.
15. The panda was chewing tender bamboo shoots.
16. I shall be leaving soon.
17. The greasy pans were soaking in the sink.
18. We wish that they had been performing.
19. In September, we shall have been living here for one year.
20. I have been hoping this movie would end.

Basic English Grammar

TRL

Activity 24

Lesson 5 Subject-Verb Agreement

A verb must agree in number (singular or plural) with its subject. The present tense of a regular verb has two forms. We use one form with a singular subject. We use another form with a plural subject.

Add *-s* or *-es* to the present tense of the verb when the subject is a singular noun.

EXAMPLE		
	Singular Subject	Melissa's puppy always cries for treats.
	Plural Subject	Both puppies cry for treats.

When the subject is a singular pronoun (he, she, it), add *-s* or *-es* to the verb.

EXAMPLE		
	Singular Subject	She likes to write.
	Plural Subject	They like to write.

When the subject is *I* or *you,* use the plural form of the verb.

EXAMPLE

I enjoy holidays with my cousins.
Do you enjoy holidays?

Activity A Write each sentence with the correct verb on your paper.

1. Jack (hope, hopes) to win the tournament.
2. They (love, loves) history class.
3. I (want, wants) a new box of colored pencils.
4. He (watch, watches) his neighbor's cat.
5. The robin (fly, flies) to the feeder.

Lesson at a Glance

Chapter 4 Lesson 5

Overview This lesson presents the rules for subject-verb agreement and explains the agreement of verbs with indefinite pronouns.

Objectives

- To explain the agreement of subject and verb.
- To understand the correct agreement of verbs with indefinite pronouns.

Student Pages 101–105

Teacher's Resource Library 

Workbook Activity 25
Activity 25
Alternative Activity 25

1 Warm-Up Activity

Write on the board the following sentence: *They ____ TV on Sundays.* Ask students to fill in the blank with a familiar verb, eliciting from them the verb *watch.* Now erase *They* and in its place write *Michael.* Ask students whether the sentence is still correct. Invite a volunteer to make the necessary correction, adding *-es* to *watch.* Ask why this change was necessary. Help students conclude that when the subject changes from singular to plural, a verb in the present tense will change to "agree" with it. Explain that this lesson will help them understand subject-verb agreement.

2 Teaching the Lesson

Write the word *everybody* on the board and ask whether it refers to many people or to one person. Students should respond that it refers to many. Have them review the definition of indefinite pronouns on page 46. Explain that indefinite pronouns may seem to be plural but often take a singular form of the verb. Point out that there is a built-in clue to help determine the number of an indefinite pronoun. If the pronoun ends in *-one, -body,* or *-thing* or if you can say "one" after the pronoun as in *another one, each one* or *either one,* it will take a singular form of the verb.

3 Reinforce and Extend

Teacher Alert

Subject-verb agreement can be confusing. Some students may think that a plural subject with an *-s* ending should take a verb with an *-s* ending. Point out that it is actually the opposite; if one (either subject or verb) has an *-s* ending, the other usually doesn't. Use the items in Activity A and additional examples, if necessary, to stress this rule.

Activity A

Invite a volunteer to read item 1 aloud twice—first with *hope* and then with *hopes.* Ask students which form of the verb belongs in the sentence and why. Then have them complete the activity on their own. When they have finished, invite them to read the sentences aloud with the answers in place. Ask students to explain how they knew which form of the verb to use.

Activity A Answers

1. Jack hopes to win the tournament. 2. They love history class. 3. I want a new box of colored pencils. 4. He watches his neighbor's cat. 5. The robin flies to the feeder.

Activity B

Write a list of the indefinite pronouns that may be either singular or plural on the board. Then have students read the activity items and identify the sentences containing these pronouns from the list. Remind them to read these sentences carefully to determine whether the pronouns are singular or plural.

Activity B Answers

1. has **2.** is **3.** go **4.** attend **5.** are **6.** travels **7.** are **8.** get **9.** eat **10.** need

At Home

Have students review the list of singular indefinite pronouns on page 46. Ask them to copy the list and keep it nearby while watching television at home. When they hear these words during their viewing, have them copy down the sentences in which they were used. Invite students to read their examples to the class, identifying the shows on which they heard them. Discuss which of these pronouns were used as subjects and whether their verbs agree with them.

Most indefinite pronouns are singular even though their meanings are plural. They take a singular form of the verb.

Correct	Everyone goes to the mountains in the fall.
Incorrect	Everyone go to the mountains in the fall.

Some indefinite pronouns may be singular or plural depending on the way we use them. They are *all, any, most,* and *none.*

EXAMPLE

Singular	All of the picnic food is in the cooler.
Plural	All of the girls are going to the mall.

Activity B On your paper, write the correct verb to complete each sentence.

1. All of the noise (has, have) stopped.
2. Anyone (is, are) welcome at the play.
3. Most of the club members (go, goes) to Angie's for snacks.
4. All of the musicians (attend, attends) the band concert.
5. None of us (are, is) going.
6. Everyone I know (travel, travels) to Nova Scotia in May.
7. All of us (is, are) going to a movie on Saturday.
8. Everyone will (gets, get) in for free.
9. Most of the teachers (eats, eat) lunch in the faculty room.
10. None of you (need, needs) braces.

Hearing the correct verb forms as they are spoken can help you write them correctly. Read aloud sentences that are correct. Listen to the sound of correct usage.

Some indefinite pronouns are always plural: *both, many, few,* and *several.* These indefinite pronouns take a plural form of the verb.

EXAMPLE Several of the students want to take the test.

Activity C Write the correct verb to complete each sentence on your paper.

1. Everyone (is, are) coming to the football game.
2. Both of the teachers (announces, announce) an exam.
3. Few of them (was, were) prepared for the exam.
4. Nothing (sound, sounds) as noisy as a hockey game.
5. Several of our student council members (decorate, decorates) the hall every year.
6. Many of the students (participate, participates) in the spring dance.
7. Both of you (need, needs) to finish getting dressed now.
8. Few of them could (identify, identifies) their bags.
9. Several of the students (chooses, choose) hot food for lunch.
10. All of the band members (wear, wears) their band uniforms for the concert.

Activity D Find the mistakes in these sentences. Then write the sentences correctly on your paper.

1. Everyone at the mall were in a hurry.
2. All of the shoppers was going to the sale.
3. Several of the people wants to buy new shoes.
4. No one are finding their size.
5. Both of my friends plans to be there soon.

LEARNING STYLES

Body/Kinesthetic

Divide the class into teams of three or four. Each team should compose five sentences with an indefinite pronoun as the subject. In some of these sentences, the verbs should agree with the subjects; in others they should not. Assign separate areas at the board for the teams. Ask each team to write its first sentence. Then say "move stations," and have all the teams move clockwise to the next station. There they should read the sentence written by the previous team, mark it right or wrong, and write their next sentence. Keep the class moving swiftly, reversing direction after two or three stops. When all of the sentences are on the board and corrected, invite the class to check the answers.

Activity C

Have students identify sentences containing the words *both, many, few,* and *several.* Remind them that the verb forms in these sentences will be plural.

Activity C Answers

1. is **2.** announce **3.** were **4.** sounds **5.** decorate **6.** participate **7.** need **8.** identify **9.** choose **10.** wear

Activity D

Ask volunteers to write their corrected sentences on the board and explain why they changed them.

Activity D Answers

1. Everyone at the mall was in a hurry. **2.** All of the shoppers were going to the sale. **3.** Several of the people want to buy new shoes. **4.** No one is finding his or her size. **5.** Both of my friends plan to be there soon.

LEARNING STYLES

Auditory/Verbal

Give students the opportunity to listen for subject-verb agreement as you read 10 sentences. Call out the number of each sentence before you read it. Students should write the number on the left on a sheet of paper if the subject and verb agree and on the right if the subject does not agree with the verb. When you have finished reading, have students compare their answers. Discuss any areas of disagreement.

Activity E

Before they begin writing, have students take turns reading the sentences aloud and identifying the collective nouns. Complete the first two items orally and discuss with students the reasons for the correct answer.

Activity E Answers

1. likes **2.** was **3.** scores **4.** flies **5.** meets **6.** eats **7.** holds **8.** gathers **9.** makes **10.** discusses

Vocabulary Builder

Point out to students that there are few perfect synonyms in the English language. Most words have slightly different meanings. Draw students' attention to the words related to laughter in their text. Ask for volunteers to demonstrate each of these forms of laughter. Have them use a dictionary if they are unsure of a definition. Ask students to use these words in sentences that indicate their meaning.

Answers to Vocabulary Builder: Sentences will vary. Possible sentences follow. **1.** The wind howled during the storm. **2.** Mr. and Mrs. Perez stroll every evening. **3.** He scrubbed the stain out of his shirt. **4.** Stefan scrambled down the basketball court. **5.** Ming peers through the telescope.

A collective noun names a group of people or things. Examples include army, audience, jury, committee, troop, and crowd. A collective noun usually takes the singular form of a verb.

EXAMPLE The jury returns to the courtroom.

Activity E Write the correct verb to complete each sentence on your paper.

1. The audience (like, likes) the performance.
2. The group (was, were) planning a party.
3. I hope the team (score, scores)!
4. The flock of birds (flies, fly) south.
5. Your club (meet, meets) on Friday.
6. The herd of cows (eat, eats) meadow grass.
7. The troop (holds, hold) an annual barbecue.
8. A crowd (gather, gathers) on the corner every day at noon.
9. The committee (make, makes) a decision.
10. The book club (discuss, discusses) a new book each month.

Vocabulary Builder

Synonyms

A synonym is a word that has the same or nearly the same meaning as another word. For example, *laugh, chortle, snicker, cackle,* and *guffaw* all have similar meanings. You can improve your writing by replacing common verbs with unusual verbs with similar meanings. A thesaurus will help you find words to use.

Rewrite each of these sentences on your paper. Replace the verb in bold with a more specific or unusual verb.

1. The wind **blew** during the storm.
2. Mr. and Mrs. Perez **walk** every evening.
3. He **washed** the stain out of his shirt.
4. Stefan **moved** down the basketball court.
5. Ming **looks** through the telescope.

Learning Styles

Logical/Mathematical

Have students read the definition of *collective noun* at the top of page 104. Then invite the class to help you make a list of collective nouns. There are 10 in Activity E. Ask students why they think that collective nouns usually take the singular form of a verb. Elicit from them that groups of people or things often act as one. Point out that sometimes, however, collective nouns are plural. Write the following sentences on the board: *The jury disagree among themselves* and *The team leave the park by different exits.* Challenge students to think of why the collective nouns in these examples take a plural form of the verb. Lead them to understand that sometimes a sentence indicates that members of a group are acting individually. Invite students to think of other examples in which collective nouns would take a plural form of the verb.

REVIEW

Write the correct verb to complete each sentence on your paper.

1. The committee (record, records) the facts.
2. The flock (flies, flys) away.
3. The troop (meets, meet) after lunch.
4. The council members (leave, leaves) for their vacations tomorrow.
5. The jury (was, were) undecided.

Find the mistakes in these sentences. Write each sentence correctly on your paper.

6. Jay teach people to play tennis.
7. Several of his students wants to play professionally.
8. Many hopes to play in college.
9. The tennis team always win.
10. Each of Jay's students learn a lot.
11. Everyone enjoy winning.
12. They practices forehands during their lessons.
13. Nothing are better than hitting a smash.
14. He participate in the tournament.
15. Both of the umpires calls the ball out.

Write the correct verb to complete each sentence on your paper.

16. All of the students (go, goes) to the pep rally.
17. None of the workers (are, is) finished.
18. Anyone (is, are) invited.
19. Most of the teachers (plan, plans) the meeting.
20. None of us (has, have) prepared.

Lesson 5 Review Answers

1. records **2.** flies **3.** meets **4.** leave **5.** was **6.** Jay teaches people to play tennis. **7.** Several of his students want to play professionally. **8.** Many hope to play in college. **9.** The tennis team always wins. **10.** Each of Jay's students learns a lot. **11.** Everyone enjoys winning. **12.** They practice forehands during their lessons. **13.** Nothing is better than hitting a smash. **14.** He participates in the tournament. **15.** Both of the umpires call the ball out. **16.** go **17.** are **18.** is **19.** plan **20.** have

LEARNING STYLES

LEP/ESL

Give students learning English extra practice with subject-verb agreement by pairing them with students whose first language is English. Assign each pair a selection of nouns and pronouns (singular and plural), including indefinite pronouns and at least one collective noun. Ask partners to compose sentences using these words as the subjects. Suggest that English language learners write the sentences. Call on pairs to share their sentences—and any problems—with the class.

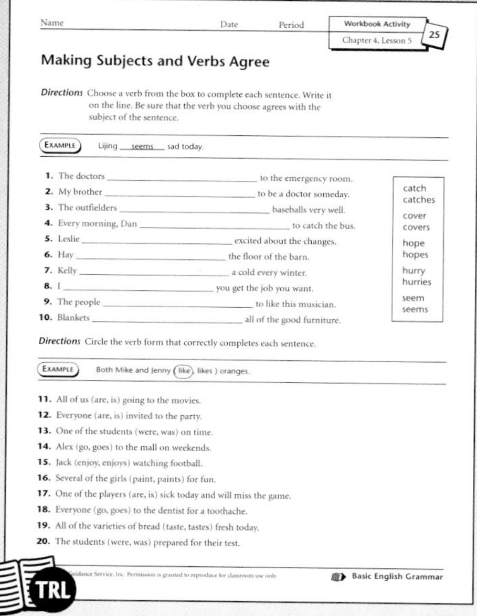

Name Date Period

Workbook Activity 25
Chapter 4, Lesson 5

Making Subjects and Verbs Agree

Directions Choose a verb from the box to complete each sentence. Write it on the line. Be sure that the verb you choose agrees with the subject of the sentence.

EXAMPLE Lijing __seems__ sad today.

1. The doctors ______ to the emergency room.
2. My brother ______ to be a doctor someday.
3. The outfielders ______ baseballs very well.
4. Every morning, Dan ______ to catch the bus.
5. Leslie ______ excited about the changes.
6. Hay ______ the floor of the barn.
7. Kelly ______ a cold every winter.
8. I ______ you get the job you want.
9. The people ______ to like this musician.
10. Blankets ______ all of the good furniture.

catch catches / cover covers / hope hopes / hurry hurries / seem seems

Directions Circle the verb form that correctly completes each sentence.

EXAMPLE Both Mike and Jenny (like, likes) oranges.

11. All of us (are, is) going to the movies.
12. Everyone (are, is) invited to the party.
13. One of the students (were, was) on time.
14. Alex (go, goes) to the mall on weekends.
15. Jack (enjoy, enjoys) watching football.
16. Several of the girls (paint, paints) for fun.
17. One of the players (are, is) sick today and will miss the game.
18. Everyone (go, goes) to the dentist for a toothache.
19. All of the varieties of bread (taste, tastes) fresh today.
20. The students (were, was) prepared for their test.

 Basic English Grammar

TRL

Workbook Activity 25

Name Date Period

Activity 25
Chapter 4, Lesson 5

Subject and Verb Agreement

Directions Use the verb that is underlined in the first sentence to complete the second sentence. Make the verb agree with its subject.

EXAMPLE Anna makes the final score. We __make__ a goal at the end of the game.

1. Jim eats dinner at six o'clock. The children ______ dinner at five o'clock.
2. The boats sink in the river. The boat ______ in the harbor.
3. The frightened child cries. You ______ when you are frightened.
4. The school of fish swim in the ocean. Maria ______ in the ocean.
5. The bird flies to the nest. The birds ______ south for the winter.
6. The boys go to the park. Everyone ______ to school.
7. Jaunita finds her music stand. All of the members ______ their chairs.
8. You jump up to the hoop. Michael ______ up to the hoop, too.
9. The delegate attends the meeting. The delegates ______ the morning session.
10. Turtles dive for the bottom. A turtle ______ into the water.
11. No one knows their lines. The actors don't ______ their lines.
12. I finish my homework before she does. Candice ______ her homework.
13. All of the water stays in the glass. The glasses ______ on the table.
14. Both girls need new coats. Jamie ______ a new hat and gloves.
15. The day was warm and sunny. The days ______ ending earlier.

 Basic English Grammar

TRL

Activity 25

Lesson at a Glance

Chapter 4 Lesson 6

Overview This lesson presents the verb *do* as a helping verb and as a main verb.

Objectives

- To identify verb phrases with the helping verb *do* in sentences.
- To distinguish between the verb *do* used as a helping verb and as a main verb in sentences.

Student Pages 106–108

Teacher's Resource Library 

Workbook Activity 26

Activity 26

Alternative Activity 26

1 Warm-Up Activity

Write the following sentence on the board: *Bob and Miwako do their homework together in the library most afternoons.* Ask students to identify the main verb of the sentence. Explain that we frequently use the verb *do* to mean "to perform an action." Now write the words *when, where, who,* and *what* on the board. Ask students to create questions about the statement beginning with one of these words. Example: *When do Bob and Miwako do their homework?* Point out that we use *do* as a helping verb in questions. Finally ask students to make a statement about Bob and Miwako using the word *not.* Example: *Bob and Miwako do not do their homework at home.* Lead them to understand that *do* is also a helping verb in negative sentences.

2 Teaching the Lesson

Write the phrase *you movies like do?* on the board. Invite students to rearrange the words to form a conventional question: *Do you like movies?* Ask students to identify the verb or verb phrase in the question. Point out that the subject of the sentence (*you*) comes between the helping verb and the main verb *do* and *like.* Demonstrate the same importance of word order in negative sentences by asking students to unscramble the phrase *not Maria eat meat does: Maria does not eat meat.* Point out that we also use the helping verb *do* in negative sentences, but that the word *not* breaks up the verb phrase in this case, *does eat.*

Explain to students that since *do* can be either a main verb or a helping verb, in some cases it can play both roles. Write *We did not do the dishes* on the board. Point out that *did* is a helping verb and *do* is the main verb. Encourage students to create other sentences in which *do* is both a helping and main verb.

Lesson  Using the Verb *Do*

The verb *do* can be a main verb. When *do* is a main verb, it means "to perform an action."

EXAMPLE Keiko does her chores on the weekend. (main verb)

We use the verb *do* in all tenses.

EXAMPLE		
	Present	Yolanda does her exercises early.
	Past	Rishi did his report well.
	Future	Everyone will do his or her best.
	Present Perfect	The team has done its work well.
	Past Perfect	We had done the chores by noon.
	Future Perfect	Soon he will have done his assignments.

The verb *do* can also be a helping verb.

EXAMPLE He did dust the cabinets.

We use the helping verbs *do* and *did* only with the present form of the main verb.

EXAMPLE Did you go home? (The verb *go* is present.)

We use the helping verbs *do* and *did* for emphasis, with the word *not,* and in questions. Notice the word order in questions.

EXAMPLE Alonzo did enjoy the match. (emphasis)
Many businesses do not close on holidays. (with the word *not*)
Do you like pears? (question)

Activity A Write the verb or verb phrase in each sentence on your paper.

1. Did you see Anita at lunch?
2. Jack never did find his gloves.
3. The family is doing the dishes.
4. Do you read the newspaper?
5. Where do you do your homework?
6. I have already done my part.
7. Did Dad rake the front yard?
8. The boys are doing the pruning.
9. They did not trim the fruit trees this year.
10. How does the yard look?

Activity B On your paper, write the verb or verb phrase in bold. Decide whether *do* is a helping verb or a main verb. Then write *helping verb* or *main verb* next to each verb or verb phrase.

Example Soon he **will have done** his speech.
will have done—main verb

1. After dinner Eric and Lakshmi **did** the dishes.
2. Finally they **had done** all their chores.
3. Lakshmi **had** already **done** her homework.
4. "**Did** you **see** my math book?" Eric asked.
5. "What **did** you **do** with it this time?" she asked.
6. "I **did** not **see** it today," he said.
7. **Did** Eric ever **find** his book?
8. Soon he **was doing** his math.
9. **Will** you **do** your part?
10. **Have** you ever **done** that before?

Activity A

Before having students complete the activity, have partners take turns asking each other questions with *do* and *did.* The listening partner should identify the main verb and helping verb in each question.

Activity A Answers

1. Did see **2.** did find **3.** is doing **4.** Do read **5.** do do **6.** have done **7.** Did rake **8.** are doing **9.** did trim **10.** does look

Activity B

Write these sentences on the board and have students identify the main verb and helping verb or verbs in each sentence.

- I did not do that.
- She does not want any help.

Activity B Answers

1. did—main verb **2.** had done—main verb **3.** had done—main verb **4.** Did see—helping verb **5.** did do—main verb and helping verb **6.** did see—helping verb **7.** Did find—helping verb **8.** was doing—main verb **9.** Will do—main verb **10.** Have done—main verb

Reinforce and Extend

Teacher Alert

Remind students that the verb *do* is an irregular verb; its past and past participle forms (*did, have done*) are not formed by adding *-d* or *-ed* to the infinitive.

Learning Styles

Visual/Spatial

An idiom is an expression whose meaning goes beyond the actual meaning of the words. The verb *do* is part of several English idioms, including *to do without; to do in; that will do; to do away with; how do you do?* Write these and other idioms with *do* on the board and discuss their meanings. Invite students to write idioms on paper and to illustrate their meanings. Students can bind their pages together in a booklet that they can place in a resource center.

Lesson 6 Review Answers

1. did—past 2. was doing—past progressive 3. will have done—future perfect 4. had done—past perfect 5. does—present

6. do—main verb 7. Did rake—helping verb 8. have done—main verb 9. Does plant—helping verb 10. will have done—main verb

Where To Find It

Point out to students that many biographical dictionaries are organized by subject. There are dictionaries of rock 'n' roll stars, athletes, writers, presidents, famous Native Americans, and many others. In the library, such books are not always kept in the reference section with general encyclopedias and dictionaries. They may be classified under subjects such as music, sports, or literature. Take students to the school or local library and have them ask the reference librarian for help in finding the appropriate biographical dictionary.

Answers to Where To Find It: Answers will vary. Make sure that students have understood the importance of the people they have researched.

Learning Styles

Auditory/Verbal

Ask partners to compose questions that use *do* as a helping verb. These might start with the words *did, do, where, what, when, why,* etc. Partners should identify and underline the verb phrases. Suggest that partners then exchange their questions with another pair and practice interviewing each other.

Lesson 6 REVIEW

Write the verb or verb phrase in each sentence on your paper. Next to each verb or verb phrase, write its tense.

1. Yesterday, Monica did her yard work.
2. She was doing yard work all afternoon.
3. Soon she will have done the entire yard.
4. She had done all of the weeding, too.
5. Who does the yard work at your house?

Write the verb or verb phrase in bold on your paper. Decide whether *do* is a helping verb or a main verb. Then write *helping verb* or *main verb* next to each verb or verb phrase.

6. In the fall, people **do** extra yard work.
7. **Did** you **rake** your leaves yet?
8. They **have** already **done** the raking.
9. **Does** your family **plant** grass seed in the fall?
10. Soon they **will have done** the whole yard.

Where To Find It

Biographical Dictionary

Suppose you want to learn more about jazz musician Louis Armstrong. One place to start is a biographical dictionary. A biographical dictionary lists entries about important historical figures. Entries are in alphabetical order and can be a single sentence or several pages.

You can locate people in a biographical dictionary by their last names. Guide words will help you find the correct page.

1. Locate the following people in a biographical dictionary: Frederick Douglass, Dr. Seuss, and Indira Gandhi. If you cannot find these entries, look up a favorite athlete from the past and someone from your history book.
2. On your paper, write the year of birth for each person you locate. Then write a brief description of his or her role in history.

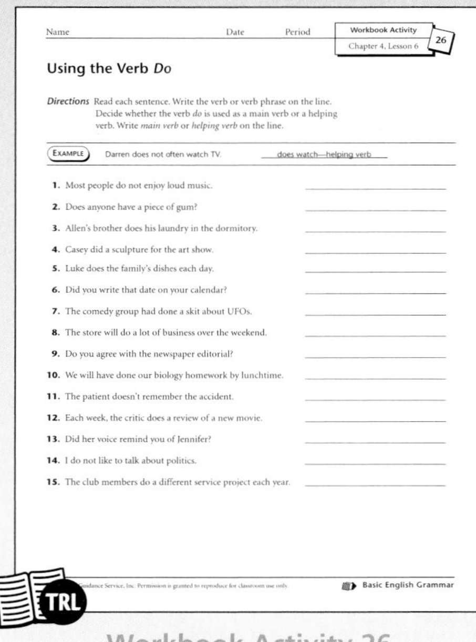

Name ____ Date ____ Period ____

Workbook Activity 26
Chapter 4, Lesson 6

Using the Verb *Do*

Directions Read each sentence. Write the verb or verb phrase on the line. Decide whether the verb *do* is used as a main verb or a helping verb. Write *main verb* or *helping verb* on the line.

EXAMPLE Darren does not often watch TV. does watch—helping verb

1. Most people do not enjoy loud music. ____
2. Does anyone have a piece of gum? ____
3. Allen's brother does his laundry in the dormitory. ____
4. Casey did a sculpture for the art show. ____
5. Luke does the family's dishes each day. ____
6. Did you write that date on your calendar? ____
7. The comedy group had done a skit about UFOs. ____
8. The store will do a lot of business over the weekend. ____
9. Do you agree with the newspaper editorial? ____
10. We will have done our biology homework by lunchtime. ____
11. The patient doesn't remember the accident. ____
12. Each week, the critic does a review of a new movie. ____
13. Did her voice remind you of Jennifer? ____
14. I do not like to talk about politics. ____
15. The club members do a different service project each year. ____

 Basic English Grammar

TRL

Workbook Activity 26

Name ____ Date ____ Period ____

Activity 26
Chapter 4, Lesson 6

Learning to Work with *Do*

Directions Insert the missing form of the word *do* on the line to correctly complete the sentence. Sometimes *do* may need helping verbs, too.

EXAMPLE Jeff and Audrey have done more than their share.

1. I ____ not take your hairbrush.
2. Andy was ____ about fifty miles-per-hour.
3. They ____ more than half of the project.
4. ____ your mother want to come to the party?
5. When will I get to ____ your hair?
6. They ____ their homework so they got to go.
7. Let me know when the painting is ____.
8. What are you ____?
9. When ____ your bus pick you up?
10. By that time, he will ____ all of the dishes.
11. ____ you finish your shopping?
12. I ____ not want any more fighting!
13. Soon, she will ____ her assignment.
14. What else are you ____ for him?
15. Before long, the list was ____.

Directions Determine how the form of *do* is being used and write *main* or *helping* on the line.

EXAMPLE She did yell, but she wasn't heard. helping

16. Did you find her at the corner? ____
17. The team did a fantastic job. ____
18. Cinderella did not sweep the floor. ____
19. What are you doing after the game? ____
20. Do you enjoy reading comics? ____

 Basic English Grammar

TRL

Activity 26

Lesson 7 The Conditional Verb

Conditional verb
A helping verb that puts a condition, or requirement, on an action

Some helping verbs put a condition on an action. We use them to express possibility or requirement. The **conditional verbs** are *may, might, can, could, shall, should, will, would,* and *must.* Look carefully at the main verbs in the verb phrases in the example. They are all present tense verbs.

EXAMPLE

may—might	She may succeed.
	She might succeed.
can—could	He can sing.
	He could sing.
shall—should	You shall leave.
	You should leave.
will—would	He will like that show.
	He would like that show.
must	I must go now.
	You must find your report.
	They must leave quickly.

Activity A Write the verb phrase in each sentence on your paper.

1. You may stay at the party until ten o'clock.
2. David can play the trombone.
3. The basket will hold a dozen tomatoes.
4. She should do her homework.
5. She must finish her report tonight.
6. I shall give her the message.
7. They could join us for dinner.
8. Jackie might try that new food.
9. Would you like some potatoes?
10. Richard must mow the lawn today.

Lesson at a Glance

Chapter 4 Lesson 7

Overview This lesson introduces helping verbs used in conditional forms.

Objective

- To identify verb phrases that express the conditional form.

Student Pages 109–112

Teacher's Resource Library 

Workbook Activity 27

Activity 27

Alternative Activity 27

Vocabulary

conditional verb

1 Warm-Up Activity

Invite students to write sentences using the words *can, may, would,* and *must.* Ask them what part of speech these words are. Explain that they are helping verbs, known as conditional verbs. Ask the class to consider how they alter the meaning of the main verb. Then have students read the information at the top of page 109. Encourage them to ask questions. Provide additional examples if necessary.

2 Teaching the Lesson

Write the following sentences on the board: *He is eating. It does not bite. She has bought a car.* Ask students to name the helping verbs (*is, has, does*). Then ask students to write sentences containing conditional helping verbs using *he, she,* and *it* as subjects. Challenge them to point out how the conditional helping verbs differ from the previous examples. (*They do not end with the letter -s when the subject is singular.*)

Demonstrate the "understood" verb by asking students a series of questions using verb phrases. Examples: *Can you swim? Are you going home this afternoon? Do you have a brother?* Elicit the short form of answer, without the main verb. (*Yes, I can. No, I'm not. Yes, I do.*) Point out that these responses use only the helping verb. The main verb does not need repeating. It is said to be understood.

Activity A

Have students use each of these verb phrases in oral sentences before they complete the activity independently: *may leave, can work, will find, should ask, must wait.*

Activity A Answers

1. may stay 2. can play 3. will hold 4. should do 5. must finish 6. shall give 7. could join 8. might try 9. Would like 10. must mow

3 Reinforce and Extend

TEACHER ALERT

Although *shall* was once the only correct form of the simple future when using first person, *will* is now used more frequently in speaking and writing. In some cases, however, *shall* is the only correct form, as in *Shall I call for help?*

Teacher Alert

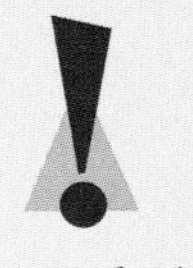

Point out that the phrasal verb *have to* means the same as *must* and often replaces *must* in ordinary speech. (*I have to work. I have to go home.*) In fact, *have to* is the more versatile of the two verbs because, unlike *must,* it has a past tense. (*I had to visit my aunt yesterday.*)

Learning Styles

Interpersonal/Group Learning

Write this on the board: *If it rained cats and dogs, . . .* Point out that this is not a complete sentence. It is the beginning of a sentence that could end in several ways, each of them using a conditional verb. Invite students to suggest ways the sentence starter could end. (Examples: *We would get very wet; Everyone could have a pet.*) Ask pairs of students to write several sentence starters like the one on the board, all beginning with the word *If.* Have pairs exchange their prompts and finish the sentences using as many different conditional verbs as make sense. Invite them to write their best completions on the board. Note: An *if* clause in the present tense is generally followed by the present conditional; an *if* clause in the past tense normally takes the past conditional.

Conditional verbs are irregular. Do not add *-s* or *-es* to the verb when you use it with a singular subject.

Example

Singular Subject	**Plural Subject**
He may go.	They may go.
Antonia must leave.	The women must leave.

For all other regular verbs and irregular verbs you need to add either *-s* or *-es* or change the verb to a different form.

Example

Singular Subject	**Plural Subject**
He sings well.	They sing well.
He has gone.	They have gone.
She is going.	They are going.

A conditional verb may be combined with the perfect tense.

Example

Present Perfect	I have gone.
Conditional	I could have gone.
	He might have gone.
Present Progressive	I am going.
Conditional Progressive	I could be going.
	They must be going.

In some sentences, the main verb is not stated. It is understood.

Example

Are you doing your assignment?
No, but I should.
(The rest of the response, *do my assignment,* is understood.)

Activity B On your paper, write the correct verb to complete each sentence.

1. Every day Deshawn will (exercise, exercises) at the gym.
2. They could (exercise, exercises) on a regular basis.
3. Julian (might, mights) exercise today.
4. He would (goes, go) every day if he had the time.
5. Carmen (must, musts) leave early.
6. I could (win, wins) if I tried.
7. They (should, shoulds) study for the test.
8. David must (get, gets) the mail now.
9. The train (will, wills) leave at noon.
10. (May, Mays) I take your picture?

Writing Tip

Use *can* when referring to ability. Use *may* when referring to permission. For example: Phil *can* play the piano. (ability); *May* I play the piano? (permission)

Activity C Write the verb phrase in each sentence on your paper.

1. Cam's backpack will hold many things.
2. She can hardly lift it.
3. She should clean it out.
4. In fact, she must clean it out.
5. She cannot find anything in it.
6. She could have looked harder.
7. Cam should have bought a new backpack.
8. She might be buying a new one.
9. Should she buy a new backpack?
10. Yes, she should.

Activity B

Have volunteers read each item aloud twice, each time with a different answer in place. Students should write the answer they think sounds correct. Afterward, students can compare and explain their answer choices.

Activity B Answers

1. exercise 2. exercise 3. might 4. go 5. must 6. win 7. should 8. get 9. will 10. May

Activity C

Write these sentences on the board:

- Would you have known the answer?
- May I come with you to the mall?
- Yes, you may.

Have students raise their hands when they have identified the verb phrase in each sentence. When all hands are raised, invite volunteers to point out each verb phrase.

Activity C Answers

1. will hold 2. can lift 3. should clean 4. must clean 5. cannot find 6. could have looked 7. should have bought 8. might be buying 9. Should buy 10. should (*buy* is understood.)

Career Connection

Have students think of a career that they would like to pursue. Ask them to write a series of eight to ten sentences about this career, using conditional verbs. Help get them started by writing leading questions on the board, underlining the conditional verbs: What sort of grades must I get? How much would the training cost? Could I get into a good college? Should I become a U.S. citizen?

Lesson 7 Review Answers

1. might be going 2. could have gone 3. must go 4. would leave 5. should pack 6. must take 7. can go 8. may take 9. might rain 10. Should take

Answers will vary. Possible answers follow. 11. should 12. may 13. might 14. could 15. should 16. will 17. can 18. might 19. will 20. could

Learning Styles

Body/Kinesthetic

Make a set of cards containing the conditional verb forms *may, might, can, could, shall, should, will, would,* and *must.* Give the set to one student. Have the student mix the cards and give one to another student. Ask that student to use the conditional verb form on the card in a sentence. Have the student write the sentence on the board and underline the verb form. Continue with this process until all the students have written a sentence on the board.

Learning Styles

Visual/Spatial

Have students make posters illustrating the conditional verbs. Ask them to cut out a selection of photographs from magazines or to make their own drawings. Each picture should have as a caption a sentence including one of the nine conditional verbs. Captions could be descriptions (*She can act well*), questions (*Should he be doing that?*), or comments (*I must get one of those.*) Have students present their conditional captions to the class and display their posters around the room.

Lesson 7 REVIEW

Write the verb phrase in each sentence on your paper.

1. Next week, I might be going to Indiana.
2. I could have gone last year.
3. This year I must go.
4. I would leave on Monday if possible.
5. I should pack my bags.
6. I must take my winter coat.
7. I can go by plane.
8. I may take only one bag.
9. It might rain.
10. Should I take an umbrella?

Write a conditional helping verb to complete each sentence on your paper.

11. Julia ________ go to the movies with Guy.
12. Guy ________ ask her to go.
13. Al ________ finish his work by noon.
14. He ________ finish sooner if he hurries.
15. Lily said that Latasha ________ use the school computer.
16. With a computer, Latasha ________ write a better paper.
17. That computer program ________ catch grammar and spelling errors.
18. Saul ________ like that program.
19. The program ________ start soon.
20. Robert ________ be late.

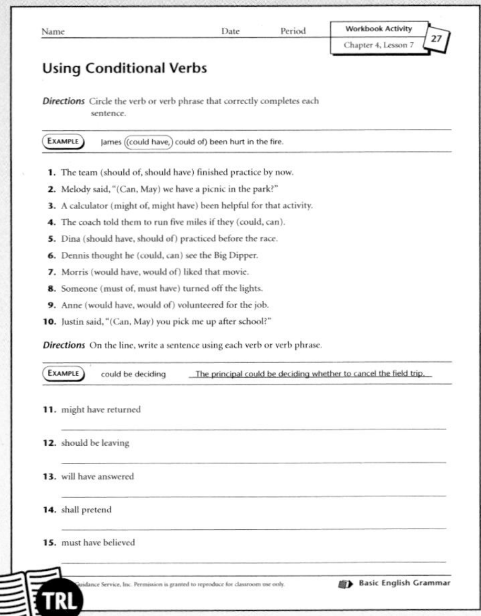

Name Date Period

Workbook Activity 27
Chapter 4, Lesson 7

Using Conditional Verbs

Directions Circle the verb or verb phrase that correctly completes each sentence.

EXAMPLE James (could have, could of) been hurt in the fire.

1. The team (should of, should have) finished practice by now.
2. Melody said, "(Can, May) we have a picnic in the park?"
3. A calculator (might of, might have) been helpful for that activity.
4. The coach told them to run five miles if they (could, can).
5. Dina (should have, should of) practiced before the race.
6. Dennis thought he (could, can) see the Big Dipper.
7. Morris (would have, would of) liked that movie.
8. Someone (must of, must have) turned off the lights.
9. Anne (would have, would of) volunteered for the job.
10. Justin said, "(Can, May) you pick me up after school?"

Directions On the line, write a sentence using each verb or verb phrase.

EXAMPLE could be deciding The principal could be deciding whether to cancel the field trip.

11. might have returned ____________________
12. should be leaving ____________________
13. will have answered ____________________
14. shall pretend ____________________
15. must have believed ____________________

Basic English Grammar

TRL

Workbook Activity 27

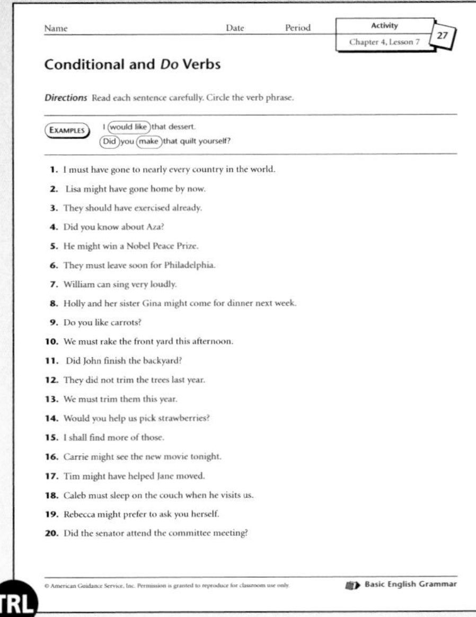

Name Date Period

Activity 27
Chapter 4, Lesson 7

Conditional and *Do* Verbs

Directions Read each sentence carefully. Circle the verb phrase.

EXAMPLES I (would like) that dessert.
(Did) you (make) that quilt yourself?

1. I must have gone to nearly every country in the world.
2. Lisa might have gone home by now.
3. They should have exercised already.
4. Did you know about Aza?
5. He might win a Nobel Peace Prize.
6. They must leave soon for Philadelphia.
7. William can sing very loudly.
8. Holly and her sister Gina might come for dinner next week.
9. Do you like carrots?
10. We must rake the front yard this afternoon.
11. Did John finish the backyard?
12. They did not trim the trees last year.
13. We must trim them this year.
14. Would you help us pick strawberries?
15. I shall find more of those.
16. Carrie might see the new movie tonight.
17. Tim might have helped Jane moved.
18. Caleb must sleep on the couch when he visits us.
19. Rebecca might prefer to ask you herself.
20. Did the senator attend the committee meeting?

Basic English Grammar

TRL

Activity 27

Lesson 8 Active and Passive Verbs

Active verb
A verb form that we use when the subject is doing the action

Passive verb
A verb form that we use when the action happens to the subject

Action verbs can be **active** or **passive.** A verb is active when the subject is doing the action.

EXAMPLE **Active** Alvaro wrote a play.

A verb is passive when the action happens to the subject.

EXAMPLE **Passive** The play was written by Alvaro.

Passive verbs use the helping verb *be* with the past participle.

EXAMPLE The song was sung by Amy.

In some sentences in which the verb is passive, we do not name the person doing the action. The person is "understood."

EXAMPLE Today the safe was robbed. (by someone)
The pass was thrown well. (by someone)

Activity A Write the verb phrase in each sentence on your paper.

1. The note was discovered by Marisa.
2. We were disturbed by a loud noise.
3. The telephone was finally answered.
4. The ball was hit to left field.
5. The car was washed last month.
6. The home run was scored by Alex.
7. All of the decorations were brought by the dance committee.
8. The annual fund-raiser was held by the chess club.
9. The picnic was prepared by Mrs. Choy.
10. The students were tested by the teacher.

Lesson at a Glance

Chapter 4 Lesson 8

Overview This lesson presents active and passive verbs.

Objectives

- To identify when verbs are active or passive.
- To use active and passive verbs in sentences.

Student Pages 113–115

Teacher's Resource Library 

Workbook Activity 28

Activity 28

Alternative Activity 28

Vocabulary

active verb
passive verb

1 Warm-Up Activity

Write *passive* on the board. Ask students if they know what the word means. Explain that *passive* is the opposite of *active.* Passive people don't act, allowing things to be done to them. Write these two sentences next to each other on the board: *Anita threw the ball. The ball was thrown by Anita.* Point out that verbs are like people; they can be active or passive. Take a class vote on which verb is active. Then have students read the definitions and examples on this page and ask them to vote again. Make sure that they have correctly identified the form of each verb before inviting them to provide additional examples.

2 Teaching the Lesson

Have students review the definition of *past participle* on page 91. Point out that passive verbs are formed with the past participle of an action verb preceded by a form of the verb *be.* Give students practice forming passive verbs by writing the following verbs on the board: *paint, clean, find, eat.* First have students find the past participle (*painted, cleaned, found, eaten*); then ask them to add some form of the verb *be.* Remind them of the chart on page 97. Invite students to write sentences using the passive verb constructions.

For further practice, have students complete these sentences with passive verbs: *The winning photograph* _______ *by a young child. Those wooden toys* _______ *by my grandfather. The movie* _______ *in Africa.*

Activity A

Remind students of the structure of passive verbs (*be* + past participle). Point out that the first word of each verb phrase will be some form of the verb *be.*

Activity A Answers

1. was discovered **2.** were disturbed **3.** was answered **4.** was hit **5.** was washed **6.** was scored **7.** were brought **8.** was held **9.** was prepared **10.** were tested

Activity B Write the verb or verb phrase in each sentence on your paper. Next to each one, write whether it is *active* or *passive.*

1. John Steinbeck wrote many stories.
2. *The Red Pony* was written by John Steinbeck.
3. Mozart composed many operas.
4. That cake was baked by my aunt.
5. My aunt baked that cake.

Activity C Write two sentences for each verb on your paper. In the first sentence, use the verb as an active verb. In the second sentence, use the verb as a passive verb.

1. cover
2. direct
3. discover
4. disturb
5. teach
6. hit
7. invent
8. cook
9. answer
10. pack

Spelling Builder

Words with *ie* or *ei*

Several action verbs include the letters *ie* or *ei.* Read aloud the following examples: *achieve, believe, receive, shriek, weigh, neigh,* and *reign.* Try memorizing this verse to help you remember which way to spell words with *ie* or *ei:*

Put *i* before *e*
Except after *c*
Or when sounded like *a*
As in *neighbor* and *weigh.*

Several exceptions to the pattern in the verse are *science, either, seize,* and *height.*

Write the correct spelling of each word on your paper.

1. friend, freind
2. cheif, chief
3. neighbor, nieghbor
4. piece, peice
5. receipt, reciept

Activity B

Students will have an easier time completing the activity if they follow this procedure for each item: **1.** read the sentence; **2.** identify the subject and the verb; **3.** decide if the subject is doing the action or if the action is happening to the subject. Remind students that if the subject is performing the action, the verb is active; if the action is happening to the subject, the verb is passive.

Activity B Answers

1. wrote—active **2.** was written—passive **3.** composed—active **4.** was baked—passive **5.** baked—active

Activity C

Do the first item in the activity to provide examples of ways to vary the sentence content and verb tense. (Active: *He should cover his book. I will cover the paper with paint.* Passive: *The pot of soup was covered by the chef. The pool will be covered for the winter.*)

Activity C Answers

Sentences will vary.

Spelling Builder

Give students further practice with the spelling patterns by writing the following incomplete words on the board: *w__rd, n__ce, f__ld, c__ling, __ght, fr__ght, w__ld, prot__n.* Have students insert the letters *i* and *e,* in either order, to spell the words correctly. Encourage them to check problem spellings in a dictionary. Ask how many of these words were exceptions to the *i* before *e* rhyme (*weird* and *protein*).

Answers to Spelling Builder: 1. friend **2.** chief **3.** neighbor **4.** piece **5.** receipt

Spelling Practice

Dictate to students a paragraph of about 100 words from a textbook or periodical. Ask students to copy their handwritten paragraphs onto a computer with a spell-checking function. Have them take note of the words they misspelled. Encourage them to correct the spelling by themselves before taking the computer's recommendations. Survey the class for the words that caused most problems.

3 Reinforce and Extend

Teacher Alert

Students should understand that active verbs generally create stronger, more interesting sentences than passive verbs. They may realize that some software writing programs consider any use of a passive verb an error. Point out, however, that sometimes a passive verb is preferable to an active one, especially when the person or thing doing the action is unknown or unimportant. The following sentences are more effective with passive verbs: *The jewels were stolen* [by an unknown thief]. *The streets were flooded* [by water].

Lesson 8 REVIEW

Write the verb or verb phrase in each sentence on your paper. Next to each one, write whether it is *active* or *passive.*

1. Eli Whitney invented the cotton gin.
2. Cotton seeds are removed from the cotton.
3. *Gone With the Wind* was written by Margaret Mitchell.
4. Her book was made into a successful movie.
5. Tecumseh, a Shawnee leader, settled Indiana in 1808.

Rewrite each sentence on your paper. Change the verb in bold from passive to active.

6. The batter **was hit** by the wild pitch.
7. John's bag **was packed** by his mother.
8. The telephone **was answered** by the receptionist.
9. The neighbors **were disturbed** by the barking dog.
10. The oil **was changed** last month by the mechanic.

Writing Project

Using Action Verbs

You can use vivid action verbs to make your writing more interesting.

Choose an activity that you enjoy.

On your paper, write 10 sentences about the actions involved in doing the activity. Use a vivid action verb in each sentence. You can use a thesaurus to find vivid action verbs.

Underline the verb in each sentence.

Pair up with a classmate and read each other's sentences.

Example Bike riding

First I <u>leap</u> on the bike.
I <u>speed</u> down the driveway.
The wind <u>rushes</u> through my hair.

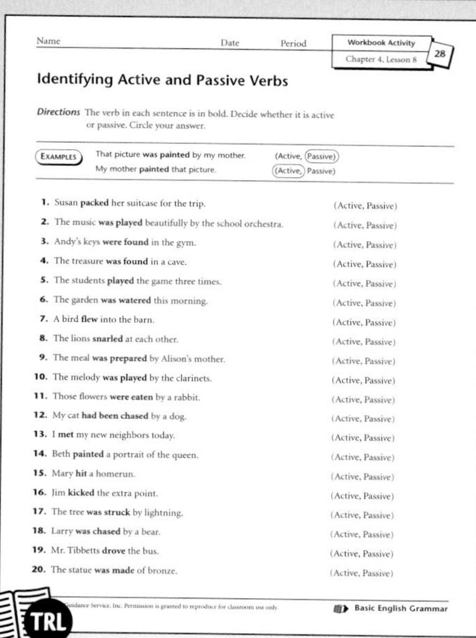

Name Date Period | Workbook Activity 28 | Chapter 4, Lesson 8

Identifying Active and Passive Verbs

Directions The verb in each sentence is in bold. Decide whether it is active or passive. Circle your answer.

EXAMPLES That picture **was painted** by my mother. (Active, Passive)
My mother **painted** that picture. (Active, Passive)

1. Susan **packed** her suitcase for the trip. (Active, Passive)
2. The music **was played** beautifully by the school orchestra. (Active, Passive)
3. Andy's keys **were found** in the gym. (Active, Passive)
4. The treasure **was found** in a cave. (Active, Passive)
5. The students **played** the game three times. (Active, Passive)
6. The garden **was watered** this morning. (Active, Passive)
7. A bird **flew** into the barn. (Active, Passive)
8. The lions **snarled** at each other. (Active, Passive)
9. The meal **was prepared** by Alison's mother. (Active, Passive)
10. The melody **was played** by the clarinets. (Active, Passive)
11. Those flowers **were eaten** by a rabbit. (Active, Passive)
12. My cat **had been chased** by a dog. (Active, Passive)
13. I **met** my new neighbors today. (Active, Passive)
14. Beth **painted** a portrait of the queen. (Active, Passive)
15. Mary **hit** a homerun. (Active, Passive)
16. Jim **kicked** the extra point. (Active, Passive)
17. The tree **was struck** by lightning. (Active, Passive)
18. Larry **was chased** by a bear. (Active, Passive)
19. Mr. Tibbetts **drove** the bus. (Active, Passive)
20. The statue **was made** of bronze. (Active, Passive)

 Basic English Grammar

TRL

Workbook Activity 28

Name Date Period | Activity 28 | Chapter 4, Lesson 8

Using Passive and Active Verbs

Directions The following sentences have passive verbs. Rewrite each sentence so it has an active verb.

EXAMPLE Passive: The wood was chopped by Douglas.
Active: Douglas chopped the wood.

1. The production was funded by Tendel and Margie.
2. A race was run by Steve.
3. The machine was operated by an engineer.
4. Sidney High School was challenged by Audley Technical.
5. The package was delivered by a courier.
6. The Saturday class was cancelled by Mr. Feinbrow.
7. The bread dough was kneaded by my mother.
8. The fire was extinguished by firefighters.
9. My bedroom was messed up by my little sisters.
10. The mess was cleaned up by Sarah.

 Basic English Grammar

TRL

Activity 28

Lesson 8 Review Answers

1. invented—active 2. are removed—passive 3. was written—passive 4. was made—passive 5. settled—active 6. The wild pitch hit the batter. 7. John's mother packed his bag. 8. The receptionist answered the telephone. 9. The barking dog disturbed the neighbors. 10. The mechanic changed the oil last month.

Writing Project

Refer students to the definition of *action verb* on page 82. Remind them that action verbs describe something that the subject does. Some common verbs—the verb *be,* for instance—do not describe an action. Have students check their sentences carefully to make sure that their main verbs express action.

After they have completed their descriptions, invite students to choose a sentence and to write it on the board.

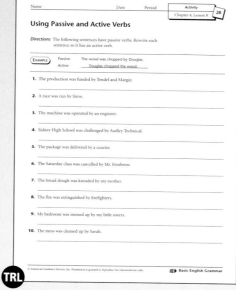

Chapter 4 Review

Use the Chapter Review to prepare students for tests and to reteach content from the chapter.

Chapter 4 Mastery Test 

The Teacher's Resource Library includes two parallel forms of the Chapter 4 Mastery Test. The difficulty level of the two forms is equivalent. You may wish to use one form as a pretest and the other form as a posttest.

Review Answers

Part A

1. tense 2. action verb 3. main verb 4. infinitive 5. verb 6. verb phrase 7. simple tenses 8. subject 9. helping verb 10. progressive form 11. conditional verb 12. active verb 13. future perfect 14. regular verb 15. passive verb 16. present perfect 17. irregular verb 18. present participle 19. past participle 20. past perfect

Chapter 4 REVIEW

Word Bank
- action verb
- active verb
- conditional verb
- future perfect
- helping verb
- infinitive
- irregular verb
- main verb
- passive verb
- past participle
- past perfect
- present participle
- present perfect
- progressive form
- regular verb
- simple tenses
- subject
- tense
- verb
- verb phrase

Part A On a sheet of paper, write the correct word or words from the Word Bank to complete each sentence.

1. The time when an action takes place is called ______ .
2. An ______ tells what someone or something does, did, or will do.
3. A ______ is the last verb in a verb phrase.
4. An ______ is *to* plus the present tense of a verb.
5. A word that expresses action or state of being is a ______ .
6. A ______ is a main verb plus one or more helping verbs.
7. The present, past, and future forms of verbs are all ______ .
8. The part of a sentence that tells who or what the sentence is about is the ______ .
9. A ______ combines with a main verb to form a verb phrase.
10. The ______ ends in *-ing* and shows continuing action.
11. A ______ puts a condition, or a requirement, on an action.
12. An ______ shows that the subject is doing the action.
13. The ______ shows an action that will be completed before a certain time in the future.
14. A verb that forms its past tense and past participle by adding *-ed* or *-d* is a ______ .
15. A ______ shows that the action happens to the subject.
16. The ______ shows an action started in the past and continuing to the present.
17. A verb that does not form its past tense and past participle by adding *-ed* or *-d* is an ______ .
18. A verb form that shows continuing action is the ______ .
19. A ______ is used to form the perfect tenses.
20. The ______ shows one action completed before another action began.

Name ______ Date ______ Period ______ | Mastery Test A, Page 1 | Chapter 4

Chapter 4 Mastery Test A

Part A Complete each sentence. Write the correct form of the verb in parentheses.

1. Juana usually ______ her bike to school. (ride)
2. Would you ______ me the spoon? (pass)
3. What are you ______ tomorrow? (do)
4. We could have ______ the floors last week. (sand)
5. Anna and Kurt have ______ Spanish for two years. (study)
6. Mike ______ his favorite pencil. (break)
7. Gerry has ______ a new car. (purchase)
8. Claudia had ______ her homework. (finish)
9. Jamal was ______ an apple. (eat)
10. Will you have ______ to the cleaners by then? (be)

Part B Circle the verb or verb phrase in each sentence.

11. I would like a second piece of bread.
12. Janice and Randy may come to dinner next week.
13. We must plant a garden this year.
14. Do you know the cost of a CD?
15. Bill plays tennis very well.

Part C Write whether the verb in these sentences is *active* or *passive*.

16. The book was written by Toni Morrison. ______
17. Rhonda put the cover on the jar. ______
18. The lawn mower was tuned up in April. ______
19. Pedro drew a sad face on the clown. ______
20. Hak was disturbed by the noise. ______

 Basic English Grammar

TRL

Name ______ Date ______ Period ______ | Mastery Test A, Page 2 | Chapter 4

Chapter 4 Mastery Test A, continued

Part D Write each verb in the tense that is shown.

	Verb	Tense	
21.	answer	past	______
22.	begin	future perfect	______
23.	go	present perfect	______
24.	call	past perfect	______
25.	plan	present progressive plural	______
26.	close	future	______
27.	practice	past progressive singular	______
28.	last	future perfect progressive	______
29.	buy	future progressive	______
30.	rake	present	______

Part E Circle the correct answer.

31. Which of these verbs is in the infinitive form?
    A will dance B to dance C danced D dance
32. Which of these verbs is in the past tense?
    A will dance B to dance C danced D will have danced
33. Which of these verbs is in the future tense?
    A has danced B will have danced C had danced D will dance
34. Which of these verbs is in the past perfect tense?
    A had danced B danced C will dance D will have danced
35. Which of these verbs is the future perfect tense?
    A has danced B will have danced C had danced D will dance

 Basic English Grammar

TRL

Chapter 4 Mastery Test A

Part B Write the verb or verb phrase in bold on your paper. Write the tense of each verb. Then write whether the verb is *active* or *passive*.

21. Mr. Torres **went** to work.
22. The Wildcats **will play** their first game today.
23. Everyone **will cheer** them on.
24. He **had hit** 60 home runs in a single year.
25. We **have been running** for an hour.
26. Your portrait **can be drawn** by Flora.
27. Damon **should leave** the room.

Part C Choose the letter of the verb that correctly completes each sentence. Write the letter on your paper.

28. Did Kim _______ home yet?
    A go B went C goes D going
29. The herd _______ over the hill.
    A runned B running C run D runs
30. There _______ jugglers and clowns at the party.
    A is B was C were D be

Part D Write the correct form of each verb on your paper.

31. Devon _______ in the passenger seat. (present progressive tense of *ride*)
32. He _______ many times. (present perfect tense of *drive*)
33. He _______ to school every day. (present tense of *drive* with the helping verb *does*)
34. Devon _______ too sick to drive today. (present tense of *be*)
35. He _______ home to rest. (present tense of *stay*)

Look over a test before you begin answering questions. See how many parts there are. Think about what you are being asked to do in each part.

Review Answers

Part B

21. went—past, active 22. will play—future, active 23. will cheer—future, active 24. had hit—past perfect, active 25. have been running—present perfect progressive, active 26. can be drawn—conditional present, passive 27. should leave—conditional present, active

Part C

28. A 29. D 30. C

Part D

31. is riding 32. has driven 33. does drive 34. is 35. stays

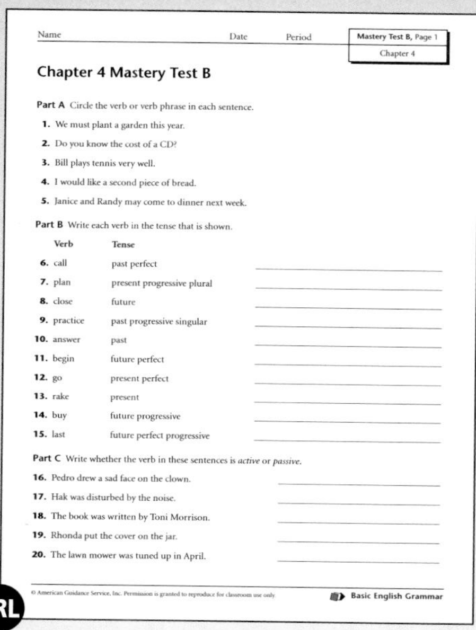

Name _______ Date _______ Period _______

Mastery Test B, Page 1
Chapter 4

Chapter 4 Mastery Test B

Part A Circle the verb or verb phrase in each sentence.

1. We must plant a garden this year.
2. Do you know the cost of a CD?
3. Bill plays tennis very well.
4. I would like a second piece of bread.
5. Janice and Randy may come to dinner next week.

Part B Write each verb in the tense that is shown.

	Verb	Tense	
6.	call	past perfect	_______
7.	plan	present progressive plural	_______
8.	close	future	_______
9.	practice	past progressive singular	_______
10.	answer	past	_______
11.	begin	future perfect	_______
12.	go	present perfect	_______
13.	rake	present	_______
14.	buy	future progressive	_______
15.	last	future perfect progressive	_______

Part C Write whether the verb in these sentences is *active* or *passive*.

16. Pedro drew a sad face on the clown. _______
17. Hak was disturbed by the noise. _______
18. The book was written by Toni Morrison. _______
19. Rhonda put the cover on the jar. _______
20. The lawn mower was tuned up in April. _______

Basic English Grammar

TRL

Name _______ Date _______ Period _______

Mastery Test B, Page 2
Chapter 4

Chapter 4 Mastery Test B, continued

Part D Circle the correct answer.

21. Which of these verbs is in the future tense?
    A has danced B will have danced C had danced D will dance
22. Which of these verbs is in the past tense?
    A will dance B to dance C danced D will have danced
23. Which of these verbs is in the infinitive form?
    A will dance B to dance C danced D dance
24. Which of these verbs is the future perfect tense?
    A has danced B will have danced C had danced D will dance
25. Which of these verbs is in the past perfect tense?
    A had danced B danced C will dance D will have danced

Part E Complete each sentence. Write the correct form of the verb in parentheses.

26. Claudia had _______ her homework. (finish)
27. Jamal was _______ an apple. (eat)
28. Will you have _______ to the cleaners by then? (be)
29. We could have _______ the floors last week. (sand)
30. Anna and Kurt have _______ Spanish for two years. (study)
31. Mike _______ his favorite pencil. (break)
32. Gerry has _______ a new car. (purchase)
33. Juana usually _______ her bike to school. (ride)
34. Would you _______ me the spoon? (pass)
35. What are you _______ tomorrow? (do)

Basic English Grammar

TRL

Chapter 4 Mastery Test B

Chapter

5

Planning Guide

The State-of-Being Verb

	Student Text Lesson				Language Skills		
	Student Pages	Vocabulary	Practice Exercises	Lesson Review	Identification Skills	Writing Skills	Punctuation Skills
Lesson 1 What Is a State-of-Being Verb?	120–124	✔	✔	✔	✔	✔	✔
Lesson 2 Action or State of Being?	125–129		✔	✔	✔	✔	✔
Lesson 3 Using State-of-Being Verbs	130–133		✔	✔	✔	✔	✔

Chapter Activities

Teacher's Resource Library

Community Connection 5: A Journal of Action and Being

Media and Literature Connection 5: State-of-Being Verbs in the Media

Assessment Options

Student Text

Chapter 5 Review

Teacher's Resource Library

Chapter 5 Mastery Tests A and B

Student Text Features						Teaching Strategies						Learning Styles						Teacher's Resource Library			
Spelling Builder	Vocabulary Builder	Where To Find It	Writing Project	Using What You've Learned	Writing Tips/Notes/ Technology Notes	Teacher Alert	Online Connection	Applications (Home, Career, Community, Global)	Speaking Practice	Spelling Practice	Writing Practice	Auditory/Verbal	Body/Kinesthetic	Interpersonal/Group Learning	Logical/Mathematical	Visual/Spatial	LEP/ESL	Workbook Activities	Activities	Alternative Activities	Self-Study Guide
124		123		123	✔	120, 124				124	121		121		122			29	29	29	✔
			129		✔	125, 127	128	129	129			126			126	127	126	30	30	30	✔
	133				✔	132		131, 132				132		131		133		31	31	31	✔

Pronunciation Key

a	hat	e	let	ī	ice	ô	order	u̇	put	sh	she	ə a	in about
ā	age	ē	equal	o	hot	oi	oil	ü	rule	th	thin	ə e	in taken
ä	far	ėr	term	ō	open	ou	out	ch	child	ᴛʜ	then	ə i	in pencil
â	care	i	it	ȯ	saw	u	cup	ng	long	zh	measure	ə o	in lemon
												ə u	in circus

Alternative Activities

The Teacher's Resource Library (TRL) contains a set of lower-level worksheets called Alternative Activities. These worksheets cover the same content as the regular Activities but are written at a second-grade reading level.

Skill Track Software

Use the Skill Track Software for Basic English Grammar for additional reinforcement of this chapter. The software program allows students using AGS textbooks to be assessed for mastery of each chapter and lesson of the textbook. Students access the software on an individual basis and are assessed with multiple-choice items.

Chapter at a Glance

Chapter 5: The State-of-Being Verb

(Answer Keys for the Teacher's Resource Library begin on page 340 of this Teacher's Edition.)

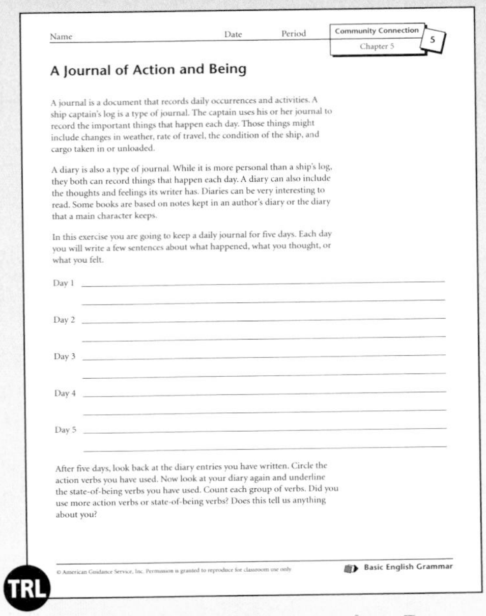

Name ____ Date ____ Period ____ Community Connection 5 Chapter 5

A Journal of Action and Being

A journal is a document that records daily occurrences and activities. A ship captain's log is a type of journal. The captain uses his or her journal to record the important things that happen each day. Those things might include changes in weather, rate of travel, the condition of the ship, and cargo taken in or unloaded.

A diary is also a type of journal. While it is more personal than a ship's log, they both can record things that happen each day. A diary can also include the thoughts and feelings its writer has. Diaries can be very interesting to read. Some books are based on notes kept in an author's diary or the diary that a main character keeps.

In this exercise you are going to keep a daily journal for five days. Each day you will write a few sentences about what happened, what you thought, or what you felt.

Day 1 ____

Day 2 ____

Day 3 ____

Day 4 ____

Day 5 ____

After five days, look back at the diary entries you have written. Circle the action verbs you have used. Now look at your diary again and underline the state-of-being verbs you have used. Count each group of verbs. Did you use more action verbs or state-of-being verbs? Does this tell us anything about you?

Basic English Grammar

TRL

Community Connection 5

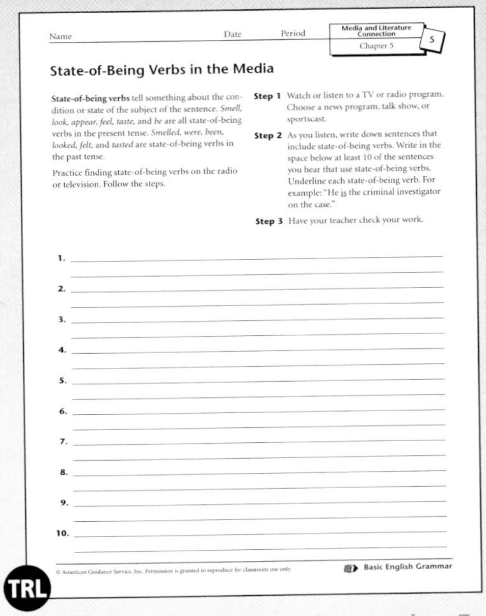

Name ____ Date ____ Period ____ Media and Literature Connection 5 Chapter 5

State-of-Being Verbs in the Media

State-of-being verbs tell something about the condition or state of the subject of the sentence. *Smell, look, appear, feel, taste,* and *be* are all state-of-being verbs in the present tense. *Smelled, were, been, looked, felt,* and *tasted* are state-of-being verbs in the past tense.

Practice finding state-of-being verbs on the radio or television. Follow the steps.

Step 1 Watch or listen to a TV or radio program. Choose a news program, talk show, or sportscast.

Step 2 As you listen, write down sentences that include state-of-being verbs. Write in the space below at least 10 of the sentences you hear that use state-of-being verbs. Underline each state-of-being verb. For example: "He is the criminal investigator on the case."

Step 3 Have your teacher check your work.

1. ____
2. ____
3. ____
4. ____
5. ____
6. ____
7. ____
8. ____
9. ____
10. ____

Basic English Grammar

TRL

Media and Literature Connection 5

Chapter

The State-of-Being Verb

How could you describe this scene? You could say "It *looks* quiet. The snow *seems* powdery and deep. The wind *feels* crisp and cold. The air *smells* clean and fresh." The verb in each of these sentences is a state-of-being verb.

A state-of-being verb tells something about the condition of the subject of a sentence.

In Chapter 5, you will learn about state-of-being verbs. Each lesson in the chapter focuses on the correct use and form of state-of-being verbs in sentences.

Goals for Learning

- To identify state-of-being verbs and verb phrases in sentences
- To distinguish between state-of-being and action verbs
- To identify the correct form of state-of-being verbs

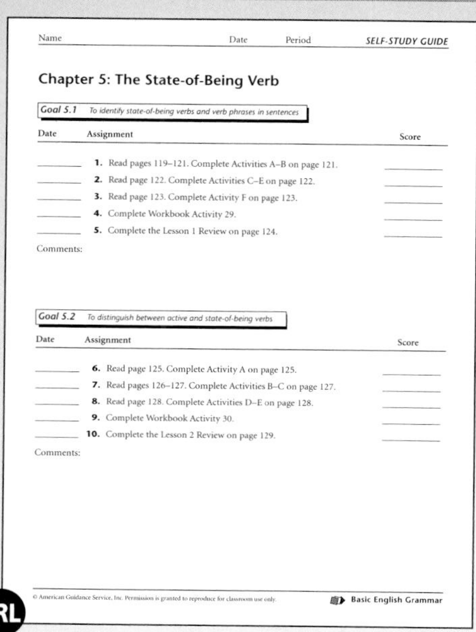

Name Date Period *SELF-STUDY GUIDE*

Chapter 5: The State-of-Being Verb

Goal 5.1 *To identify state-of-being verbs and verb phrases in sentences*

Date	Assignment	Score
______	**1.** Read pages 119–121. Complete Activities A–B on page 121.	______
______	**2.** Read page 122. Complete Activities C–E on page 122.	______
______	**3.** Read page 123. Complete Activity F on page 123.	______
______	**4.** Complete Workbook Activity 29.	______
______	**5.** Complete the Lesson 1 Review on page 124.	______

Comments:

Goal 5.2 *To distinguish between active and state-of-being verbs*

Date	Assignment	Score
______	**6.** Read page 125. Complete Activity A on page 125.	______
______	**7.** Read pages 126–127. Complete Activities B–C on page 127.	______
______	**8.** Read page 128. Complete Activities D–E on page 128.	______
______	**9.** Complete Workbook Activity 30.	______
______	**10.** Complete the Lesson 2 Review on page 129.	______

Comments:

 Basic English Grammar

TRL

Name Date Period *SELF-STUDY GUIDE*

Chapter 5: The State-of-Being Verb, continued

Goal 5.3 *To identify the correct form of state-of-being verbs*

Date	Assignment	Score
______	**11.** Read page 130. Complete Activity A on page 130.	______
______	**12.** Read page 131. Complete Activity B on page 131.	______
______	**13.** Read page 132. Complete Activities C–D on page 132.	______
______	**14.** Complete the Workbook Activity 31.	______
______	**15.** Complete the Lesson 3 Review on page 133.	______
______	**16.** Complete the Chapter 5 Review on pages 134–135.	______

Comments:

Student's Signature ______________________ Date ________

Instructor's Signature ______________________ Date ________

 Basic English Grammar

TRL

Chapter 5 Self-Study Guide, Pages 1–2

Introducing the Chapter

Have students examine the picture of the snow-covered landscape. Ask students questions that will encourage them to use state-of-being verbs, such as *What season is shown in the photograph? What is the weather like?* Write the students' responses on the board and underline the verbs. Remind students of the definition of an action verb (*a word that expresses action*). Ask if the verbs you underlined are action verbs. Then explain that the verbs are state-of-being verbs, or verbs that tell the condition or state of the subject. Explain to students that in Chapter 5 they will learn about state-of-being verbs.

Writing Tips, Notes, and Technology Notes

Ask volunteers to read the tips and notes that appear in the margins throughout the chapter. Then discuss them with the class.

Teacher's Resource

The AGS Teaching Strategies in English Transparencies may be used with this chapter. The transparencies add an interactive dimension to expand and enhance the *Basic English Grammar* program content.

Career Interest Inventory

The AGS Harrington-O'Shea Career Decision-Making System–Revised (CDM) may be used with this chapter. Students can use the CDM to explore their interests and identify careers. The CDM defines career areas that are indicated by students' responses on the inventory.

Lesson at a Glance

Chapter 5 Lesson 1

Overview This lesson introduces state-of-being verbs.

Objectives

- To use state-of-being verbs in sentences.
- To find verbs and verb phrases in sentences and identify their tense.
- To distinguish between action verbs and state-of-being verbs.

Student Pages 120–124

Teacher's Resource Library 

Workbook Activity 29

Activity 29

Alternative Activity 29

Vocabulary

state-of-being verb

Lesson 1 What Is a State-of-Being Verb?

> ***State-of-being verb***
> *A verb that tells something about the condition of the subject of a sentence*

A **state-of-being verb** tells something about the condition or state of the subject of a sentence. A state-of-being verb does not tell what the subject is doing.

Example

State-of-Being Verb	Dan is a tackle on the football team. (The verb *is* helps to make a statement about Dan.)
Action Verb	Dan plays on the football team. (The verb *plays* tells an action that Dan does.)

The most common state-of-being verb is *be*. Other forms of the verb include *am, are, is, was, were, being,* and *been. To be* means "to exist, to live, or to happen."

Forms of *Be*

Present	(singular)	(I) am, (he, she, it) is
	(plural)	are
Past	(singular)	was
	(plural)	were
Future		will be
Present Perfect	(singular)	has been
	(plural)	have been
Past Perfect		had been
Future Perfect		will have been
Present Progressive	(singular)	(I) am being, (he, she, it) is being
	(plural)	are being
Past Progressive	(singular)	was being
	(plural)	were being
Future Progressive		will be being

1 Warm-Up Activity

Ask students to write two brief sentences beginning with the word *I* on a piece of paper. One sentence should name something that they do; the other should make a statement about themselves. Have students write their sentences on the board. When they have finished, number the sentences containing action verbs 1 and the sentences containing state-of-being verbs 2. Then ask students why you classified the sentences in this way. Lead them to understand that the verbs are of two types. Explain that the state-of-being verbs are an important tool in effective communication. This lesson explains their use.

2 Teaching the Lesson

Have students read the text and examples on page 120. Then write the following sentence on the board: *Alex's sister is very young.* Point out that the verb *be* is the most common state-of-being verb. It makes a direct connection between the subject and the information that follows, almost as an equal sign does in math. Ask students if they can think of other verbs to use in place of *is* in this sentence. If they fail to come up with any, have them look at the list on page 121. Try some of these verbs out. Point out that they all have slightly different meanings but many of them fit in the model sentence.

Explain that an easy way to identify a state-of-being verb is to put some form of the verb *be* in its place. (Example: *That tastes awful* becomes *That is awful.*) If the new sentence makes sense and means almost the same thing, then the original verb is a state-of-being verb.

 Reinforce and Extend

Teacher Alert

Students should understand that the terms *state-of-being verb* and *linking verb* are interchangeable.

Activity A On your paper, write the verb or verb phrase in each sentence. Then, write the verb tense next to it.

Example My brother is sick today.
is—present

1. Alex and Jennifer have been at the museum.
2. Mike was at the mall.
3. Mike and Alex are good friends.
4. They have been friends since second grade.
5. Mike and Alex will be at practice this evening.

Here are some other state-of-being verbs.

appear	grow	seem
become	keep	smell
feel	look	stay
get	remain	taste

Activity B Read the example. On your paper, write five more sentences about Alex. Use state-of-being verbs. Underline the verb in each sentence.

Example Alex seems nice.

Writing Tip

The words *seem* and *seam* sound alike. *Seem* is a state-of-being verb. A *seam* is a line formed when two or more items are joined together.

The verb *be* can also be a helping verb. We use *be* with a main verb to form progressive tenses. We use the present participle form *(-ing)* of the verb to do that.

EXAMPLE Pedro is cooking dinner.
Yumi was talking softly.

Activity A

Before students start to write, invite volunteers to read aloud the chart of tenses for the verb *be* on page 120.

Activity A Answers

1. have been—present perfect **2.** was—past **3.** are—present **4.** have been—present perfect **5.** will be—future

Activity B

Before they start the activity, have students compose model sentences using *appear* and *become,* with *Alex* as the subject.

Activity B Answers

Sentences will vary. Each verb should be underlined.

Writing Practice

Have students write a paragraph about their families or themselves using at least five state-of-being verbs. Have them underline the verbs and exchange their papers with a partner for checking. Invite volunteers to read their paragraphs to the class. Ask students in the audience to identify the state-of-being verbs.

LEARNING STYLES

Body/Kinesthetic

Have students print the present and perfect forms of the verb *be* on the board, leaving space between each item. Then divide the class into two teams and have them stand facing the board. Read them sentences using different forms of the verb *be.* Instead of saying the verb, however, ring a bell or buzzer. If a student identifies the missing verb form, he or she should quickly go to the appropriate station at the board and stand there. Award two points for the correct answer; deduct a point for an incorrect answer.

Activity C

If necessary, remind students that the progressive forms of verbs express continuing action. You may also wish to write the six progressive forms on the board with examples. As students do Activity C, point out that they can use any of the progressive forms in their sentences.

Activity C Answers

Sentences will vary. Sample sentences are given. **1.** be—being You are being very stubborn. **2.** seem—seeming The boys are seeming to like the play. **3.** look—looking You are looking well today. **4.** feel—feeling I am feeling much better today. **5.** appear—appearing Storm clouds are appearing dark and threatening.

Activity D

Remind students that a verb phrase is made up of a main verb and one or more helping verbs. If necessary, help students identify the verb phrase in each sentence and determine whether *be* is a main verb or a helping verb.

Activity D Answers

1. was feeling—helping verb **2.** is—main verb **3.** is going—helping verb **4.** will be—main verb **5.** will be—main verb

Activity E

Have students review the examples of conditional verbs on page 109. Remind them that the main verb following a conditional verb will always be in the present tense.

Activity E Answers

1. must be **2.** may appear **3.** could become **4.** Will be **5.** must feel

---

We also use *be* to form passive verbs. *Be* is a helping verb in these verb phrases, too. For example: The mural was painted by Pablo Picasso.

Activity C On your paper, write the present participle for each of these state-of-being verbs. Then write a sentence using each verb.

Example grow—growing
I am growing taller this year.

1. be
2. seem
3. look
4. feel
5. appear

Activity D On your paper, write the verb or verb phrase in each sentence. Next to each verb or verb phrase, write whether the verb *be* is a *main verb* or a *helping verb.*

1. Carlita was feeling fine yesterday.
2. Today she is sick.
3. She is going to the doctor.
4. Carlita will be absent from school.
5. She probably will be better tomorrow.

We can use the conditional helping verbs with state-of-being verbs. Remember, the conditional helping verbs are *may, can, should, might, could, will, must, shall,* and *would.*

Activity E On your paper, write the state-of-being verb or verb phrase in each sentence.

1. The team must be early.
2. The pitcher may appear nervous.
3. He could become tired.
4. Will our team be a winner?
5. Emily must feel happy today.

Learning Styles

Logical/Mathematical

Point out that state-of-being verbs are sometimes known as linking verbs because they indicate a connection between the subject and the rest of the sentence. Write on the board *Ivan is good at math,* and have students identify the verb. Then erase *is* and replace it with the mathematical equal sign (=). Point out that if the verb is a state-of-being verb, the equal sign will make sense in the sentence. Write other sample sentences on the board, inviting volunteers to test state-of-being verbs with the equal sign. Have students test themselves by writing and exchanging original sentences.

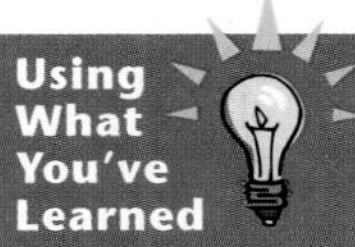

On your paper, draw a picture of yourself. Then write a caption using three to five sentences. Use state-of-being verbs in your sentences to tell about yourself.

State-of-being verbs have the same verb tenses as action verbs.

Present	The blanket feels warm.
Past	He looked good yesterday.
Future	Maria will be 15 next week.
Present Perfect	I have been hungry all morning.
Past Perfect	Jack had seemed tired by evening.
Future Perfect	Madison will have been sick for three days tomorrow.

Activity F On your paper, write the verb or verb phrase in each sentence. Next to each verb or verb phrase, write its tense.

1. Sam will not be happy about that.
2. Mrs. Franco has been our neighbor for two years.
3. She was a Spanish teacher.
4. We had been the winners twice.
5. We will have become tired by then.

Where To Find It

Atlas

What kind of book would you use to look at maps or to gather facts about geography? The answer is an atlas.

To find information in an atlas, use the table of contents. Look up the state or country about which you want to learn. Read the map titles to find the map you need. You can also look in the index for the names of particular cities, land features, or bodies of water.

1. On your paper, write three places you would like to visit.
2. Use an atlas to find these places on a map. Then write a short description of each place, using facts from the atlas.

Activity F

Write the six tenses on the board. Then ask partners to work together to write a sentence with a state-of-being verb for each tense. Students can use the example sentences as models. When students have finished, point to a tense and invite volunteers to read their sentences for that tense. Ask the class to identify the verb or verb phrase in each sentence. Then have students work independently to complete Activity F.

Activity F Answers

1. will be—future **2.** has been—present perfect **3.** was—past **4.** had been—past perfect **5.** will have become—future perfect

Using What You've Learned

After students have drawn their self-portraits, have them turn to the list of state-of-being verbs on page 121. Ask students leading questions, using a selection of verbs, to help them think about themselves: *How do you look? How do you seem to others? Have you grown taller this year? Will you appear the same next year?* Encourage students to use a variety of tenses in their sentences.

Where To Find It

Point out that atlases are not all the same. World atlases give general information about all the countries and oceans on Earth. Other atlases are specialized. There are atlases of individual countries, states, and cities. There are even atlases of the moon.

Before beginning the exercise, students should understand that maps do not always give the same information. Some maps may show natural features, such as mountains and rivers; some may show roads or national boundaries; still others may give information about natural resources, population, religion, or climate. Students should read the title in order to understand the purpose of the map.

Answers to Where To Find It: Answers will vary. Encourage students to find facts that interest them.

Lesson 1 Review Answers

1. is—main verb **2.** is looking—helping verb **3.** has been—main verb **4.** is—main verb **5.** has been keeping—helping verb **6.** smells—present **7.** was—past **8.** looks—present **9.** is—present **10.** tasted—past

Sentences will vary. Each sentence should contain a state-of-being verb. Each verb should be underlined.

Spelling Builder

Write the homonyms in the Spelling Builder box on the board. Give each like-sounding word a letter—*a, b,* or *c.* Then say aloud sentences using these words. Challenge students to identify the word you are using by letter. Have them give an explanation for their choice. Invite students to use these words in sentences of their own, and write model sentences on the board.

Answers to Spelling Builder: 1. break **2.** past **3.** through **4.** plane **5.** their

Spelling Practice

Give students extra practice with the commonly confused homonyms *its/it's* and *their/they're/there.* Read the following paragraph, omitting the italicized words. Have students insert the appropriate homonyms.

Every morning before *it's* light, I let the dogs out of *their* kennels and give the cat *its* breakfast. *It's* not afraid of the dogs. If *there* is time, I take the dogs out for *their* run. *They're* very fast. After that, *they're* ready for *their* food.

Teacher Alert

Point out to students that the homonyms in this lesson are *homophones,* or words that sound alike but have different meanings and spellings. Another kind of homonym is the *homograph,* or words with the same spelling but with different meanings and sometimes different pronunciations. (Example: *The performers took a* bow. *Angelique tied the laces into a* bow.) *Bow* and *bow* are homographs.

Lesson 1 REVIEW

On your paper, write the verb or verb phrase in each sentence. Then write whether the verb *be* is a *main verb* or a *helping verb.*

1. My aunt is 80 years old.
2. She is looking well.
3. She always has been healthy.
4. Aunt Marie is a good cook.
5. She has been keeping very active.

On your paper, write the verb or verb phrase in each sentence. Then write the verb tense next to it.

6. Dinner smells very inviting.
7. The food was wonderful.
8. That turkey looks delicious.
9. The drumstick is my favorite part.
10. Nothing tasted better than the stuffing.

On your paper, write five sentences using state-of-being verbs in the box on page 121. Then underline the verb in each sentence.

Spelling Builder

Homonyms (Words That Sound Alike)

Words that sound alike but have different meanings and spellings are *homonyms.* Examples of homonyms include *break, brake; past, passed; through, threw; plain, plane;* and *their, they're, there.*

On your paper, write the correct word to complete each sentence. Use a dictionary if you need help.

1. Have you given the workers a (break, brake) yet?
2. He forgives her for her (past, passed) mistakes.
3. We drove (through, threw) a long tunnel.
4. The passengers boarded the (plain, plane).
5. Teachers should help (their, they're, there) students.

124 Chapter 5 The State-of-Being Verb

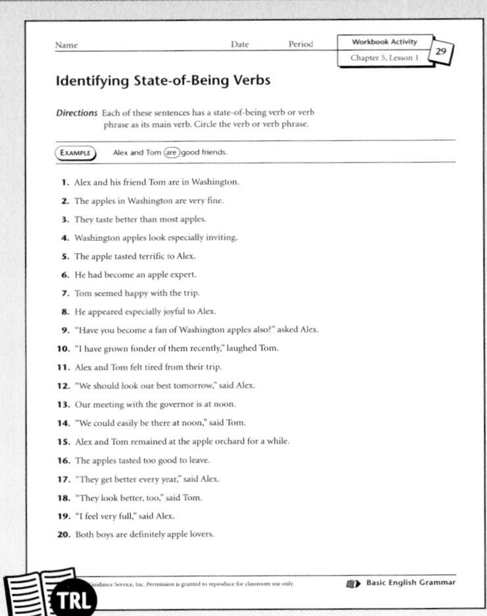

Name Date Period | Workbook Activity 29 | Chapter 5, Lesson 1

Identifying State-of-Being Verbs

Directions Each of these sentences has a state-of-being verb or verb phrase as its main verb. Circle the verb or verb phrase.

EXAMPLE Alex and Tom (are) good friends.

1. Alex and his friend Tom are in Washington.
2. The apples in Washington are very fine.
3. They taste better than most apples.
4. Washington apples look especially inviting.
5. The apple tasted terrific to Alex.
6. He had become an apple expert.
7. Tom seemed happy with the trip.
8. He appeared especially joyful to Alex.
9. "Have you become a fan of Washington apples also?" asked Alex.
10. "I have grown fonder of them recently," laughed Tom.
11. Alex and Tom felt tired from their trip.
12. "We should look our best tomorrow," said Alex.
13. Our meeting with the governor is at noon.
14. "We could easily be there at noon," said Tom.
15. Alex and Tom remained at the apple orchard for a while.
16. The apples tasted too good to leave.
17. "They get better every year," said Alex.
18. "They look better, too," said Tom.
19. "I feel very full," said Alex.
20. Both boys are definitely apple lovers.

 Basic English Grammar

TRL

Workbook Activity 29

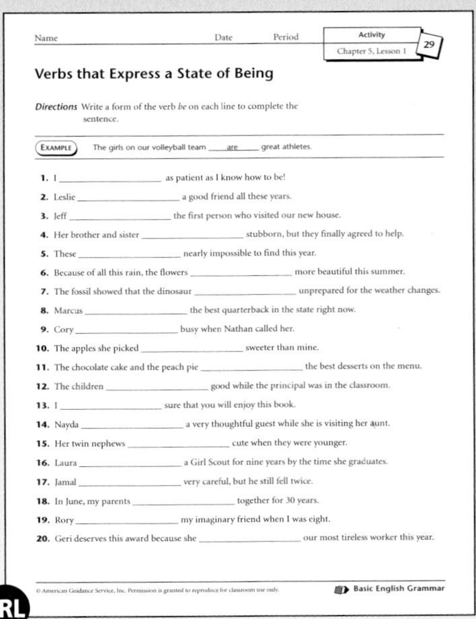

Name Date Period | Activity 29 | Chapter 5, Lesson 1

Verbs that Express a State of Being

Directions Write a form of the verb *be* on each line to complete the sentence.

EXAMPLE The girls on our volleyball team __are__ great athletes.

1. I ________ as patient as I know how to be!
2. Leslie ________ a good friend all these years.
3. Jeff ________ the first person who visited our new house.
4. Her brother and sister ________ stubborn, but they finally agreed to help.
5. These ________ nearly impossible to find this year.
6. Because of all this rain, the flowers ________ more beautiful this summer.
7. The fossil showed that the dinosaur ________ unprepared for the weather changes.
8. Marcus ________ the best quarterback in the state right now.
9. Cory ________ busy when Nathan called her.
10. The apples she picked ________ sweeter than mine.
11. The chocolate cake and the peach pie ________ the best desserts on the menu.
12. The children ________ good while the principal was in the classroom.
13. I ________ sure that you will enjoy this book.
14. Nayda ________ a very thoughtful guest while she is visiting her aunt.
15. Her twin nephews ________ cute when they were younger.
16. Laura ________ a Girl Scout for nine years by the time she graduates.
17. Jamal ________ very careful, but he still fell twice.
18. In June, my parents ________ together for 30 years.
19. Rory ________ my imaginary friend when I was eight.
20. Geri deserves this award because she ________ our most tireless worker this year.

 Basic English Grammar

TRL

Activity 29

Lesson 2 Action or State of Being?

The verb *be* expresses state of being when it is the main verb in a sentence.

EXAMPLE The chicken is golden brown.
The chicken was delicious.

Many state-of-being verbs can also be action verbs. To decide whether a verb expresses action or a state of being, think about the meaning of the sentence.

EXAMPLE

Action Verb	Gabi tasted the mashed potatoes. (*Tasted* expresses action. Gabi did something.)
State-of-Being Verb	The mashed potatoes tasted salty. (*Tasted* expresses a state of being. The condition of the mashed potatoes was salty.)

Activity A On your paper, write the verb in each sentence. Next to each one, write whether the verb expresses *action* or a *state of being*. Ask yourself "Is the subject doing something?" If it is, the verb is an action verb.

Example The other players are tired.
are—state of being

1. The sky looks very stormy.
2. My jacket keeps me warm.
3. Corey appeared calm.
4. Jamal and Kim became ill after the trip.
5. Everyone smelled the burning rubber.

3 Reinforce and Extend

TEACHER ALERT

You may wish to point out that the verb *be* is always a state-of-being, or linking, verb except when it is followed by certain adverbs and adverb phrases. (Examples: *Alice is here. They have been away. We were at the party.*) The verb *be* is never an action verb.

Activity A

Have students complete this exercise in pairs. Encourage partners to discuss the reasons for their answers before writing them down.

Activity A Answers

1. looks—state of being 2. keeps—action 3. appeared—state of being 4. became—state of being 5. smelled—action

Lesson at a Glance

Chapter 5 Lesson 2

Overview This lesson focuses on state-of-being verbs that can also function as action verbs.

Objectives

- To locate verbs and verb phrases in sentences.
- To determine whether a verb expresses a state of being or an action.

Student Pages 125–129

Teacher's Resource Library 

Workbook Activity 30
Activity 30
Alternative Activity 30

1 Warm-Up Activity

Have students review the state-of-being verbs in the box on page 121. Then write the following sentence on the board: *Benjamin looked great in that suit.* Ask students how they know that *looked* is a state-of-being verb. (*They may answer that it tells something about the subject or that it can be replaced with the verb* be.) Then write *Benjamin looked at the suit in the window.* Invite students to explain how the verb *looked* is used differently. Lead them to understand that in the second sentence the verb describes something Benjamin is doing. In this case, *looked* is an action verb. Point out that many state-of-being verbs can double as action verbs. This lesson explains how to determine the differences between them.

2 Teaching the Lesson

Read the examples on page 126 aloud with the class. Make sure that students understand each definition and how the word is used in the model sentence. Test their understanding by asking for other examples expressing action and state of being. Remind students that if the verbs *be* or *seem*, or the mathematical equal sign, can replace the main verb without creating a nonsense sentence, then the verb is a state-of-being verb.

Learning Styles

LEP/ESL

Ask English-language learners to look at the boxed words on this page. Encourage them to make a chart with the labels *State of Being* and *Action.* Ask them to work with English-proficient students to write sentences for each verb as both a state-of-being verb and an action verb and to place the sentences in their charts. They can use their charts as a study tool.

Learning Styles

Auditory/Verbal

Invite volunteers to read the model sentences on this page in random order to the class. Students listening should identify the verb and tell whether it expresses action or state of being.

Learning Styles

Logical/Mathematical

Give students a brief passage from a book or magazine to read. Ask them to list all the verbs, separating them into columns headed *Action* and *State of Being.* Have students calculate what percentage, or fraction, of all the verbs expresses state of being. As a further refinement, have students determine the percentage of the state-of-being verbs represented by the verb *be.*

Verbs often have more than one meaning. Some meanings express action and some express state of being.

Example

APPEAR	**Action:** to come into view; to become visible The firefighters appeared quickly. **State of Being:** to seem; to look The firefighters appeared strong.
FEEL	**Action:** to touch; to think or believe Ling felt the heat of the sun on her face. **State of Being:** to be aware of a physical or mental sensation Ling felt relaxed.
GROW	**Action:** to cause to grow; to develop Colin grows corn. The vegetables grew in the garden. **State of Being:** to pass into a condition (become) The sky grew darker.
SMELL	**Action:** to catch the scent or odor of something Freida smelled the baking bread. **State of Being:** to have a certain scent or odor The bread smells delicious.
LOOK	**Action:** to use one's sense of sight Ling looked at the ocean. **State of Being:** to appear a certain way Ling looks worried.
TASTE	**Action:** to test the flavor of something Colin tasted the juice. **State of Being:** to have a certain flavor The juice tasted sour.
GET	**Action:** to fetch; to arrive at I got my tennis racket at the mall. We got to the play late. **State of Being:** to be; to become or possess It gets windy during a storm.
BECOME	**Action:** to suit or be suitable to This color becomes you. **State of Being:** to pass into a condition Devon became angry.

Some computer grammar checkers may highlight state-of-being verbs. This is to remind you to replace them with action verbs whenever possible. If your computer has a thesaurus, you can use it to find more interesting and specific action verbs.

Activity B On your paper, write whether the verb in bold expresses *action* or a *state of being.*

1. She could **smell** the smoke in the air.
2. The warm rolls **smelled** inviting.
3. The oven **felt** too hot.
4. She **appeared** to have a good time.
5. She **has grown** as tall as I.
6. Mary **felt** a hole in her pocket.
7. Joe **grows** orange trees in Arizona.
8. Our cat **smells** his food before he **tastes** it.
9. Brad **felt** wonderful about his perfect score.
10. Cary suddenly **appeared** at the party.

If you are not sure whether a verb is a state-of-being verb, try this test. Substitute a form of the verb *be* for the verb. If the meaning of the sentence is almost the same, the verb is a state-of-being verb. You cannot substitute a form of *be* for an action verb.

EXAMPLE

State-of-Being Verb	They remained members. (You could say: They were members.)
Action Verb	He got a new hat. (You could not say: He was a new hat.)

Activity C On your paper, write two sentences for each verb in the box on page 126. In the first sentence, use the verb as an action verb. In the second sentence, use the verb as a state-of-being verb.

LEARNING STYLES

Visual/Spatial

Point out that thank-you cards, valentine cards, sympathy cards, birthday cards, and others often use state-of-being verbs in their messages. (Examples: *Each year you become more special. I hope you feel better.*) Have students design a card for an occasion and compose a message using one of the words discussed in this lesson. Suggest that they review the box on page 126 for examples.

Activity B

Do the first two items as a class to be sure students understand when a verb expresses action and when it expresses a state of being. Then have students complete the activity on their own.

Activity B Answers

1. action **2.** state of being **3.** state of being **4.** state of being **5.** state of being **6.** action **7.** action **8.** action, action **9.** state of being **10.** action

Activity C

Suggest that as they do Activity C, students apply the test described in the text to their own sentences. This will help them check that they have used each verb first as an action verb and then as a state-of-being verb.

Activity C Answers

Sentences will vary. Sample sentences follow. When the sun set, mosquitoes appeared out of nowhere. (action) The tea appears strong. (state of being) Sam felt the bee sting. (action) Dana feels tired. (state of being)

TEACHER ALERT

Read the Technology Note on this page with the students. Point out that a computer's thesaurus, like a print thesaurus, does not give accurate guidance about which synonym to use. Advise students not to substitute a thesaurus word for one of their own until they look it up in a dictionary and thoroughly understand its meaning.

Activity D

Have students identify the subject in the first two items. Suggest that students picture each sentence as you read it aloud. Ask them which sentence describes the subject doing something that requires movement or action. (#2) Remind students that a state-of-being verb does not express action.

Activity D Answers

1. state of being **2.** action **3.** action **4.** state of being **5.** state of being

Activity E

After they complete the activity, have students pair up and compose sentences using the same verbs in the alternative form. (For example, *Smell* in item 1 would become a state-of-being verb.)

Activity E Answers

1. Smell—action **2.** seems—state of being **3.** is watching—action **4.** appeared—state of being **5.** Did taste—action

Online Connection

Point out that most cities and towns have their own Web sites, providing information about their history, education systems, local government, commercial opportunities, and tourist attractions. Have students log on to the Web site of their community or one for a large city, such as **www.ci.chi.il.us** for Chicago, Illinois. Ask them to print out a page that interests them and to circle the state-of-being verbs that they find in the content. Invite students to share their research with the class.

The verb *seem* is always a state-of-being verb.

Example **Seem** to be; to appear
Alex seems afraid.

Activity D On your paper, write whether each verb in bold expresses *action* or a *state of being.*

1. Their whole family **seems** athletic.
2. Mrs. Jones **smelled** something burning.
3. The boys **grew** beans, squash, and corn in their garden.
4. Ron **seems** tired this evening.
5. Flora **feels** sick.

Activity E On your paper, write the verb or verb phrase in each sentence. Next to each verb or verb phrase, write whether it expresses *action* or a *state of being.*

1. Smell these beautiful flowers.
2. The grass seems greener this time of year.
3. That cute little puppy in the window is watching us.
4. The plants in our garden appeared yellow and shriveled.
5. Did you taste the vegetable pizza?

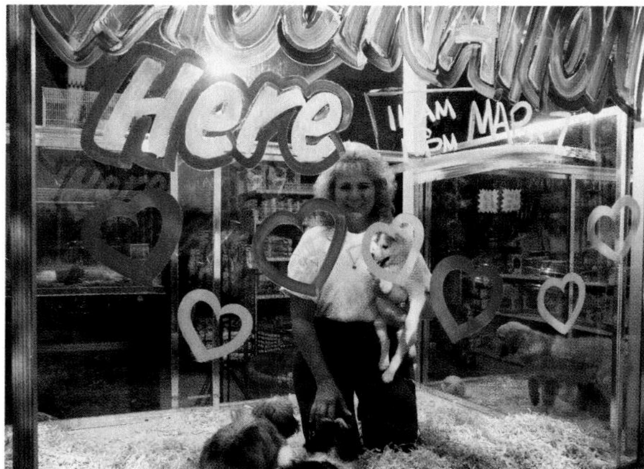

The puppies in the window look so cute.

On your paper, write whether the verb in bold expresses *action* or a *state of being.*

1. Howard finally **appeared.**
2. He **seems** strong and healthy.
3. The cloth **felt** soft to me.
4. I **felt** the soft cloth.
5. The taco sauce **tasted** spicy.

On your paper, write the verb or verb phrase in each sentence. Next to each verb or verb phrase, write whether it expresses *action* or a *state of being.*

6. Mr. Klein was looking for the newspaper.
7. Suddenly the newspaper appeared!
8. The newspaper appeared wrinkled.
9. Mr. Klein grew thoughtful for a moment.
10. He spotted the dog under the table.

Writing Project

Using State-of-Being Verbs

Interviewers often use state-of-being verbs in the questions they ask the people they interview.

Imagine you are an interviewer. On your paper, write 10 questions you can use to interview a classmate, neighbor, or friend. Use both state-of-being and action verbs in your questions.

When you finish, go back and underline the verb or verb phrase in each question. Then, identify each verb as *action* or *state of being.*

Example What is your name? is—state of being
Do you enjoy school? Do enjoy—action

When you are finished, share your questions with a classmate.

Lesson 2 Review Answers

1. action 2. state of being 3. state of being 4. action 5. state of being 6. was looking—action 7. appeared—action 8. appeared—state of being 9. grew—state of being 10. spotted—action

Writing Project

Point out that many interview questions include some form of the verb *be.* Encourage students to use a variety of state-of-being verbs in their questions. Before they begin writing, have them review the list in the box on page 121. Ask them to include at least one of these verbs in their interview questions.

Speaking Practice

Have students conduct an interview, using the questions they wrote for the Writing Project on this page. Encourage them to depart from their prepared questions if the person they are interviewing says something unexpected or intriguing.

Remind students that the interviewer must speak clearly and with expression. Have them tape-record their interviews. Invite volunteers to play their tapes for the class.

Career Connection

Help students conduct mock job interviews. Have one student take the role of the employer while the other takes the role of the job candidate. Beforehand, students should work together to write a list of questions for the interviewers to ask. Stress that students should use state-of-being verbs in their questions and responses. Point out that using correct grammar during a real job interview can create a favorable impression on a potential employer.

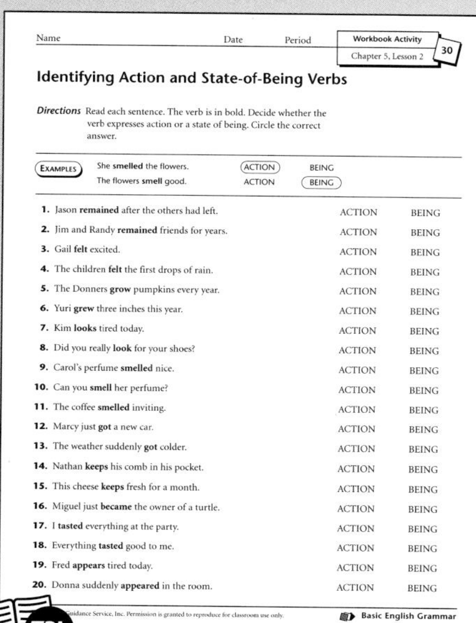

Name Date Period

Workbook Activity 30
Chapter 5, Lesson 2

Identifying Action and State-of-Being Verbs

Directions Read each sentence. The verb is in bold. Decide whether the verb expresses action or a state of being. Circle the correct answer.

EXAMPLES She **smelled** the flowers. (ACTION) BEING
The flowers **smell** good. ACTION (BEING)

1. Jason **remained** after the others had left. ACTION BEING
2. Jim and Randy **remained** friends for years. ACTION BEING
3. Gail **felt** excited. ACTION BEING
4. The children **felt** the first drops of rain. ACTION BEING
5. The Donners **grow** pumpkins every year. ACTION BEING
6. Yuri **grew** three inches this year. ACTION BEING
7. Kim **looks** tired today. ACTION BEING
8. Did you really **look** for your shoes? ACTION BEING
9. Carol's perfume **smelled** nice. ACTION BEING
10. Can you **smell** her perfume? ACTION BEING
11. The coffee **smelled** inviting. ACTION BEING
12. Marcy just **got** a new car. ACTION BEING
13. The weather suddenly **got** colder. ACTION BEING
14. Nathan **keeps** his comb in his pocket. ACTION BEING
15. This cheese **keeps** fresh for a month. ACTION BEING
16. Miguel just **became** the owner of a turtle. ACTION BEING
17. I **tasted** everything at the party. ACTION BEING
18. Everything **tasted** good to me. ACTION BEING
19. Fred **appears** tired today. ACTION BEING
20. Donna suddenly **appeared** in the room. ACTION BEING

 Basic English Grammar

TRL

Workbook Activity 30

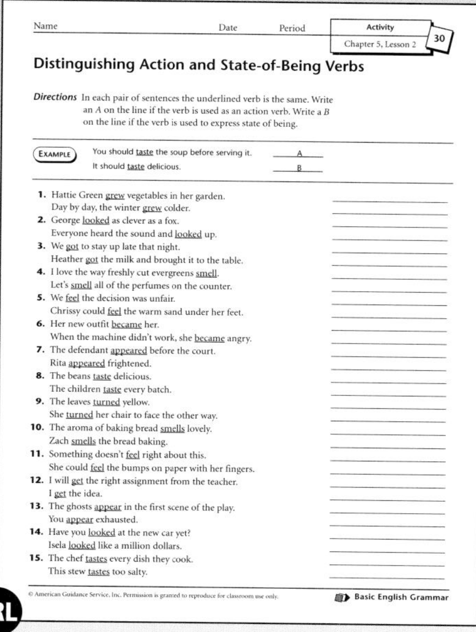

Name Date Period

Activity 30
Chapter 5, Lesson 2

Distinguishing Action and State-of-Being Verbs

Directions In each pair of sentences the underlined verb is the same. Write an *A* on the line if the verb is used as an action verb. Write a *B* on the line if the verb is used to express state of being.

EXAMPLE You should taste the soup before serving it. A
It should taste delicious. B

1. Hattie Green grew vegetables in her garden. ______
   Day by day, the winter grew colder. ______
2. George looked as clever as a fox. ______
   Everyone heard the sound and looked up. ______
3. We got to stay up late that night. ______
   Heather got the milk and brought it to the table. ______
4. I love the way freshly cut evergreens smell. ______
   Let's smell all of the perfumes on the counter. ______
5. We feel the decision was unfair. ______
   Chrissy could feel the warm sand under her feet. ______
6. Her new outfit became her. ______
   When the machine didn't work, she became angry. ______
7. The defendant appeared before the court. ______
   Rita appeared frightened. ______
8. The beans taste delicious. ______
   The children taste every batch. ______
9. The leaves turned yellow. ______
   She turned her chair to face the other way. ______
10. The aroma of baking bread smells lovely. ______
    Zach smells the bread baking. ______
11. Something doesn't feel right about this. ______
    She could feel the bumps on paper with her fingers. ______
12. I will get the right assignment from the teacher. ______
    I get the idea. ______
13. The ghosts appear in the first scene of the play. ______
    You appear exhausted. ______
14. Have you looked at the new car yet? ______
    Isela looked like a million dollars. ______
15. The chef tastes every dish they cook. ______
    This stew tastes too salty. ______

 Basic English Grammar

TRL

Activity 30

Lesson at a Glance

Chapter 5 Lesson 3

Overview This lesson focuses on the correct usage of the forms of the irregular verb *be.*

Objectives

- To identify the forms of the verb *be.*
- To use the correct form of the verb *be* in sentences.

Student Pages 130–133

Teacher's Resource Library 

Workbook Activity 31

Activity 31

Alternative Activity 31

1 Warm-Up Activity

Remind students that the verb *be* is an irregular verb by writing the following sentences on the board: *It looks like a duck. It quacks like a duck. It ___ a duck.* Invite students to supply the missing word. Point out that *is* is the present tense of the verb *be* when the subject is *he, she,* or *it.* Now change the subject of the sentences to *they,* and challenge students to make the necessary alterations. Explain that the verb must agree with the subject in number. Continue with *I, we,* and *you.* When all the forms of *be* are on the board, have students look at the chart on page 131.

2 Teaching the Lesson

Point out that the past participle of a verb is the form used with the helping verb *have.* Write on the board the following sentence: *She has looked ill all day.* Ask students to identify the past participle (*looked*)and ask them to substitute the verb *be* for *look.* Elicit from them that *been* is the past participle of the verb *be.* Have students compose other examples using *been* with the helping verb *have.*

Remind students that the present participle of a verb is the form that ends in *-ing.* Write on the board *The children were being very noisy.* Ask students to identify the verb phrase and the present participle (*were being/being*). Invite them to write other examples.

Activity A

Before students complete the activity, have them identify the subjects and say whether they are singular or plural.

Activity A Answers

1. Alex feels sure that his answer is correct. 2. Jennifer appears pleased with the results of the test. 3. Alex and Mike look sad. 4. The bread cooling on the counter smells delicious. 5. The hot apple cider tastes good.

Lesson 3 Using State-of-Being Verbs

In a sentence, the verb must agree in number (singular or plural) with its subject. The rules for subject-verb agreement for state-of-being verbs and action verbs are the same. Add *-s* or *-es* to the present tense when the subject is singular. *Be* is the only verb that does not follow this rule.

EXAMPLE		
	Singular Subject	Will looks happy.
	Plural Subject	They look happy.

The past tense of the verb stays the same for singular and plural subjects.

EXAMPLE		
	Singular Subject	Laura looked nice.
	Plural Subject	Both girls looked nice.

Activity A On your paper, write each sentence using the present tense of the verb in parentheses. Be sure the subject and the verb agree.

1. Alex (feel) sure that his answer is correct.
2. Jennifer (appear) pleased with the results of the test.
3. Alex and Mike (look) sad.
4. The bread cooling on the counter (smell) delicious.
5. The hot apple cider (taste) good.

Fresh homemade bread tastes great.

The verb *be* is an irregular verb. Its form depends on whether it is used with a singular or plural subject. It also depends on whether the subject is first, second, or third person.

Writing Tip

Put state-of-being verbs in the correct tense. When writing about past events, make all your verbs past tense. When writing about present events, use present tense verbs.

Present and Past Forms of *Be*

Singular	Present	Past
First person	I **am**	I **was**
Second person	you **are**	you **were**
Third person	he **is**	he **was**
	she **is**	she **was**
	it **is**	it **was**
Plural	**Present**	**Past**
First person	we **are**	we **were**
Second person	you **are**	you **were**
Third person	they **are**	they **were**

Activity B Each of these sentences contains a form of the verb *be*. On your paper, write each verb.

1. I am busy today.
2. They were happy to get the award.
3. They are friends of mine.
4. She is a careful driver.
5. The crowd was anxious for the game to be over.

The past participle of *be* is *been*. Use *been* with *have, has,* and *had* to form the perfect tenses.

EXAMPLE Mrs. Fong has been sick.
They have been busy all week.
Seth had been their coach.

Activity B

When students have completed the activity, have them use the chart on this page to identify the person, number, and tense of the verbs.

Activity B Answers

1. am **2.** were **3.** are **4.** is **5.** was

Reinforce and Extend

Global Connection

Challenge students to find as many ways of saying *I am* internationally as they can. Suggest that they ask family members or acquaintances who speak a language other than English to write the words and explain how to say them. Have students make a chart on the board with the languages listed across the top and the words and their pronunciations below.

In the Community

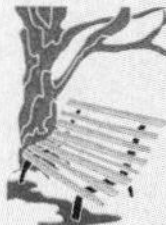

Have students compose an e-mail or letter about their community to a pen pal or friend who has never visited. Encourage students to describe the place they live and to express what they like or don't like about it. Have them underline the state-of-being verbs that they used. Invite volunteers to read their letters to the class.

Learning Styles

Interpersonal/Group Learning

Have pairs of students write two sentences in the past tense and two in the present, using state-of-being verbs. Invite partners to read a sentence of their choice aloud and challenge another pair to repeat the sentence in the other tense—changing the verb from past to present or vice versa. Remind students that they may have to alter words other than the verb in order for the sentence to make sense. (*Today* would become *yesterday,* for example.)

Activity C

Write the first activity item on the board and have students tell you what to write in the blank. Ask students to explain why *was* is correct. Then erase the verb and replace the word *yesterday* with *today.* Ask a volunteer to write the correct form of the verb *be* in the sentence. After students complete Activity C on their own, invite them to read aloud each sentence with the verb in place.

Activity C Answers

1. was 2. being 3. been 4. is 5. being

Activity D

Have students provide additional examples of sentences with the verb *be* that show future tense and simple conditional forms.

Activity D Answers

1. be 2. be 3. be 4. be 5. be

Teacher Alert

Point out that people sometimes use the word *be* instead of the correct form of the verb *be:*

They be good friends.

I be going now.

Remind students that *be* is never used by itself as a verb in a sentence.

Writing Tip

When using *be,* do not leave out the verb or verb phrase. For example, *He tall* is incorrect. *He is tall* is correct. Do not use *be* instead of the correct present form. For example, *He be tall* is incorrect. *He is tall* is correct.

The present participle of *be* is *being.* Use *being* with the helping verb *be* to show the progressive form.

Example Kim is being nice.
Shanice was being friendly.

Activity C On your paper, write the correct form of the verb *be* to complete each sentence.

1. Megan's report ______ due yesterday.
2. They were ______ stubborn about the decision.
3. Has he ever ______ a teacher?
4. Yellowstone Park ______ a national park.
5. The children were ______ silly.

Use the verb *be* to show future tense.

Example

Future	He will be home soon.
Conditional	Jamie must be late.

Activity D On your paper, write the correct form of the verb *be* to complete each sentence.

1. Will you ______ my project partner?
2. I should ______ more careful.
3. Must I always ______ the first one?
4. Can I ______ the last one?
5. Howard will ______ disappointed about the game.

At Home

Encourage students to use the correct form of the verb *be* whenever they speak or write at home or in the community-at-large. Remind students that all people, especially young children, tend to imitate those people that they admire most. The students' correct use of verb forms can serve as an example for younger siblings and friends who look up to them.

Learning Styles

Auditory/Verbal

Call on volunteers to read aloud the completed sentences in Parts C and D on this page. As each volunteer completes a sentence, invite the class to call out the form of the verb *be* used.

On your paper, write the correct form of the verb *be* to complete each sentence. There may be more than one correct answer.

1. In November there ________ a contest at Wilson High School.
2. Mitsu ________ entering the contest.
3. Her talent ________ playing the tuba.
4. On the night of the contest, Mitsu's parents ________ excited.
5. Before the contest, Mitsu had ________ nervous.

On your paper, write each sentence using the correct form of the verb in parentheses. Be sure the subject and the verb agree.

6. Tanya should (keep) warm in that jacket.
7. We will (feel) tired after the hike.
8. The teacher (seem) happy with the students.
9. Her perfume (smell) wonderful!
10. The hearty stew (taste) delicious.

Vocabulary Builder

Replacing the *Be* Verb

The verb *be* means "to exist, to live, or to happen." You can make your writing more interesting by replacing the *be* verb with more specific verbs.

When will the play *be*? When will the play *occur*?

On your paper, rewrite each of these sentences. Replace each verb in bold with a word that has a more specific meaning. You may need to change other parts of the sentence.

1. Will Frances and Brandon **be** here very long?
2. That ham **is** too salty.
3. Tanya **is** my best friend.
4. Zach **was** responsible for the goal.
5. Alex **is** in need of a backpack.

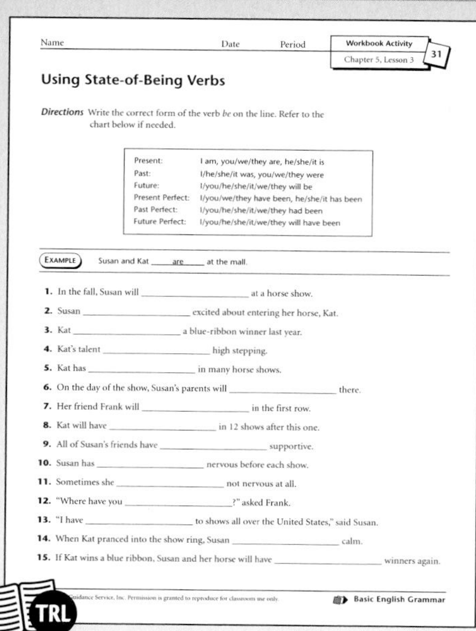

Name Date Period

Workbook Activity 31 — Chapter 5, Lesson 3

Using State-of-Being Verbs

Directions Write the correct form of the verb *be* on the line. Refer to the chart below if needed.

Present:	I am, you/we/they are, he/she/it is
Past:	I/he/she/it was, you/we/they were
Future:	I/you/he/she/it/we/they will be
Present Perfect:	I/you/we/they have been, he/she/it has been
Past Perfect:	I/you/he/she/it/we/they had been
Future Perfect:	I/you/he/she/it/we/they will have been

EXAMPLE Susan and Kat __are__ at the mall.

1. In the fall, Susan will ____________ at a horse show.
2. Susan ____________ excited about entering her horse, Kat.
3. Kat ____________ a blue-ribbon winner last year.
4. Kat's talent ____________ high stepping.
5. Kat has ____________ in many horse shows.
6. On the day of the show, Susan's parents will ____________ there.
7. Her friend Frank will ____________ in the first row.
8. Kat will have ____________ in 12 shows after this one.
9. All of Susan's friends have ____________ supportive.
10. Susan has ____________ nervous before each show.
11. Sometimes she ____________ not nervous at all.
12. "Where have you ____________?" asked Frank.
13. "I have ____________ to shows all over the United States," said Susan.
14. When Kat pranced into the show ring, Susan ____________ calm.
15. If Kat wins a blue ribbon, Susan and her horse will have ____________ winners again.

Basic English Grammar

TRL

Workbook Activity 31

Name Date Period

Activity 31 — Chapter 5, Lesson 3

State-of-Being Verbs Express Tense

Directions On the line, write the state-of-being verb or verb phrase in each sentence. Write the verb tense next to each one.

EXAMPLE Maria will have been a teacher for nine years in June. __will have been—future perfect tense__

1. Will the leaves turn red or yellow? ____________
2. Liza is becoming a wonderful dancer. ____________
3. Barbara looks beautiful in blue. ____________
4. Diana felt tired yesterday. ____________
5. *The Red Pony* is a short novel by John Steinbeck. ____________
6. Have you looked this silly before? ____________
7. August will have been the busiest month. ____________
8. Patty has been nice today. ____________
9. Eric will be fifteen on his next birthday. ____________
10. Tyler became a plumber like his uncle. ____________
11. Cheese keeps fresh in the refrigerator. ____________
12. The prices seem higher than the last time. ____________
13. Will Malcolm be in your way here? ____________
14. Jane will be here at six o'clock. ____________
15. Fire safety was the topic at the assembly today. ____________
16. Stephanie will not be here in May. ____________
17. The water had looked cleaner in the past. ____________
18. Next week, Carla will be on vacation. ____________
19. Bruce felt refreshed after his nap. ____________
20. Is your tuxedo ready? ____________

Basic English Grammar

TRL

Activity 31

Lesson 3 Review Answers

1. was/will be **2.** is/will be **3.** is/was **4.** were/will be **5.** been **6.** Tanya should keep warm in that jacket. **7.** We will feel tired after the hike. **8.** The teacher seems/seemed happy with the students. **9.** Her perfume smells/smelled wonderful! **10.** The hearty stew tastes/tasted delicious.

Vocabulary Builder

Point out that *be* is the most commonly used verb in the language. Encourage students to find alternatives to give their writing and speech variety. Before they begin the written exercises, invite students to replace the verb *be* in the sentences below. (Suggested answers are in parentheses.)

- It is taller every day. (*grows*)
- I've been well since I started jogging. (*felt*)
- The day will be sunny later. (*will become*)

Answers to Vocabulary Builder: Sentence will vary. Sample sentences are given. **1.** Will Frances and Brandon stay here very long? **2.** That ham tastes too salty. **3.** Tanya remains my best friend. **4.** Zach scored the goal. **5.** Alex needs a backpack.

Learning Styles

Visual/Spatial

Encourage students to work together to create a classroom chart of the different forms of the verb *be*, with example sentences for each form. Students should try to work from memory but can look through the lesson if they have difficulty recalling a particular form. Have students display their posters throughout the classroom.

Chapter 5 Review

Use the Chapter Review to prepare students for tests and to reteach content from the chapter.

Chapter 5 Mastery Test 

The Teacher's Resource Library includes two parallel forms of the Chapter 5 Mastery Test. The difficulty level of the two forms is equivalent. You may wish to use one form as a pretest and the other form as a posttest.

Review Answers

Part A

1. state-of-being verb

Part B

2. grow—present 3. are feeling—present progressive 4. will have been growing—future perfect progressive 5. had become—past perfect 6. was smelling—past progressive 7. has been—present perfect 8. was—past 9. could be—future 10. will be feeling—future progressive

Part C

11. state of being 12. action 13. action 14. state of being 15. action

Part D

16. is—main verb 17. is studying—helping verb 18. has been—main verb 19. is—main verb 20. had been—main verb

Chapter 5 REVIEW

Part A On your paper, write the correct words to complete the sentence.

1. A ________ tells something about the condition of the subject of the sentence.

Part B On your paper, write the verb or verb phrase in each sentence. Then write the verb tense next to it.

2. The last days of November grow cold.
3. Winter winds are feeling chilly.
4. The days will have been growing shorter.
5. The sky had become dark early in the evening.
6. The cool air was smelling fresh and clean.
7. On most days the sky has been clear.
8. There was little rain that autumn.
9. Soon the first snowfall could be here.
10. Everyone will be feeling full of energy.

Part C On your paper, write whether each verb in bold expresses *action* or a *state of being.*

11. The weather in December **stayed** cold.
12. People **got** out their winter coats.
13. "It gets cold earlier every year," Dave **complained.**
14. One day the sky **looked** gray.
15. "I can **smell** snow in the air," said Eli.

Part D On your paper, write the verb or verb phrase in each sentence. Then write whether the word *be* is a *main verb* or a *helping verb.*

16. The test is tomorrow.
17. Angela is studying her notes.
18. She always has been a good student.
19. Angela is good at math.
20. She had been captain of the math team.

Name Date Period | Mastery Test A, Page 1 | Chapter 5

Chapter 5 Mastery Test A

Part A Circle the verb or verb phrase in each sentence. Write the tense on the line.

1. Jessica had felt fine all week. ________
2. *The Joy Luck Club* is a novel by Amy Tan. ________
3. Sam appeared happy today. ________
4. Ruby will have been a teacher 10 years. ________
5. Andrea has become a nurse. ________
6. Raoul is an actor in California. ________
7. We keep food outside for the birds. ________
8. Keith will not be here tomorrow. ________
9. Pia felt rested after her vacation. ________
10. The flowers grew tall this spring. ________
11. Are you ready? ________
12. Drug education was the topic. ________
13. The air seems colder today. ________
14. The stew will taste better tomorrow. ________
15. Tyrone had become class president. ________

Part B Write the form of the verb *be* that makes each sentence correct.

16. In the spring, there will ________ a flower show.
17. Binh Pham ________ our family dentist.
18. He ________ born in Vietnam.
19. Mr. and Ms. Pettus ________ looking for a new apartment.
20. Mom ________ watching television tonight.

Basic English Grammar

TRL

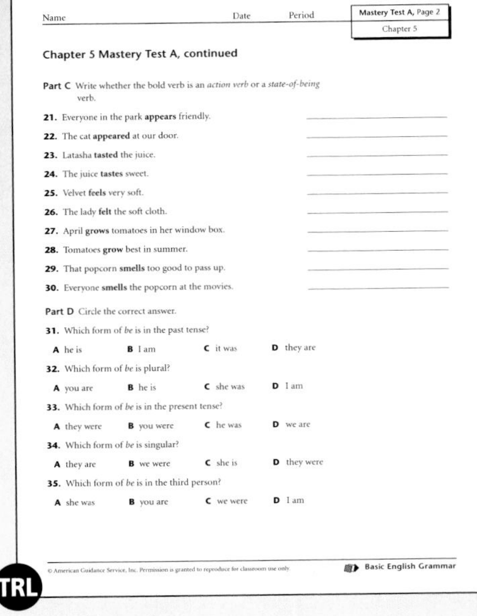
Name Date Period | Mastery Test A, Page 2 | Chapter 5

Chapter 5 Mastery Test A, continued

Part C Write whether the bold verb is an *action verb* or a *state-of-being* verb.

21. Everyone in the park **appears** friendly. ________
22. The cat **appeared** at our door. ________
23. Latasha **tasted** the juice. ________
24. The juice **tastes** sweet. ________
25. Velvet **feels** very soft. ________
26. The lady **felt** the soft cloth. ________
27. April **grows** tomatoes in her window box. ________
28. Tomatoes **grow** best in summer. ________
29. That popcorn **smells** too good to pass up. ________
30. Everyone **smells** the popcorn at the movies. ________

Part D Circle the correct answer.

31. Which form of *be* is in the past tense?
   A he is **B** I am **C** it was **D** they are
32. Which form of *be* is plural?
   A you are **B** he is **C** she was **D** I am
33. Which form of *be* is in the present tense?
   A they were **B** you were **C** he was **D** we are
34. Which form of *be* is singular?
   A they are **B** we were **C** she is **D** they were
35. Which form of *be* is in the third person?
   A she was **B** you are **C** we were **D** I am

Basic English Grammar

Chapter 5 Mastery Test A

Part E Each of these sentences contains a form of the verb *be.* On your paper, write each verb or verb phrase.

21. Lee is being stubborn.
22. I am frustrated.
23. Usually he is open minded.
24. Will he always be this difficult?
25. He has never been so angry.

Part F On your paper, write a correct form of the verb *be* in each sentence. There may be more than one correct answer.

26. "It definitely ______ snowing," Eli said.
27. "I ______ ready to go sledding," Dave said.
28. Soon the snow ______ deep enough.
29. They had ______ sledding for an hour.
30. They should ______ going home for dinner.

Part G Choose the verb form that correctly completes each sentence. On your paper, write the letter of the correct form.

31. Will Carol ______ at the meeting tomorrow?
A be **B** been **C** being **D** is

32. She ______ almost always on time.
A be **B** been **C** is **D** being

33. They ______ old friends of Antonio's.
A is **B** be **C** was **D** are

34. Everyone ______ happy about the news.
A were **B** be **C** was **D** been

35. Janaya ______ glad about the new car.
A seem **B** seems **C** seeming **D** do seem

Test-Taking Tip When studying for a test, review any tests or quizzes you took earlier that cover the same information. Make sure you have the correct answers for any items you missed.

Review Answers

Part E

21. is being **22.** am **23.** is **24.** Will be **25.** has been

Part F

26. is/was/will be **27.** am/was/will be **28.** is/was/will be **29.** been **30.** be

Part G

31. A **32.** C **33.** D **34.** C **35.** B

Name Date Period | **Mastery Test B,** Page 1 | Chapter 5

Chapter 5 Mastery Test B

Part A Write the form of the verb *be* that makes each sentence correct.

1. Mom ______ watching television tonight.
2. In the spring, there will ______ a flower show.
3. Mr. and Ms. Pettus ______ looking for a new apartment.
4. Binh Pham ______ our family dentist.
5. He ______ born in Vietnam.

Part B Circle the verb or verb phrase in each sentence. Write the tense on the line.

6. Raoul is an actor in California. ______
7. We keep food outside for the birds. ______
8. Keith will not be here tomorrow. ______
9. Jessica had felt fine all week. ______
10. *The Joy Luck Club* is a novel by Amy Tan. ______
11. Sam appeared happy today. ______
12. The air seems colder today. ______
13. The stew will taste better tomorrow. ______
14. Tyrone had become class president. ______
15. Ruby will have been a teacher 10 years. ______
16. Andrea has become a nurse. ______
17. Pia felt rested after her vacation. ______
18. The flowers grew tall this spring. ______
19. Are you ready? ______
20. Drug education was the topic. ______

 Basic English Grammar

TRL

Name Date Period | **Mastery Test B,** Page 2 | Chapter 5

Chapter 5 Mastery Test B, continued

Part C Circle the correct answer.

21. Which form of *be* is singular?
A they are **B** we were **C** she is **D** they were

22. Which form of *be* is in the third person?
A she was **B** you are **C** we were **D** I am

23. Which form of *be* is in the past tense?
A he is **B** I am **C** it was **D** they are

24. Which form of *be* is plural?
A you are **B** he is **C** she was **D** I am

25. Which form of *be* is in the present tense?
A they were **B** you were **C** he was **D** we are

Part D Write whether the bold verb is an *action verb* or a *state-of-being* verb.

26. The lady **felt** the soft cloth. ______
27. Velvet **feels** very soft. ______
28. The cat **appeared** at our door. ______
29. Everyone in the park **appears** friendly. ______
30. That popcorn **smells** too good to pass up. ______
31. Everyone **smells** the popcorn at the movies. ______
32. Tomatoes **grow** best in summer. ______
33. April **grows** tomatoes in her window box. ______
34. Latasha **tasted** the juice. ______
35. The juice **tastes** sweet. ______

 Basic English Grammar

TRL

Chapter 5 Mastery Test B

Chapter

Planning Guide

The Adverb

	Student Text Lesson				Language Skills		
	Student Pages	Vocabulary	Practice Exercises	Lesson Review	Identification Skills	Writing Skills	Punctuation Skills
Lesson 1 What Is an Adverb?	138–141	✔	✔	✔	✔	✔	✔
Lesson 2 Adverbs of Degree	142–145		✔	✔	✔	✔	✔
Lesson 3 Adverbs of Negation	146–147	✔	✔	✔	✔	✔	✔
Lesson 4 Recognizing Adverbs	148–151		✔	✔	✔	✔	✔
Lesson 5 Comparing with Adverbs	152–154		✔	✔	✔	✔	✔
Lesson 6 Using Adverbs Correctly	155–157		✔	✔	✔	✔	✔

Chapter Activities

Teacher's Resource Library

Community Connection 6: Finding Adverbs in Editorials

Media and Literature Connection 6: Adverb Poetry

Assessment Options

Student Text

Chapter 6 Review

Teacher's Resource Library

Chapter 6 Mastery Tests A and B

Student Text Features						Teaching Strategies						Learning Styles						Teacher's Resource Library			
Spelling Builder	Vocabulary Builder	Where To Find It	Writing Project	Using What You've Learned	Writing Tips/Notes/ Technology Notes	Teacher Alert	Online Connection	Applications (Home, Career, Community, Global)	Speaking Practice	Spelling Practice	Writing Practice	Auditory/Verbal	Body/Kinesthetic	Interpersonal/Group Learning	Logical/Mathematical	Visual/Spatial	LEP/ESL	Workbook Activities	Activities	Alternative Activities	Self-Study Guide
						138, 140		140			139		140	139	141			32	32	32	✔
145				143	✔		142	143, 144		145					144			33	33	33	✔
		147			✔										147			34	34	34	✔
	151											149, 150	150			149	151	35	35	35	✔
													153	153		154	153	36	36	36	✔
			157			156		157	157									37	37	37	✔

Pronunciation Key

a	hat	e	let	ī	ice	ô	order	ù	put	sh	she	ə { a	in about
ā	age	ē	equal	o	hot	oi	oil	ü	rule	th	thin	e	in taken
ä	far	ėr	term	ō	open	ou	out	ch	child	ŦH	then	i	in pencil
â	care	i	it	ȯ	saw	u	cup	ng	long	zh	measure	o	in lemon
												u	in circus

Alternative Activities

The Teacher's Resource Library (TRL) contains a set of lower-level worksheets called Alternative Activities. These worksheets cover the same content as the regular Activities but are written at a second-grade reading level.

Skill Track Software

Use the Skill Track Software for Basic English Grammar for additional reinforcement of this chapter. The software program allows students using AGS textbooks to be assessed for mastery of each chapter and lesson of the textbook. Students access the software on an individual basis and are assessed with multiple-choice items.

Chapter at a Glance

Chapter 6: The Adverb

pages 136–159

Skill Track Software for Basic English Grammar

Teacher's Resource Library TRL

- Workbook Activities 32–37
- Activities 32–37
- Alternative Activities 32–37
- Community Connection 6
- Media and Literature Connection 6
- Chapter 6 Self-Study Guide
- Chapter 6 Mastery Tests A and B

(Answer Keys for the Teacher's Resource Library begin on page 340 of this Teacher's Edition.)

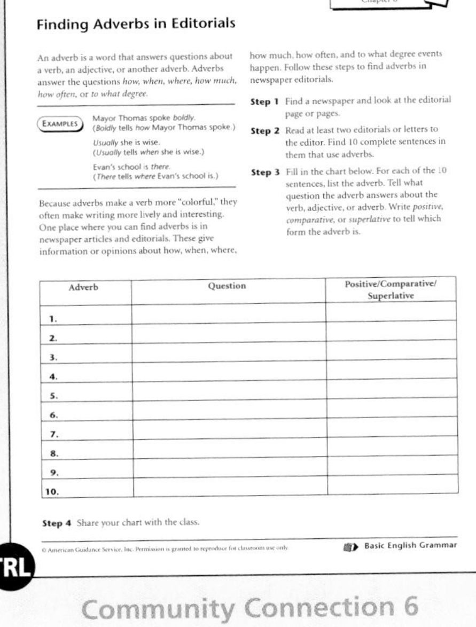

Name Date Period | Community Connection 6 | Chapter 6

Finding Adverbs in Editorials

An adverb is a word that answers questions about a verb, an adjective, or another adverb. Adverbs answer the questions *how, when, where, how much, how often,* or *to what degree.*

EXAMPLES Mayor Thomas spoke *boldly.*
(*Boldly* tells *how* Mayor Thomas spoke.)
Usually she is wise.
(*Usually* tells *when* she is wise.)
Evan's school is *there.*
(*There* tells *where* Evan's school is.)

Because adverbs make a verb more "colorful," they often make writing more lively and interesting. One place where you can find adverbs is in newspaper articles and editorials. These give information or opinions about how, when, where, how much, how often, and to what degree events happen. Follow these steps to find adverbs in newspaper editorials.

Step 1 Find a newspaper and look at the editorial page or pages.

Step 2 Read at least two editorials or letters to the editor. Find 10 complete sentences in them that use adverbs.

Step 3 Fill in the chart below. For each of the 10 sentences, list the adverb. Tell what question the adverb answers about the verb, adjective, or adverb. Write *positive, comparative,* or *superlative* to tell which form the adverb is.

Adverb	Question	Positive/Comparative/ Superlative
1.		
2.		
3.		
4.		
5.		
6.		
7.		
8.		
9.		
10.		

Step 4 Share your chart with the class.

 Basic English Grammar

TRL

Community Connection 6

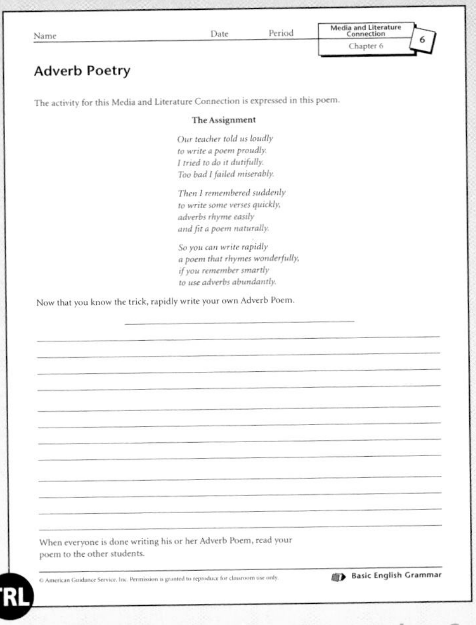

Name Date Period | Media and Literature Connection 6 | Chapter 6

Adverb Poetry

The activity for this Media and Literature Connection is expressed in this poem.

The Assignment

Our teacher told us loudly
to write a poem proudly.
I tried to do it dutifully.
Too bad I failed miserably.

Then I remembered suddenly
to write some verses quickly,
adverbs rhyme easily
and fit a poem naturally.

So you can write rapidly
a poem that rhymes wonderfully,
if you remember smartly
to use adverbs abundantly.

Now that you know the trick, rapidly write your own Adverb Poem.

When everyone is done writing his or her Adverb Poem, read your poem to the other students.

 Basic English Grammar

TRL

Media and Literature Connection 6

Chapter

The Adverb

What would you think if you saw this scene out your window? You might think, "The storm is approaching *quickly*. Lightning is striking in the distance *already*. Maybe it will strike *here next*. The tornado looks *extremely* dangerous. It has touched down on *very* open land. Maybe I should take shelter *immediately*."

The words in italics are adverbs. Adverbs answer questions about verbs, adjectives, or other adverbs.

In Chapter 6, you will learn about adverbs. Each lesson in the chapter focuses on recognizing and using adverbs correctly in sentences.

Goals for Learning

- To recognize adverbs in sentences
- To identify the word that the adverb answers questions about
- To understand adverbs of degree and adverbs of negation
- To use adverbs correctly to make comparisons

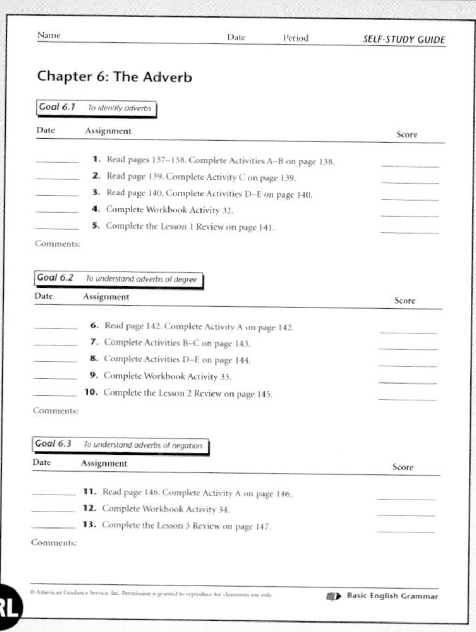

Name Date Period SELF-STUDY GUIDE

Chapter 6: The Adverb

Goal 6.1 To identify adverbs

Date	Assignment	Score
____	**1.** Read pages 137–138. Complete Activities A–B on page 138.	____
____	**2.** Read page 139. Complete Activity C on page 139.	____
____	**3.** Read page 140. Complete Activities D–E on page 140.	____
____	**4.** Complete Workbook Activity 32.	____
____	**5.** Complete the Lesson 1 Review on page 141.	____

Comments:

Goal 6.2 To understand adverbs of degree

Date	Assignment	Score
____	**6.** Read page 142. Complete Activity A on page 142.	____
____	**7.** Complete Activities B–C on page 143.	____
____	**8.** Complete Activities D–E on page 144.	____
____	**9.** Complete Workbook Activity 33.	____
____	**10.** Complete the Lesson 2 Review on page 145.	____

Comments:

Goal 6.3 To understand adverbs of negation

Date	Assignment	Score
____	**11.** Read page 146. Complete Activity A on page 146.	____
____	**12.** Complete Workbook Activity 34.	____
____	**13.** Complete the Lesson 3 Review on page 147.	____

Comments:

Basic English Grammar

TRL

Name Date Period SELF-STUDY GUIDE

Chapter 6: The Adverb, continued

Goal 6.4 To recognize adverbs in sentences

Date	Assignment	Score
____	**14.** Read page 148. Complete Activity A on page 148.	____
____	**15.** Read page 149. Complete Activities B–C on page 149.	____
____	**16.** Read page 150. Complete Activity D on page 150.	____
____	**17.** Complete Workbook Activity 35.	____
____	**18.** Complete the Lesson 4 Review on page 151.	____

Comments:

Goal 6.5 To use adverbs correctly to make comparisons

Date	Assignment	Score
____	**19.** Read page 152. Complete Activity A on page 152.	____
____	**20.** Complete Activities B–C on page 153.	____
____	**21.** Complete Workbook Activity 36.	____
____	**22.** Complete the Lesson 5 Review on page 154.	____

Comments:

Goal 6.6 To use adverbs correctly in sentences

Date	Assignment	Score
____	**23.** Read page 155. Complete Activities A–B on page 155.	____
____	**24.** Read page 156. Complete Activity C on page 156.	____
____	**25.** Complete Workbook Activity 37.	____
____	**26.** Complete the Lesson 6 Review on page 157.	____
____	**27.** Complete the Chapter 6 Review on pages 158–159.	____

Comments:

Student's Signature ____________ Date ______

Instructor's Signature ____________ Date ______

Basic English Grammar

TRL

Chapter 6 Self-Study Guide, Pages 1–2

Introducing the Chapter

Have students examine and describe the picture of the storm. Write this sentence on the board: *The funnel cloud suddenly touched the ground and raced across the land.* Ask a volunteer to circle the word that tells how the tornado touched the ground. (*suddenly*) Explain to students that *suddenly* is an adverb, or a word that tells about a verb, adjective, or another adverb. Have students read the first paragraph on page 137 and help them identify the words in italics as adverbs. Tell students that in Chapter 6 they will learn about different kinds of adverbs.

Writing Tips, Notes, and Technology Notes

Ask volunteers to read the tips and notes that appear in the margins throughout the chapter. Then discuss them with the class.

Teacher's Resource

The AGS Teaching Strategies in English Transparencies may be used with this chapter. The transparencies add an interactive dimension to expand and enhance the *Basic English Grammar* program content.

Career Interest Inventory

The AGS Harrington-O'Shea Career Decision-Making System–Revised (CDM) may be used with this chapter. Students can use the CDM to explore their interests and identify careers. The CDM defines career areas that are indicated by students' responses on the inventory.

Lesson at a Glance

Chapter 6 Lesson 1

Overview This lesson introduces adverbs as words that answer questions about verbs, adjectives, or adverbs.

Objectives

- To identify adverbs in sentences.
- To use adverbs in sentences.

Student Pages 138–141

Teacher's Resource Library 

- Workbook Activity 32
- Activity 32
- Alternative Activity 32

Vocabulary

adverb

1 Warm-Up Activity

Lead students to understand that adverbs are an essential part of our everyday language by writing the following incomplete passage on the board:

It took me _____ to get to sleep because the band was playing so _____. _____ I will sleep _____.

Ask students to fill in the blanks from the following word bank: *upstairs, tomorrow, forever, loudly.* Then have students read the definition of adverb on page 138.

2 Teaching the Lesson

Explain to students that many adverbs provide sentences with the important information *how, when,* and *where.* Remind them of the story "The Tortoise and the Hare." Ask these questions about the story: *How did the turtle race? When did the race take place? Where did the race end?*

Ask students to name single words that answer these questions from the list of "Some Common Adverbs" on page 138.

Activity A

Before students do the activity, help them identify the action verb in each sentence.

Lesson 1 What Is an Adverb?

Adverb
A word that answers questions about a verb, an adjective, or another adverb

An **adverb** is a word that answers questions about a verb, an adjective, or another adverb.

Some Common Adverbs			
again	lately	previously	today
already	next	quickly	tomorrow
badly	now	shortly	upstairs
easily	once	slowly	usually
forever	often	soon	well
here	presently	there	yesterday

We use adverbs that answer the question *how* with action verbs. These adverbs tell something about the way the action happened.

EXAMPLE
The bird chirped loudly.
Marty guessed right.
Deion works quickly.

Activity A On your paper, write the adverb that answers the question *how did the action happen.*

1. The ballerina danced gracefully.
2. The acrobat climbed the ladder quickly.
3. Kiera helped us gladly.
4. Slowly Tiffany found the answers.
5. Jorge played the game hard.

Activity B Write these sentences on your paper. Add an adverb that answers the question *how* about each verb in bold.

1. The children **ate** their dinner _______.
2. Willis **drives** his car _______.
3. Amanda **sews** _______.
4. Mrs. Barrett **sang** _______.
5. We **cleaned** the house _______.

Activity A Answers

1. gracefully 2. quickly 3. gladly
4. Slowly 5. hard

Activity B

Do the first item with the class. Give several students a chance to respond to emphasize that there are many possible answers for each item.

Activity B Answers

Sentences will vary. Adverbs should answer the question *how* about each verb in bold.

3 Reinforce and Extend

TEACHER ALERT

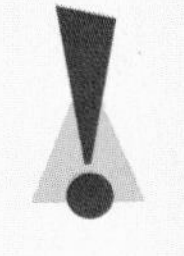

Point out that the word most commonly misused as an adverb is *good.* In everyday speech *good* is the answer to almost any *how* question. *How did you do on the test? Good. How did the baby sleep? Good. How did the team play? Good.* Explain to students that *good* is an adjective. *Well,* not *good,* properly describes action verbs.

Adverbs also answer the questions *when, how often, how long,* or *how many times.* They tell something about the time of the action or state of being.

EXAMPLE Dora will be home soon.
Kyle will speak next.
Ramon is usually happy.

Activity C Write the adverb in each sentence on your paper. The adverbs in these sentences answer the questions *when* or *how often.*

1. Please begin immediately!
2. I will go first.
3. They jumped up instantly.
4. Luis hit a home run today.
5. I saw the movie before.
6. The weather has been nice lately.
7. Sometimes I enjoy baseball.
8. Occasionally we visit our relatives in Texas.
9. The newspaper is delivered daily.
10. We trim our trees yearly.

The varsity baseball team wins often.

Activity C

Suggest that students follow these steps to help identify the adverbs in each sentence: **1.** find the verb; **2.** ask *when* or *how often* about the verb. As an example, do item 1 with students. Help them identify the verb *begin.* Then ask the question *Begin when? Begin immediately.*

Activity C Answers

1. immediately **2.** first **3.** instantly **4.** today **5.** before **6.** lately **7.** Sometimes **8.** Occasionally **9.** daily **10.** yearly

Writing Practice

Have students review the adverbs in Activity C on page 139. Then encourage them to think of other adverbs that answer the questions *when, how often, how long,* or *how many times.* Ask them to choose five of these adverbs and to use them in sentences about their own lives.

LEARNING STYLES

Interpersonal/Group Learning

Point out that adverbs may come at the beginning, middle, or end of a sentence. Have students form pairs and ask them to compose three sentences in which adverbs appear in different places. Invite partners to write model sentences on the board.

Activity D

Write these sentences on the board: *Put your books there. Go straight for one mile.* Help students find the verb in each sentence. Have them ask *where* about the verb in the first sentence and *in what direction* about the verb in the second sentence. Then have students complete Activity D on their own.

Activity D Answers

1. forward 2. near 3. high 4. backwards 5. outside 6. right 7. here 8. upstairs 9. away 10. above

Activity E

Have students complete Activity E alone or with a partner. When students have finished, invite them to share their sentences with the class.

Activity E Answers

Sentences will vary. Sentences should include the listed words used as adverbs. Adverbs should be underlined.

Global Connection

Every language has equivalent terms for such directions as *turn left, go straight,* and so on. Invite students who speak another language to give these terms in their primary language. Then encourage students to create universal signs for these directions, using pictures and symbols. Beneath each sign, students can write its meaning in English and another language.

Teacher Alert

You may wish to point out that the words *tomorrow, yesterday,* and *today* can also be nouns, as in the sentence "Tomorrow is another day." Students should check their sentences to be sure that they have used *tomorrow, yesterday,* and *today* as adverbs, not as nouns.

Adverbs also answer the questions *where* or *in what direction.* They tell something about the place of the action or state of being.

Logan lives here.
Leave your parka downstairs.
You should turn left.

Activity D Write the adverb in each sentence on your paper. The adverbs in these sentences answer the questions *where* or *in what direction.*

1. The team advanced the ball forward.
2. The storm was near.
3. Luis hit the ball high in the air.
4. He wore his baseball cap backwards.
5. Luis and Fredrick played tennis outside.
6. Turn right at the corner.
7. Hang your coat here.
8. The bedrooms are upstairs.
9. Please go away.
10. We looked at the stars above.

Activity E Write each adverb in a sentence on your paper. Then underline the adverb in each sentence.

1. tomorrow
2. never
3. still
4. yesterday
5. today
6. now
7. always
8. later
9. already
10. again

Learning Styles

Body/Kinesthetic

Ask each student to print an action verb on an index card. Collect and mix the cards. Distribute the cards and have each student make up a sentence that uses the verb and an adverb that modifies the verb on their card. Volunteers should physically demonstrate the action of the verb and the adverb as they read their sentences to the class.

140 *Chapter 6 The Adverb*

Lesson 1 REVIEW

Write the adverbs in these sentences on your paper. A sentence may have more than one adverb. Then write the question each adverb answers.

1. Yesterday, the dog happily buried his bone.
2. Today, he looked for it.
3. He barked loudly at Carla.
4. "I bet you lost your bone again," Carla scolded gently.
5. The dog jumped up and down constantly.

On your paper, complete each sentence by adding an adverb. The adverb should answer the question in parentheses about each verb in bold.

6. The students **rushed** to their desks (how?).
7. (How often?) their teacher **gave** them a surprise quiz.
8. Otis **came** in late (how often?).
9. Mr. Wong **walked** (where?).
10. The silence seemed to **last** (how long?).

On your paper, write the adverb that answers the question *how did the action happen.*

11. The gymnast jumped powerfully.
12. Gradually he learned the rules.
13. We jogged steadily for an hour.
14. He held the kitten gently.
15. Eliza sang loudly.

Write each adverb in a sentence on your paper. Then underline the adverb in each sentence.

16. first
17. here
18. inside
19. next
20. usually

Lesson 1 Review Answers

1. Yesterday—when, happily—how **2.** Today—when **3.** loudly—how **4.** again—how often, gently—how **5.** up—in what direction, down—in what direction, constantly—how often **6–10.** Responses will vary. Responses should answer the question in parentheses about the word in bold. **11.** powerfully **12.** Gradually **13.** steadily **14.** gently **15.** loudly **16–20.** Sentences will vary. Sentences should include the listed words used as adverbs. Adverbs should be underlined.

Learning Styles

Logical/Mathematical

Appoint a small group of students to serve as a "design team." They should design symbols to represent adverbs that answer the questions *how, when, how often,* and *where.* At the same time, have other groups of students compose sentences using adverbs from this lesson. Have the design team write their symbols on the board; then invite a volunteer from another group to write a sentence on the board, replacing the adverb with the appropriate symbol. Challenge the class to guess the missing adverb.

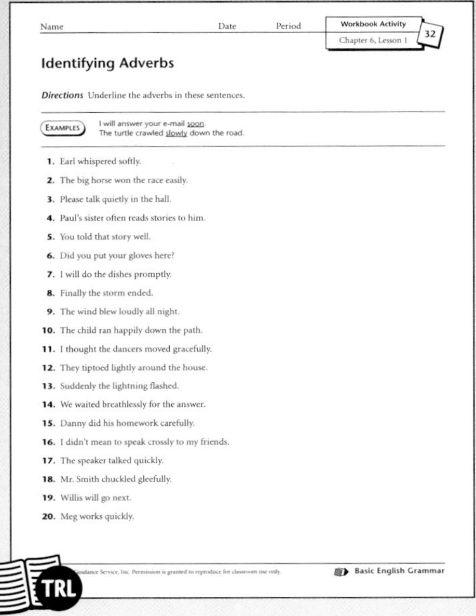

Name Date Period | Workbook Activity 32 | Chapter 6, Lesson 1

Identifying Adverbs

Directions Underline the adverbs in these sentences.

EXAMPLES I will answer your e-mail soon.
The turtle crawled slowly down the road.

1. Earl whispered softly.
2. The big horse won the race easily.
3. Please talk quietly in the hall.
4. Paul's sister often reads stories to him.
5. You told that story well.
6. Did you put your gloves here?
7. I will do the dishes promptly.
8. Finally the storm ended.
9. The wind blew loudly all night.
10. The child ran happily down the path.
11. I thought the dancers moved gracefully.
12. They tiptoed lightly around the house.
13. Suddenly the lightning flashed.
14. We waited breathlessly for the answer.
15. Danny did his homework carefully.
16. I didn't mean to speak crossly to my friends.
17. The speaker talked quickly.
18. Mr. Smith chuckled gleefully.
19. Willis will go next.
20. Meg works quickly.

 Basic English Grammar

TRL

Workbook Activity 32

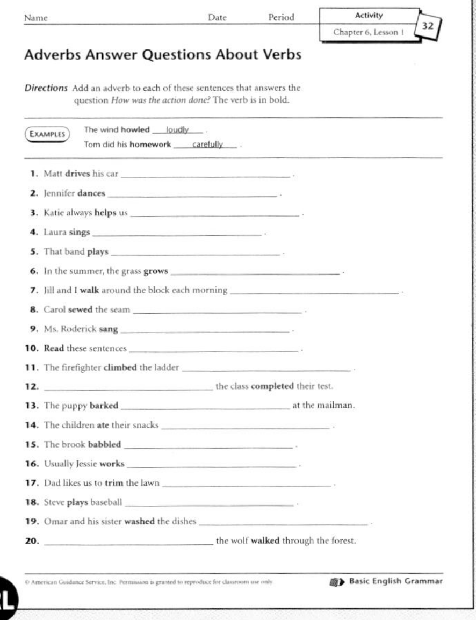

Name Date Period | Activity 32 | Chapter 6, Lesson 1

Adverbs Answer Questions About Verbs

Directions Add an adverb to each of these sentences that answers the question *How was the action done?* The verb is in bold.

EXAMPLES The wind **howled** __loudly__.
Tom did his **homework** __carefully__.

1. Matt **drives** his car __________.
2. Jennifer **dances** __________.
3. Katie always **helps** us __________.
4. Laura **sings** __________.
5. That band **plays** __________.
6. In the summer, the grass **grows** __________.
7. Jill and I **walk** around the block each morning __________.
8. Carol **sewed** the seam __________.
9. Ms. Roderick **sang** __________.
10. **Read** these sentences __________.
11. The firefighter **climbed** the ladder __________.
12. __________ the class **completed** their test.
13. The puppy **barked** __________ at the mailman.
14. The children **ate** their snacks __________.
15. The brook **babbled** __________.
16. Usually Jessie **works** __________.
17. Dad likes us to **trim** the lawn __________.
18. Steve **plays** baseball __________.
19. Omar and his sister **washed** the dishes __________.
20. __________ the wolf **walked** through the forest.

 Basic English Grammar

TRL

Activity 32

Lesson at a Glance

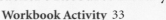

Chapter 6 Lesson 2

Overview This lesson presents adverbs of degree.

Objectives

- To identify adverbs of degree in sentences.
- To use adverbs of degree in sentences.

Student Pages 142–145

Teacher's Resource Library 

Workbook Activity 33

Activity 33

Alternative Activity 33

1 Warm-Up Activity

Write on the board the following sentence: *The car is new.* Help students identify *new* as an adjective describing the subject *car.* Then ask the class whether they can think of words that might describe *new*. Elicit from them words such as *very, almost, completely,* and *too* and write them on the board. Invite students to say the sentence with these words added. Point out that each word changes the meaning of the original sentence to some degree. Explain to students that the words they have added are known as adverbs of degree.

2 Teaching the Lesson

Have students read the definition and examples of adverbs of degree on page 142.

Then write on the board a number of simple sentences containing unmodified adjectives or adverbs. (Examples: *That car goes fast. School is over.*) Invite students to experiment with adverbs of degree that will fit in these sentences and to list them on the board. Have students check to see which words from the box on this page they have not used. Ask them to write sentences using one of the words.

Lesson 2 Adverbs of Degree

Adverbs that answer questions about adjectives and other adverbs are adverbs of degree. They answer these questions: *how much, how little, how often,* and *to what degree.*

Adverbs of Degree		
almost	extremely	rather
altogether	just	so
awfully	little	sometime
completely	nearly	too
entirely	partly	unusually
especially	quite	very

Technology Note

Using a variety of adverbs will make your writing more interesting. The thesaurus in your word processing software can help you find adverbs to replace common adverbs such as *very* or *especially.* If your software doesn't have a thesaurus, you can use an online thesaurus. Use an Internet search engine to find an online thesaurus.

The adverb of degree comes before the adjective or adverb.

EXAMPLE

How Cold?	It is very cold here. (The adverb *very* tells about the adjective *cold.*)
How Fast?	I work extremely fast. (The adverb *extremely* tells about the adverb *fast.*)

Activity A Write these sentences on your paper. Then circle the adverbs of degree.

1. His old truck is so noisy.
2. Your puppy is quite friendly.
3. That is an unusually large pumpkin.
4. He has an extremely bad headache.
5. Mark has a rather interesting idea for the project.

Activity A

Write *This is very easy* on the board. Draw an arrow from *very* to *easy* and explain that *very* answers the question *How easy?* Then have the class identify the adverb of degree and the word it tells about in the first item. (*so, noisy*) Have students complete the rest of Activity A on their own.

Activity A Answers

1. His old truck is (so) noisy. 2. Your puppy is (quite) friendly. 3. That is an (unusually) large pumpkin. 4. He has an (extremely) bad headache. 5. Mark has a (rather) interesting idea for the project.

3 Reinforce and Extend

ONLINE CONNECTION

Have students read the Technology Note on page 142. Point out that it is easy to find a thesaurus on the Internet by typing the keyword *thesaurus* into a search engine. Students should understand, however, that not all thesauruses are equally easy to use. One of the most user friendly is the Wordsmyth Educational Dictionary-Thesaurus at **www.wordsmyth.net.**

Activity B Write the adverb that tells about each adjective in bold on your paper.

1. I am almost **ready** to go.
2. Fernando was rather **happy.**
3. That coat is too **small** for you.
4. Ms. Ramos was quite **pleased** with the class.
5. They were completely **satisfied** with their new stove.
6. An extremely **strong** wind blew down the old oak tree.
7. That was a very **odd** thing for him to do.
8. She spoke in an unusually **soft** voice.
9. I'm not entirely **sure** of my plans.
10. Your kitten is so **energetic**!

Activity C Write the adverb that tells about each adverb in bold on your paper.

1. Do your homework very **carefully.**
2. Alissa works too **quickly.**
3. The band played unusually **well.**
4. I am leaving sometime **today.**
5. He went far **away.**
6. Rita left much **later** than Donya.
7. Carlo swims rather **often.**
8. The children walked quite **slowly.**
9. Ellie gets up so **early** for work.
10. She tried awfully **hard** to win the race.

Using What You've Learned

On your paper, write directions telling a friend how to do a task you know well. Use at least three adverbs in your directions. When you finish, circle each adverb and underline the verb, adjective, or adverb it tells about.

Activity B

Read through all the sentences in Activity B with students. Ask students to read aloud the adjective in bold in each sentence and to find the noun or pronoun the adjective describes. Then have students complete Activity B on their own.

Activity B Answers

1. almost **2.** rather **3.** too **4.** quite **5.** completely **6.** extremely **7.** very **8.** unusually **9.** entirely **10.** so

Activity C

Before they complete Activity C on their own, have students read aloud the adverb in bold in each sentence and tell what question it answers about the verb.

Activity C Answers

1. very **2.** too **3.** unusually **4.** sometime **5.** far **6.** much **7.** rather **8.** quite **9.** so **10.** awfully

Using What You've Learned

Before they begin writing their directions, have students practice describing their task orally to partners. Encourage partners to ask questions that will elicit adverbs in reply. Students should take note of the adverbs they use to answer these questions and employ them when they write their directions.

In the Community

Point out to students that people who participate in community programs are often asked their opinions of these programs. Whenever students are asked to evaluate community programs in which they participate, they can use adverbs of degree to effectively describe the positive and negative aspects of a program. Have students brainstorm a list of adverbs of degree that they could use.

Activity D

Ask students to tell whether the word in bold in each sentence is an adjective or adverb. Then ask for volunteers to give sample answers for the first two items in the activity.

Activity D Answers

Sentences will vary. Each sentence should include a different adverb of degree. Sample sentences follow. **1.** The extremely strong man lifted 500 pounds. **2.** Pedro is almost ready. **3.** Your new sweater is very pretty. **4.** Rhoda does her work especially well. **5.** Anne plays tennis quite often.

Activity E

Remind students that adverbs of degree answer questions about adjectives and other adverbs. Then invite volunteers to write sentences for the first two or three items in Activity E on the board. Ask them to underline the adverb of degree in each sentence. Then have the class identify the adjective or adverb each underlined adverb tells about in the sentences on the board.

Activity E Answers

Sentences will vary. Sentences should include the listed adverbs of degree. Sample sentences follow. **1.** You look very nice today. **2.** The water is too cold for swimming. **3.** Susan was quite happy when she got a raise. **4.** He is rather clumsy. **5.** Dan was somewhat surprised by the barking dog.

Activity D Write these sentences on your paper. Add an adverb of degree before each adjective or adverb in bold. Use a different adverb in each sentence.

1. The **strong** man lifted 500 pounds.
2. Pedro is **ready.**
3. Your new sweater is **pretty.**
4. Rhoda does her work **well.**
5. Anne plays tennis **often.**
6. Lin works **quickly.**
7. Dana is **late.**
8. The bus arrived **early.**
9. We watched the **small** bug crawl across the table.
10. Mom is **happy** about her new job.

Activity E Use each adverb of degree in a sentence. Write the sentences on your paper.

1. very
2. too
3. quite
4. rather
5. somewhat
6. extremely
7. unusually
8. completely
9. so
10. almost

144 Chapter 6 The Adverb

At Home

The word *very* may be one of the most over-used words in the English language. Encourage students to note how many times they use or hear the word *very* in a single conversation. Suggest that students avoid the use of *very* by using more precise language when they speak and write. For example, instead of saying, "He is very angry," they might say, "He was furious."

Learning Styles

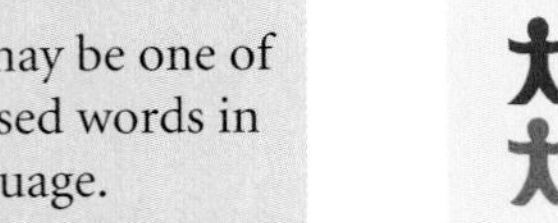

Logical/Mathematical

Divide the class into groups of four. Give each group a colorful magazine picture. Ask the groups to use their pictures to write five sentences that represent the following pattern: adjective/noun/verb/adverb of degree/adverb. (For example, a group might write *The best runner ran extremely fast.*) Afterward, invite the groups to share their pictures and sentences.

Lesson 2 REVIEW

Write the adverbs of degree in each sentence on your paper. Then use each adverb of degree in sentences of your own.

1. Rashid enjoyed his job at the bookstore very much.
2. Saturday was an unusually busy day.
3. Rashid worked quite hard.
4. Mrs. Hemsi was completely satisfied with Rashid's work.
5. "You are an exceptionally good worker," she told him.

Write each sentence on your paper. Add an adverb of degree to tell about each adjective or adverb in bold. Try to use a different adverb in each sentence.

6. I will be ready to go shopping **tomorrow.**
7. The wind was **noisy** all night.
8. Reggie was **proud** of his accomplishment.
9. Everyone was **happy** about the holiday.
10. Jia Li arrived **later.**

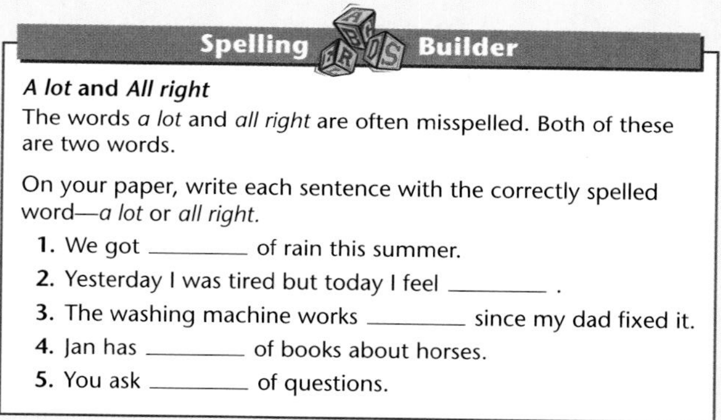

Spelling Builder

A lot* and *All right

The words *a lot* and *all right* are often misspelled. Both of these are two words.

On your paper, write each sentence with the correctly spelled word—*a lot* or *all right.*

1. We got ________ of rain this summer.
2. Yesterday I was tired but today I feel ________ .
3. The washing machine works ________ since my dad fixed it.
4. Jan has ________ of books about horses.
5. You ask ________ of questions.

Lesson 2 Review Answers

1. very 2. unusually 3. quite 4. completely 5. exceptionally Sentences will vary. Sentences should include the adverbs of degree listed in sentences 1–5. 6–10. Sentences will vary. Each sentence should have a different adverb of degree.

Spelling Builder

Point out that the misspellings *alot* and *allright* are very common because these expressions are used as one word in a sentence—*a lot* meaning "many" and *all right* meaning "well." Suggest that students who have trouble spelling these words recall the phrases with the opposite meanings. Point out that no one writes *a little* or *all wrong* as one word. Students who like rhymes might enjoy the following:

When allright is eight letters long
Someone has spelled it all wrong.

Answers to Spelling Builder: 1. a lot 2. all right 3. all right 4. a lot 5. a lot

Spelling Practice

Students frequently confuse the adverb *then,* meaning "at that time" or "next," with the conjunction *than,* meaning "in comparison with." Write these words and their definitions on the board. Then give students the following sentence to complete: *At first, our team captain ran faster* ____ (than) *any other runner, but* ____ (then) *another runner sped up and passed him.* ____ (Then) *he sped up and ran faster* ____ (than) *he'd ever run before.*

Name Date Period Workbook Activity 33 Chapter 6, Lesson 2

Finding Adverbs of Degree

Directions Underline the adverb of degree in each sentence. Then write the word that the adverb answers a question about on the line. Decide whether that word is an adjective or an adverb. Write *adjective* or *adverb* on the line next to each word.

EXAMPLE The monument was rather large. large—adjective

1. Your eyes look so blue when you wear that shirt.
2. Maurice seemed extremely angry about the accident.
3. Karen only occasionally remembers to call.
4. Caleb very rarely goes to the movies.
5. She was completely sure they were planning a surprise.
6. Norm just barely fit in the small car.
7. Laura was especially tired after the track meet.
8. Just two rooms are available at the hotel.
9. Luke nearly always forgets to carry an umbrella.
10. Very little help is available for this problem.

Directions On the line, rewrite each sentence, adding an adverb of degree. The adverb may answer a question about an adjective or about an adverb.

EXAMPLE The lemonade is refreshing. The lemonade is quite refreshing.

11. A quiet woman sat down beside me.
12. Donald and his brother ride that bus frequently.
13. The weather became cool.
14. The divers came to the surface rapidly.
15. Laura's painting seemed old-fashioned.

 Basic English Grammar

TRL

Workbook Activity 33

Name Date Period Activity 33 Chapter 6, Lesson 2

Adverbs of Degree

Directions In these sentences, the word in bold is an adjective. Circle the adverb of degree—the word that tells about the adjective.

EXAMPLE The dancers are (nearly) **ready** to perform.

1. The castle we visited is so **beautiful.**
2. Matthew was rather **tired** after working all weekend.
3. The very **powerful** waves crashed against the seashore.
4. Anna was extremely **happy** about receiving the award.
5. These pants are too **long** for my brother.

Directions In these sentences, the word in bold is an adverb. Circle the adverb of degree—the word that tells about the adverb.

EXAMPLE He is singing (unusually) **loudly** today.

6. We arrived at the party too **late.**
7. The ship sank extremely **quickly** in the harbor.
8. Pilar plays the piano exceedingly **well.**
9. The truck moved unusually **slowly.**
10. The machine breaks extraordinarily **often.**
11. Donna plays tennis quite **often.**
12. Jimmy concentrates very **hard** when he is writing.
13. Todd left for work much **sooner** than Ron.
14. Lorie speaks very **softly.**
15. We will receive his answer sometime **today.**

 Basic English Grammar

TRL

Activity 33

Lesson at a Glance

Chapter 6 Lesson 3

Overview This lesson presents adverbs of negation.

Objective

- To identify adverbs of negation.

Student Pages 146–147

Teacher's Resource Library 

Workbook Activity 34

Activity 34

Alternative Activity 34

Vocabulary

adverb of negation

1 Warm-Up Activity

Ask students what is meant when someone is said to be negative. Elicit that a negative person tends to say *no* to ideas and proposals. Point out that a sentence can be negative too. Write *We are having a great time* on the board. Challenge students to demonstrate a simple way of changing this positive sentence to a negative one. (Insert *not* after *are.*) Now write a second sentence on the board: *She always finishes first.* Ask students to replace the positive word *always* with a negative one (*never*). Encourage students to write other negative sentences using *not* and *never* on the board.

2 Teaching the Lesson

Point out that many adverbs of negation are concealed in contractions, made by combining a helping verb with the negative adverb *not.* The apostrophe takes the place of letters that are dropped when the two words are joined; for example, *did + not – o = didn't.* Then write *is, are, do, does, would, could, have,* and *has* on the board. Invite students to demonstrate how these words form contractions with *not.* Point out that *won't* for *will not* is an exception to how contractions are formed.

Lesson 3 Adverbs of Negation

Never and *not* are **adverbs of negation.** A negative adverb tells that the action will not happen or that the state of being is not present. The adverb *not* is often hidden in a contraction.

Adverb of negation
The adverbs never and not, which tell that an action in a sentence will not happen or that a state of being is not present

EXAMPLE
She is never lazy.
Anita is not at practice today.
They didn't find the key. (did not)

Remember that adverbs tell something about a verb, an adjective, or another adverb.

Writing Tip
When writing or speaking, do not use *can't* and *won't* with the adverb *hardly.* When used together, these words create a double negative.

Activity A Write these sentences on your paper. Then circle the adverbs of negation.

1. There is not enough snow to ski.
2. Fernando couldn't find his pencil.
3. It was not his fault.
4. I have never met him.
5. They haven't been there before.
6. Isn't that a beautiful painting?
7. She never answers the phone during dinner.
8. Susan would never quit her job.
9. The play didn't start on time.
10. Lynn has never been on an airplane.
11. The grocery store never closes on holidays.
12. The store won't be busy today.
13. Alex couldn't find his car keys.
14. Jennifer didn't have time to see her friends.
15. Susan doesn't live next door to Alex.

Activity A

Do the first two items on the board, having students circle just the *n't* in *couldn't.* Then have students work on their own.

Activity A Answers

1. There is (not) enough snow to ski. **2.** Fernando could(n't) find his pencil. **3.** It was (not) his fault. **4.** I have (never) met him. **5.** They have(n't) been there before. **6.** Is(n't) that a beautiful painting? **7.** She (never) answers the phone during dinner. **8.** Susan would (never) quit her job. **9.** The play did(n't) start on time. **10.** Lynn has (never) been on an airplane. **11.** The grocery store (never) closes on holidays. **12.** The store wo(n't) be busy today. **13.** Alex could(n't) find his car keys. **14.** Jennifer did(n't) have time to see her friends. **15.** Susan does(n't) live next door to Alex.

On your paper, write the adverb of negation in each sentence.

1. Ahmed won't be at play practice tonight.
2. He does not think he's good enough.
3. The director never praised Ahmed.
4. He should never quit acting.
5. We mustn't let him quit.

Rewrite these sentences on your paper. Add an adverb of negation to each sentence.

6. Greg could swim across the pool.
7. Valerie goes to the beach.
8. I have time for lunch.
9. Our neighbors have been here before.
10. Yoko did find her book.

Where To Find It

Table of Contents

You can find information in a book by reading the table of contents. A table of contents lists in order a book's chapters or sections and page numbers. The table of contents usually appears at the front of the book.

Some tables of contents will also include details about the information in the chapter.

1. Choose a book that interests you. Find the table of contents. Make sure the book has chapters or sections. Write the title of the book on your paper.
2. Write some of the chapter or section titles and the page numbers.
3. Now pick a chapter or section. Using the table of contents, find the first page of the chapter or section. Turn to that page.
4. Using the table of contents, find the first page of the next chapter or section. Continue to use the table of contents to find other chapters or sections in the book.

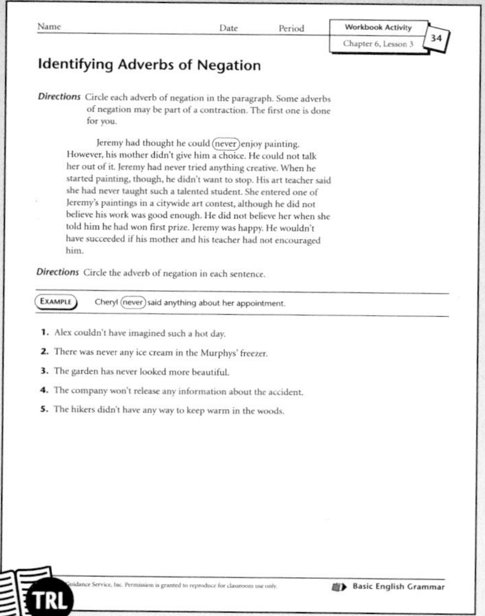

Name Date Period | Workbook Activity 34 | Chapter 6, Lesson 3

Identifying Adverbs of Negation

Directions Circle each adverb of negation in the paragraph. Some adverbs of negation may be part of a contraction. The first one is done for you.

Jeremy had thought he could (never) enjoy painting. However, his mother didn't give him a choice. He could not talk her out of it. Jeremy had never tried anything creative. When he started painting, though, he didn't want to stop. His art teacher said she had never taught such a talented student. She entered one of Jeremy's paintings in a citywide art contest, although he did not believe his work was good enough. He did not believe her when she told him he had won first prize. Jeremy was happy. He wouldn't have succeeded if his mother and his teacher had not encouraged him.

Directions Circle the adverb of negation in each sentence.

EXAMPLE Cheryl (never) said anything about her appointment.

1. Alex couldn't have imagined such a hot day.
2. There was never any ice cream in the Murphys' freezer.
3. The garden has never looked more beautiful.
4. The company won't release any information about the accident.
5. The hikers didn't have any way to keep warm in the woods.

 Basic English Grammar

TRL

Workbook Activity 34

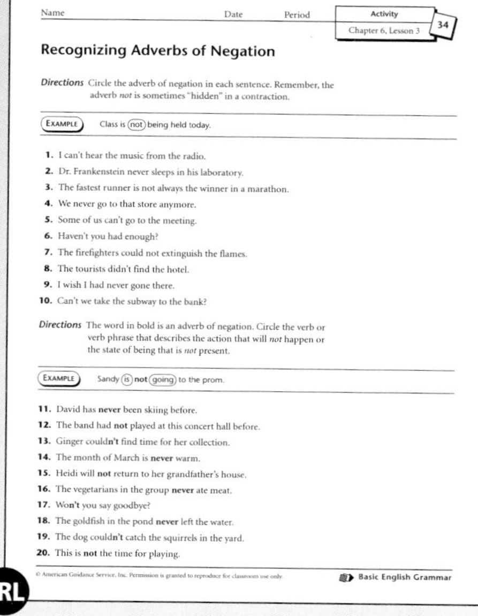

Name Date Period | Activity 34 | Chapter 6, Lesson 3

Recognizing Adverbs of Negation

Directions Circle the adverb of negation in each sentence. Remember, the adverb *not* is sometimes "hidden" in a contraction.

EXAMPLE Class is (not) being held today.

1. I can't hear the music from the radio.
2. Dr. Frankenstein never sleeps in his laboratory.
3. The fastest runner is not always the winner in a marathon.
4. We never go to that store anymore.
5. Some of us can't go to the meeting.
6. Haven't you had enough?
7. The firefighters could not extinguish the flames.
8. The tourists didn't find the hotel.
9. I wish I had never gone there.
10. Can't we take the subway to the bank?

Directions The word in bold is an adverb of negation. Circle the verb or verb phrase that describes the action that will *not* happen or the state of being that is *not* present.

EXAMPLE Sandy (is) **not** (going) to the prom.

11. David has **never** been skiing before.
12. The band had **not** played at this concert hall before.
13. Ginger could**n't** find time for her collection.
14. The month of March is **never** warm.
15. Heidi will **not** return to her grandfather's house.
16. The vegetarians in the group **never** ate meat.
17. Wo**n't** you say goodbye?
18. The goldfish in the pond **never** left the water.
19. The dog could**n't** catch the squirrels in the yard.
20. This is **not** the time for playing.

 Basic English Grammar

TRL

Activity 34

Lesson 3 Review Answers

1. n't **2.** not **3.** never **4.** never **5.** n't **6–10.** Answers for will vary. Possible answers follow. **6.** Greg could not swim across the pool. **7.** Valerie never goes to the beach. **8.** I don't have time for lunch. **9.** Our neighbors have never been here before. **10.** Yoko didn't find her book.

Where To Find It

Point out that some books have long tables of contents; others have none at all. Ask students what might account for this difference. Where would they expect to find a detailed table of contents? (*in a textbook with many section headings*) What sort of book might have no table of contents? (*a novel with untitled chapters*) Have students locate the table of contents of this book. Ask them to find the reference to this lesson.

3 Reinforce and Extend

Learning Styles

Logical/Mathematical

Point out that the unintentional use of two negative adverbs may mean the opposite of what a speaker intended. Have small groups of students prove with sentences of their own what a double negative logically means. (Example: *"If a person is not going nowhere," he or she must be going somewhere.*) Invite students to use negative words including *nowhere, nothing,* and *no one* and the prefixes *un-* and *in-*.

Lesson at a Glance

Chapter 6 Lesson 4

Overview This lesson explains how some adverbs are formed. It also provides practice in distinguishing adverbs from adjectives.

Objective

- To distinguish between adjectives and adverbs in sentences.

Student Pages 148–151

Teacher's Resource Library 

Workbook Activity 35

Activity 35

Alternative Activity 35

Warm-Up Activity

Write the words *beautiful* and *beautifully* on the board. Ask students to write sentences using these words. Have them identify what these two words describe in their sentences. Remind them that an adjective describes a noun or a pronoun and an adverb answers questions about a verb, adjective, or another adverb. Lead students to understand that *beautiful* is an adjective and *beautifully* is an adverb. Explain that this chapter will help them distinguish adjectives from adverbs.

Teaching the Lesson

If they have trouble identifying the word that an adjective or adverb describes or tells about, remind students that an adverb answers the questions *how, when, where,* or *how much.* Encourage them to ask these questions when the identity of a word is unclear. Have students look back at the examples in Lesson 1 (pages 138–141) to review the role of adverbs.

Activity A

Do this activity orally with the class. If necessary, help students figure out which word the bold word tells about.

Lesson 4 Recognizing Adverbs

Sometimes people are not sure whether a word is an adjective or an adverb. Review the definitions of these two parts of speech.

An adjective describes a noun or pronoun.

 Nina is tall.
(*Tall* describes the noun *Nina.*)

An adverb answers a question about a verb, an adjective, or another adverb.

 Nina walked outside.
(*Outside* tells where Nina *walked.*)

Activity A Write the words in bold on your paper. Next to each word, write whether it is an *adjective* or an *adverb.*

1. Baiko is **late.**
2. He is **here.**
3. That house is **large.**
4. She works **hard.**
5. He is a **hard** worker.
6. Brad lives **here.**
7. **Today** we ran.
8. We arrived **late.**
9. They arrived **later.**
10. We looked **up.**
11. He runs **fast.**
12. He's a **fast** runner.
13. He is **fast.**
14. The answer is **clear.**
15. Speak **clearly!**
16. We practice **daily.**
17. Do **daily** exercises.
18. Let's leave **early.**
19. Is this the **early** show?
20. We **usually** eat at noon.

Activity A Answers

1. late—adjective **2.** here—adverb **3.** large—adjective **4.** hard—adverb **5.** hard—adjective **6.** here—adverb **7.** Today—adverb **8.** late—adverb **9.** later—adverb **10.** up—adverb **11.** fast—adverb **12.** fast—adjective **13.** fast—adjective **14.** clear—adjective **15.** clearly—adverb **16.** daily—adverb **17.** daily—adjective **18.** early—adverb **19.** early—adjective **20.** usually—adverb

We can change many adjectives into adverbs by adding the ending *-ly.*

EXAMPLE	Adjectives	Adverbs
	The blanket is soft.	He sang softly.
	The fruit is sweet.	She smiled sweetly.
	Alex looks happy.	Fernando laughed happily.

Activity B Write the words in bold on your paper. Next to each word, write whether it is an *adjective* or an *adverb.*

1. The sea was very **calm** today.
2. The boy **quietly** watched the movie.
3. "This is an **extremely** difficult case," the lawyer said.
4. "This is an **extreme** case," the lawyer said.
5. The hikers ate lunch **hungrily.**

We can change some nouns into adverbs by adding the ending *-ly.*

EXAMPLE	Noun	Adverb
	May I have part of that?	He is partly finished.

Activity C Write the words in bold on your paper. Next to each word, write whether it is a *noun* or an *adverb.*

1. The books were in alphabetical **order.**
2. Please do things **orderly.**
3. The family shops **weekly.**
4. The bills arrive every **month.**
5. We pay our bills **monthly.**

Activity B

Write these adjectives on the board: *bad, sad, calm, brave, quick,* and *lucky.* Ask students to use each adjective in a sentence. Then ask volunteers to make each adjective an adverb by adding *-ly.* If necessary, remind students to change *y* to *i* before adding *-ly* to words that end in consonant + *y.* Ask students to use the adverbs in sentences. Students can then complete Activity B on their own.

Activity B Answers

1. calm—adjective **2.** quietly—adverb **3.** extremely—adverb **4.** extreme—adjective **5.** hungrily—adverb

Activity C

Before students complete Activity C, have them explain the difference between a noun and an adverb in their own words.

Activity C Answers

1. order—noun **2.** orderly—adverb **3.** weekly—adverb **4.** month—noun **5.** monthly—adverb

Reinforce and Extend

LEARNING STYLES

Auditory/Verbal

Ask students to listen carefully as you read each of the following sentences. Tell them to identify the phrase in each sentence that answers the question *how* or *when.* Encourage students to repeat the sentence after substituting an appropriate adverb for the phrase.

- He ran with great speed. (*fast*)
- We donate to that charity every twelve months. (*yearly*)
- She shouted in an angry way. (*angrily*)
- They ate with a great appetite. (*hungrily*)

LEARNING STYLES

Visual/Spatial

Have students find pictures in magazines that illustrate the following adverbs: *gracefully, smoothly, slowly, happily, loudly, fast, cautiously.* Ask them to write two sentences describing each picture: one using the adverb, the other using the adjective form of the same word. Invite volunteers to present their pictures, explaining how they used the adverbs and adjectives differently.

Activity D

Write these words on the board: *jolly, silly, hourly, unfriendly, nightly*. Help students identify the words that are just adjectives (*jolly, silly, unfriendly*) and those that can be used as adjectives and adverbs (*hourly, nightly*). Have students use these two words in sentences as adjectives and then as adverbs.

Activity D Answers

1. costly—adjective **2.** Only—adjective **3.** ugly—adjective **4.** quietly—adverb **5.** timely—adjective **6.** lovely—adjective **7.** early—adjective **8.** easily—adverb **9.** dangerously—adverb **10.** lively—adjective

Learning Styles

Auditory/Verbal

Read the following passage aloud and ask students to jot down words ending in *-ly* that they hear:

> The lovely Ms. Lopez sang beautifully. Usually I fall asleep at concerts, but this time I listened eagerly and applauded wildly. The tickets were not costly. Ms. Lopez performs here regularly. I look forward to her next yearly visit.

Explain to students that this passage includes eight words ending in *-ly*. Read it to them again slowly. This time ask students to identify whether the *-ly* words are adjectives or adverbs. Have pairs of students compare their answers.

Not all words ending in *-ly* are adverbs. Some common adjectives end in *-ly*, too.

Ryan received some fatherly advice from Mr. Baines.
(*Fatherly* is an adjective that describes the noun *advice*.)
Elizabeth is a friendly person.
(*Friendly* is an adjective that describes the noun *person*.)

Other words that end in *-ly* can be adjectives or adverbs.

Adjectives	Adverbs
He did the daily report.	He reported daily.
We left in the early afternoon.	We left early.

Activity D Write the words in bold on your paper. Next to each word, write whether it is an *adjective* or an *adverb*.

1. New cars are very **costly.**
2. **Only** Vanessa arrived on time.
3. That is an **ugly** cut.
4. They sat **quietly** and waited.
5. Donna's report was **timely.**
6. That is a **lovely** song.
7. Mr. Santos missed his **early** class.
8. They **easily** won first prize.
9. The car skidded **dangerously** close to us.
10. The music has a **lively** beat.

Learning Styles

Body/Kinesthetic

Prepare a set of index cards with a variety of adverbs describing *how* an action is performed. Think of actions that students would find easy to mime. (*happily, slowly, angrily, proudly,* etc.) Invite a volunteer to pick one of the cards and then give him or her a simple instruction. (Examples: *Sharpen a pencil. Read this paragraph.*) The volunteer should add the adverb on the card to the instruction given and mime it for the class. Have other students guess the adverb that was on the volunteer's card.

Lesson 4 REVIEW

Write the words in bold on your paper. Next to each word, write whether it is an *adverb,* a *noun,* or an *adjective.*

1. This **deadly** poison will get rid of all kinds of bugs.
2. Mr. Ozawa prepared his **yearly** report.
3. We receive a newspaper every **day.**
4. Please try to come to class **early.**
5. Carla smiled **happily.**

Write two sentences for each word on your paper. In the first sentence, use the word as an adjective. In the second sentence, use the word as an adverb.

6. fast
7. early
8. late
9. weekly
10. hard

Biannually* and *Biennially

Two adverbs that answer the question *when* are *biannually* and *biennially.* Say each word aloud to hear the difference in how they sound. Each has a different meaning and spelling, but people often confuse the two words. Both are adjectives when spelled without the final *-ly.*

Biannual means "twice in one year." For example: We do a *biannual* feeding of the lawn. We feed our lawn *biannually.*

Biennial means "every two years." For example: Next fall is the *biennial* election for mayor. We vote for mayor *biennially.*

On your paper, complete each sentence by adding *biannual, biennial, biannually,* or *biennially.*

1. We hold meetings ________ , or every other year.
2. The store has a ________ sale in spring and fall.
3. We get our report cards ________ , in January and June.
4. I help paint park benches every other year, during the ________ town cleanup.
5. Our trip to my aunt's house twice a year is a ________ event.

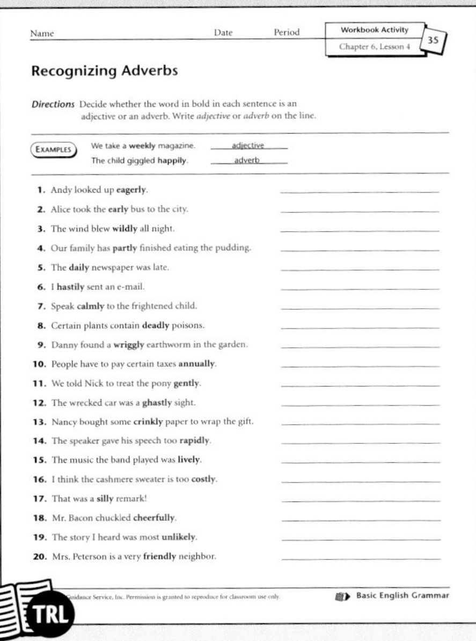

Name Date Period — Workbook Activity 35, Chapter 6, Lesson 4

Recognizing Adverbs

Directions Decide whether the word in bold in each sentence is an adjective or an adverb. Write *adjective* or *adverb* on the line.

EXAMPLES We take a **weekly** magazine. adjective
The child giggled **happily**. adverb

1. Andy looked up **eagerly**.
2. Alice took the **early** bus to the city.
3. The wind blew **wildly** all night.
4. Our family has **partly** finished eating the pudding.
5. The **daily** newspaper was late.
6. I **hastily** sent an e-mail.
7. Speak **calmly** to the frightened child.
8. Certain plants contain **deadly** poisons.
9. Danny found a **wriggly** earthworm in the garden.
10. People have to pay certain taxes **annually**.
11. We told Nick to treat the pony **gently**.
12. The wrecked car was a **ghastly** sight.
13. Nancy bought some **crinkly** paper to wrap the gift.
14. The speaker gave his speech too **rapidly**.
15. The music the band played was **lively**.
16. I think the cashmere sweater is too **costly**.
17. That was a **silly** remark!
18. Mr. Bacon chuckled **cheerfully**.
19. The story I heard was most **unlikely**.
20. Mrs. Peterson is a very **friendly** neighbor.

Basic English Grammar

TRL

Workbook Activity 35

Name Date Period — Activity 35, Chapter 6, Lesson 4

Distinguishing Adjectives and Adverbs

Directions Write an adjective or adverb to correctly complete the sentence. On the line to the right of the sentence, write whether the word you used to complete the sentence is an adjective or adverb.

EXAMPLE We practice daily. adverb

1. Sumi is ________.
2. We left ________.
3. The violin sang ________.
4. The children are ________.
5. ________ we are going.
6. We ate ________.
7. The garden is ________.
8. We are traveling ________.
9. Is this the ________ bus?
10. Her voice was ________.
11. She sang ________.
12. The sky was ________.
13. Harriet jumped ________.
14. The homework was ________.
15. Stephen lives ________.
16. Let's leave ________.
17. Brian is ________.
18. Sonja is a ________ musician.
19. She studied ________.
20. ________ he left the room.

Basic English Grammar

TRL

Activity 35

Lesson 4 Review Answers

1. deadly—adjective **2.** yearly—adjective **3.** day—noun **4.** early—adverb **5.** happily—adverb **6–10.** Sentences will vary. The first sentence in each pair should include the listed word as an adjective. The second sentence should include the listed word as an adverb.

Vocabulary Builder

Explain that the prefix *bi-* means "two." Invite students to think of words that begin with this syllable. Elicit from them familiar words such as *biweekly, bicycle,* and *bifocal.* Invite students to explain the structure of these words.

Have students form small groups, and ask them to look up the following words in a dictionary: *biathlon, bicentennial, binary, binocular, biped, biplane,* and *bivalve.* Discuss the definitions of these words with the class.

Answers to Vocabulary Builder:
1. biennially **2.** biannual **3.** biannually **4.** biennial **5.** biannual

Learning Styles

LEP/ESL

On separate note cards, write each adverb and adjective printed in bold on pages 148–151. Have students who are learning English work with English-proficient partners. Ask partners to choose a card and compose a sentence that uses the word on the card. One partner writes the sentence on the board and the other reads the sentence aloud and tells whether the word on the card was used as an adjective or an adverb.

Lesson at a Glance

Chapter 6 Lesson 5

Overview This lesson presents the positive, comparative, and superlative forms of adverbs.

Objectives

- To identify adverbs in sentences.
- To write the three degrees of comparison of adverbs.
- To use adverbs correctly to make comparisons.

Student Pages 152–154

Teacher's Resource Library 

Workbook Activity 36

Activity 36

Alternative Activity 36

1 Warm-Up Activity

Write *6 minutes, 7 minutes,* and *8 minutes* on the board under the headings *A, B,* and *C.* Explain to students that these are the times it takes students A, B, and C to run a mile. Invite students to compare B and C using a form of the word *fast.* (*B runs faster than C.*) Then ask them to compose a statement about student C using *slowly.* (*C runs most slowly* or *C runs more slowly than B and A.*) Continue to ask questions about the three "runners," using the adverbs *fast* and *slowly.*

Teaching the Lesson

Point out that the word *comparative* comes from the verb *compare.* Remind students that you compare one thing with another. When there are more than two items, the comparison becomes a superlative.

Explain to students that the endings *-er* and *-est* are never used when one item is less than the other. The words *less* and *least* apply in all cases. Have them practice using *less* and *least* in original sentences.

Lesson 5 Comparing with Adverbs

We use adverbs to make comparisons. The three forms of comparison are positive, comparative, and superlative.

EXAMPLE

Positive	Comparative	Superlative
fast	faster	fastest
slowly	more slowly	most slowly
happily	less happily	least happily
well	better	best

Use these rules to form comparisons.

Rule 1 Use the positive form to describe one person or thing.

Rule 2 Use the comparative form to compare two people or things.

Rule 3 Use the superlative form to compare more than two people or things.

Most adverbs of more than one syllable use *more* and *most* or *less* and *least* to form the comparative and superlative.

A few adverbs, such as *well,* are irregular. The comparative and superlative of *well* are *better* and *best.*

EXAMPLE Keisha finished more quickly than Zach.
Tobey worked most quickly of them all.

Activity A Write the adverbs in each of these sentences on your paper.

1. This shoe fits more comfortably than that one.
2. Of the three, that shoe fits most comfortably.
3. Victor is speaking calmly.
4. He speaks most calmly when he has practiced his speech.
5. Mr. Hong changes the oil in his car regularly.

Activity A

Invite volunteers to read aloud the three rules for forming comparisons. Encourage students to compose model sentences for each rule and to write them on the board. Then have students complete activity A on their own.

Activity A Answers

1. more comfortably **2.** most comfortably **3.** calmly **4.** most calmly **5.** regularly

Activity B Write each adverb on your paper. Next to each adverb, write its comparative and superlative forms.

Example softly—more softly, most softly

1. loudly
2. brightly
3. fast
4. well
5. gladly
6. clearly
7. skillfully
8. angrily
9. hard
10. cheerfully

Activity C Write the correct form of each adverb on your paper. Next to each one, write the form of comparison.

Example He writes (well) this year than last year.
better—comparative

1. The lights shone (brightly) tonight than any night this week.
2. Elsa sings (well) of all the soloists.
3. Dan works (hard) when he is interested.
4. Of all the students, Kim worked (quickly).
5. Zeke played the trumpet (loudly) than his brother.

This band plays more beautifully than the last band.

Activity B

You may wish to have students write their responses for Activity B in a chart similar to the one in the first example on page 152.

Activity B Answers

1. loudly—more loudly, most loudly 2. brightly—more brightly, most brightly 3. fast—faster, fastest 4. well—better, best 5. gladly—more gladly, most gladly 6. clearly—more clearly, most clearly 7. skillfully—more skillfully, most skillfully 8. angrily—more angrily, most angrily 9. hard—harder, hardest 10. cheerfully—more cheerfully, most cheerfully

Activity C

Before they complete Activity C, ask students to identify the comparative and superlative forms of the adverbs in parentheses.

Activity C Answers

1. more brightly—comparative 2. best—superlative 3. hard—positive 4. most quickly—superlative 5. more loudly—comparative

Reinforce and Extend

Learning Styles

Interpersonal/Group Learning

Write on the board the following formula: *Subject + action verb + adverb + the word* because + *noun + verb + adverb of degree + adjective.* Beneath it write the following sentence: *Ahmed swam slowly because the water was very rough.* Point out that the model sentence follows the word order of the formula. Now have students form small groups and ask them to construct sentences following the same pattern. Encourage them to add adverbs of negation (*not* and *never*) when they are appropriate. Invite groups to write model sentences on the board.

Learning Styles

Body/Kinesthetic

Divide the class into groups of five. Ask each group to choose one adverb from the list in Activity B on page 153 and to write a skit in which they use the positive, comparative, and superlative forms of the chosen adverb. Afterward, have each group perform its skit. Encourage the other students to raise their hands as they hear the three uses of the adverb.

Learning Styles

LEP/ESL

Have students form groups including English language learners and fluent English speakers. Each group should choose five adverbs that answer the question *how* and write them on index cards. Prepare a set of prompt cards on which you have written *positive, comparative,* and *superlative.* Have groups exchange cards with each other. Then ask each group to choose a prompt card and to create sentences using their adverbs and the prompts. Have groups share their sentences.

Lesson 5 Review Answers

1. faster—comparative **2.** hard—positive **3.** best—superlative **4.** less quickly—comparative **5.** more loudly—comparative **6.** least happily—superlative **7.** better—comparative **8.** most loudly—superlative **9.** more quietly—comparative **10.** well—positive **11.** bravely—more bravely, most bravely **12.** slowly—more slowly, most slowly **13.** well—better, best **14.** gracefully—more gracefully, most gracefully **15.** politely—more politely, most politely **16.** sweetly—more sweetly, most sweetly **17.** noisily—more noisily, most noisily **18.** briskly—more briskly, most briskly **19.** sadly—more sadly, most sadly **20.** kindly—more kindly, most kindly

LEARNING STYLES

Visual/Spatial

Ask students to write 10 sentences about a subject that interests them, using a variety of positive, comparative, and superlative adverbs. Encourage them to stick to one theme—music, sports, movies—and to refer to real people and events. Have students exchange their papers for peer editing. Suggest that students reinforce their sentences with illustrations. Have them display their work on a bulletin board.

Lesson 5 REVIEW

Write the adverb in each sentence on your paper. Next to each adverb, write the form of comparison.

1. Gordon runs the mile faster than Rafael.
2. Everyone in class worked hard.
3. I work best when I am rested.
4. Hans reads less quickly than Mike.
5. The choir sang the chorus more loudly than the verses.
6. Everyone worked least happily at the end of the day.
7. I like apples better than pears.
8. The winds howled most loudly at midnight.
9. The children played more quietly after lunch.
10. Irene plays the drums well.

Write these adverbs on your paper. Next to each adverb, write its comparative and superlative forms.

11. bravely
12. slowly
13. well
14. gracefully
15. politely
16. sweetly
17. noisily
18. briskly
19. sadly
20. kindly

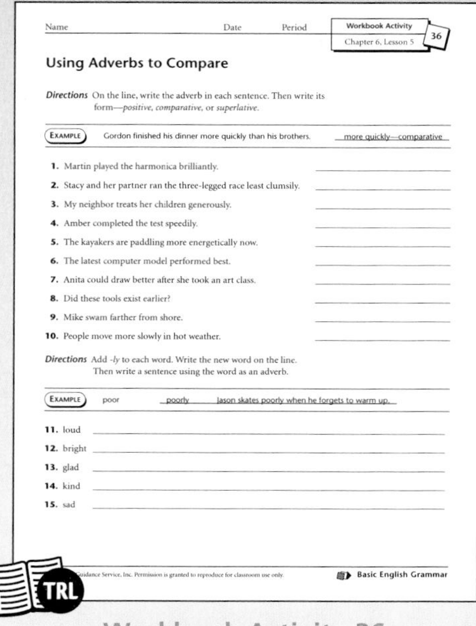

Name ____ Date ____ Period ____

Workbook Activity 36
Chapter 6, Lesson 5

Using Adverbs to Compare

Directions On the line, write the adverb in each sentence. Then write its form—*positive, comparative,* or *superlative.*

EXAMPLE Gordon finished his dinner more quickly than his brothers. more quickly—comparative

1. Martin played the harmonica brilliantly. ____
2. Stacy and her partner ran the three-legged race least clumsily. ____
3. My neighbor treats her children generously. ____
4. Amber completed the test speedily. ____
5. The kayakers are paddling more energetically now. ____
6. The latest computer model performed best. ____
7. Anita could draw better after she took an art class. ____
8. Did these tools exist earlier? ____
9. Mike swam farther from shore. ____
10. People move more slowly in hot weather. ____

Directions Add *-ly* to each word. Write the new word on the line. Then write a sentence using the word as an adverb.

EXAMPLE poor poorly Jason skates poorly when he forgets to warm up.

11. loud ____
12. bright ____
13. glad ____
14. kind ____
15. sad ____

Basic English Grammar

TRL

Workbook Activity 36

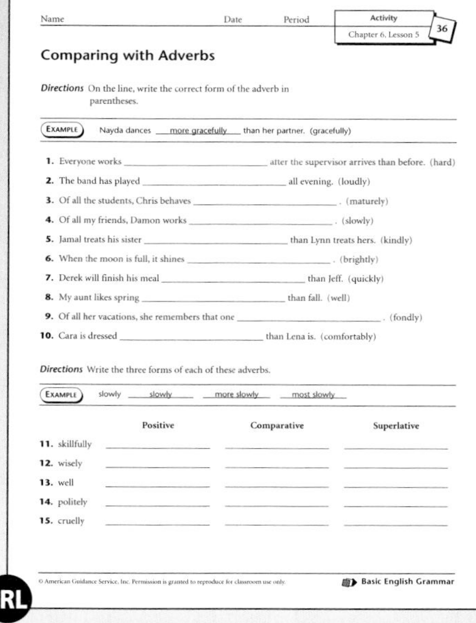

Name ____ Date ____ Period ____

Activity 36
Chapter 6, Lesson 5

Comparing with Adverbs

Directions On the line, write the correct form of the adverb in parentheses.

EXAMPLE Nayda dances more gracefully than her partner. (gracefully)

1. Everyone works ____ after the supervisor arrives than before. (hard)
2. The band has played ____ all evening. (loudly)
3. Of all the students, Chris behaves ____. (maturely)
4. Of all my friends, Damon works ____. (slowly)
5. Jamal treats his sister ____ than Lynn treats hers. (kindly)
6. When the moon is full, it shines ____. (brightly)
7. Derek will finish his meal ____ than Jeff. (quickly)
8. My aunt likes spring ____ than fall. (well)
9. Of all her vacations, she remembers that one ____. (fondly)
10. Cara is dressed ____ than Lena is. (comfortably)

Directions Write the three forms of each of these adverbs.

EXAMPLE slowly slowly more slowly most slowly

	Positive	Comparative	Superlative
11. skillfully	____	____	____
12. wisely	____	____	____
13. well	____	____	____
14. politely	____	____	____
15. cruelly	____	____	____

Basic English Grammar

TRL

Activity 36

Lesson 6 Using Adverbs Correctly

Adverbs often tell when the action in a sentence is taking place. *Ago* indicates past time. *Later* indicates future time. The tense of the verb in a sentence and the adverb must agree.

Lila sang long ago.	(past action)
Sarah sang yesterday.	(past action)
Reggie will sing later.	(future action)
Troy will sing next.	(future action)

Activity A In these sentences, the adverbs are in bold. On your paper, write each sentence using the correct tense of the verb in parentheses. Use helping verbs if needed.

1. We (go) there a year **ago.**
2. **Yesterday** we (be) late to class.
3. Felice (arrive) **soon.**
4. The dog (eat) his dinner **now.**
5. We (paint) the house **before.**

Use an adverb in a sentence when answering a question about a verb.

EXAMPLE

Correct	She sighed softly. (How did she sigh? *softly*)
Incorrect	She sighed soft. (*Soft* is an adjective.)

Activity B Write the correct word to complete each sentence on your paper. Check your answers by reading the sentences aloud.

1. Fernando laughed (happy, happily).
2. The rain fell (rapid, rapidly).
3. She left home (quick, quickly).
4. Sit there (quiet, quietly)!
5. Melissa dances (graceful, gracefully).

Lesson at a Glance

Chapter 6 Lesson 6

Overview This lesson focuses on using adverbs correctly.

Objectives

- To use the correct verb tense with adverbs of time.
- To use an adverb to tell about a verb.
- To use *good* and *well* correctly.

Student Pages 155–157

Teacher's Resource Library 

Workbook Activity 37

Activity 37

Alternative Activity 37

1 Warm-Up Activity

Write on the board *Me speaks English good.* Challenge students to make the necessary corrections to turn this sentence into standard English. (*I speak English well.*) Have the class explain each change. Point out that some people would leave the word *good* unaltered. Lead students to understand that *good* is an adjective and cannot describe the way a person speaks. Ask students what they do well, and have them answer in complete sentences. (Example: *I play basketball well.*) Point out that while *good* is often used as an adverb in conversation, it is not acceptable in writing or in formal speech.

2 Teaching the Lesson

Write *tomorrow, ago,* and *now* on the board in one column. In a second column, write *am eating, will play,* and *went bowling.* Invite students to write a sentence using an item in column 1 in combination with an item in column 2. (Example: *Tomorrow I will play lacrosse.*) Ask students what the words in column 1 have in common. Help students conclude that they are all adverbs indicating time. Lead students to understand that adverbs can determine the tense of a verb. Have students compose other sentences with *yesterday, later, next,* and *soon.*

Activity A

Suggest that students read each sentence to themselves with the answer in place to see whether it makes sense. Point out that some items have more than one correct answer.

Activity A Answers

1. We went there a year ago. 2. Yesterday we were late to class. 3. Felice will arrive soon. 4. The dog eats/is eating/will eat his dinner now. 5. We painted/have painted the house before.

Activity B

Do the first item with students. Encourage them to explain why happily is the correct answer. (*The word must describe* laughed, *which is a verb, therefore, the adverb* happily *is the correct choice.*)

Activity B Answers

1. happily 2. rapidly 3. quickly 4. quietly 5. gracefully

Activity C

Be sure students have a clear understanding of when to use *good* and *well.* Then do the first two items in Activity C with the class. Help students determine why *good* is the correct answer for item 1 and *well* is the correct answer for item 2. Then have students complete Activity C on their own. Some students may benefit from working with a partner. Encourage partners to discuss each item before writing their responses.

Activity C Answers

1. good **2.** well **3.** good **4.** well **5.** well/good **6.** well **7.** well **8.** good **9.** well **10.** well/good

Reinforce and Extend

TEACHER ALERT

The use of *good* and *well* causes problems for many students. Check students' responses to Activity C to get an indication of which students need additional support with this skill. Offer one-on-one instruction or suggest that students work in small groups with students who have mastered the usage of *good* and *well.*

Good is always an adjective and describes a noun. Do not use *good* to answer questions about a verb.

Correct	We had a good day. (What kind of day? We had a *good* day.)
Incorrect	They worked good together. (Do not use the adjective *good* to answer the question *how did they work.*)

Well is usually an adverb. *Well* means to do something correctly.

She speaks well.
(How does she speak? She speaks *well.*)

Well is an adjective when it describes someone's health. *Good* and *well* can follow state-of-being verbs. Either *good* or *well* will work in the following example sentence.

EXAMPLE

I feel good today.	(describes emotions)
I feel well today.	(describes health)

Activity C Decide whether to complete each sentence with *good* or *well.* Write your answers on your paper.

1. Carol is ______ at arithmetic.
2. Dan dances very ______ .
3. She did her ______ deed for the day.
4. Mike always does his work ______ .
5. Larry isn't feeling ______ today.
6. Billy does everything ______ .
7. Ellie paints very ______ .
8. Ming had a ______ game yesterday.
9. Ashley sings ______ .
10. Do you feel ______ enough to go to school?

156 Chapter 6 The Adverb

Lesson 6 REVIEW

Rewrite each of these sentences correctly on your paper.

1. Yesterday we are late to class.
2. Yo-Yo Ma plays the cello very good.
3. Owen and I are well friends.
4. "Julio spoke now," the teacher reminds the class.
5. Sandy always talks very soft.

The word in bold in each sentence is an adverb. Write the correct verb to complete each sentence on your paper. Next to each verb, write its tense.

6. **Tomorrow** we (go) to work.
7. We (eat) at that restaurant a long time **ago.**
8. Our friends (arrive) **soon.**
9. The men (clean) our rug **yesterday.**
10. I (wash) the car **now.**

Writing Project

Using Adverbs

We use adverbs to answer questions about verbs, adjectives, and other adverbs.

On your paper, write a paragraph that describes a job you think you would enjoy. Your paragraph should have at least five sentences. When you finish, go back and underline all of the adverbs in your paragraph. Then share your paragraph with a classmate.

Answer these questions in your paragraph:

- Where does someone do this job?
- When does someone do this job?
- What do these workers do at work? Be specific.
- Why does this job seem interesting?
- How is this job different from or better than other jobs?

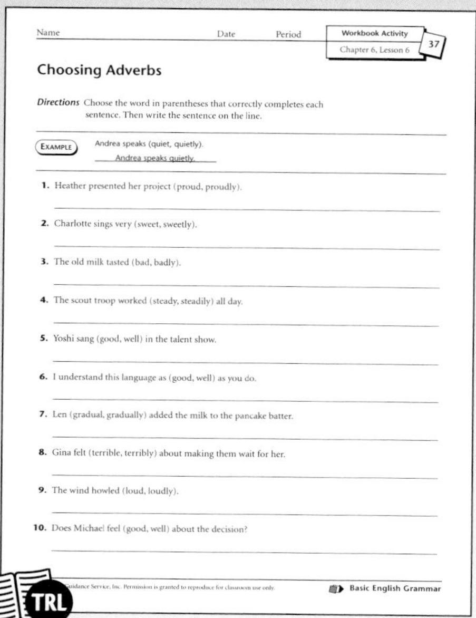

Name Date Period

Workbook Activity 37
Chapter 6, Lesson 6

Choosing Adverbs

Directions Choose the word in parentheses that correctly completes each sentence. Then write the sentence on the line.

EXAMPLE Andrea speaks (quiet, quietly).
Andrea speaks quietly.

1. Heather presented her project (proud, proudly).
2. Charlotte sings very (sweet, sweetly).
3. The old milk tasted (bad, badly).
4. The scout troop worked (steady, steadily) all day.
5. Yoshi sang (good, well) in the talent show.
6. I understand this language as (good, well) as you do.
7. Len (gradual, gradually) added the milk to the pancake batter.
8. Gina felt (terrible, terribly) about making them wait for her.
9. The wind howled (loud, loudly).
10. Does Michael feel (good, well) about the decision?

Basic English Grammar

TRL

Workbook Activity 37

Name Date Period

Activity 37
Chapter 6, Lesson 6

Using Adverbs Correctly

Directions On the line, rewrite the verb that is in the parentheses, using the correct tense. Remember, the tense of the verb must agree with the adverb, which appears in bold.

EXAMPLE I (call) you **yesterday**. called

1. We (go) **later**.
2. Rosie and I (tell) him **tomorrow**.
3. Harry will (find) it **soon**.
4. We (take) the train **before**.
5. **Now** the teacher (show) the class.
6. Chuckie (sing) with the microphone **next**.
7. **After** Ben goes, Jared (go).
8. Stephanie **already** (go).
9. Thomas (drive) **yesterday**.
10. **Long ago** the pioneers (travel) west.

Directions Underline the word that is used incorrectly and write the corrected adverb on the line.

EXAMPLE The train moved swift. swiftly

11. Trudy sings beautiful.
12. The ice melted slow.
13. The baby slept peaceful.
14. The rabbit ran rapid.
15. The rain fell gentle to the ground.
16. Geraldo ate hearty.
17. The children eager asked for more.
18. That performance was nice done.
19. The music soft lulled her to sleep.
20. We cheered loud.

Basic English Grammar

TRL

Activity 37

Lesson 6 Review Answers

1. Yesterday we were late to class.
2. Yo-Yo Ma plays the cello very well.
3. Owen and I are good friends.
4. "Julio is speaking now," the teacher reminds the class. 5. Sandy always talks very softly. 6. will go—future 7. ate—past 8. will arrive—future 9. cleaned—past 10. wash—present, will wash—future, am washing—present

Speaking Practice

Call on volunteers to read aloud sentences 1–5 as they appear on page 157. Invite other volunteers to repeat each sentence aloud but to improve it by using the correct verb form.

Writing Project

Before they begin to write, have students form small groups and describe to each other the jobs they have in mind. Ask them to make sure that they have precise answers to the five questions in the Writing Project. Remind students that specific details make writing interesting.

CAREER CONNECTION

Engage students in a discussion of the kinds of things people can do to help themselves get a job. Then divide the class into small groups and have each group of students create a poster with a list of guidelines or tips for successful job hunting. Tell students to try to use at least one adverb in each tip or guideline. Offer the following as examples: *Dress neatly. Speak confidently. Arrive early for your interview.*

Chapter 6 Review

Use the Chapter Review to prepare students for tests and to reteach content from the chapter.

Chapter 6 Mastery Test 

The Teacher's Resource Library includes two parallel forms of the Chapter 6 Mastery Test. The difficulty level of the two forms is equivalent. You may wish to use one form as a pretest and the other form as a posttest.

Review Answers

Part A

1. adverb of negation **2.** adverb

Part B

3. early **4.** not, so **5.** anyway **6.** extremely

Part C

7. lately—adverb **8.** early—adjective **9.** daily—adjective **10.** well—adverb **11.** order—noun **12.** orderly—adjective **13.** orderly—adverb **14.** weekly—adjective **15.** weekly—adverb

Part D

16–20. Answers will vary. Adverbs should answer the question in parentheses. Sample answers follow. **16.** Gordon is going fishing today. **17.** Put the paper here. **18.** Fran has been to the restaurant frequently. **19.** Keisha plays the piano beautifully. **20.** I will call you tomorrow.

Chapter 6 REVIEW

Word Bank
adverb
adverb of negation

Part A On a sheet of paper, write the correct word or words from the Word Bank to complete each sentence.

1. An ________ tells that an action in a sentence will not happen or that a state of being is not present.

2. An ________ answers questions about a verb, an adjective, or another adverb.

Part B Write all the adverbs in these sentences on your paper. A sentence may have more than one adverb.

3. A heavy snowfall arrived early in December.

4. At home Alex was not so pleased.

5. He went to work anyway.

6. He knew the roads would be extremely slippery.

Part C Write the words in bold on your paper. Next to each word, write whether it is an *adjective*, a *noun*, or an *adverb*.

7. Where have you been **lately**?

8. They went to Winnipeg on the **early** train.

9. We listened to the **daily** weather report.

10. Dan plays the guitar very **well.**

11. I put the files in **order.**

12. Carmen's desk is very **orderly.**

13. Please get in line **orderly.**

14. Did you get the **weekly** report?

15. They turn in the assignments **weekly.**

Part D On your paper, complete each sentence with an adverb that answers the question in parentheses.

16. Gordon is going fishing (when?).

17. Put the paper (where?).

18. Fran has been to the restaurant (how many times?).

19. Keisha plays the piano (how?).

20. I will call you (when?).

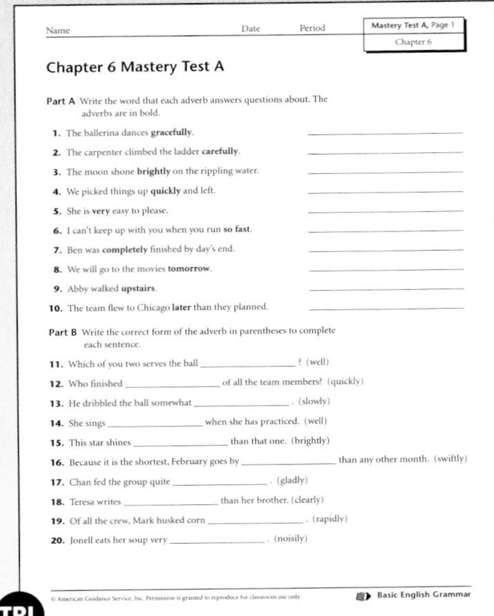

Name ______ Date ______ Period ______ Mastery Test A, Page 1 Chapter 6

Chapter 6 Mastery Test A

Part A Write the word that each adverb answers questions about. The adverbs are in bold.

1. The ballerina dances **gracefully**. ________

2. The carpenter climbed the ladder **carefully**. ________

3. The moon shone **brightly** on the rippling water. ________

4. We picked things up **quickly** and left. ________

5. She is **very** easy to please. ________

6. I can't keep up with you when you run **so fast**. ________

7. Ben was **completely** finished by day's end. ________

8. We will go to the movies **tomorrow**. ________

9. Abby walked **upstairs**. ________

10. The team flew to Chicago **later** than they planned. ________

Part B Write the correct form of the adverb in parentheses to complete each sentence.

11. Which of you two serves the ball ________? (well)

12. Who finished ________ of all the team members? (quickly)

13. He dribbled the ball somewhat ________. (slowly)

14. She sings ________ when she has practiced. (well)

15. This star shines ________ than that one. (brightly)

16. Because it is the shortest, February goes by ________ than any other month. (swiftly)

17. Chan fed the group quite ________. (gladly)

18. Teresa writes ________ than her brother. (clearly)

19. Of all the crew, Mark husked corn ________. (rapidly)

20. Jonell eats her soup very ________. (noisily)

 Basic English Grammar

TRL

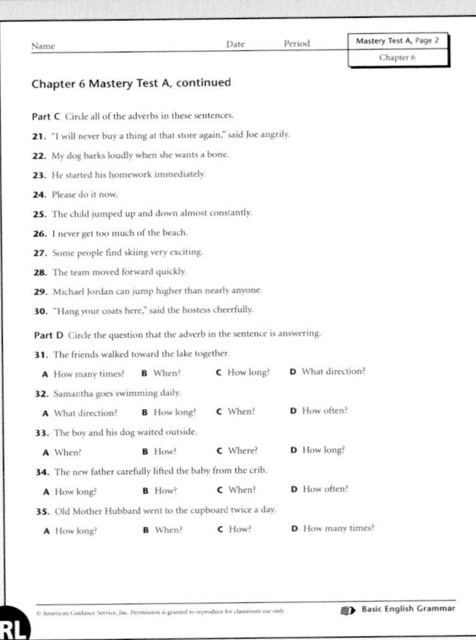

Name ______ Date ______ Period ______ Mastery Test A, Page 2 Chapter 6

Chapter 6 Mastery Test A, continued

Part C Circle all of the adverbs in these sentences.

21. "I will never buy a thing at that store again," said Joe angrily.

22. My dog barks loudly when she wants a bone.

23. He started his homework immediately.

24. Please do it now.

25. The child jumped up and down almost constantly.

26. I never get too much of the beach.

27. Some people find skiing very exciting.

28. The team moved forward quickly.

29. Michael Jordan can jump higher than nearly anyone.

30. "Hang your coats here," said the hostess cheerfully.

Part D Circle the question that the adverb in the sentence is answering.

31. The friends walked toward the lake together.

A How many times? **B** When? **C** How long? **D** What direction?

32. Samantha goes swimming daily.

A What direction? **B** How long? **C** When? **D** How often?

33. The boy and his dog waited outside.

A When? **B** How? **C** Where? **D** How long?

34. The new father carefully lifted the baby from the crib.

A How long? **B** How? **C** When? **D** How often?

35. Old Mother Hubbard went to the cupboard twice a day.

A How long? **B** When? **C** How? **D** How many times?

 Basic English Grammar

TRL

Chapter 6 Mastery Test A

Part E Write these sentences on your paper. Add an adverb of degree before each adjective or adverb in bold. Use a different adverb in each sentence.

21. The chili was **salty.**

22. He was a **dedicated** student.

23. They are **interested** in buying the car.

24. She will be **happy** to hear that.

Part F Write the adverbs of negation in these sentences on your paper.

25. The boys never went to a meeting.

26. We shouldn't jump to conclusions.

27. She won't be attending class today.

Part G On your paper, write the letter of the adverb that correctly completes each sentence.

28. The class did ________ on the test.

A good **B** well **C** bad **D** gooder

29. The truck was moving ________ .

A fast **B** fastly **C** good **D** quick

30. Russ spoke ________ to the reporter.

A calm **B** calmlier **C** calmly **D** more calm

Part H Write each adverb on your paper. Next to each adverb, write its comparative and superlative forms. Then use each adverb in sentences of your own.

31. smoothly

32. lovely

33. easily

34. regularly

35. lively

Test-Taking Tip Count the number of answers on your paper. Make sure the number of answers matches the number of items on the test.

Review Answers

Part E

Answers will vary. Possible responses are given. **21.** The chili was too salty. **22.** He was an extremely dedicated student. **23.** They are quite interested in buying the car. **24.** She will be so happy to hear that.

Part F

25. never **26.** n't **27.** n't

Part G

28. B **29.** A **30.** C

Part H

31. smoothly—more smoothly, most smoothly **32.** lovely—lovelier, loveliest **33.** easily—more easily, most easily **34.** regularly—more regularly, most regularly **35.** lively—livelier, liveliest Sentences will vary.

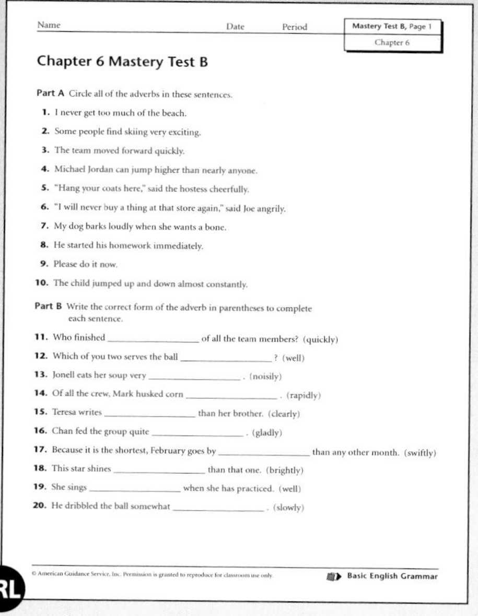

Name Date Period | Mastery Test B, Page 1 | Chapter 6

Chapter 6 Mastery Test B

Part A Circle all of the adverbs in these sentences.

1. I never get too much of the beach.

2. Some people find skiing very exciting.

3. The team moved forward quickly.

4. Michael Jordan can jump higher than nearly anyone.

5. "Hang your coats here," said the hostess cheerfully.

6. "I will never buy a thing at that store again," said Joe angrily.

7. My dog barks loudly when she wants a bone.

8. He started his homework immediately.

9. Please do it now.

10. The child jumped up and down almost constantly.

Part B Write the correct form of the adverb in parentheses to complete each sentence.

11. Who finished ________ of all the team members? (quickly)

12. Which of you two serves the ball ________ ? (well)

13. Jonell eats her soup very ________ . (noisily)

14. Of all the crew, Mark husked corn ________ . (rapidly)

15. Teresa writes ________ than her brother. (clearly)

16. Chan fed the group quite ________ . (gladly)

17. Because it is the shortest, February goes by ________ than any other month. (swiftly)

18. This star shines ________ than that one. (brightly)

19. She sings ________ when she has practiced. (well)

20. He dribbled the ball somewhat ________ . (slowly)

 Basic English Grammar

TRL

Name Date Period | Mastery Test B, Page 2 | Chapter 6

Chapter 6 Mastery Test B, continued

Part C Circle the question that the adverb in the sentence is answering.

21. The boy and his dog waited outside.

A When? **B** How? **C** Where? **D** How long?

22. The new father carefully lifted the baby from the crib.

A How long? **B** How? **C** When? **D** How often?

23. Old Mother Hubbard went to the cupboard twice a day.

A How long? **B** When? **C** How? **D** How many times?

24. The friends walked toward the lake together.

A How many times? **B** When? **C** How long? **D** What direction?

25. Samantha goes swimming daily.

A What direction? **B** How long? **C** When? **D** How often?

Part D Write the word that each adverb answers questions about. The adverbs are in bold.

26. We will go to the movies **tomorrow**. ________

27. Abby walked **upstairs**. ________

28. The team flew to Chicago **later** than they planned. ________

29. We picked things up **quickly** and left. ________

30. She is **very** easy to please. ________

31. I can't keep up with you when you run **so fast**. ________

32. Ben was **completely** finished by day's end. ________

33. The ballerina dances **gracefully**. ________

34. The carpenter climbed the ladder **carefully**. ________

35. The moon shone **brightly** on the rippling water. ________

 Basic English Grammar

TRL

Chapter 6 Mastery Test B

Chapter

7

Planning Guide

The Preposition

	Student Text Lesson				Language Skills		
	Student Pages	Vocabulary	Practice Exercises	Lesson Review	Identification Skills	Writing Skills	Punctuation Skills
Lesson 1 What Is a Preposition?	162–165	✔	✔	✔	✔	✔	✔
Lesson 2 The Object of the Preposition	166–169		✔	✔	✔	✔	✔
Lesson 3 The Prepositional Phrase Used as an Adjective	170–172	✔	✔	✔	✔	✔	✔
Lesson 4 The Prepositional Phrase Used as an Adverb	173–175	✔	✔	✔	✔	✔	✔
Lesson 5 Preposition or Adverb?	176–177		✔	✔	✔	✔	✔

Chapter Activities

Teacher's Resource Library

Community Connection 7:
Using Prepositions to Give Directions

Media and Literature Connection 7:
My Great Adventure Getting Here

Assessment Options

Student Text

Chapter 7 Review

Teacher's Resource Library

Chapter 7 Mastery Tests A and B

Student Text Features						Teaching Strategies						Learning Styles						Teacher's Resource Library			
Spelling Builder	Vocabulary Builder	Where To Find It	Writing Project	Using What You've Learned	Writing Tips/Notes/Technology Notes	Teacher Alert	Online Connection	Applications (Home, Career, Community, Global)	Speaking Practice	Spelling Practice	Writing Practice	Auditory/Verbal	Body/Kinesthetic	Interpersonal/Group Learning	Logical/Mathematical	Visual/Spatial	LEP/ESL	Workbook Activities	Activities	Alternative Activities	Self-Study Guide
165								164	164	165		163	163			164	164	38	38	38	✔
	169			167	✔	167		167, 168						169	168			39	39	39	✔
		172			✔	171		171								172		40	40	40	✔
					✔	175					175	173	174	174			174	41	41	41	✔
			177				177											42	42	42	✔

Pronunciation Key

a	hat	e	let	ī	ice	ô	order	ů	put	sh	she	ə { a	in about
ā	age	ē	equal	o	hot	oi	oil	ü	rule	th	thin	e	in taken
ä	far	ėr	term	ō	open	ou	out	ch	child	ŦH	then	i	in pencil
â	care	i	it	ȯ	saw	u	cup	ng	long	zh	measure	o	in lemon
												u	in circus

Alternative Activities

The Teacher's Resource Library (TRL) contains a set of lower-level worksheets called Alternative Activities. These worksheets cover the same content as the regular Activities but are written at a second-grade reading level.

Skill Track Software

Use the Skill Track Software for Basic English Grammar for additional reinforcement of this chapter. The software program allows students using AGS textbooks to be assessed for mastery of each chapter and lesson of the textbook. Students access the software on an individual basis and are assessed with multiple-choice items.

Chapter at a Glance

Chapter 7: The Preposition

Skill Track Software for Basic English Grammar

Teacher's Resource Library

- **Workbook Activities** 38–42
- **Activities** 38–42
- **Alternative Activities** 38–42
- **Community Connection** 7
- **Media and Literature Connection** 7
- **Chapter 7 Self-Study Guide**
- **Chapter 7 Mastery Tests A and B**

(Answer Keys for the Teacher's Resource Library begin on page 340 of this Teacher's Edition.)

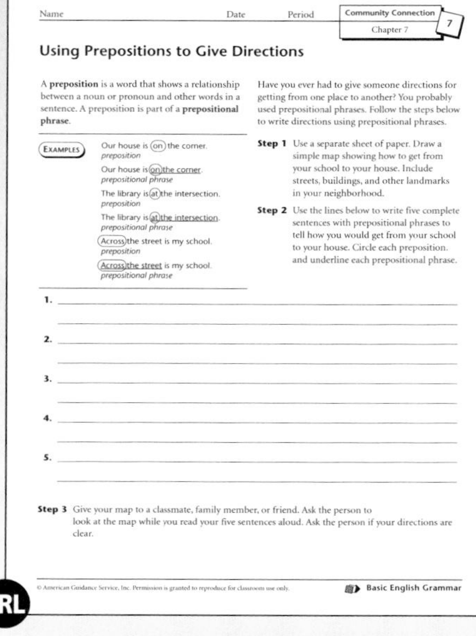

Name Date Period | Community Connection 7 | Chapter 7

Using Prepositions to Give Directions

A **preposition** is a word that shows a relationship between a noun or pronoun and other words in a sentence. A preposition is part of a **prepositional phrase**.

EXAMPLES
Our house is (on) the corner.
preposition
Our house is (on) the corner.
prepositional phrase
The library is (at) the intersection.
preposition
The library is (at) the intersection.
prepositional phrase
(Across) the street is my school.
preposition
(Across) the street is my school.
prepositional phrase

Have you ever had to give someone directions for getting from one place to another? You probably used prepositional phrases. Follow the steps below to write directions using prepositional phrases.

Step 1 Use a separate sheet of paper. Draw a simple map showing how to get from your school to your house. Include streets, buildings, and other landmarks in your neighborhood.

Step 2 Use the lines below to write five complete sentences with prepositional phrases to tell how you would get from your school to your house. Circle each preposition. and underline each prepositional phrase.

1. ______________________
2. ______________________
3. ______________________
4. ______________________
5. ______________________

Step 3 Give your map to a classmate, family member, or friend. Ask the person to look at the map while you read your five sentences aloud. Ask the person if your directions are clear.

Basic English Grammar

Community Connection 7

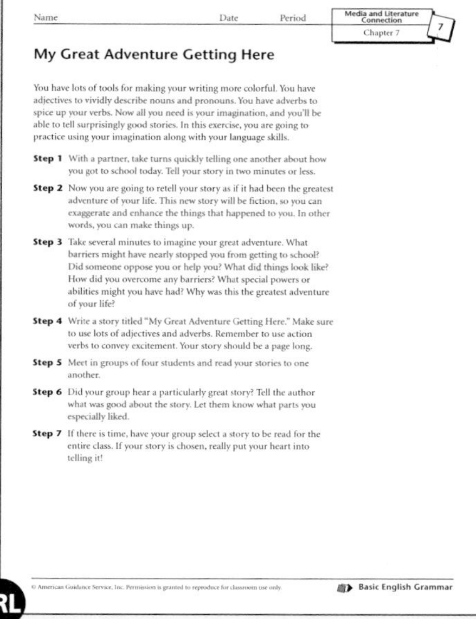

Name Date Period | Media and Literature Connection 7 | Chapter 7

My Great Adventure Getting Here

You have lots of tools for making your writing more colorful. You have adjectives to vividly describe nouns and pronouns. You have adverbs to spice up your verbs. Now all you need is your imagination, and you'll be able to tell surprisingly good stories. In this exercise, you are going to practice using your imagination along with your language skills.

Step 1 With a partner, take turns quickly telling one another about how you got to school today. Tell your story in two minutes or less.

Step 2 Now you are going to retell your story as if it had been the greatest adventure of your life. This new story will be fiction, so you can exaggerate and enhance the things that happened to you. In other words, you can make things up.

Step 3 Take several minutes to imagine your great adventure. What barriers might have nearly stopped you from getting to school? Did someone oppose you or help you? What did things look like? How did you overcome any barriers? What special powers or abilities might you have had? Why was this the greatest adventure of your life?

Step 4 Write a story titled "My Great Adventure Getting Here." Make sure to use lots of adjectives and adverbs. Remember to use action verbs to convey excitement. Your story should be a page long.

Step 5 Meet in groups of four students and read your stories to one another.

Step 6 Did your group hear a particularly great story? Tell the author what was good about the story. Let them know what parts you especially liked.

Step 7 If there is time, have your group select a story to be read for the entire class. If your story is chosen, really put your heart into telling it!

Basic English Grammar

Media and Literature Connection 7

Chapter

The Preposition

In this photograph, the turtle is *under* the water. The fish swim *through* the water and *around* the turtle. The island appears *above* the turtle, but it is really *in* the distance *beyond* the turtle. Words such as *under, through, around, above, in,* and *beyond* are prepositions.

A preposition is a word that shows a relationship between a noun or pronoun and other words in a sentence. A preposition is the first word of a prepositional phrase. A prepositional phrase is a group of words made up of a preposition, an object, and adjectives and adverbs that describe the object.

In Chapter 7, you will learn about prepositions, prepositional phrases, and their purposes. Knowing how a preposition works in a sentence will help you understand relationships among ideas.

Goals for Learning

- To identify prepositions in sentences
- To identify prepositional phrases in sentences
- To recognize the object of a preposition
- To identify the form of pronouns used as objects of prepositions
- To distinguish between adjective and adverb phrases
- To distinguish between prepositions and adverbs

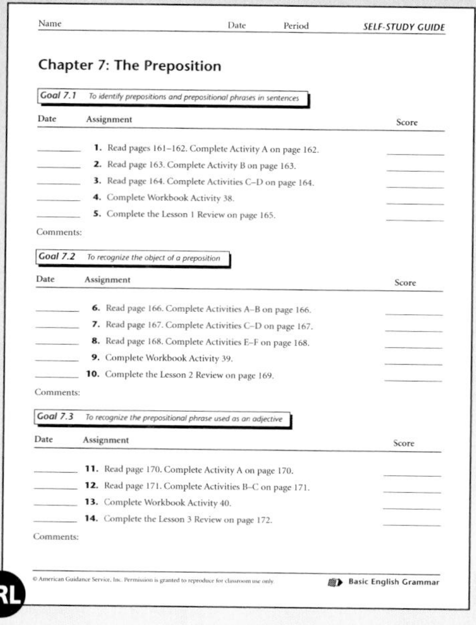

Name ______ Date ______ Period ______ ***SELF-STUDY GUIDE***

Chapter 7: The Preposition

Goal 7.1 *To identify prepositions and prepositional phrases in sentences*

Date	Assignment	Score
______	**1.** Read pages 161–162. Complete Activity A on page 162.	______
______	**2.** Read page 163. Complete Activity B on page 163.	______
______	**3.** Read page 164. Complete Activities C–D on page 164.	______
______	**4.** Complete Workbook Activity 38.	______
______	**5.** Complete the Lesson 1 Review on page 165.	______

Comments:

Goal 7.2 *To recognize the object of a preposition*

Date	Assignment	Score
______	**6.** Read page 166. Complete Activities A–B on page 166.	______
______	**7.** Read page 167. Complete Activities C–D on page 167.	______
______	**8.** Read page 168. Complete Activities E–F on page 168.	______
______	**9.** Complete Workbook Activity 39.	______
______	**10.** Complete the Lesson 2 Review on page 169.	______

Comments:

Goal 7.3 *To recognize the prepositional phrase used as an adjective*

Date	Assignment	Score
______	**11.** Read page 170. Complete Activity A on page 170.	______
______	**12.** Read page 171. Complete Activities B–C on page 171.	______
______	**13.** Complete Workbook Activity 40.	______
______	**14.** Complete the Lesson 3 Review on page 172.	______

Comments:

 Basic English Grammar

TRL

Name ______ Date ______ Period ______ ***SELF-STUDY GUIDE***

Chapter 7: The Preposition, continued

Goal 7.4 *To recognize the prepositional phrase used as an adverb*

Date	Assignment	Score
______	**15.** Read page 173. Complete Activity A on page 173.	______
______	**16.** Read page 174. Complete Activities B–C on page 174.	______
______	**17.** Complete Workbook Activity 41.	______
______	**18.** Complete the Lesson 4 Review on page 175.	______

Comments:

Goal 7.5 *To distinguish between prepositions and adverbs*

Date	Assignment	Score
______	**19.** Read page 176. Complete Activities A–B on page 176.	______
______	**20.** Complete Workbook Activity 42.	______
______	**21.** Complete the Lesson 5 Review on page 177.	______
______	**22.** Complete the Chapter 7 Review on pages 178–179.	______

Comments:

Student's Signature ______________________ Date ________

Instructor's Signature ______________________ Date ________

 Basic English Grammar

TRL

Chapter 7 Self-Study Guide, Pages 1–2

Introducing the Chapter

Use the photograph to introduce the idea that some words can describe the positional relationship between two things. Encourage students to identify the turtle in the picture and to suggest sentences that describe its position in relation to the water, land, trees, and so on. Write the prepositional phrases students use on the board and circle the prepositions. Then ask students if they could discuss the turtle's position without words like those you circled. Point out that the circled words are called prepositions, or words that show a relationship between a noun or pronoun and other words in a sentence. Tell students that in Chapter 7 they will learn about prepositions and prepositional phrases.

Writing Tips, Notes, and Technology Notes

Ask volunteers to read the tips and notes that appear in the margins throughout the chapter. Then discuss them with the class.

Teacher's Resource

The AGS Teaching Strategies in English Transparencies may be used with this chapter. The transparencies add an interactive dimension to expand and enhance the *Basic English Grammar* program content.

Career Interest Inventory

The AGS Harrington-O'Shea Career Decision-Making System–Revised (CDM) may be used with this chapter. Students can use the CDM to explore their interests and identify careers. The CDM defines career areas that are indicated by students' responses on the inventory.

Lesson at a Glance

Chapter 7 Lesson 1

Overview This lesson defines a preposition, the object of the preposition, a prepositional phrase, a compound object, and a compound preposition and gives examples of each.

Objectives

- To use prepositions and compound prepositions in sentences.
- To identify prepositional phrases.
- To identify objects and compound objects of prepositions.

Student Pages 162–165

Teacher's Resource Library 

Workbook Activity 38

Activity 38

Alternative Activity 38

Lesson 1 What Is a Preposition?

Preposition

A word that shows a relationship between a noun or pronoun and other words in a sentence

Object of the preposition

The noun or pronoun that follows the preposition in a prepositional phrase

Prepositional phrase

A group of words made up of a preposition, an object, and adjectives and adverbs that describe the object

A **preposition** shows a relationship between a noun or pronoun and other words in a sentence. The noun or pronoun that follows the preposition is the **object of the preposition.**

The preposition, the object of the preposition, and any words in between make up a **prepositional phrase.**

EXAMPLE Michael gave his notebook to Daphne. (The preposition *to* shows the relationship of *Daphne,* the object of the preposition, to *gave.*)

Carl read the note from Maria. (The preposition *from* shows the relationship of *Maria,* the object of the preposition, to *note.*)

When the preposition changes, the relationship between the words in the sentence changes. Notice how the relationship between *spoke* and *Alexis* changes in the following sentences.

EXAMPLE Charles spoke to Alexis.
Charles spoke about Alexis.

Common Prepositions						
about	around	beneath	for	near	out	to
above	at	beside	from	of	over	under
across	before	down	in	off	past	until
after	behind	during	into	on	through	with

Activity A Complete each sentence with a preposition. Write each complete sentence on your paper.

1. The apples ______ the tree are ripe.
2. The story ______ pirates was exciting.
3. The girl ______ the picture is my sister.
4. The boots ______ the chair are mine.
5. The girl ______ Ken is a good dancer.

Vocabulary

compound object
compound preposition
object of the preposition
preposition
prepositional phrase

1 Warm-Up Activity

Hold a pencil in a variety of locations, such as over your head or beside a desk. Ask students to use a sentence to describe where the pencil is. As prepositions such as *over, beside,* and *between* are used, write the words on the board. Point out that the words describe the relationship of the pencil to its position.

Then write this sentence on the board:

The mouse crept ___ the bed.

Ask pairs of students to list five words that could be used to complete the sentence. Write their words on the board as the pairs share them. Explain that the words on the board are examples of prepositions.

Teaching the Lesson

With the class, read the definition of the word *preposition.* Return to the sentence *The mouse crept ___ the bed.* Fill in the blank with a preposition from the board. Ask students to identify what two words in the sentence are linked and how they are related. Help students recognize that the preposition links the words *mouse* and *bed* by describing where the mouse is in relation to the bed.

Next read the definitions for *object of the preposition* and *prepositional phrase.* Once again, focus on the sentence *The mouse crept ___ the bed.* Ask a student to suggest a preposition for the blank and to underline the prepositional phrase. Challenge the class to create new sentences by changing both the preposition and the object in the sentence. Let volunteers write the new sentences on the board, circling the preposition in each sentence.

Activity A

Ask students to read the first sentence. Encourage students to suggest a preposition that would fit in the blank. Help students realize that more that one preposition may work in the sentence and that they may choose the one they prefer.

Activity A Answers

Answers will vary. Possible answers follow. **1.** on *or* under **2.** about **3.** in *or* beside **4.** under *or* on **5.** with *or* near

Compound object
Two or more objects

In a prepositional phrase, the preposition may have a **compound object.** A compound object is two or more objects.

EXAMPLE Austin works with Noah and Yuri. (*Noah* and *Yuri* is the compound object of the preposition *with.*)

In a prepositional phrase, the object of the preposition may have adjectives in front of it.

EXAMPLE across the muddy grass

Because adverbs can answer questions about adjectives, a prepositional phrase can also have an adverb.

EXAMPLE after the very long appointment

The object of the preposition can be a pronoun. When the object is a pronoun, no other words come between the preposition and its object or objects.

EXAMPLE to him beside it between you and me

A sentence may have more than one prepositional phrase.

EXAMPLE We bought vegetables for supper at the market.

Activity B Write the prepositional phrases in these sentences on your paper. Underline the preposition once and its object or objects twice. A sentence may have more than one prepositional phrase.

1. Write your name in the left-hand corner.
2. They live near a very busy highway.
3. Would you please sit on the bench with Laura and me?
4. Give this book about Mexico to him.
5. Early in the day, the sun shines through the front window.

Activity B

Write this sentence on the board: *Come to the play with Barry and me.* Ask students to identify the prepositional phrases in the sentence, inviting volunteers to underline the prepositions once and their objects twice. Let other volunteers tell whether the objects are nouns or pronouns and which prepositional phrase has a compound object.

Activity B Answers

1. in the left-hand corner **2.** near a very busy highway **3.** on the bench, with Laura and me **4.** about Mexico, to him **5.** in the day, through the front window

3 Reinforce and Extend

Learning Styles

Body/Kinesthetic

Mime is a universal language. Students may benefit from seeing and acting out how different prepositions can change the meaning of a sentence. Write this sentence on the board: *She walked ___ him.* Then have pairs of students think of prepositions to complete the sentence and mime the sentence. Have the class guess the preposition that completes the sentence being mimed.

Learning Styles

Auditory/Verbal

Ask students to select one or more paragraphs from a story, book, or newspaper article to read to a group of classmates. Explain that as one student reads, the other members of the group list the prepositions and prepositional phrases they hear. After the reading, let group members discuss what they wrote. Have the group experiment with the prepositions by substituting some of the prepositions used in the selection with others. Have the group discuss the effect the change of prepositions had on the selection.

Activity C

Invite students to use the compound prepositions listed in the box to compose sentences of their own. Ask volunteers to write their sentences on the board. Have the class identify the compound prepositional phrase in each sentence. Then have students complete Activity C.

Activity C Answers

1. According to Jorge 2. instead of Tim 3. in place of Judy 4. In spite of the heavy rain 5. as far as the Pacific Ocean

Activity D

Have students take turns making up sentences for item 1. Ask volunteers to identify the prepositional phrase and the object or objects of the preposition in each sentence.

Activity D Answers

Sentences will vary. Sample sentences follow. 1. Sam moved out of the country. 2. The train went through the tunnel. 3. Come with me to the mall. 4. During the performance, the lead actor sang. 5. The tree grew beside the pond.

Speaking Practice

After students have written their sentences for Activity D, invite them to work in pairs. Have one student read a sentence and the partner identify the preposition in the sentence. Ask the partner to find the sentence he or she wrote that uses the same preposition and to read the sentence. Then let the partner choose a sentence to read.

Compound preposition
A preposition made up of more than one word

A **compound preposition** is made up of more than one word.

Compound Prepositions			
according to	in spite of	because of	instead of
in addition to	out of	in front of	as far as
in place of	along with		

Activity C Write each prepositional phrase on your paper. Then underline the compound preposition.

Example Alex stood in front of Frieda.—<u>in front of</u> Frieda

1. According to Jorge, the party was fun.
2. I am going instead of Tim.
3. Jorge will speak in place of Judy.
4. In spite of the heavy rain, they played the soccer game.
5. Jack traveled as far as the Pacific Ocean.

Activity D Write a sentence using each preposition on your paper.

Example around—Her house is **around the bend.**

1. out of
2. through
3. with
4. during
5. beside
6. down
7. under
8. in front of
9. across
10. according to

The students hang the party decorations in front of the gymnasium.

Learning Styles

LEP/ESL

Encourage English language learners and English-proficient students to work together to prepare an illustrated book of prepositions. Students should list each preposition in the example box on page 162, write a phrase using the preposition, and draw a picture illustrating the phrase. Have students bind their pages into a booklet that they can use for reference.

Learning Styles

Visual/Spatial

Divide the class into pairs, giving each pair a colorful magazine picture. Point out the list of compound prepositions in the box on page 164. Ask partners to compose 10 sentences about their picture, using one of the compound prepositions in each sentence. When the sentences have been written, let each pair read their sentences to the class. Ask class members to raise their hands when they hear a compound preposition.

Career Connection

Many jobs require workers to write reports and evaluations. The use of prepositional phrases can make these reports and evaluations precise and informative as well as interesting to read. Let students work in small groups to brainstorm a list of careers in which reports or evaluations are written. Ask each student to write the list that the group creates. Afterward, have students mark one or more careers of interest to them. Provide time for them to explain to their group why they might like that career.

Lesson 1 REVIEW

Write each prepositional phrase on your paper. Underline the preposition once and its object or objects twice. A sentence may have more than one prepositional phrase.

1. My dog Honey was sleeping in the shade under a tree.
2. Suddenly, a loud noise in the street frightened her.
3. Honey ran around the bush and the tree wildly.
4. From the porch, I called her inside the house.
5. She dashed up the stairs instantly.

Complete each sentence with a compound preposition. Write each complete sentence on your paper. More than one compound preposition may make sense. Choose a different compound preposition for each sentence.

6. The chair ________ the window is yellow.
7. ________ the loud music, Kelly fell asleep.
8. I'll have salad ________ soup.
9. Peter felt happy ________ his good grades.
10. Jennifer will go to the movie ________ Alex and Deion.

Spelling Builder

Spelling Demons

The preposition *across* is one of many words that are often misspelled. People call words that are often misspelled "spelling demons." Here are some examples of other spelling demons:

beneath past through since

On your paper, practice spelling *beneath, past, through,* and *since* several times to learn how to spell them. Then look at the following words. Say each word and spell it aloud. Then write each word on your paper.

1. surprise
2. false
3. doctor
4. once
5. library

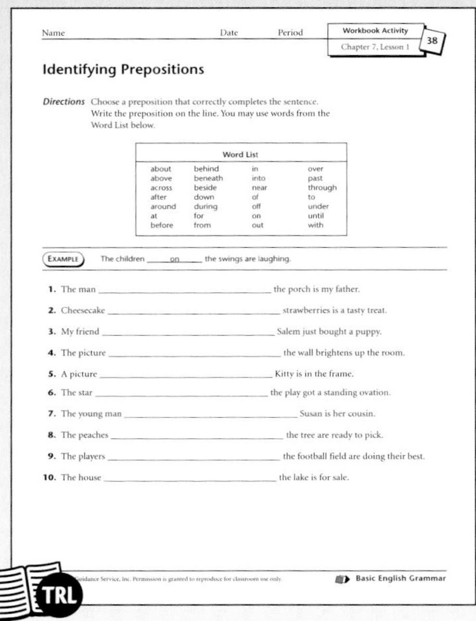

Name Date Period

Workbook Activity 38
Chapter 7, Lesson 1

Identifying Prepositions

Directions Choose a preposition that correctly completes the sentence. Write the preposition on the line. You may use words from the Word List below.

Word List			
about	behind	in	over
above	beneath	into	past
across	beside	near	through
after	down	of	to
around	during	off	under
at	for	on	until
before	from	out	with

EXAMPLE The children ___on___ the swings are laughing.

1. The man ________________ the porch is my father.
2. Cheesecake ________________ strawberries is a tasty treat.
3. My friend ________________ Salem just bought a puppy.
4. The picture ________________ the wall brightens up the room.
5. A picture ________________ Kitty is in the frame.
6. The star ________________ the play got a standing ovation.
7. The young man ________________ Susan is her cousin.
8. The peaches ________________ the tree are ready to pick.
9. The players ________________ the football field are doing their best.
10. The house ________________ the lake is for sale.

Basic English Grammar

TRL

Workbook Activity 38

Name Date Period

Activity 38
Chapter 7, Lesson 1

Recognizing Prepositional Phrases

Directions Underline the prepositional phrase in each of these sentences. Some sentences may have more than one prepositional phrase.

EXAMPLE The small village lay over the hill.

1. "Please put your wet boots in the closet," said my mother.
2. At the end of the rainbow is a pot of gold.
3. Salvadore took notes during the lecture.
4. Over the river and through the woods, to grandmother's house we go.
5. I would like to have coffee with my breakfast.
6. The Underground Railroad helped enslaved people escape to freedom.
7. This occurred before the Civil War ended slavery.
8. We had to drive around the closed road and across the bridge.
9. The whole class has a present for you.
10. Rachel went to the party on Saturday.

Directions Underline the prepositional phrases in the following sentences. Circle the word each phrase describes.

EXAMPLE Jack (went) to the picnic.

11. Katie went to a class. ________
12. She looked through her notebook. ________
13. Open the textbook to page 72. ________
14. Katie began reading from the chapter. ________
15. She asked a question about the material. ________
16. She went to her room. ________
17. Katie went to her sister's recital. ________
18. She talked with the children happily. ________
19. The children talked to Katie. ________
20. She decided to become a teacher of young children. ________

Basic English Grammar

TRL

Activity 38

Lesson 1 Review Answers

1. in the shade, under a tree 2. in the street 3. around the bush and the tree 4. From the porch, inside the house 5. up the stairs

Sentences will vary. Possible answers follow. 6. The chair in front of the window is yellow. 7. In spite of the loud music, Kelly fell asleep. 8. I'll have salad instead of soup. 9. Peter felt happy because of his good grades. 10. Jennifer will go to the movie along with Alex and Deion.

Spelling Builder

Call attention to the prepositions in the box and ask students why these words are called spelling demons. Help students notice that *across* might be mistakenly spelled *a cross*, *beneath* has a silent letter, *past* can be confused with *passed* and *through* with *threw*, and the *c* in *since* may be written as an *s* if a person is spelling by sound. Invite volunteers to choose a word and suggest a way to remember how to spell it.

Answers to Spelling Builder: Each word should be spelled correctly.

Spelling Practice

Point out that words that are spelling demons to one person may not be a problem to others. Ask volunteers to describe the method they use when learning to spell a word. Then help students set aside blank pages in a notebook where they can write their personal spelling demons. Explain that by having a handy list, students can easily check the spellings of words as they write. Encourage students to start their list by writing words from the Spelling Builder activity.

Lesson at a Glance

Chapter 7 Lesson 2

Overview This lesson explains the difference between an infinitive and a prepositional phrase that begins with *to* and also explains how to identify the correct form of pronouns used as objects of prepositions.

Objectives

- To distinguish an infinitive from a prepositional phrase.
- To identify the correct form of pronouns used as objects of prepositions.

Student Pages 166–169

Teacher's Resource Library TRL

Workbook Activity 39

Activity 39

Alternative Activity 39

Lesson 2 The Object of the Preposition

The object of the preposition is a noun or a pronoun.

EXAMPLE
Alex threw the ball into the basket. (*Basket* is a noun.)
The players cheered for him. (*Him* is a pronoun.)

Technology Note

A search engine examines information on the Internet and identifies related Web sites. You can type key words into a search engine to find Web sites about specific topics.

Activity A Write the object of the preposition on your paper. Identify it as a *noun* or a *pronoun*.

Example They played softball in the park.
park—noun

1. Kevin plays the drums in the band.
2. He practices every night before dinner.
3. Hoshi looked at her coin collection.
4. She checked some Web sites for information.
5. Is Berto sitting with you?

Do not confuse a prepositional phrase with an infinitive, which begins with the word *to.* The word that follows *to* in an infinitive is a verb.

EXAMPLE

Infinitive	He wants to leave early. He hopes to have a party.
Prepositional Phrase	Nidal went to the store. Amber wrote to her uncle.

Activity B Write five sentences using the word *to* on your paper. Next to each sentence, write whether *to* introduces a prepositional phrase or an infinitive.

1 Warm-Up Activity

Write this pair of sentences on the board: *I tossed the ball to Leah. I tossed the ball to her.* Have volunteers circle the prepositional phrase and underline the preposition once and the object of the preposition twice in each sentence. Ask how the objects in the sentences are different. Help students recognize that *Leah* is a noun and *her* is a pronoun. Point out that objects of prepositional phrases may be nouns or pronouns.

2 Teaching the Lesson

Write this pair of sentences on the board: *I will go to the store. I want to go now.* Circle the word *to* in each sentence. Ask students which sentence contains a prepositional phrase and why. Help students realize that the first sentence contains the prepositional phrase *to the store.* It is a prepositional phrase because it begins with a preposition and includes an object of the preposition.

Next focus on the second sentence. Ask why *to go* is not a prepositional phrase. Help students recall that a prepositional phrase must include an object and this phrase has none. Point out that *to go* is an infinitive and that the word that follows *to* in an infinitive is a verb. Ask volunteers to write sentences on the board that contain either a prepositional phrase or an infinitive. Have classmates identify the prepositional phrase or the infinitive in each sentence.

Activity A

Write these prepositional phrases on the board: *to the store, next to her, between the rows, along with him.* Ask volunteers to tell whether the object of the preposition is a noun or a pronoun.

Activity A Answers

1. band—noun 2. dinner—noun 3. collection—noun 4. information—noun 5. you—pronoun

Activity B

Before having students do Activity B on their own, ask each student to say one infinitive and one prepositional phrase that begins with *to* to a partner.

Activity B Answers

Sentences will vary. Check to see that students have identified prepositional phrases and infinitives correctly.

Activity C Write on your paper whether the phrase in bold is an *infinitive* or a *prepositional phrase.*

1. Alex went **to his class.**
2. He likes **to work** with computers.
3. "Turn **to page 8,**" the teacher said.
4. Alex began **to read** his lesson.
5. He wanted **to ask** the teacher a question.

If the object of the preposition is a pronoun, it must be in the object form.

EXAMPLE		
	Incorrect	She sat between Gabriela and I.
	Correct	She sat between Gabriela and me.

Possessive nouns and pronouns cannot be objects of prepositions.

EXAMPLE		
	Incorrect	Rashid went home with his.
	Correct	Rashid went home with him.
		Rashid went home with his friend.

Activity D Write these sentences on your paper. Correct any mistakes.

1. Please bring coats for Pete and I.
2. Sam bought an apple for his.
3. Susan passed out papers to theirs.
4. Let's keep this a secret between you and I.
5. Jennifer sat between Sara and she.

Alex brought his completed assignment to class.

Using What You've Learned

On your paper, draw a diagram of a place (such as your room). Then write five sentences about your diagram. Use prepositions in your sentences. Then underline all the prepositions and circle their objects.

Activity C

Before students begin the activity, ask volunteers to explain the difference between a prepositional phrase that begins with *to* and an infinitive.

Activity C Answers

1. prepositional phrase 2. infinitive 3. prepositional phrase 4. infinitive 5. infinitive

Activity D

Before students complete Activity D, review object pronouns with them. On the board, write the sentence *She sat between Juan and me.* Have students replace *me* with other object pronouns including *her, him, it, you, us,* and *them.* Then have the class read aloud the sentences in the activity, listening for mistakes in the use of object pronouns.

Activity D Answers

1. Please bring coats for Pete and me. 2. Sam bought an apple for him. 3. Susan passed out papers to them. 4. Let's keep this a secret between you and me. 5. Jennifer sat between Sara and her.

Using What You've Learned

Have students choose partners and show their drawings to one another. As one partner exhibits his or her drawing, the other should suggest possible prepositional phrases that could be used with the picture. Then the person who drew the picture can read his or her sentences. Have students discuss why their phrases may have been the same or different.

3 Reinforce and Extend

AT HOME

Suggest that students listen to a news item presented in a television newscast and list prepositional phrases and infinitives used in the story. Students may want to videotape the newscast in order to be able to listen more carefully. Invite students to bring in their lists. Help students notice that prepositional phrases and infinitives are common in oral language.

TEACHER ALERT

If students are unclear about which pronoun to use in a compound construction, such as *Please bring a coat for Pete and ___,* suggest that they drop part of the compound. For example, *Please bring a coat for me.* By dropping part of the compound, it is often easier to hear and see mistakes.

Activity E

Write this sentence on the board: *What is she staring at?* Help students identify the preposition and its object by asking students to rephrase the sentence as a statement like this: *She is staring at what.* Students can use this strategy as they do Activity E on their own.

Activity E Answers

1. about—Whom **2.** with—Whom **3.** about—What **4.** of—What **5.** to—Whom

Activity F

Read the paragraph with students before having them work independently.

Activity F Answers

1. of Mary Lyon **2.** in the education **3.** of women **4.** in 1797 **5.** in 1849 **6.** in schools **7.** in New Hampshire **8.** in Massachusetts **9.** In those days **10.** for middle-class women **11.** In 1837 **12.** in Massachusetts **13.** of the school **14.** At this school **15.** about mathematics, science, and Latin **16.** in themselves **17.** of everyone **18.** through her work

LEARNING STYLES

Logical/Mathematical

Create a set of preposition cards with one of these prepositions printed on each card: *after, before, near, with, past, beside.* Invite students to play a pattern game. Divide the class into two teams. Let a volunteer choose a card and read it. Each team member should create a prepositional phrase using the preposition and give the prepositional phrase orally. Points are scored based on the object of the preposition used. Give students one point if the object is a noun, two points if it is a pronoun, and three points if it is a compound object made of a noun and pronoun or two pronouns.

The object of the preposition usually comes after the preposition. However, sometimes the preposition and its object are separated in sentences that ask questions.

	Object	**Preposition**
	What did you do that for?	

Activity E Write the prepositions and their objects on your paper.

1. Whom are you talking about?
2. Whom are Dionne and Len with?
3. What is that book about?
4. What was she thinking of?
5. Whom will you give it to?

Activity F Write all the prepositional phrases in this paragraph on your paper. Do *not* include the three infinitives that are in the paragraph.

Have you ever heard of Mary Lyon? She was a pioneer in the education of women. Mary Lyon was born in 1797. She died in 1849. She taught in schools in New Hampshire and in Massachusetts. In those days, only rich women could get a good education. She raised money to begin a school for middle-class women. In 1837, she opened a school in Massachusetts. The name of the school was Mount Holyoke. At this school, women learned about mathematics, science, and Latin. Mary Lyon's only goal was to teach. Mary Lyon wanted to give women confidence in themselves. She won the love of everyone through her work.

GLOBAL CONNECTION

Emphasize that Mary Lyons helped provide women in the United States with a higher education. Then ask students to find out about education in other countries. Have students choose a country and find out about its minimum education requirements for boys and girls and the number of colleges and universities in the country. Have students use the information to complete these sentences.

In [name of country], [all children, boys, girls] between the ages of ___ and ___ must attend school. The country has [number] of colleges and universities.

Students may present their research information to the class and discuss the importance that nations around the world place on education.

Write on your paper whether the phrase in bold is an *infinitive* or a *prepositional phrase*.

1. Alex had **to study** for a test.
2. He went with Anita and me **to the library**.
3. The students had **to concentrate** hard on the questions.

Write each object of the preposition on your paper. Identify each one as a *noun* or a *pronoun*.

4. Rishi hoped to sing with them.
5. Tamara tossed the ball over the fence.
6. We walked through the exhibit.
7. Whom are you studying with?

Write these sentences on your paper. Correct any mistakes.

8. Jeff gave the present to hers.
9. Will you come with Trina and I?
10. Bob gave a card to she.

Vocabulary Builder

Among* and *Between

We use *among* when we discuss a group of three or more people or things. For example: The students whispered *among* themselves. We use *between* when we discuss two people or things. For example: Just *between* you and me, I didn't care for the band.

Choose the correct word in each sentence. Write each correct word on your paper.

1. Please arrive (among, between) one and two o'clock.
2. (Among, Between) milk and juice, I prefer juice.
3. You may choose (among, between) all of these dishes.
4. During the summer (among, between) ninth and tenth grade, I visited the Grand Canyon.
5. We spotted Lee (among, between) the 10 dancers.

Lesson 2 Review Answers

1. infinitive 2. prepositional phrase 3. infinitive 4. them—pronoun 5. fence—noun 6. exhibit—noun 7. Whom—pronoun 8. Jeff gave the present to her. 9. Will you come with Trina and me? 10. Bob gave a card to her.

Vocabulary Builder

Write these phrases on the board in two columns: *between = two, among = three or more.* Ask students to write prepositional phrases in each column. Work together to make sure *between* and *among* were used correctly in each phrase. You might suggest that students use this device to remember when to use each word: Both *between* and *two* have *tw*, which leaves *among* with a group.

Answers to Vocabulary Builder:
1. between 2. Between 3. among 4. between 5. among

Learning Styles

Interpersonal/Group Learning

Divide the class into small groups. Write a noun or pronoun, such as *team*, on the board. Tell each group to create a word web, putting the noun in the center circle and writing prepositional phrases around the center circle. Use *team* as the object of the preposition in each phrase. The group with the most correctly written prepositional phrases wins the round. If students need help remembering prepositions, have them refer to page 162. Other nouns and pronouns that might be used for the center circle include *computer, elephant, me, him, her, shelf,* and *foot*.

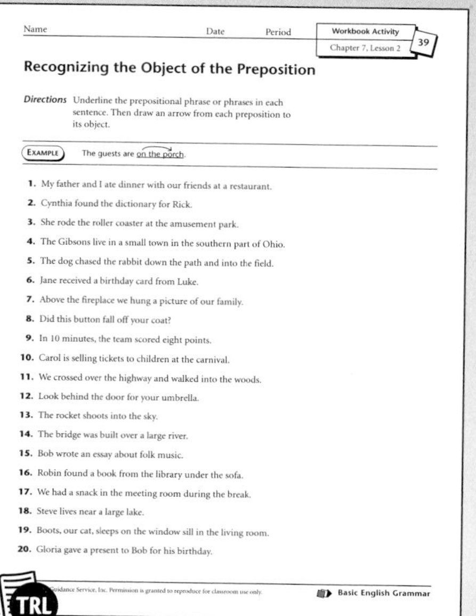

Name Date Period Workbook Activity 39 Chapter 7, Lesson 2

Recognizing the Object of the Preposition

Directions Underline the prepositional phrase or phrases in each sentence. Then draw an arrow from each preposition to its object.

EXAMPLE The guests are on the porch.

1. My father and I ate dinner with our friends at a restaurant.
2. Cynthia found the dictionary for Rick.
3. She rode the roller coaster at the amusement park.
4. The Gibsons live in a small town in the southern part of Ohio.
5. The dog chased the rabbit down the path and into the field.
6. Jane received a birthday card from Luke.
7. Above the fireplace we hung a picture of our family.
8. Did this button fall off your coat?
9. In 10 minutes, the team scored eight points.
10. Carol is selling tickets to children at the carnival.
11. We crossed over the highway and walked into the woods.
12. Look behind the door for your umbrella.
13. The rocket shoots into the sky.
14. The bridge was built over a large river.
15. Bob wrote an essay about folk music.
16. Robin found a book from the library under the sofa.
17. We had a snack in the meeting room during the break.
18. Steve lives near a large lake.
19. Boots, our cat, sleeps on the window sill in the living room.
20. Gloria gave a present to Bob for his birthday.

Guidance Service, Inc. Permission is granted to reproduce for classroom use only. Basic English Grammar

TRL

Workbook Activity 39

Name Date Period Activity 39 Chapter 7, Lesson 2

Prepositions and Their Objects

Directions If the word *to* is used in a prepositional phrase, write *P* on the line. If the word *to* is used as an infinitive, write *I* on the line.

EXAMPLES I want to go. I
We went to the park. P

1. Our team members need to have new uniforms.
2. The truck driver took the north exit to Livingston.
3. It is always hard to find a lost sock.
4. Is this the bus to Main Street?
5. The trip to the zoo was rained out.
6. Jared can't wait to jump on the trampoline.
7. My mother and I are going to the store.
8. Are you going to wait here for me?
9. The flowers of spring look beautiful to the bees.
10. Please give it to me.

Directions Circle the word that is used incorrectly in the prepositional phrase. Write the correct word on the line.

EXAMPLE Jill sat between Franklin and I. me

11. Billy went to the park with he.
12. The secret is between the teacher and she.
13. We hope there are enough sandwiches for Clarence and I.
14. Are you going to the party with they?
15. The policeman walked right past she.

© American Guidance Service, Inc. Permission is granted to reproduce for classroom use only. Basic English Grammar

TRL

Activity 39

Lesson at a Glance

Chapter 7 Lesson 3

Overview This lesson presents adjective phrases.

Objectives

- To identify adjective phrases and the words they describe.
- To add adjective phrases to sentences.

Student Pages 170–172

Teacher's Resource Library 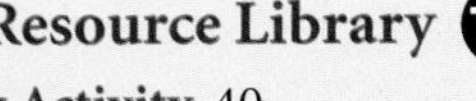

Workbook Activity 40

Activity 40

Alternative Activity 40

Vocabulary

adjective phrase

1 Warm-Up Activity

Ask students to recall what an adjective is (*a word that describes a noun or pronoun*). Then play the opening of Beethoven's *Fifth Symphony* or another piece of music with a strong recurring phrase or melody. Ask volunteers to write adjectives describing the music on the board. Then ask students to use the words on the board to compose prepositional phrases that could describe the music, such as *with a strong beat, after three identical notes, by Beethoven,* or *from firm to lively.* Point out that prepositional phrases may be used as adjectives or adverbs and that in this lesson, students will focus on using prepositional phrases as adjectives.

2 Teaching the Lesson

Review with students how a prepositional phrase begins (*with a preposition*) and how it ends (*with a noun or pronoun*). Write the words *adjective phrase* on the board. Ask students what they think an adjective phrase is (*a group of words that describes a noun or pronoun*) and how a prepositional phrase might be used as an adjective phrase. Help students conclude that a prepositional phrase used to describe a noun or pronoun is functioning as an adjective phrase. Use the sentences in the example boxes on the page to provide students with examples of adjective phrases.

Activity A

Do the activity orally with the class. Then encourage students to replace the adjective phrase in each sentence with a different adjective phrase.

Activity A Answers

1. with me—boy **2.** on the table—flowers **3.** of bricks and stone—house **4.** of the girls—None **5.** by Maya Angelou—poem

Lesson 3 The Prepositional Phrase Used as an Adjective

Adjective phrase
A prepositional phrase that answers the question which one, what kind, *or* how many *about the noun or pronoun in a sentence*

A prepositional phrase begins with a preposition and ends with a noun or a pronoun. A prepositional phrase is either an adjective phrase or an adverb phrase.

An adjective is a word that describes a noun or pronoun. An **adjective phrase** does the same thing as an adjective. The phrase tells *which one, what kind,* or *how many* about the noun or pronoun in a sentence.

In writing, a *phrase* is a group of words that work together. The word *phrase* also describes a group of notes in music. A small part of a song's tune or melody is a *phrase.*

EXAMPLE

The store across the road is open. (*Which* store is open? The one *across the road* is open.)

This book by Katherine Paterson is popular. (*Which* book is popular? The one *by Katherine Paterson* is popular.)

An adjective usually comes *before* the noun it describes. An adjective phrase *follows* the noun it describes.

EXAMPLE

Adjective	The Wilson High band won.
Adjective Phrase	The band from Wilson High won.

Activity A Write each adjective phrase in bold on your paper. Next to each phrase, write the noun or pronoun it describes.

Example A cousin **of mine** called.
of mine—cousin

1. The boy **with me** is my brother.
2. The flowers **on the table** are beautiful.
3. We built a house **of bricks and stone.**
4. None **of the girls** left early.
5. The poem **by Maya Angelou** was beautiful.

Writing Tip

Reread your prepositional phrases to be sure the relationships between the words are clear.

An adjective phrase can describe the object of another preposition.

The woman at the front of the store is Mrs. Jackson. (The adjective phrase *of the store* describes the noun *front*. *Front* is the object of the preposition in the phrase *at the front*.)

Activity B Write the adjective phrases in these sentences on your paper. Next to each phrase, write the noun or pronoun it describes.

1. The woods beside the lake near our house are dark.
2. Elvin's dad owns a shoe store in the mall beside Jones River.
3. The woman with the baby in her arms is my aunt.
4. The lamp on the table beside your bed needs a new lightbulb.
5. All of the people in the auditorium cheered.

Activity C Rewrite these sentences on your paper. Add an adjective phrase after each noun or pronoun in bold.

1. **Everyone** enjoys the football **games.**
2. Several **friends** are coming to the **party.**
3. The **dish** fell from the **counter**.
4. The **man** bought a new **car.**
5. The **teacher** liked that **book.**
6. I read the **story** to the **class.**
7. The **girl** bought **tickets.**
8. **Many** studied the **map.**
9. The **lamp** needed a new **bulb.**
10. The **customers** entered the **store.**

Activity B

Do Activity B as a whole class activity. Let volunteers write a sentence on the board. Have students underline each prepositional phrase. Then invite volunteers to draw an arrow from each prepositional phrase in the sentence to the noun or pronoun it describes.

Activity B Answers

1. beside the lake—woods, near our house—lake **2.** in the mall—store, beside Jones River—mall **3.** with the baby—woman, in her arms—baby **4.** on the table—lamp, beside your bed—table **5.** of the people—All, in the auditorium—people

Activity C

Do the first item on the board. Have students supply adjective phrases to describe the words in bold. Help students check that the phrase tells *which one, what kind,* or *how many* about the word in bold.

Activity C Answers

Sentences will vary. Each sentence should include an adjective phrase after each noun or pronoun in bold.

Reinforce and Extend

In the Community

Point out that using prepositions correctly when giving directions can make the difference between someone getting where they are going and someone getting lost. Have small groups of students select two or three specific sites in the community. These places may include historical sites, public buildings, parks, theaters, or any well-known place. Students can work together to write directions from the school to these sites. When all the groups are finished, review each set of directions as a class. Have prepositional phrases used in the directions identified. Then assemble the directions in a booklet to place in the school library.

Teacher Alert

You may wish to point out that when one adjective phrase follows another adjective phrase, both phrases may be describing the same noun or pronoun. For example, *Read this poem by my sister about city life.*

The Preposition *Chapter 7* 171

Lesson 3 Review Answers

1. in Alaska—temperatures **2.** of Alaska—explorer **3.** from Russia—people **4.** in the corner—tree, of our yard—corner **5.** of the members—All, in the club—members **6–10.** Sentences will vary. Each sentence should include an adjective phrase after each noun or pronoun in bold.

Where To Find It

Help students locate the Index in their textbooks. Ask them to describe the features of an index. Students should note that the index is arranged alphabetically by topics, some topics have subtopics, and page references follow each entry. Together choose a topic in the index and locate the page numbers related to it. Discuss with students where else they might find an index. Ask them to find other books that contain an index.

Answers to Where To Find It: Students should list a grammar topic from the Index and any related subtopics. Each topic and subtopic should be followed by one or more page references.

Learning Styles

Visual/Spatial

Give students objects, such as books, plants, pieces of chalk, and erasers. Ask each student to compose a sentence with an adjective phrase about his or her object. Afterward, ask students to display their objects, write their sentences on the board, and explain whether the sentences tell *which one, what kind,* or *how many* about the object.

Lesson 3 REVIEW

Write the adjective phrases in these sentences on your paper. Next to each phrase, write the noun or pronoun it describes.

1. January temperatures in Alaska are very cold.
2. Vitus Bering was the first explorer of Alaska.
3. People from Russia also explored Alaska.
4. The tree in the corner of our yard is blooming.
5. All of the members in the club voted.

Rewrite these sentences on your paper. Add an adjective phrase after each noun or pronoun in bold.

6. The **dog** ran under the **porch.**
7. The **students** liked that **teacher.**
8. The **meeting** is on **Friday.**
9. Several **players** are coming to the **field.**
10. **Everyone** loved the **play.**

Where To Find It

Index

An index is at the back of a book and lists topics alphabetically with page numbers. To use an index, first choose a topic such as a person, a historical event, or a subject like "video cameras." If you can't find your topic, try a more general topic, like "cameras." Some topic listings will have subtopics, which also appear alphabetically. Find your topic, and then read the pages listed to find the information you need.

Think of a grammar topic that has confused you recently. Use the index of this book to find information about that topic. On your paper, write the topic's index heading. Also write any subheadings and page numbers listed under the heading.

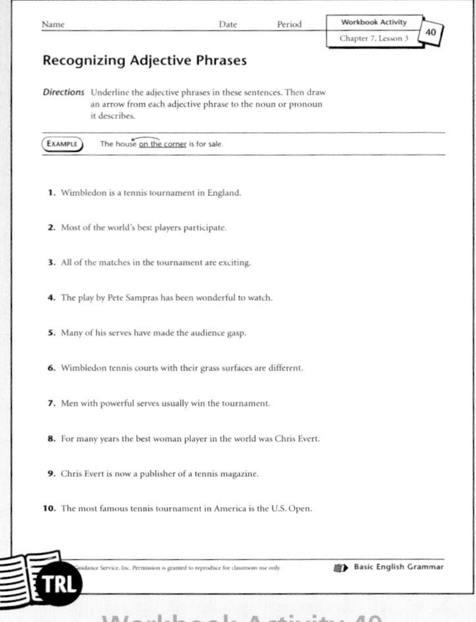

Name Date Period

Workbook Activity 40
Chapter 7, Lesson 3

Recognizing Adjective Phrases

Directions Underline the adjective phrases in these sentences. Then draw an arrow from each adjective phrase to the noun or pronoun it describes.

EXAMPLE The house on the corner is for sale.

1. Wimbledon is a tennis tournament in England.
2. Most of the world's best players participate.
3. All of the matches in the tournament are exciting.
4. The play by Pete Sampras has been wonderful to watch.
5. Many of his serves have made the audience gasp.
6. Wimbledon tennis courts with their grass surfaces are different.
7. Men with powerful serves usually win the tournament.
8. For many years the best woman player in the world was Chris Evert.
9. Chris Evert is now a publisher of a tennis magazine.
10. The most famous tennis tournament in America is the U.S. Open.

Basic English Grammar

TRL

Workbook Activity 40

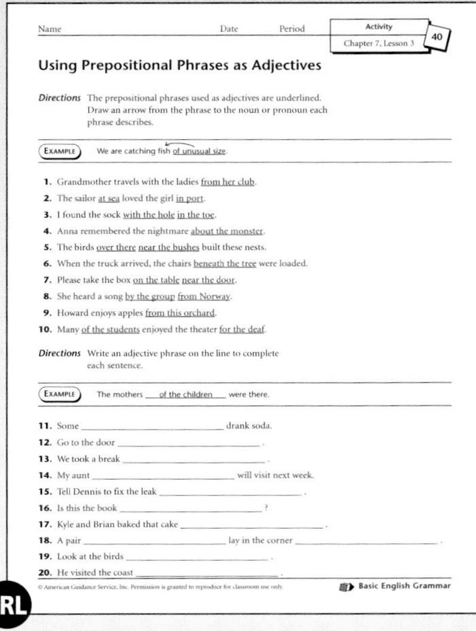

Name Date Period

Activity 40
Chapter 7, Lesson 3

Using Prepositional Phrases as Adjectives

Directions The prepositional phrases used as adjectives are underlined. Draw an arrow from the phrase to the noun or pronoun each phrase describes.

EXAMPLE We are catching fish of unusual size.

1. Grandmother travels with the ladies from her club.
2. The sailor at sea loved the girl in port.
3. I found the sock with the hole in the toe.
4. Anna remembered the nightmare about the monster.
5. The birds over there near the bushes built these nests.
6. When the truck arrived, the chairs beneath the tree were loaded.
7. Please take the box on the table near the door.
8. She heard a song by the group from Norway.
9. Howard enjoys apples from this orchard.
10. Many of the students enjoyed the theater for the deaf.

Directions Write an adjective phrase on the line to complete each sentence.

EXAMPLE The mothers __of the children__ were there.

11. Some __________ drank soda.
12. Go to the door __________ .
13. We took a break __________ .
14. My aunt __________ will visit next week.
15. Tell Dennis to fix the leak __________ .
16. Is this the book __________ ?
17. Kyle and Brian baked that cake __________ .
18. A pair __________ lay in the corner __________ .
19. Look at the birds __________ .
20. He visited the coast __________ .

Basic English Grammar

TRL

Activity 40

Lesson 4 The Prepositional Phrase Used as an Adverb

Adverb phrase
A prepositional phrase that answers the question how, when, where, how much, *or* how long *about the verb in a sentence*

An adverb is a word that answers questions about a verb. You can use a prepositional phrase as an adverb. An **adverb phrase** does the same thing as an adverb. It is a group of words that tells *how, when, where, how much,* or *how long* about the verb in a sentence.

EXAMPLE

Adverb	They shopped rapidly.
Adverb Phrase	They shopped in a hurry. *(How did they shop? They shopped in a hurry.)*

An adverb phrase may appear in different places in a sentence.

EXAMPLE After lunch we napped.
We napped after lunch.

Writing Tip
Try putting adverb phrases at the beginning or at the end of your sentences. Varying your sentences will make your writing more lively.

Activity A On your paper, write each adverb phrase in bold. Next to each phrase, write the question the adverb phrase answers about the verb. Write *how, when, where, how much,* or *how long.*

1. **For three hours** the band played.
2. Ling ironed her dress **with great care.**
3. Dad put the roast **into the oven.**
4. **Before midnight** Parker wrote the report.
5. They stayed **about an hour.**
6. **During the winter** we enjoy skiing.
7. Honey chased the neighbor's cat **up a tree.**
8. The day **after tomorrow** is Alex's birthday.
9. She beat the record **by 30 seconds.**
10. **After dinner** Lisa walked her dog.

Lesson at a Glance

Chapter 7 Lesson 4

Overview This lesson presents adverb phrases.

Objectives

- To identify adverb phrases in sentences.
- To add adverb phrases to sentences.

Student Pages 173–175

Teacher's Resource Library 

Workbook Activity 41
Activity 41
Alternative Activity 41

Vocabulary
adverb phrase

1 Warm-Up Activity

Before starting the lesson, write the words *adverb phrase* on the board. Remind students that they learned about adverbs in Chapter 6. Ask them to use their understanding of what an adverb is to tell what an adverb phrase is. Elicit from students that an adverb phrase is a group of words that tells about the verb, an adjective, or an adverb in a sentence. Write these questions on the board: *how, when, where, how much, how long,* and *why.* Ask students to compose prepositional phrases that answer each question.

2 Teaching the Lesson

Write this sentence on the board: I *painted around the window frame carefully.* Underline the word *carefully* and have students identify it as an adverb. Then have a volunteer change the adverb to an adverb phrase, such as *with care.* Review the examples on the page with students. Point out that an adverb phrase need not always come after the verb in a sentence.

3 Reinforce and Extend

LEARNING STYLES

Auditory/Verbal
Have partners practice asking and answering questions, using the sentences in Activity A. For example, one partner takes the answer to the first item, *how long,* and uses it in a question related to the sentence: *How long did the band play?* The partner responds using the adverb phrase that answers the question: *for three hours.* Have partners take turns asking and answering the questions.

Activity A

Ask students to find the verb in the first item (*played*). Then have them apply each question to the verb to figure out which one the phrase answers. In the first item, the phrase answers the question *how long.* Suggest that students use this strategy to help them do Activity A.

Activity A Answers

1. For three hours—how long 2. with great care—how 3. into the oven—where 4. Before midnight—when 5. about an hour—how long 6. During the winter—when 7. up a tree—where 8. after tomorrow—when 9. by 30 seconds—how much 10. After dinner—when

Activity B

Write the first item on the board and have a volunteer underline the adverb phrase that answers the question *why*. Point out that the word *because* is often a signal of an adverb phrase that tells *why*.

Activity B Answers

1. because of the rain 2. for dinner 3. for me 4. Because of his fever 5. for her aunt

Activity C

Do the activity orally with the class. Then encourage students to replace the adverb phrase or phrases in each sentence with different adverb phrases.

Activity C Answers

1. in the trash can 2. by two hours 3. with her mother, at the store 4. for the school newspaper 5. Because of the weather

Learning Styles

Body/Kinesthetic

Ask each student to think of an action to do in the classroom, to write a sentence with the action and an adverb phrase, and to demonstrate the sentence. For example, a student could demonstrate the sentence *I picked up a paper off the floor.* As each person demonstrates his or her sentence, have the class decide what action and adverb phrase is being demonstrated.

An adverb phrase can answer the question *why* about a verb.

They were crying because of the sad story. (*Why* were they crying? They were crying *because of the sad story.*)

Activity B On your paper, write the adverb phrase that answers the question *why* in each sentence.

1. I ran inside because of the rain.
2. She shopped for dinner.
3. Will you sing for me?
4. Because of his fever, Jeff stayed home.
5. Janet bought a gift for her aunt.

An adverb phrase can describe an adjective or another adverb.

Monique is now taller by three inches. (*Taller* is an adjective. The adverb phrase *by three inches* tells how much taller Monique is.)

In the tryouts, Leigh ran faster than Johnny by one minute. (*Faster* is an adverb. The adverb phrase *by one minute* tells how much faster Leigh ran.)

Activity C Write the adverb phrases on your paper.

1. Put the paper in the trash can.
2. Constance stayed longer than Zack by two hours.
3. She shopped with her mother at the store.
4. Carol wrote for the school newspaper.
5. Because of the weather, officials ended the game.

Learning Styles

Interpersonal/Group Learning

Write the following verbs on the board: *studied, explored, ran.* Organize students into small groups and ask each group to write six adverb phrases to go with each verb. Each adverb phrase should answer one of these questions: *how, when, where, how much, how long,* and *why.* When students have written their sentences, let pairs of groups share their adverb phrases with each other.

Learning Styles

LEP/ESL

Encourage students to create a personal dictionary of adjective and adverb phrases. As they read in class or on their own, they can jot down adjective and adverb phrases that they think add interest to the story or article they are reading. They can also include the noun, pronoun, or verb that the phrase describes. Students can refer to their lists for ideas when they write.

Lesson 4 REVIEW

Write the adverb phrases in these sentences on your paper. A sentence may have more than one adverb phrase. Next to each phrase, write the question the adverb phrase answers about the verb.

1. Alex studies computer technology at Hanover Community College.
2. He will attend classes there for two years.
3. Someday Alex might use computers in a bank.
4. At school Alex studies in a computer lab.
5. Because of the programmer's directions, the computer performs its job without a problem.

Identify the prepositional phrase in bold as an adjective phrase or an adverb phrase. Write *adjective phrase* or *adverb phrase* on your paper.

6. **At the concert** the orchestra played the music **of Brahms.**
7. Both boys go **to Hanover Community College.**
8. Bess plays soccer **in the spring.**
9. The gift **from my aunt** arrived **before my birthday.**
10. A girl **in my class** wrote a short story **during her summer vacation.**

Rewrite these sentences on your paper. Add an adverb phrase that answers *how, when, where, how much, how long,* or *why* about each word in bold.

11. The chorus **sang.**
12. Jennifer **stayed** home.
13. My cousins **went** home.
14. Kate **missed** the bus.
15. The fans **cheered.**

Lesson 4 Review Answers

1. at Hanover Community College—where **2.** for two years—how long **3.** in a bank—where **4.** At school—where, in a computer lab—where **5.** Because of the programmer's directions—why, without a problem—how **6.** adverb phrase, adjective phrase **7.** adverb phrase **8.** adverb phrase **9.** adjective phrase, adverb phrase **10.** adjective phrase, adverb phrase

11–15. Sentences will vary. Each sentence should include an adverb phrase that answers the question *how, when, where, how much, how long,* or *why* about the word in bold.

Writing Practice

Have small groups of students brainstorm lists of possible story ideas. Then each group can choose one idea from its list to develop into a group story. Encourage each group to write 10 prepositional phrases to use in their story. In choosing the prepositional phrases, groups should think about who the characters will be and what actions they will perform. Then ask groups to write their stories, using the prepositional phrases they wrote. Tell the groups they may change or replace or add prepositional phrases as needed. Ask the groups to read their stories aloud. Have listeners jot down prepositional phrases they hear.

TEACHER ALERT

Ending a sentence with a preposition was once discouraged in formal grammar. However, this rule has been ignored so often that ending a sentence with a preposition has become acceptable to most writers and speakers. Nevertheless, students can avoid this issue by reworking their sentences or by dropping unnecessary prepositions. For example, in the sentence *What was she thinking of?*, the *of* could be dropped.

Name Date Period — Workbook Activity 41 — Chapter 7, Lesson 4

Adding Adverb Phrases

Directions Each verb or verb phrase in these sentences is in bold. Add an adverb phrase to each sentence and write the new sentence on the line. Then underline the adverb phrase in each sentence.

EXAMPLE We **left**.
We **left** in a hurry.

1. The lady **bought** a new bike.
2. Everyone **joined** the exercise class.
3. The snow **was falling** lightly.
4. The puppy **barked** excitedly.
5. The store **opens** early.
6. Sally **will be** there.
7. Bully, the St. Bernard puppy, **barked** loudly.
8. **Bake** us a chocolate cake.
9. Carla **wrote** a short story.
10. The teacher **asked** the class a question.

 Basic English Grammar

TRL

Workbook Activity 41

Name Date Period — Activity 41 — Chapter 7, Lesson 4

Distinguishing Adverb and Adjective Phrases

Directions Circle the prepositional phrase in each sentence. Decide whether it is an adverb phrase or an adjective phrase. Write *adverb* or *adjective* on the line.

EXAMPLES Alicia Silverstone is the star (of that movie). adjective
She acts (with great enthusiasm). adverb

1. We will march in the parade.
2. The clowns in the parade were very funny.
3. Bob and his wife walked through the woods.
4. You must walk over the bridge to get there.
5. The covering over the bridge should be repaired.
6. Everyone bought a ticket for the concert.
7. The girl from Iowa won first prize.
8. This family moved here from Iowa.
9. Randy bought his groceries at the supermarket.
10. Will Greg open the door on the left side?
11. They drive on the left side there.
12. During the storm, the tree blew down.
13. Carrie likes to cruise in the fast lane.
14. The truck in the fast lane is speeding.
15. The train to Boise arrived late.
16. After dinner we can leave.
17. The show after dinner will be wonderful.
18. Sarah threw her clothes across the bed.
19. She heated the food in the microwave oven.
20. The popcorn in the microwave oven is Peter's.

 Basic English Grammar

TRL

Activity 41

Lesson at a Glance

Chapter 7 Lesson 5

Overview This lesson explains the difference between prepositions and adverbs.

Objectives

- To distinguish between adverbs and prepositions in sentences.
- To add prepositional phrases to sentences.

Student Pages 176–177

Teacher's Resource Library 

Workbook Activity 42

Activity 42

Alternative Activity 42

Warm-Up Activity

Write these words on cards: *along, around, below, down, inside.* On the board write these headings: *Prepositional Phrase, Adverb.* Have students choose a word card, read the word, and then write on the board a prepositional phrase using the word. Then have students use the word as an adverb by writing a verb followed by the word. For example, for *along,* students might write *along the river* and *move along.* Then discuss the differences between the prepositions and the adverbs. Help students conclude that a preposition begins a phrase and has an object and that an adverb describes a verb and has no object.

Teaching the Lesson

Point out that some words are used as both adverbs and prepositions and that a preposition has an object. Write these sentences on the board: *Climb inside the ___. Climb inside.* Ask what is missing in the first sentence. When students note that the object is missing, ask if the word inside is used as a preposition or an adverb in the first sentence. When students indicate that *inside* is used as a preposition, have a volunteer complete the sentence with an object. Point out that the second sentence has no object and that *inside* is being used as an adverb.

Lesson 5 Preposition or Adverb?

Some words can be either a preposition or an adverb. A preposition always has an object. An adverb does not.

EXAMPLE		
	Adverb	Estella climbed aboard. (*Aboard* is not followed by a noun or a pronoun.)
	Preposition	Estella climbed aboard the bus. (*Aboard* relates its object, the noun *bus,* to the rest of the sentence.)

Activity A Write each word in bold on your paper. Next to it, write *adverb* or *preposition.*

1. Please come **in.**
2. Howard walked **in** the woods.
3. Turn the lights **off** when you leave.
4. Jane jumped **off** the stage.
5. I will come **by** later.

Activity B Write these sentences on your paper. Add at least one prepositional phrase to each sentence to make it more interesting. Be sure to add only prepositional phrases.

Example The man arrived.
The man **from Los Angeles** arrived **in the morning.**

1. My aunt wrote me a letter.
2. The principal spoke.
3. My neighbor bought a new car.
4. The quarterback threw the ball.
5. The crowd cheered.

Activity A

Do the first two items orally with the class. Ask students to explain how they know that *in* is an adverb in item 1 and a preposition in item 2. Then have students complete the activity on their own.

Activity A Answers

1. in—adverb 2. in—preposition 3. off—adverb 4. off—preposition 5. by—adverb

Activity B

Read and discuss the example. Then have students take turns adding different prepositional phrases to this sentence: *The train arrived.*

Activity B Answers

Sentences will vary. Each sentence should include at least one prepositional phrase. Sample sentences follow. 1. My aunt wrote me a letter about her Hawaiian vacation. 2. The principal spoke at the assembly. 3. My neighbor bought a new car at the closeout sale. 4. The quarterback threw the ball to the nearest receiver. 5. The crowd cheered for the home team.

Lesson 5 REVIEW

Write each word in bold on your paper. Next to it, write *adverb* or *preposition.*

1. The dog sat **outside** and barked all afternoon.
2. Leave the package **outside** the door.
3. Haven't we met **before?**
4. The elephant disappeared **before** our eyes!
5. The old car rumbled **down** the highway.

On your paper, write two sentences for each word. In the first sentence, use the word as a preposition. In the second sentence, use the word as an adverb.

6. in
7. on
8. below
9. around
10. about
11. up
12. underneath
13. inside
14. near
15. through

Writing Project

Writing Prepositional Phrases

We use prepositional phrases to show the relationship between a noun or pronoun and other words in a sentence. Sentences can have more than one prepositional phrase.

On your paper, write a paragraph describing an event that you have attended. Include a prepositional phrase in each sentence. Your paragraph should have at least five sentences.

Some possible topics:

- A concert
- A birthday party
- A picnic
- A school meeting
- A sporting event
- A play

When you have finished, underline the prepositional phrases in your paragraph. Then read your paragraph to a classmate. Ask him or her to identify the prepositional phrase in each sentence.

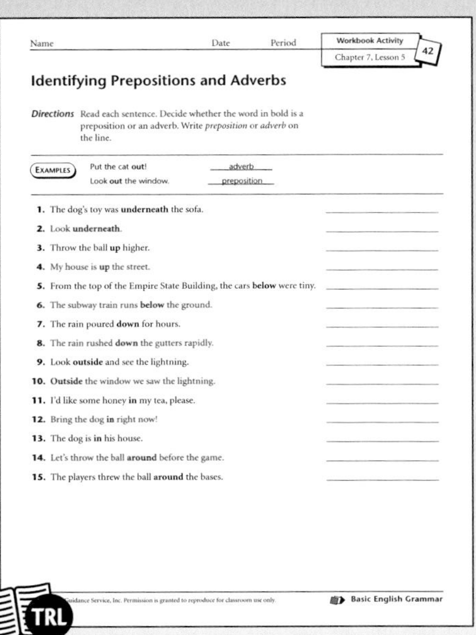

Name Date Period

Workbook Activity 42
Chapter 7, Lesson 5

Identifying Prepositions and Adverbs

Directions Read each sentence. Decide whether the word in bold is a preposition or an adverb. Write *preposition* or *adverb* on the line.

EXAMPLES
Put the cat **out**! adverb
Look **out** the window. preposition

1. The dog's toy was **underneath** the sofa. ____
2. Look **underneath**. ____
3. Throw the ball **up** higher. ____
4. My house is **up** the street. ____
5. From the top of the Empire State Building, the cars **below** were tiny. ____
6. The subway train runs **below** the ground. ____
7. The rain poured **down** for hours. ____
8. The rain rushed **down** the gutters rapidly. ____
9. Look **outside** and see the lightning. ____
10. **Outside** the window we saw the lightning. ____
11. I'd like some honey **in** my tea, please. ____
12. Bring the dog **in** right now! ____
13. The dog is **in** his house. ____
14. Let's throw the ball **around** before the game. ____
15. The players threw the ball **around** the bases. ____

Basic English Grammar

TRL

Workbook Activity 42

Name Date Period

Activity 42
Chapter 7, Lesson 5

Distinguishing Adverbs and Prepositions

Directions Determine if the word in bold is an adverb or a preposition. Write *adverb* or *preposition* on the line. If the word is used as a preposition, circle the object of the prepositional phrase.

EXAMPLES
Please step **inside**. adverb
Hiram found stones **inside** the (bottle.) preposition

1. Hang your coat on the hook **behind** the door. ____
2. I'm running **behind**, but I'll be there. ____
3. When you get to the exit, turn **off**. ____
4. Henry and Jeff jumped **off** the diving board together ____
5. The Sheffield sisters invited her **in**. ____
6. She had been invited to the party **in** the park. ____
7. The sound of wolves howling drew **near**. ____
8. The wolf packs **near** the river howl at night. ____
9. Alice put **down** the tiny bottle and began growing. ____
10. She ran **down** the hallway. ____
11. After work, the officer will come **by**. ____
12. The officer standing **by** the squad car is filing the report. ____
13. She ran **through** the gate. ____
14. Open the gate and let her **through**. ____
15. **After** the race everyone will drink water. ____
16. Scott raced ahead and Trent ran **after**. ____
17. Trent passed Scott at the bridge and ran **across**. ____
18. Scott ran **across** the bridge after Trent. ____
19. The crowd cheered for Trent as he ran **past** the finish line. ____
20. Trent cheered as Scott ran **past**. ____

Basic English Grammar

TRL

Activity 42

Lesson 5 Review Answers

1. outside—adverb 2. outside—preposition 3. before—adverb 4. before—preposition 5. down—preposition

6–15. Sentences will vary. Students should write two sentences for each word. One sentence should use the word in a prepositional phrase, and the other should use the word as an adverb. Sample sentences follow. 6. My car is in the garage. The mechanic will be in by 10 A.M.

Writing Project

Point out that prepositional phrases are helpful in showing relationships between words in a sentence and are sometimes necessary for a sentence to make sense. Help students notice how these sentences change when the prepositional phrase is omitted: *Write your name on the top line. Write your name. The sun blazed through the kitchen window. The sun blazed.* In the writing exercise on the page, urge students to use prepositional phrases to help make connections between the parts of the sentence.

Answers to Writing Project: Sentences will vary. Remind students to underline the prepositional phrases.

3 Reinforce and Extend

Online Connection

Suggest that students log on to **iteslj.org/quizzes/grammar.** Once at the site, students should scroll down to "Prepositions." Here they will have an opportunity to select different quizzes at two difficulty levels. The quizzes provide practice in selecting prepositions to complete sentences. Although designed for ESL students, the site offers all students an opportunity to check their understanding of and skill in using prepositions.

The Preposition Chapter 7 177

Chapter 7 Review

Use the Chapter Review to prepare students for tests and to reteach content from the chapter.

Chapter 7 Mastery Test 

The Teacher's Resource Library includes two parallel forms of the Chapter 7 Mastery Test. The difficulty level of the two forms is equivalent. You may wish to use one form as a pretest and the other form as a posttest.

Review Answers

Part A

1. prepositional phrase
2. compound preposition
3. preposition 4. adverb phrase
5. compound object 6. object of the preposition 7. adjective phrase

Part B

Sentences will vary. Possible sentences follow. 8. The books in front of the shelf and couch are heavy. shelf, couch—nouns 9. Play the CD after dinner. dinner—noun 10. Walk with me to the beach. me—pronoun

Part C

11. prepositional phrase—adjective phrase 12. infinitive
13. prepositional phrase—adverb phrase, prepositional phrase—adverb phrase 14. prepositional phrase—adjective phrase, prepositional phrase—adverb phrase

Chapter 7 REVIEW

Word Bank
adjective phrase
adverb phrase
compound object
compound preposition
object of the preposition
preposition
prepositional phrase

Part A On a sheet of paper, write the correct word or words from the Word Bank to complete each sentence.

1. A group of words made up of a preposition, an object, and adjectives and adverbs that describe the object is a ________.
2. A ________ is a preposition made up of more than one word.
3. A ________ is a word that shows a relationship between a noun or pronoun and other words in a sentence.
4. An ________ answers the question *how, when, where, how much,* or *how long* about the verb in a sentence.
5. Two or more objects form a ________.
6. An ________ follows the preposition in a prepositional phrase.
7. An ________ answers the question *which one, what kind, or how many* about the noun or pronoun.

Part B Complete each sentence with a preposition. Write the complete sentence on your paper. More than one preposition may make sense in the sentence. Use at least one compound preposition. Then write the object or objects of each preposition. Identify them as *nouns* or *pronouns.*

8. The books ________ the shelf and couch are heavy.
9. Play the CD ________ dinner.
10. Walk ________ me to the beach.

Part C On your paper, write whether the phrase or phrases in bold are *infinitives* or *prepositional phrases.* Next to each prepositional phrase, write whether it is an *adjective phrase* or an *adverb phrase.*

11. The letter **from Aunt Vera** arrived yesterday.
12. Carol waited **to leave.**
13. Jiro traveled **across the country in a bus** last summer.
14. I put my homework **for math class inside my book.**

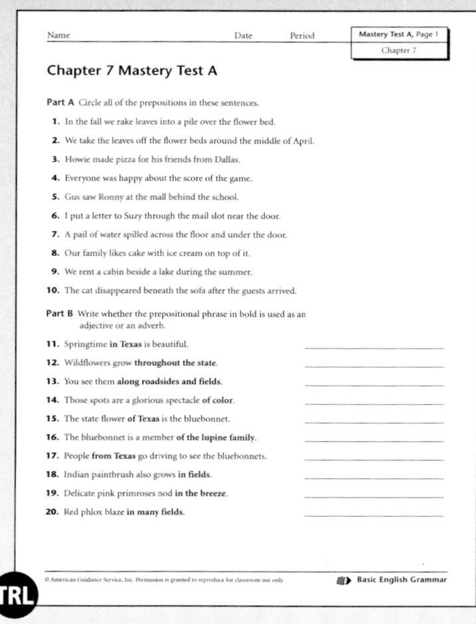

Name Date Period | Mastery Test A, Page 1 | Chapter 7

Chapter 7 Mastery Test A

Part A Circle all of the prepositions in these sentences.

1. In the fall we rake leaves into a pile over the flower bed.
2. We take the leaves off the flower beds around the middle of April.
3. Howie made pizza for his friends from Dallas.
4. Everyone was happy about the score of the game.
5. Gus saw Ronny at the mall behind the school.
6. I put a letter to Suzy through the mail slot near the door.
7. A pail of water spilled across the floor and under the door.
8. Our family likes cake with ice cream on top of it.
9. We rent a cabin beside a lake during the summer.
10. The cat disappeared beneath the sofa after the guests arrived.

Part B Write whether the prepositional phrase in bold is used as an adjective or an adverb.

11. Springtime **in Texas** is beautiful. ________
12. Wildflowers grow **throughout the state**. ________
13. You see them **along roadsides and fields**. ________
14. Those spots are a glorious spectacle **of color**. ________
15. The state flower **of Texas** is the bluebonnet. ________
16. The bluebonnet is a member **of the lupine family**. ________
17. People **from Texas** go driving to see the bluebonnets. ________
18. Indian paintbrush also grows **in fields**. ________
19. Delicate pink primroses nod **in the breeze**. ________
20. Red phlox blaze **in many fields**. ________

 Basic English Grammar

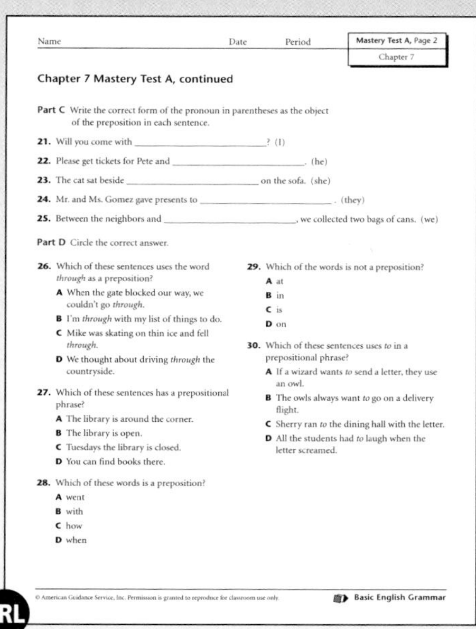

Name Date Period | Mastery Test A, Page 2 | Chapter 7

Chapter 7 Mastery Test A, continued

Part C Write the correct form of the pronoun in parentheses as the object of the preposition in each sentence.

21. Will you come with ________? (I)
22. Please get tickets for Pete and ________. (he)
23. The cat sat beside ________ on the sofa. (she)
24. Mr. and Ms. Gomez gave presents to ________. (they)
25. Between the neighbors and ________, we collected two bags of cans. (we)

Part D Circle the correct answer.

26. Which of these sentences uses the word *through* as a preposition?
    - **A** When the gate blocked our way, we couldn't go *through.*
    - **B** I'm *through* with my list of things to do.
    - **C** Mike was skating on thin ice and fell *through.*
    - **D** We thought about driving *through* the countryside.
27. Which of these sentences has a prepositional phrase?
    - **A** The library is around the corner.
    - **B** The library is open.
    - **C** Tuesdays the library is closed.
    - **D** You can find books there.
28. Which of these words is a preposition?
    - **A** went
    - **B** with
    - **C** how
    - **D** when
29. Which of the words is not a preposition?
    - **A** at
    - **B** in
    - **C** is
    - **D** on
30. Which of these sentences uses *to* in a prepositional phrase?
    - **A** If a wizard wants *to* send a letter, they use an owl.
    - **B** The owls always want *to* go on a delivery flight.
    - **C** Sherry ran *to* the dining hall with the letter.
    - **D** All the students had *to* laugh when the letter screamed.

 Basic English Grammar

Chapter 7 Mastery Test A

Part D Write the prepositional phrases in these sentences on your paper. Then write the question the prepositional phrase answers about each word in bold.

15. Michaela **came** to see me for a minute.
16. **Some** of the trails are steep and difficult to climb.
17. Still, Carrie should **make** it to the top with no problem.

Part E Write the letter of the prepositional phrase that correctly completes each sentence on your paper.

18. Nathan watched TV ________.
A with he father
B with his father
C with him's father
D with he's father

19. Mario wrote a letter ________.
A to Alex and me
B to I and him
C to he and I
D to Alex and I

20. ________ did Elsa talk to?
A Who
B What
C Whom
D Which

Part F Write these sentences on your paper. Add at least one prepositional phrase to each one to make the sentence more interesting. Be sure to add only prepositional phrases. Then write the noun or pronoun each prepositional phrase describes.

21. Everyone was happy.
22. The weather was good.
23. The family went out.
24. They came home.
25. The family was tired.

When taking a test, read the question twice to make sure you understand what is being asked.

Review Answers

Part D

15. for a minute—how long **16.** of the trails—what kind **17.** to the top—where, with no problem—how

Part E

18. B **19.** A **20.** C

Part F

21–25. Sentences will vary.

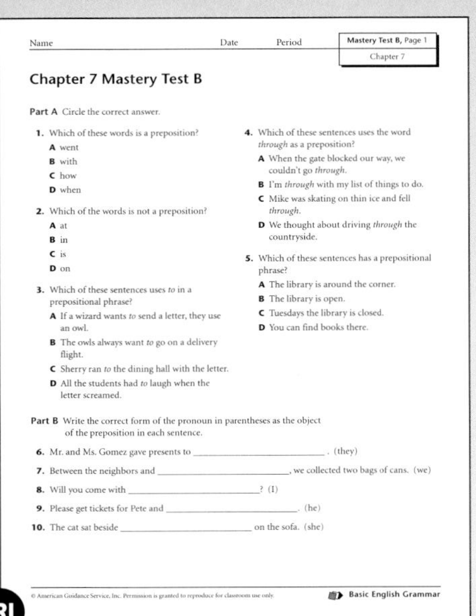

Name Date Period | **Mastery Test B,** Page 1 | Chapter 7

Chapter 7 Mastery Test B

Part A Circle the correct answer.

1. Which of these words is a preposition?
A went
B with
C how
D when

2. Which of the words is not a preposition?
A at
B in
C is
D on

3. Which of these sentences uses *to* in a prepositional phrase?
A If a wizard wants *to* send a letter, they use an owl.
B The owls always want *to* go on a delivery flight.
C Sherry ran *to* the dining hall with the letter.
D All the students had *to* laugh when the letter screamed.

4. Which of these sentences uses the word *through* as a preposition?
A When the gate blocked our way, we couldn't go *through*.
B I'm *through* with my list of things to do.
C Mike was skating on thin ice and fell *through*.
D We thought about driving *through* the countryside.

5. Which of these sentences has a prepositional phrase?
A The library is around the corner.
B The library is open.
C Tuesdays the library is closed.
D You can find books there.

Part B Write the correct form of the pronoun in parentheses as the object of the preposition in each sentence.

6. Mr. and Ms. Gomez gave presents to ________________. (they)
7. Between the neighbors and ________________, we collected two bags of cans. (we)
8. Will you come with ________________? (I)
9. Please get tickets for Pete and ________________. (he)
10. The cat sat beside ________________ on the sofa. (she)

 Basic English Grammar

TRL

Name Date Period | **Mastery Test B,** Page 2 | Chapter 7

Chapter 7 Mastery Test B, continued

Part C Circle all of the prepositions in these sentences.

11. In the fall we rake leaves into a pile over the flower bed.
12. We take the leaves off the flower beds around the middle of April.
13. Howie made pizza for his friends from Dallas.
14. A pail of water spilled across the floor and under the door.
15. Our family likes cake with ice cream on top of it.
16. We rent a cabin beside a lake during the summer.
17. The cat disappeared beneath the sofa after the guests arrived.
18. Everyone was happy about the score of the game.
19. Gus saw Ronny at the mall behind the school.
20. I put a letter to Suzy through the mail slot near the door.

Part D Write whether the prepositional phrase in bold is used as an adjective or an adverb.

21. The state flower **of Texas** is the bluebonnet. ________________
22. The bluebonnet is a member **of the lupine family**. ________________
23. People **from Texas** go driving to see the bluebonnets. ________________
24. Indian paintbrush also grows **in fields**. ________________
25. Delicate pink primroses nod **in the breeze**. ________________
26. Red phlox blaze **in many fields**. ________________
27. Springtime **in Texas** is beautiful. ________________
28. Wildflowers grow **throughout the state**. ________________
29. You see them **along roadsides and fields**. ________________
30. Those spots are a glorious spectacle **of color**. ________________

 Basic English Grammar

TRL

Chapter 7 Mastery Test B

Chapter

8

Planning Guide

The Conjunction and the Interjection

	Student Text Lesson				Language Skills		
	Student Pages	Vocabulary	Practice Exercises	Lesson Review	Identification Skills	Writing Skills	Punctuation Skills
Lesson 1 What Is a Coordinating Conjunction?	182–186	✔	✔	✔	✔	✔	✔
Lesson 2 Subordinating Conjunctions	187–191	✔	✔	✔	✔	✔	✔
Lesson 3 Correlative Conjunctions	192–194	✔	✔	✔	✔	✔	✔
Lesson 4 Using Interjections	195–197	✔	✔	✔	✔	✔	✔

Chapter Activities

Teacher's Resource Library

Community Connection 8: Your Product Endorsement

Media and Literature Connection 8: Conjunctions and Interjections in Magazines

Assessment Options

Student Text

Chapter 8 Review

Teacher's Resource Library

Chapter 8 Mastery Tests A and B

Student Text Features						Teaching Strategies						Learning Styles						Teacher's Resource Library			
Spelling Builder	Vocabulary Builder	Where To Find It	Writing Project	Using What You've Learned	Writing Tips/Notes/ Technology Notes	Teacher Alert	Online Connection	Applications (Home, Career, Community, Global)	Speaking Practice	Spelling Practice	Writing Practice	Auditory/Verbal	Body/Kinesthetic	Interpersonal/Group Learning	Logical/Mathematical	Visual/Spatial	LEP/ESL	Workbook Activities	Activities	Alternative Activities	Self-Study Guide
	186			184	✔	184, 185	183							183	185		182	43	43	43	✔
		191			✔	187		188, 190			189			190	188	190		44	44	44	✔
194								193		194		193	192		193			45	45	45	✔
			197		✔	196		197	196							195		46	46	46	✔

Pronunciation Key

a	hat	e	let	ī	ice	ô	order	u̇	put	sh	she	ə { a	in about
ā	age	ē	equal	o	hot	oi	oil	ü	rule	th	thin	e	in taken
ä	far	ėr	term	ō	open	ou	out	ch	child	ᴛʜ	then	i	in pencil
â	care	i	it	ȯ	saw	u	cup	ng	long	zh	measure	o	in lemon
												u	in circus

Alternative Activities

The Teacher's Resource Library (TRL) contains a set of lower-level worksheets called Alternative Activities. These worksheets cover the same content as the regular Activities but are written at a second-grade reading level.

Skill Track Software

Use the Skill Track Software for Basic English Grammar for additional reinforcement of this chapter. The software program allows students using AGS textbooks to be assessed for mastery of each chapter and lesson of the textbook. Students access the software on an individual basis and are assessed with multiple-choice items.

Chapter at a Glance

Chapter 8: The Conjunction and the Interjection

pages 180–199

Lessons

1. What Is a Coordinating Conjunction?
   pages 182–186
2. Subordinating Conjunctions
   pages 187–191
3. Correlative Conjunctions
   pages 192–194
4. Using Interjections
   pages 195–197

Chapter 8 Review

pages 198–199

Skill Track Software for Basic English Grammar

Teacher's Resource Library

Workbook Activities 43–46

Activities 43–46

Alternative Activities 43–46

Community Connection 8

Media and Literature Connection 8

Chapter 8 Self-Study Guide

Chapter 8 Mastery Tests A and B

(Answer Keys for the Teacher's Resource Library begin on page 340 of this Teacher's Edition.)

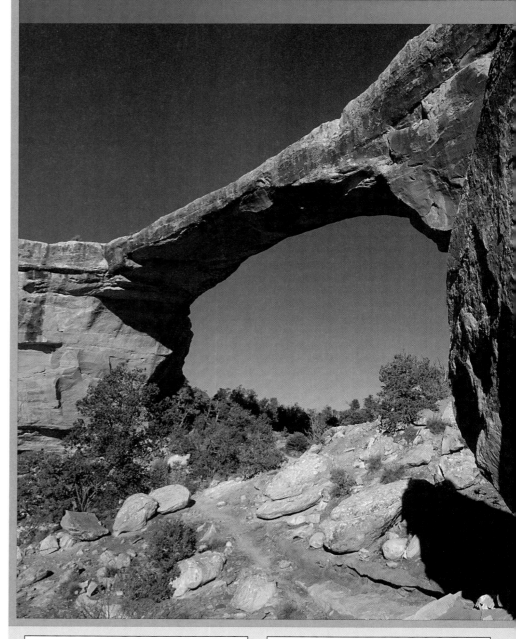

Name Date Period — Community Connection 8, Chapter 8

Your Product Endorsement

An endorsement is when someone gives their personal approval of a product in order to increase the product's sales. We've all heard and seen endorsements on radio, television, and in print advertising. An example of an endorsement is when a famous sports figure like Michael Jordan says that a product is great. If someone we respect endorses a type of car, piece of equipment, style of clothing, or kind of food, then we may be interested in driving, using, wearing, or eating that product.

Step 1 Make up a famous personality. Imagine that you are actually that person. What are you known for? Why would people respect your opinion?

Step 2 Decide on a product that you will endorse. It should be something you would really like to let other people know about. You can select from a wide range of products including music, movies, vehicles, equipment, games, activities, foods, or places to go.

Step 3 Write a product endorsement that would be used on the radio. Make it interesting and persuasive. One of the ways that you will do this is to use lots of interjections. Hey! It's natural to use interjections when we are enthusiastic! Remember to write your endorsement as if you are speaking directly to the audience.

Step 4 Remember to include information about who you are, why we should listen to you, what the product is, and why we should buy this product.

Step 5 When everyone is done writing, read your product endorsement aloud to the class.

Step 6 Discuss some of the benefits and drawbacks of product endorsements with your classmates.

 Basic English Grammar

TRL Community Connection 8

Name Date Period — Media and Literature Connection 8, Chapter 8

Conjunctions and Interjections in Magazines

A conjunction is a word that connects parts of a sentence. Conjunctions connect words, phrases, or ideas.

EXAMPLES Ron *and* Natalie went outside.
He wanted to help, *but* he couldn't.
They would have done well on the test *if* they had studied.

And, but, and *if* are all conjunctions.

An **interjection** is a word or phrase that expresses feeling. It is not key to the meaning of the sentence.

EXAMPLES *Well!* It's about time you got here.
Really? I didn't think he was that old.
Sorry. I didn't mean to interrupt

Well, really, and *sorry* are the interjections in these sentences.

Conjunctions are used in most things you read. Some things will have interjections, too. Follow these steps to find conjunctions and interjections in a magazine.

Step 1 Find a magazine at the library or at home.

Step 2 Read through the magazine. Find 10 sentences with conjunctions or interjections. Write each sentence below. Circle the conjunction or interjection in each sentence.

Step 3 Look at each sentence. Decide whether each conjunction is a coordinating, subordinating, or correlative conjunction. After each sentence, write *coordinating, subordinating, correlative,* or *interjection.*

EXAMPLE You will be late (unless) you hurry. subordinating

1.
2.
3.
4.
5.
6.
7.
8.
9.
10.

 Basic English Grammar

TRL Media and Literature Connection 8

Chapter

The Conjunction and the Interjection

You could walk on this bridge from one rock formation to another. Conjunctions work the same way in sentences. They help you link words and ideas together. Words such as *and, but,* and *for* can connect words, phrases, or ideas. Using conjunctions when you write and speak can help you create sentences that are smooth and easy to understand.

A person first seeing this rock bridge might say "Wow!" or "My goodness!" He or she would be using an interjection. Interjections are words or phrases that express strong feeling.

In Chapter 8, you will learn about conjunctions and interjections. Each lesson in the chapter focuses on recognizing and using conjunctions and different kinds of interjections in sentences.

Goals for Learning

- To identify conjunctions in sentences
- To write compound sentences using coordinating conjunctions
- To write complex sentences using subordinating conjunctions
- To write sentences using correlative conjunctions
- To punctuate sentences with conjunctions
- To use interjections in sentences
- To write and punctuate sentences that contain interjections

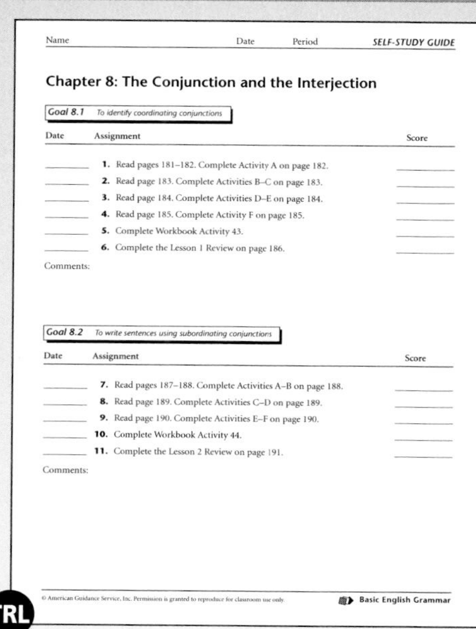

Name Date Period *SELF-STUDY GUIDE*

Chapter 8: The Conjunction and the Interjection

Goal 8.1 *To identify coordinating conjunctions*

Date	Assignment	Score
______	**1.** Read pages 181–182. Complete Activity A on page 182.	______
______	**2.** Read page 183. Complete Activities B–C on page 183.	______
______	**3.** Read page 184. Complete Activities D–E on page 184.	______
______	**4.** Read page 185. Complete Activity F on page 185.	______
______	**5.** Complete Workbook Activity 43.	______
______	**6.** Complete the Lesson 1 Review on page 186.	______

Comments:

Goal 8.2 *To write sentences using subordinating conjunctions*

Date	Assignment	Score
______	**7.** Read pages 187–188. Complete Activities A–B on page 188.	______
______	**8.** Read page 189. Complete Activities C–D on page 189.	______
______	**9.** Read page 190. Complete Activities E–F on page 190.	______
______	**10.** Complete Workbook Activity 44.	______
______	**11.** Complete the Lesson 2 Review on page 191.	______

Comments:

 Basic English Grammar

TRL

Name Date Period *SELF-STUDY GUIDE*

Chapter 8: The Conjunction and the Interjection, continued

Goal 8.3 *To write sentences using correlative conjunctions*

Date	Assignment	Score
______	**12.** Read page 192. Complete Activity A on page 192.	______
______	**13.** Read page 193. Complete Activity B on page 193.	______
______	**14.** Complete Workbook Activity 45.	______
______	**15.** Complete the Lesson 3 Review on page 194.	______

Comments:

Goal 8.4 *To use interjections in sentences*

Date	Assignment	Score
______	**16.** Read pages 195–196. Complete Activities A–B on page 196.	______
______	**17.** Complete Workbook Activity 46.	______
______	**18.** Complete the Lesson 4 Review on page 197.	______
______	**19.** Complete the Chapter 8 Review on pages 198–199.	______

Comments:

Student's Signature ______________ Date ______

Instructor's Signature ______________ Date ______

 Basic English Grammar

TRL

Chapter 8 Self-Study Guide, Pages 1–2

Introducing the Chapter

Focus students' attention on the rock bridge in the photograph. Then engage them in a discussion about the main purpose of a bridge. Ask students what the function of a bridge is. Elicit that a bridge connects two divided pieces of land. Then write the word *and* on the board. Ask students if they recognize any similarity between the bridge and the word *and.* Accept any reasonable response. Help students conclude that the word *and* acts like a bridge to connect ideas. Explain that *and* is a conjunction.

Point out that when looking at this scene of natural beauty, a person might be at a loss for words. The person might utter an interjection such as "Gosh!," "Wow!," or "Magnificent!" Explain that interjections express more than wonder. There is an interjection for nearly every occasion when we are otherwise left speechless. By the end of Chapter 8, students will understand how they can use conjunctions to connect their ideas and interjections to express themselves.

Writing Tips, Notes, and Technology Notes

Ask volunteers to read the tips and notes that appear in the margins throughout the chapter. Then discuss them with the class.

Teacher's Resource

The AGS Teaching Strategies in English Transparencies may be used with this chapter. The transparencies add an interactive dimension to expand and enhance the *Basic English Grammar* program content.

Career Interest Inventory

The AGS Harrington-O'Shea Career Decision-Making System–Revised (CDM) may be used with this chapter. Students can use the CDM to explore their interests and identify careers. The CDM defines career areas that are indicated by students' responses on the inventory.

Lesson at a Glance

Chapter 8 Lesson 1

Overview This lesson introduces the concept of conjunctions, focusing on coordinating conjunctions.

Objectives

- To identify and use coordinating conjunctions in sentences.
- To punctuate sentences with coordinating conjunctions.
- To distinguish between prepositions and conjunctions.

Student Pages 182–186

Teacher's Resource Library 

Workbook Activity 43

Activity 43

Alternative Activity 43

Vocabulary

clause
comma
conjunction
coordinating conjunction
series

Warm-Up Activity

Write on the board the following incomplete sentence: *Paulo his mother got on the bus went to town.* Invite a volunteer to read this passage. Ask the class to turn it into a sentence by adding two words. Elicit that the word *and* should be inserted after *Paulo* and after *bus.* Point out that *and* is a coordinating conjunction, a word that connects ideas.

Teaching the Lesson

Point out that all coordinating conjunctions serve the same purpose—to connect parts of a sentence—but that they can also contribute to a sentence's meaning. On the left of the board, write the clause *We ran hard.* On the right side, write *we were late, we missed the bus,* and *we got there on time.* Between these clauses write the conjunctions *and, but,* and *for.* Have students connect the clause on the left with each clause on the right, using the most appropriate conjunction.

Emphasize the role of punctuation by writing the following example on the board: *Would you rather watch birds rent a movie or go for a walk.* Make sure that students appreciate the ridiculous image in this sentence (watching birds rent a movie). Ask them to make the simple corrections (commas after *birds* and *movie*).

Activity A

Before students start this activity, invite a volunteer to read aloud the coordinating conjunctions in the box on this page.

Activity A Answers

1. and 2. and 3. and 4. as well as 5. but

Reinforce and Extend

Learning Styles

LEP/ESL

Invite students learning English to list the eight coordinating conjunctions on page 182. Ask volunteers to create English sentences that use these eight conjunctions and to say the sentences aloud. Then have each volunteer repeat the sentence but pause by the conjunction. Have the student learning English say aloud the conjunction that goes in the sentence. Then have the volunteer complete the sentence.

Lesson 1 What Is a Coordinating Conjunction?

Conjunction
A word that connects parts of a sentence

Clause
A group of words with a subject and a verb

Coordinating conjunction
A word that connects two or more equal parts of a sentence

A **conjunction** is a word that connects parts of a sentence. A conjunction can connect words, phrases, or clauses. A **clause** is a group of words with a subject and a verb.

There are three kinds of conjunctions: the **coordinating conjunction,** the subordinating conjunction, and the correlative conjunction.

A coordinating conjunction connects words, phrases, or sentences that are equal.

Example

Conjunctions Connect Words	Robert plays hockey and soccer.
Conjunctions Connect Phrases	He ran down the street and into Joe's house.
Conjunctions Connect Sentences	I'd like to help you, but I'm busy.

Here are the most common coordinating conjunctions.

Coordinating Conjunctions			
and	but	nor	so
as well as	for	or	yet

Activity A On your paper, write the coordinating conjunction in each sentence.

1. Eight and eight make 16.
2. All night the winds blew and the snow fell.
3. The referee blew her whistle and stopped the game.
4. Mike is coming to the party as well as Tim.
5. The actor sang well, but he could not dance.

Comma

A punctuation mark (,) used to separate words, phrases, or clauses in a series

Series

A group of three or more words, phrases, or clauses

Activity B Complete each sentence with a coordinating conjunction. On your paper, write the conjunctions.

1. I will have milk ________ water with my dinner.
2. Paco hits well, ________ he cannot throw a curve ball.
3. Vic tried hard ________ made the team.
4. Louisa studies hard, ________ she has time for her friends.
5. After school we played CDs ________ relaxed.

A coordinating conjunction may connect two or more complete ideas.

To coordinate means to bring into proper order or relation. When you use a coordinating conjunction, you are bringing ideas into proper order.

EXAMPLE I will drink water. I will drink lemonade.
I will drink water or lemonade.
(*Or* connects *water* and *lemonade.* We do not repeat the words that appear in both sentences.)

Activity C Use coordinating conjunctions to connect the ideas in the following pairs of sentences. On your paper, write the new sentences. You may need to change the verb form.

1. Lena likes oranges. Andy likes oranges.
2. Lloyd plays football. Lloyd plays baseball.
3. Langston Hughes wrote short stories. He also wrote poetry.
4. I grew okra in my garden. I grew beans in my garden.
5. Laura plays basketball. Her sister plays basketball.

Use a **comma** to separate words, phrases, or clauses in a **series.** A series is three or more words, phrases, or clauses. Place the comma after each item in the series except the last one.

EXAMPLE

Words in a Series	Rajeeva, Annie, and Phil arrived late. (Three people are in this series. Use commas.)
Phrases in a Series	Tamika jogged down the street, across the park, and around the lake. (Three phrases are in this series. Use commas.)

Activity B

Point out that more than one conjunction may make sense in each sentence before doing the first two items orally with students. Then have students complete the activity on their own.

Activity B Answers

1. and *or* or 2. but *or* yet 3. and 4. but *or* yet 5. and

Activity C

Write these sentences on the board: *Joe enjoys watching old movies. Edie enjoys watching old movies.* Help students recognize the related ideas in these sentences. Elicit that both Joe and Edie enjoy watching old movies. Then help students combine these sentences, using a conjunction. (*Joe and Edie enjoy watching old movies.*) Be sure students note the verb form change. After students complete Activity B, invite them to share their sentences with the class.

Activity C Answers

1. Lena and Andy like oranges. 2. Lloyd plays football and baseball. 3. Langston Hughes wrote short stories and poetry. 4. I grew okra and beans in my garden. 5. Laura and her sister play basketball.

ONLINE CONNECTION

Have students visit **www.chompchomp.com/terms/** and select "Coordinating Conjunction" from the Index. Here they will find more information about coordinating conjunctions with example sentences. Suggest that pairs of students use the information to prepare their own lesson on coordinating conjunctions. Invite volunteer pairs to teach their lesson to the class.

LEARNING STYLES

Interpersonal/Group Learning

Ask students to name foods that people often eat. Write their selections on the board. Then have students compose simple sentences describing their own preferences, using items from the list. (Examples: *I like ice cream. I don't like rice.*) Have students read and record each other's statements. Then ask them to write five sentences in the following pattern using *and* and *but: Jamal and I like pizza and peanut butter but not snails and spinach.* Encourage them to add more names and food items to their sentences, linking them in series with commas and coordinating conjunctions. Invite volunteers to read their sentences.

Activity D

Write the first item on the board and help students find the three items in a series and the conjunction that connects them in the sentence. Help students determine where to place commas. Have students work with partners to complete the remaining items in Activity D.

Activity D Answers

1. We planted bushes, trees, (and) flowers around the house. 2. Later we washed up, changed our clothes, (and) went out to dinner. 3. I ordered a salad (and) milk. 4. My brother, sister, father, (and) mother ordered the soup. 5. After dinner we talked about going to a movie, playing miniature golf, (or) taking a walk around the lake.

Activity E

Invite volunteers to write sample sentences for items 1 and 2 on the board. Encourage one or two of the volunteers to write a sentence with items in a series, punctuated correctly. Then have students work independently to complete Activity E.

Activity E Answers

Answers will vary. Possible answers follow. 1. Tiffany, Amber, and Ramon went to the park. 2. They looked for Tisha, but she had already left. 3. You may wash the dishes or clean your room. 4. Tim did not go to the play, nor did Gina. 5. I wanted to go to the coffee house, yet I had homework to do.

Using What You've Learned

Give students practice listening for where commas should occur by having them read aloud their sentences to the class. Invite a volunteer to repeat the sentence after hearing it read, saying the word *comma* at the appropriate points in the series. Ask the reader to write the sentence on the board to confirm the volunteer's punctuation.

Activity D On your paper, write these sentences. Add commas only where needed. Circle the conjunctions.

1. We planted bushes trees and flowers around the house.
2. Later we washed up changed our clothes and went out to dinner.
3. I ordered a salad and milk.
4. My brother sister father and mother ordered the soup.
5. After dinner we talked about going to a movie playing miniature golf or taking a walk around the lake.

Using What You've Learned

Use coordinating conjunctions and commas to list words in a series correctly. Write a sentence in which you group your classmates by hair color, birth dates, or first names. For example, *Jill, Jared, and Jorge all have names that start with J.*

Activity E Use each of these conjunctions in a sentence. Write your sentences on your paper. Try to write at least two sentences that contain items in a series. Use correct punctuation.

1. and
2. but
3. or
4. nor
5. yet

Rule 1 Use *and* to connect two items when both are true. Lisa and Kylie entered the marathon. (Both of them entered.)

Rule 2 Use *but* to point out a difference between two ideas.
Lisa entered the marathon, but Ethan did not. (Only Lisa entered.)

Rule 3 Use *or* to connect ideas that are choices or differences.
Lisa or Kylie will enter the marathon. (One of them will enter. We don't know which one yet.)

Rule 4 Use *nor* to point out that neither of the subjects did the action.
Ethan did not enter the marathon, nor did Leon. (Ethan did not enter. Leon did not enter.)

Teacher Alert

You may wish to explain that a comma is used in writing to show a pause in thought. Commas separate ideas so that readers do not get confused.

When you join complete sentences with any of the following conjunctions, use a semicolon (;) before it and a comma (,) after it.

More Conjunctions		
accordingly	furthermore	nevertheless
also	however	otherwise
besides	instead	therefore
consequently	moreover	

Grace likes to play the violin; however, she doesn't like to practice.

Alex worked all weekend; nevertheless, he didn't finish.

The words *but* and *for* can be either conjunctions or prepositions.

EXAMPLE

Conjunction Angie feeds her puppy dog food, but he prefers steak!
Trevor brought the CDs, for he was the disc jockey.

Preposition No one was hungry but Jennifer.
We knew that Lee would work hard for the group.

Activity F Write these sentences on your paper. Add punctuation where it is needed. Then write whether the word in bold is a *preposition* or a *conjunction.*

1. Everyone liked the story **but** Yolanda.
2. We wanted to go shopping **instead** we stayed home.
3. After dinner Lisa read a book Marco did homework Mr. Martinez watched TV **and** Mrs. Martinez relaxed.
4. Karl rode the bus to school **but** he walked home.
5. The students cheered loudly **for** their team.

Activity F

You may wish to do activity F as a class. Write the first item on the board and work through it with students, helping them to distinguish between conjunctions and prepositions and to punctuate the sentence correctly. Follow the same procedure with the remaining items.

Activity F Answers

1. Everyone liked the story but Yolanda. preposition **2.** We wanted to go shopping; instead, we stayed home. conjunction **3.** After dinner Lisa read a book, Marco did homework, Mr. Martinez watched TV, and Mrs. Martinez relaxed. conjunction **4.** Karl rode the bus to school, but he walked home. conjunction **5.** The students cheered loudly for their team. preposition

Teacher Alert

Remind students that a prepositional phrase begins with a preposition and ends with the object of the preposition, which is always a noun or pronoun. Emphasize that a prepositional phrase never has a verb.

Learning Styles

Logical/Mathematical

Draw students' attention to the words in the More Conjunctions box on page 185. Point out that like the conjunctions *and* and *but,* these words are used for different purposes. Write *also, besides, furthermore, however, nevertheless,* and *moreover* on the board. Ask students to divide these conjunctions into two groups: those that can replace *but* and those that can replace *and.* With the use of model sentences, help students understand that *nevertheless* and *however* serve a similar role to *but,* while the remaining four can replace *and.* Encourage students to use these conjunctions in sentences of their own.

Lesson 1 Review Answers

1. Sue is hard of hearing, (but) she signs (and) reads lips. 2. She learned sign language (and) lip reading at a special class. 3. Lisa (and) Becky wanted to learn sign language, (for) they wanted to be able to communicate with Sue. 4. Some words are spelled out letter by letter; (therefore,) Lisa (and) Becky learned the finger alphabet. 5. There are 26 hand symbols in the finger alphabet, (and) each symbol stands for a letter of the alphabet. 6. conjunction 7. conjunction 8. preposition 9. conjunction, preposition 10. conjunction

Vocabulary Builder

Before students read the information in the box, ask them to write two sentences—one using *and* as a coordinating conjunction, the other using *but*. Invite volunteers to write their sentences on the board, and ask the class to define the difference between these two common conjunctions. Then read the contents of the Vocabulary Builder box aloud with the class, and have students complete the exercise. Afterward, invite students to write their solutions on the board and to explain the reasons for their choices.

Answers to Vocabulary Builder: 1. but 2. and 3. but 4. and 5. and

Lesson 1 REVIEW

Write these sentences on your paper. Circle the coordinating conjunctions. Add any missing punctuation.

1. Sue is hard of hearing but she signs and reads lips.
2. She learned sign language and lip reading at a special class.
3. Lisa and Becky wanted to learn sign language for they wanted to be able to communicate with Sue.
4. Some words are spelled out letter by letter therefore Lisa and Becky learned the finger alphabet.
5. There are 26 hand symbols in the finger alphabet and each symbol stands for a letter of the alphabet.

Write on your paper whether the word in bold is a *conjunction* or a *preposition.*

6. Paul played tennis well **for** he practiced every day.
7. The new apartment was beautiful, **but** the rent was high.
8. Bring a lunch **for** me.
9. Lisa hurried, **but** she was still late **for** work.
10. Today is rainy **but** tomorrow we should see the sun.

Vocabulary Builder

And* or *But

And and *but* are both coordinating conjunctions, but their meanings are different.

We use *and* when we connect things of similar value. For example:
Jennifer likes the colors red and blue equally.

We use *but* to introduce an exception or a different point of view. For example:
Antonio enjoys reading, but he did not like that book.

Complete each sentence by adding either *and* or *but.*

1. A frog begins life as a tadpole, ________ a turtle does not.
2. Alonzo enjoys both painting ________ drawing.
3. Our football team played well, ________ the other team won.
4. Let's go to the movies ________ skateboard in the park.
5. Both cars ________ trucks can drive on the new highway.

Name Date Period | Workbook Activity 43 | Chapter 8, Lesson 1

Using Coordinating Conjunctions

Directions Connect the ideas in the following pairs of sentences, using coordinating conjunctions. Follow the example. You may need to change the verb form. Write your sentences on the lines.

EXAMPLE Toby had soup for lunch. Toby also had salad.
Toby had soup and salad for lunch.

1. Plain water is sugar-free. It is also caffeine-free.
2. My older brother, Casey, plays soccer. My little brother, Jimmy, plays soccer.
3. My favorite baseball player is Derek Jeter. My other favorite player is Roger Clements.
4. Toni Morrison wrote *Beloved*. She wrote *Tar Baby*.
5. I have a poodle named Velvet. I have a poodle named Buffy.
6. Velvet is black. Buffy is white.
7. My garden has roses. It has ivy. It has herbs.
8. Our telephone is a cell phone. Our telephone is very small.
9. For the picnic, we bought potato salad. We bought hot dogs.
10. Betty likes hot dogs. She doesn't like hamburgers.

 Basic English Grammar

TRL

Workbook Activity 43

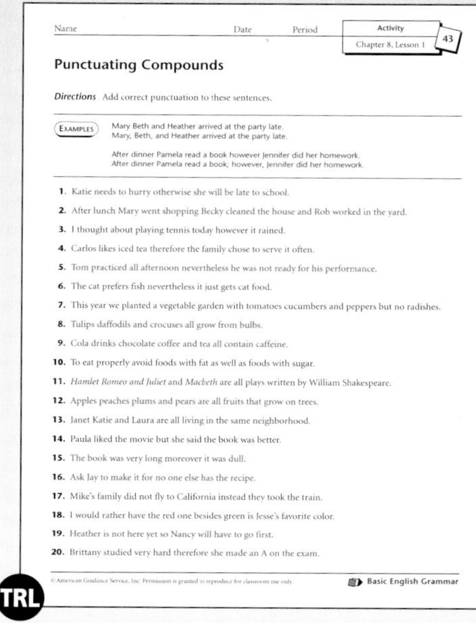

Name Date Period | Activity 43 | Chapter 8, Lesson 1

Punctuating Compounds

Directions Add correct punctuation to these sentences.

EXAMPLES Mary Beth and Heather arrived at the party late.
Mary, Beth, and Heather arrived at the party late.

After dinner Pamela read a book however Jennifer did her homework.
After dinner Pamela read a book; however, Jennifer did her homework.

1. Katie needs to hurry otherwise she will be late to school.
2. After lunch Mary went shopping Becky cleaned the house and Rob worked in the yard.
3. I thought about playing tennis today however it rained.
4. Carlos likes iced tea therefore the family chose to serve it often.
5. Tom practiced all afternoon nevertheless he was not ready for his performance.
6. The cat prefers fish nevertheless it just gets cat food.
7. This year we planted a vegetable garden with tomatoes cucumbers and peppers but no radishes.
8. Tulips daffodils and crocuses all grow from bulbs.
9. Cola drinks chocolate coffee and tea all contain caffeine.
10. To eat properly avoid foods with fat as well as foods with sugar.
11. *Hamlet Romeo and Juliet* and *Macbeth* are all plays written by William Shakespeare.
12. Apples peaches plums and pears are all fruits that grow on trees.
13. Janet Katie and Laura are all living in the same neighborhood.
14. Paula liked the movie but she said the book was better.
15. The book was very long moreover it was dull.
16. Ask Jay to make it for no one else has the recipe.
17. Mike's family did not fly to California instead they took the train.
18. I would rather have the red one besides green is Jesse's favorite color.
19. Heather is not here yet so Nancy will have to go first.
20. Brittany studied very hard therefore she made an A on the exam.

 Basic English Grammar

TRL

Activity 43

Lesson 2 Subordinating Conjunctions

Subordinating conjunction
A word that connects a dependent clause to an independent clause in a sentence

Independent clause
A clause that expresses a complete thought

Dependent clause
A clause that does not express a complete thought

A **subordinating conjunction** connects an **independent clause** to a **dependent clause.** An independent clause expresses a complete thought. A dependent clause is a group of words that has a subject and a verb but does not express a complete thought. Since a dependent clause does not express a complete thought by itself, it cannot stand alone as a sentence. A dependent clause depends on the main, or independent, clause to make sense.

EXAMPLE

When the cheers stop we can continue the basketball game. (The subordinating conjunction *when* connects the incomplete idea *when the cheers stop* to the main clause *we can continue.*)

A dependent clause may begin or end a sentence. When a dependent clause begins a sentence, use a comma to separate that clause from the independent clause.

EXAMPLE

Dependent Clause **Independent Clause**
After the game was over, we went to Tim's house.

Independent Clause **Dependent Clause**
We went to Tim's house after the game was over.

A subordinating conjunction introduces an adverb clause. Like adverbs, these clauses answer the questions *when, where, why,* and *how.*

Lesson at a Glance

Chapter 8 Lesson 2

Overview This lesson presents subordinating conjunctions and independent and dependent clauses.

Objectives

- To identify dependent clauses introduced by subordinating conjunctions.
- To connect independent and dependent clauses with subordinating conjunctions.
- To distinguish between prepositions and conjunctions.

Student Pages 187–191

Teacher's Resource Library 

Workbook Activity 44
Activity 44
Alternative Activity 44

Vocabulary

dependent clause
independent clause
subordinating conjunction

1 Warm-Up Activity

Write on the board the following clauses: *I go to school at seven* and *If I go to school at seven.* Ask students to identify the subject and verb of each clause. Establish that they are the same (*I* and *go*). Then explain that one of these clauses is a sentence. Ask students to identify which one and to explain what makes it a sentence. Elicit that the first clause is a sentence because it expresses a complete thought. Lead students to understand that the second clause requires more information to express a complete thought. Substitute the word *if* with *after, since,* and *whenever.* Explain that each of these words is a subordinating conjunction. A clause that begins with one of these words is called a dependent clause because it needs another clause to form a complete sentence.

2 Teaching the Lesson

Help students understand that dependent clauses introduced by subordinating conjunctions have their own specific meanings that must relate to the sense of the independent clause. Write on the board *I will go to hockey practice.* Then ask students to add to this sentence a dependent clause beginning with one of the following subordinating conjunctions: *although, because, if,* and *after.* (Example: *I will go to hockey practice although I have a sprained ankle.)* Point out that their dependent clauses all have different content determined by the meaning of the subordinating conjunction.

3 Reinforce and Extend

TEACHER ALERT

The concepts presented in this lesson assume that students have a basic understanding of the meanings of *subject, predicate,* and *sentence.* It may be helpful for students if you review simple definitions of these terms.

Activity A

Write this sentence on the board: *While you were out, Amy called twice.* Work with students to identify and label the main, or independent, clause and dependent clause in this sentence. Discuss how students determined which was which. Then invite a volunteer to circle the subordinating conjunction in the dependent clause, *While you were out.* After students complete Activity A on their own, discuss their answers.

Activity A Answers

1. (If) you want to play the piano better 2. (until) I finish 3. (because) he wanted to go to college 4. (When) Lisa gets here 5. (while) they watched the movie

Activity B

Have volunteers do items 1 and 2 on the board. Encourage the class to check that the students have introduced the dependent clauses with subordinating conjunctions, and that the sentences have been punctuated correctly. Then have students complete Activity B on their own.

Activity B Answers

Answers will vary. Sample sentences follow. **1.** Dan would like to visit California (when) he graduates from high school. **2.** Darryl saved 25 dollars a week (because) he wanted to go to France. **3.** My neighbors asked me to water their garden (while) they are on vacation. **4.** Anne's report was late (because) she was sick for a week. **5.** Marcus went to the new computer store (where) he bought three new software packages. **6.** The storm forced people to stay home (until) the crew could fix the bridge. **7.** Cassie watched a nature program about crocodiles (after) she finished her homework. **8.** While the storm raged outside, a strange noise woke me from a deep sleep. **9.** (Although) he finished his report, Lee left his school books at the library. **10.** The front door slammed shut (when) the wind blew.

When you save files while working on your computer, keep the file names short. It will be easier to locate the files on your computer later on. One way to have shorter file names is to leave out the conjunctions. A file called *Justin saves money so he can go to college* could have the name *College Fund.*

Here are some common subordinating conjunctions.

Subordinating Conjunctions		
after	in order that	when
although	since	whenever
as	so that	where
because	unless	wherever
if	until	while

Activity A On your paper, write the dependent clause in each sentence. Circle the subordinating conjunctions.

1. If you want to play the piano better, you have to practice.
2. I plan to study until I finish.
3. Justin saved his money because he wanted to go to college.
4. When Lisa gets here, we will leave.
5. They ate popcorn while they watched the movie.

Activity B Add a dependent clause to each sentence. Write the new sentences on your paper. Circle the subordinating conjunctions. Add commas where needed.

1. Dan would like to visit California.
2. Darryl saved 25 dollars a week.
3. My neighbors asked me to water their garden.
4. Anne's report was late.
5. Marcus went to the new computer store.
6. The storm forced people to stay home.
7. Cassie watched a nature program about crocodiles.
8. A strange noise woke me up from a deep sleep.
9. Lee left his school books at the library.
10. The front door slammed shut.

Global Connection

Have each student choose a continent, research information about it, and write five sentences that detail information about the continent without using its name. Ask students to use subordinating conjunctions in their sentences. Have students read their sentences to the class and have the class use a map to identify the continent the sentences describe. Have students identify the clues that helped them name the continent.

Learning Styles

Logical/Mathematical

Have students form small groups and assign them the following subordinating conjunctions: *after, where, because, while, so that, wherever.* Explain that each of these words introduces clauses that answer the questions *when, where,* or *why.* Ask students to classify their six subordinating conjunctions under these three headings: *when, where, why.* (Answers: when: *after, while;* where: *where, wherever;* why: *because, so that.*) Ask groups to compose sentences using each of these words. Invite volunteers to read their sentences.

> **Writing Tip**
>
> Use subordinating conjunctions to connect two short sentences. Use a mixture of short and long sentences to add variety to your writing.

Activity C Add an independent clause (a complete thought) to each dependent clause to make a sentence. Write the sentences on your paper.

1. Although we had just eaten breakfast,
2. Until the other team scored,
3. Because my mom is at work,
4. Since I flew on an airplane,
5. When I finish this book,

Activity D Connect each pair of sentences with a subordinating conjunction. Write the new sentences on your paper. Add commas where needed.

1. Zack is lifting weights. He wants to be on the baseball team.
2. Pete went to the library. He needed a book.
3. I was asleep. A storm blew down our tree.
4. Lisa wants to see the movie. We will buy tickets ahead of time.
5. The baseball team won the championship. The town celebrated.

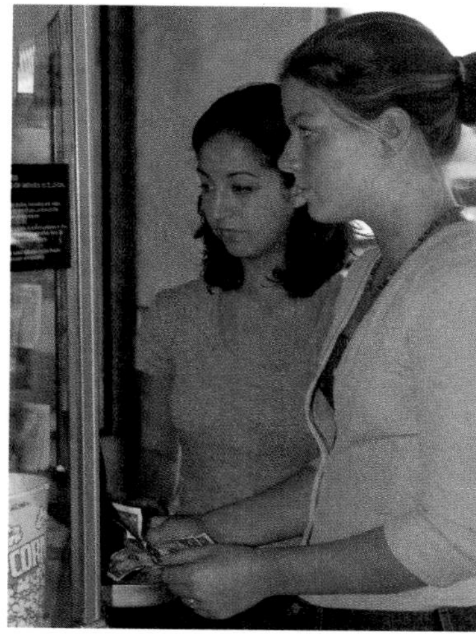

Cassie and Lisa bought popcorn because it was going to be a long movie.

Activity C

Have a volunteer do item 1 on the board. Encourage the class to check that the student has added an independent clause that expresses a complete thought. Then erase the independent clause and invite another volunteer to complete the sentence. Repeat this process until you are sure students can complete Activity C on their own.

Activity C Answers

Answers will vary. Sample sentences follow. **1.** Although we had just eaten breakfast, Brandon and I were still hungry. **2.** Until the other team scored, the fans sat quietly in the stands. **3.** Because my mom is at work, I can't go with you to the mall. **4.** Since I flew on an airplane, my ears have been ringing. **5.** When I finish this book, I'll lend it to you.

Activity D

Encourage students to use a different subordinating conjunction in each sentence and to vary the position of the conjunction. Then do item 1 together as a class before having students complete Activity D on their own.

Activity D Answers

Sentences may vary. Possible answers follow. **1.** Zack is lifting weights because he wants to be on the baseball team. **2.** Pete went to the library whenever he needed a book. **3.** While I was asleep, a storm blew down our tree. **4.** Since Lisa wants to see the movie, we will buy tickets ahead of time. **5.** After the baseball team won the championship, the town celebrated.

Writing Practice

Invite a volunteer to read the following paragraph aloud. Lead students to understand that so many short sentences create a monotonous style. Have them pair up and rewrite the passage using subordinating and coordinating conjunctions to give the sentences more variety. Point out that there are several possible revisions.

It was a warm, sunny day. We went to the beach. It was still only March. The weather was warm. We arrived at the beach. We saw something unexpected. Our English teacher was there before us. He had come to the beach. The weather was so beautiful. He said, "I hope you have finished your homework. Tomorrow's a school day."

Activity E

Write these words on the board: *after, before, until, because of,* and *since.* Have students choose partners and ask the partners to select a word from the list and write two sentences for that word, using the word once as a subordinating conjunction and once as a preposition. Invite students to read their sentences aloud. Ask the class to identify the sentence with the preposition and the sentence with the conjunction. Then have students complete Activity E independently.

Activity E Answers

1. conjunction **2.** preposition **3.** conjunction **4.** preposition **5.** preposition

Activity F

Before students do Activity F on their own, suggest that they review the list of subordinating conjunctions on page 188.

Activity F Answers

1. because **2.** although **3.** If **4.** when **5.** Where **6.** When **7.** as **8.** While **9.** since **10.** when

Learning Styles

Visual/Spatial

Divide the class into groups of five. Ask each group to choose five subordinating conjunctions from the box on page 188. Then have the group create 10 sentences, two for each conjunction. One of the two sentences should begin with a dependent clause that uses the conjunction; the other should end with a dependent clause that uses the conjunction. Ask each group to create a chart of their conjunctions and sentence examples. Display the charts and encourage the students to read the various charts to review the subordinating conjunctions.

We can use some words as subordinating conjunctions or prepositions.

Conjunction	The test was put off until we finished our projects.
Preposition	The test was put off until Friday.

Activity E On your paper, write whether the word in bold is a *conjunction* or a *preposition.*

1. We went home **after** school was over.
2. **Because** of Marco, we won the game.
3. I like that coat **because** it is warm.
4. I haven't heard from her **since** Monday.
5. **Before** lunch, I have Spanish class.

Activity F On your paper, write the subordinating conjunction in each sentence.

1. We drove home carefully because it was snowing.
2. We had classes until noon, although the weather was bad.
3. If the snow is deep enough, there will be no school tomorrow.
4. School is closed only when the snow is deep.
5. Where Lisa and Marco live, there are usually two deep snows each year.
6. When Tony walked into the room, everyone began to clap.
7. We walked around the lake as the sun was setting.
8. While I am drying the dishes, you can pick out a movie.
9. Tina has been my best friend since she moved here 10 years ago.
10. Sally's dog barks at the door when he wants to go outside.

Learning Styles

Interpersonal/Group Learning

Have students form teams of three or four, and assign each team a different station at the board. Read a short sentence aloud. The teams should quickly confer and write on the board a dependent clause that would work with the sentence you read. (Example: If you read, "The first bell rang," students might write "as I hurried to class.") Encourage students to refer to the list of subordinating conjunctions on page 188 as they work.

Career Connection

Job application forms often contain coordinating and subordinate conjunctions. If possible, obtain copies of application forms from local businesses. Review the forms with students, pointing out the conjunctions. Discuss the meanings of the conjunctions and how they affect the information an applicant should provide. You might acquire permission from an employer to duplicate the company's application form and provide practice in filling out the forms.

Lesson 2 REVIEW

Write these sentences on your paper, adding commas where needed. Circle the subordinating conjunction in each sentence.

1. Kathy will hold dinner until everyone gets here.
2. If you will help we can finish early.
3. When warm weather arrives Marco and Anthony will go fishing.
4. Until the team scored the fans were quiet.
5. Everyone cheered as the band played the school song.

Connect each pair of sentences with a subordinating conjunction. Write the new sentences on your paper. Add commas where needed. Be sure the sentences make sense.

6. Mai got an excellent grade on her test. She studied hard.
7. I will clean the house. You do the shopping.
8. Jon got hungry about three o'clock. He ate an apple.
9. The weather is too cold. I can't go outside.
10. He lost the election. He didn't have enough help.

Where To Find It

Telephone Book

The yellow pages of a telephone book list businesses in alphabetical order by the type of business.

The white pages of a telephone book include alphabetical listings of

- government agencies (These listings are easy to find. The pages have a blue border.)
- residents
- businesses

Use the guide words at the top of each page to locate listings. The guide words tell you the first and last listings on the page.

1. Look at the table of contents in the white pages of a local telephone book. What kind of information does the book include? List at least four kinds of information.
2. Look up your phone number or the phone number of someone you know. Write down the page number on which you found it. Write down the name, address, and phone number of the people who are listed above and below the name you looked up.

Name Date Period **Workbook Activity** Chapter 8, Lesson 2 **44**

Recognizing Subordinating Conjunctions

Directions Underline the subordinating conjunction in each sentence.

EXAMPLE Ms. Rodriguez will ride in the parade since she is on the city council.

1. Lisa bought paints so that she could create a sign for the garage sale.
2. Rob said he would go wherever we want to go.
3. No planes will be able to take off tonight if the blizzard strikes.
4. Will you call me when you arrive?
5. After he left office, President George Washington retired to Mount Vernon, his home in Virginia.
6. Even though it is the largest state in land area, Alaska has a very small population.
7. Because it was raining, the baseball game was canceled.
8. The relay runner grabbed the baton as it was passed to her.
9. The artist did not want anyone to see her painting before it was completed.
10. Although she was a student at the time, Maya Ying Lin won the design competition for the Vietnam Veterans Memorial.

Directions Use a subordinating conjunction to connect each pair of sentences. Write the sentences on the line. Then circle the dependent clause in each new sentence.

EXAMPLE Our team cannot win. They score another touchdown.
Our team cannot win unless they score another touchdown.

11. Sara baby-sat for three hours. She can earn enough money to by a CD.
12. The movie began at 7:00 P.M. We didn't arrive at the theater until 7:10 P.M.
13. I met Jose at the library. We could study together.
14. The President gave a speech. He took the oath of office.
15. The groundhog saw its shadow. It came out of its hole on February 2.

 Basic English Grammar

TRL

Workbook Activity 44

Name Date Period **Activity** Chapter 8, Lesson 2 **44**

Dependent Clauses

Directions Underline the dependent clause in each sentence. Circle the subordinating conjunction. The words in the box below will help you.

Common Subordinating Conjunctions				
after	because	so that	when	in order that
although	if	unless	where	whenever
as	since	until	while	wherever

EXAMPLE If you want to stay fit, exercise often.

1. Because margarine and butter are mostly fat, they should be eaten sparingly.
2. I would like to continue until I finish.
3. When Keesha arrives, we will be able to leave.
4. Since the party was over, everyone went home.
5. In order that everyone might have a chance to speak, comments must be limited to one minute.
6. Whenever I am sad, I try to think happy thoughts.
7. Although it was raining, we went for our morning walk.
8. Everyone wanted popcorn while they watched the movie.
9. If Jacob is late again, we will be very angry.
10. Because an education leads to a better job, Alex wanted to go to college.
11. In order that the workers look the same, they were issued uniforms.
12. Unless you save your money, you will never get ahead.
13. While my brother is in the Navy I am using his bedroom.
14. Wherever Ramona goes her little brother will follow her.
15. After the rain comes, the ground will be too muddy.

 Basic English Grammar

TRL

Activity 44

Lesson 2 Review Answers

1. Kathy will hold dinner (until) everyone gets here. **2.** (If) you will help, we can finish early. **3.** (When) warm weather arrives, Marco and Anthony will go fishing. **4.** (Until) the team scored, the fans were quiet. **5.** Everyone cheered (as) the band played the school song. **6–10.** Sentences may vary. Sample sentences follow. **6.** Mai got an excellent grade on her test because she studied hard. **7.** I will clean the house if you do the shopping. **8.** Since Jon got hungry about three o'clock, he ate an apple. **9.** When the weather is too cold, I can't go outside. **10.** He lost the election because he didn't have enough help.

Where To Find It

Give students a telephone book for their area. Have them identify the sections of the book that include government agencies, residents, and businesses. Point out that residential numbers under the same last name are listed alphabetically by first name. Choose a last name that is common in your area; then specify a first name and ask students to locate that person's entry.

Assign students businesses to look up in the yellow pages. Give them general headings—*carpets, locks, painting*—and ask them to find numbers for businesses near them.

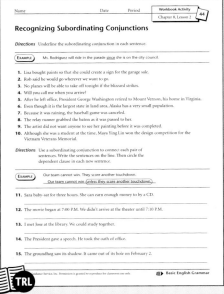

Lesson at a Glance

Chapter 8 Lesson 3

Overview This lesson introduces correlative conjunctions.

Objectives

- To identify correlative conjunctions in sentences.
- To use the correct verb form in sentences with correlative conjunctions.

Student Pages 192–194

Teacher's Resource Library 

Workbook Activity 45

Activity 45

Alternative Activity 45

Vocabulary

correlative conjunctions

Warm-Up Activity

Ask students if they have ever heard of an "either-or situation." Invite volunteers to come up with sentences a parent might say to a child using the words *either* and *or.* (Example: *Either clean your room or you're not going out tonight.*) Point out that they have just made use of a correlative conjunction. Draw students' attention to the conjunctions listed in the box on page 192. Ask them to compose sentences using these words.

Lesson 3 Correlative Conjunctions

Correlative conjunctions

A pair of conjunctions that connects words or groups of words

Correlative conjunctions express a shared relationship. Use correlative conjunctions in pairs.

Neither Ethan nor Leon enjoyed that book.
Both the characters and the plot were weak.

Correlative Conjunctions		
both . . . and	neither . . . nor	whether . . . or
either . . . or	not only . . . but also	

Activity A On your paper, write the correlative conjunctions in each sentence.

1. Ann Marie will write her report on either James Polk or Benjamin Harrison.
2. Both Polk and Harrison were presidents of the United States.
3. Not only Ann Marie but also Susan must write a report.
4. Susan doesn't know whether to write about Chester Arthur or Franklin Pierce.
5. She had heard of neither Arthur nor Pierce before.
6. Chester Arthur enjoyed not only entertaining but also traveling.
7. Neither Pierce nor Arthur served a second term.
8. Ramon will use either his laptop or a computer at school to write his report.
9. He is researching the terms of both Nixon and Reagan.
10. Sally is not only writing her speech but also videotaping it for the class.

2 Teaching the Lesson

Write on the board *Either Miguel or Lisa has won the prize.* Have students identify the verb *has won* and ask why it is not *have won,* the plural form. Point out that normally when referring to two people we would say *They have won.* Lead students to understand that when using *either . . . or,* we are referring to each subject individually. Now change the original sentence to *Either Miguel or the twins have won the prize.* Point out that *twins* is plural and the verb will agree with the subject that is closest to it.

Activity A

Invite students to read all the sentences in Activity A aloud, emphasizing the correlative conjunctions in each sentence. Then ask students to complete the activity on their own.

Activity A Answers

1. either . . . or **2.** Both . . . and **3.** Not only . . . but also **4.** whether . . . or **5.** neither . . . nor **6.** not only . . . but also **7.** Neither . . . nor **8.** either . . . or **9.** both . . . and **10.** not only . . . but also

3 Reinforce and Extend

LEARNING STYLES

Body/Kinesthetic

Write each pair of correlative conjunctions in the box on page 192 on a separate card. Mix up the cards and invite students to choose cards and use the pair of conjunctions in sentences. Ask students to use their classroom as the context for their sentences. Encourage them to pick up or point to objects to demonstrate their sentences and the correlative conjunctions.

When subjects are joined with correlative conjunctions, the verb agrees with the subject closer to the verb.

EXAMPLE Neither **Justin** nor **Mark** has signed up for that class. (*Justin* and *Mark* are singular.)

Not only **the porch** but also **the shed** needs cleaning. (*Shed* is singular.)

Either **fruit** or **vegetables** are a good snack. (*Vegetables* is plural.)

However, when *and* joins subjects, the verb takes the plural form.

EXAMPLE Both **Lisa** and **Chris** take photography classes.

Activity B Write the correct verb on your paper. Then say the sentences aloud to hear correct usage.

1. Either a pencil or a pen (is, are) all right to use.
2. Neither the coat nor the shoes (is, are) on sale.
3. Neither the car nor the truck (is, are) working today.
4. If I'm right, either your photographs or his sculpture (have, has) received an award.
5. Both Yvette and her brother (loves, love) cooking.
6. Not only my father but also my uncle (is, are) going to Florida next week.
7. Both oranges and grapefruit (is, are) excellent sources of vitamin C.
8. Not only the team but also the fans (is, are) running out of the stadium.
9. Neither the band nor the chorus (has, have) practice tonight.
10. Either a bracelet or a necklace (is, are) a good gift for Mitsu's birthday.

IN THE COMMUNITY

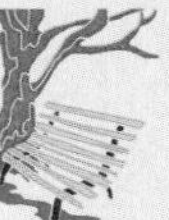

Encourage students to write an article for the school or local newspaper about community organizations and services that need volunteers. Remind students to use conjunctions in their sentences to connect related thoughts and ideas.

Activity B

Be sure students understand subject/verb agreement before having them do Activity B independently. If necessary, provide additional examples. As they complete Activity B, encourage students to read each item to themselves twice, with a different answer in place each time. They should choose the answer that sounds most correct to them.

Activity B Answers

1. is **2.** are **3.** is **4.** has **5.** love **6.** is **7.** are **8.** are **9.** has **10.** is

LEARNING STYLES

Auditory/Verbal

Read sentences containing correlative conjunctions aloud to the class. (Items from Activity A or B in this lesson are suitable.) Ask students to repeat the sentence and identify the correlative conjunction.

LEARNING STYLES

Logical/Mathematical

Write the names of two students on the board. Underneath each name, list information about that student. Make sure that some of the information is the same for both of them. (Both might have black hair, for example.) Then have students compose sentences using this information and as many of the correlative conjunctions as they can. (Examples: *Both Sam and Maria have black hair. Neither Sam nor Maria has blond hair.*) Invite students to write their sentences on the board.

Lesson 3 Review Answers

1. not only . . . but also **2.** either . . . or **3.** Both . . . and **4.** neither . . . nor **5.** not only . . . but also **6–10.** Answers will vary. Possible answers follow. **6.** Both . . . and **7.** both . . . and **8.** Not only . . . but also **9.** either . . . or **10.** both . . . and

Spelling Builder

Students should understand that few rules in English are without exception, particularly those involving spelling. After they have completed the spelling exercise, write the following on the board:

awe + -ful =
judge + -ment =
mile + -age =
change + -able =

Ask students to add the suffixes to the words. Encourage them to consult a dictionary if necessary. (Answers: *awful, judgment, mileage, changeable*) Elicit that all of these words represent exceptions to the general rule about the silent *e*.

Answers to Spelling Builder:
1. surprising **2.** useful **3.** noisy **4.** careless **5.** baker

Spelling Practice

Give students practice in another spelling rule involving a suffix.

> When a word ends in a consonant + *y*, change the *y* to *i* when adding a suffix unless the suffix begins in *i*.

Write the following words and suffixes on the board and ask students to spell them by applying this rule: *try + -ed, copy + -ing, happy + -ness, silly + -er.* (Answers: *tried, copying, happiness, sillier.*)

Lesson 3 REVIEW

On your paper, write the correlative conjunctions in each sentence.

1. The football team scored not only the touchdown but also the extra point.
2. Would you like either milk or juice?
3. Both Chandra and her sister speak three languages.
4. She bought neither the dress nor the suit.
5. Kate, Inez, and Dwight are not only in the same homeroom but also in all the same classes.

Complete these sentences with correlative conjunctions. On your paper, write the complete sentences. There may be more than one correct answer.

6. _______ Mark _______ Justin have part-time jobs.
7. Susan thinks _______ the jeans _______ the shirt fit her well.
8. _______ Estelle _______ her brother is a talented artist.
9. Mr. Wu _______ drives to work _______ takes the bus.
10. Ann knows _______ the reports _______ the outlines are due.

Spelling Builder

Dropping the Final *e*

Many words have suffixes or endings. To add an ending to a word, you may first need to make a change in the spelling. For example, you may need to drop a silent final *e,* or you may need to keep the silent final *e*.

Follow these rules when adding an ending to a word that has a silent final *e*.

- Keep the *e* before adding an ending that begins with a consonant.
  safe + ty = safety
  excite + ment = excitement
- Drop the *e* before adding an ending that begins with a vowel.
  choose + ing = choosing
  use + able = usable

Put the word and ending together. On your paper, write the new word on your paper.

1. surprise + ing = _______
2. use + ful = _______
3. noise + y = _______
4. care + less = _______
5. bake + er = _______

Name Date Period **Workbook Activity 45** Chapter 8, Lesson 3

Using Correlative Conjunctions

Directions On the line, write the correlative conjunction in each sentence.

EXAMPLE Both the time and the place of the next meeting will be posted on the board. Both . . . and

1. Sasha has exams Tuesday in both algebra and biology. _______
2. You may use either a clock with a second hand or a stopwatch for this activity. _______
3. Neither the bank nor the post office is open on Thanksgiving. _______
4. Mr. Yan is both my advisor and my history teacher. _______
5. Dad said to turn off either the CD player or the TV set. _______
6. Alex not only played in the game but he also made the winning goal. _______
7. Both my brother and my sister like to sing. _______
8. You may either take this bus or wait for a later one. _______
9. Whether you catch the first bus or you catch the next one, you should get there on time. _______
10. Not only is Sarah the class president, but she is also on the soccer team. _______

Directions Read each pair of sentences. Underline the correct sentence in each pair.

EXAMPLE Both the national anthem and "America, the Beautiful" were sung.
Both the national anthem and "America, the Beautiful" was sung.

11. Neither the gym nor the cafeteria is open now.
Neither the gym nor the cafeteria are open now.
12. Not only Luke but also his younger sisters take violin lessons.
Not only Luke but also his younger sisters takes violin lessons.
13. Neither the Senate nor the House of Representatives meet today.
Neither the Senate nor the House of Representatives meets today.
14. Both Stephen and Maria tutor younger students.
Both Stephen and Maria tutors younger students.
15. Either Liza or Scott live in that house.
Either Liza or Scott lives in that house.

 Basic English Grammar

TRL

Workbook Activity 45

Name Date Period **Activity 45** Chapter 8, Lesson 3

Finding Conjunctions

Directions Find the conjunction in each sentence. Underline the word or words. Write the type of conjunction—*coordinating, subordinating,* or *correlative*—on the line.

EXAMPLES Both Jefferson and Adams were vice presidents. correlative
I like tea, but I don't like coffee. coordinating
Pam always eats pretzels while she watches a movie. subordinating

1. Unless you hurry, you won't finish. _______
2. Either roses or petunias will look pretty there. _______
3. Dan was hungry; however, he was too tired to eat. _______
4. We will leave when it is ten o'clock. _______
5. Darleen has owned Tiny since she was twelve. _______
6. Candy couldn't decide whether to go swimming or fishing. _______
7. Poodles, collies, and shepherds are all types of dogs. _______
8. Both Sue and Darleen came for dinner. _______
9. Whenever you are ready, we will go. _______
10. Pat liked the movie, but the book was better. _______
11. Because the report was due, they worked all evening. _______
12. I like cookies, but I prefer ice cream. _______
13. "Kelly and I are leaving now," said Janet. _______
14. Do you need help, or can you do it yourself? _______
15. Neither Fido nor Rover has fleas. _______
16. Either Tom will come or he will send a replacement. _______
17. This recipe requires butter, sugar, and vanilla extract. _______
18. Erica bought not only a bicycle but also safety gear. _______
19. Stanley did not know whether to turn left or turn right. _______
20. Kayla did not feel well; nevertheless, she performed beautifully. _______

 Basic English Grammar

TRL

Activity 45

Lesson 4 Using Interjections

Interjection
A word or phrase that shows strong feeling

An **interjection** is a word or phrase that expresses a strong feeling. Always separate the interjection from the rest of the sentence with a punctuation mark. Use a comma, a question mark, or an exclamation mark. Use an exclamation mark after a strong interjection.

EXAMPLE

Hurry! I'll be late again.
Oh? I didn't know you were sick.
Say, could you help me?
Hey, don't ask me again.
Yes, indeed! That's really nice.

Here are some common interjections.

Interjections			
ah	hurrah	oh, boy	stop
alas	hurry	ouch	terrific
fine	hush	please	thanks
gosh	listen	quick	well
great	look out	quiet	what
ha	my goodness	really	whew
hello	nonsense	so	wow
hey	oh	so what	yes

When end punctuation comes after an interjection, capitalize the first word that follows.

So? Who wants to drive?
Wow! That is lovely.
Whew! I'm glad I am finished!

Lesson at a Glance

Chapter 8 Lesson 4

Overview This lesson introduces interjections.

Objectives

- To punctuate sentences with interjections.
- To add interjections to sentences.

Student Pages 195–197

Teacher's Resource Library 

Workbook Activity 46

Activity 46

Alternative Activity 46

Vocabulary

interjection

Warm-Up Activity

Draw several speech balloons on the board, each containing an interjection: *Oh no! Really? Wow! Yikes! Hey! Whew!* Ask students to think of situations in which people might use these words. Explain to students that words, such as these, that express strong feeling are called interjections. Explain that this lesson will help them use interjections effectively and correctly in sentences.

2 Teaching the Lesson

Help students understand that what makes an interjection special is the emotion that goes with it and the fact that it is separate from the rest of the sentence. Point out that the words in the box on page 195 are not always used as interjections. Write on the board, *What is that?* and *What? You crashed the car?* Ask students to explain the difference between these two uses of *what.* Elicit that one is used to create a question; the other to express shock. Have students read the two examples expressively. Explain that the second use of *what* is a typical interjection. Invite students to compose their own sentences using the words listed, both as interjections and as other parts of speech.

Reinforce and Extend

Learning Styles

Visual/Spatial

Divide the class into groups of five. Ask each group to choose five interjections from the boxed list on page 195. Encourage each group to create an icon, or symbol, for each of the five interjections. Afterward, have the groups draw their icons on an "Interjection" poster for the classroom.

Activity A

Different students may read each sentence with different feeling. As a result, they may punctuate each sentence differently. It may be helpful to do Activity A together as a class so that you can discuss the different options for punctuating each sentence correctly.

Activity A Answers

End punctuation may vary. Possible answers follow. **1.** Quick! I need help fast! **2.** Wow! What a great party this is! **3.** Really, I was surprised. **4.** Well, you finally got here. **5.** Whew! That was fun.

Activity B

Invite volunteers to provide sample sentences orally before students complete the activity on their own. When students have finished, have them exchange sentences with partners who can check for correct punctuation.

Activity B Answers

Sentences will vary. Sample sentences follow. **1.** Thanks, I will need a ride to the game. **2.** Hurry! There are only three tickets left. **3.** Great! We have good seats! **4.** Whew, what a day I have had. **5.** Excellent! Tomorrow is a holiday. **6.** Hey, what time are you going home? **7.** Oops, I didn't know that was your jacket. **8.** Hello, is this the home of Mrs. Li? **9.** Ha! That's a great joke. **10.** Hurrah! I passed my driving test.

Speaking Practice

Give students practice speaking sentences with interjections by reading to them the following prompts:

- You've just run 10 miles.
- You see a beautiful sunset.
- You burn your finger.
- You win a prize.

After each prompt invite volunteers to respond expressively, using one of the interjections listed on page 195 or another of their choice. Encourage students to compose their own prompts and to continue eliciting responses from their peers.

Writing Tip

You probably use interjections in conversations with your friends and do not realize it. You can use them in your writing, too. Interjections help make written conversations sound natural. Use interjections in your writing to express strong emotions.

If you use a comma, do not capitalize the next word of the sentence unless it is a proper noun.

EXAMPLE Ah, that project looks great!
Yes, indeed! That's really nice.

Activity A Write these sentences on your paper. Add punctuation after the interjection and at the end of each sentence. Capitalize the first words of sentences.

1. quick I need help fast
2. wow what a great party this is
3. really I was surprised
4. well you finally got here
5. whew that was fun

Activity B On your paper, write 10 sentences that use interjections. Be sure to punctuate each sentence correctly.

Oh, no! Tamika forgot Josh's gift.

TEACHER ALERT

Some students may mistakenly add a question mark at the end of exclamatory sentences that begin with the word *what,* which frequently begins questions. Caution students to read each sentence carefully and remind them that only sentences that ask questions end in question marks.

Lesson 4 REVIEW

Write these sentences on your paper. Add punctuation after each interjection and at the end of each sentence.

1. no I can't help you
2. ouch that hurts
3. whew that has a strong smell
4. well what's new
5. hey I had better get home

Write these sentences on your paper. Add an interjection and any punctuation needed. Remember to capitalize the first word of each sentence.

6. Isn't that beautiful?
7. We're having a test.
8. That ladder is going to fall.
9. I ripped my best shirt.
10. I won!

Writing Project

Using Conjunctions and Interjections

Write a letter to a friend or family member telling about a time when you were surprised. Include conjunctions and interjections in your sentences. You may use words from the lists below or choose others.

When you finish writing your letter, go back and underline the conjunctions. Circle any interjections.

Then exchange papers with a classmate, and read each other's letters.

Suggested conjunctions	Suggested interjections
and	Wow!
or	Oh, yes!
but	Whew!
nevertheless	Yippee!
however	Really!
while	Cool!

Lesson 4 Review Answers

Punctuation may vary. Possible answers follow. **1.** No, I can't help you. **2.** Ouch! That hurts! **3.** Whew! That has a strong smell! **4.** Well? What's new? **5.** Hey, I had better get home. **6–10.** Answers may vary. Sample answers follow. **6.** Oh, isn't that beautiful? **7.** Quiet, we're having a test. **8.** Look out! That ladder is going to fall. **9.** Oops, I ripped my best shirt. **10.** Hurrah! I won!

Writing Project

Point out that people frequently use interjections in their everyday speech. Encourage students to imagine that they are actually talking to a friend or family member when they write their letters. Have them review the list of interjections on page 195, but point out that there are many others—some of them unique to individuals. Encourage students to be imaginative and entertaining in their use of interjections.

At Home

Have students listen for the use of interjections in family conversations or on radio or television. Ask them to write, to the best of their memory, the exact sentences in which the interjections were used. Encourage students to make a record of at least five of these examples. Invite them to share their findings with the class.

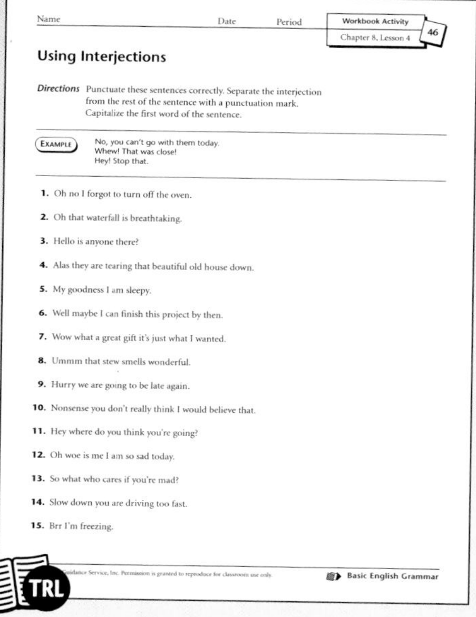

Name Date Period | Workbook Activity 46 | Chapter 8, Lesson 4

Using Interjections

Directions Punctuate these sentences correctly. Separate the interjection from the rest of the sentence with a punctuation mark. Capitalize the first word of the sentence.

EXAMPLE No, you can't go with them today.
Whew! That was close!
Hey! Stop that.

1. Oh no I forgot to turn off the oven.
2. Oh that waterfall is breathtaking.
3. Hello is anyone there?
4. Alas they are tearing that beautiful old house down.
5. My goodness I am sleepy.
6. Well maybe I can finish this project by then.
7. Wow what a great gift it's just what I wanted.
8. Ummm that stew smells wonderful.
9. Hurry we are going to be late again.
10. Nonsense you don't really think I would believe that.
11. Hey where do you think you're going?
12. Oh woe is me I am so sad today.
13. So what who cares if you're mad?
14. Slow down you are driving too fast.
15. Brr I'm freezing.

 Basic English Grammar

TRL Workbook Activity 46

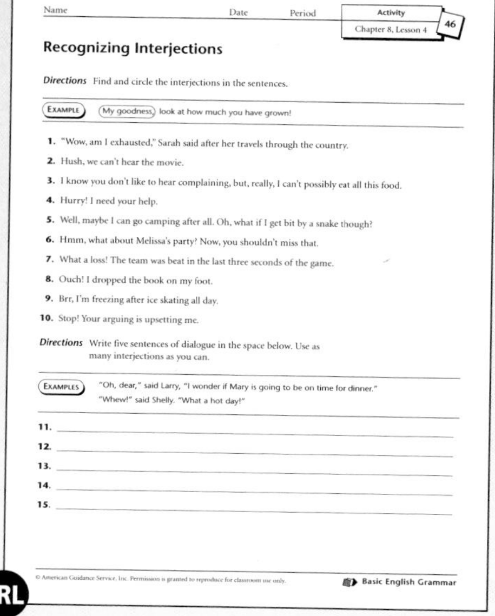

Name Date Period | Activity 46 | Chapter 8, Lesson 4

Recognizing Interjections

Directions Find and circle the interjections in the sentences.

EXAMPLE (My goodness) look at how much you have grown!

1. "Wow, am I exhausted," Sarah said after her travels through the country.
2. Hush, we can't hear the movie.
3. I know you don't like to hear complaining, but, really, I can't possibly eat all this food.
4. Hurry! I need your help.
5. Well, maybe I can go camping after all. Oh, what if I get bit by a snake though?
6. Hmm, what about Melissa's party? Now, you shouldn't miss that.
7. What a loss! The team was beat in the last three seconds of the game.
8. Ouch! I dropped the book on my foot.
9. Brr, I'm freezing after ice skating all day.
10. Stop! Your arguing is upsetting me.

Directions Write five sentences of dialogue in the space below. Use as many interjections as you can.

EXAMPLES "Oh, dear," said Larry, "I wonder if Mary is going to be on time for dinner."
"Whew!" said Shelly. "What a hot day!"

11. ______
12. ______
13. ______
14. ______
15. ______

 Basic English Grammar

TRL Activity 46

Chapter 8 Review

Use the Chapter Review to prepare students for tests and to reteach content from the chapter.

Chapter 8 Mastery Test 

The Teacher's Resource Library includes two parallel forms of the Chapter 8 Mastery Test. The difficulty level of the two forms is equivalent. You may wish to use one form as a pretest and the other form as a posttest.

Review Answers

Part A

1. dependent clause **2.** correlative conjunction **3.** conjunction **4.** series **5.** interjection **6.** coordinating conjunction **7.** subordinating conjunction **8.** comma **9.** clause **10.** independent clause

Part B

Answers may vary. Sample sentences follow. **11.** They were hungry, but they were not tired. **12.** Both Liang and Anthony ordered sandwiches **13.** Lisa wanted something hot, so she ordered soup **14.** Neither Lisa nor Tamara wanted desert. **15.** They talked about the dance, and then they went home.

Part C

16. Lisa, Anthony, Tamara, and Liang went to the dance together.
17. Because the night was warm, they opened the car windows.
18. "The dance committee wanted a band; however, they got a disc jockey," Lisa said.

Chapter 8 REVIEW

Word Bank
clause
comma
conjunction
coordinating conjunction
correlative conjunctions
dependent clause
independent clause
interjection
series
subordinating conjunction

Part A On a sheet of paper, write the correct word or words from the Word Bank to complete each sentence.

1. A clause that does not express a complete thought is a ______.
2. A ______ is a pair of conjunctions that connects words or groups of words.
3. A word that connects parts of a sentence is a ______.
4. A group of more than two words or phrases is a ______.
5. An ______ is a word or phrase that shows strong feeling.
6. A word that connects two or more equal parts of a sentence is a ______.
7. A ______ connects a dependent clause to an independent clause in a sentence.
8. A ______ separates words, phrases, or ideas in a series.
9. A ______ is a group of words with a subject and a verb.
10. A clause that expresses a complete thought is an ______.

Part B Add conjunctions to complete these sentences. On your paper, write the sentences. There is more than one correct answer.

11. They were hungry, ______ they were not tired.
12. ______ Liang ______ Anthony ordered sandwiches.
13. Lisa wanted something hot ______ she ordered soup.
14. Neither Lisa ______ Tamara wanted dessert.
15. They talked about the dance, ______ then they went home.

Part C On your paper, write these sentences. Add punctuation where needed.

16. Lisa Anthony Tamara and Liang went to the dance together.
17. Because the night was warm they opened the car windows.
18. "The dance committee wanted a band however they got a disc jockey," Lisa said.

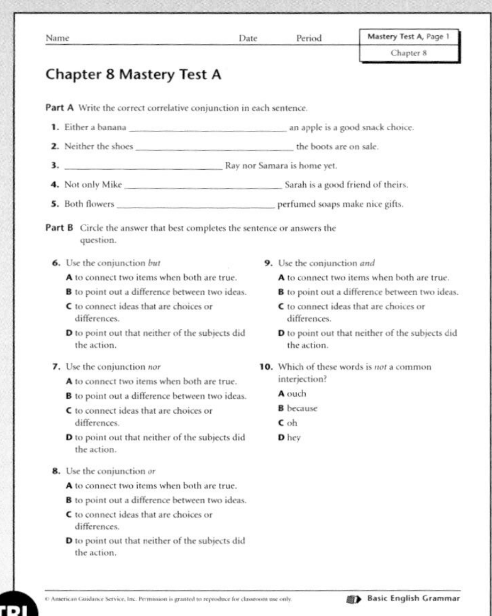

Name ______ Date ______ Period ______ Mastery Test A, Page 1 / Chapter 8

Chapter 8 Mastery Test A

Part A Write the correct correlative conjunction in each sentence.

1. Either a banana ______ an apple is a good snack choice.
2. Neither the shoes ______ the boots are on sale.
3. ______ Ray nor Samara is home yet.
4. Not only Mike ______ Sarah is a good friend of theirs.
5. Both flowers ______ perfumed soaps make nice gifts.

Part B Circle the answer that best completes the sentence or answers the question.

6. Use the conjunction *but*
A to connect two items when both are true.
B to point out a difference between two ideas.
C to connect ideas that are choices or differences.
D to point out that neither of the subjects did the action.

7. Use the conjunction *nor*
A to connect two items when both are true.
B to point out a difference between two ideas.
C to connect ideas that are choices or differences.
D to point out that neither of the subjects did the action.

8. Use the conjunction *or*
A to connect two items when both are true.
B to point out a difference between two ideas.
C to connect ideas that are choices or differences.
D to point out that neither of the subjects did the action.

9. Use the conjunction *and*
A to connect two items when both are true.
B to point out a difference between two ideas.
C to connect ideas that are choices or differences.
D to point out that neither of the subjects did the action.

10. Which of these words is *not* a common interjection?
A ouch
B because
C oh
D hey

 Basic English Grammar

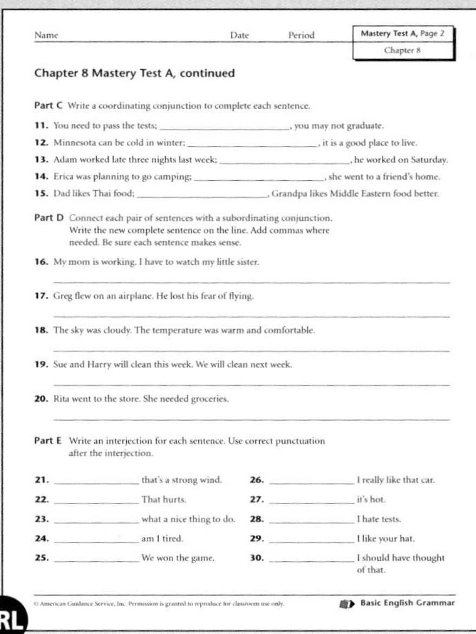

Name ______ Date ______ Period ______ Mastery Test A, Page 2 / Chapter 8

Chapter 8 Mastery Test A, continued

Part C Write a coordinating conjunction to complete each sentence.

11. You need to pass the tests; ______, you may not graduate.
12. Minnesota can be cold in winter; ______, it is a good place to live.
13. Adam worked late three nights last week; ______, he worked on Saturday.
14. Erica was planning to go camping; ______, she went to a friend's home.
15. Dad likes Thai food; ______, Grandpa likes Middle Eastern food better.

Part D Connect each pair of sentences with a subordinating conjunction. Write the new complete sentence on the line. Add commas where needed. Be sure each sentence makes sense.

16. My mom is working. I have to watch my little sister.
17. Greg flew on an airplane. He lost his fear of flying.
18. The sky was cloudy. The temperature was warm and comfortable.
19. Sue and Harry will clean this week. We will clean next week.
20. Rita went to the store. She needed groceries.

Part E Write an interjection for each sentence. Use correct punctuation after the interjection.

21. ______ that's a strong wind.
22. ______ That hurts.
23. ______ what a nice thing to do.
24. ______ am I tired.
25. ______ We won the game.
26. ______ I really like that car.
27. ______ it's hot.
28. ______ I hate tests.
29. ______ I like your hat.
30. ______ I should have thought of that.

 Basic English Grammar

Chapter 8 Mastery Test A

Part D On your paper, write the letter of the sentence that is correct.

19. **A** Paul bought a coat, he bought a scarf, He bought some gloves.
B Paul bought a coat. A scarf. Some gloves.
C Paul bought a coat, a scarf, and some gloves.
D Paul bought a coat, He bought a scarf, he bought some gloves

20. **A** It rained on Monday, it rained on Tuesday.
B It rained on Monday while it rained on Tuesday.
C It rained on Monday, nor it rain on Tuesday.
D It rained on Monday and Tuesday.

21. **A** Dan was absent, nor Abby was absent.
B Dan and Abby were absent.
C Dan but Abby was absent.
D Dan or Abby are absent.

Part E On your paper, write these sentences. Add an interjection and any punctuation needed. Remember to capitalize the first word of each sentence.

22. What a funny story that was.
23. I ran a mile in less than eight minutes.
24. I bumped my elbow again.
25. The traffic light is changing.

Test-Taking Tip Do not wait until the night before a test to begin studying for it. Plan your study time so that you can get a good night's sleep the night before the test.

Review Answers

Part D

19. C **20.** D **21.** B

Part E

Answers may vary. Possible answers follow. **22.** Ha! What a funny story that was. **23.** Whew! I ran a mile in less than eight minutes! **24.** Ouch! I bumped my elbow again. **25.** Stop! The traffic light is changing.

Name ______ Date ______ Period ______ Mastery Test B, Page 1 Chapter 8

Chapter 8 Mastery Test B

Part A Write a coordinating conjunction to complete each sentence.

1. Adam worked late three nights last week; ______, he worked on Saturday.
2. Erica was planning to go camping; ______, she went to a friend's home.
3. Dad likes Thai food; ______, Grandpa likes Middle Eastern food better.
4. You need to pass the tests; ______, you may not graduate.
5. Minnesota can be cold in winter; ______, it is a good place to live.

Part B Connect each pair of sentences with a subordinating conjunction. Write the new complete sentence on the line. Add commas where needed. Be sure each sentence makes sense.

6. Greg flew on an airplane. He lost his fear of flying.
______
7. The sky was cloudy. The temperature was warm and comfortable.
______
8. Sue and Harry will clean this week. We will clean next week.
______
9. Rita went to the store. She needed groceries.
______
10. My mom is working. I have to watch my little sister.
______

Part C Write the correct correlative conjunction in each sentence.

11. ______ Ray nor Samara is home yet.
12. Not only Mike ______ Sarah is a good friend of theirs.
13. Both flowers ______ perfumed soaps make nice gifts.
14. Either a banana ______ an apple is a good snack choice.
15. Neither the shoes ______ the boots are on sale.

 Basic English Grammar

TRL

Name ______ Date ______ Period ______ Mastery Test B, Page 2 Chapter 8

Chapter 8 Mastery Test B, continued

Part D Circle the answer that best completes the sentence or answers the question.

16. Which of these words is *not* a common interjection?
A ouch
B because
C oh
D hey

17. Use the conjunction *and*
A to connect two items when both are true.
B to point out a difference between two ideas.
C to connect ideas that are choices or differences.
D to point out that neither of the subjects did the action.

18. Use the conjunction *or*
A to connect two items when both are true.
B to point out a difference between two ideas.
C to connect ideas that are choices or differences.
D to point out that neither of the subjects did the action.

19. Use the conjunction *nor*
A to connect two items when both are true.
B to point out a difference between two ideas.
C to connect ideas that are choices or differences.
D to point out that neither of the subjects did the action.

20. Use the conjunction *but*
A to connect two items when both are true.
B to point out a difference between two ideas.
C to connect ideas that are choices or differences.
D to point out that neither of the subjects did the action.

Part E Write an interjection for each sentence. Use correct punctuation after the interjection.

21. ______ I really like that car.
22. ______ it's hot.
23. ______ I hate tests.
24. ______ I like your hat.
25. ______ I should have thought of that.
26. ______ that's a strong wind.
27. ______ That hurts.
28. ______ what a nice thing to do.
29. ______ am I tired.
30. ______ We won the game.

 Basic English Grammar

TRL

Chapter 8 Mastery Test B

Part

Sentence Construction

The bulldozers in the photograph are working together to accomplish a goal—building a road. Each machine has a job or a purpose. Each is important to the overall construction of the road. By working together, these machines will create the road.

Building sentences works in a similar way. A sentence must express a complete thought. Your goal is to put parts of speech together in a sentence to express that thought. The sentences you create can have different patterns. They can also have different purposes. There are four different purposes of sentences.

Statement	States a fact or tells about something
Question	Asks a question
Command	Gives an order or makes a request
Exclamation	Shows surprise or other strong feelings

You can arrange and combine sentence parts in different ways. There are four basic sentence structures.

Simple	One subject and one predicate
Compound	Two or more independent clauses joined by a conjunction
Complex	One independent and one dependent clause
Compound-Complex	At least two independent clauses and at least one dependent clause

In Part 2, you will learn about sentence purposes and patterns. You will learn to capitalize and punctuate a sentence. You will learn to recognize sentence parts and put them together. With these skills, you can speak and write clearly.

Introducing Part 2

Ask students to look at the different heavy equipment in the picture on page 200. Ask them to consider what type of work each piece of equipment might do. (Some students may be able to name each piece of equipment or might enjoy finding out what each piece can do. Encourage them to do so.) Point out that each piece of heavy equipment is being used for a single purpose (to build a road), but each has a different function. Together they can get the work done.

Ask students to compare sentences to the different pieces of equipment. Help them conclude that the different kinds of sentences are very much like the different pieces of heavy equipment. Together the sentences work together to help people express themselves (a single purpose), yet each has its own function. Then have students read page 201 and explain to them that by the end of Part 2 of this book, they will understand how to construct sentences in a variety of ways so that they can express themselves effectively.

Chapter 9

Planning Guide

Sentences: Subjects and Predicates

	Student Text Lesson				Language Skills		
	Student Pages	Vocabulary	Practice Exercises	Lesson Review	Identification Skills	Writing Skills	Punctuation Skills
Lesson 1 What Is a Sentence?	204–206	✔	✔	✔	✔	✔	✔
Lesson 2 The Subject of the Sentence	207–211	✔	✔	✔	✔	✔	✔
Lesson 3 The Predicate of the Sentence	212–215	✔	✔	✔	✔	✔	✔
Lesson 4 Purposes of Sentences	216–218		✔	✔	✔	✔	✔
Lesson 5 Simple and Compound Sentences	219–221	✔	✔	✔	✔	✔	✔

Chapter Activities

Teacher's Resource Library

Community Connection 9: Writing a Letter to the Editor

Media and Literature Connection 9: The Purposes of Sentences

Assessment Options

Student Text

Chapter 9 Review

Teacher's Resource Library

Chapter 9 Mastery Tests A and B

Student Text Features						Teaching Strategies						Learning Styles						Teacher's Resource Library			
Spelling Builder	Vocabulary Builder	Where To Find It	Writing Project	Using What You've Learned	Writing Tips/Notes/ Technology Notes	Teacher Alert	Online Connection	Applications (Home, Career, Community, Global)	Speaking Practice	Spelling Practice	Writing Practice	Auditory/Verbal	Body/Kinesthetic	Interpersonal/Group Learning	Logical/Mathematical	Visual/Spatial	LEP/ESL	Workbook Activities	Activities	Alternative Activities	Self-Study Guide
	206				✔	204, 205		205, 206						205				47	47	47	✔
		211			✔			210	209		210			208		211	209	48	48	48	✔
215					✔	212	214	213		215		214	213			214		49	49	49	✔
			218		✔	216		217				218						50	50	50	✔
				220									220		221			51	51	51	✔

Pronunciation Key

a	hat	e	let	ī	ice	ô	order	ù	put	sh	she	ə { a	in about
ā	age	ē	equal	o	hot	oi	oil	ü	rule	th	thin	e	in taken
ä	far	ėr	term	ō	open	ou	out	ch	child	ŦH	then	i	in pencil
â	care	i	it	ȯ	saw	u	cup	ng	long	zh	measure	o	in lemon
												u	in circus

Alternative Activities

The Teacher's Resource Library (TRL) contains a set of lower-level worksheets called Alternative Activities. These worksheets cover the same content as the regular Activities but are written at a second-grade reading level.

Skill Track Software

Use the Skill Track Software for Basic English Grammar for additional reinforcement of this chapter. The software program allows students using AGS textbooks to be assessed for mastery of each chapter and lesson of the textbook. Students access the software on an individual basis and are assessed with multiple-choice items.

Chapter at a Glance

Chapter 9: Sentences: Subjects and Predicates

Skill Track Software for Basic English Grammar

Teacher's Resource Library

Workbook Activities 47–51

Activities 47–51

Alternative Activities 47–51

Community Connection 9

Media and Literature Connection 9

Chapter 9 Self-Study Guide

Chapter 9 Mastery Tests A and B

(Answer Keys for the Teacher's Resource Library begin on page 340 of this Teacher's Edition.)

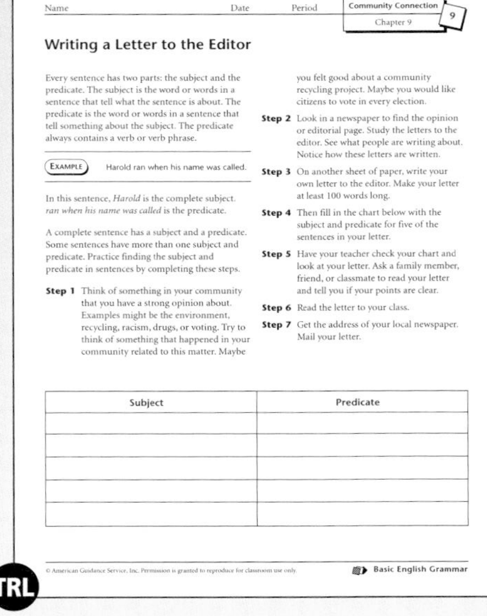

Name Date Period | Community Connection 9 | Chapter 9

Writing a Letter to the Editor

Every sentence has two parts: the subject and the predicate. The subject is the word or words in a sentence that tell what the sentence is about. The predicate is the word or words in a sentence that tell something about the subject. The predicate always contains a verb or verb phrase.

EXAMPLE Harold ran when his name was called.

In this sentence, *Harold* is the complete subject. *ran when his name was called* is the predicate.

A complete sentence has a subject and a predicate. Some sentences have more than one subject and predicate. Practice finding the subject and predicate in sentences by completing these steps.

Step 1 Think of something in your community that you have a strong opinion about. Examples might be the environment, recycling, racism, drugs, or voting. Try to think of something that happened in your community related to this matter. Maybe you felt good about a community recycling project. Maybe you would like citizens to vote in every election.

Step 2 Look in a newspaper to find the opinion or editorial page. Study the letters to the editor. See what people are writing about. Notice how these letters are written.

Step 3 On another sheet of paper, write your own letter to the editor. Make your letter at least 100 words long.

Step 4 Then fill in the chart below with the subject and predicate for five of the sentences in your letter.

Step 5 Have your teacher check your chart and look at your letter. Ask a family member, friend, or classmate to read your letter and tell you if your points are clear.

Step 6 Read the letter to your class.

Step 7 Get the address of your local newspaper. Mail your letter.

Subject	Predicate

 Basic English Grammar

TRL

Community Connection 9

Name Date Period | Media and Literature Connection 9 | Chapter 9

The Purposes of Sentences

Each sentence has a purpose. Sentences can make a statement, ask a question, give a command, or make a request. An exclamation can show strong feelings.

Read the following excerpt from the novel *Great Expectations*, by the British author Charles Dickens, to yourself. Then with a partner, read the excerpt aloud, alternating paragraphs with your partner. As you read, notice the purpose of the sentences.

> "Hold your noise!" cried a terrible voice, as a man started up from among the graves at the side of the church porch. "Keep still, you little devil, or I'll cut your throat!"
>
> A fearful man, all in coarse grey, with a great iron on his leg. A man with no hat, and with broken shoes, and with an old rag tied round his head. A man who had been soaked in water, and smothered in mud, and lamed by stones, and cut by flints, and stung by nettles, and torn by briars; who limped, and shivered, and glared and growled; and whose teeth chattered in his head as he seized me by the chin.
>
> "O! Don't cut my throat, sir," I pleaded in terror. "Pray don't do it, sir."
>
> "Tell us your name!" said the man. "Quick!"
>
> "Pip, sir."
>
> "Once more," said the man, staring at me. "Give it mouth!"
>
> "Pip. Pip, sir."
>
> "Show us where you live," said the man. "Pint [point] out the place!"
>
> I pointed to where our village lay, on the flat in-shore among the alder-trees and pollards, a mile or more from the church.
>
> The man, after looking at me for a moment, turned me upside down, and emptied my pockets. There was nothing in them but a piece of bread. When the church came to itself—for he was so sudden and strong that he made it go head over heels before me, and I saw the steeple under my feet—when the church came to itself, I say, I was seated on a high tombstone, trembling, while he ate the bread ravenously.

Discuss this excerpt with your classmates. How are sentences used in this excerpt? What are the main purposes of the sentences? What affect do these sentences have on you as the reader?

 Basic English Grammar

TRL

Media and Literature Connection 9

Chapter

Sentences: Subjects and Predicates

Without the key, this lock is useless. Without the lock, the key is also useless. Subjects and predicates work the same way. You need both to express a complete thought. They work together to form a sentence.

Every sentence has these two parts: a subject and a predicate. The subject of a sentence is who or what the sentence is about. The predicate tells what the subject did or what happened to the subject.

However, just as there are different types of locks, there are different types of sentences. In Chapter 9, you will unlock the key to identifying the different types of sentences. In doing so, you will also open up new ways of expressing yourself.

Goals for Learning

- To identify a sentence
- To identify the subject and predicate in a simple sentence
- To identify the noun or pronoun in a subject
- To identify the verb or verb phrase in a predicate
- To identify different types of sentences
- To identify the subject and predicate in a compound sentence

Name Date Period **SELF-STUDY GUIDE**

Chapter 9: Sentences: Subjects and Predicates

Goal 9.1 *To identify a sentence*

Date	Assignment	Score
______	**1.** Read pages 203–205. Complete Activities A–B on page 205.	______
______	**2.** Complete Workbook Activity 47.	______
______	**3.** Complete the Lesson 1 Review on page 206.	______

Comments:

Goal 9.2 *To identify the subject in simple sentences and to identify the noun or pronoun in subjects*

Date	Assignment	Score
______	**4.** Read page 207. Complete Activity A on page 207.	______
______	**5.** Read page 208. Complete Activities B–C on page 208.	______
______	**6.** Read page 209. Complete Activities D–E on page 209.	______
______	**7.** Read page 210. Complete Activities F–G on page 210.	______
______	**8.** Complete Workbook Activity 48.	______
______	**9.** Complete the Lesson 2 Review on page 211.	______

Comments:

Goal 9.3 *To identify the predicate in simple sentences and to identify the verb in predicates*

Date	Assignment	Score
______	**10.** Read page 212. Complete Activities A–B on page 212.	______
______	**11.** Read page 213. Complete Activity C on page 213.	______
______	**12.** Read page 214. Complete Activities D–E on page 214.	______
______	**13.** Complete Workbook Activity 49.	______
______	**14.** Complete the Lesson 3 Review on page 215.	______

Comments:

 Basic English Grammar

TRL

Name Date Period **SELF-STUDY GUIDE**

Chapter 9: Sentences: Subjects and Predicates, continued

Goal 9.4 *To identify different types of sentences*

Date	Assignment	Score
______	**15.** Read pages 216–217. Complete Activity A on page 217.	______
______	**16.** Complete Workbook Activity 50.	______
______	**17.** Complete the Lesson 4 Review on page 218.	______

Comments:

Goal 9.5 *To identify the subject and predicate in compound sentences*

Date	Assignment	Score
______	**18.** Read page 219. Complete Activity A on page 219.	______
______	**19.** Complete Activities B–C on page 220.	______
______	**20.** Complete Workbook Activity 51.	______
______	**21.** Complete the Lesson 5 Review on page 221.	______
______	**22.** Complete the Chapter 9 Review on pages 222–223.	______

Comments:

Student's Signature ______________ Date ______

Instructor's Signature ______________ Date ______

 Basic English Grammar

TRL

Chapter 9 Self-Study Guide, Pages 1–2

Introducing the Chapter

Use the photograph to introduce the idea that certain things go together and that one without the other means that neither is useful. Encourage students to name other things besides a lock or an ignition switch and a key that must be used together. Students might mention a can opener and a can, a computer and software, or a light bulb and a lamp. Then focus students' attention on the area of grammar by writing these sentence fragments on the board: *The shiny car* and *opened the door.* Ask students what is wrong with each set of words. When they point out that each group of words is an incomplete sentence, explain that a sentence expresses a complete thought. It must have a subject—a word or words that tell who or what the sentence is about—and a predicate—a word or words that tell what the subject did or what happened to the subject. Point out that by the end of Chapter 9, students will be able to recognize a sentence and its two basic parts.

Writing Tips, Notes, and Technology Notes

Ask volunteers to read the tips and notes that appear in the margins throughout the chapter. Then discuss them with the class.

Teacher's Resource

The AGS Teaching Strategies in English Transparencies may be used with this chapter. The transparencies add an interactive dimension to expand and enhance the *Basic English Grammar* program content.

Career Interest Inventory

The AGS Harrington-O'Shea Career Decision-Making System–Revised (CDM) may be used with this chapter. Students can use the CDM to explore their interests and identify careers. The CDM defines career areas that are indicated by students' responses on the inventory.

Lesson at a Glance

Chapter 9 Lesson 1

Overview This lesson presents the definition of a sentence.

Objectives

- To distinguish between a sentence and a sentence fragment.
- To write complete sentences from fragments.

Student Pages 204–206

Teacher's Resource Library 

Workbook Activity 47

Activity 47

Alternative Activity 47

Vocabulary

capital letter
end punctuation
sentence

Warm-Up Activity

Write *What is a sentence?* on the board and ask students to suggest definitions. If the terms *subject* and *predicate* are mentioned, ask students to define those terms also.

When the class has determined a definition for *sentence,* discuss with them the mechanics of sentence writing. Prompt students with questions related to how a sentence begins (with a capital letter) and how it ends (with an end punctuation mark). Finally discuss why knowing what a sentence is and how it is written is important in writing.

Teaching the Lesson

Use the first set of examples on page 204 to discuss what makes each sentence complete. Help students notice that each sentence expresses a complete thought. Call attention to the capital letter at the beginning of each sentence and the end punctuation mark.

Next focus on the second set of examples and discuss what is missing in each example that is not a sentence. Have volunteers explain how the incomplete sentences were made complete. Finally, ask students to give additional examples of complete sentences.

Reinforce and Extend

TEACHER ALERT

You may wish to point out that another name for *incomplete sentences* is *sentence fragments.*

Lesson 1 What Is a Sentence?

Sentence
A group of words that expresses a complete thought

Capital letter
The uppercase form of a letter such as A, B, C

End punctuation
A mark at the end of a sentence that tells the reader where a sentence ends:
- *a period (.)*
- *a question mark (?)*
- *an exclamation mark (!)*

A **sentence** is a group of words that expresses a complete thought. Every sentence begins with a **capital letter** and ends with an **end punctuation mark.**

Mr. Okada sold his truck to Reggie.
What did he pay for the truck?
Stop right there!

A group of words may look like a sentence, but if it does not express a complete thought, it is not a sentence.

EXAMPLE

Not a Sentence	The bicycle with the wide tires. (This group of words does not express a complete thought. What happened to the bicycle with the wide tires?)
Sentence	Mr. Stamos sold the bicycle with the wide tires to Joe.
Not a Sentence	Looked all over school for Latasha. (This group of words does not express a complete thought. Who looked all over school for Latasha?)
Sentence	Mario looked all over school for Latasha.
Not a Sentence	Before Ming bought the scooter. (This group of words does not express a complete thought. What happened before Ming bought the scooter?)
Sentence	Before Ming bought the scooter, her brother looked it over.

Arranging documents on your computer is a little like arranging words into sentences. You take small parts like words and put them into a larger place like a sentence. On the computer, the smallest part is a document such as your letter or school report. You can put your documents into a folder on the hard drive.

Activity A Read each group of words. Write *S* on your paper if the group of words is a sentence. Write *NS* if the group of words is not a sentence.

1. Stop for the red light!
2. Before the storm was over.
3. In the house across the street.
4. That's nice.
5. Where does he work?
6. Searching for a new job.
7. She laughed.
8. Jack went fishing.
9. Because of the cold weather.
10. Each day before the sun rises.

Activity B Write each group of words from Activity A that you marked *NS*. Add words to each group to make it a complete sentence. Be sure that each sentence begins with a capital letter and ends with a period, question mark, or exclamation mark.

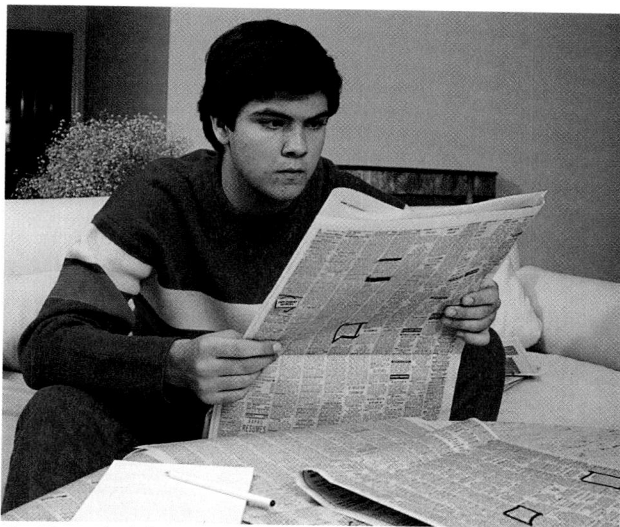

David searched the newspaper for a job.

Activity A

Do Activity A orally with the class. Invite students to read each item aloud with you, listening to hear whether the words express a complete thought. If students decide the item is a sentence, they should raise their hands; if it is not a sentence, they should keep their hands down. Students should be ready to explain why the group of words is or is not a sentence.

Activity A Answers

1. S **2.** NS **3.** NS **4.** S **5.** S **6.** NS **7.** S **8.** S **9.** NS **10.** NS

Activity B

If you did not do Activity A together as a class, you may wish to check answers for Activity A now. This will ensure that students have correctly identified all of the incomplete sentences. Then ask volunteers to suggest different ways to complete items 2 and 3 in Activity A before having students complete Activity B on their own.

Activity B Answers

Answers will vary. Possible answers follow. **2.** Before the storm was over, a tree had crashed into our house. **3.** Julio lives in the house across the street. **6.** Tom spent the day searching for a new job. **9.** Schools were closed because of the cold weather. **10.** Do you hear the birds sing each day before the sun rises?

At Home

Encourage students to check recent writing assignments, personal writing, and work they may have done on the computer for incomplete sentences, capitalization errors, and missing end punctuation.

Teacher Alert

Refer students to the Technology Note on this page. If possible have a computer available for demonstration purposes. Ask volunteers to demonstrate or explain how to create documents and files. Encourage students to use examples from their personal experiences.

Learning Styles

Interpersonal/Group Learning

Divide the class into groups of four. Ask each group to write eight sets of words that do not form a sentence. On a different sheet of paper, they should write sentences using the eight sets of words. Then have each group exchange its sets of words with another group, who will write their own sentences for the set of words. Afterward, groups compare all of the sentences. Discuss how the same set of words can make different sentences.

Lesson 1 Review Answers

Answers for items 1 and 5 will vary. Possible answers follow. **1.** NS Our neighbors in the house across the street finished painting last night. **2.** S **3.** S **4.** S **5.** NS They stopped painting when dark clouds appeared in the sky.

6–10. Answers will vary. Possible answers follow. **6.** Yesterday's homework is under the papers on my desk. **7.** Have you seen any deer in the woods near the lake? **8.** Tony is walking to the game with friends. **9.** The girl on the bus rode all the way to Main Street. **10.** If anyone calls while I'm out, take a message.

Vocabulary Builder

Point out to students that one way to decide which word to use—*if* or *whether*—is to ask "Is there a choice described in the sentence?" If the answer to their question is "Yes," then the word they need is *whether.*

Write *whether* and *weather* on the board. Tell students that *whether* and *weather* are homonyms, or words that sound alike but have different spellings and meanings. Remind them to use the correct spelling—*whether*—when dealing with sentences in which a choice is described.

Answers to Vocabulary Builder:
1. whether **2.** if **3.** if **4.** whether **5.** if

Career Connection

The ability to write and recognize a complete sentence is important for many careers. Administrative assistants and any other employees who must type or edit a supervisor's work as well as compose original letters will not be successful if they cannot write, capitalize, and punctuate a sentence correctly.

Lesson 1 REVIEW

Write *S* on your paper if the group of words is a sentence. If the group of words is not a sentence, add words to make a complete sentence.

1. Our neighbors in the house across the street.
2. They painted the house a light shade of brown.
3. The entire family picked out the color.
4. They needed a two-story ladder.
5. When dark clouds appeared in the sky.

Write each group of words on your paper. Add words to make each one a complete sentence. Begin each sentence with a capital letter and end it with an end punctuation mark.

6. the papers on my desk
7. seen in the woods near the lake
8. walking to the game with friends
9. the girl on the bus
10. if anyone calls while I'm out

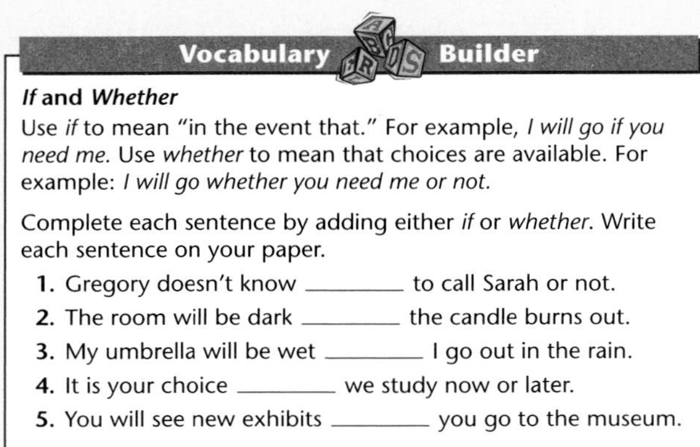

Vocabulary Builder

If* and *Whether
Use *if* to mean "in the event that." For example, *I will go if you need me.* Use *whether* to mean that choices are available. For example: *I will go whether you need me or not.*

Complete each sentence by adding either *if* or *whether*. Write each sentence on your paper.

1. Gregory doesn't know ________ to call Sarah or not.
2. The room will be dark ________ the candle burns out.
3. My umbrella will be wet ________ I go out in the rain.
4. It is your choice ________ we study now or later.
5. You will see new exhibits ________ you go to the museum.

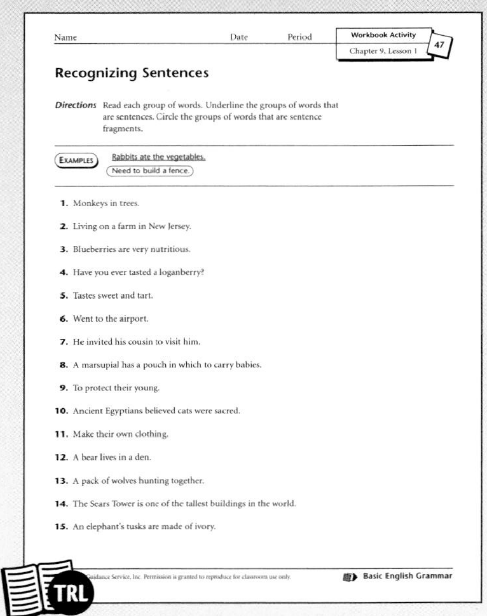

Name Date Period | Workbook Activity 47 | Chapter 9, Lesson 1

Recognizing Sentences

Directions Read each group of words. Underline the groups of words that are sentences. Circle the groups of words that are sentence fragments.

EXAMPLES Rabbits ate the vegetables.
Need to build a fence.

1. Monkeys in trees.
2. Living on a farm in New Jersey.
3. Blueberries are very nutritious.
4. Have you ever tasted a loganberry?
5. Tastes sweet and tart.
6. Went to the airport.
7. He invited his cousin to visit him.
8. A marsupial has a pouch in which to carry babies.
9. To protect their young.
10. Ancient Egyptians believed cats were sacred.
11. Make their own clothing.
12. A bear lives in a den.
13. A pack of wolves hunting together.
14. The Sears Tower is one of the tallest buildings in the world.
15. An elephant's tusks are made of ivory.

 Basic English Grammar

TRL

Workbook Activity 47

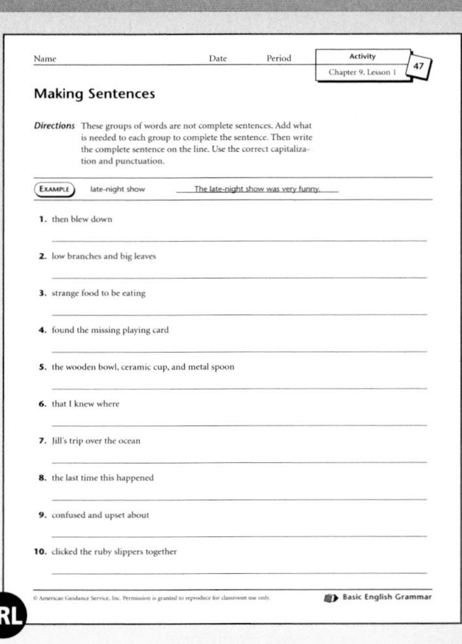

Name Date Period | Activity 47 | Chapter 9, Lesson 1

Making Sentences

Directions These groups of words are not complete sentences. Add what is needed to each group to complete the sentence. Then write the complete sentence on the line. Use the correct capitalization and punctuation.

EXAMPLE late-night show ___The late-night show was very funny.___

1. then blew down
2. low branches and big leaves
3. strange food to be eating
4. found the missing playing card
5. the wooden bowl, ceramic cup, and metal spoon
6. that I knew where
7. Jill's trip over the ocean
8. the last time this happened
9. confused and upset about
10. clicked the ruby slippers together

 Basic English Grammar

TRL

Activity 47

Lesson 2 The Subject of the Sentence

Complete subject
All the words in the subject

Simple subject
The noun or pronoun that the sentence is about

Every sentence has two parts: the subject and the predicate. You will learn more about the predicate in the next lesson. The subject is the part of the sentence that tells what the sentence is about. The main word in a subject is usually a noun or pronoun. The noun or pronoun and all the words that describe it make up the **complete subject.** The complete subject may be one word or many words.

EXAMPLE Amir opened the window. (Who opened the window? *Amir* opened it.)
The man who taught us math in sixth grade became principal. (Who became principal? *The man who taught us math in sixth grade.*)

The **simple subject** is the noun or pronoun that the sentence is about.

EXAMPLE The test in history was easy. (The simple subject is the noun *test.* The complete subject is *the test in history.*)
Mr. Torres is our principal this year. (The simple subject is the proper noun *Mr. Torres.* The complete subject is also *Mr. Torres.*)

Activity A Write the complete subject of each sentence on your paper. Circle the simple subject. A complete subject may be only one word.

1. Mr. Rojas comes from Mexico City, Mexico.
2. The entire class speaks in Spanish every day.
3. The teacher asks the students questions in Spanish.
4. They must answer him in Spanish.
5. The students in this class learn quickly.

Lesson at a Glance

Chapter 9 Lesson 2

Overview This lesson introduces the concept of simple subject and complete subject.

Objectives

- To identify the complete subject.
- To identify the simple subject.
- To find the subject in questions and commands.
- To identify compound subjects.

Student Pages 207–211

Teacher's Resource Library 

Workbook Activity 48
Activity 48
Alternative Activity 48

Vocabulary

complete subject
compound subject
simple subject

1 Warm-Up Activity

Ask volunteers to select an object, hold it up, and give a complete sentence about the object. (Example: *My pencil needs sharpening.*) Write each sentence on the board. Remind students that who or what the sentence is about is called the subject of the sentence. Ask what one word tells who or what each sentence is about. Circle words such as *pencil* that students identify and explain that these words are called the simple subject. Underline the complete subject, such as *My pencil,* in each sentence. Explain that the underlined words are called the complete subject. Have students suggest a definition for complete subject. Help them recognize that the simple subject is part of the *complete subject* and that the additional words in the complete subject tell about the simple subject.

2 Teaching the Lesson

Focus on the first example box. Have students identify the simple subject in each sentence. Ask them what question the simple subject of each sentence answers. (*Who*) Then have students read the second set of examples and identify the simple subject in each sentence. Ask what question the simple subject in each sentence answers. (*The first sentence answers* What. *The second sentence answers* Who.) Point out that one way students can find the simple subject is by asking themselves, "Who or what is this sentence about?"

Activity A

Before students complete Activity A on their own, ask volunteers to read each sentence. When a sentence has been read, ask, "Who or what is this sentence about?" Then have students do the activity on their own.

Activity A Answers

1. (Mr. Rojas) 2. The entire (class) 3. The (teacher) 4. (They) 5. The (students) in this class

Activity B

Ask volunteers to identify the prepositional phrase in each subject. Emphasize that the object of a preposition is never the simple subject of a sentence. Then have students do Activity B on their own.

Activity B Answers

1. Each 2. All 3. Eight 4. secretary 5. Two

Activity C

Ask volunteers to find the complete subjects in these sentences: *The woman in the front row laughed out loud. All of the eggs were cracked.* Then ask students to find the simple subject in each sentence. Elicit through discussion how students knew which noun or pronoun was the simple subject in each sentence.

Activity C Answers

1. I 2. A friend of Mr. Torres 3. Three of our classmates 4. The car with the flat tire 5. Everyone in the band

3 Reinforce and Extend

Learning Styles

Interpersonal/Group Learning

Organize students into groups of three, and challenge each group to create sentences with the longest complete subjects that they can think of. Explain that each complete subject must contain at least one prepositional phrase. For example, *The large, tan filing cabinet near the window at the back of the room is full.* Let groups exchange sentences. Have each group underline the complete subject, circle the simple subject, and bracket each prepositional phrase in the complete subject of each sentence. Finally determine which group created the longest complete subject.

The simple subject cannot be the object of the preposition.

EXAMPLE One of the twins was late.
(*One of the twins* is the complete subject. The prepositional phrase *of the twins* describes the simple subject *one. Twins* is the object of the preposition *of;* therefore, *twins* cannot be the subject of the sentence.)

Writing Tip

Use the words in the complete subject to help your readers understand the simple subject. If you write *Eight were absent yesterday,* readers might wonder "Were eight students or eight teachers absent?"

Activity B The complete subject in each sentence is in bold. Write each simple subject on your paper.

1. **Each of the students** wrote the answer on the board.
2. **All of my friends** like music.
3. **Eight of the students** were absent yesterday.
4. **The secretary in the principal's office** has the flu.
5. **Two of the students** were ill.

Activity C On your paper, write the complete subject in each sentence.

1. I am going to the store.
2. A friend of Mr. Torres visited from Mexico.
3. Three of our classmates went on the field trip.
4. The car with the flat tire pulled off the road.
5. Everyone in the band practiced for the concert.

The subject of a sentence usually comes before the verb, but it may come after the verb. When a sentence begins with the words *here* or *there,* the subject comes after the verb.

EXAMPLE There will be a train at eleven-thirty. (What will be there? A *train* will be there.)
Here comes Antonia now. (Who comes now? *Antonia* does.)

Activity D On your paper, write the simple subject in each sentence.

1. There is a good program on TV tonight.
2. Here is the bus stop.
3. There are no sandwiches left.
4. There is my school.
5. Here is the correct answer.

Writing Tip

When you collect information for your writing, use the interrogative pronouns *who, what,* and *which* to help you gather facts.

In a question, the subject may come between a helping verb and a main verb. Or it may come between parts of a verb phrase.

When does Margot have history? (The subject *Margot* comes between the helping verb *does* and the main verb *have.*)

Are you leaving soon? (The subject *you* comes between the verb phrase *are leaving.*)

When the interrogative pronoun *what, who,* or *which* begins a sentence that asks a question, the interrogative pronoun may be the subject.

Who called? What is happening?
Which of these backpacks is yours?

Activity E Write the simple subject in each sentence on your paper.

1. Will you be going to the meeting?
2. Which of the members will speak?
3. Who will lead the discussion?
4. Has this group ever met before?
5. Where will the meeting be?

Activity D

Have students practice finding the simple subject in the following sentences before having them do Activity D on their own: *There are three of my friends in that play. Here is Emilio.* Help students rephrase each sentence before having them look for the simple subject. (*Three of my friends are in that play. Emilio is here.*) Suggest that students apply this strategy as they do Activity D.

Activity D Answers

1. program **2.** stop **3.** sandwiches **4.** school **5.** answer

Activity E

Invite students to make up a variety of questions, including some that begin with *what, who,* and *which.* Write students' questions on the board and help them find the simple subject in each sentence. Then have students do Activity E on their own.

Activity E Answers

1. you **2.** Which **3.** Who **4.** group **5.** meeting

Speaking Practice

Have students work Activity E with partners. Explain that one partner is to read a question and the other partner is to rephrase the question as a statement. Then the first partner is to name the simple subject.

Learning Styles

LEP/ESL

Have students learning English as a second language work with partners who are fluent in English. Give each pair a section from a newspaper. Tell them to select an article to read and identify the simple subjects in its sentences. In this way both students can benefit from practicing locating simple subjects in real-world materials.

Activity F

Point to a student and say, "Stand up." After the student stands up, ask the person why he or she stood up. Elicit that the student understood you were talking to him or her. Write *Stand up.* on the board. Ask what the simple subject is. Help students understand that the subject is *You,* which is understood. Write *You stand up.* Point out that in commands and requests, *you* is the understood simple subject. Then have students complete Activity F independently.

Activity F Answers

1. you 2. you 3. you 4. you 5. you

Activity G

Ask students to read aloud the sentences in the activity. Then ask other volunteers to identify the words that join the compound subjects in each sentence. (*Neither, nor; and; and; or; and*) Ask students what these words are called. Help them identify the words as conjunctions.

Activity G Answers

1. Freddie, Tricia 2. hat, gloves 3. Spring, summer 4. books, papers 5. sandwiches, juice

Writing Practice

Point out that using compound subjects in a sentence can help students avoid repetition in their writing. Use these examples: *My book is lost. My lunch is lost.* Let students explain how to use a compound subject to avoid the repetition. (*My book and my lunch are lost.*)

Ask students to look through their portfolio or other writing for examples of places where sentences could be combined with a compound subject. Have students write each original sentence and its revision. Provide time for students to share the results with the class.

Compound subject

Two or more subjects connected by a conjunction

In a command or a request, the subject is *you.* Even though the word *you* may not appear in the sentence, it is understood. The subject is understood to be the person spoken to.

Please help me arrange the flowers.
(You) Please help me arrange the flowers.

Eduardo, come here right now.
Eduardo, (you) come here right now.
(Although the person spoken to is named, the subject *you* is understood.)

Activity F On your paper, write the simple subject in each sentence.

1. Pedro, help me carry these bags into the house.
2. Open your books to page 45.
3. Denise, please come home right after school.
4. Don't touch that!
5. Please hurry!

The subject of a sentence can be compound. A **compound subject** is two or more subjects connected by a conjunction.

David and Brittany went to the park.
The boy and his cousin went skating.

Activity G On your paper, write the compound subject in each sentence.

1. Neither Freddie nor Tricia went to the concert.
2. Both my hat and my gloves are blue.
3. Spring and summer are my favorite seasons.
4. Are my books or my papers in your locker?
5. There are enough sandwiches and juice for everyone.

In the Community

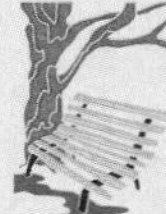

Ask pairs of students to list 10 businesses in the community and to write an advertising statement that includes a compound subject for each business. (Example: *Soup or salad is only $2.50 at the Highway Diner. Spring sweaters and jackets have arrived at Value Mart.*) Have partners share their statements with the class.

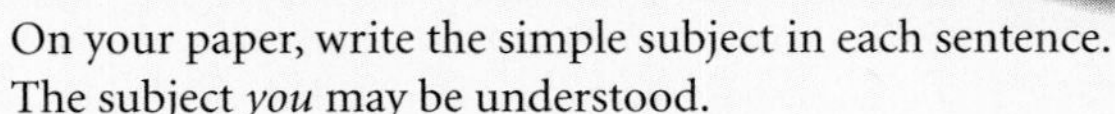

Lesson 2 REVIEW

On your paper, write the simple subject in each sentence. The subject *you* may be understood.

1. On Saturday Christa looked at CD players in the store.
2. Her birthday was in two weeks.
3. "Would Christa like anything special for her birthday?"
4. "Get her a CD player."
5. Who is coming to Christa's party?

Write each sentence on your paper. Underline the complete subject. Then circle the simple subject. Some of the subjects may be compound.

6. Baseball season begins soon.
7. Are James and Darren on the team?
8. They usually play infield.
9. There will be tryouts for all positions on Friday.
10. Where will the practices be held?

Where To Find It

Internet Search Engine

Imagine that you want to learn about major league baseball. You can look on the Internet for information. Use a search engine to find Web sites.

- First, log on to the Internet.
- Type in a search engine's Internet address to reach its home page. For example, you could try www.yahoo.com, www.google.com, or www.search.com.
- Enter a key word in the search window. A key word is one or more words that narrow your search. The engine searches Internet sites for those words.
- Click on *Search* or *Go*.
- A list of Internet Web sites will appear. Read the summaries to pick the best Web site for your topic. Click on a site.
- To exit a site and go back to the list, click on the *Back* button.

Sometimes search engines find Web sites that do not match your key words. If you reach a Web site that is inappropriate, use the *Back* button to return to the search engine's home page.

Use a search engine to gather information about a topic that interests you. On your paper, list the Web sites you find.

Lesson 2 Review Answers

1. Christa 2. birthday 3. Christa 4. you (understood) 5. Who 6. Baseball season begins soon. 7. Are James and Darren on the team? 8. They usually play infield. 9. There will be tryouts for all positions on Friday. 10. Where will the practices be held?

Where To Find It

Invite students to suggest topics to research on the Internet. Then have one student read the directions for using a search engine to find Web sites while another student follows the directions. During and after the search, ask students to discuss any problems they may have encountered in attempting to research topics. They might mention the need to narrow topics or the problem of spending time investigating sites that prove not to be useful. Encourage students to offer suggestions on how to solve some of the problems that they encounter.

Answers to Where To Find It: Lists of Web sites will vary.

Learning Styles

Visual/Spatial

Give pairs of students a colorful magazine picture and ask them to write on a sheet of paper all the nouns—people, places, things—they see in the picture. On the board, print the following pattern: adjective/noun/prepositional phrase. Have each pair make a poster with the pattern as a heading. Then have them write under the heading 10 complete subjects, using the pattern, for a possible sentence. Note: Keep the pictures and the posters for use with the Visual/ Spatial Learning Styles activity on page 214.

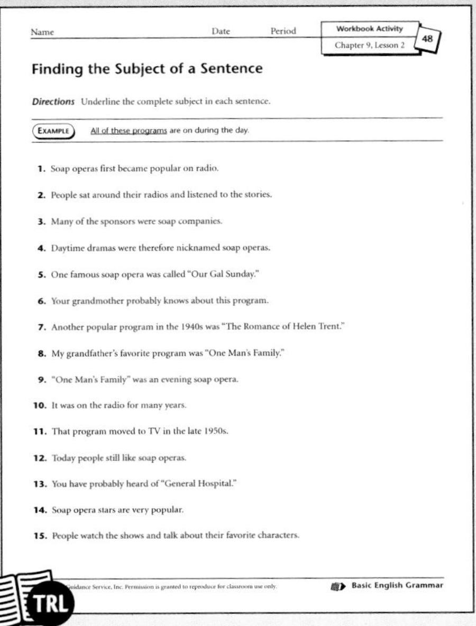

Name Date Period | Workbook Activity 48 | Chapter 9, Lesson 2

Finding the Subject of a Sentence

Directions Underline the complete subject in each sentence.

EXAMPLE All of these programs are on during the day.

1. Soap operas first became popular on radio.
2. People sat around their radios and listened to the stories.
3. Many of the sponsors were soap companies.
4. Daytime dramas were therefore nicknamed soap operas.
5. One famous soap opera was called "Our Gal Sunday."
6. Your grandmother probably knows about this program.
7. Another popular program in the 1940s was "The Romance of Helen Trent."
8. My grandfather's favorite program was "One Man's Family."
9. "One Man's Family" was an evening soap opera.
10. It was on the radio for many years.
11. That program moved to TV in the late 1950s.
12. Today people still like soap operas.
13. You have probably heard of "General Hospital."
14. Soap opera stars are very popular.
15. People watch the shows and talk about their favorite characters.

 Basic English Grammar

TRL

Workbook Activity 48

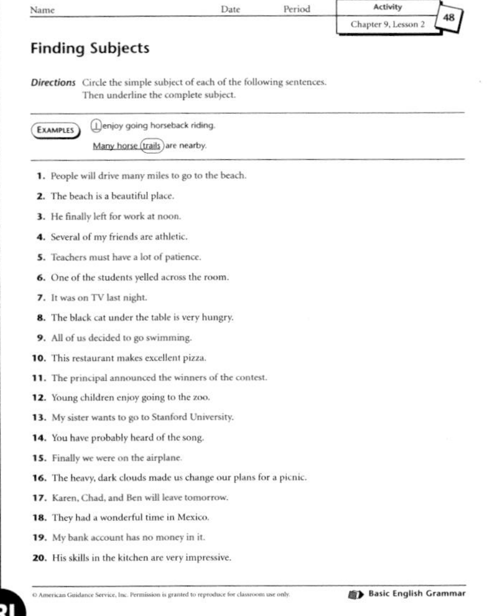

Name Date Period | Activity 48 | Chapter 9, Lesson 2

Finding Subjects

Directions Circle the simple subject of each of the following sentences. Then underline the complete subject.

EXAMPLES I enjoy going horseback riding.
Many horse trails are nearby.

1. People will drive many miles to go to the beach.
2. The beach is a beautiful place.
3. He finally left for work at noon.
4. Several of my friends are athletic.
5. Teachers must have a lot of patience.
6. One of the students yelled across the room.
7. It was on TV last night.
8. The black cat under the table is very hungry.
9. All of us decided to go swimming.
10. This restaurant makes excellent pizza.
11. The principal announced the winners of the contest.
12. Young children enjoy going to the zoo.
13. My sister wants to go to Stanford University.
14. You have probably heard of the song.
15. Finally we were on the airplane.
16. The heavy, dark clouds made us change our plans for a picnic.
17. Karen, Chad, and Ben will leave tomorrow.
18. They had a wonderful time in Mexico.
19. My bank account has no money in it.
20. His skills in the kitchen are very impressive.

 Basic English Grammar

TRL

Activity 48

Lesson at a Glance

Chapter 9 Lesson 3

Overview This lesson explains predicates.

Objectives

- To identify the predicate.
- To identify the main verb or verb phrase.

Student Pages 212–215

Teacher's Resource Library 

Workbook Activity 49

Activity 49

Alternative Activity 49

Vocabulary

compound predicate
compound verb
predicate

1 Warm-Up Activity

Write the words *Subject* and *Predicate* as headings on the board. Ask students to name some action words, such as *walked, followed,* and *wrote.* Write the words for the actions under the *Predicate* heading. Then have volunteers use each verb in a sentence. Write the subject portion of their sentences under the *Subject* heading and the predicate portion under the *Predicate* heading. Review with students that the subject is who or what the sentence is about. Ask them to tell what the predicate must be. Through discussion, lead students to conclude that the predicate is the part of the sentence that tells what the subject did or what happened to the subject.

2 Teaching the Lesson

Begin by asking students to explain subject and predicate. (*The subject tells about the doer of the action and the predicate tells about the action.*) Refer to the two example boxes on page 212. Ask volunteers to identify the verb or verb phrase in each example. Remind students that like the subject, the predicate may be one word or many words. However, every predicate must contain a verb or verb phrase.

Lesson 3 The Predicate of the Sentence

Predicate
The part of a sentence that tells something about the subject; it always contains a verb

The **predicate** of a sentence tells what the subject did or what happened to the subject. The predicate can be one word or many words. It always contains a verb.

EXAMPLE
We studied.
Andy will look at the videotapes this weekend.

Activity A On your paper, write the predicate in each sentence.

1. Lena lost her earring yesterday.
2. Denise found the earring today.
3. One of the stones was missing.
4. Someone had apparently stepped on it.
5. A jeweler can replace the stone in Lena's earring.

The main part of the predicate is the verb or verb phrase. The verb or verb phrase in the predicate is the simple predicate.

EXAMPLE
Jessica helped her mother in the kitchen. (The main word in the predicate is the verb *helped.*)
Latasha will meet us at the mall. (The main words in the predicate form the verb phrase *will meet.*)

Activity B On your paper, write the predicate in each sentence. Underline the verb or verb phrase.

1. Mrs. Barry gave Christa a surprise birthday party.
2. Christa's brother Will invited her friends.
3. Her friends had decorated the house.
4. Christa was arriving home at six-thirty.
5. Everyone yelled "surprise!"

Activity A

Before they complete Activity A on their own, ask students to identify the complete subject in each item.

Activity A Answers

1. lost her earring yesterday 2. found the earring today 3. was missing 4. had apparently stepped on it 5. can replace the stone in Lena's earring

Activity B

Do the first item on the board with students. Then have them complete Activity B independently.

Activity B Answers

1. gave Christa a surprise birthday party 2. invited her friends 3. had decorated the house 4. was arriving home at six-thirty 5. yelled "surprise"

Teacher Alert

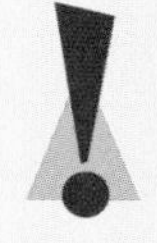

Students may see *complete predicate* in some books. Explain that *complete predicate* is another term for *predicate,* or the part of the sentence that contains the main verb or verb phrase and all the words that describe it.

Usually the predicate part of the sentence comes after the subject.

EXAMPLE The whole school enjoyed the game.

In a question, part of the predicate comes before the subject.

EXAMPLE Did you bring Sita the tapes?
Where did you buy them?
Are you having fun?

Adverbs and prepositional phrases that are part of the predicate may come at the beginning of the sentence.

The word *o'clock* is a contraction of the words *of the clock.*

EXAMPLE At twelve o'clock everyone went to lunch.
Then Akira helped his sisters clean up.

Activity C On your paper, write the predicate in each sentence. Underline the verb or verb phrase.

1. Did you talk to Christa after the party?
2. Why did Elena leave early?
3. Maybe she was feeling sick.
4. After the party, Christa called Elena.
5. What was wrong?
6. Her mother needed her at home.
7. At the last minute, Mrs. Grasso was called in to work.
8. Usually, Mrs. Grasso does not work on weekends.
9. Because of a computer problem, she was needed in the office.
10. Luckily for Elena, the party was almost over.

Activity C

Write these sentences on the board: *Will I see you at the party? What can I do for you? In the morning, we are leaving on vacation.* Help students find the predicate and the verb or verb phrase in each sentence. Suggest that they begin by finding the complete subject. Remind them that all the words not in the complete subject are in the predicate. Be sure students notice that part of the predicate may come before the subject and part of the predicate may come after the subject. Then have them complete Activity C.

Activity C Answers

1. Did talk to Christa after the party **2.** Why did leave early **3.** Maybe was feeling sick **4.** After the party called Elena **5.** was wrong **6.** needed her at home **7.** At the last minute was called in to work **8.** Usually does not work on weekends **9.** Because of a computer problem was needed in the office **10.** Luckily for Elena was almost over

3 Reinforce and Extend

LEARNING STYLES

Body/Kinesthetic

Review the definitions of *subject* and *predicate.* Then ask a volunteer to think of a simple action such as to stand or to wave and then to do that action. Ask a student to say aloud in a sentence what the volunteer did. (*Juan stood up. Keesha waved.*) Write the sentences on the board. Have students underline the complete subject once and the predicate twice. Ask them to expand the basic sentences by adding words to the subject and predicate. Have students write their ideas on paper. Invite volunteers to read and act out their new sentences. Have the class identify the complete subjects and predicates in the new sentences.

GLOBAL CONNECTION

Ask students who speak and write another language to write sentences in that language on the board. Have them tell what the sentence means in English. Ask the students who wrote sentences to underline the complete subjects once and the predicates twice. Then have them circle the verbs or verb phrases and tell what they mean in English. Help students recognize that subjects and predicates are a part of every language's sentences.

Activity D

Write the first item on the board and help students identify the predicate. Then ask them to name the conjunction (*but*) and to find the verbs or verb phrases connected by the conjunction. If necessary, help students eliminate other parts of speech in the predicate to find the compound verb.

Activity D Answers

1. looked at new cars but did not buy one **2.** cost too much and used too much gas **3.** got good gas mileage but remained out of his price range **4.** showed rust spots and needed repairs **5.** Should buy that car or look some more

Activity E

Invite volunteers to provide examples of sentences with compound predicates. Ask other students to identify each part of the compound predicate and the conjunction that joins them. Then have students complete Activity E.

Activity E Answers

1. thought about it but could not decide **2.** talked to him and gave him some advice **3.** would save some more money and look again in the spring **4.** called Alex and asked for a ride **5.** will meet Andy and take him home

Compound verb
Two or more verbs or verb phrases connected by a conjunction

Compound predicate
Two or more predicates connected by a conjunction

A verb can be compound. A **compound verb** is two or more verbs or verb phrases joined by a conjunction such as *and, but,* or *or.* The subject of both verbs is the same.

The deer moved behind the trees and disappeared.
The parents clapped and cheered.
The actors looked calm but were very nervous.

Activity D On your paper, write the predicate in each sentence. Underline the verb or verb phrase in each predicate.

1. Andy looked at new cars but did not buy one.
2. The big cars cost too much and used too much gas.
3. The small cars got good gas mileage but remained out of his price range.
4. The used cars showed rust spots and needed repairs.
5. Should he buy that car or look some more?

The predicate of a sentence can be compound. A **compound predicate** is two or more predicates that are connected by a conjunction.

The band members marched well and played their instruments with precision.

Activity E On your paper, write the compound predicate in each sentence.

1. He thought about it but could not decide.
2. His parents talked to him and gave him some advice.
3. He would save some more money and look again in the spring.
4. Andy called Alex and asked for a ride.
5. Alex will meet Andy and take him home.

Learning Styles

Visual/Spatial
Give students who worked on the Visual/Spatial activity on page 211 their poster from that activity. On the board, print this pattern: verb/adverb/prepositional phrase. Ask the pairs to write the pattern on the poster as a heading. Then have them write 10 action verbs they can use for their picture on the poster under the heading. Tell them to use these verbs and the new pattern to write predicates. Then have them combine these predicates with the subjects on their posters to make complete sentences. Note: Save the posters for use in the Auditory/Verbal Learning Styles activity on page 218.

Learning Styles

Auditory/Verbal
Ask students to write a short paragraph of three or four sentences that each have a compound predicate. Encourage students to videotape or audiotape their reading of their paragraphs. Select a time to play the tapes. Ask the class to listen for and identify the compound predicates.

Online Connection

Suggest that students log on to **www.uottawa.ca/academic/arts/writcent/ hypergrammer/partse.html** for more information about subjects and predicates. Have students click on *Subjects and Predicates* to read about these topics. Then ask students to use the *Back* Button to return to the *Parts of a Sentence* page. There students can choose *Review: The Subjects* or *Review: The Predicate* or both.

Lesson 3 REVIEW

Write these sentences on your paper. Underline the predicate in each sentence.

1. Will you come to our apple picking party this Sunday?
2. When does it start?
3. Around two o'clock, all of my relatives will arrive.
4. Usually we walk around the orchard and pick apples.
5. Bring a big appetite!

Write each sentence on your paper. Underline the predicate. Then circle each verb or verb phrase.

6. I always know the first day of spring.
7. My neighbor Matt takes out his fishing gear.
8. He cleans his gear and practices his casting.
9. Every year he goes on a fishing vacation and returns with a lot of fish.
10. He has already invited us to a fish dinner.

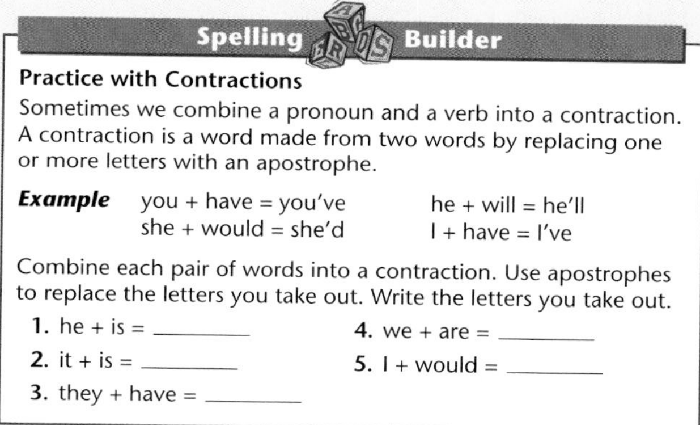

Spelling Builder

Practice with Contractions

Sometimes we combine a pronoun and a verb into a contraction. A contraction is a word made from two words by replacing one or more letters with an apostrophe.

Example you + have = you've he + will = he'll
she + would = she'd I + have = I've

Combine each pair of words into a contraction. Use apostrophes to replace the letters you take out. Write the letters you take out.

1. he + is = ________
2. it + is = ________
3. they + have = ________
4. we + are = ________
5. I + would = ________

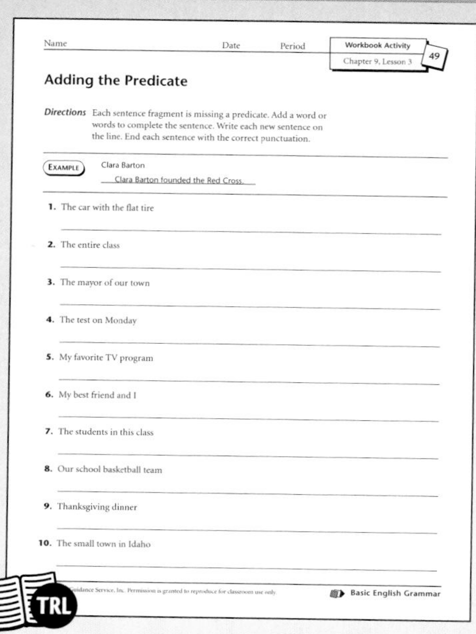

Name Date Period Workbook Activity 49 Chapter 9, Lesson 3

Adding the Predicate

Directions Each sentence fragment is missing a predicate. Add a word or words to complete the sentence. Write each new sentence on the line. End each sentence with the correct punctuation.

EXAMPLE Clara Barton
Clara Barton founded the Red Cross.

1. The car with the flat tire
2. The entire class
3. The mayor of our town
4. The test on Monday
5. My favorite TV program
6. My best friend and I
7. The students in this class
8. Our school basketball team
9. Thanksgiving dinner
10. The small town in Idaho

Basic English Grammar

TRL

Workbook Activity 49

Name Date Period Activity 49 Chapter 9, Lesson 3

A Sentence Has Two Parts

Directions Find the complete subject of each sentence. Underline it once. Then find the complete predicate of each sentence. Underline it twice.

EXAMPLES Many of the students went home after school.
(You) Go get the dog.

1. The teacher opened the package.
2. Where is my homework?
3. Everyone on the trip was ready for lunch.
4. The mailbox was entirely full of letters.
5. Stop that right now!
6. Both Heather and I were late for class.
7. My exam for English is scheduled to be at one o'clock.
8. The bus driver missed our bus stop today.
9. Two candy bars were left.
10. Ice cream will melt fast in warm weather.
11. The award committee's final decisions were made.
12. I am very excited about college.
13. We should go out to dinner tonight.
14. Did one of you see that movie?
15. They ran off in a hurry.
16. The program had ended.
17. The whole dozen eggs fell to the floor.
18. Europe, Asia, and Africa are connected by land.
19. The shuttle flight crew repaired the solar panels.
20. Please find my slippers.

Basic English Grammar

TRL

Activity 49

Lesson 3 Review Answers

1. Will you come to our apple picking party this Sunday? 2. When does it start? 3. Around two o'clock, all of my relatives will arrive. 4. Usually we walk around the orchard and pick apples. 5. Bring a big appetite! 6. I always know the first day of spring. 7. My neighbor Matt takes out his fishing gear. 8. He cleans his gear and practices his casting. 9. Every year he goes on a fishing vacation and returns with a lot of fish. 10. He has already invited us to a fish dinner.

Spelling Builder

Point out to students that if they know how to spell each word that goes into forming a contraction, they will most likely be able to spell the contraction. The key to spelling contractions is to know what letters to replace with an apostrophe. Together make a reminder chart on the board, using the examples in the activity like this: *have* = *'ve will* = *'ll would* = *'d*. Let students add other words to the chart that form contractions, such as *is, are,* and *not.* Finally ask students to suggest contractions and write them on the board.

Answers to Spelling Builder: 1. he's, i **2.** it's, i **3.** they've, ha **4.** we're, a **5.** I'd, woul

Spelling Practice

Point out to students that contractions should be avoided in formal writing. However, in informal writing and in speech, contractions are important. Oral language in particular sounds stiff and robotic when contractions are not used. In fact, screenwriters often omit contractions when writing dialogue for robots. Invite students to write a short dialogue without contractions. Ask them to mark each place where a contraction could be used and to write the contraction correctly above that place. Then let volunteers read their dialogue, first without contractions and then with contractions. Invite the class to comment on the difference.

Lesson at a Glance

Chapter 9 Lesson 4

Overview This lesson presents different types of sentences and explains their purposes.

Objectives

- To identify types of sentences.
- To write different types of sentences correctly.

Student Pages 216–218

Teacher's Resource Library 

Workbook Activity 50

Activity 50

Alternative Activity 50

1 Warm-Up Activity

Review with students how a sentence begins (*with a capital letter*) and ends (*with end punctuation*). Also have students identify the three punctuation marks that are used at the end of sentences. Then provide students with a topic, such as favorite music, recycling, and homework. Ask them to suggest a statement, a question, a command or request, and an exclamation related to each topic. As each sentence is suggested, write it on the board and ask students to tell what mark of end punctuation you should use.

2 Teaching the Lesson

Focus on the sentences in the first example box and how they are punctuated. Ask students to give additional examples of each kind of sentence and to tell what punctuation mark would be used at the end of the sentence. In addition, have them identify the complete subject and predicate for each sentence. For questions, focus on the word order of the subject and predicate. For commands and requests, remind students that the subject *you* is understood. For exclamations, help students note that part of the predicate may come first.

Lesson 4 Purposes of Sentences

Writing Tip

A sentence that expresses a command can add excitement to your writing. It can also allow you to speak directly to the reader. Use a command when you want readers to take action: for example, *Save the park!*

Every sentence has a purpose. A sentence can make a statement. A sentence can ask a question. A sentence can give a command or make a request. A sentence can show strong feelings.

EXAMPLE

Statement	They went to the soccer game.
Question	Are you going to the soccer game?
Command	Go to the soccer game with them.
Exclamation	What a great soccer game that was!

A sentence that makes a statement usually begins with the subject. A statement ends with a period.

EXAMPLE The play began at seven o'clock.

A sentence that asks a question begins with either a helping verb or an interrogative pronoun or adverb. A question ends with a question mark.

EXAMPLE

Are you ready yet? Who is she?
Did you like the play? Where are my books?

A sentence that makes a command or request begins with a verb. The subject *you* is understood. The subject is understood to be the person spoken to. A command usually ends with a period. A strong command may end with an exclamation mark.

EXAMPLE

(You) Please give me two CDs.
(You) Take your pen.
(You) Do it now!

3 Reinforce and Extend

TEACHER ALERT

Sentences showing strong feeling are often called exclamatory sentences as well as exclamations. Commands are also called imperative sentences.

We use different kinds of sentences in writing and in speaking. Listen to the way people use their voices. You can hear the differences among questions, statements, commands, and exclamations.

A sentence that shows strong feeling or excitement ends with an exclamation mark.

EXAMPLE I can't believe our class won!
What a great race that was!

Activity A Decide the purpose of each sentence. Write *S* on your paper if the sentence makes a statement. Write *Q* if the sentence asks a question. Write *C* if the sentence states a command or request. Write *E* if the sentence is an exclamation.

1. Are you hungry?
2. I am starved!
3. We can eat at this restaurant.
4. Melissa and her parents had lunch here last week.
5. Do you know what you want?
6. Please order something for both of us.
7. I'm having the soup and sandwich special.
8. That sounds good to me.
9. What kind of sandwich would you like?
10. Decide quickly!

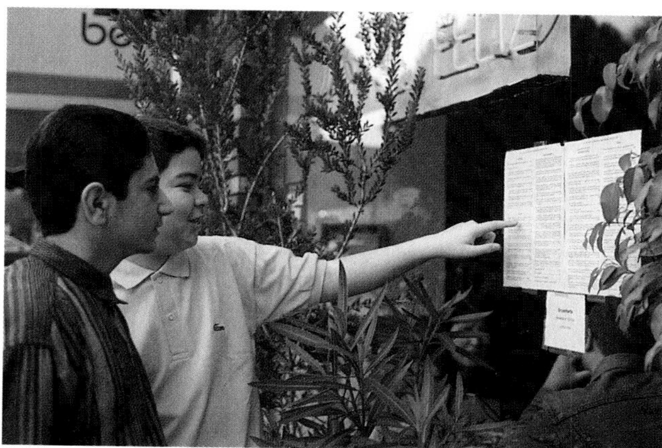

Mark pointed out the restaurant's special sandwiches.

Activity A

Before students do Activity A, ask them to look at the end punctuation of each sentence. Ask what clues the end punctuation gives about the purpose of each sentence. Then have volunteers read each sentence aloud. Encourage readers to think about the words and to use good oral expression as they read. Listeners should pay attention to the meaning of the words and the expression, for expression can give clues to the purpose of a sentence. For example, when reading aloud or speaking a sentence that is a statement, the voice of the speaker often drops in pitch. However, in a question, the voice often goes up. Exclamations are usually spoken with excitement and commands with more force.

Activity A Answers

1. Q **2.** E **3.** S **4.** S **5.** Q **6.** C **7.** S **8.** S **9.** Q **10.** C or E

GLOBAL CONNECTION

Explain to students that punctuation of sentences may vary from language to language. For example, in Spanish, an inverted question mark comes at the beginning of a question and an inverted exclamation mark comes at the beginning of an exclamation. Regular end punctuation appears at the end of each type of sentence. To illustrate, write these sentences on the board or invite a student fluent in Spanish to do so: ¿Qué podemos hacer? (*What can we do?*) ¡Claro que podrás! (*Of course, you can!*) You might ask students who can write languages other than English to explain how the different kinds of sentences are punctuated in those languages.

IN THE COMMUNITY

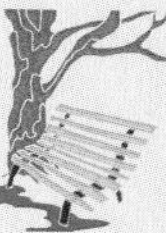

Students may enjoy sharing their knowledge with younger people in the community. Encourage students to volunteer at youth centers, day-care centers, homework clubs, and other organizations where they might work with school-age children to help them write short stories, letters, and simple articles. Students can also help review younger children's school writing assignments to check for complete sentences and correct capitalization and end punctuation.

Lesson 4 Review Answers

1. Listen to the new CD.—command or request **2.** What a terrific sound that is!—exclamation **3.** Where do you buy your CDs?—question **4.** The music store at Crosstown Mall has the best prices.—statement **5.** What is the average price of a tape or CD at the store near our school?—question **6–10.** Answers will vary. Possible answers follow. **6.** Charles Dickens is my favorite author. **7.** Did he write *A Tale of Two Cities*? **8.** Please hand me that book. **9.** Give me your full attention while I read a summary of it. **10.** What a great story that was!

Writing Project

Remind students that using compound subjects and compound predicates can help them avoid repetition in their writing. Using a variety of sentence types, especially questions, commands and requests, and exclamations can add interest and excitement. Suggest that they look for ways to avoid repetition and to use a variety of sentences in their paragraphs.

Answers to Writing Project: Paragraphs will vary. Students should have underlined the subject in each sentence once and the predicate twice. There should be no sentence fragments. Invite students to read their paragraphs to the class.

Learning Styles

Auditory/Verbal

Return posters and pictures from the activities on pages 211 and 214 to the pairs of students who made them. Have one student read the complete subject of each sentence on the poster to the other student, who then reads the complete predicate. Ask the pairs to name the purpose of each sentence—statement, question, command or request, or exclamation. Then have the partners change three of their sentences to another purpose. Have the pairs read these sentences to class members, who then state the purpose of each sentence.

Lesson 4 REVIEW

Write the sentences on your paper. Add correct end punctuation marks. Next to each sentence, write its purpose (*statement, question, command or request, exclamation*).

1. Listen to this new CD
2. What a terrific sound that is
3. Where do you buy your CDs
4. The music store at Crosstown Mall has the best prices
5. What is the average price of a tape or CD at the store near our school

On your paper, write an example of each kind of sentence. Be sure to begin each sentence with a capital letter and end it with the correct end punctuation mark.

6. a statement
7. a question
8. a request
9. a command
10. a sentence that shows strong feeling or excitement

Writing Project

Using Subjects and Predicates

What is your dream vacation? Is it a camping trip or a visit to a distant place? Is it a vacation to see a family member? Write a paragraph about your dream vacation that answers these questions:

- Where would you go?
- How long would you stay?
- What would you do?
- How would you travel?

After you write your paragraph, underline the subject in each sentence once. Underline the predicates twice. If you have sentence fragments, add subjects or predicates to make them complete sentences. Then read your paragraph to the class.

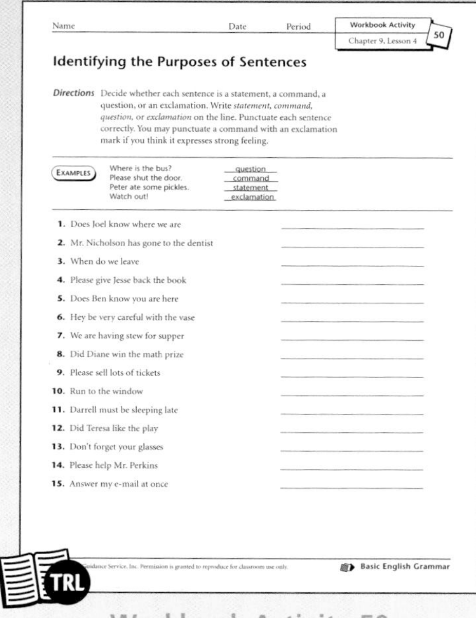

Name Date Period Workbook Activity 50 Chapter 9, Lesson 4

Identifying the Purposes of Sentences

Directions Decide whether each sentence is a statement, a command, a question, or an exclamation. Write *statement, command, question,* or *exclamation* on the line. Punctuate each sentence correctly. You may punctuate a command with an exclamation mark if you think it expresses strong feeling.

EXAMPLES
Where is the bus? — question
Please shut the door. — command
Peter ate some pickles. — statement
Watch out! — exclamation

1. Does Joel know where we are
2. Mr. Nicholson has gone to the dentist
3. When do we leave
4. Please give Jesse back the book
5. Does Ben know you are here
6. Hey be very careful with the vase
7. We are having stew for supper
8. Did Diane win the math prize
9. Please sell lots of tickets
10. Run to the window
11. Darrell must be sleeping late
12. Did Teresa like the play
13. Don't forget your glasses
14. Please help Mr. Perkins
15. Answer my e-mail at once

 Basic English Grammar

TRL

Workbook Activity 50

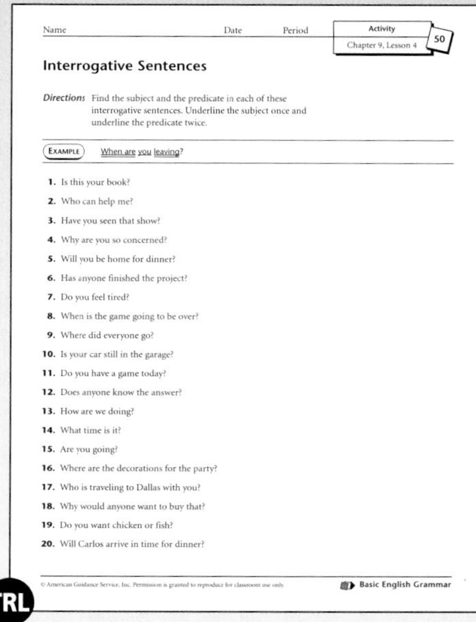

Name Date Period Activity 50 Chapter 9, Lesson 4

Interrogative Sentences

Directions Find the subject and the predicate in each of these interrogative sentences. Underline the subject once and underline the predicate twice.

EXAMPLE When are you leaving?

1. Is this your book?
2. Who can help me?
3. Have you seen that show?
4. Why are you so concerned?
5. Will you be home for dinner?
6. Has anyone finished the project?
7. Do you feel tired?
8. When is the game going to be over?
9. Where did everyone go?
10. Is your car still in the garage?
11. Do you have a game today?
12. Does anyone know the answer?
13. How are we doing?
14. What time is it?
15. Are you going?
16. Where are the decorations for the party?
17. Who is traveling to Dallas with you?
18. Why would anyone want to buy that?
19. Do you want chicken or fish?
20. Will Carlos arrive in time for dinner?

 Basic English Grammar

TRL

Activity 50

Lesson 5 Simple and Compound Sentences

Simple sentence
A sentence with one subject and one predicate; an independent clause

Compound sentence
Two independent clauses joined by a conjunction such as and, but, *or* or

A **simple sentence** has one subject and one predicate. A simple sentence is an independent clause. An independent clause expresses a complete thought.

A **compound sentence** has two or more independent clauses joined together with a conjunction. Each clause has a subject and a predicate and expresses a complete idea. A comma comes before the conjunction in a compound sentence.

EXAMPLE

S P Conj. S P
Jennifer went to the party, and Sue met her there.

A compound sentence tells about two or more related events.

EXAMPLE

Correct Jennifer went to the party, but Alex stayed home.
Incorrect Jennifer went to the party, but I like grapes.

Remember that a simple sentence may have a compound subject or a compound verb. A compound sentence has two or more complete ideas, each with its own subject and verb.

Activity A Write these compound sentences on your paper. Circle the complete subject in each independent clause. Underline the predicate in each independent clause.

1. They were hungry, but all of the restaurants were closed.
2. Alice has a cat, Mike has a gerbil, and Sandy has a hamster.
3. Mr. Barry likes apples, but Mrs. Barry prefers pears.
4. Lori plays the piano, and her sister plays the flute.
5. Ms. Ray gives a lot of homework, but her tests are easy.

Lesson at a Glance

Chapter 9 Lesson 5

Overview This lesson presents simple and compound sentences.

Objectives

- To find subjects and predicates in compound sentences.
- To distinguish between simple and compound sentences.
- To write compound sentences.

Student Pages 219–221

Teacher's Resource Library 

Workbook Activity 51
Activity 51
Alternative Activity 51

Vocabulary

compound sentence
simple sentence

Warm-Up Activity

On the board, write the sentence *Jason walked to the store.* Have students identify the subject and predicate. Next write this sentence: *Jason and Consuelo walked to the store and bought oranges.* Ask students to identify the subjects and predicates in this sentence. Students should notice that there is a compound subject and a compound predicate. Then write *Jason bought oranges, but Consuelo bought apples.* Have the subjects and predicates identified. Cover *but Consuelo bought apples.* Ask students if *Jason bought oranges* is a complete sentence. Then cover *Jason bought oranges, but.* Ask if *Consuelo bought apples* is a complete sentence. Then call attention to *but* and ask what kind of word it is. (*coordinating conjunction*) Explain that the sentence *Jason bought oranges, but Consuelo bought apples* is an example of a compound sentence, or two or more independent clauses connected by a coordinating conjunction.

Teaching the Lesson

Write this compound sentence on the board: *Llamas are found in Peru, and camels are found in Arabia.* Have volunteers identify the two simple sentences that make up the compound sentence. Then write *They carry large loads.* Ask volunteers to compose oral compound sentences, using this sentence as one of the simple sentences. Have volunteers identify each simple sentence and the conjunction that joins them.

Activity A

Complete Activity A orally as a class. Ask students to identify the conjunction used to separate each simple sentence.

Activity A Answers

1. (They) were hungry, but (all of the restaurants) were closed. 2. (Alice) has a cat, (Mike) has a gerbil, and (Sandy) has a hamster. 3. (Mr. Barry) likes apples, but (Mrs. Barry) prefers pears. 4. (Lori) plays the piano, and (her sister) plays the flute. 5. (Ms. Ray) gives a lot of homework, but (her tests) are easy.

Activity B

Challenge volunteers to give examples of simple sentences with compound subjects, simple sentences with compound verbs, and compound sentences. Write each sentence on the board and have the class identify the complete subjects and predicates. Then have students do Activity B on their own.

Activity B Answers

1. S **2.** S **3.** C **4.** C **5.** S **6.** C **7.** C **8.** S **9.** C **10.** S

Activity C

Write these sentences on the board: *The team was tired, but they played well anyway. A new Italian restaurant opened in our neighborhood, and I like grapes.* Help students identify the independent clauses in each sentence. Then ask students which sentence is correct and which is incorrect. Elicit that the ideas in the first sentence are related; the ideas in the second sentence are not. Then invite students to correct the second sentence by suggesting an independent clause that relates to the other independent clause.

Activity C Answers

Each sentence should be a compound sentence with related independent clauses and should be punctuated correctly. Answers will vary. Sample answers follow. **1.** The room was yellow, but Carrie painted it light green. **2.** Brad and Mia enjoy listening to music, but they listen to different kinds of music. **3.** Dan hit a homerun, and his team finally won a game. **4.** This weekend, the drama club will perform *A Midsummer Night's Dream,* and the band will hold a concert. **5.** Rosa cooked dinner, and Mario did the dishes.

Using What You've Learned

Have volunteers write on the board one of their compound sentences from the activity. Ask other students to underline the first independent clause and to circle the second. Then ask a volunteer to identify the conjunction.

Activity B Read the sentences. Write *S* if the sentence is simple. Write *C* if it is compound.

1. Andrea and Michelle signed up for the play.

2. He goes fishing every spring but has never caught the big one.

3. The phone rang three times, and then it stopped.

4. The girls hurried, but they were late anyway.

5. After school, we came right home and did our homework.

6. The driver stomped hard on the brakes, and the bus skidded.

7. I met Lydia at the corner, and we walked to school together.

8. My brother sold his car and bought a van.

9. Kate and two of her friends signed up for swimming lessons, but the class was full.

10. The Sunday newspaper has a section designed and written completely by teens.

Activity C Write five compound sentences. Be sure the ideas in each sentence are related. Punctuate each sentence correctly.

Using What You've Learned

Write a short note to a friend or family member. Tell this person what you did this week. Use at least three compound sentences in your note. Then circle the complete subjects and underline the predicates in each compound sentence.

Reinforce and Extend

Learning Styles

Body/Kinesthetic

Let volunteers choose two action verbs such as *waved* and *cried.* Ask the volunteers to act out a short scene in which they pantomime the two actions. Have the class guess the action words and then compose oral compound sentences in which they use the two verbs. For example, *Kara waved good-bye, and then she cried her eyes out.*

Lesson 5 REVIEW

Number your paper from 1 to 5. Next to each number, write *S* if the sentence is simple. Write *C* if it is compound.

1. Alex plays on the basketball team and works part time at the grocery store.
2. The store manager hired him as a bagger, but Alex wanted more responsibility.
3. After two months, Mr. Alvarez and Alex talked.
4. Mr. Alvarez offered Alex the job in the deli, and Alex accepted it.
5. It meant more responsibility, but it also meant a raise in pay.

Write these sentences on your paper. Underline a compound subject once. Underline a compound predicate twice. Circle any independent clauses.

6. Latasha called me after school and asked for help with her project.
7. I met her at the library, and we went over the assignment.
8. Most of the students in the class were writing research papers, but she made a different decision.
9. Latasha was designing and building a model city.
10. One of our teachers and several of our classmates were also at the library.
11. Andrea spotted us and came over to our table.
12. Andrea, Latasha, and I are in the same math class.
13. We walked to the bus stop together, but Andrea did not get on the bus with Latasha and me.
14. Andrea lives close to the library, so she walked home.
15. We waved good-bye and then got on the bus.

Lesson 5 Review Answers

1. S **2.** C **3.** S **4.** C **5.** C **6.** Latasha called me after school and asked for help with her project. **7.** (I met her at the library,) and (we went over the assignment.) **8.** (Most of the students in the class were writing research papers,) but (she made a different decision.) **9.** Latasha was designing and building a model city. **10.** One of our teachers and several of our classmates were also at the library. **11.** Andrea spotted us and came over to our table. **12.** Andrea, Latasha, and I are in the same math class. **13.** (We walked to the bus stop together,) but (Andrea did not get on the bus with Latasha and me.) **14.** (Andrea lives close to the library,) so (she walked home.) **15.** We waved good-bye and then got on the bus.

LEARNING STYLES

Logical/Mathematical

On the board, write these headings: *compound subject, compound predicate, compound sentence/two independent clauses.* Invite each student to write sentences that illustrate the formulas represented by the headings on the board. Ask volunteers to read aloud one or more of their sentences. Call on other volunteers to go to the board and put a check under the heading each sentence represents.

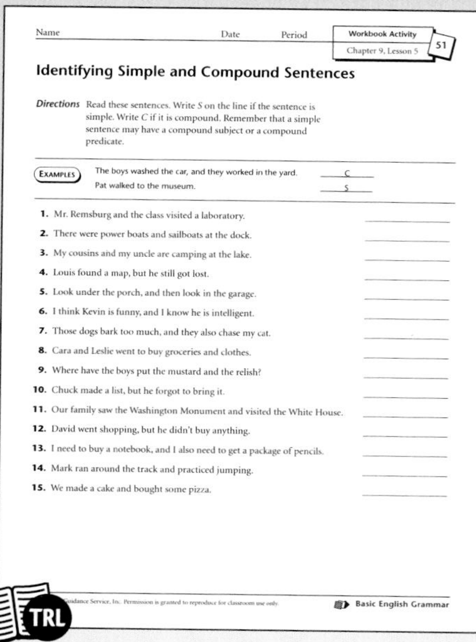

Name Date Period | Workbook Activity 51 | Chapter 9, Lesson 5

Identifying Simple and Compound Sentences

Directions Read these sentences. Write *S* on the line if the sentence is simple. Write *C* if it is compound. Remember that a simple sentence may have a compound subject or a compound predicate.

EXAMPLES The boys washed the car, and they worked in the yard. ___C___
Pat walked to the museum. ___S___

1. Mr. Remsburg and the class visited a laboratory. ______
2. There were power boats and sailboats at the dock. ______
3. My cousins and my uncle are camping at the lake. ______
4. Louis found a map, but he still got lost. ______
5. Look under the porch, and then look in the garage. ______
6. I think Kevin is funny, and I know he is intelligent. ______
7. Those dogs bark too much, and they also chase my cat. ______
8. Cara and Leslie went to buy groceries and clothes. ______
9. Where have the boys put the mustard and the relish? ______
10. Chuck made a list, but he forgot to bring it. ______
11. Our family saw the Washington Monument and visited the White House. ______
12. David went shopping, but he didn't buy anything. ______
13. I need to buy a notebook, and I also need to get a package of pencils. ______
14. Mark ran around the track and practiced jumping. ______
15. We made a cake and bought some pizza. ______

 Basic English Grammar

TRL

Workbook Activity 51

Name Date Period | Activity 51 | Chapter 9, Lesson 5

Using Compound Sentences

Directions Add an independent clause that expresses a related event or idea to each sentence to make it a compound sentence. Remember to use a conjunction to connect the two clauses. Use correct capitalization and punctuation.

EXAMPLE At night, Hannah has trouble sleeping, and in the morning she is tired.

1. ______________ Pilar and Kurt won't help us.
2. Alex found two extra bottles ______________.
3. Some people thought Mr. Snuffles was a toy ______________.
4. ______________ Ronnie liked winter's snow and ice.
5. I haven't been to Rome ______________.
6. ______________ my sister still listens to Nirvana.
7. The restaurant was known for its good food ______________.
8. ______________ Spiderman can climb up buildings.
9. ______________ I like dancing more than she does.
10. Movies sometimes make me cry ______________.
11. I wanted to play the violin ______________.
12. ______________ Webster beat him to the finish line.
13. Dr. Zimmerman performed tests on the blood ______________.
14. ______________ I haven't had lunch yet.
15. There are two boats to the island ______________.
16. ______________ Stephen wants to travel.
17. When the house is messy, mom is not happy ______________.
18. She started out in Kansas ______________.
19. ______________ pink is my favorite color.
20. The assignment seemed long ______________.

 Basic English Grammar

TRL

Activity 51

Chapter 9 Review

Use the Chapter Review to prepare students for tests and to reteach content from the chapter.

Chapter 9 Mastery Test 

The Teacher's Resource Library includes two parallel forms of the Chapter 9 Mastery Test. The difficulty level of the two forms is equivalent. You may wish to use one form as a pretest and the other form as a posttest.

Review Answers

Part A

1. capital letter **2.** end punctuation **3.** simple sentence **4.** predicate **5.** compound sentence **6.** compound predicate **7.** sentence **8.** simple subject **9.** compound verb **10.** compound subject **11.** complete subject

Part B

Answers for items 13 and 14 will vary. Possible answers are given. **12.** S **13.** As usual, each of the boys on the team had a chance to hit the ball. **14.** The team will be practicing at four instead of three on Monday. **15.** S

Chapter 9 REVIEW

Word Bank
capital letter
complete subject
compound predicate
compound sentence
compound subject
compound verb
end punctuation
predicate
sentence
simple sentence
simple subject

Part A On a sheet of paper, write the correct word or words from the Word Bank to complete each sentence.

1. The uppercase form of a letter such as *A* is a ______ .
2. A period, a question mark, and an exclamation mark are all ______ marks.
3. A ______ is an independent clause.
4. The part of a sentence that tells something about the subject and always contains a verb is the ______ .
5. Two independent clauses joined by a conjunction such as *and, but,* or *or* form a ______ .
6. Two or more predicates connected by a conjunction form a ______ .
7. A ______ is a group of words that expresses a complete thought.
8. The ______ is the noun or pronoun that the sentence is about.
9. A ______ is two or more verbs connected by a conjunction.
10. Two or more subjects connected by a conjunction form a ______ .
11. A ______ is all the words in the subject.

Part B Write *S* on your paper if the group of words is a sentence. If it is not a sentence, write the words on your paper, and add other words to make it a sentence.

12. The ball landed in the field.
13. As usual, each of the boys on the team.
14. Practicing at four instead of three on Monday.
15. How does it feel to have a winning record?

Name ______ Date ______ Period ______ | Mastery Test A, Page 1 | Chapter 9

Chapter 9 Mastery Test A

Part A Write *S* if the words are a sentence. Write *N* if the words are not a sentence.

1. ______ Before you start the test.
2. ______ We stopped at the store.
3. ______ We bought groceries.
4. ______ When Sheila gets home.
5. ______ On the day of the victory celebration.
6. ______ Mr. Nguyen tilled the field.
7. ______ Although we were tired.
8. ______ Ed and his friend are coming.
9. ______ The red-berried elder is lovely.
10. ______ After the play at the theater.

Part B In each sentence, underline the complete subject. Circle the nouns or pronouns in each subject.

11. Irene and I do not agree about that.
12. Neither the television nor the radio was working.
13. Grandfather and the entire family had to go out for dinner.
14. Our friends Howard and Heidi live in a walk-up.
15. Everything in the freezer thawed out.

Part C Review the words in bold and circle the answer that most correctly identifies them.

16. **Maggie, April, and Adrienne** ate lunch together every weekday.
A simple subject **B** predicate **C** compound subject **D** compound predicate
17. Adrienne thought the food **was delicious but needed salt**.
A simple subject **B** verb phrase **C** compound subject **D** compound predicate
18. Does **our friend Maggie** like salsa and chips?
A complete subject **B** predicate **C** simple subject **D** compound predicate
19. Adrienne told April that she **ate ketchup on her hotdog**.
A simple subject **B** predicate **C** compound subject **D** verb phrase
20. We **cheered for the cook and ate every bite**.
A simple subject **B** verb phrase **C** compound subject **D** compound predicate

 Basic English Grammar

TRL

Name ______ Date ______ Period ______ | Mastery Test A, Page 2 | Chapter 9

Chapter 9 Mastery Test A, continued

Part D In each sentence, underline the complete predicate. Circle the verb or verb phrase in each predicate.

21. The storm had knocked out the electrical power.
22. No one had electricity or telephones for three days.
23. My neighbor fly casts in summer and ice fishes in winter.
24. The highway crews are working day and night to plow the roads.
25. My aunt and uncle have been married for years.

Part E Identify the purpose of each sentence. Write *statement, question, command/request,* or *exclamation.*

26. Who was that masked man? ______
27. Tell me about your vacation. ______
28. We drove to the North Shore last week. ______
29. I am all worn out! ______
30. When do you think you will be back here? ______

Part F On the line, write *S* if the sentence is a simple sentence and *C* if it is a compound sentence. Draw a line between the complete subject and the complete predicate in each independent clause.

31. ______ Jo plays the drums, and her mother plays the banjo.
32. ______ The very small child sang sweetly.
33. ______ A motorcycle is not as expensive as a car, but it is trusty transportation.
34. ______ We stopped at the mall, and we came home after that.
35. ______ Liza and her brothers play soccer.
36. ______ Dennis read six books last month.
37. ______ Donna has not had any piano lessons, but she plays very well.
38. ______ Frank is coming for dinner, and he is bringing the salad.
39. ______ We hiked to the lake, and we spent the whole afternoon there.
40. ______ Matt assembled his new computer in the den.

 Basic English Grammar

TRL

Chapter 9 Mastery Test A

Part C Write each sentence on your paper. Underline the complete subject once and the predicate twice. Circle the simple subject and the verb or verb phrase.

16. The car sputtered and came to a stop.

17. What was that strange noise?

18. His parents and the mechanic at the garage had warned him.

19. Don't buy the car!

20. He did not take their advice but bought the car.

Part D Write the letter of the word that identifies the purpose of each sentence.

21. Listen to this.

A statement **C** command or request
B question **D** exclamation

22. Do you want to be a stand-up comic?

A statement **C** command or request
B question **D** exclamation

23. Experience and talent are the keys to success.

A statement **C** command or request
B question **D** exclamation

Part E Write each sentence on your paper. Next to each sentence, write whether it is *simple* or *compound.* Underline the complete subject once and the predicate twice in each independent clause.

24. Each summer, the Dawsons and the Ortegas vacation together.

25. Mrs. Ortega and Mrs. Dawson met in college, and they have remained friends since then.

Test-Taking Tip

When you read test directions, restate them in your own words. Think about what you are expected to do. That way, your answer is more likely to be complete and correct.

Review Answers

Part C

16. The (car) (sputtered) and (came) to a stop. **17.** What (was) that strange (noise)? **18.** His (parents) and the (mechanic) at the garage (had warned) him. **19.** ((You)) (Don't buy) the car! **20.** (He) (did) not (take) their advice but (bought) the car.

Part D

21. C **22.** B **23.** A

Part E

24. Each summer, the Dawsons and the Ortegas vacation together. simple

25. Mrs. Ortega and Mrs. Dawson met in college, and they have remained friends since then. compound

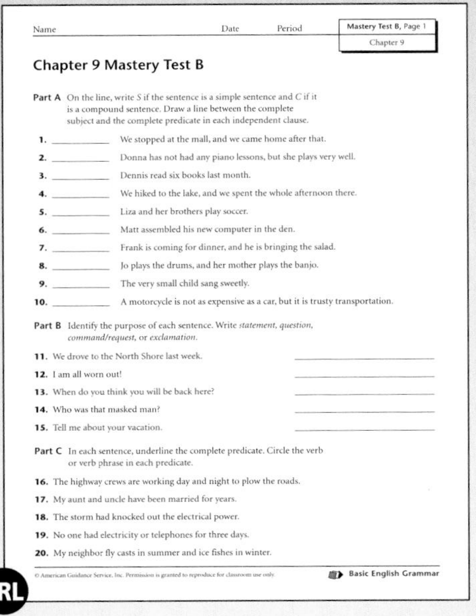

Name ______ Date ______ Period ______ | Mastery Test B, Page 1 | Chapter 9

Chapter 9 Mastery Test B

Part A On the line, write *S* if the sentence is a simple sentence and *C* if it is a compound sentence. Draw a line between the complete subject and the complete predicate in each independent clause.

1. ______ We stopped at the mall, and we came home after that.

2. ______ Donna has not had any piano lessons, but she plays very well.

3. ______ Dennis read six books last month.

4. ______ We hiked to the lake, and we spent the whole afternoon there.

5. ______ Liza and her brothers play soccer.

6. ______ Matt assembled his new computer in the den.

7. ______ Frank is coming for dinner, and he is bringing the salad.

8. ______ Jo plays the drums, and her mother plays the banjo.

9. ______ The very small child sang sweetly.

10. ______ A motorcycle is not as expensive as a car, but it is trusty transportation.

Part B Identify the purpose of each sentence. Write *statement, question, command/request,* or *exclamation.*

11. We drove to the North Shore last week. ______

12. I am all worn out! ______

13. When do you think you will be back here? ______

14. Who was that masked man? ______

15. Tell me about your vacation. ______

Part C In each sentence, underline the complete predicate. Circle the verb or verb phrase in each predicate.

16. The highway crews are working day and night to plow the roads.

17. My aunt and uncle have been married for years.

18. The storm had knocked out the electrical power.

19. No one had electricity or telephones for three days.

20. My neighbor fly casts in summer and ice fishes in winter.

Basic English Grammar

TRL

Name ______ Date ______ Period ______ | Mastery Test B, Page 2 | Chapter 9

Chapter 9 Mastery Test B, continued

Part D Review the words in bold and circle the answer that most correctly identifies them.

21. **Maggie, April, and Adrienne** ate lunch together every weekday.
A simple subject **B** predicate **C** compound subject **D** compound predicate

22. Adrienne told April that she **ate ketchup on her hotdog**.
A simple subject **B** predicate **C** compound subject **D** verb phrase

23. Does **our friend Maggie** like salsa and chips?
A complete subject **B** predicate **C** simple subject **D** compound predicate

24. Adrienne thought the food **was delicious but needed salt**.
A simple subject **B** verb phrase **C** compound subject **D** compound predicate

25. We **cheered for the cook and ate every bite**.
A simple subject **B** verb phrase **C** compound subject **D** compound predicate

Part E In each sentence, underline the complete subject. Circle the nouns or pronouns in each subject.

26. Everything in the freezer thawed out.

27. Our friends Howard and Heidi live in a walk-up.

28. Grandfather and the entire family had to go out for dinner.

29. Neither the television nor the radio was working.

30. Irene and I do not agree about that.

Part F Write *S* if the words are a sentence. Write *N* if the words are not a sentence.

31. ______ Mr. Nguyen tilled the field.

32. ______ Although we were tired.

33. ______ Ed and his friend are coming.

34. ______ The red-berried elder is lovely.

35. ______ After the play at the theater.

36. ______ Before you start the test.

37. ______ We stopped at the store.

38. ______ We bought groceries.

39. ______ When Sheila gets home.

40. ______ On the day of the victory celebration.

Basic English Grammar

TRL

Chapter 9 Mastery Test B

Chapter

10

Planning Guide

Sentence Patterns

	Student Text Lesson				Language Skills		
	Student Pages	Vocabulary	Practice Exercises	Lesson Review	Identification Skills	Writing Skills	Punctuation Skills
Lesson 1 What Are Pattern 1 Sentences?	226–232	✔	✔	✔	✔	✔	✔
Lesson 2 Pattern 2 Sentences (Direct Objects)	233–241	✔	✔	✔	✔	✔	✔
Lesson 3 Pattern 3 Sentences (Indirect Objects)	242–249	✔	✔	✔	✔	✔	✔
Lesson 4 Pattern 4 Sentences (Object Complements)	250–255	✔	✔	✔	✔	✔	✔
Lesson 5 Pattern 5 Sentences (Predicate Nouns)	256–263	✔	✔	✔	✔	✔	✔
Lesson 6 Pattern 6 Sentences (Predicate Adjectives)	264–271	✔	✔	✔	✔	✔	✔

Chapter Activities

Teacher's Resource Library

Community Connection 10: Sentence Patterns in Newspapers

Media and Literature Connection 10: Finding Sentence Patterns in Fiction

Assessment Options

Student Text

Chapter 10 Review

Teacher's Resource Library

Chapter 10 Mastery Tests A and B

Student Text Features						Teaching Strategies						Learning Styles						Teacher's Resource Library			
Spelling Builder	Vocabulary Builder	Where To Find It	Writing Project	Using What You've Learned	Writing Tips/Notes/ Technology Notes	Teacher Alert	Online Connection	Applications (Home, Career, Community, Global)	Speaking Practice	Spelling Practice	Writing Practice	Auditory/Verbal	Body/Kinesthetic	Interpersonal/Group Learning	Logical/Mathematical	Visual/Spatial	LEP/ESL	Workbook Activities	Activities	Alternative Activities	Self-Study Guide
232				230	✔	231						230	227	228		229		52	52	52	✔
					✔	236		237, 239			240	238	235, 237	234	239	241		53	53	53	✔
	248				✔	243		243		246					247	244	245	54	54	54	✔
		252			✔	255		252	251			253	253					55	55	55	✔
					✔	257	260	261, 263						261	258	257	259	56	56	56	✔
			270		✔	267		268				265		266	268	268	267	57	57	57	✔

Pronunciation Key

a	hat	e	let	ī	ice	ô	order	u̇	put	sh	she	ə { a	in about
ā	age	ē	equal	o	hot	oi	oil	ü	rule	th	thin	e	in taken
ä	far	ėr	term	ō	open	ou	out	ch	child	ŦH	then	i	in pencil
â	care	i	it	ȯ	saw	u	cup	ng	long	zh	measure	o	in lemon
												u	in circus

Alternative Activities

The Teacher's Resource Library (TRL) contains a set of lower-level worksheets called Alternative Activities. These worksheets cover the same content as the regular Activities but are written at a second-grade reading level.

Skill Track Software

Use the Skill Track Software for Basic English Grammar for additional reinforcement of this chapter. The software program allows students using AGS textbooks to be assessed for mastery of each chapter and lesson of the textbook. Students access the software on an individual basis and are assessed with multiple-choice items.

Chapter at a Glance

Chapter 10: Sentence Patterns

pages 224–273

Lessons

Skill Track Software for Basic English Grammar

Teacher's Resource Library

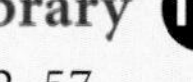

- Workbook Activities 52–57
- Activities 52–57
- Alternative Activities 52–57
- Diagramming Activities 1–6
- Community Connection 10
- Media and Literature Connection 10
- Chapter 10 Self-Study Guide
- Chapter 10 Mastery Tests A and B

(Answer Keys for the Teacher's Resource Library begin on page 340 of this Teacher's Edition.)

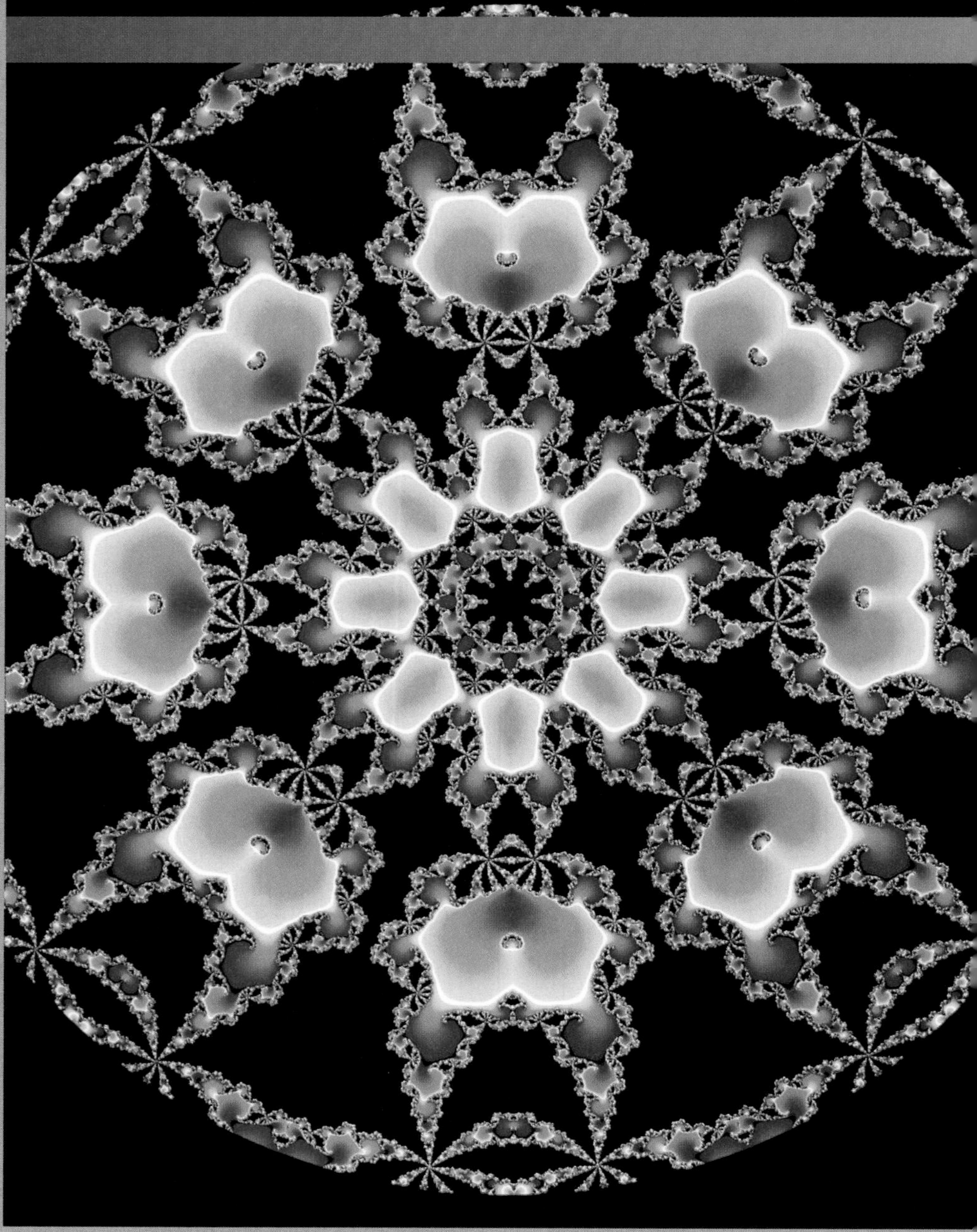

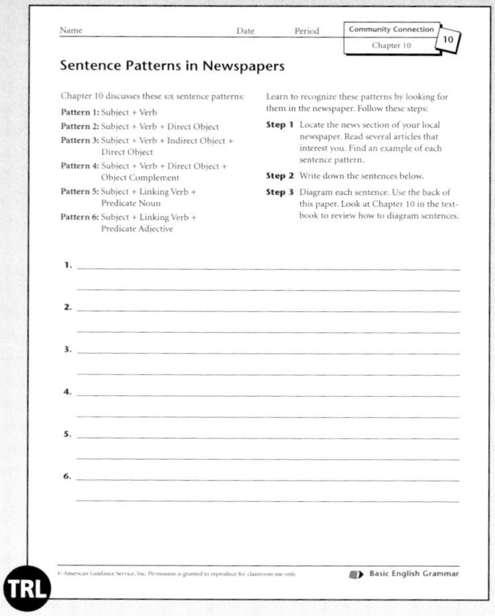

Name Date Period **Community Connection** Chapter 10 **10**

Sentence Patterns in Newspapers

Chapter 10 discusses these six sentence patterns:

Pattern 1: Subject + Verb
Pattern 2: Subject + Verb + Direct Object
Pattern 3: Subject + Verb + Indirect Object + Direct Object
Pattern 4: Subject + Verb + Direct Object + Object Complement
Pattern 5: Subject + Linking Verb + Predicate Noun
Pattern 6: Subject + Linking Verb + Predicate Adjective

Learn to recognize these patterns by looking for them in the newspaper. Follow these steps:

Step 1 Locate the news section of your local newspaper. Read several articles that interest you. Find an example of each sentence pattern.

Step 2 Write down the sentences below.

Step 3 Diagram each sentence. Use the back of this paper. Look at Chapter 10 in the textbook to review how to diagram sentences.

1. ______
2. ______
3. ______
4. ______
5. ______
6. ______

 Basic English Grammar

Community Connection 10

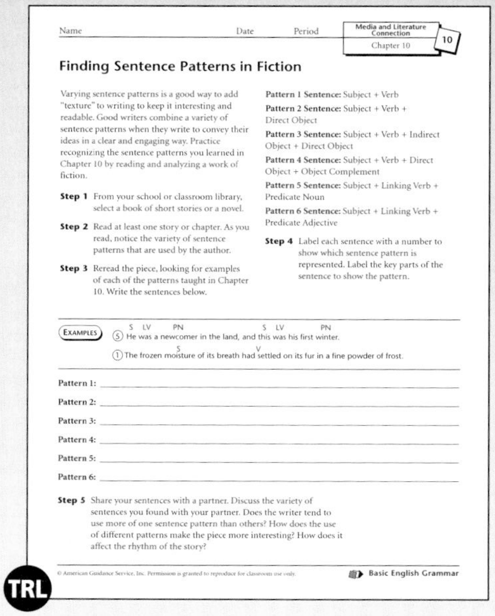

Name Date Period **Media and Literature Connection** Chapter 10 **10**

Finding Sentence Patterns in Fiction

Varying sentence patterns is a good way to add "texture" to writing to keep it interesting and readable. Good writers combine a variety of sentence patterns when they write to convey their ideas in a clear and engaging way. Practice recognizing the sentence patterns you learned in Chapter 10 by reading and analyzing a work of fiction.

Step 1 From your school or classroom library, select a book of short stories or a novel.

Step 2 Read at least one story or chapter. As you read, notice the variety of sentence patterns that are used by the author.

Step 3 Reread the piece, looking for examples of each of the patterns taught in Chapter 10. Write the sentences below.

Pattern 1 Sentence: Subject + Verb
Pattern 2 Sentence: Subject + Verb + Direct Object
Pattern 3 Sentence: Subject + Verb + Indirect Object + Direct Object
Pattern 4 Sentence: Subject + Verb + Direct Object + Object Complement
Pattern 5 Sentence: Subject + Linking Verb + Predicate Noun
Pattern 6 Sentence: Subject + Linking Verb + Predicate Adjective

Step 4 Label each sentence with a number to show which sentence pattern is represented. Label the key parts of the sentence to show the pattern.

EXAMPLES
(5) He (S) was (LV) a newcomer (PN) in the land, and this (S) was (LV) his first winter (PN).
(1) The frozen moisture (S) of its breath had settled (V) on its fur in a fine powder of frost.

Pattern 1: ______
Pattern 2: ______
Pattern 3: ______
Pattern 4: ______
Pattern 5: ______
Pattern 6: ______

Step 5 Share your sentences with a partner. Discuss the variety of sentences you found with your partner. Does the writer tend to use more of one sentence pattern than others? How does the use of different patterns make the piece more interesting? How does it affect the rhythm of the story?

 Basic English Grammar

Media and Literature Connection 10

Chapter

Sentence Patterns

Can you find the pattern in this kaleidoscope image? From the colors in a rainbow and the shape of a honeycomb to patchwork quilts, you can see patterns in nature and in things people do. Sentences have patterns, too. Understanding those patterns can help you choose sentences that make your writing both clear and colorful.

The English language has several basic sentence patterns. Chapter 10 focuses on six of them.

Goals for Learning

- ◆ To identify and write simple and compound sentences
- ◆ To recognize transitive and intransitive verbs in sentences
- ◆ To recognize direct and indirect objects in sentences
- ◆ To identify object complements in sentences
- ◆ To identify predicate nouns and predicate adjectives
- ◆ To diagram sentences from each of the six sentence patterns

225

Introducing the Chapter

Ask students to draw a pattern on the board and to explain what makes their drawing a pattern. Lead them to conclude that a pattern includes a predictable sequence of images or events. Explain that when we say, "A pattern is developing," we mean that we are beginning to know what to expect.

Ask students to look at the innermost circle of the kaleidoscopic image on this page and identify the pattern within it. Elicit that as this shape expands, the pattern remains the same: a circle divided into eight equal segments. Then point out that sentences have patterns too. Writers use different sentence patterns for different purposes to achieve different effects. Explain that by the end of Chapter 10, students will recognize different sentence patterns and learn how to diagram them to show how their parts go together.

Writing Tips, Notes, and Technology Notes

Ask volunteers to read the tips and notes that appear in the margins throughout the chapter. Then discuss them with the class.

Teacher's Resource

The AGS Teaching Strategies in English Transparencies may be used with this chapter. The transparencies add an interactive dimension to expand and enhance the *Basic English Grammar* program content.

Career Interest Inventory

The AGS Harrington-O'Shea Career Decision-Making System–Revised (CDM) may be used with this chapter. Students can use the CDM to explore their interests and identify careers. The CDM defines career areas that are indicated by students' responses on the inventory.

Name Date Period ***SELF-STUDY GUIDE***

Chapter 10: Sentence Patterns

Goal 10.1 *To recognize intransitive verbs and diagram Pattern 1 sentences*

Date	Assignment	Score
______	**1.** Read pages 225–226. Complete Activity A on page 226. Read page 227. Complete Activities B–C on page 227.	______
______	**2.** Read page 228. Complete Activities D–F on page 228. Read page 229. Complete Activities G–H on page 229.	______
______	**3.** Complete Workbook Activity 52.	______
______	**4.** Read page 230. Complete Activity I on page 230. Read page 231. Complete Activity J on page 231.	______
______	**5.** Complete the Lesson 1 Review on page 232.	______

Comments:

Goal 10.2 *To identify direct objects and transitive verbs and diagram Pattern 2 sentences*

Date	Assignment	Score
______	**6.** Read page 233. Complete Activity A on page 233. Read page 234. Complete Activities B–C on page 234.	______
______	**7.** Read page 235. Complete Activities D–E on page 235. Read page 236. Complete Activities F–G on page 236.	______
______	**8.** Read page 237. Complete Activities H–I on page 237. Read page 238. Complete Activity J on page 238.	______
______	**9.** Complete Workbook Activity 53.	______
______	**10.** Read pages 239–240. Complete Activity K on page 240.	______
______	**11.** Complete the Lesson 2 Review on page 241.	______

Comments:

 Basic English Grammar

TRL

Name Date Period ***SELF-STUDY GUIDE***

Chapter 10: Sentence Patterns, continued

Goal 10.3 *To identify indirect objects and diagram Pattern 3 sentences*

Date	Assignment	Score
______	**12.** Read page 242. Complete Activity A on page 242. Read page 243. Complete Activities B–C on page 243.	______
______	**13.** Read page 244. Complete Activities D–E on page 244. Read page 245. Complete Activity F on page 245.	______
______	**14.** Read page 246. Complete Activities G–H on page 246.	______
______	**15.** Complete Workbook Activity 54.	______
______	**16.** Read pages 247–248. Complete Activity I on page 248.	______
______	**17.** Complete the Lesson 3 Review on page 249.	______

Comments:

Goal 10.4 *To identify object complements and diagram Pattern 4 sentences*

Date	Assignment	Score
______	**18.** Read page 250. Complete Activities A–B on page 250.	______
______	**19.** Read page 251. Complete Activities C–D on page 251.	______
______	**20.** Read page 252. Complete Activity E on page 252.	______
______	**21.** Complete Workbook Activity 55.	______
______	**22.** Read pages 253–254. Complete Activity F on page 254.	______
______	**23.** Complete the Lesson 4 Review on page 255.	______

Comments:

 Basic English Grammar

TRL

Chapter 10 Self-Study Guide, Pages 1–3

Lesson at a Glance

Chapter 10 Lesson 1

Overview This lesson introduces simple Pattern 1 sentences and diagramming.

Objectives

- To identify the subject and verb in Pattern 1 sentences.
- To write Pattern 1 sentences.
- To diagram Pattern 1 sentences.

Student Pages 226–232

Teacher's Resource Library TRL

Workbook Activity 52

Activity 52

Alternative Activity 52

Diagramming Activity 1

Vocabulary

intransitive verb
simple predicate

Warm-Up Activity

Write the following sentences on the board: *Jacob is listening. Birds fly. We waited.* Ask students what they notice about these examples. Elicit that each sentence has the same subject/verb order. Point out that this is a basic pattern of English speech, one that we have known since we first began to talk. Now underline each sentence and draw a vertical line between subjects and verbs. Point out that you have made a simple diagram of the sentences. Explain that diagrams can help us understand how words relate to each other by showing sentence patterns in graphic form.

Teaching the Lesson

Review the terms *simple subject* and *complete subject* and *simple predicate* and *complete predicate.* Explain to students that all the words in a Pattern 1 sentence are either part of the subject or part of the predicate.

Help students understand the logic behind sentence diagrams by pointing out that important words, such as nouns and verbs, get a place on a solid horizontal line. Adjectives and adverbs, whose purpose is to describe nouns and verbs, are given sloping lines. It may help students think of nouns and verbs as first-class words, important travelers who get first-class seats on an airplane.

Activity A

Write these sentences on the board: *Marie laughed. The dog under the chair is sleeping.* Help students identify the complete subject and verb in each sentence and draw a line between the subject and verb. Then review the example provided for Activity A before having students complete Activity A on their own.

Activity A Answers

1. The ball / bounced. 2. My best friend / moved. 3. Donna / laughed. 4. They / were singing. 5. The people on our block / are meeting.

Lesson 1 What Are Pattern 1 Sentences?

Intransitive verb
A verb that does not transfer action from the subject to an object

A Pattern 1 sentence is the simplest kind of sentence. It expresses a complete thought with a subject and a verb.

Pattern 1 Sentence: Subject + Verb

EXAMPLE

S V S V
Julian smiled. The stars were shining.

Sometimes we use abbreviations in place of longer words. Take a look at these abbreviations. You will see them in this lesson.

S = subject

V = verb

Adj. = adjective

Adv. = adverb

Adj. Phrase = adjective phrase

Adv. Phrase = adverb phrase

Activity A Write each of these Pattern 1 sentences on your paper. Draw a line between the subject and the verb.

Example The lion / was growling.

1. The ball bounced.
2. My best friend moved.
3. Donna laughed.
4. They were singing.
5. The people on our block are meeting.

Pattern 1 sentence verbs are intransitive. An **intransitive verb** does not transfer an action from the subject to another person or thing.

EXAMPLE She is laughing. The rowboat sank.

Pattern 1 sentences may have adjectives and adverbs. The adjectives describe the subject. An adverb tells more about the verb. In a Pattern 1 sentence, an adverb may come at the beginning of a sentence. It may come between the helping verb and the main verb.

EXAMPLE

Adj. Adj. S V Adv.
The newborn baby cried loudly.

S Adv. V Adv.
Mrs. Stamos often arrives early.

Activity B Write these Pattern 1 sentences on your paper. Write *S* above the subject, *V* above the verb or verb phrase, *Adj.* above any adjectives, and *Adv.* above any adverbs.

Example Adj. S V Adv.
The candle was burning brightly.

1. Victor can run fast.
2. That little baby is always smiling.
3. Alison practices often.
4. The old radio works.
5. Yesterday it rained hard.

Activity C Write a Pattern 1 sentence with each of these verbs. Underline the complete subject once and the predicate twice in each sentence.

1. go
2. inquire
3. work
4. laugh
5. walk
6. cry
7. fall
8. scream
9. think
10. live

A Pattern 1 sentence may have a prepositional phrase. The prepositional phrase may be an adjective phrase that describes the subject. It may be an adverb phrase that tells more about the verb.

EXAMPLE

S Adj. Phrase V
The woman behind me coughed. (Which woman coughed? *The woman behind me* coughed.)
S V Adv. Phrase
Carlos is walking to the library. (Where is Carlos walking? He is walking *to the library.*)

Activity B

After discussing the example, write item 1 on the board. Help students identify and label the sentence parts. Then have students work with partners to complete the remaining items in the activity.

Activity B Answers

1. S—Victor, V—can run, Adv.—fast
2. Adj.—That, Adj.—little, S—baby, V—is smiling, Adv.—always **3.** S—Alison, V—practices, Adv.—often **4.** Adj.—The, Adj.— old, S—radio, V—works
5. Adv.—Yesterday, S—it, V—rained, Adv.—hard

Activity C

Invite volunteers to write sentences for the first three verbs on the board. Encourage the class to identify the complete subject and complete predicate in each sentence. Then have students complete Activity C independently.

Activity C Answers

Answers will vary. Five sample sentences are given. **1.** The Johnsons go there often. **2.** She inquired about the job. **3.** Those students work hard. **4.** The children laughed loudly. **5.** Maggie walks daily.

3 Reinforce and Extend

LEARNING STYLES

Body/Kinesthetic

Have students print several Pattern 1 sentences on strips of paper. Ask them to draw a line between the complete subject and complete predicate and to cut the strips in half at that point. Collect the cut strips, mix them, and put them on a desk facedown. Then invite students to take one of the strips. Each student should read the fragment and find the person with the fragment that completes the sentence. Have the partners come up to the front of the room, read their sentence, and identify the subject and verb and any adjectives and adverbs.

Activity D

Write these phrases on the board: *in the park, at home, from Mexico.* Invite volunteers to make up sentences for each phrase, making sure they have at least one example of an adverb phrase and one of an adjective phrase. After discussing the sentences, have students complete activity D on their own.

Activity D Answers

1. Madison / went to school. 2. Mr. DeLeo / works at the post office. 3. The gas station on the corner / closed. 4. Our friends from Ohio / are visiting for two weeks. 5. The basket of flowers / fell from the porch.

Activity E

Write the following example on the board: *The band marched.* Ask students to add an adjective and an adjective phrase to the subject. (Example: *The big band from the high school marched.*) Then ask for an adverb and an adverb phrase. (Example: *The band marched slowly down the street.*) Before they begin Activity E, have students tell whether the word in bold in each of the items is the subject or the verb.

Activity E Answers

Answers will vary. Possible answers follow. 1. The dog barked angrily at the cat. 2. The boys left hurriedly for the game. 3. The young woman beside me listened. 4. They ate in the cafeteria yesterday. 5. Athletic Roberto from our health club is running.

Activity F

Before having students complete Activity F on their own, encourage them to work with a partner to write a Pattern 1 sentence that is a question. Invite students to share their sentences, and have the class identify the verb or verb phrase in each sentence.

Activity F Answers

1. Which (book) fell off the shelf?
2. Where does (Mr. Davis) work?
3. Is (Annette) still practicing?
4. Are (you) listening to the radio?
5. Did (anyone) call?

Activity D Write each of these Pattern 1 sentences on your paper. Draw a line between the complete subject and predicate. Underline the prepositional phrase or phrases in each sentence.

Example Everyone in the classroom / listened to Rachel.

1. Madison went to school.
2. Mr. DeLeo works at the post office.
3. The gas station on the corner closed.
4. Our friends from Ohio are visiting for two weeks.
5. The basket of flowers fell from the porch.

Activity E Write these Pattern 1 sentences on your paper. Add adjectives and adjective phrases if the subject is bold. Add adverbs and adverb phrases if the verb is bold.

1. The dog **barked.**
2. The boys **left.**
3. **The woman** listened.
4. They **ate.**
5. **Roberto** is running.

A Pattern 1 sentence can ask a question. Part of the verb phrase can help form the question. It will come before the subject.

S V — Who is driving?
V S V — Is the actor crying?

Activity F Write these Pattern 1 sentences on your paper. Circle the subject. Underline the verb or verb phrase.

1. Which book fell off the shelf?
2. Where does Mr. Davis work?
3. Is Annette still practicing?
4. Are you listening to the radio?
5. Did anyone call?

Learning Styles

Interpersonal/Group Learning

Have students pair up and give each pair three familiar prepositions. Ask students to use each preposition in two Pattern 1 sentences: one as an adjective phrase describing the subject and one as an adverb phrase telling more about the verb. Have partners underline and identify their prepositional phrases and then exchange their six sentences with another pair for checking.

A Pattern 1 sentence can be a command or request. The subject *you* is understood. The entire sentence in a command or a request is the predicate.

S V S V
(You) Come to the park. (You) Stop here!

Activity G In each sentence, the subject *you* is understood. Write the verb or verb phrase in each sentence.

1. Hang up your coat.
2. Come with me to the movie.
3. Take off your shoes.
4. Do not play with matches.
5. Listen to the teacher.

A Pattern 1 sentence may have a compound subject or a compound verb.

Compound Subject	Alma and Hector will rehearse next.
Compound Verb	The band will march and play in a parade.

We can join two Pattern 1 sentences with a conjunction to form a compound sentence.

EXAMPLE Dr. Taylor laughed loudly, but Mr. Wilson only smiled.

Activity H These Pattern 1 sentences have a compound subject or a compound verb. Some sentences are compound. Write each sentence on your paper. Then, underline the subject or subjects once. Underline the predicate or predicates twice.

1. The book and the pencil fell on the floor.
2. Marilyn laughed first and then cried.
3. Lisa and Rico were on time, but Alex wasn't.
4. Clarissa studied for her test, and then she read a book.
5. The actors and director came on stage for a final bow, but the writer stayed behind the curtain.

Activity G

Have students read the examples of commands or requests. Make sure they understand that commands or requests are instructions made directly to another person. Ask students to read aloud each activity item twice: once as written and once with the subject *you* inserted at the beginning (Example: *You hang up your coat.*). Remind them that the person they are addressing is the subject.

Activity G Answers

1. Hang 2. Come 3. Take 4. Do play 5. Listen

Activity H

Depending on the needs of your class, do Activity H together or have students work on their own.

Activity H Answers

1. The book and the pencil fell on the floor. 2. Marilyn laughed first and then cried. 3. Lisa and Rico were on time, but Alex wasn't. 4. Clarissa studied for her test, and then she read a book. 5. The actors and director came on stage for a final bow, but the writer stayed behind the curtain.

LEARNING STYLES

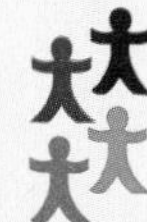

Visual/Spatial

Invite students to draw a variety of objects and actions on the board using stick figures, simple drawings, or symbols. Have them explain to the class what their pictures depict. Then have students pair up and ask the pairs to combine the objects and actions represented on the board in sentences. Encourage students to compose compound sentences and sentences with compound subjects or predicates. Invite volunteers to write model sentences on the board.

Activity I

Review the example diagram in the text and the example given for Activity I. Ask students to explain why *Josie* is to the left of the vertical line and *has been working* is to the right of the line. Be sure students understand that *Josie* is the simple subject and *has been working* is the verb phrase. Have students identify the subject and verb in each of the activity items before they diagram the sentences.

Activity I Answers

1. Snow | fell
2. Susan | is smiling
3. Dogs | are barking
4. Jennifer | will dance
5. Rain | is falling

Using What You've Learned

Help students understand that Pattern 1 sentences are everywhere, from elementary readers to college texts. Have students identify at least two Pattern 1 sentences from a newspaper or magazine passage. Invite volunteers to diagram their examples on the board.

Learning Styles

Auditory/Verbal

Have students practice identifying parts of a sentence aurally by asking a volunteer to come to the board and to draw the horizontal line for a sentence outline. Then read a very simple subject/verb sentence (Example: *Firefighters are working.*) Invite the class to instruct the volunteer where to write the subject and verb. Then read the sentence again, this time with an adjective or adverb. (Example: *Brave firefighters are working.*) Again, have students coach the volunteer in how to expand the outline. Continue adding to the sentence with simple modifiers.

Simple predicate
The verb or verb phrase

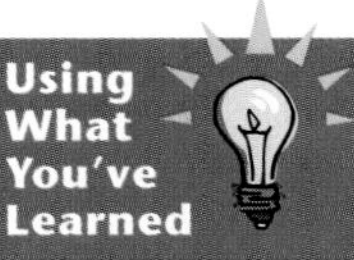

Using What You've Learned

Look at a few pages from a book you are reading. Find two examples of Pattern 1 sentences. Write the sentences on your paper and diagram them.

Diagramming Pattern 1 Sentences

A sentence diagram is a picture of a sentence. It helps us see the parts of the sentence more clearly. When you diagram, you identify the parts to see how they work together.

To diagram a Pattern 1 sentence, start with these steps.

1. Find the simple subject (noun or pronoun) and the **simple predicate** (verb or verb phrase) in the sentence.

The daring woman in the blue jumpsuit skied expertly down the mountain.

2. Write the simple subject and the simple predicate on a horizontal line.
3. Draw a short vertical line between the subject and predicate.

woman | skied

Activity I Diagram these Pattern 1 sentences.

Example Josie has been working. Josie | has been working.

1. Snow fell.
2. Susan is smiling.
3. Dogs are barking.
4. Jennifer will dance.
5. Rain is falling.

Follow these steps to add other words to Pattern 1 sentence diagrams.

1. Write the adjectives and prepositional phrases that describe the subject below the subject.
2. Place adjectives (including articles) on slanted lines.
3. Write the adverbs and prepositional phrases that describe the verb below it.

woman | skied
The
daring
in
jumpsuit
the
blue
expertly
down
mountain
the

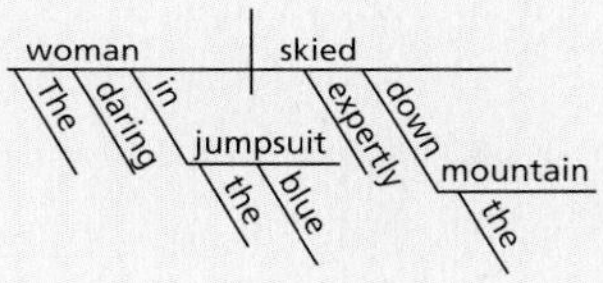

A Pattern 1 sentence can have a compound subject and a compound verb. Some Pattern 1 sentences are compound sentences.

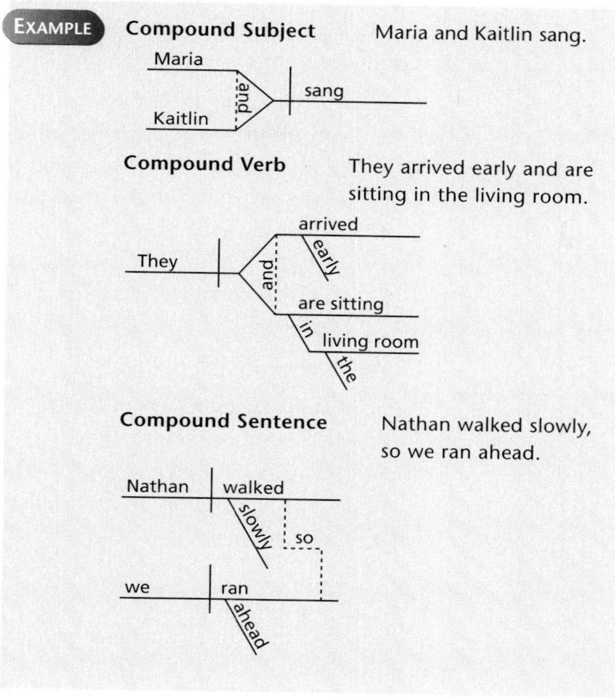

Activity J Diagram these Pattern 1 sentences on your paper. Follow the directions for diagramming that begin on page 230.

1. The school band went on a trip.
2. Everyone on the bus was laughing and singing.
3. Students and parents had been gone for a week.
4. Photographers were everywhere, and reporters wrote quickly.
5. Band members beamed happily into the camera.

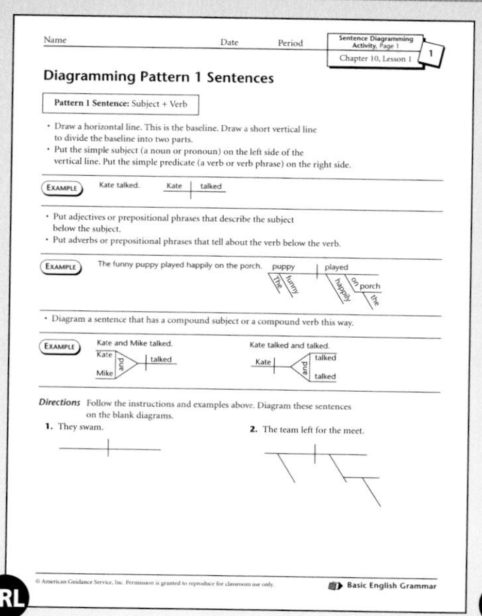

Name Date Period Sentence Diagramming Activity, Page 1 Chapter 10, Lesson 1 1

Diagramming Pattern 1 Sentences

Pattern 1 Sentence: Subject + Verb

- Draw a horizontal line. This is the baseline. Draw a short vertical line to divide the baseline into two parts.
- Put the simple subject (a noun or pronoun) on the left side of the vertical line. Put the simple predicate (a verb or verb phrase) on the right side.

EXAMPLE Kate talked. Kate | talked

- Put adjectives or prepositional phrases that describe the subject below the subject.
- Put adverbs or prepositional phrases that tell about the verb below the verb.

EXAMPLE The funny puppy played happily on the porch. puppy | played The funny happily on porch the

- Diagram a sentence that has a compound subject or a compound verb this way.

EXAMPLE Kate and Mike talked. Kate and Mike talked. Kate talked and talked. Kate and talked talked

Directions Follow the instructions and examples above. Diagram these sentences on the blank diagrams.

1. They swam.
2. The team left for the meet.

© American Guidance Service, Inc. Permission is granted to reproduce for classroom use only. Basic English Grammar

TRL

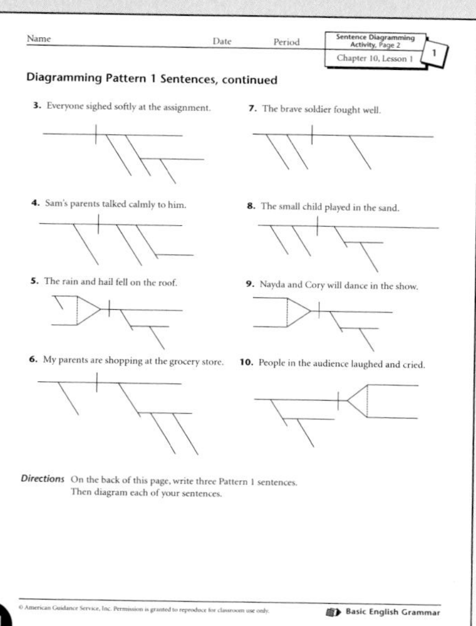

Name Date Period Sentence Diagramming Activity, Page 2 Chapter 10, Lesson 1 1

Diagramming Pattern 1 Sentences, continued

3. Everyone sighed softly at the assignment.
4. Sam's parents talked calmly to him.
5. The rain and hail fell on the roof.
6. My parents are shopping at the grocery store.
7. The brave soldier fought well.
8. The small child played in the sand.
9. Nayda and Cory will dance in the show.
10. People in the audience laughed and cried.

Directions On the back of this page, write three Pattern 1 sentences. Then diagram each of your sentences.

© American Guidance Service, Inc. Permission is granted to reproduce for classroom use only. Basic English Grammar

TRL

Diagramming Activity 1

Activity J

Diagram the first item in Activity J as a class. Draw the baseline on the board. Invite volunteers to write in the different parts of the diagram as the class identifies them, beginning with the simple subject and verb. Then suggest that students work with partners to complete Activity J.

Activity J Answers

1.
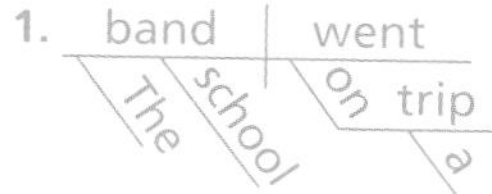

2.
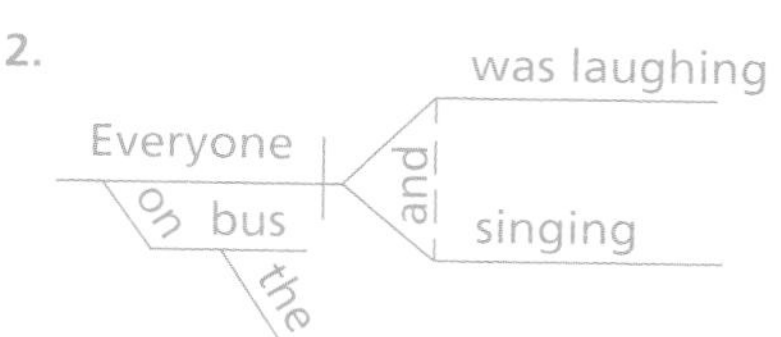

3.
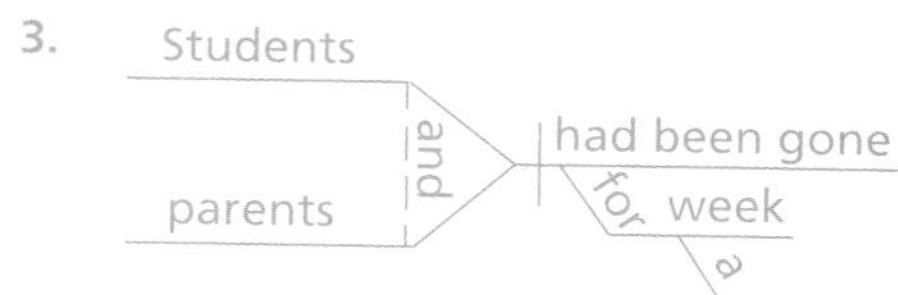

4.
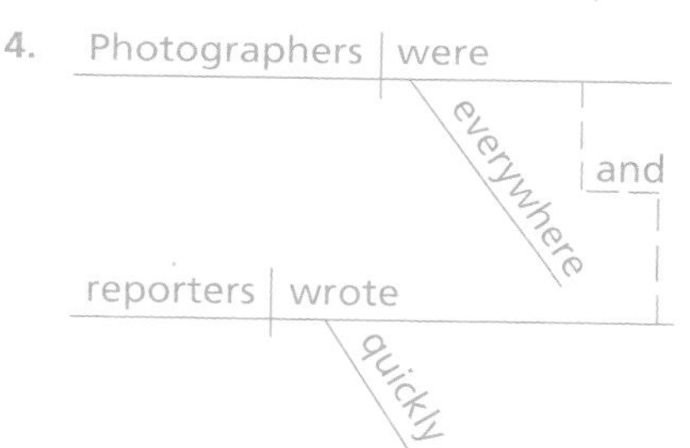

5.
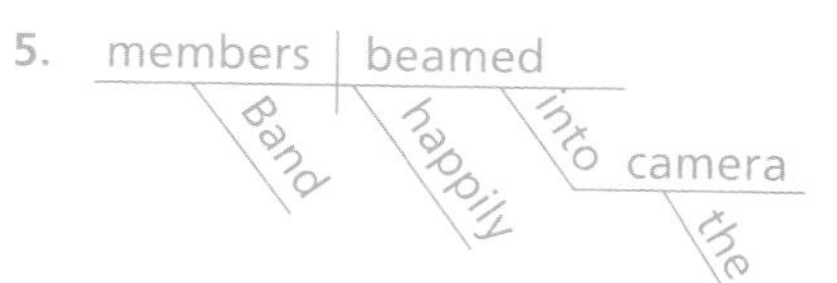

TEACHER ALERT

Take this opportunity to review coordinating conjunctions. Use the diagram for item 4 to point out that in a compound sentence, the conjunction is a connector and not part of either of the subjects or predicates.

Lesson 1 Review Answers

1. Which students are in the band room? S—students, V—are 2. Everyone in the band will ride on the bus. S—Everyone, V—will ride 3. The plate slid off the table, and my dinner crashed to the floor. S—plate, V—slid, S—dinner, V—crashed 4. Liz and her friend from Ottawa are eating at my favorite restaurant. S—Liz, friend; V—are eating 5. We have been practicing and preparing for this trip for a long time. S—We, V—have been practicing, preparing

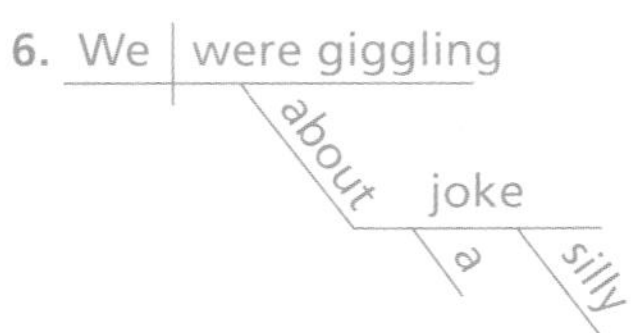

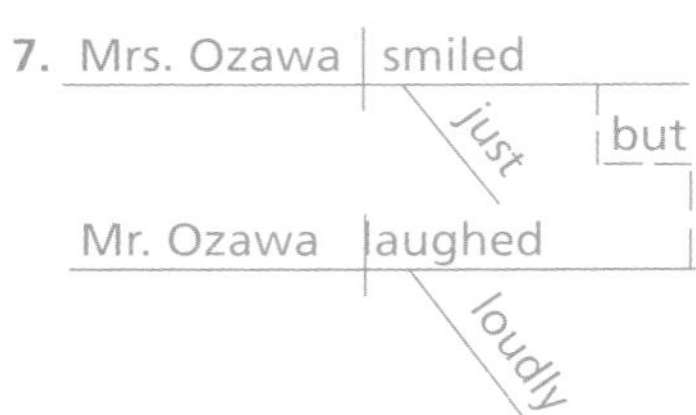

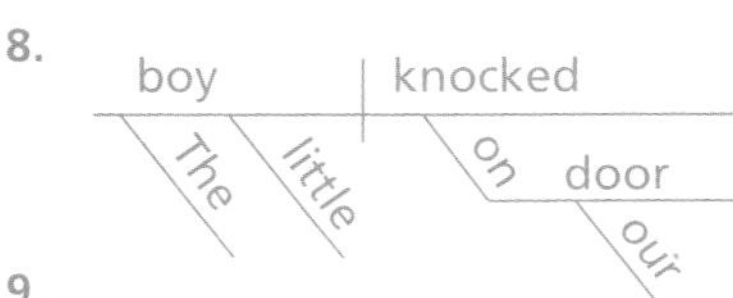

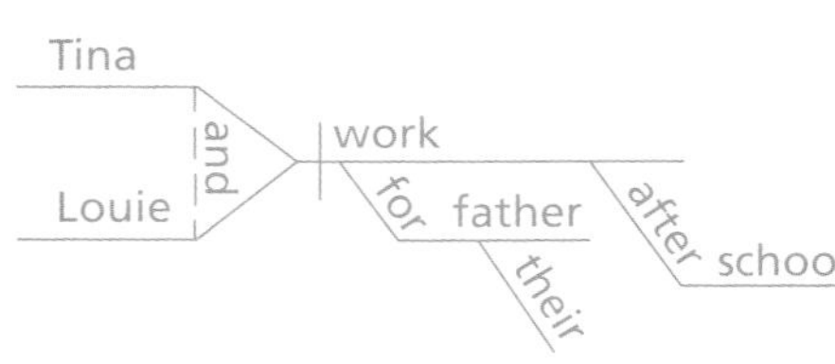

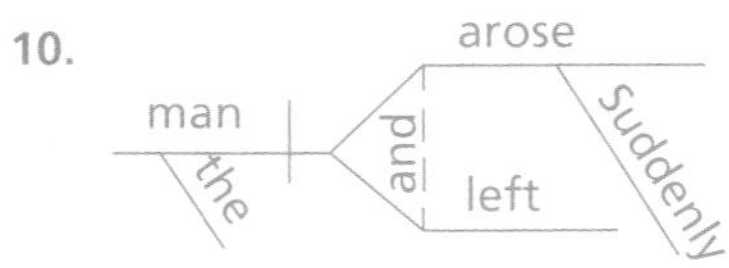

Spelling Builder

Point out that consonant-vowel-consonant words are very common in English.

Answers to Spelling Builder:
1. digging, dropping 2. redder, winner 3. shipped, controlled Sentences will vary.

Lesson 1 REVIEW

Write each of these sentences on your paper. Write *S* above the subject and *V* above the verb or verb phrase. Underline the complete subject once and the complete predicate twice.

1. Which students are in the band room?
2. Everyone in the band will ride on the bus.
3. The plate slid off the table, and my dinner crashed to the floor.
4. Liz and her friend from Ottawa are eating at my favorite restaurant.
5. We have been practicing and preparing for this trip for a long time.

Diagram these Pattern 1 sentences.

6. We were giggling about a silly joke.
7. Mrs. Ozawa just smiled, but Mr. Ozawa laughed loudly.
8. The little boy knocked on our door.
9. Tina and Louie work for their father after school.
10. Suddenly, the man arose and left.

Spelling Builder

Doubling the Final Consonant

Read these words: hopping, bigger.

Note the double consonants before the *-ing* and *-er* endings. The endings *-ing* and *-er* begin with vowels. To add an ending that begins with a vowel to a consonant-vowel-consonant word, first double the final consonant. Then add the ending.

1. Add *-ing* to *dig* and *drop.*
2. Add *-er* to *red* and *win.*
3. Add *-ed* to *ship* and *control.*

Then use each word in a sentence.

Name Date Period | Workbook Activity 52 | Chapter 10, Lesson 1

Using Pattern 1 Sentences

Directions Read the sentences. Then complete the chart below. Write the simple subject and verb or verb phrase of each sentence on the line in the correct column.

EXAMPLE The train to Baltimore has departed already.

Subject	Verb or Verb Phrase
train	has departed

1. The president's speech will be televised.
2. Some birds outside the window chirped noisily.
3. My friend Janet will study with me in the library.
4. Who can work at the bake sale on Saturday?
5. We will walk in the parade with the clowns.
6. Plates and glasses suddenly crashed onto the floor.
7. Did the team practice yesterday?
8. George Washington was born and raised in Virginia.
9. Many doctors were treating patients.
10. Our music teacher has performed on Broadway.

	Subject	Verb or Verb Phrase
1.		
2.		
3.		
4.		
5.		
6.		
7.		
8.		
9.		
10.		

 Basic English Grammar

TRL

Workbook Activity 52

Name Date Period | Activity 52 | Chapter 10, Lesson 1

Recognizing Pattern 1 Sentences

Pattern 1 Sentence: Subject + Verb

Directions Read the sentences. Write *S* above the subject, *V* above the verb or verb phrase, *Adj.* above any adjectives, and *Adv.* above any adverbs.

EXAMPLE
Adj. S V Adv.
The sad boy is walking slowly.

1. Mike will arrive tomorrow.
2. Your sisters have learned quickly.
3. The last bus to Detroit will leave soon.
4. The sun set behind the hill.
5. Marla and Greg are traveling to Phoenix next week.
6. Is Jenny coming early?
7. Rob yelled loudly when the Ravens scored.
8. Sheila draws and paints beautifully.
9. The temperature has dropped since this morning.
10. Nayda's younger sisters laughed and played.
11. Who runs fastest?
12. The patient coughs frequently.
13. The old, brown dog sat lazily by the door.
14. My grandmother's rocking chair squeaks loudly.
15. Toni and Andrea drove across Indiana.

 Basic English Grammar

TRL

Activity 52

Lesson 2 Pattern 2 Sentences (Direct Objects)

> ***Transitive verb***
> *A verb that shows action passed from the subject of the sentence toward another person or thing*
>
> ***Direct object***
> *The noun or pronoun that receives the action from a transitive verb*

The two main kinds of verbs are transitive and intransitive. A **transitive verb** transfers the action from the subject of a sentence to another person or thing. The person or thing that receives the action is the **direct object.** The direct object is a noun or pronoun.

EXAMPLE Jake mowed the backyard.
(What did Jake mow? He *mowed the backyard.*)

The store manager has changed the displays.
(What has the store manager changed? She has *changed the displays.*)

> Sometimes we use abbreviations in place of longer words. Take a look at this abbreviation. You will see it in this lesson.
>
> DO = direct object

A Pattern 2 sentence has a transitive verb and a direct object. The direct object of the verb is a noun or pronoun. The direct object answers *what* or *whom* after the verb.

Pattern 2 Sentence: Subject + Verb + Direct Object

EXAMPLE

S V DO
Dr. Ramirez made breakfast.

Activity A Write the direct object in each sentence on your paper. The verb is in bold.

1. He **found** the book.
2. Rosa **took** notes.
3. The teacher **praised** him.
4. The farmer **planted** corn.
5. Len **raised** his hand.
6. Jennifer **has made** waffles.
7. Alex **caught** the ball.
8. The coach **changed** pitchers again.
9. Sara **has cleaned** her room.
10. The musician **played** his guitar.

Lesson at a Glance

Chapter 10 Lesson 2

Overview This lesson explains transitive verbs and introduces Pattern 2 sentences and direct objects.

Objectives

- To identify direct objects in Pattern 2 sentences.
- To write Pattern 2 sentences.
- To diagram Pattern 2 sentences.

Student Pages 233–241

Teacher's Resource Library TRL

Workbook Activity 53
Activity 53
Alternative Activity 53
Diagramming Activity 2

Vocabulary

direct object
transitive verb

Warm-Up Activity

Draw one student's attention to you, say "Catch," and gently toss a beanbag to the student. Ask him or her, "What did you just do?" Elicit the answer, "I caught a beanbag." Invite a volunteer to write this sentence on the board. Ask students to look at it closely. Ask them how this sentence differs from the Pattern 1 sentences in Lesson 1. Help them conclude that the sentence has a direct object. Underline the sentence on the board, and draw vertical lines between the three major parts. Explain that this is the diagram of a simple Pattern 2 sentence.

2 Teaching the Lesson

Point out that all the sentences in this lesson follow the same subject/verb/direct object pattern. Encourage students to keep their eyes on this shape by writing the diagram of a simple Pattern 2 sentence on the board. (Example: *Students played games.*) If possible, use colored chalk for this skeleton sentence. Then gradually add, in white chalk, adjectives, adverbs, and prepositional phrases to the diagram. (Example: *The 18 young students in Ms. Esler's class played many games on the playground.*) For each addition, point out that the basic shape has remained the same. When students are ready, show how parts of a Pattern 2 sentence can become compound without fundamentally altering the three-part skeleton.

Activity A

Write these Pattern 2 sentences on the board and work with students to identify the direct object in each sentence: *That artist paints flowers. Ali will like you. Lightning struck the house.* Then have students complete Activity A on their own.

Activity A Answers

1. book 2. notes 3. him 4. corn 5. hand 6. waffles 7. ball 8. pitchers 9. room 10. guitar

Activity B

Before they complete Activity B on their own, help students identify the adjectives that describe the direct object in each sentence. If necessary, point out that *mom's* in item 3 is a possessive noun.

Activity B Answers

1. wallet 2. supper 3. car 4. house 5. song

Activity C

Have students take turns completing each of the following sentences with a pronoun in the object form: *I met* ______. *The teacher chose* ______. *Maria found* ______. Suggest that students refer to the chart on page 234 before responding. Then, have students complete Activity C on their own.

Activity C Answers

1. him 2. her 3. them 4. us 5. me

3 Reinforce and Extend

Learning Styles

Interpersonal/Group Learning

Write on the board *The crossing guard stopped I.* Ask students what is wrong with this sentence. Elicit that the pronoun *I* is the direct object and should be in the object form *me.* Now write *The crossing guard stopped my brother and I/me.* Ask students to select the correct pronoun form. Lead them to understand that nothing has changed: the pronoun *me* is still the direct object. Have students pair up and ask them to find the correct pronoun form for the following sentences: *Jared and I/me are going home.* (*I*) *The teacher didn't see you and I/me arriving late.* (*me*) *I/Me like anyone who likes my friends and I/me.* (*I, me*) *Mr. Jeter helped my mother and I/me.* (*me*) *My sister and I/me will come if you phone Sarah and I/me at home.* (*I, me*)

We can use adjectives to describe nouns used as direct objects.

S V Adj. Adj. DO
David sold his old car.

Activity B Write the direct object in each sentence on your paper. The verb is in bold. Do not include adjectives.

1. Len **lost** his wallet.
2. They **ate** an early supper.
3. He **is washing** his mom's car.
4. The next door neighbors **are painting** their house.
5. She **sang** a beautiful song.

When a pronoun is the direct object, use the object form.

S V DO
Susan drove them to the park.

Personal Pronouns		
Singular	**Subject**	**Object**
First person	I	me
Second person	you	you
Third person	he, she, it	him, her, it
Plural		
First person	we	us
Second person	you	you
Third person	they	them

Activity C Write the correct pronoun on your paper. Remember when a pronoun is a direct object, use the object form.

1. Did you see (he, him)?
2. Fred saw (she, her) at the library.
3. Before he put on his sneakers, he cleaned (they, them).
4. Tina helped (we, us) with our math homework.
5. He likes (I, me).

Activity D Create three columns on your paper with the headings *Subject, Verb,* and *Direct Object.* Then identify the simple subject, the verb, and the direct object in each sentence, and write them in the correct column.

Example Sarah bought a new necklace.

Subject	Verb	Direct Object
Sarah	bought	necklace

1. The cat chased the mouse.
2. I have been studying a new language.
3. The brave firefighters climbed the ladders.
4. Mr. Cha loves that old song!
5. We did not see her.

The predicate of a Pattern 2 sentence must have a verb and an object. It may also have an adverb.

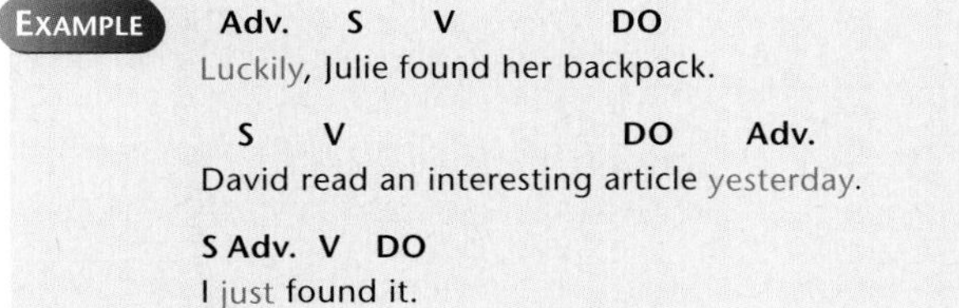

EXAMPLE
Adv. S V DO
Luckily, Julie found her backpack.
S V DO Adv.
David read an interesting article yesterday.
S Adv. V DO
I just found it.

Activity E Write the predicate in each sentence on your paper. Find the complete subject first. All of the words left over make up the predicate.

1. Leon bought his tickets early.
2. You can make dinner now.
3. Kevin ate his dinner quickly.
4. She just answered the phone.
5. Yesterday Dan lost his favorite baseball cap.

Activity D

You may wish to do this activity together as a class. If so, draw a chart on the board with the headings *Subject, Verb,* and *Direct Object.* Then invite volunteers to fill in the chart as students identify the subject, verb, and direct object in each sentence.

Activity D Answers

1. S—cat, V—chased, DO—mouse **2.** S—I, V—have been studying, DO—language **3.** S—firefighters, V—climbed, DO—ladders **4.** S—Mr. Cha, V—loves, DO—song **5.** S—We, V—did see, DO—her

Activity E

Remind students that adverbs may come anywhere in a sentence. Then write this sentence on the board: *Tomorrow, Erica is starting a new job.* Ask students to find the complete predicate in the sentence and to identify the different parts of the complete predicate. Then have students complete Activity E on their own.

Activity E Answers

1. bought his tickets early **2.** can make dinner now **3.** ate his dinner quickly **4.** just answered the phone **5.** Yesterday lost his favorite baseball cap

Learning Styles

Body/Kinesthetic

Have students form groups of three and ask them to compose a simple Pattern 2 sentence. Then have them print the subject, verb, and direct object on three separate index cards. Collect the cards and distribute them randomly to individual students. Students should examine each other's cards and decide how to recreate the original sentences. When they have found their missing sentence parts, invite each group of three students to line up in order. Each student reads a part of the reconstructed sentence and identifies themselves as subject, verb, or direct object.

Activity F

Review the example given for Activity F, making sure that students understand the directions and what they are to do. Encourage students to discuss each item before writing their answers.

Activity F Answers

1. wrote a letter (to her Uncle Albert) (arrow: letter—Uncle Albert) 2. bought the blue sneakers (with the white trim) (arrow: trim—sneakers) 3. carried the two bags (of groceries) (into the house) (arrow: groceries—bag, house—carried) 4. (Before school) fed the fish (in the tank) (arrow: school—fed, tank—fish) 5. filled the fish tank (with water) (arrow: water—tank)

Activity G

Invite volunteers to give sample Pattern 2 sentences for the verbs *eat* and *watch* before they complete Activity G on their own.

Activity G Answers

Answers will vary. Possible answers follow. 1. The winner broke a school record. 2. Carlos will buy the groceries for dinner. 3. Mrs. Chan will dig a hole for that tree. 4. My brother drinks milk with every meal. 5. Every morning, my dog brings the newspaper to me.

Teacher Alert

Explain to students that a prepositional phrase telling about the verb can often be moved from place to place in a sentence. A prepositional phrase describing a noun cannot be separated from the word it modifies. Write the following sentence on the board: *I am meeting the person in charge at two o'clock.* Have students identify the two prepositional phrases (*in charge* and *at two o'clock*). Then invite students to put each of these phrases at the beginning of the sentence. They will discover that only one of them (*at two o'clock*) can be moved. This is the adverb phrase.

A direct object cannot be the object of the preposition.

The predicate part of a Pattern 2 sentence may have a prepositional phrase that tells about the verb, the direct object, or both.

Example

S V DO Adv. Phrase
Matt ate an apple at lunch.
(*For lunch* is an adverb phrase that tells about the verb *ate.* When did Matt eat an apple? He ate it *at lunch.*)

S V DO Adj. Phrase
Matt ate both apples in his lunch. (*In his lunch* is an adjective phrase that describes *apples.* Which apples? He ate the ones *in his lunch.*)

Adv. Phrase S V DO Adj. Phrase
After school, we played two sets of tennis.
(*After school* tells when we played. What kind of sets? We played two sets *of tennis.*)

Activity F Write the complete predicate in each sentence on your paper. Then underline the verb once and the direct object twice. Circle each prepositional phrase. Draw an arrow from the prepositional phrase to the word it tells about.

Example Angie painted the shed in her backyard on Thursday.
painted the shed (in her backyard) (on Thursday.)

1. Carol wrote a letter to her Uncle Albert.
2. Sara bought the blue sneakers with the white trim.
3. He carried the two bags of groceries into the house.
4. Before school, we fed the fish in the tank.
5. We filled the fish tank with water.

Activity G Write Pattern 2 sentences for each of these verbs. Each sentence must have a subject, a verb, and an object. You may also add adjectives, adverbs, and prepositional phrases.

1. break
2. buy
3. dig
4. drink
5. bring

Pattern 2 sentences can be questions. Part of the verb may come before the subject to help form the question. To find the subject, change the question to a statement.

EXAMPLE

V S V DO
Did I see a cat on your porch? (I did see a cat.)
DO V S V Adv.
What is he doing today? (He is doing what today.)

Activity H Find the verb or verb phrase and the direct object in each sentence. Write them on your paper.

1. Have you read that article?
2. May I have a piece of fruit?
3. Can you type my report?
4. What will he do after graduation?
5. Which of these do you want?

Pattern 2 sentences can also be commands or requests. Remember that the subject of a command or request is understood to be *you.*

S V DO
(You) Finish your homework.
S V DO
(You) Take the cat inside the house.

Activity I Write each sentence on your paper. Circle the verb. Underline the direct object.

1. Take this book to the library.
2. Make vegetable soup for supper, please.
3. Complete your essay at home.
4. Hang your coat in the closet.
5. Have some more soup.

Activity H

Work with students to turn each question in Activity H into a statement. Write the statements on the board. Then have students do the activity.

Activity H Answers

1. V—Have read, DO—article **2.** V—May have, DO—piece **3.** V—Can type, DO—report **4.** V—will do, DO—What **5.** V—do want, DO—Which

Activity I

Encourage students to provide additional examples of Pattern 2 sentences that are commands or requests. Write the sentences on the board and have the class check that the sentences are commands or requests and they are Pattern 2 sentences with verbs and direct objects. Then have students complete Activity I independently.

Activity I Answers

1. Take this book to the library. **2.** Make vegetable soup for supper, please. **3.** Complete your essay at home. **4.** Hang your coat in the closet. **5.** Have some more soup.

Learning Styles

Body/Kinesthetic

On the board, print the following pattern: *subject/predicate/direct object/prepositional phrase.* Ask volunteers to use classroom objects to demonstrate this pattern and to create a sentence that represents the doer of the action, the action, the receiver of the action, and a prepositional phrase that describes the receiver. (For example, a student might pick up a book and say, "Tom picked up a book from the floor.")

At Home

Point out that instructions for assembling or operating household items frequently take the form of Pattern 2 commands. (Example: *Insert a blank videotape.*) Have students find a Pattern 2 sentence in an instruction booklet at home. Encourage each of them to bring their example sentence to class, write it on the board, and explain its structure.

Activity J

After reading page 238 with the class, discuss the example provided for Activity J. Complete Activity J orally as a class.

Activity J Answers

1. compound object—book, one
2. compound verb—has, takes
3. compound object—wallet, contents
4. compound object —piano, violin
5. compound verb—fed, walked

Learning Styles

Auditory/Verbal

Have students form a circle, and give them the following oral prompt: *When I went home, I . . .* Invite a volunteer to complete the prompt with a verb and a direct object. (Example: *When I went home, I ate a snack.*) The student to the volunteer's left should then repeat the sentence, adding another verb and direct object. (Example: *When I went home, I ate a snack and fed the dog.*) Continue around the circle, adding to the series. Encourage students to listen closely so that they can remember the sequence of actions. When a student forgets a link in the chain, have him or her write the entire sentence on the board, coached by the class. Label the compound verbs and direct objects.

The word *compound* comes from a French word that means "put together." It has many meanings that all share the idea of blending several things into one.

A Pattern 2 sentence can have a compound verb and a compound object. A compound object is more than one direct object in a sentence connected by a conjunction. You may join two Pattern 2 sentences together with a conjunction to make a compound sentence.

Example

Compound Verb	We cooked and served lunch.
Compound Direct Object	She will play baseball or hockey.
Compound Sentence	I saw Brad, but he didn't have my coat.

Each part of a compound verb may have its own direct object.

Example

S V DO V DO
We arranged the flowers and put them on the table.

Activity J Read each Pattern 2 sentence. Decide whether it has a compound verb or a compound object. Write the compound verb or compound object on your paper.

Example We did our homework and then played video games.
compound verb—did, played

1. Are you reading that book or this one?
2. Tim has a part-time job and takes classes at a community college.
3. They returned the wallet and its contents to the owner.
4. Virginia plays the piano and the violin.
5. Alex fed and walked his dog.

Diagramming Pattern 2 Sentences

To diagram a Pattern 2 sentence:

1. Identify the subject, verb, and direct object.
2. Place the object on the baseline with the subject and verb.
3. Draw a short vertical line to separate the verb and the direct object.
4. Put each adverb, adjective, or prepositional phrase under the word it describes or tells about.

Example Amber baked potatoes for dinner.

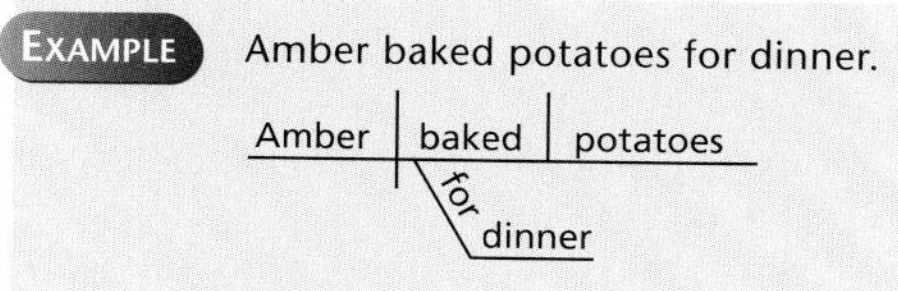

5. If a Pattern 2 sentence is a question, change the question to a statement. Then draw the diagram.

Example

Question		Statement
Did you find your backpack?	→	You did find your backpack.

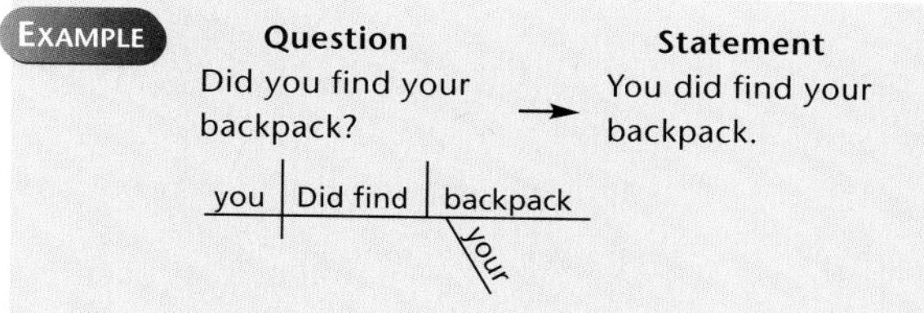

6. In a command or a request when the subject *you* is understood, put it in parentheses.

Example Change that dirty shirt immediately.

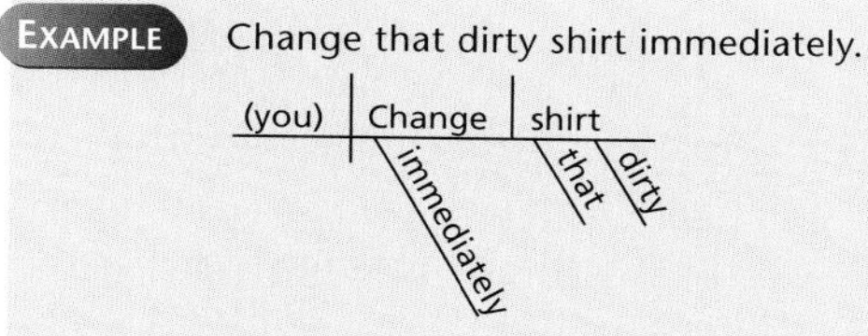

Learning Styles

Logical/Mathematical

Write on the board the following Pattern 2 sentence: *People with green hair eat apples.* Help students diagram this sentence on the board. Then write a second sentence: *Happy people have green hair.* Have students form pairs and ask them to diagram this sentence. Then explain to students that the two sentences you have given them lead to a logical conclusion. (*Happy people eat apples.*) Challenge partners to find this conclusion and to write it as a Pattern 2 sentence. Invite volunteers to put their diagrams for sentences two and three on the board.

Career Connection

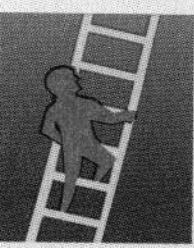

Many different kinds of diagrams are used in the workplace. Being able to read a diagram can be a helpful and sometimes essential skill for some occupations and professions. For example, many construction workers, plumbers, and electricians must read diagrams to complete a project; architects must be able to draw and understand diagrams to design houses; and car mechanics must be able to read and understand diagrams in automobile manuals. Engage students in a discussion about different careers they hope to pursue and the types of diagrams they might use in these careers. If possible, provide examples of different diagrams for students to examine and discuss.

Activity K

Before students start work on Activity K, have the class identify the subject, verb, and direct object in items 1 and 2.

Activity K Answers

1.
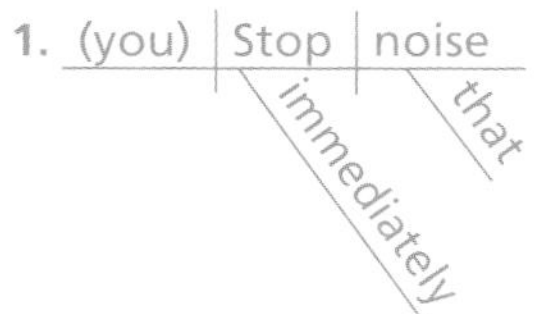

2.
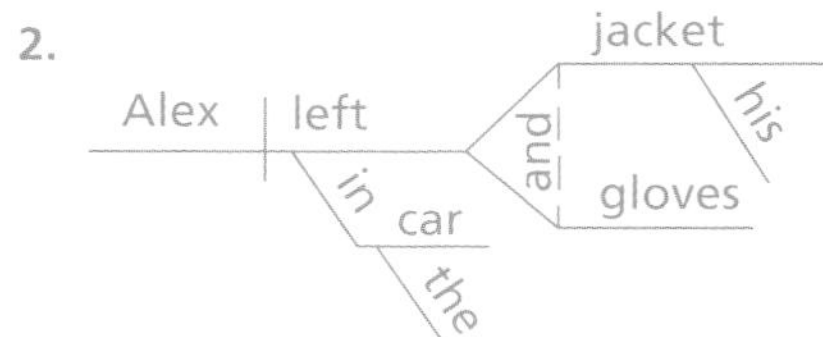

3. you | Have seen | Sally

4.
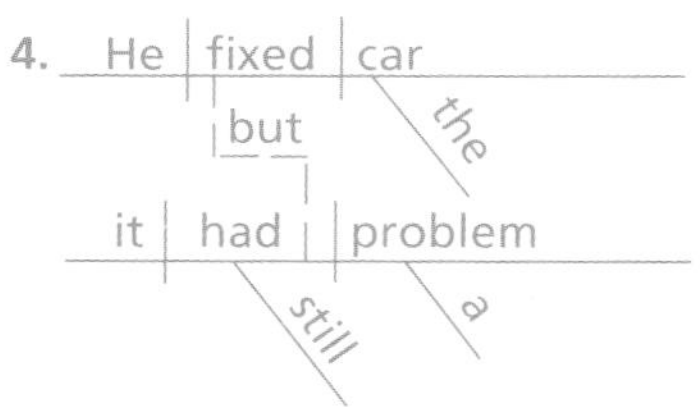

5.
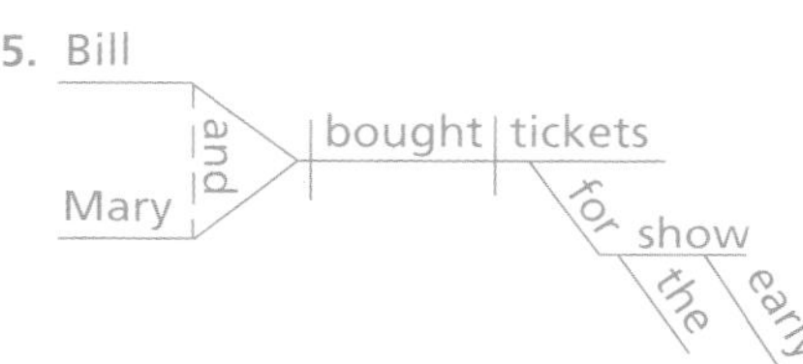

Writing Practice

Have students study the six types of Pattern 2 sentences diagrammed on pages 239 and 240. Point out that each sentence has at its center a baseline containing subject, verb, and direct object. Examples 5 to 9 are simply variations on this basic pattern. Then have students pair up and ask them to write six original sentences modeled on these diagrams. Invite pairs to share their sentences with the class. Work with students to diagram one example of each type of sentence on the board.

7. Diagram a Pattern 2 sentence that has a compound verb this way.

EXAMPLE Alex bought a new sweater and wore it to the game.

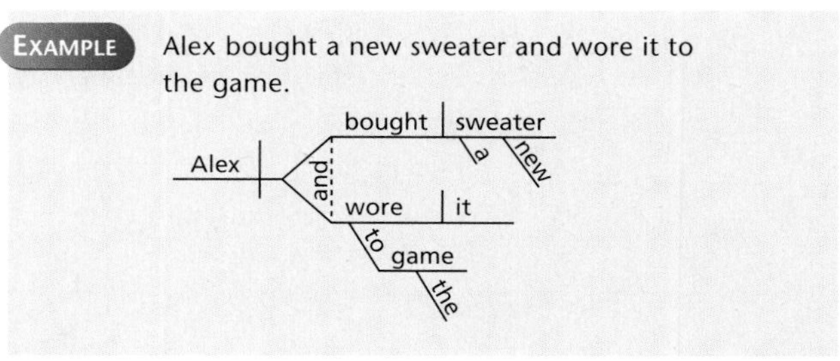

8. Diagram a Pattern 2 sentence that has a compound object this way.

EXAMPLE Jack left his notebook and pen in his locker.

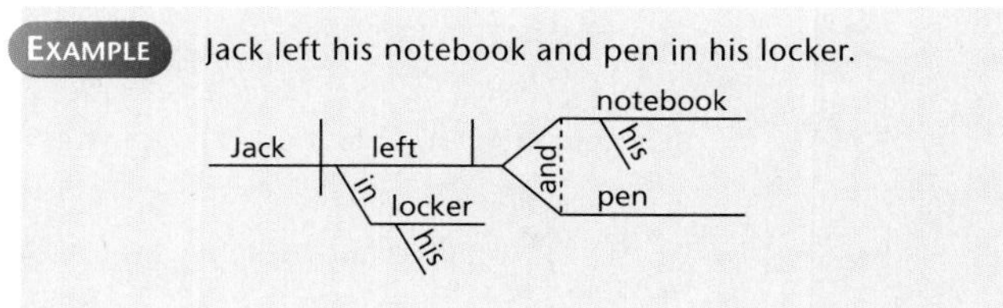

9. Diagram a compound Pattern 2 sentence this way.

EXAMPLE Kaitlin wrote a poem, and Devon painted a mural.

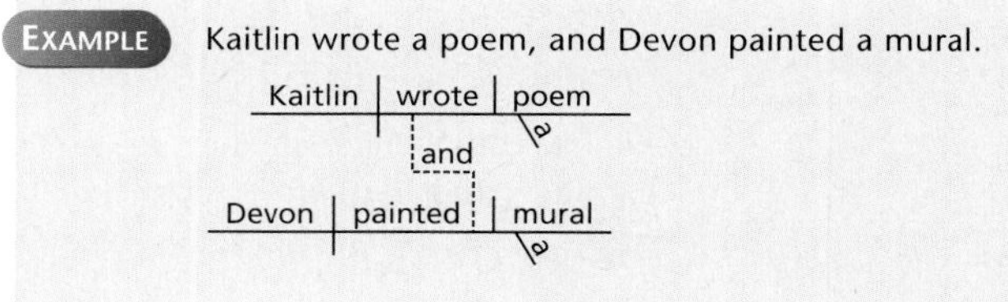

Activity K Diagram these sentences. Look at the examples that begin on page 239.

1. Stop that noise immediately!
2. Alex left his jacket and gloves in the car.
3. Have you seen Sally?
4. He fixed the car, but it still had a problem.
5. Bill and Mary bought tickets for the early show.

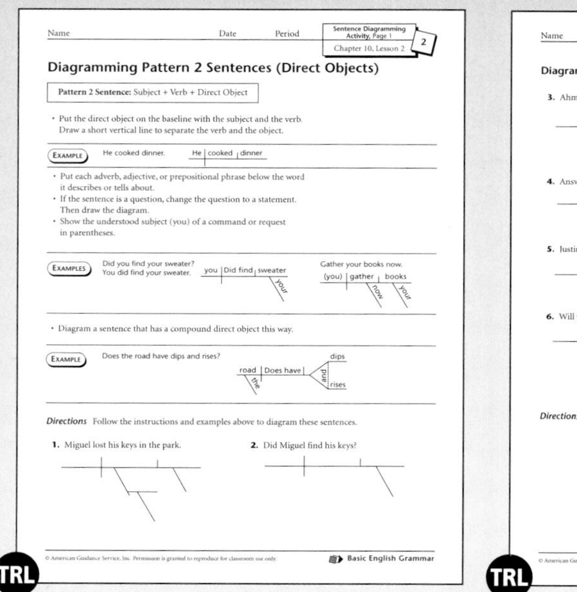

Name Date Period — Sentence Diagramming Activity, Page 1 — Chapter 10, Lesson 2 — 2

Diagramming Pattern 2 Sentences (Direct Objects)

Pattern 2 Sentence: Subject + Verb + Direct Object

- Put the direct object on the baseline with the subject and the verb. Draw a short vertical line to separate the verb and the object.

EXAMPLE He cooked dinner. He | cooked | dinner

- Put each adverb, adjective, or prepositional phrase below the word it describes or tells about.
- If the sentence is a question, change the question to a statement. Then draw the diagram.
- Show the understood subject (you) of a command or request in parentheses.

EXAMPLES Did you find your sweater? You did find your sweater. you | Did find | sweater your — Gather your books now. (you) | gather | books now your

- Diagram a sentence that has a compound direct object this way.

EXAMPLE Does the road have dips and rises? road | Does have | dips and rises the

Directions Follow the instructions and examples above to diagram these sentences.

1. Miguel lost his keys in the park.
2. Did Miguel find his keys?

 Basic English Grammar

TRL

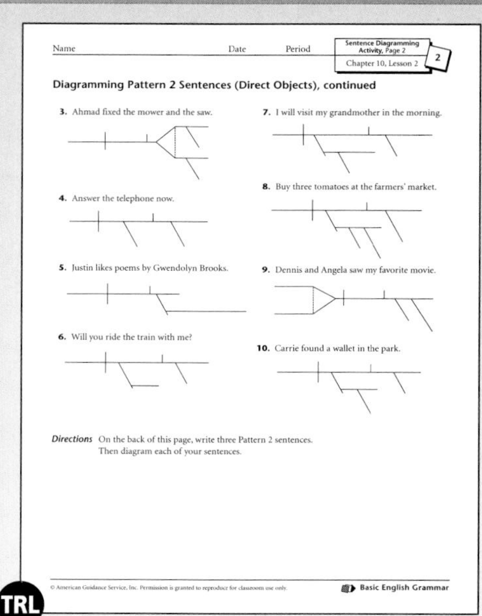

Name Date Period — Sentence Diagramming Activity, Page 2 — Chapter 10, Lesson 2 — 2

Diagramming Pattern 2 Sentences (Direct Objects), continued

3. Ahmad fixed the mower and the saw.
4. Answer the telephone now.
5. Justin likes poems by Gwendolyn Brooks.
6. Will you ride the train with me?
7. I will visit my grandmother in the morning.
8. Buy three tomatoes at the farmers' market.
9. Dennis and Angela saw my favorite movie.
10. Carrie found a wallet in the park.

Directions On the back of this page, write three Pattern 2 sentences. Then diagram each of your sentences.

 Basic English Grammar

TRL

Diagramming Activity 2

Lesson 2 REVIEW

Create three columns on your paper with the headings *Subject*, *Verb*, and *Direct Object*. Then identify the simple subject, the verb, and the direct object in each sentence. Write them in the correct column. Some sentences may have a compound direct object.

1. Fax the contract on Tuesday.

2. Alex used his computer for his school project.

3. Did Jennifer purchase a new CD at the mall?

4. Our family likes apples and oranges for dessert.

5. We installed a new ceiling fan in the kitchen.

Write these sentences on your paper. Write *S* above the subject, *V* above the verb, and *DO* above the direct object.

6. Evan's dad sells computers.

7. The teacher answered the questions.

8. Laura described her new dress to her friends.

9. The museum guard checked our tickets.

10. Loni ordered shrimp and broccoli for lunch.

Diagram these Pattern 2 sentences.

11. Have you seen that movie?

12. We bought a ticket for the early show.

13. First, read the book, and then see the movie.

14. He read an interesting article about UFOs recently.

15. Otis recited the long poem without a single mistake.

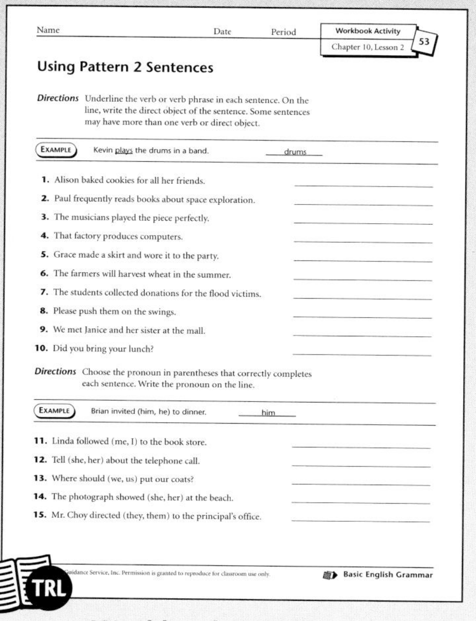

Name Date Period

Workbook Activity 53
Chapter 10, Lesson 2

Using Pattern 2 Sentences

Directions Underline the verb or verb phrase in each sentence. On the line, write the direct object of the sentence. Some sentences may have more than one verb or direct object.

EXAMPLE Kevin plays the drums in a band. ___drums___

1. Alison baked cookies for all her friends. ______

2. Paul frequently reads books about space exploration. ______

3. The musicians played the piece perfectly. ______

4. That factory produces computers. ______

5. Grace made a skirt and wore it to the party. ______

6. The farmers will harvest wheat in the summer. ______

7. The students collected donations for the flood victims. ______

8. Please push them on the swings. ______

9. We met Janice and her sister at the mall. ______

10. Did you bring your lunch? ______

Directions Choose the pronoun in parentheses that correctly completes each sentence. Write the pronoun on the line.

EXAMPLE Brian invited (him, he) to dinner. ___him___

11. Linda followed (me, I) to the book store. ______

12. Tell (she, her) about the telephone call. ______

13. Where should (we, us) put our coats? ______

14. The photograph showed (she, her) at the beach. ______

15. Mr. Choy directed (they, them) to the principal's office. ______

 Basic English Grammar

TRL

Workbook Activity 53

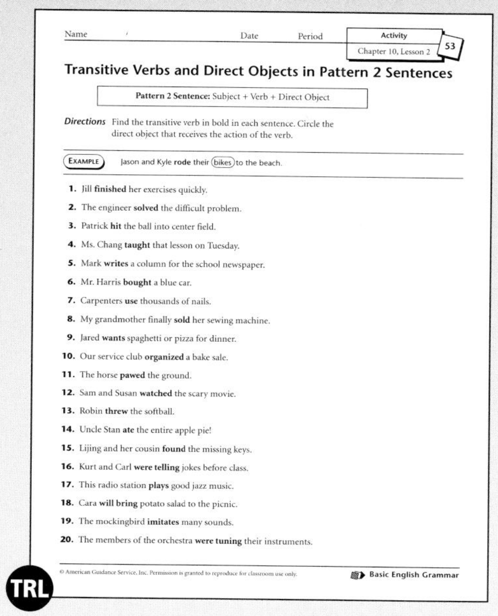

Name Date Period

Activity 53
Chapter 10, Lesson 2

Transitive Verbs and Direct Objects in Pattern 2 Sentences

Pattern 2 Sentence: Subject + Verb + Direct Object

Directions Find the transitive verb in bold in each sentence. Circle the direct object that receives the action of the verb.

EXAMPLE Jason and Kyle **rode** their (bikes) to the beach.

1. Jill **finished** her exercises quickly.

2. The engineer **solved** the difficult problem.

3. Patrick **hit** the ball into center field.

4. Ms. Chang **taught** that lesson on Tuesday.

5. Mark **writes** a column for the school newspaper.

6. Mr. Harris **bought** a blue car.

7. Carpenters **use** thousands of nails.

8. My grandmother finally **sold** her sewing machine.

9. Jared **wants** spaghetti or pizza for dinner.

10. Our service club **organized** a bake sale.

11. The horse **pawed** the ground.

12. Sam and Susan **watched** the scary movie.

13. Robin **threw** the softball.

14. Uncle Stan **ate** the entire apple pie!

15. Lijing and her cousin **found** the missing keys.

16. Kurt and Carl **were telling** jokes before class.

17. This radio station **plays** good jazz music.

18. Cara **will bring** potato salad to the picnic.

19. The mockingbird **imitates** many sounds.

20. The members of the orchestra **were tuning** their instruments.

 Basic English Grammar

TRL

Activity 53

Lesson 2 Review Answers

1. S—(you), V—Fax, DO—contract 2. S—Alex, V—used, DO—computer 3. S—Jennifer, V—Did purchase, DO—CD 4. S—family; V—likes; DO—apples, oranges 5. S—We, V—installed, DO—fan 6. S—dad, V—sells, DO—computers 7. S—teacher, V—answered, DO—questions 8. S—Laura, V—described, DO—dress 9. S—guard, V—checked, DO—tickets 10. S—Loni; V—ordered; DO—shrimp, broccoli

11. 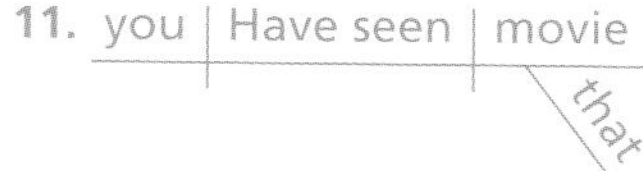

12. 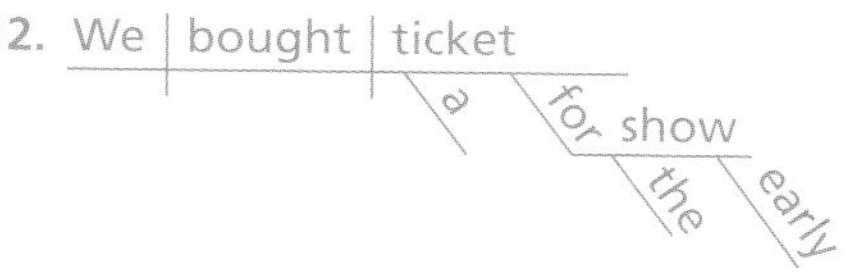

13. 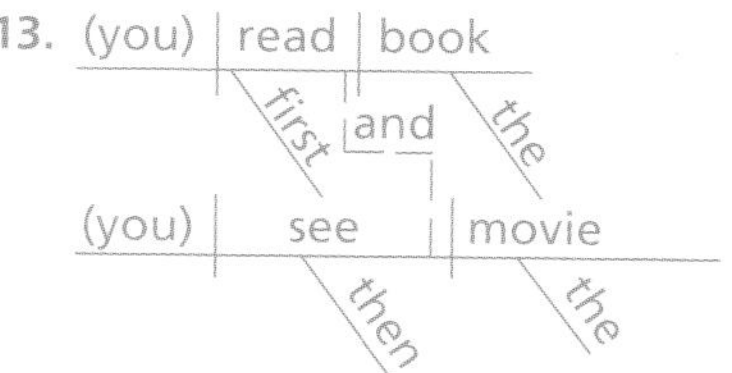

14. 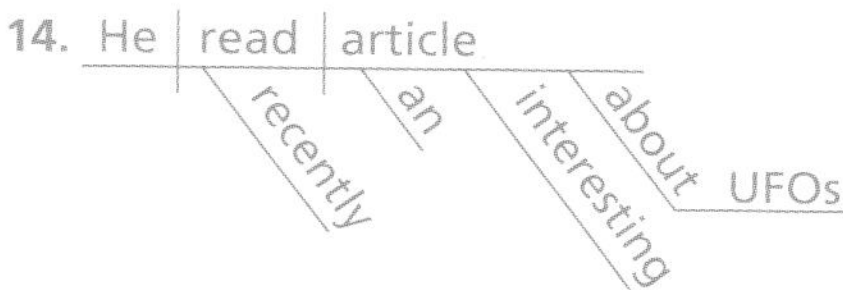

15. 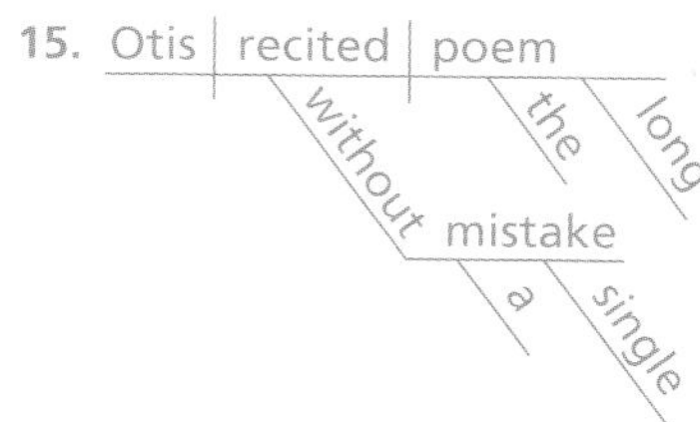

LEARNING STYLES

Visual/Spatial

Write on the board the outline diagrams of several Pattern 2 sentences. The first should simply be a baseline divided into three. Others could include sloping lines for adjectives, adverbs, or prepositional phrases. Challenge students to write sentences that match any or all of these empty outlines. Invite them to fill in the diagrams with their original sentences.

Sentence Patterns *Chapter 10* 241

Lesson at a Glance

Chapter 10 Lesson 3

Overview This lesson introduces Pattern 3 sentences and indirect objects.

Objectives

- To identify indirect objects in Pattern 3 sentences.
- To complete Pattern 3 sentences with indirect objects.
- To diagram Pattern 3 sentences.

Student Pages 242–249

Teacher's Resource Library 

Workbook Activity 54
Activity 54
Alternative Activity 54
Diagramming Activity 3

Vocabulary

indirect object

Warm-Up Activity

Write *Enrico handed the money* on the board. Ask students what important information is missing from this sentence. Point out that most people would want to know who received Enrico's money. Then complete the sentence with the words *to the ticket agent.* Elicit from students that this is a prepositional phrase. Now erase the word *to* and ask students to read the sentence again. (*Enrico handed the money the ticket agent.*) Challenge students to make a proper English sentence using just those words. When a volunteer has inserted *the ticket agent* between *handed* and *the,* point out that he or she has just used an indirect object and created a Pattern 3 sentence, the subject of this lesson.

Teaching the Lesson

Help students identify indirect objects by suggesting that they use them in prepositional phrases beginning with *to* or *for.* Write on the board the following Pattern 3 sentences: *I prepared my mother dinner. Did Rosa send Trevor a letter?* Ask students which words answer the questions *for whom* or *to whom.* Lead them to rearrange the sentences to include a prepositional phrase. (*I prepared dinner for my mother. Did Rosa send a letter to Trevor?*) Help students understand that they have identified *mother* and *Trevor* as indirect objects. Encourage them to compose examples of their own.

Lead students to understand that prepositional phrases and adjectives often describe indirect objects. Write *That movie gave the town a reputation* on the board and encourage students to practice adding modifiers to *town* (*the old town in the hollow by route 2,* etc.).

Activity A

Do the first item with the class before having students complete Activity A. Suggest that students turn each sentence into a question, such as *Joanna gave a gift to whom?*

Activity A Answers

1. mother 2. myself 3. students 4. Chan 5. me 6. me 7. Mr. Nakai 8. Maya 9. Jon 10. daughters

---

Lesson 3 Pattern 3 Sentences (Indirect Objects)

Indirect object
A noun or pronoun that tells who receives the direct object of a verb

A Pattern 3 sentence has a transitive verb, a direct object, and an **indirect object.** An indirect object is a noun or pronoun. It tells who will receive the direct object of the verb.

The indirect object comes *after* the verb and *before* the direct object in a sentence. An indirect object answers the question *to whom* or *for whom* about the verb.

Pattern 3 Sentence: Subject + Verb + Indirect Object + Direct Object

Sometimes we use abbreviations in place of longer words. Take a look at this abbreviation. You will see it in this lesson.

IO = indirect object

EXAMPLE
S V IO DO
Christa wrote Paul a note.
(Christa wrote a note *to whom?* She wrote to Paul.)

Activity A Write the indirect object in each sentence on your paper. To find the indirect object, ask the question *to whom, to what, for whom,* or *for what* about the verb.

1. Joanna gave her mother a gift.
2. I wrote myself a reminder.
3. The school mailed students their final report cards.
4. I offered Chan some assistance.
5. Mrs. Lopez brought me my homework.
6. Marlene showed me her baseball card collection.
7. The bank lent Mr. Nakai money.
8. The salesclerk handed Maya the change.
9. Joseph sold Jon his old bike.
10. The woman bought her twin daughters matching outfits.

A sentence cannot have an indirect object unless it has a direct object.

An indirect object is never part of a prepositional phrase.

EXAMPLE

Indirect Object	He sent me an e-mail message.
Object of the Preposition	He sent an e-mail message to me.

Activity B Decide whether the word in bold is an indirect object or the object of the preposition. Write *indirect object* or *object of the preposition* on your paper.

1. Lou gave his **dog** a bone.
2. Helena poured some milk for her **cat.**
3. The store sent coupons to their best **customers.**
4. The server brought **us** lunch.
5. Mrs. Jenkins handed my paycheck to **me.**

Activity C Create four columns on your paper with the headings *Subject, Verb, Indirect Object,* and *Direct Object.* Identify the simple subject, the verb, the indirect object, and the direct object in each sentence. Write each in the correct column.

Example The coach gave Deion a clean towel.

Subject	Verb	Indirect Object	Direct Object
coach	gave	Deion	towel

1. The director gave the band members their music.
2. Fred asked Mr. Smith a question.
3. The music company sent the school a bill.
4. Mrs. Arloff offered the students her help.
5. She taught her friend sign language.

Activity B

Write these sentences on the board: *Madison sang us a song. Madison sang a song for us.* Help students identify the sentence in which *us* is an indirect object and the sentence in which *us* is an object of a preposition. Then have students complete Activity B independently.

Activity B Answers

1. indirect object 2. object of the preposition 3. object of the preposition 4. indirect object 5. object of the preposition

Activity C

Discuss the example and do the first item as a class before having students complete Activity C on their own.

Activity C Answers

1. S—director, V—gave, IO—members, DO—music 2. S—Fred, V—asked, IO—Mr. Smith, DO—question 3. S—company, V—sent, IO—school, DO—bill 4. S—Mrs. Arloff, V—offered, IO—students, DO—help 5. S—She, V—taught, IO—friend, DO—sign language

3 Reinforce and Extend

TEACHER ALERT

Draw students' attention to the box at the top left of this page. Point out that while a sentence with an indirect object always has a direct object, sometimes the direct object is understood, just as the word *you* is the understood subject in a command. Write the sentences *Karyn wrote Mark* and *I told her* on the board. In these sentences *Mark* and *her* are indirect objects; the direct objects are understood.

GLOBAL CONNECTION

Ask the class to examine the sentences in Activity C on page 243 to discover where the indirect object usually comes in a statement (after the verb and before the direct object). Give students who speak another language a sentence from Activity C to print in English on the board. Then ask them to print the same sentence in the other language. Have the student circle the indirect object and underline the direct object. Use these sentences to discover if the indirect object-direct object pattern is the same or different in different languages.

Activity D

Ask students to listen carefully as you read the first item in Activity D aloud twice, each time with a different answer in place. Ask students which sentence is correct, the one with *I* or the one with *me.* Have students explain their choice. Point out that reading each sentence in the activity to themselves twice with each of the answer choices in place will help them "hear" the correct answer.

Activity D Answers

1. me 2. him 3. her 4. us 5. them

Activity E

Write the first item in Activity E on the board. Encourage students to take turns adding an adjective or prepositional phrase to the sentence to describe the indirect object *friend.* Then have students complete Activity E on their own. When they have finished, invite them to share their sentences with the class.

Activity E Answers

Answers will vary. Possible answers follow. 1. Pat sent her new friend from school a message. 2. Marcus offered the elderly woman his seat. 3. The teacher told the boy in the third row the answer. 4. We made our neighbor on Elm Street an offer. 5. We asked the mechanic at the garage a question about the car.

When the indirect object is a pronoun, the pronoun must be in the object form. If you need help, refer to the chart on page 234.

S V IO DO
His teacher offered him some help.

Activity D Write the correct pronoun on your paper. Remember when the indirect object is a pronoun, always use the object form.

1. Tom gave (I, me) the message.
2. Fred sent (he, him) a letter.
3. Martha told (she, her) the answer.
4. That teacher taught (we, us) Spanish.
5. We served (they, them) dinner.

Pattern 3 sentences can have adjectives and adjective phrases that describe the indirect object.

S V Adj. IO DO
Amanda wrote her boss a memo.

S V Adj. IO Adj. Phrase DO
She gave her cousin from Idaho a necklace.

Activity E Rewrite each sentence on your paper. Add an adjective or adjective phrase to describe the indirect object in bold.

1. Pat sent her **friend** from school a message.
2. Marcus offered the **woman** his seat.
3. The teacher told the **boy** the answer.
4. We made our **neighbor** an offer.
5. We asked the **mechanic** a question about the car.

Learning Styles

Visual/Spatial

Have students form pairs, and ask them to write four or five prepositional phrases and the same number of adjectives on small pieces of paper. (Refer them to the list of common prepositions on page 162.) Have students put their phrases facedown in one pile and their adjectives in another. Write on the board a simple Pattern 3 sentence. (Example: *I gave the car a wash.*) Then invite students to take one adjective and one phrase from the piles, read their choices aloud, and use them to modify the indirect object in the sample sentence. (Example: *I gave the lazy car under the table a wash.*) Write their sentences on the board. Have students vote on which examples are the most serious and the silliest.

A Pattern 3 sentence can be a question. Part of the verb phrase can come before the subject. The question can begin with an interrogative pronoun.

EXAMPLE

V S V IO DO
Will you give Dana a present?

S V IO DO
Who sent you that sweater?

A command or request can have an indirect object. Pattern 3 sentences can be commands or requests.

EXAMPLE

S V IO DO
(You) Show the doctor your bruise.

S V IO DO
(You) Give me his new coat.

Activity F Write the indirect objects in these sentences on your paper.

1. Tell me the answer.
2. Did Amanda give Jeff the volleyball?
3. Would you lend me your sweater for the evening?
4. Please teach me Spanish.
5. When did Anna write you that note?

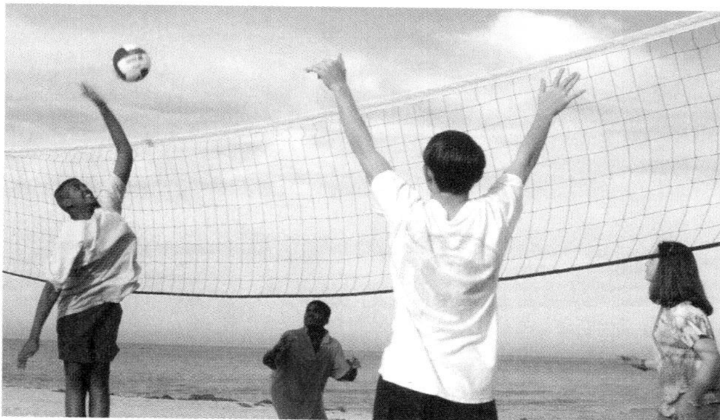

Pass me the ball!

Activity F

Remind students that one way to identify the indirect object in a sentence is to imagine the word *to* or *for* before the noun or pronoun that follows the verb. Additionally, they can reverse the position of the direct object and the indirect object in the sentence. To illustrate this, write the first item in Activity F on the board as follows: *Tell the answer <to> me.* Students who are having difficulty recognizing the indirect object may wish to use this method, writing the entire sentence as they complete Activity F.

Activity F Answers

1. me **2.** Jeff **3.** me **4.** me **5.** you

LEARNING STYLES

LEP/ESL

Have students form small groups of English language learners and students fluent in English. Point out that Pattern 3 sentences consist of just four basic elements and write these on the board: *subject, verb, indirect object, direct object.* Ask groups to construct simple sentences in this pattern. Simplify the process by giving each group a number of familiar transitive verbs (*show, give, read, tell, lend*) and by instructing group members to use the names of fellow students for the indirect object. Encourage English language learners to represent their groups, saying model sentences and writing them on the board. Extend the exercise by having students change the proper names in their sentences to the object form of pronouns.

Activity G

Write these sentences on the board: *Sing ____ a song. Jason told ____ his latest joke.* Have students take turns filling in the blanks with compound indirect objects. Then have students work independently to complete Activity G.

Activity G Answers

Answers will vary. Possible answers follow. **1.** Uncle Bill and Aunt Sue **2.** Tom and me **3.** Maria and Alyssa **4.** his nephew and niece **5.** Judy and Tom **6.** Alex and Jennifer **7.** Mom and Mya **8.** Bret and Bart **9.** Maria and Tony **10.** Ana and me

Activity H

Write the first item in Activity H on the board. Ask students to see how fast they can rearrange the words to make a Pattern 3 sentence. Invite a volunteer to read the sentence and identify the indirect object.

Activity H Answers

1. We served them the dinner. **2.** Julio gave Erica a rose. / Erica gave Julio a rose. **3.** The announcer told the audience the score. **4.** I fixed myself a snack. **5.** He handed him a dollar.

Spelling Practice

Ask students to identify the verbs in the five sentences of Activity H. Write the verbs on the board. Help students note that all of the verbs are in the past tense and ask them to identify the present tense of each verb. Point out to students that the verbs *give* (*gave*) and *tell* (*told*) are irregular. Then have them tell you how the past tense of most verbs are formed (*by adding* -ed *to the present tense*). Identify rules for adding *-ed* to regular verbs: If a verb ends in consonant + *e*, drop the *e* before adding *-ed*; if a verb ends in consonant + *y*, change the *y* to *i* and add *-ed*; if a verb has a consonant-vowel-consonant pattern, double the final consonant before adding *-ed*; for all other regular verbs, just add *-ed*. Give students a list of regular verbs, such as *spy, hurry, offer, rain, race, serve, spot,* and *fan,* to practice spelling the past tense, using these rules.

The indirect object of a Pattern 3 sentence can be compound.

Fix Tom and Lin a sandwich.
Will you give Greg and Sharon some milk?
Jorge read his cousin and his neighbor a folktale.

Activity G Complete each sentence with a compound indirect object. Write the sentences on your paper.

1. Write ________ a letter.
2. Give ________ more time.
3. Please tell ________ the answer.
4. Uncle Fred made ________ a model airplane.
5. Would you lend ________ five dollars?
6. I offered ________ more juice.
7. Mac gave ________ a lovely gift.
8. Kim sent ________ birthday gifts.
9. Bill handed ________ an apple.
10. Eric served ________ soup.

Activity H Rearrange each group of words to make a Pattern 3 sentence. Write the sentences on your paper.

1. them served we dinner the
2. gave rose Erica Julio a
3. the score told audience the announcer the
4. myself snack fixed I a
5. a him he handed dollar

Diagramming Pattern 3 Sentences

To diagram a Pattern 3 sentence:

1. Draw a slanted line and a horizontal line under the verb.
2. Leave the slanted line blank.
3. Write the indirect object on the horizontal line.

EXAMPLE Emilio gave me a warm jacket.

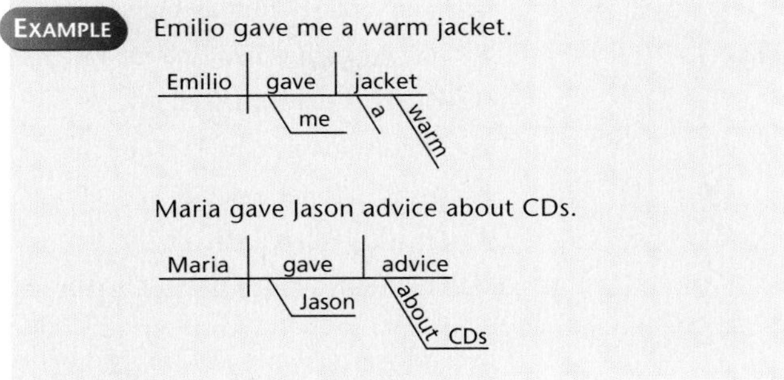

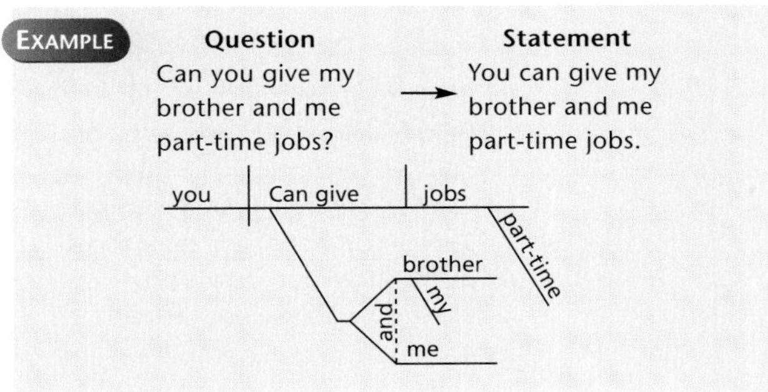

4. If a Pattern 3 sentence is a question, change the question to a statement. Diagram a compound indirect object this way.

EXAMPLE

Question		Statement
Can you give my brother and me part-time jobs?	→	You can give my brother and me part-time jobs.

LEARNING STYLES

Logical/Mathematical

Copy one of the sentence diagrams on this page on the board and have students close their books. Invite a volunteer to point out the principal parts of the sentence. Then challenge him or her to reconstruct the original sentence based on its diagram. Next copy two or three diagrammed Pattern 3 sentences on the board. (Examples from Activity I on page 248 will serve this purpose.) Have students formulate the original statement or question represented by the diagrams. Invite volunteers to write their sentences on the board and to give reasons for their solutions.

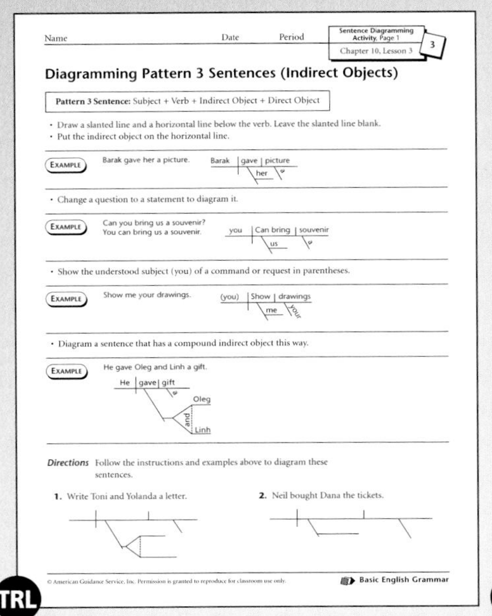

Name Date Period | Sentence Diagramming Activity, Page 1 | Chapter 10, Lesson 3 | 3

Diagramming Pattern 3 Sentences (Indirect Objects)

Pattern 3 Sentence: Subject + Verb + Indirect Object + Direct Object

- Draw a slanted line and a horizontal line below the verb. Leave the slanted line blank.
- Put the indirect object on the horizontal line.

EXAMPLE Barak gave her a picture.

- Change a question to a statement to diagram it.

EXAMPLE Can you bring us a souvenir? You can bring us a souvenir.

- Show the understood subject (you) of a command or request in parentheses.

EXAMPLE Show me your drawings.

- Diagram a sentence that has a compound indirect object this way.

EXAMPLE He gave Oleg and Linh a gift.

Directions Follow the instructions and examples above to diagram these sentences.

1. Write Toni and Yolanda a letter.
2. Neil bought Dana the tickets.

Basic English Grammar

TRL

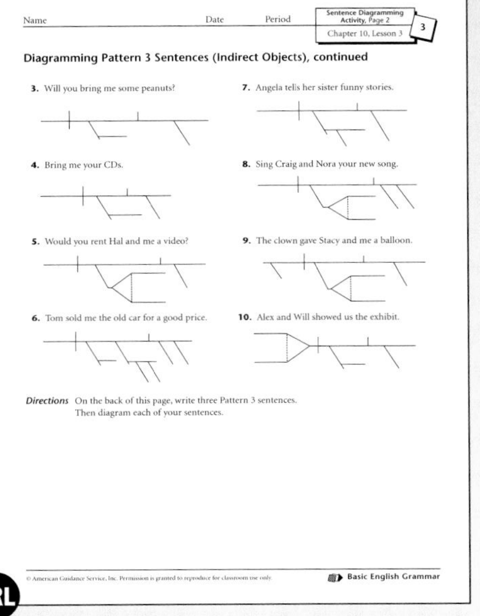

Name Date Period | Sentence Diagramming Activity, Page 2 | Chapter 10, Lesson 3 | 3

Diagramming Pattern 3 Sentences (Indirect Objects), continued

3. Will you bring me some peanuts?
4. Bring me your CDs.
5. Would you rent Hal and me a video?
6. Tom sold me the old car for a good price.
7. Angela tells her sister funny stories.
8. Sing Craig and Nora your new song.
9. The clown gave Stacy and me a balloon.
10. Alex and Will showed us the exhibit.

Directions On the back of this page, write three Pattern 3 sentences. Then diagram each of your sentences.

Basic English Grammar

TRL

Diagramming Activity 3

Activity I

Review what students have learned about diagramming previously in the chapter. Then discuss the steps and diagram examples presented on page 247. If necessary, have students work together to diagram the first item in Activity I. Ask a volunteer to write the diagram on the board. Then have students complete Activity I on their own.

Activity I Answers

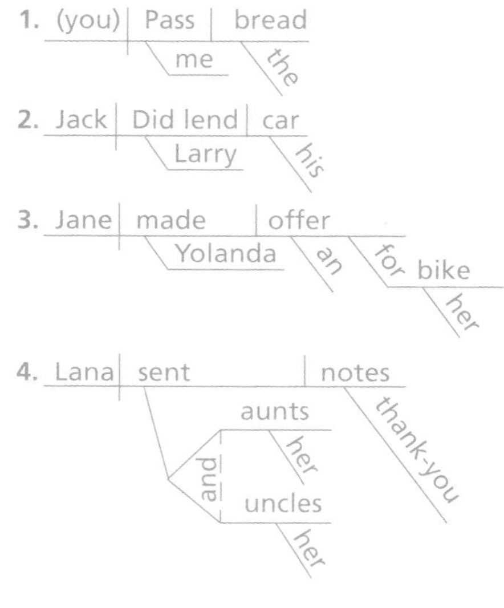

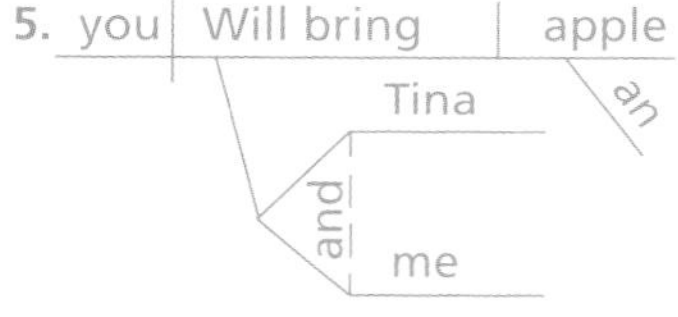

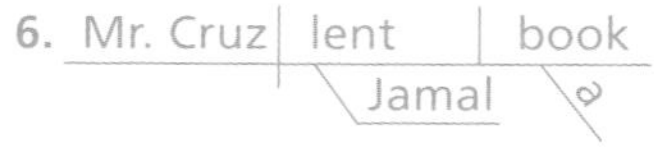

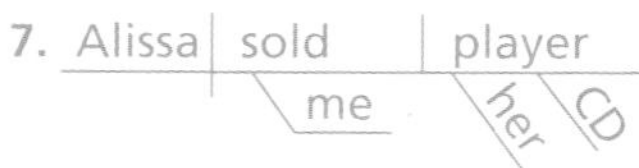

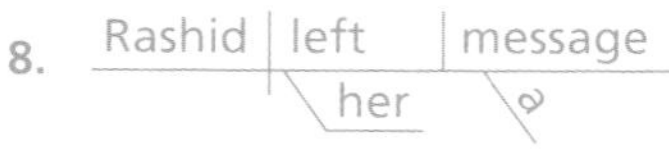

9. chef | reserved | table
The
us
a

10. Mrs. Hemsi | assigned | homework
students
her
extra

Activity I Diagram these Pattern 3 sentences on your paper. Look at the examples on page 247.

1. Pass me the bread.
2. Did Jack lend Larry his car?
3. Jane made Yolanda an offer for her bike.
4. Lana sent her aunt and her uncles thank-you notes.
5. Will you bring Tina and me an apple?
6. Mr. Cruz lent Jamal a book.
7. Alissa sold me her CD player.
8. Rashid left her a message.
9. The chef reserved us a table.
10. Mrs. Hemsi assigned her students extra homework.

Vocabulary Builder

Unique **and** ***Unusual***

People often confuse the words *unique* and *unusual.* Use *unique* when you mean "one of a kind."

Example Each snowflake is *unique.*

Use *unusual* when you mean "out of the ordinary."

Example The warm weather is *unusual* for December.

Complete each sentence by adding either *unique* or *unusual.* Write the new sentences on your paper.

1. Each human being in the world is ________.
2. The sunset last evening was ________.
3. Every person's fingerprints are ________.
4. What an ________ choice—to wear boots in June!
5. It is ________ today for people to live in one town their whole lives.

Vocabulary Builder

Point out that the prefix *uni-* means single. Something that is unique is the single example of its kind. Ask students what other words begin with the prefix *uni-*. Have them form pairs and use a dictionary to find the meaning of the following words: *unicorn, unicycle, unify, United Nations, union, unisex, unison, universe.* Ask students to identify what is singular about each term.

Answers to Vocabulary Builder:
1. unique 2. unusual 3. unique 4. unusual 5. unusual

Lesson 3 REVIEW

Write these sentences on your paper. Write *S* above the subject, *V* above the verb, *IO* above the indirect object, and *DO* above the direct object.

1. Sue brought Rita and Pam some books.
2. After dinner, Grandpa told the family some old stories.
3. The members of the team gave Kerry an award for her outstanding effort.
4. Give me another chance at the game, please.
5. Will you make Sam and me some lunch?

Decide whether the word in bold is an indirect object or an object of the preposition. Write *indirect object* or *object of the preposition* on your paper.

6. Alicia paid me for the **tickets.**
7. She gave the money to **me** yesterday.
8. Latisha cooked **us** a special meal.
9. He gave his **mother** a birthday present.
10. He gave a birthday present to his **mother.**

Diagram these Pattern 3 sentences.

11. Dan gave Meg and Lian a ride to work.
12. Who gave you that book?
13. Father prepared Danny and Anna their lunch.
14. Will you give Sean my phone number?
15. Nancy asked Joan a question.

Lesson 3 Review Answers

1. S—Sue; V—brought; IO—Rita, Pam; DO—books **2.** S—Grandpa, V—told, IO—family, DO—stories **3.** S—members, V—gave, IO—Kerry, DO—award **4.** S—(you), V—Give, IO—me, DO—chance **5.** V—Will make; S—you; IO—Sam, me; DO—lunch **6.** object of the preposition **7.** object of the preposition **8.** indirect object **9.** indirect object **10.** object of the preposition

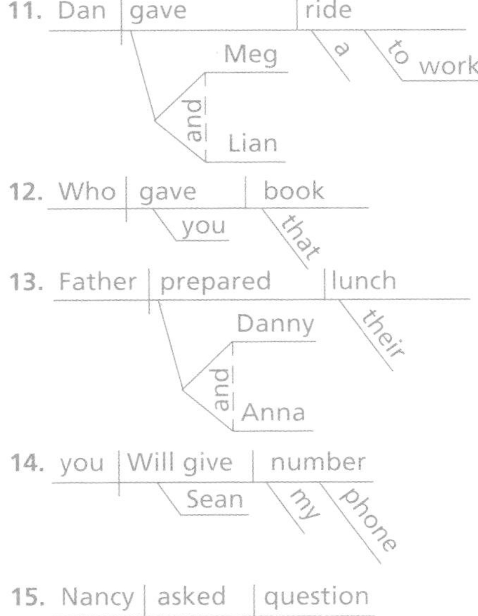

Name Date Period

Workbook Activity 54
Chapter 10, Lesson 3

Using Pattern 3 Sentences

Directions Circle the direct object in each sentence. On the line, write the indirect object in each sentence.

EXAMPLE Samantha poured him a (glass) of iced tea. ___him___

1. Send your mother some flowers. ______
2. Did that movie give you the chills? ______
3. Jessica showed Kurt and me her art project. ______
4. Ryan read his friends a story by Mark Twain. ______
5. Her grandmother wrote her a poem for her birthday. ______
6. The weather report gave us an idea of what to pack. ______
7. The pitcher threw the batter a curveball. ______
8. Sasha wrote her cousin a long letter. ______
9. The librarian brought them several books. ______
10. Todd tossed Jason the ball. ______

Directions Add an indirect object to each sentence. Write the sentences on the line.

EXAMPLE Beth told a good joke. ___Beth told us a good joke.___

11. John sold his old computer.
12. That university offered a scholarship.
13. The store issued a refund.
14. Please lend your support.
15. Mr. Giles built a swing set.

 Basic English Grammar

TRL

Workbook Activity 54

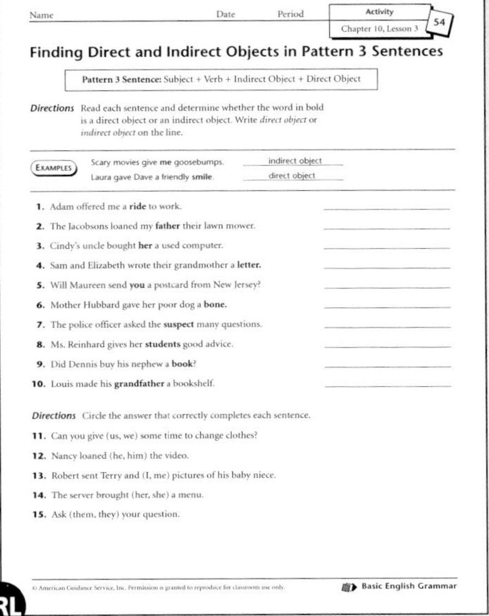

Name Date Period

Activity 54
Chapter 10, Lesson 3

Finding Direct and Indirect Objects in Pattern 3 Sentences

Pattern 3 Sentence: Subject + Verb + Indirect Object + Direct Object

Directions Read each sentence and determine whether the word in bold is a direct object or an indirect object. Write *direct object* or *indirect object* on the line.

EXAMPLES Scary movies give **me** goosebumps. ___indirect object___
Laura gave Dave a friendly **smile**. ___direct object___

1. Adam offered me a **ride** to work. ______
2. The Jacobsons loaned my **father** their lawn mower. ______
3. Cindy's uncle bought **her** a used computer. ______
4. Sam and Elizabeth wrote their grandmother a **letter.** ______
5. Will Maureen send **you** a postcard from New Jersey? ______
6. Mother Hubbard gave her poor dog a **bone.** ______
7. The police officer asked the **suspect** many questions. ______
8. Ms. Reinhard gives her **students** good advice. ______
9. Did Dennis buy his nephew a **book**? ______
10. Louis made his **grandfather** a bookshelf. ______

Directions Circle the answer that correctly completes each sentence.

11. Can you give (us, we) some time to change clothes?
12. Nancy loaned (he, him) the video.
13. Robert sent Terry and (I, me) pictures of his baby niece.
14. The server brought (her, she) a menu.
15. Ask (them, they) your question.

 Basic English Grammar

TRL

Activity 54

Sentence Patterns *Chapter 10* 249

Lesson at a Glance

Chapter 10 Lesson 4

Overview This lesson explains object complements and introduces Pattern 4 sentences.

Objectives

- To identify object complements in Pattern 4 sentences.
- To write Pattern 4 sentences.
- To diagram Pattern 4 sentences.

Student Pages 250–255

Teacher's Resource Library TRL

- Workbook Activity 55
- Activity 55
- Alternative Activity 55
- Diagramming Activity 4

Vocabulary

complement
object complement

1 Warm-Up Activity

Write the following sentences on the board: *They named the dog* and *They made the room.* Ask students to identify the pattern of these sentences. Elicit that they are Pattern 2 sentences, consisting of a subject, verb, and direct object. Now challenge students to add a single word to the end of each sentence providing extra information about the direct objects *dog* and *room.* Compile a list of possible nouns and adjectives (*Spot, Fluffy, Fang; green, messy, bigger*) Lead students to understand that the words they have added are object complements, nouns or adjectives referring to a direct object. Explain that a Pattern 4 sentence is a Pattern 2 sentence with an object complement following the direct object.

2 Teaching the Lesson

Review with students the diagrams for Sentence Patterns 1 and 2. Point out that Pattern 4 sentences simply represent an extension of the baseline to include the object complement. Make sure that students understand that compound subjects, verbs, direct objects, and object complements all involve the same technique in sentence diagramming: a fork in the baseline with the compound items written one above the other. Give students practice diagramming sentences, encouraging them to fill in all the baseline items before adding modifiers.

Lesson 4 Pattern 4 Sentences (Object Complements)

Complement
A word that completes the meaning of the verb

Object complement
A noun or an adjective that follows the verb and refers to a direct object

A Pattern 4 sentence has a transitive verb, a direct object, and an **object complement.** A **complement** is a word that completes an idea expressed by a verb. An **object complement** is a noun or an adjective that follows the verb and refers to the direct object. The object complement comes after the direct object in the sentence.

Pattern 4 Sentence:
Subject + Verb + Direct Object + Object Complement

EXAMPLE

S V DO OC
The Rands named their daughter Olivia.
(*Olivia* is a noun that renames the direct object *daughter.*)

S V DO OC
My uncle painted his garage white.
(*White* is an adjective that describes the direct object *garage.*)

Sometimes we use abbreviations in place of longer words. Take a look at this abbreviation. You will see it in this lesson.

OC = object complement

Activity A Write the object complements on your paper.

1. The people elected George Washington president in 1788.
2. The frost turned the leaves bright red.
3. Happiness made the girl beautiful.
4. Everyone calls him a great actor.
5. Emilio considers Alison smart.

Activity B Write these sentences on your paper. Add an object complement. Be sure your sentences make sense.

1. Don't make the soup ______.
2. Students in Mr. Alvarez's class find his tests ______.
3. The hot oven turned the dough ______.
4. The new parents named their baby ______.
5. Andy considers the comic strip ______.

Activity A

Do the first item in Activity A as a class, having students identify the object complement and the direct object that it renames. Then have students complete Activity A on their own.

Activity A Answers

1. president 2. red 3. beautiful 4. actor 5. smart

Activity B

Write item 1 in Activity B on the board. Invite volunteers to take turns adding an object complement. When you are sure they understand the concept, have students complete Activity B on their own.

Activity B Answers

Answers will vary. Possible answers follow. 1. Don't make the soup too salty. 2. Students in Mr. Alvarez's class find his tests easy. 3. The hot oven turned the dough golden brown. 4. The new parents named their baby Emily. 5. Andy considers that comic strip funny.

A Pattern 4 sentence can be a question.

EXAMPLE V S V DO OC
Will that dark room make you sleepy?

A Pattern 4 sentence can be a command or request.

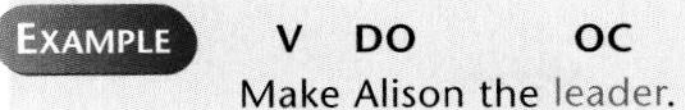

EXAMPLE V DO OC
Make Alison the leader.

Activity C Write the object complements on your paper.

1. Will you make the cake chocolate?
2. Did the polls name him the winner?
3. Has Samantha found the instructions helpful?
4. Make the chili spicier please.
5. The heat in the oven turned the rolls brown.

Activity D Find the object complements in the paragraphs below. List them on your paper in order. Not every sentence will have an object complement.

> Alex and his friend Ted found the spring day irresistible. The sun had turned the air warm and inviting.
>
> "I award this day the grand prize," said Ted.
>
> They both considered the situation perfect for a fishing trip.
>
> "I consider myself an outstanding fisherman," said Alex. "I will catch a dozen fish today."
>
> "I would call you an optimist," said Ted.

The object complement can be compound.

EXAMPLE S V DO OC OC
They painted the garage beige and brown.

Activity C

Write *They call him Tom* on the board. Have students identify the object complement (*Tom*). Then invite a volunteer to rewrite this statement as a question. (*Do they call him Tom?*) Point out that the subject and verb have altered position but that the place of the object complement remains unchanged.

Activity C Answers

1. chocolate **2.** winner **3.** helpful **4.** spicier **5.** brown

Activity D

Have students complete this activity in small groups. Encourage group members to take turns reading individual sentences aloud. Others should listen and decide whether the sentence includes an object complement.

Activity D Answers

irresistible; warm, inviting; perfect; fisherman; optimist

Speaking Practice

Have students form pairs and ask them to practice reading the paragraph in Activity D aloud to each other. Encourage them to read with expression, emphasizing important words. Invite volunteers to read aloud to the class.

Sentence Patterns Chapter 10 251

Activity E

Ask students to work on the first sentence with partners. When they have completed item 1, invite a volunteer to write the solution on the board. Have students complete the activity with their partners.

Activity E Answers

1. DO—players; OC—hot, tired 2. DO—computer studies, OC—interesting, DO—class, OC—helpful 3. DO—Jason, OC—most valuable player, DO—him, OC—captain 4. DO—leaves; OC—gold, orange 5. DO—him, OC—anxious, DO—passengers, OC—angry

Where To Find It

Provide students with copies of local or regional newspapers. Discuss with them the types of articles newspapers often contain. Write on the board the following list: *news stories, feature stories, editorials, sports stories, reviews, letters to the editor.* Have students pair up and challenge them to find and cut out an example of each of these items. Invite students to mount their articles by type on poster board and put them on display in the classroom.

3 Reinforce and Extend

Global Connection

Some students may receive foreign newspapers in their home. Invite these students to share a newspaper article from one of these papers with the class. You might wish to use an overhead projector or have the students copy sample sentences from the article onto the board. Have students point out different sentence patterns in the article and tell how they compare to sentence patterns in English.

If the sentence has a compound direct object, each direct object can have an object complement.

S V DO OC DO OC
They elected Corey president and Vonetta treasurer.

If the sentence has a compound verb, each verb can have a direct object. Each direct object can have an object complement.

EXAMPLE

V DO OC V DO OC
Don't make the soup spicy and don't serve it cold.

Activity E Write these sentences on your paper. Write *DO* over each direct object and *OC* over each object complement.

Example DO OC DO OC
Brian painted the walls yellow and the door blue.

1. The exercise made the players hot and tired.
2. Many students find computer studies interesting and keyboarding class helpful.
3. The team named Jason the most valuable player and elected him captain.
4. The cool weather turned the leaves gold and orange.
5. The flight delay made him anxious and other passengers angry.

Where To Find It

Newspaper

Newspapers in small towns may have only one section. You can usually find a table of contents on the first or second page. It will tell you the section and page number for listings such as classified ads, movie times, or local news. Newspapers in large cities usually have several sections. These are usually named by topic, for example, sports, news, business, and travel.

1. Look at your local newspaper. Write its name, and list the sections it has. Bring the newspaper to class with you.
2. Find and read an article that interests you. Look at the sentences in the first paragraph of the article. Identify the patterns and write the patterns on your paper.

Diagramming Pattern 4 Sentences

To diagram a Pattern 4 sentence:

1. Place the object complement on the baseline of the diagram next to the direct object.
2. Separate the object complement from the direct object with a line slanted toward the direct object.

EXAMPLE Jennifer dyed the yarn red.

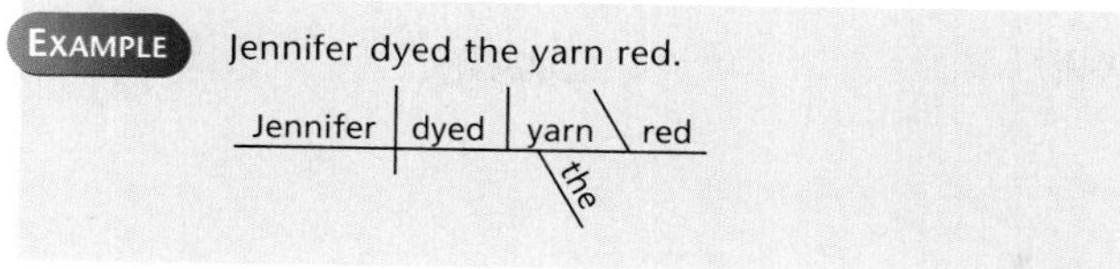

3. If a Pattern 4 sentence is a question, change the question to a statement. Then draw the diagram.

EXAMPLE

Question		Statement
Did Brittany find it interesting?	→	Brittany did find it interesting.

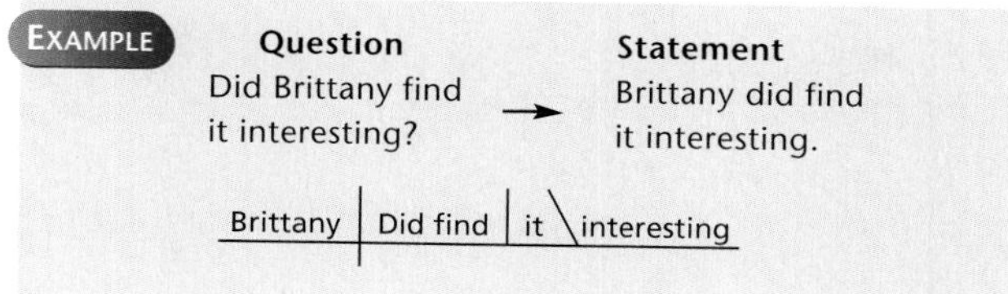

4. Remember, if a Pattern 4 sentence is a command or request, the subject *you* is understood. Put *you* in parentheses.

EXAMPLE Make Sarah the leader.

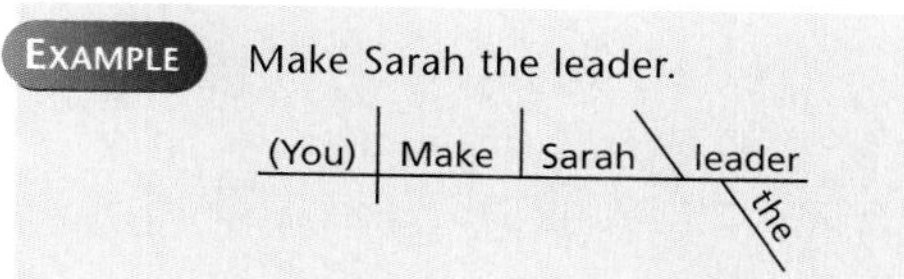

5. Diagram a Pattern 4 sentence that has a compound subject or compound verb this way.

EXAMPLE Runners and bikers consider the new trail excellent.

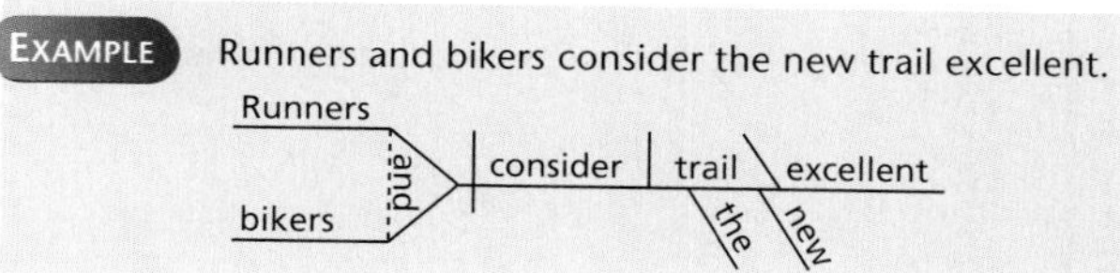

LEARNING STYLES

Auditory/Verbal

Give students practice adding the understood subject *you* to commands and rewording questions as statements by reading aloud the following sentences:

Did they find him unconscious?

Make her president.

Does Mr. Sanchez consider me a genius?

Paint my face red, white, and blue.

After each example, invite volunteers to reword the sentence, saying it the way it would appear in a sentence diagram. (Example: *They did find him unconscious. You make her president.*) Repeat the exercise, calling on others to rephrase the examples orally. Finally, ask students to compose their own Pattern 4 questions and commands. Encourage them to test the class orally with their examples.

LEARNING STYLES

Body/Kinesthetic

Give each student a sign with S, V, DO, or OC printed on it. Have them team up with three other students so that their signs combine to create the four parts of a Pattern 4 sentence. Then ask each team to choose any one sentence from the activities or examples in this lesson. Have them each adopt the part of the sentence described by their sign and line up in order in front of the class, first reading the sentence, then introducing the words they represent.

Activity F

Discuss the steps for diagramming a Pattern 4 sentence. Then have students work alone or with partners to complete Activity F.

Activity F Answers

1.

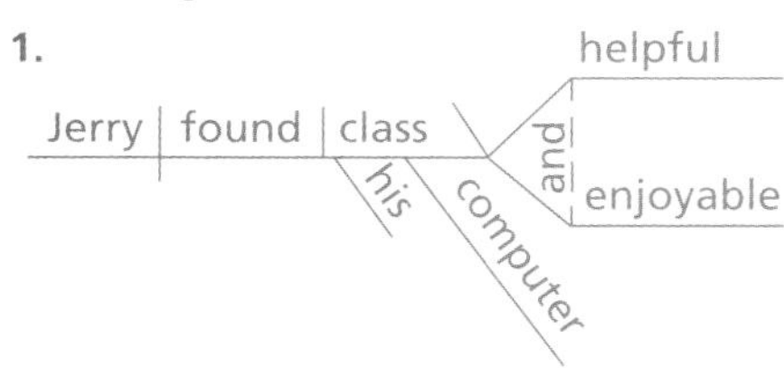

2. students | elected | Jack \ treasurer
The

3. (you) | Make | chili \ spicier
this

4. They | named | Mrs. Santiago \ Woman of the Year

5. Grace | Did paint | room \ yellow
her

6. They | called | cottage \ Our Escape
the

7. we | Should declare | Jodie \ winner
the

8. water | turned | lips \ blue
The cold her

9. They | judged | act \ excellent
his

10. Who | considers | book \ dull
her latest

6. Diagram a Pattern 4 sentence with a compound direct object this way.

EXAMPLE The city council chose Mrs. Ozawa president and Mr. Hemsi secretary.

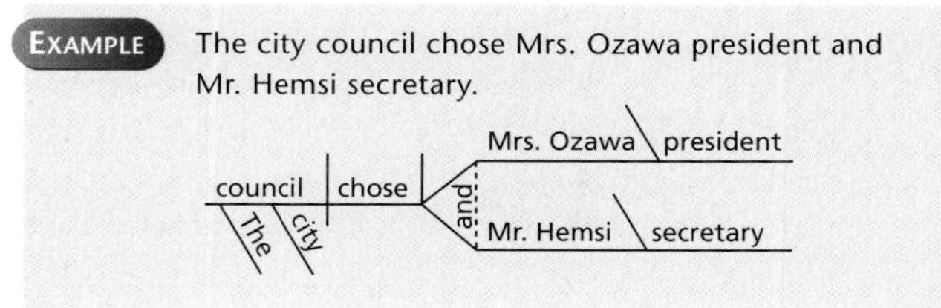

7. Diagram a Pattern 4 sentence with a compound object complement this way.

EXAMPLE Mr. Santos considered our project interesting and educational.

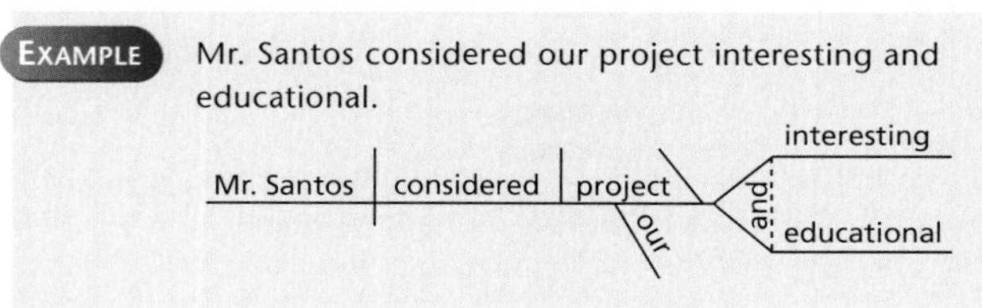

Activity F Diagram these Pattern 4 sentences on your paper.

1. Jerry found his computer class helpful and enjoyable.
2. The students elected Jack treasurer.
3. Make this chili spicier.
4. They named Mrs. Santiago "Woman of the Year."
5. Did Grace paint her room yellow?
6. They called the cottage "Our Escape."
7. Should we declare Jodie the winner?
8. The cold water turned her lips blue.
9. They judged his act excellent.
10. Who considers her latest book dull?

254 *Chapter 10 Sentence Patterns*

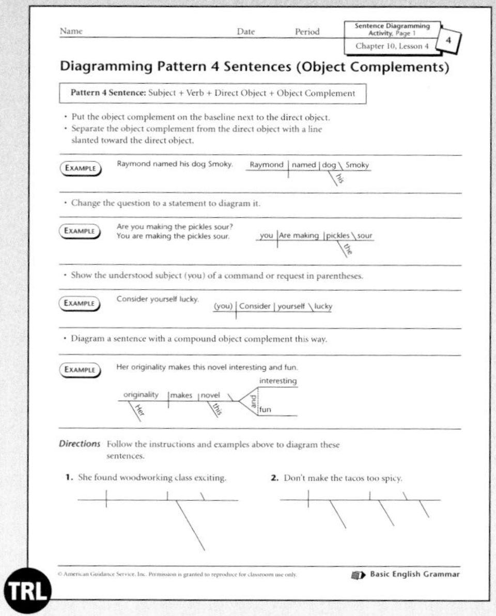

Name Date Period Sentence Diagramming Activity, Page 1 Chapter 10, Lesson 4

Diagramming Pattern 4 Sentences (Object Complements)

Pattern 4 Sentence: Subject + Verb + Direct Object + Object Complement

- Put the object complement on the baseline next to the direct object.
- Separate the object complement from the direct object with a line slanted toward the direct object.

EXAMPLE Raymond named his dog Smoky.

- Change the question to a statement to diagram it.

EXAMPLE Are you making the pickles sour? You are making the pickles sour.

- Show the understood subject (you) of a command or request in parentheses.

EXAMPLE Consider yourself lucky.

- Diagram a sentence with a compound object complement this way.

EXAMPLE Her originality makes this novel interesting and fun.

Directions Follow the instructions and examples above to diagram these sentences.

1. She found woodworking class exciting.
2. Don't make the tacos too spicy.

© American Guidance Service, Inc. Permission is granted to reproduce for classroom use only. Basic English Grammar

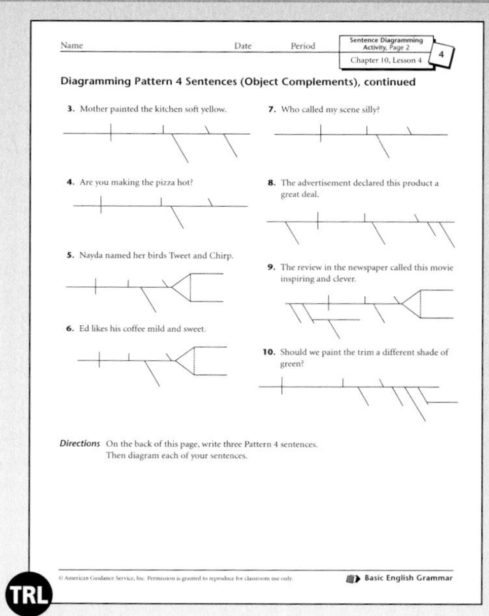

Name Date Period Sentence Diagramming Activity, Page 2 Chapter 10, Lesson 4

Diagramming Pattern 4 Sentences (Object Complements), continued

3. Mother painted the kitchen soft yellow.
4. Are you making the pizza hot?
5. Nayda named her birds Tweet and Chirp.
6. Ed likes his coffee mild and sweet.
7. Who called my scene silly?
8. The advertisement declared this product a great deal.
9. The review in the newspaper called this movie inspiring and clever.
10. Should we paint the trim a different shade of green?

Directions On the back of this page, write three Pattern 4 sentences. Then diagram each of your sentences.

© American Guidance Service, Inc. Permission is granted to reproduce for classroom use only. Basic English Grammar

TRL

Diagramming Activity 4

Lesson 4 REVIEW

Write the object complements in these sentences on your paper.

1. They declared the young boy the winner.
2. We made Joe group leader.
3. They call their hamster Swifty.
4. Old age has turned the dog's hair silver.
5. They dyed the wool brown.

Write these sentences on your paper. Write *S* above the subject, *V* above the verb, *DO* above the direct object, and *OC* above the object complement.

6. You made that meal delicious!
7. We named the white kitten Snowball and the black kitten Midnight.
8. Did you find that program interesting?
9. What makes him so shy?
10. Do you consider yourself an expert on the subject?

Diagram these Pattern 4 sentences.

11. The wind turned the day cold.
12. The class will elect Carlotta president.
13. Can we call the puppy Pooch?
14. Mya and Danzel found the play boring.
15. Paint the inside of your closet purple.

Lesson 4 Review Answers

1. winner **2.** leader **3.** Swifty **4.** silver **5.** brown **6.** S—You, V—made, DO—meal, OC—delicious **7.** S—We, V—named, DO—kitten, OC—Snowball, DO—kitten, OC—Midnight **8.** V—Did, S—you, V—find, DO—program, OC—interesting **9.** S—What, V—makes, DO—him, OC—shy **10.** V—Do, S—you, V—consider, DO—yourself, OC—expert

11.

12.
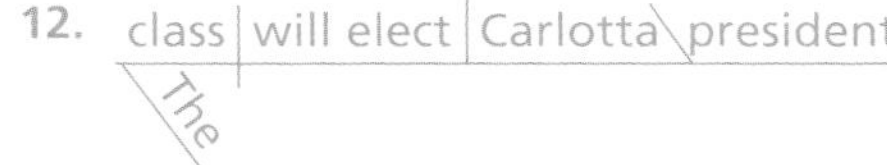

13.
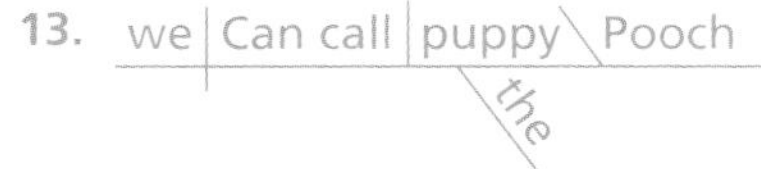

14.
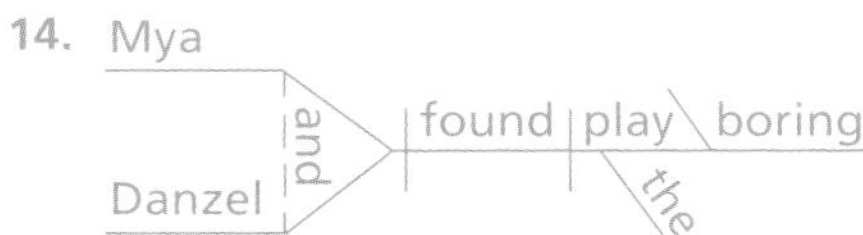

15.

Teacher Alert

Help students avoid leaving words out of their diagrams. Suggest that they count the number of words in their sentence diagrams and compare that to the number of words in the original sentence. Except for commands or requests (which have the added subject *you*) the number must be the same.

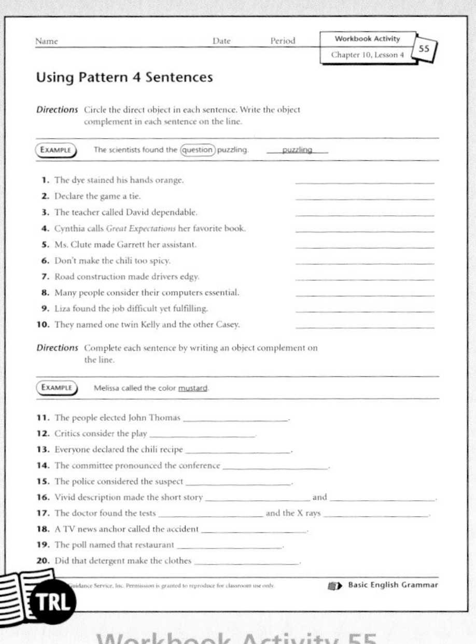

Name Date Period | Workbook Activity 55 | Chapter 10, Lesson 4

Using Pattern 4 Sentences

Directions Circle the direct object in each sentence. Write the object complement in each sentence on the line.

EXAMPLE The scientists found the (question) puzzling. puzzling

1. The dye stained his hands orange. ______
2. Declare the game a tie. ______
3. The teacher called David dependable. ______
4. Cynthia calls *Great Expectations* her favorite book. ______
5. Ms. Clute made Garrett her assistant. ______
6. Don't make the chili too spicy. ______
7. Road construction made drivers edgy. ______
8. Many people consider their computers essential. ______
9. Liza found the job difficult yet fulfilling. ______
10. They named one twin Kelly and the other Casey. ______

Directions Complete each sentence by writing an object complement on the line.

EXAMPLE Melissa called the color mustard.

11. The people elected John Thomas ______.
12. Critics consider the play ______.
13. Everyone declared the chili recipe ______.
14. The committee pronounced the conference ______.
15. The police considered the suspect ______.
16. Vivid description made the short story ______ and ______.
17. The doctor found the tests ______ and the X rays ______.
18. A TV news anchor called the accident ______.
19. The poll named that restaurant ______.
20. Did that detergent make the clothes ______.

 Basic English Grammar

TRL

Workbook Activity 55

Name Date Period | Activity 55 | Chapter 10, Lesson 4

Finding Object Complements in Pattern 4 Sentences

Pattern 4 Sentence: Subject + Verb + Direct Object + Object Complement

Directions In the following paragraph, circle each direct object and underline each object complement.

EXAMPLE The cooler weather turned the (leaves) red and gold.

The weather made the day perfect for a long walk. Jennifer had long considered walking one of the best kinds of exercise. She found it energizing and refreshing. The trees that lined the street kept the sidewalk shady. Nevertheless, as time passed, the walking made her thirstier and thirstier. The sun was also making the air warmer. She considered a rest necessary, and she found the neighborhood park an inviting place to stop for a while. As she sat under a tree, she considered herself lucky to have the time to be outside that day. As the sun was setting, a mild breeze turned the air cooler. Jennifer headed for home, and she declared the day very enjoyable.

Directions Complete each sentence by writing an object complement on the line. Make sure the sentence makes sense.

EXAMPLE Did Kimberly find my directions helpful?

1. Lena called Marcus ______.
2. Do you consider Shakespeare ______?
3. The judges declared her performance ______.
4. The wind turned the air ______.
5. The blazing campfire made us ______.
6. The large window made the room ______.
7. My sister painted her bedroom ______.
8. He nicknamed his car ______.
9. On a hot day, I find ice cream ______.
10. The mayor named Mr. Rodriguez ______.

 Basic English Grammar

TRL

Activity 55

Lesson 5 Pattern 5 Sentences (Predicate Nouns)

> ***Predicate noun***
> *A noun or pronoun that follows a linking verb and renames the subject*
>
> ***Linking verb***
> *A verb that joins the subject with a noun, pronoun, or adjective in the predicate; it is always a state-of-being verb*

A Pattern 5 sentence has a **linking verb** and a **predicate noun.** A linking verb joins the subject to a word in the predicate part of the sentence. A linking verb is always a state-of-being verb. *Feel, look, become, remain,* and *be* are some examples of linking verbs.

EXAMPLE

Action Verb	Hector studies art.
Linking Verb	Hector is an art student.

A linking verb joins the subject to a predicate noun. The predicate noun is a noun or pronoun that renames the subject. A predicate noun always follows a linking verb. A predicate noun helps the sentence express a complete thought.

> Sometimes we use abbreviations in place of longer words. Take a look at these abbreviations. You will see them in this lesson.
>
> LV = linking verb
>
> PN = predicate noun

Pattern 5 Sentence:
Subject + Linking Verb + Predicate Noun

EXAMPLE

S LV PN
That neighborhood was once a farm.

S LV PN
Vanessa is an excellent runner.

Activity A Add a predicate noun to each sentence that renames the subject.

1. Alex and Jason are ______.
2. Please be my ______ always.
3. Tennessee is a southern ______.
4. Alex is the ______ on the team.
5. Agatha Christie is a famous ______.

Lesson at a Glance

Chapter 10 Lesson 5

Overview This lesson explains linking verbs and predicate nouns used in Pattern 5 sentences.

Objectives

- To identify linking verbs and predicate nouns.
- To identify the parts of a Pattern 5 sentence
- To write Pattern 5 sentences.
- To diagram Pattern 5 sentences.

Student Pages 256–263

Teacher's Resource Library 

Workbook Activity 56

Activity 56

Alternative Activity 56

Diagramming Activity 5

Vocabulary

linking verb
predicate noun

1 Warm-Up Activity

Write the following sentences on the board:

1. We laughed.
2. Tony hit the ball
3. She read us the book.
4. Larissa named her rabbit Bugs.
5. My name is Hahn.

Explain to students that four of these sentences represent patterns they have already studied. Invite volunteers to identify them and draw their diagrams on the board. (*Sentences 1–4 are in Patterns 1–4.*) Lead students to understand that the last sentence on your list is a new type. The subject is not completing an action, and the verb is simply connecting, or linking, the subject with the noun that follows. Point out that this is a Pattern 5 sentence.

Teaching the Lesson

Students may have difficulty identifying the predicate noun when it is modified with adjectives and prepositional phrases. First make sure that students can identify prepositional phrases by brainstorming a list with the class. Point out that the predicate noun can never be the object of a preposition. Then write a simple Pattern 5 sentence on the board. (Example: *Julia is an actor.*) Invite students to add on modifiers to the predicate noun. (Example: *Julia is an extremely talented actor with a lot of experience.*) Point out that the basic diagram of the sentence remains unchanged. Have students write their own simple Pattern 5 sentences, and invite the class to add adjectives and phrases to the predicate noun.

Activity A

Help students complete the first item. Point out that the subject and the predicate noun must agree in number. If the subject is plural the predicate noun must be plural.

Activity A Answers

Answers will vary. Possible answers follow. **1.** classmates **2.** friend **3.** state **4.** captain **5.** mystery writer

Activity B Write these sentences on your paper. Write *S* above the subject, *LV* above the linking verb, and *PN* above the predicate noun.

Example   S   LV   PN
Dr. Turner has been our mayor.

1. In 1968, Pierre Elliot Trudeau became prime minister of Canada.
2. She became my friend in first grade.
3. My favorite horror story is *The Tell-Tale Heart.*
4. The song writer is also a poet.
5. The winner of the race was Emily.
6. They are athletes.
7. The woman in the picture is a neighbor.
8. Charles will be the director.
9. My choice for class president is you.
10. The title of that play is *A Raisin in the Sun.*

In a Pattern 5 sentence, adjectives often come before the predicate noun. The adjective describes the predicate noun.

S LV Adj. Adj. PN
Ling is a good auto mechanic.
(The adjectives *good* and *auto* describe the noun *mechanic.*)

Activity C Write these sentences on your paper. Circle the predicate noun and underline the adjectives that describe it in each sentence. Do not include the articles *the, a,* or *an.*

1. George Washington was the first president.
2. Aunt Marie is a great cook.
3. Carol has always been a friendly, helpful person.
4. Ted has become an excellent soccer coach.
5. Ms. Marino is a popular teacher.

Activity B

Discuss the example. Then have students complete Activity B on their own.

Activity B Answers

1. S—Pierre Elliot Trudeau, LV—became, PN—prime minister 2. S—She, LV—became, PN—friend 3. S—story, LV—is, PN—"The Tell-Tale Heart" 4. S—writer, LV—is, PN—poet 5. S—winner, LV—was, PN—Emily 6. S—They, LV—are, PN—athletes 7. S—woman, LV—is, PN—neighbor 8. S—Charles, LV—will be, PN—director 9. S—choice, LV—is, PN—you 10. S—title, LV—is, PN—*A Raisin in the Sun*

Activity C

Do the first item orally with the class. Then ask students to complete Activity C on their own. Have students who need extra support work with partners. Suggest that they first identify the subject and linking verb in each sentence before they try to find the predicate noun.

Activity C Answers

1. George Washington was the first president. 2. Aunt Marie is a great cook. 3. Carol has always been a friendly, helpful person. 4. Ted has become an excellent soccer coach. 5. Ms. Marino is a popular teacher.

3 Reinforce and Extend

Learning Styles

Visual/Spatial

Give each pair of students a photograph from a magazine or newspaper. Ask the pairs to write a Pattern 5 sentence about their photograph, including at least one adjective describing the predicate noun. (Example: *This is a beautiful, snowy mountain.*) When they have written their sentences, have pairs exchange photographs and write a sentence describing the next picture. Continue until each pair has described all the pictures. Invite volunteers to write sample sentences on the board.

Teacher Alert

You may wish to point out that words that follow a linking verb and tell about the subject are sometimes called *subject complements.* Be sure students understand the distinction between subject complements and object complements, which they learned about in Lesson 4.

Activity D

Write the following sentences on the board: *Those fans enjoy baseball. Baseball is a fun sport.* Help students determine which sentence has the direct object and which has the predicate noun. Then have students complete Activity D independently.

Activity D Answers

1. direct object 2. predicate noun 3. predicate noun 4. direct object 5. predicate noun

Learning Styles

Logical/Mathematical

Write the equal sign on the board, followed by the unequal sign (≠), and invite volunteers to use these symbols in mathematical equations. Now point out that Pattern 5 sentences can be expressed as equations. Write on the board *Franklin Roosevelt was president.* Then write the sentence again, using the equal sign in place of the word *was.* Explain that sentences with direct objects cannot be expressed in this way. Write on the board *She fed the cat;* then replace *fed* with ≠. Have pairs of students complete the items in Activity D, using these two symbols instead of verbs. Finally ask the pairs to write sentences of their own, indicating predicate nouns and direct objects by the use of symbols.

Do not confuse a noun or pronoun used as a direct object with a predicate noun. Remember, a direct object receives the action of a transitive verb. A predicate noun follows an intransitive verb and renames the subject.

Example

Direct Object	Alicia introduced the new student. (*Student* receives the action of the transitive verb *introduced.*)
Predicate Noun	Alicia is a new student. (*Student* renames the subject *Alicia.*)

Activity D Write on your paper whether the word in bold is a *direct object* or a *predicate noun.*

1. James plays **baseball** in the spring.
2. He is the team **captain.**
3. Tony is the league's best **catcher.**
4. He can also hit the **ball** a mile.
5. He is a good **hitter.**

Alicia is a new student in Mr. Martinez's class.

A predicate noun is never part of a prepositional phrase.

Most computer grammar checkers will remind you about overusing the verb *be.* Highlight the underlined text, and click on the grammar checker. Action verbs will appear in the window that opens.

A Pattern 5 sentence can have an adverb or a prepositional phrase that answers questions about the linking verb.

EXAMPLE
S LV PN
Sara is always a good student. (When is Sara a good student? Sara is *always* a good student.)
S LV PN
She has been my neighbor for years. (How long has she been a neighbor? She has been a neighbor *for years.*)

A Pattern 5 sentence can have a prepositional phrase that describes the predicate noun.

EXAMPLE
S LV PN
A woman from Ohio became the president of our company. (She became the president of what? She became the president *of our company.*)

Activity E Write the predicate noun in each sentence on your paper. The predicate noun is never the object of a preposition.

1. Uruguay is a country in South America.
2. Jimmy Stewart was a popular actor.
3. Pasta is a common food in the United States.
4. *Gone With the Wind* was the most popular movie in 1939.
5. *Star Wars* is still Andy's favorite movie.

Activity F Write five Pattern 5 sentences on your paper. Add as many adverbs, adjectives, and prepositional phrases as you wish. For each sentence, write *S* above the subject, *LV* above the linking verb, and *PN* above the predicate noun.

Example S LV PN
Sara has been Eric's neighbor since kindergarten.

A Pattern 5 sentence can also be a question.

EXAMPLE
LV S PN
Were you the one in the newspaper photo?

Activity E

Read through each item in the activity with students. Work with them to identify the prepositional phrases and objects of the prepositions in each sentence. Then have students complete Activity E on their own.

Activity E Answers

1. country **2.** actor **3.** food **4.** movie **5.** movie

Activity F

Discuss the directions and example given for Activity F. Then invite a volunteer to write another Pattern 5 sentence modeled on the example. Have the class identify the subject, linking verb, and predicate noun in the sentence for the student to label. Then have students write and label their own sentences to complete Activity F.

Activity F Answers

Answers will vary. Possible answers follow. **1.** Alicia is my best friend. S—Alicia, LV—is, PN—friend **2.** She has been my best friend since first grade. S—She, LV—has been, PN—friend **3.** Ann is my only sister. S—Ann, LV—is, PN—sister **4.** Toronto is my favorite city in Canada. S—Toronto, LV—is, PN—city **5.** The Joneses have been our neighbors. S—Joneses, LV—have been, PN—neighbors

LEARNING STYLES

LEP/ESL

Point out that the most common linking verb is the verb *be.* Give English language learners practice recognizing the verb *be* in its various forms by having them form small groups with students who are proficient in English. Each group should appoint one member to read aloud from a school text or magazine. Students should identify different uses of the verb *be* as they hear it read to them and copy the sentence or phrase in which the word occurred. When groups have found five different examples, invite English language learners to write their model phrases or sentences on the board. Challenge the class to identify these examples according to their tense.

Activity G

Before they begin the activity, have students read the sentences, identifying them as statements, questions, or commands. Review the examples for each of these forms. Then have students complete the activity on their own.

Activity G Answers

1. LV—Was, S—Franklin Pierce, PN—president 2. S—Canada, LV—is, PN—country 3. S—(you), LV—be, PN—friend 4. S—Picasso, LV—is, PN—artist 5. LV—Is, S—that, PN—house

Activity H

Remind students that the coordinating conjunctions *and, but,* and *or* are common linking words in sentences with compound parts. Before students start to work on Activity H, have them look through the activity items for these three words.

Activity H Answers

1. S—Joyce Carol Oates; LV—is; PN—poet, novelist 2. LV—Are; S—trees; PN—oaks, maples 3. S—Alex, father; LV—are; PN—night owls 4. S—*The Good Earth*; LV—is; PN—movie, book 5. S—Phil, LV—is, PN—student, S—he, LV—will be, PN—architect

ONLINE CONNECTION

Introduce students to the world of sentence diagramming by suggesting that they log on to **webster.commnet.edu/grammar.** Have them select *word and sentence level* and click on *Diagramming Sentences.* Encourage students to print out diagrams featured on the site, including examples of sentences in Patterns 1 to 5.

A Pattern 5 sentence can be a command or a request.

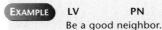

EXAMPLE LV PN
Be a good neighbor.

Activity G Write these sentences on your paper. Write *S* above the subject, *LV* above the linking verb, and *PN* above the predicate noun. If the subject *you* is understood, write it in.

1. Was Franklin Pierce a U.S. president?
2. Canada is a country in North America.
3. Please be my friend.
4. Picasso is a famous Spanish artist.
5. Is that your house?

A Pattern 5 sentence can have compound parts.

EXAMPLE
S S LV PN PN
Alvaro and Sita are excellent musicians and talented artists.

You can combine two Pattern 5 sentences with a conjunction to form a compound sentence.

EXAMPLE
S LV PN S LV PN
Deshawn is a quarterback now, but last year he was a fullback.

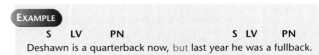

Activity H Write these sentences on your paper. Write *S* above the subject, *LV* above the linking verb, and *PN* above the predicate noun. Some sentences may have compound parts or may be compound sentences.

1. Joyce Carol Oates is a poet and a novelist.
2. Are those trees oaks or maples?
3. Alex and his father are the night owls in the family.
4. *The Good Earth* is a movie and a book.
5. Phil is a student now, but he will be an architect some day.

260 Chapter 10 Sentence Patterns

Diagramming Pattern 5 Sentences

To diagram a Pattern 5 sentence:

1. Place the predicate noun on the baseline of the diagram.
2. Separate the predicate noun from the verb with a line slanted toward the verb.

EXAMPLE Mr. Stamos is an excellent principal.

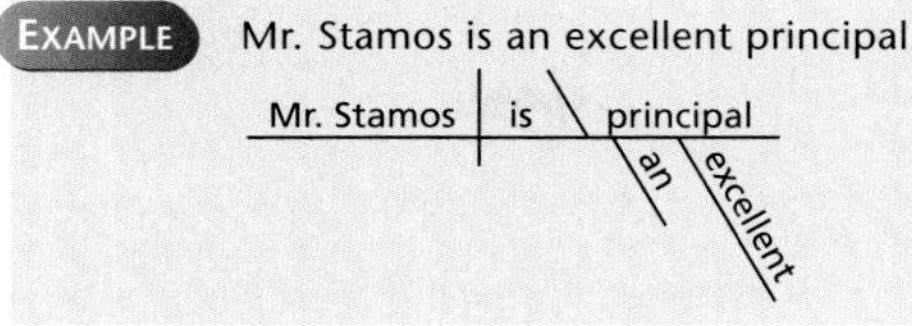

3. If a Pattern 5 sentence is a question, change the question to a statement. Then draw the diagram.

EXAMPLE

Question		Statement
Is that your brown jacket?	→	That is your brown jacket.

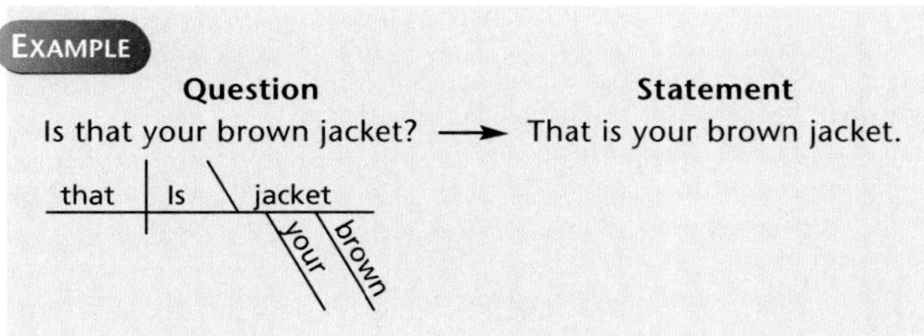

4. In a command or request, the subject *you* is understood. Put *you* in parentheses.

EXAMPLE Be a good student.

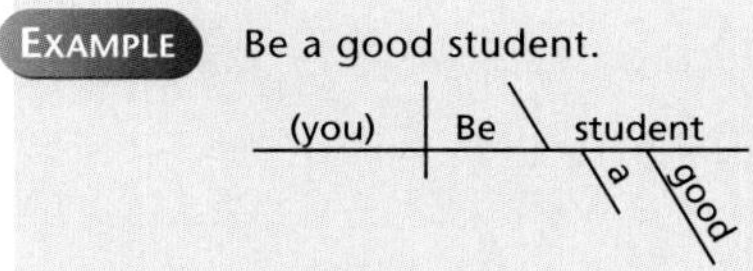

CAREER CONNECTION

Point out to students that employers use organizational charts to show the structure of their companies and how each employee fits into that structure. If possible, obtain a transparency of an organizational chart for a company near you. Project the transparency and explain how the different positions in the company relate to one another. Point out to students that a company's organizational chart is much like a sentence diagram. Both show how parts are related to one another and to the whole.

LEARNING STYLES

Interpersonal/Group Learning

Determine how many groups of three are in your class. Then draw a diagram pattern for each group. (Use the patterns on page 261.) Give each group one pattern and ask the group to create a sentence that will fit its diagram pattern. Afterward, have each group print its sentence and its diagram on the board.

Activity I

Do the first two items on the board with students before having them complete Activity I on their own.

Activity I Answers

1. Who | is \ she

2. Kim | became \ secretary
   our
   class

3.

4.

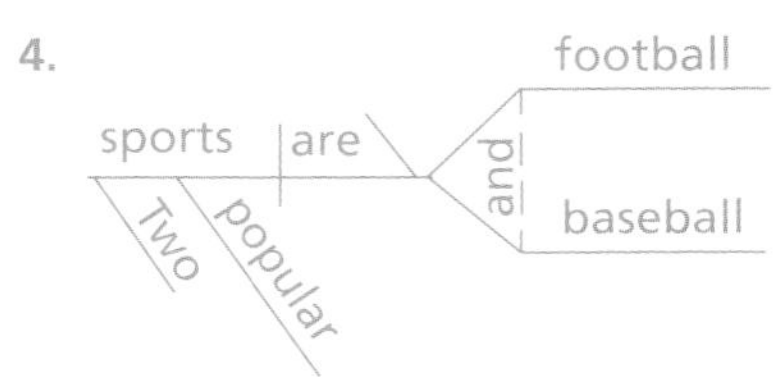

5.

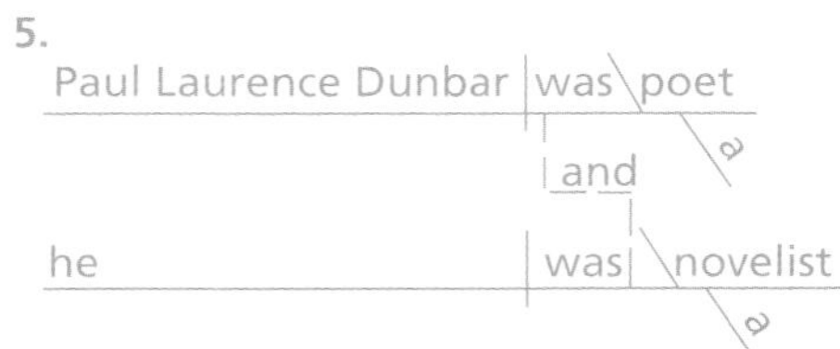

6. Dana | has been \ friend
   for years
   two
   Anne's
   best

7.

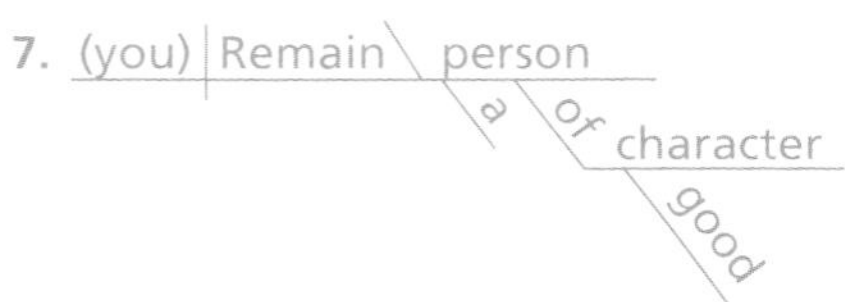

8.

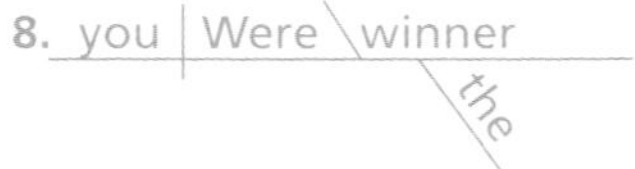

9.

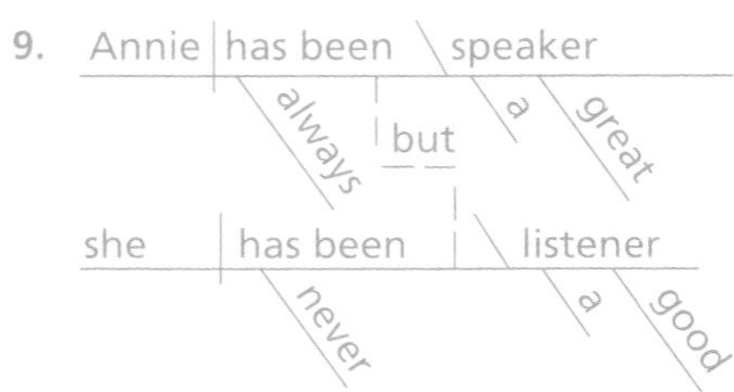

10.

5. Diagram a compound predicate noun this way.

EXAMPLE Janine is a musician and an artist.

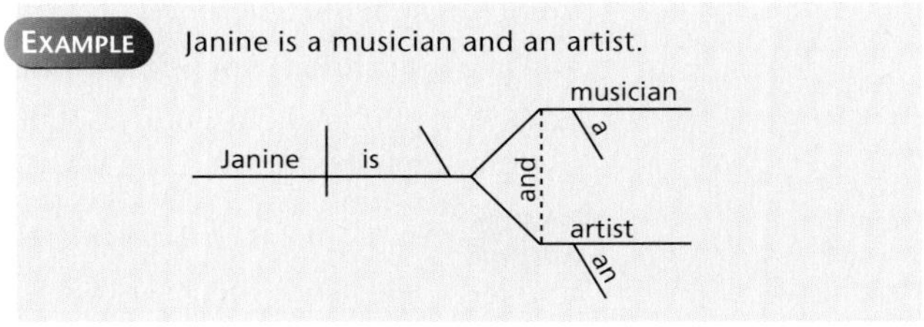

6. Diagram a compound Pattern 5 sentence this way.

EXAMPLE New York is my favorite city, but my home is Los Angeles.

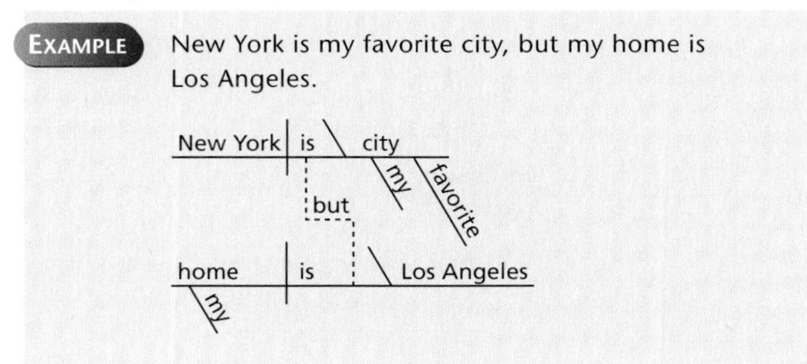

Activity I Diagram these Pattern 5 sentences on your paper.

1. Who is she?
2. Kim became our class secretary.
3. Sue and Kelly have become good friends.
4. Two popular sports are football and baseball.
5. Paul Laurence Dunbar was a poet, and he was a novelist.
6. Dana has been Anne's best friend for two years.
7. Remain a person of good character.
8. Were you the winner?
9. Annie has always been a great speaker, but she has never been a good listener.
10. Michael J. Fox is a popular actor.

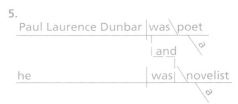

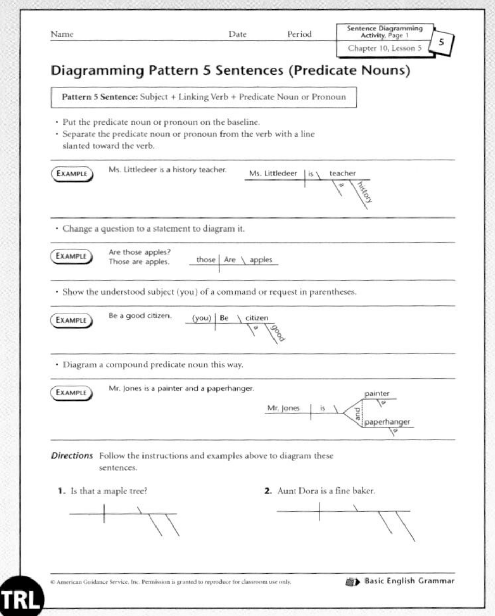

Name Date Period | Sentence Diagramming Activity, Page 1 | Chapter 10, Lesson 5 | 5

Diagramming Pattern 5 Sentences (Predicate Nouns)

Pattern 5 Sentence: Subject + Linking Verb + Predicate Noun or Pronoun

- Put the predicate noun or pronoun on the baseline.
- Separate the predicate noun or pronoun from the verb with a line slanted toward the verb.

EXAMPLE Ms. Littledeer is a history teacher. Ms. Littledeer | is \ teacher / a / history

- Change a question to a statement to diagram it.

EXAMPLE Are those apples? Those are apples. those | Are \ apples

- Show the understood subject (you) of a command or request in parentheses.

EXAMPLE Be a good citizen. (you) | Be \ citizen / a / good

- Diagram a compound predicate noun this way.

EXAMPLE Mr. Jones is a painter and a paperhanger. Mr. Jones | is \ painter / a / and / paperhanger / a

Directions Follow the instructions and examples above to diagram these sentences.

1. Is that a maple tree?
2. Aunt Dora is a fine baker.

 Basic English Grammar

TRL

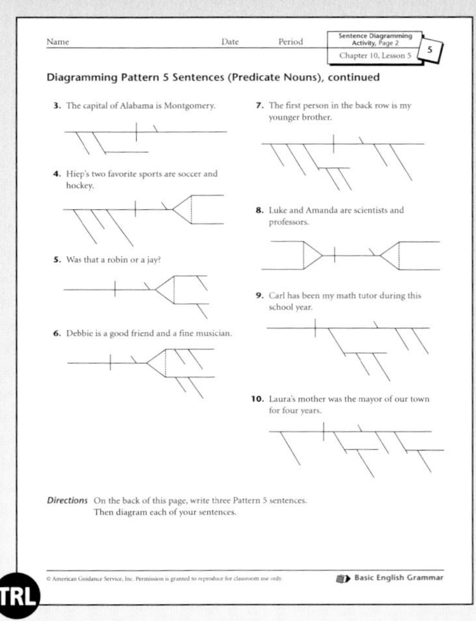

Name Date Period | Sentence Diagramming Activity, Page 2 | Chapter 10, Lesson 5 | 5

Diagramming Pattern 5 Sentences (Predicate Nouns), continued

3. The capital of Alabama is Montgomery.
4. Hiep's two favorite sports are soccer and hockey.
5. Was that a robin or a jay?
6. Debbie is a good friend and a fine musician.
7. The first person in the back row is my younger brother.
8. Luke and Amanda are scientists and professors.
9. Carl has been my math tutor during this school year.
10. Laura's mother was the mayor of our town for four years.

Directions On the back of this page, write three Pattern 5 sentences. Then diagram each of your sentences.

 Basic English Grammar

TRL

Diagramming Activity 5

Lesson 5 REVIEW

On your paper, write whether the verb in bold is a *linking verb* or an *action verb.* Remember, a linking verb never takes a direct object.

1. **Be** a good friend.
2. Later I **am going** to the movies.
3. **Taste** this stew for me.
4. You **are** a good cook.
5. I **like** dinner at your house.

Write these sentences on your paper. Write *S* above the subject, *LV* above the linking verb, and *PN* above the predicate noun.

6. Two popular Mexican foods are tacos and burritos.
7. Jupiter is the largest planet in the solar system.
8. Is Dan a friend of yours?
9. Who was that?
10. Lima is the capital of Peru.

Diagram these Pattern 5 sentences on your paper.

11. Janelle is a good artist.
12. Be a responsible student and worker.
13. I am an unemployed singer, and Sal is the owner of a small theater.
14. Are they the champions?
15. Jack is a friend of mine.

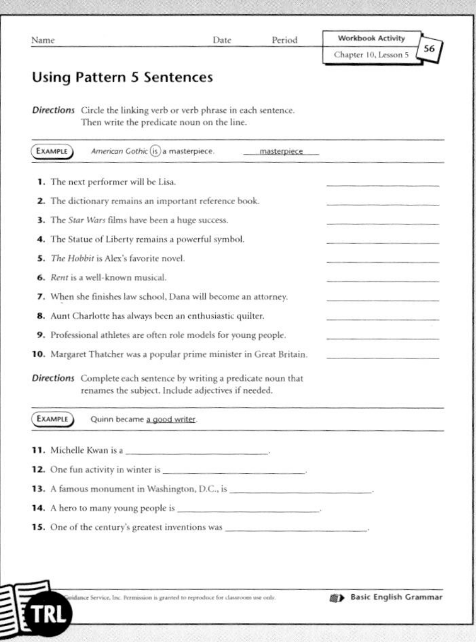

Name Date Period

Workbook Activity 56
Chapter 10, Lesson 5

Using Pattern 5 Sentences

Directions Circle the linking verb or verb phrase in each sentence. Then write the predicate noun on the line.

EXAMPLE *American Gothic* (is) a masterpiece. masterpiece

1. The next performer will be Lisa. ______
2. The dictionary remains an important reference book. ______
3. The *Star Wars* films have been a huge success. ______
4. The Statue of Liberty remains a powerful symbol. ______
5. *The Hobbit* is Alex's favorite novel. ______
6. *Rent* is a well-known musical. ______
7. When she finishes law school, Dana will become an attorney. ______
8. Aunt Charlotte has always been an enthusiastic quilter. ______
9. Professional athletes are often role models for young people. ______
10. Margaret Thatcher was a popular prime minister in Great Britain. ______

Directions Complete each sentence by writing a predicate noun that renames the subject. Include adjectives if needed.

EXAMPLE Quinn became a good writer.

11. Michelle Kwan is a ______.
12. One fun activity in winter is ______.
13. A famous monument in Washington, D.C., is ______.
14. A hero to many young people is ______.
15. One of the century's greatest inventions was ______.

Basic English Grammar

TRL

Workbook Activity 56

Name Date Period

Activity 56
Chapter 10, Lesson 5

Object or Predicate Noun?

Pattern 5 Sentence: Subject + Linking Verb + Predicate Noun

Directions Look at the word in bold in each sentence. Decide whether it is a direct object or a predicate noun. Write *direct object* or *predicate noun* on the line.

EXAMPLES My mother is an accomplished **musician**. predicate noun
Mr. Deans has taught **history** for years. direct object

1. Paul is the best **player** on the football team. ______
2. My aunt makes chewy **cookies**. ______
3. Sky diving is a dangerous **sport**. ______
4. Uncle Tom is the tallest **member** of our family. ______
5. The yearbook staff has many hard **tasks** ahead of them. ______
6. Will our baseball team become the **victors**? ______
7. Your dog licked my best **friend**. ______
8. Spring is my favorite **season**. ______
9. Gerald Ford was a **president** of the United States. ______
10. Geography is a very interesting **subject**. ______
11. Jill is the **drummer** in a rock band. ______
12. Morris mailed the **letter** on Friday. ______
13. Terry will become a **doctor** someday. ______
14. Thomas is the friendliest **person** in this school. ______
15. Leslie and John gave their **presentation** yesterday. ______

Basic English Grammar

TRL

Activity 56

Lesson 5 Review Answers

1. linking verb 2. action verb 3. action verb 4. linking verb 5. action verb 6. S—foods; LV—are; PN—tacos, burritos 7. S—Jupiter, LV—is, PN—planet 8. LV—Is, S—Dan, PN—friend 9. S—Who, LV—was, PN—that 10. S—Lima, LV—is, PN—capital

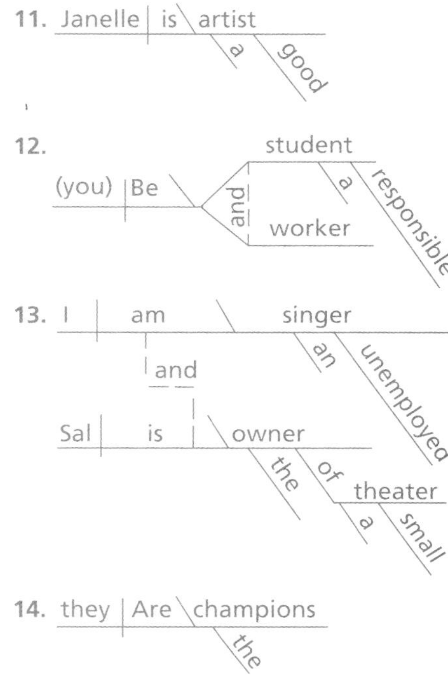

14. they | Are \ champions
the

15. Jack | is \ friend
a
of
mine

At Home

Have students interview a parent or sibling, copying down responses or using a tape recorder. Ask them to choose two or three Pattern 5 sentences from the interview and to diagram them following the instructions on pages 261 and 262. Invite volunteers to draw their interview diagrams on the board.

Lesson at a Glance

Chapter 10 Lesson 6

Overview This lesson explains predicate adjectives used in Pattern 6 sentences.

Objectives

- To identify predicate adjectives.
- To write Pattern 6 sentences.
- To diagram Pattern 6 sentences.

Student Pages 264–271

Teacher's Resource Library TRL

- **Workbook Activity** 57
- **Activity** 57
- **Alternative Activity** 57
- **Diagramming Activity** 6

Vocabulary

predicate adjective

1 Warm-Up Activity

Write on the board the following sentences: *She is a doctor. She is interesting.* Ask students to identify the Pattern 5 sentence. Elicit that the first example, with the linking verb *is* and the predicate noun *doctor*, fits this pattern. Then ask students how the second sentence is different from the first. They should understand that the only difference is that the adjective *interesting* has replaced the noun *doctor.* Write *subject, linking verb,* and *predicate adjective* on the board. Explain that this sequence represents a Pattern 6 sentence. Invite students to create Pattern 6 sentences about themselves, friends, or members of their family.

2 Teaching the Lesson

Write the following Pattern 6 sentence on the board: *Ramon is intelligent.* Invite students to think of other verbs that could substitute for *is* and still make sense. Elicit words such as *appears, seems,* and *looks.* Point out that these are also linking verbs, relating the subject to the predicate of the sentence. Remind students that linking verbs are always state-of-being verbs. Refer them to the definition of state-of-being verbs on page 120. Point out that while the verb *be* is still the principal linking verb, Pattern 6 sentences may use any of the verbs listed in the box on page 121. Invite students to use a selection of these words as linking verbs in Pattern 6 sentences.

Activity A

Write the first item in Activity A on the board. Invite volunteers to take turns completing the sentence with different predicate adjectives. After students complete Activity A on their own, invite them to share their sentences with the class.

Activity A Answers

Answers will vary. Possible answers follow. **1.** Today the air feels cool. **2.** The sky looks overcast. **3.** The day has been long. **4.** Everyone seems happy. **5.** They appear content. **6.** Jim looks unhappy. **7.** That painting is beautiful. **8.** The taco tastes bland. **9.** The music sounds loud. **10.** Amanda seems bored.

Lesson 6 Pattern 6 Sentences (Predicate Adjectives)

> ***Predicate adjective***
> *An adjective that follows a linking verb and tells about the subject*

A Pattern 6 sentence has a linking verb and a **predicate adjective.** When an adjective appears after a linking verb, the adjective describes the subject. This adjective is called a predicate adjective. It is part of the complete predicate, but it describes the subject of the sentence.

> Sometimes we use abbreviations in place of longer words. Take a look at this abbreviation. You will see it used in this lesson.
>
> PA = predicate adjective

Pattern 6 Sentence:
Subject + Linking Verb + Predicate Adjective

EXAMPLE

S LV PA PA
The orange is juicy and sweet.
(*Juicy* and *sweet* are adjectives. What *is juicy and sweet?* The *orange* is juicy and sweet.)

Activity A Complete each sentence with a predicate adjective. Write the new sentences on your paper.

Example S LV PA
This video game is expensive.

1. Today the air feels ______.
2. The sky looks ______.
3. The day has been ______.
4. Everyone seems ______.
5. They appear ______.
6. Jim looks ______.
7. That painting is ______.
8. The taco tastes ______.
9. The music sounds ______.
10. Amanda seems ______.

Activity B Create three columns on your paper with the titles *Subject, Linking Verb,* and *Predicate Adjective.* Then identify the simple subject, the linking verb, and the predicate adjective in each sentence. Write them in the correct column.

Example Kiara's project was interesting.

Subject	Linking Verb	Predicate Adjective
project	was	interesting

1. My cousin is artistic.
2. The sauce tasted spicy.
3. That note sounds flat.
4. The little girl became sleepy.
5. The young actor appeared nervous.

A Pattern 6 sentence may have an adverb that tells about the predicate adjective. Adverbs of degree answer questions about adjectives.

S LV Adv. PA
Her plan sounded very risky.

Activity C Write these sentences on your paper. Add an adverb of degree to each sentence that tells about the predicate adjective in bold.

Example I feel **good** today.
I feel extremely good today.

1. She looks **happy.**
2. He sounds **tired.**
3. The day turned **cold.**
4. They appeared **calm.**
5. You seem **worried.**

Activity B

Do this activity together as a class. Discuss the example. Then draw a chart on the board with the headings: *Subject, Linking Verb,* and *Predicate Adjective.* Invite volunteers to fill in the chart as students identify the subject, linking verb, and predicate adjective in each sentence. As a follow-up to this activity, you might invite students to replace the predicate adjective in each sentence with another adjective that changes the meaning of the sentence.

Activity B Answers

1. S—cousin, LV—is, PA—artistic **2.** S—sauce, LV—tasted, PA—spicy **3.** S—note, LV—sounds, PA—flat **4.** S—girl, LV—became, PA—sleepy **5.** S—actor, LV—appeared, PA—nervous

Activity C

Before they complete Activity C on their own, work with students to create a list of adverbs of degree. Suggest that students refer to the list as they complete Activity C and try to use a different adverb in each sentence.

Activity C Answers

Answers will vary. Possible answers follow. **1.** She looks extremely happy. **2.** He sounds very tired. **3.** The day turned rather cold. **4.** They appeared somewhat calm. **5.** You seem really worried.

3 Reinforce and Extend

Learning Styles

Auditory/Verbal

Invite a volunteer to be a television meteorologist and read the following forecast to the class:

Today is cloudy and cool. Tomorrow will be overcast. Temperatures will be around 50 degrees. Expect to see some rain tomorrow night. Temperatures on Friday will be much warmer. From here, the weekend looks good. Have a great day.

Ask students to listen closely for Pattern 6 sentences. Then have the volunteer repeat the forecast slowly, stopping after each sentence. Students should identify the sentences containing predicate adjectives. Write their selections on the board and discuss any difficulties.

Sentence Patterns Chapter 10 265

Activity D

Write these sentences on the board: *The children became restless. That girl seems shy.* Ask students to identify the predicate adjective in each sentence. Invite volunteers to add adverbs or prepositional phrases to each sentence to tell about the predicate adjective. Following this, have students complete Activity D on their own.

Activity D Answers

Answers will vary. Possible answers follow. **1.** Yvonne looks amused by the story. **2.** The sky grew dark before the storm. **3.** This salad tastes delicious with our meal. **4.** Lydia seems very quiet. **5.** Her notebook is extremely neat.

Learning Styles

Interpersonal/Group Learning

Have students form small groups, and ask them to compose three original Pattern 6 sentences. (If students need help, suggest that they alter one of the activity items in this lesson.) Then instruct them to work together to write each sentence as a question. Invite a spokesperson from each group to read aloud one of the original statements. Give the listening groups a brief period to confer and to repeat the statement as a question.

A Pattern 6 sentence can have adverbs and prepositional phrases. They give more information about the predicate adjective.

She is always busy on Saturday.
How often is she busy? *She is* always *busy.* When is she always busy? *She is always busy* on Saturday.

Activity D Write these sentences on your paper. Underline the predicate adjectives in each sentence. Then add adverbs or prepositional phrases that tell about the predicate adjective.

1. Yvonne looks amused.
2. The sky grew dark.
3. This salad tastes delicious.
4. Lydia seems quiet.
5. Her notebook is neat.

A Pattern 6 sentence may be a question. In a Pattern 6 question, the predicate adjective may come right after the subject. Use the verb or part of a verb phrase to form the question.

LV S LV PA
Did his speech seem short?

A Pattern 6 sentence may be a command or request. Commands are always in the present tense. Use the infinitive form of linking verbs in commands.

LV PA
Be quiet.

Activity E Write these sentences on your paper. Circle the subject. Underline the linking verb once and the predicate adjective twice.

Example Is your friend upset about something?

1. Look friendly during the job interview.
2. Does the school day seem longer to you?
3. Was she excited about the play?
4. Will these flowers stay fresh until Friday?
5. Remain loyal and true to your friends.

In a Pattern 6 sentence, the predicate adjective may be compound.

EXAMPLE

S LV PA PA
Roberto's speech was short and funny.

Activity F Complete each sentence with compound predicate adjectives. Write the new sentences on your paper.

1. The new curtains were _______ and _______.
2. It was not an easy victory for _______ or _______.
3. Andy's new bike is _______ but not _______.
4. The month of May is _______ and _______.
5. After a big dinner, I am usually _______ and _______.

A compound sentence has two complete thoughts.

Add a conjunction to two Pattern 6 sentences to form a compound sentence.

EXAMPLE

S LV PA S LV PA
Mrs. Cruz is usually serious, but Mr. Santos is always funny.

Activity G First, write two related Pattern 6 sentences. Then use one of these conjunctions—and, for, or, but—to create a compound sentence.

Learning Styles

LEP/ESL

Help students who are learning English understand the role of coordinating conjunctions. Have them work in groups with students who are proficient in English. Give them the following Pattern 6 sentences. *He looks old. Michelle was chilly. The sun is bright. Be quiet.* Ask groups to write related sentences (in any pattern) and to connect them to the given sentences with *and, or, but,* or *for.* Have groups write one compound sentence for each of the conjunctions.

Teacher Alert

Remind students to put a comma before the conjunction in a compound sentence.

Activity E

Some students may have trouble identifying the subject or the verb in questions. Suggest that these students change each question into a statement and then try to find the subject, verb, and predicate adjective.

Activity E Answers

1. (You) Look friendly during the job interview. **2.** Does the school day seem longer to you? **3.** Was she excited about the play? **4.** Will these flowers stay fresh until Friday? **5.** (You) Remain loyal and true to your friends.

Activity F

Remind students that the coordinating conjunctions *and, but,* and *or* connect words that do the same job in a sentence. Then write the first item in Activity F on the board and have volunteers take turns completing the sentence with different compound adjectives. After students complete Activity F on their own, invite them to share their sentences with the class.

Activity F Answers

Answers will vary. Possible answers follow. **1.** The new curtains were crisp and flowery. **2.** It was not an easy victory for the coach or the team. **3.** Andy's new bike is sleek but not expensive. **4.** The month of May is sunny and warm. **5.** After a big dinner, I am usually full and sleepy.

Activity G

Before having students complete Activity G on their own, emphasize that the two ideas expressed in a compound sentence must be related. If necessary, illustrate this concept with the following examples:

Incorrect: The test was long, and the day grew cold.

Correct: The test was long, and the questions were difficult.

Activity G Answers

Answers will vary. Possible answers follow. Their smiles were bright. Their voices sounded cheerful. Their smiles were bright, and their voices sounded cheerful.

Learning Styles

Logical/Mathematical

Have students study the Pattern 6 sentence diagrams on pages 268 and 269, while you copy the example sentences on the board. Then invite volunteers to draw the six diagram outlines on the board. Ask students to close their books and match the sentences to the diagrams, putting the words into the correct spaces. Finally, erase all the words except the linking verbs from the diagrams, and invite students to create new sentences using the same diagram outlines.

Learning Styles

Visual/Spatial

Have students draw on the board a chart with columns headed *Subject, Verb, Predicate Adjective,* and *Other.* Then invite students to read aloud 10 sentences from the activities in this lesson while a volunteer writes the words in the correct column. Include adverbs, prepositional phrases, and other adjectives, in the *Other* column. Now have pairs of students compose two original Pattern 6 sentences from the items on the chart. Encourage them to create one serious and one nonsensical sentence and to diagram both of them. Invite students to draw their diagrams on the board.

In the Community

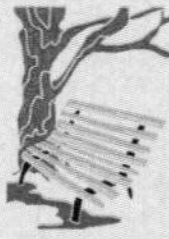

Invite a community service representative to speak to the class about the work his or her organization does to benefit the community. Suggest that the speaker use diagrams and other graphic aids, such as a slide presentation, to create interest for student listeners.

Diagramming Pattern 6 Sentences

To diagram a Pattern 6 sentence:

1. Place the predicate adjective on the baseline of the diagram.
2. Separate the predicate adjective from the verb with a line slanted toward the verb.

EXAMPLE The lilacs smelled sweet.

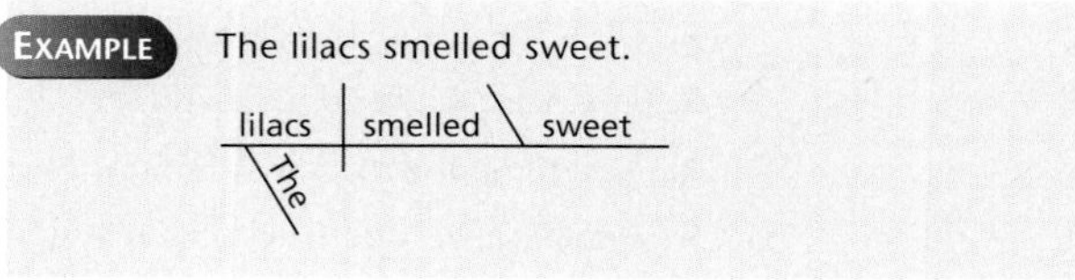

3. Place an adverb of degree under the adjective on a slanted line.

EXAMPLE The salad was very tasty.

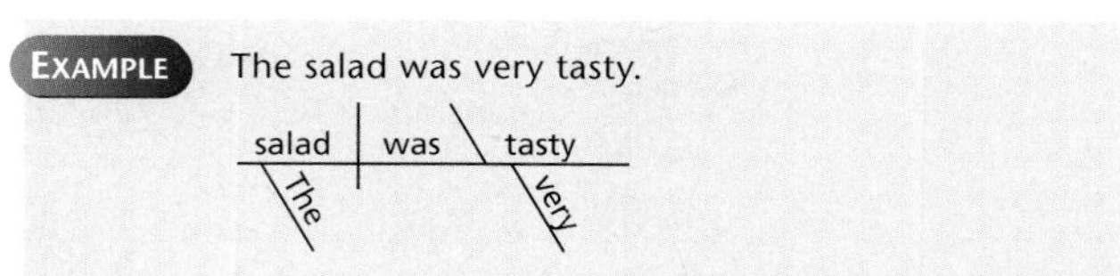

4. If a Pattern 6 sentence is a question, change the question to a statement. Then draw the diagram.

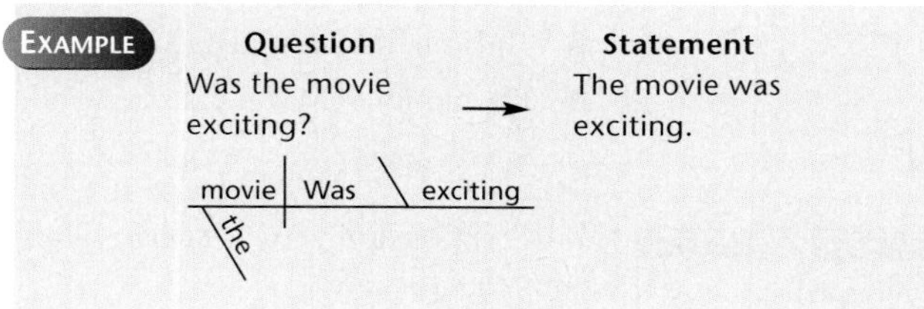

5. In a command or request, the subject *you* is understood. Put *you* in parentheses.

EXAMPLE Be kind.

6. Diagram a compound predicate adjective this way.

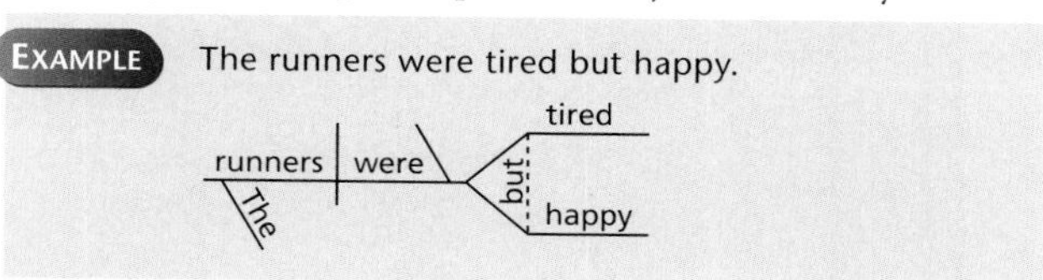

7. Diagram a compound Pattern 6 sentence this way.

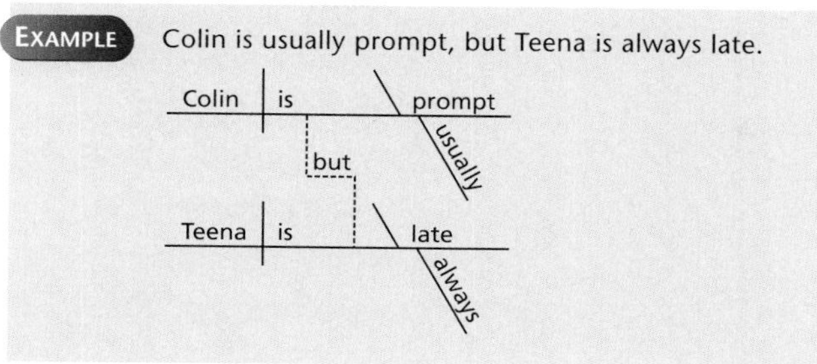

Activity H Diagram these Pattern 6 sentences on your paper. If you need help, look at the rules and examples that begin on page 268.

1. Monday morning was extremely windy, but the air was warm.
2. Stay quiet and absolutely still.
3. Is your puppy afraid of loud noises?
4. Is Emily usually calm during a thunderstorm?
5. The audience grew quiet.

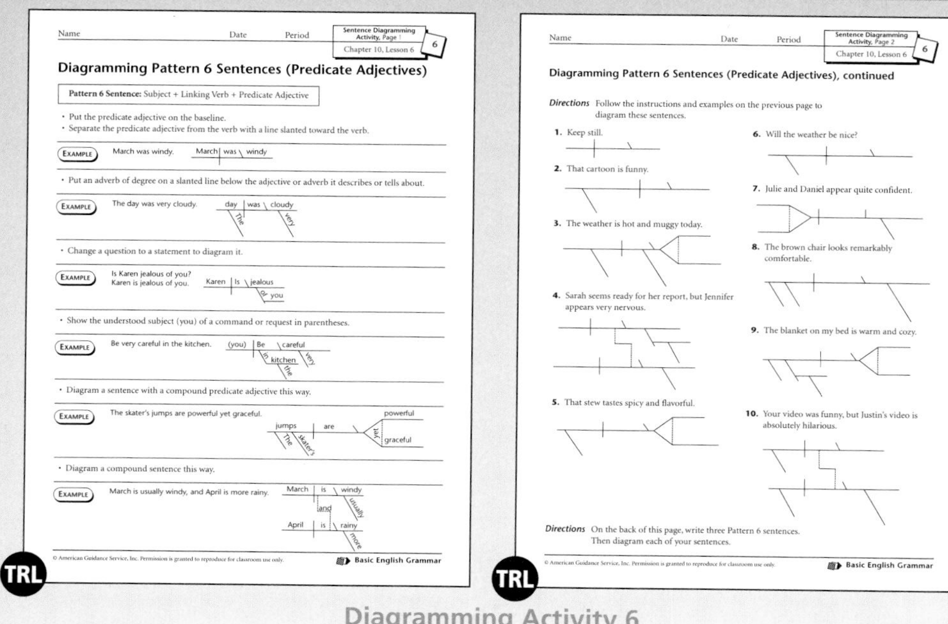

Name Date Period

Sentence Diagramming Activity, Page 1 — Chapter 10, Lesson 6 — 6

Diagramming Pattern 6 Sentences (Predicate Adjectives)

Pattern 6 Sentence: Subject + Linking Verb + Predicate Adjective

- Put the predicate adjective on the baseline.
- Separate the predicate adjective from the verb with a line slanted toward the verb.

EXAMPLE March was windy. March | was \ windy

- Put an adverb of degree on a slanted line below the adjective or adverb it describes or tells about.

EXAMPLE The day was very cloudy. day | was \ cloudy / The / very

- Change a question to a statement to diagram it.

EXAMPLE Is Karen jealous of you? Karen is jealous of you. Karen | Is \ jealous / of you

- Show the understood subject (you) of a command or request in parentheses.

EXAMPLE Be very careful in the kitchen. (you) | Be \ careful / in kitchen / the / very

- Diagram a sentence with a compound predicate adjective this way.

EXAMPLE The skater's jumps are powerful yet graceful. jumps | are \ powerful / yet / graceful / The / skater's

- Diagram a compound sentence this way.

EXAMPLE March is usually windy, and April is more rainy. March | is \ windy / usually / and / April | is \ rainy / more

 Basic English Grammar

Name Date Period

Sentence Diagramming Activity, Page 2 — Chapter 10, Lesson 6 — 6

Diagramming Pattern 6 Sentences (Predicate Adjectives), continued

Directions Follow the instructions and examples on the previous page to diagram these sentences.

1. Keep still.
2. That cartoon is funny.
3. The weather is hot and muggy today.
4. Sarah seems ready for her report, but Jennifer appears very nervous.
5. That stew tastes spicy and flavorful.
6. Will the weather be nice?
7. Julie and Daniel appear quite confident.
8. The brown chair looks remarkably comfortable.
9. The blanket on my bed is warm and cozy.
10. Your video was funny, but Justin's video is absolutely hilarious.

Directions On the back of this page, write three Pattern 6 sentences. Then diagram each of your sentences.

 Basic English Grammar

TRL TRL

Diagramming Activity 6

Activity H

Write these sentences in a row across the top of the board. *She seemed terribly sorry about the accident. Stay warm and dry. Is dinner finally ready?* Then ask for pairs of volunteers to diagram each sentence on the board. Have the class check each diagram and point out any mistakes to be corrected. Then have students complete Activity H on their own.

Activity H Answers

1.

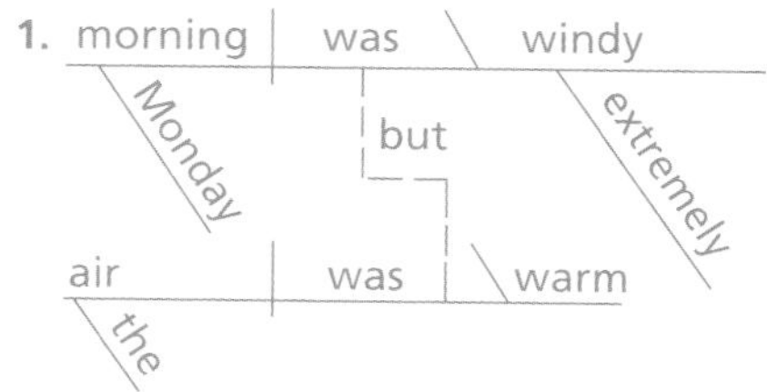

2.

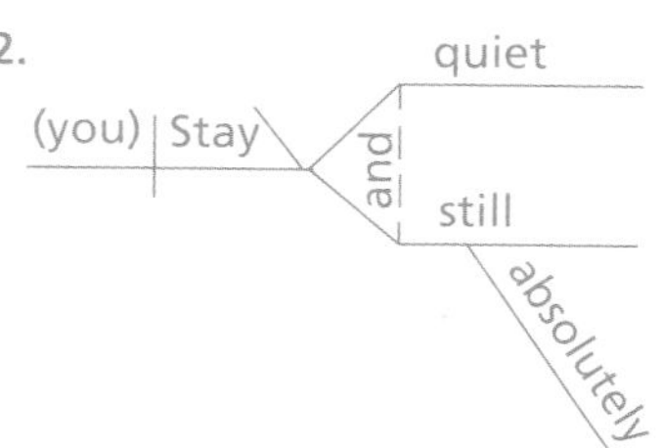

3.

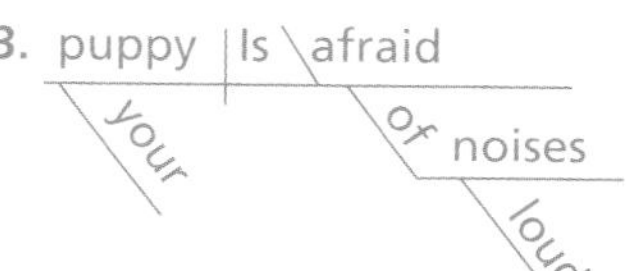

4.

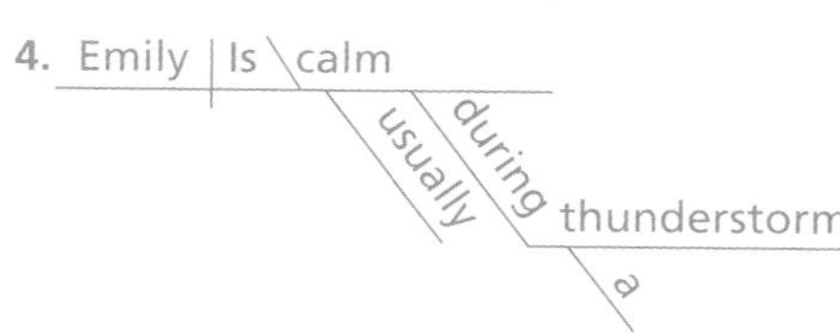

5. audience | grew \ quiet / The

Sentence Patterns Chapter 10 269

Lesson 6 Review Answers

1. S—lemon, LV—tasted, PA—sour
2. S—Sue, LV—appears, PA—friendly
3. S—James, LV—is, PA—athletic 4. LV—Have been, S—they, PA—active
5. S—computer; LV—is; PA—small, powerful

6.

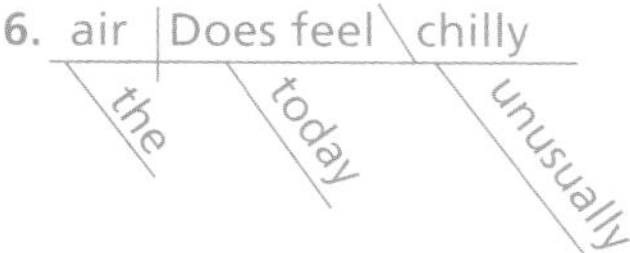

7.

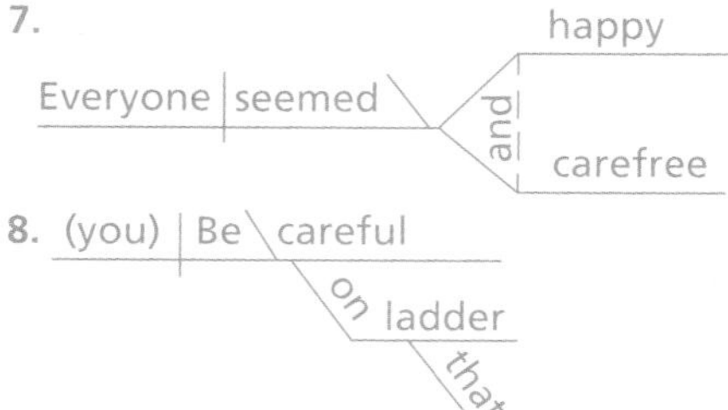

9.

10.

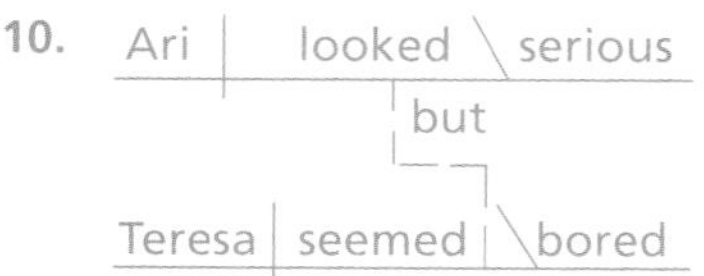

Writing Project

Review with students the six sentence patterns they have studied. Write on the board a sample sentence for each pattern and invite volunteers to draw diagrams for the samples.

Have the class make a list that identifies things a creature from another planet might notice if it visited your school. Suggest to students that items familiar to them—clothing, food, books, desks, hairstyles—would be strange to an extraterrestrial. Encourage students to refer to the list when writing their sentences.

Lesson 6 REVIEW

Write these sentences on your paper. Write *S* above the subject, *LV* above the linking verb, *PA* above the predicate adjective.

1. The lemon tasted sour.
2. Sue appears friendly.
3. James is very athletic.
4. Have they always been so active?
5. That computer is small but powerful.

Diagram these Pattern 6 sentences on your paper.

6. Does the air feel unusually chilly today?
7. Everyone seemed happy and carefree.
8. Be careful on that ladder!
9. Was my speech too long?
10. Ari looked serious, but Teresa seemed bored.

Writing Project

Using Different Sentence Patterns

Use different sentence patterns to make your writing more interesting.

1. Imagine that a creature from another planet visited your school. Use all six sentence patterns to write sentences about the things and activities the creature would see.
2. When you have finished writing, go back and identify the main parts of each of your sentences.

Example S V
Pattern 1 People in the halls are laughing.

S V DO
Pattern 2 The students carry books to their lockers.

This activity will help you identify parts of speech, and also help you see the sentence patterns you use most often. Try to add new patterns to your writing to add interest and variety.

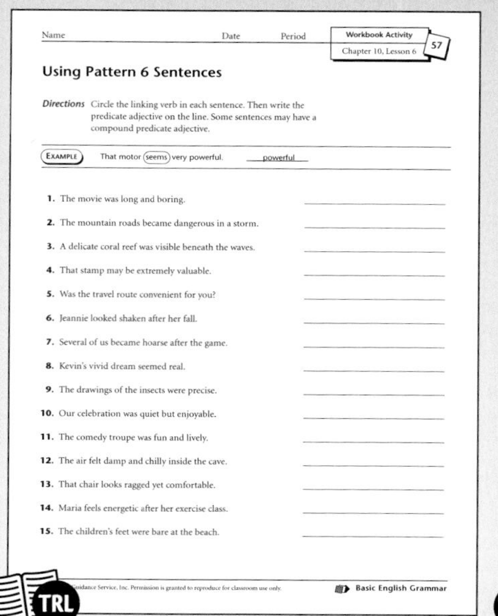

Name Date Period **Workbook Activity** Chapter 10, Lesson 6 57

Using Pattern 6 Sentences

Directions Circle the linking verb in each sentence. Then write the predicate adjective on the line. Some sentences may have a compound predicate adjective.

EXAMPLE That motor (seems) very powerful. powerful

1. The movie was long and boring. ______
2. The mountain roads became dangerous in a storm. ______
3. A delicate coral reef was visible beneath the waves. ______
4. That stamp may be extremely valuable. ______
5. Was the travel route convenient for you? ______
6. Jeannie looked shaken after her fall. ______
7. Several of us became hoarse after the game. ______
8. Kevin's vivid dream seemed real. ______
9. The drawings of the insects were precise. ______
10. Our celebration was quiet but enjoyable. ______
11. The comedy troupe was fun and lively. ______
12. The air felt damp and chilly inside the cave. ______
13. That chair looks ragged yet comfortable. ______
14. Maria feels energetic after her exercise class. ______
15. The children's feet were bare at the beach. ______

 Basic English Grammar

TRL

Workbook Activity 57

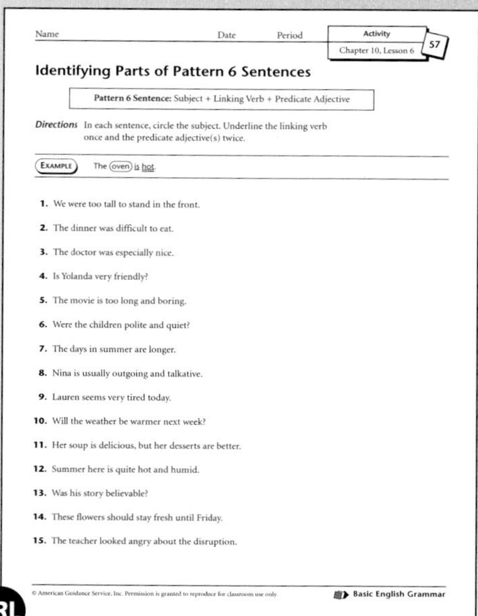

Name Date Period **Activity** Chapter 10, Lesson 6 57

Identifying Parts of Pattern 6 Sentences

Pattern 6 Sentence: Subject + Linking Verb + Predicate Adjective

Directions In each sentence, circle the subject. Underline the linking verb once and the predicate adjective(s) twice.

EXAMPLE The (oven) is hot.

1. We were too tall to stand in the front.
2. The dinner was difficult to eat.
3. The doctor was especially nice.
4. Is Yolanda very friendly?
5. The movie is too long and boring.
6. Were the children polite and quiet?
7. The days in summer are longer.
8. Nina is usually outgoing and talkative.
9. Lauren seems very tired today.
10. Will the weather be warmer next week?
11. Her soup is delicious, but her desserts are better.
12. Summer here is quite hot and humid.
13. Was his story believable?
14. These flowers should stay fresh until Friday.
15. The teacher looked angry about the disruption.

 Basic English Grammar

TRL

Activity 57

Sentence Pattern REVIEW

Diagram these sentences. There are at least two of each of the six sentence patterns.

1. Is Mrs. Simpson your math teacher?
2. The Smiths named their puppy Fluffy.
3. The blue van skidded right suddenly.
4. Sara ate a sandwich for lunch.
5. Did Rebecca seem nervous?
6. Send Jake a birthday card today and tell him about the party.
7. Janna painted the mural blue.
8. The football team will travel to Columbus and will play for the championship.
9. That house looks shabby and old.
10. Teresa won a set, but Jack won the match.
11. Did Rico send you an e-mail message?
12. Be nice to your sister!
13. After lunch, we played basketball for two hours.
14. Give me the hammer and then hand me some nails.
15. Her speech was lively and entertaining.

Sentence Pattern Review Answers

1.

2.

3.
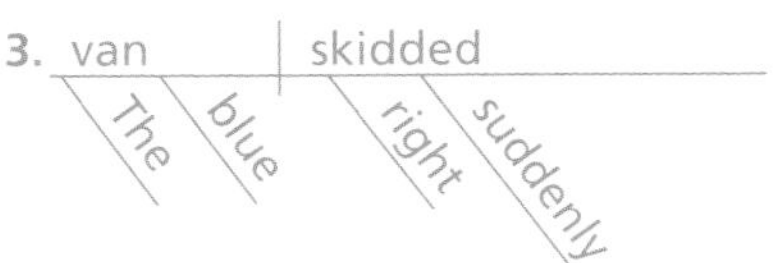

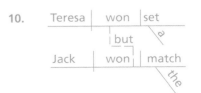

4. Sara | ate | sandwich — for lunch — a

5. Rebecca | Did seem \ nervous

6.
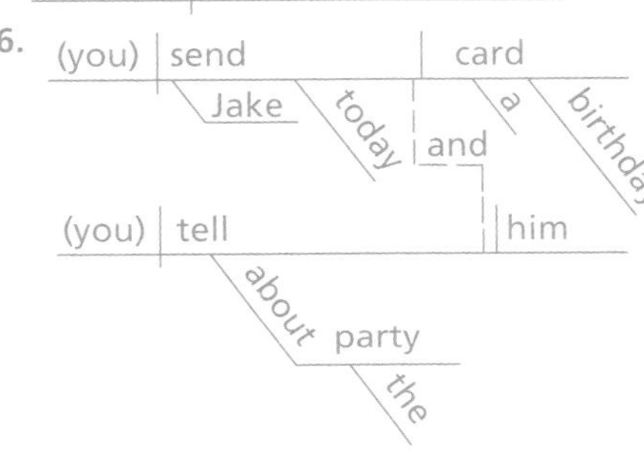

7.

8.
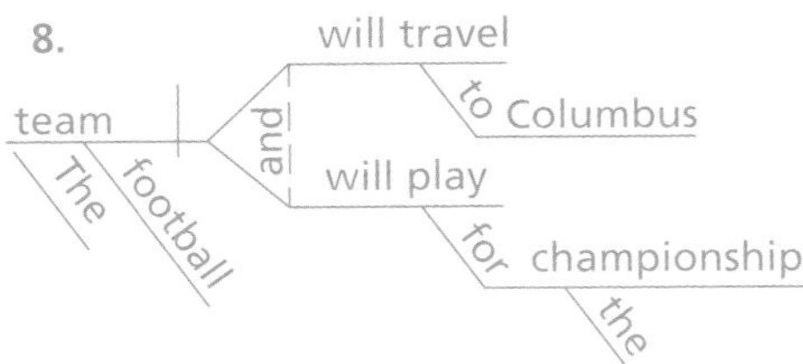

9.
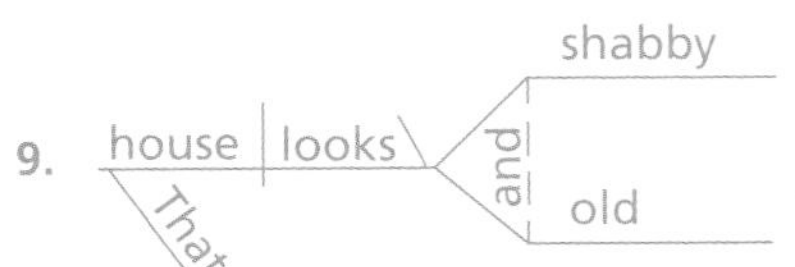

10.
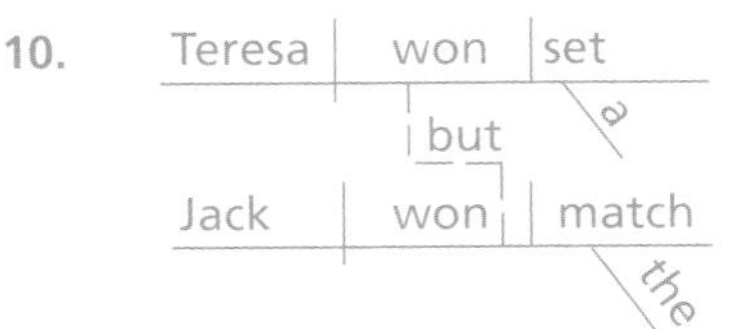

11.

12. 13.
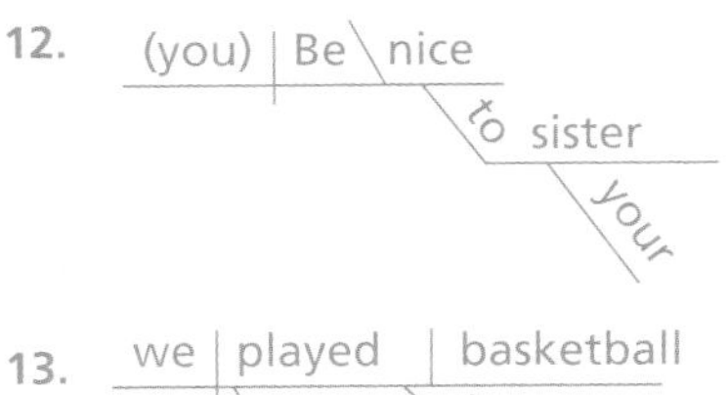

14.
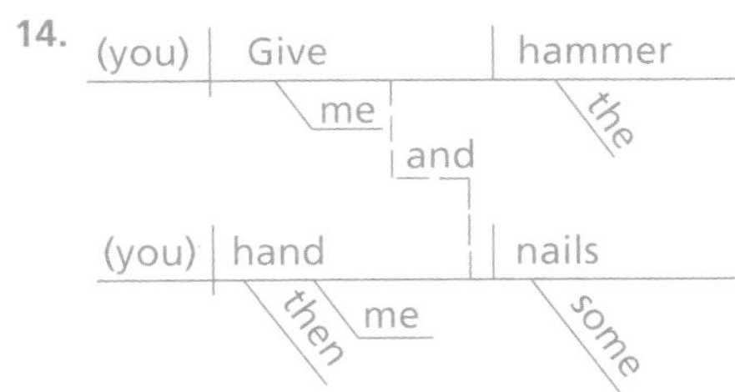

15.
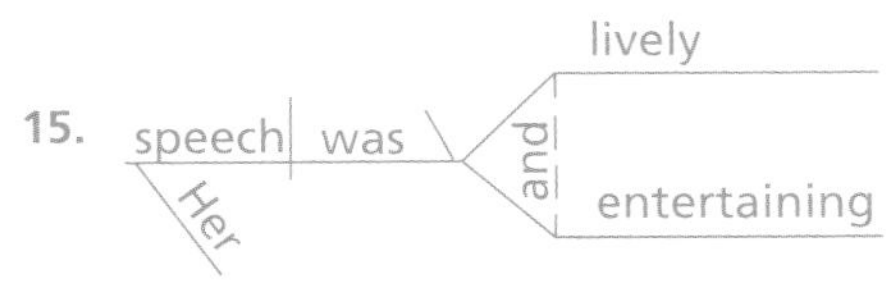

Chapter 10 Review

Use the Chapter Review to prepare students for tests and to reteach content from the chapter.

Chapter 10 Mastery Test 

The Teacher's Resource Library includes two parallel forms of the Chapter 10 Mastery Test. The difficulty level of the two forms is equivalent. You may wish to use one form as a pretest and the other form as a posttest.

Review Answers

Part A

1. transitive verb **2.** intransitive verb **3.** direct object **4.** simple predicate **5.** indirect object **6.** complement **7.** object complement **8.** linking verb **9.** predicate noun **10.** predicate adjective

Part B

11. transitive **12.** intransitive **13.** intransitive **14.** transitive

Part C

15. Jiro—indirect object **16.** president—object complement **17.** money—direct object **18.** Have read—verb phrase **19.** song—direct object

Chapter 10 REVIEW

Word Bank
complement
direct object
indirect object
intransitive verb
linking verb
object complement
predicate adjective
predicate noun
simple predicate
transitive verb

Part A On a sheet of paper, write the correct word or words from the Word Bank to complete each sentence.

1. A ________ shows action passed from the subject of the sentence toward a person or thing.

2. An ________ does not transfer action from the subject to an object.

3. A ________ is a noun or pronoun that receives the action from a transitive verb.

4. A ________ is the verb or verb phrase.

5. An ________ is a noun or pronoun that tells who receives the direct object of a verb.

6. A ________ is a word that completes the meaning of the verb.

7. A noun or an adjective that follows the verb and refers to a direct object is an ________ .

8. A state-of-being verb that links the subject to a noun, pronoun, or adjective in the predicate is a ________ .

9. A ________ follows a linking verb and renames the subject.

10. A ________ follows a linking verb and tells about the subject.

Part B Write these sentences on your paper. Decide whether the verb in bold is *transitive* or *intransitive*. Write *transitive* or *intransitive* on your paper.

11. One day Mr. Ellis **bought** a computer.

12. The child **stared** at the computer screen.

13. That program **ran** all evening.

14. Mrs. Ellis **keeps** a daily journal on the computer.

Part C Write the word or words in bold on your paper. Identify each word as the *subject, verb or verb phrase, direct object, indirect object, object of the preposition,* or *object complement.*

15. We gave **Jiro** a CD for his birthday.

16. We elected John **president.**

17. The band raised **money** for the trip.

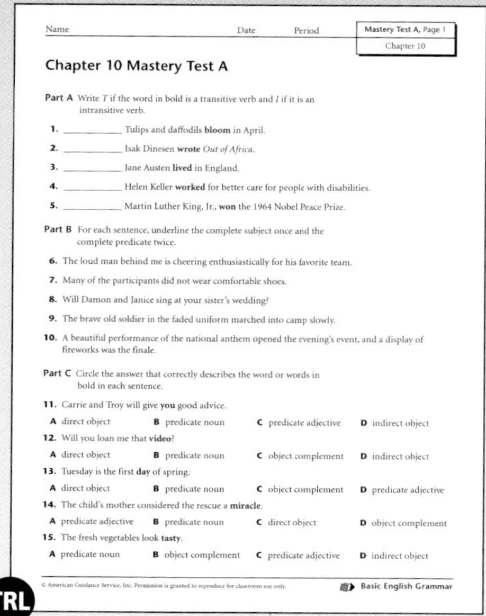

Name Date Period | Mastery Test A, Page 1 | Chapter 10

Chapter 10 Mastery Test A

Part A Write *T* if the word in bold is a transitive verb and *I* if it is an intransitive verb.

1. __________ Tulips and daffodils **bloom** in April.

2. __________ Isak Dinesen **wrote** *Out of Africa.*

3. __________ Jane Austen **lived** in England.

4. __________ Helen Keller **worked** for better care for people with disabilities.

5. __________ Martin Luther King, Jr., **won** the 1964 Nobel Peace Prize.

Part B For each sentence, underline the complete subject once and the complete predicate twice.

6. The loud man behind me is cheering enthusiastically for his favorite team.

7. Many of the participants did not wear comfortable shoes.

8. Will Damon and Janice sing at your sister's wedding?

9. The brave old soldier in the faded uniform marched into camp slowly.

10. A beautiful performance of the national anthem opened the evening's event, and a display of fireworks was the finale.

Part C Circle the answer that correctly describes the word or words in bold in each sentence.

11. Carrie and Troy will give **you** good advice.
A direct object **B** predicate noun **C** predicate adjective **D** indirect object

12. Will you loan me that **video**?
A direct object **B** predicate noun **C** object complement **D** indirect object

13. Tuesday is the first **day** of spring.
A direct object **B** predicate noun **C** object complement **D** predicate adjective

14. The child's mother considered the rescue a **miracle**.
A predicate adjective **B** predicate noun **C** direct object **D** object complement

15. The fresh vegetables look **tasty**.
A predicate noun **B** object complement **C** predicate adjective **D** indirect object

Basic English Grammar

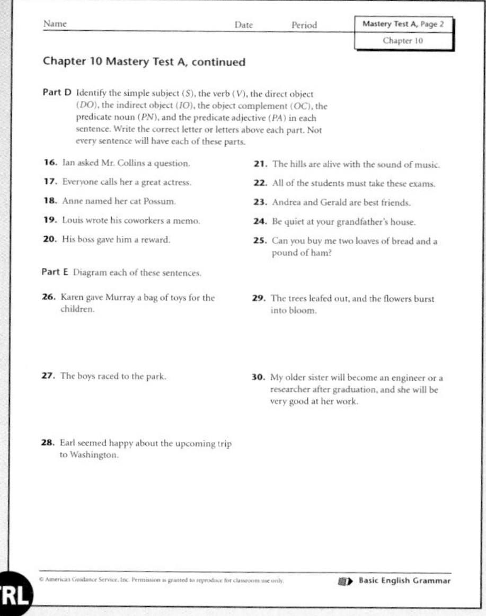

Name Date Period | Mastery Test A, Page 2 | Chapter 10

Chapter 10 Mastery Test A, continued

Part D Identify the simple subject (*S*), the verb (*V*), the direct object (*DO*), the indirect object (*IO*), the object complement (*OC*), the predicate noun (*PN*), and the predicate adjective (*PA*) in each sentence. Write the correct letter or letters above each part. Not every sentence will have each of these parts.

16. Ian asked Mr. Collins a question.

17. Everyone calls her a great actress.

18. Anne named her cat Possum.

19. Louis wrote his coworkers a memo.

20. His boss gave him a reward.

21. The hills are alive with the sound of music.

22. All of the students must take these exams.

23. Andrea and Gerald are best friends.

24. Be quiet at your grandfather's house.

25. Can you buy me two loaves of bread and a pound of ham?

Part E Diagram each of these sentences.

26. Karen gave Murray a bag of toys for the children.

27. The boys raced to the park.

28. Earl seemed happy about the upcoming trip to Washington.

29. The trees leafed out, and the flowers burst into bloom.

30. My older sister will become an engineer or a researcher after graduation, and she will be very good at her work.

Basic English Grammar

Chapter 10 Mastery Test A

18. **Have** you **read** that book?

19. The Rolling Stones recorded that **song.**

Part D Identify the pattern of each sentence. Write the letter of the correct answer on your paper.

20. Try it for yourself.
    - **A** Pattern 1
    - **B** Pattern 2
    - **C** Pattern 3
    - **D** Pattern 6

21. Tamika and Andrea asked their mother a question.
    - **A** Pattern 1
    - **B** Pattern 2
    - **C** Pattern 3
    - **D** Pattern 6

22. Their mother is a well-known lawyer.
    - **A** Pattern 3
    - **B** Pattern 4
    - **C** Pattern 5
    - **D** Pattern 6

23. *Camelot* will always be one of my favorite movies.
    - **A** Pattern 1
    - **B** Pattern 2
    - **C** Pattern 4
    - **D** Pattern 5

24. The message was short but very important.
    - **A** Pattern 3
    - **B** Pattern 4
    - **C** Pattern 5
    - **D** Pattern 6

25. Will you give Sandy some help with her math homework?
    - **A** Pattern 3
    - **B** Pattern 4
    - **C** Pattern 5
    - **D** Pattern 6

Test-Taking Tip

When you don't know the answer to a question, put a check mark beside it and go on. After you finish the test, go back to the check marked questions. Try again to answer them.

Review Answers

Part D

20. B 21. C 22. C 23. D 24. D 25. A

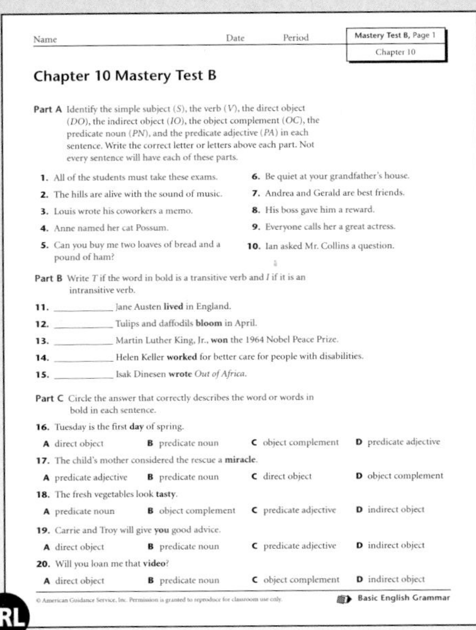

Name Date Period | Mastery Test B, Page 1 | Chapter 10

Chapter 10 Mastery Test B

Part A Identify the simple subject (*S*), the verb (*V*), the direct object (*DO*), the indirect object (*IO*), the object complement (*OC*), the predicate noun (*PN*), and the predicate adjective (*PA*) in each sentence. Write the correct letter or letters above each part. Not every sentence will have each of these parts.

1. All of the students must take these exams.
2. The hills are alive with the sound of music.
3. Louis wrote his coworkers a memo.
4. Anne named her cat Possum.
5. Can you buy me two loaves of bread and a pound of ham?
6. Be quiet at your grandfather's house.
7. Andrea and Gerald are best friends.
8. His boss gave him a reward.
9. Everyone calls her a great actress.
10. Ian asked Mr. Collins a question.

Part B Write *T* if the word in bold is a transitive verb and *I* if it is an intransitive verb.

11. __________ Jane Austen **lived** in England.
12. __________ Tulips and daffodils **bloom** in April.
13. __________ Martin Luther King, Jr., **won** the 1964 Nobel Peace Prize.
14. __________ Helen Keller **worked** for better care for people with disabilities.
15. __________ Isak Dinesen **wrote** *Out of Africa*.

Part C Circle the answer that correctly describes the word or words in bold in each sentence.

16. Tuesday is the first **day** of spring.
    - **A** direct object
    - **B** predicate noun
    - **C** object complement
    - **D** predicate adjective
17. The child's mother considered the rescue a **miracle**.
    - **A** predicate adjective
    - **B** predicate noun
    - **C** direct object
    - **D** object complement
18. The fresh vegetables look **tasty**.
    - **A** predicate noun
    - **B** object complement
    - **C** predicate adjective
    - **D** indirect object
19. Carrie and Troy will give **you** good advice.
    - **A** direct object
    - **B** predicate noun
    - **C** predicate adjective
    - **D** indirect object
20. Will you loan me that **video**?
    - **A** direct object
    - **B** predicate noun
    - **C** object complement
    - **D** indirect object

 Basic English Grammar

TRL

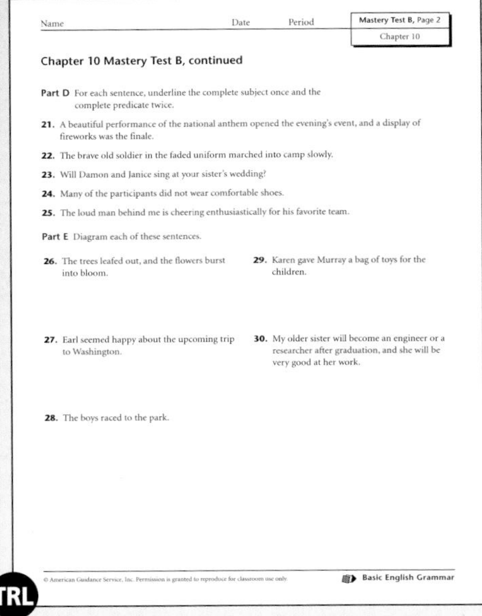

Name Date Period | Mastery Test B, Page 2 | Chapter 10

Chapter 10 Mastery Test B, continued

Part D For each sentence, underline the complete subject once and the complete predicate twice.

21. A beautiful performance of the national anthem opened the evening's event, and a display of fireworks was the finale.
22. The brave old soldier in the faded uniform marched into camp slowly.
23. Will Damon and Janice sing at your sister's wedding?
24. Many of the participants did not wear comfortable shoes.
25. The loud man behind me is cheering enthusiastically for his favorite team.

Part E Diagram each of these sentences.

26. The trees leafed out, and the flowers burst into bloom.
27. Earl seemed happy about the upcoming trip to Washington.
28. The boys raced to the park.
29. Karen gave Murray a bag of toys for the children.
30. My older sister will become an engineer or a researcher after graduation, and she will be very good at her work.

 Basic English Grammar

TRL

Chapter 10 Mastery Test B

Chapter

11

Planning Guide

Complex Sentences

	Student Text Lesson				Language Skills		
	Student Pages	Vocabulary	Practice Exercises	Lesson Review	Identification Skills	Writing Skills	Punctuation Skills
Lesson 1 What Are Phrases and Clauses?	276–278	✔	✔	✔	✔	✔	✔
Lesson 2 The Adverb Clause	279–281	✔	✔	✔	✔	✔	✔
Lesson 3 The Noun Clause	282–286	✔	✔	✔	✔	✔	✔
Lesson 4 The Adjective Clause	287–289	✔	✔	✔	✔	✔	✔
Lesson 5 Complex & Compound-Complex Sentences	290–295	✔	✔	✔	✔	✔	✔

Chapter Activities

Teacher's Resource Library

Community Connection 11: Searching for Complex Sentences in Manuals

Media and Literature Connection 11: Complex Sentences in Magazine Articles

Assessment Options

Student Text

Chapter 11 Review

Teacher's Resource Library

Chapter 11 Mastery Tests A and B

Student Text Features						Teaching Strategies						Learning Styles						Teacher's Resource Library			
Spelling Builder	Vocabulary Builder	Where To Find It	Writing Project	Using What You've Learned	Writing Tips/Notes/ Technology Notes	Teacher Alert	Online Connection	Applications (Home, Career, Community, Global)	Speaking Practice	Spelling Practice	Writing Practice	Auditory/Verbal	Body/Kinesthetic	Interpersonal/Group Learning	Logical/Mathematical	Visual/Spatial	LEP/ESL	Workbook Activities	Activities	Alternative Activities	Self-Study Guide
	278							277				278						58	58	58	✔
				281	✔	280								281	280			59	59	59	✔
286					✔	282, 283		284		286		284				283	285	60	60	60	✔
		289							288		289				288			61	61	61	✔
			295		✔		293	292, 294				291	292			294	291	62	62	62	✔

Pronunciation Key

a	hat	e	let	ī	ice	ô	order	u̇	put	sh	she	ə { a	in about
ā	age	ē	equal	o	hot	oi	oil	ü	rule	th	thin	e	in taken
ä	far	ėr	term	ō	open	ou	out	ch	child	ŦH	then	i	in pencil
â	care	i	it	ȯ	saw	u	cup	ng	long	zh	measure	o	in lemon
												u	in circus

Alternative Activities

The Teacher's Resource Library (TRL) contains a set of lower-level worksheets called Alternative Activities. These worksheets cover the same content as the regular Activities but are written at a second-grade reading level.

Skill Track Software

Use the Skill Track Software for Basic English Grammar for additional reinforcement of this chapter. The software program allows students using AGS textbooks to be assessed for mastery of each chapter and lesson of the textbook. Students access the software on an individual basis and are assessed with multiple-choice items.

Chapter at a Glance

Chapter 11: Complex Sentences

pages 274–297

Skill Track Software for Basic English Grammar

Teacher's Resource Library TRL

- Workbook Activities 58–62
- Activities 58–62
- Alternative Activities 58–62
- Community Connection 11
- Media and Literature Connection 11
- Chapter 11 Self-Study Guide
- Chapter 11 Mastery Tests A and B

(Answer Keys for the Teacher's Resource Library begin on page 340 of this Teacher's Edition.)

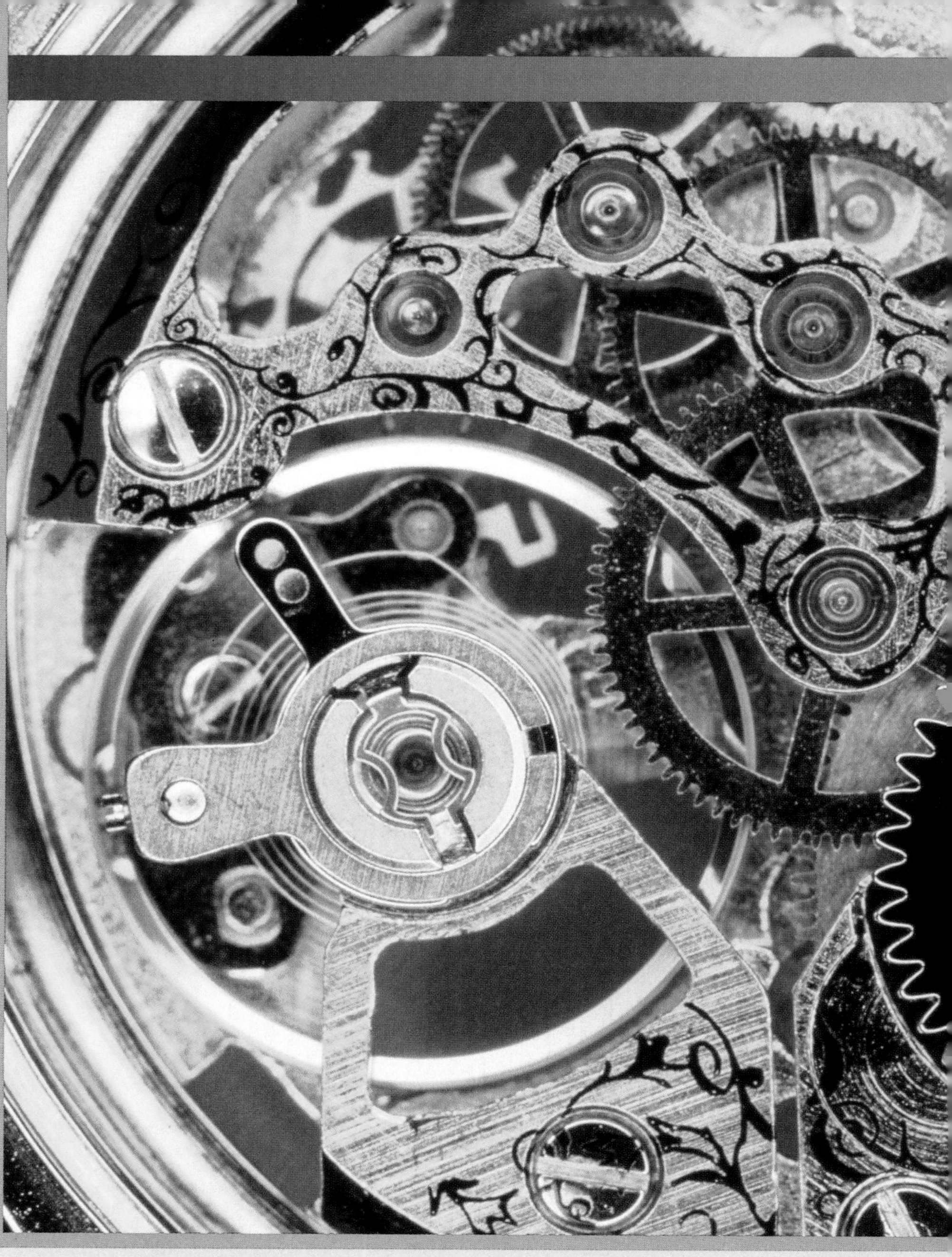

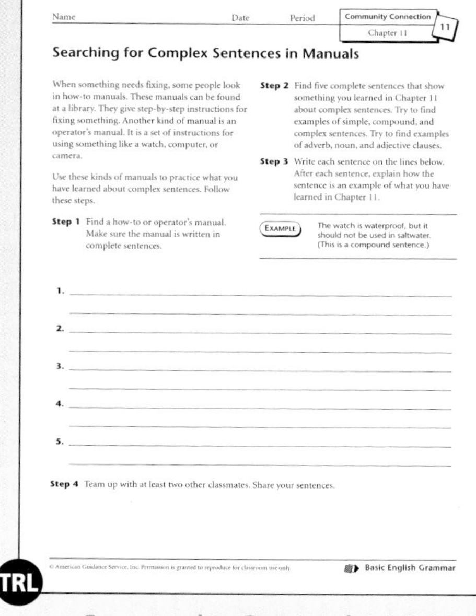

Name Date Period — Community Connection 11, Chapter 11

Searching for Complex Sentences in Manuals

When something needs fixing, some people look in how-to manuals. These manuals can be found at a library. They give step-by-step instructions for fixing something. Another kind of manual is an operator's manual. It is a set of instructions for using something like a watch, computer, or camera.

Use these kinds of manuals to practice what you have learned about complex sentences. Follow these steps.

Step 1 Find a how-to or operator's manual. Make sure the manual is written in complete sentences.

Step 2 Find five complete sentences that show something you learned in Chapter 11 about complex sentences. Try to find examples of simple, compound, and complex sentences. Try to find examples of adverb, noun, and adjective clauses.

Step 3 Write each sentence on the lines below. After each sentence, explain how the sentence is an example of what you have learned in Chapter 11.

EXAMPLE The watch is waterproof, but it should not be used in saltwater. (This is a compound sentence.)

1. ____________
2. ____________
3. ____________
4. ____________
5. ____________

Step 4 Team up with at least two other classmates. Share your sentences.

 Basic English Grammar

TRL Community Connection 11

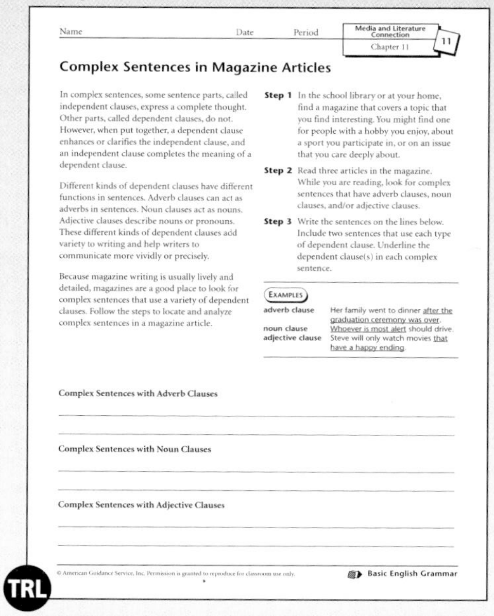

Name Date Period — Media and Literature Connection 11, Chapter 11

Complex Sentences in Magazine Articles

In complex sentences, some sentence parts, called independent clauses, express a complete thought. Other parts, called dependent clauses, do not. However, when put together, a dependent clause enhances or clarifies the independent clause, and an independent clause completes the meaning of a dependent clause.

Different kinds of dependent clauses have different functions in sentences. Adverb clauses can act as adverbs in sentences. Noun clauses act as nouns. Adjective clauses describe nouns or pronouns. These different kinds of dependent clauses add variety to writing and help writers to communicate more vividly or precisely.

Because magazine writing is usually lively and detailed, magazines are a good place to look for complex sentences that use a variety of dependent clauses. Follow the steps to locate and analyze complex sentences in a magazine article.

Step 1 In the school library or at your home, find a magazine that covers a topic that you find interesting. You might find one for people with a hobby you enjoy, about a sport you participate in, or on an issue that you care deeply about.

Step 2 Read three articles in the magazine. While you are reading, look for complex sentences that have adverb clauses, noun clauses, and/or adjective clauses.

Step 3 Write the sentences on the lines below. Include two sentences that use each type of dependent clause. Underline the dependent clause(s) in each complex sentence.

EXAMPLES

adverb clause	Her family went to dinner after the graduation ceremony was over.
noun clause	Whoever is most alert should drive.
adjective clause	Steve will only watch movies that have a happy ending.

Complex Sentences with Adverb Clauses

Complex Sentences with Noun Clauses

Complex Sentences with Adjective Clauses

 Basic English Grammar

TRL Media and Literature Connection 11

Chapter

Complex Sentences

A watch has several parts. Some parts can work alone. Some parts will not work without the help of other parts. This is also true of complex sentences. In a complex sentence, some sentence parts can work independently and others cannot. To write complex sentences that readers will understand, you must put the parts together correctly.

You know that a simple sentence is an independent clause. An independent clause expresses one complete thought and can stand alone. You have learned that a compound sentence has two independent clauses joined by a conjunction. You also know that a dependent clause is a group of words with a subject and a verb. Because a dependent clause does not express a complete idea, it *cannot* stand alone as a sentence.

In Chapter 11, you will learn more about dependent clauses and sentence structure. This chapter focuses on different kinds of dependent clauses. You will learn that you can use them to form complex and compound-complex sentences.

Goals for Learning

- To distinguish among a word, a phrase, and a clause
- To recognize simple, compound, complex, and compound-complex sentences
- To identify adverb, noun, and adjective clauses
- To distinguish between a complex and a compound-complex sentence

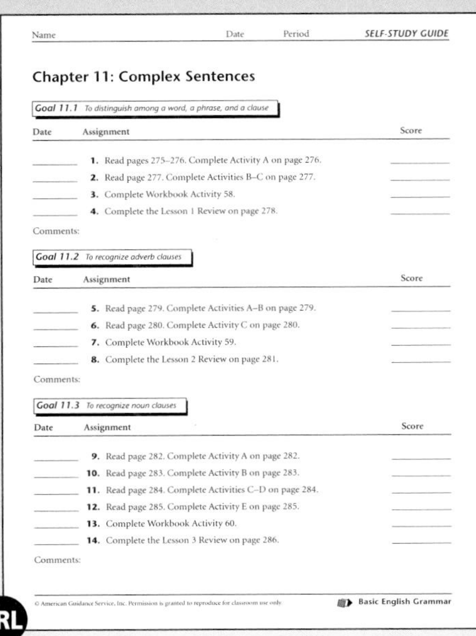

Name Date Period ***SELF-STUDY GUIDE***

Chapter 11: Complex Sentences

Goal 11.1 *To distinguish among a word, a phrase, and a clause*

Date	Assignment	Score
______	**1.** Read pages 275–276. Complete Activity A on page 276.	______
______	**2.** Read page 277. Complete Activities B–C on page 277.	______
______	**3.** Complete Workbook Activity 58.	______
______	**4.** Complete the Lesson 1 Review on page 278.	______

Comments:

Goal 11.2 *To recognize adverb clauses*

Date	Assignment	Score
______	**5.** Read page 279. Complete Activities A–B on page 279.	______
______	**6.** Read page 280. Complete Activity C on page 280.	______
______	**7.** Complete Workbook Activity 59.	______
______	**8.** Complete the Lesson 2 Review on page 281.	______

Comments:

Goal 11.3 *To recognize noun clauses*

Date	Assignment	Score
______	**9.** Read page 282. Complete Activity A on page 282.	______
______	**10.** Read page 283. Complete Activity B on page 283.	______
______	**11.** Read page 284. Complete Activities C–D on page 284.	______
______	**12.** Read page 285. Complete Activity E on page 285.	______
______	**13.** Complete Workbook Activity 60.	______
______	**14.** Complete the Lesson 3 Review on page 286.	______

Comments:

Basic English Grammar

TRL

Name Date Period ***SELF-STUDY GUIDE***

Chapter 11: Complex Sentences, continued

Goal 11.4 *To recognize adjective clauses*

Date	Assignment	Score
______	**15.** Read page 287. Complete Activities A–B on page 287.	______
______	**16.** Read page 288. Complete Activities C–D on page 288.	______
______	**17.** Complete Workbook Activity 61.	______
______	**18.** Complete the Lesson 4 Review on page 289.	______

Comments:

Goal 11.5 *To recognize simple, compound, complex, and compound-complex sentences*

Date	Assignment	Score
______	**19.** Read page 290. Complete Activity A on page 290.	______
______	**20.** Read page 291. Complete Activity B on page 291.	______
______	**21.** Read pages 292–293. Complete Activities C–D on page 293.	______
______	**22.** Read page 294. Complete Activities E–F on page 294.	______
______	**23.** Complete Workbook Activity 62.	______
______	**24.** Complete the Lesson 5 Review on page 295.	______
______	**25.** Complete the Chapter 11 Review on pages 296–297.	______

Comments:

Student's Signature ______________________ Date ________

Instructor's Signature ______________________ Date ________

Basic English Grammar

TRL

Chapter 11 Self-Study Guide, Pages 1–2

Introducing the Chapter

Use the photograph to introduce the idea that in order for something to work properly all the parts must be there and running correctly. Explain that the gears shown are those of a watch. Discuss what would happen if one of the gears were removed. Ask why a watchmaker needs to know which parts to use and where to put them. Then ask students to explain why the parts of a sentence might be compared with the parts of a watch and why writers might be compared with watchmakers. Help students conclude that just as watchmakers need to know how to construct a watch so it will run properly, writers must understand how to construct interesting, varied sentences if they want readers to understand and enjoy what they write. Point out that in Chapter 11, students will identify how to form complex and compound-complex sentences.

Writing Tips, Notes, and Technology Notes

Ask volunteers to read the tips and notes that appear in the margins throughout the chapter. Then discuss them with the class.

Teacher's Resource

The AGS Teaching Strategies in English Transparencies may be used with this chapter. The transparencies add an interactive dimension to expand and enhance the *Basic English Grammar* program content.

Career Interest Inventory

The AGS Harrington-O'Shea Career Decision-Making System–Revised (CDM) may be used with this chapter. Students can use the CDM to explore their interests and identify careers. The CDM defines career areas that are indicated by students' responses on the inventory.

Lesson 1 What Are Phrases and Clauses?

> **Phrase**
> *A group of words that does not contain a subject and predicate, such as a prepositional phrase or a verb phrase*

Before you learn about complex sentences, it is important to understand the meanings of three important terms: *word, phrase,* and *clause.*

A word is a set of letters that has meaning.

A **phrase** is a group of words that does not have a subject and predicate.

Example

Prepositional Phrase	across the street
Verb Phrase	has been

A clause is a group of words with a subject and a verb. There are two kinds of clauses: independent clauses (complete ideas) and dependent clauses (incomplete ideas).

An independent clause is a sentence. It has a subject and a verb and expresses a complete thought.

A dependent clause has a subject and a verb, but it is not a sentence.

Example

Independent Clause	James was happy.
Dependent Clause	Because he passed the test.

Activity A Write on your paper whether each group of words is a *phrase* or a *clause.*

1. over the river
2. if he leaves
3. will have been late
4. the youngest girl in school
5. whoever wants an apple

Lesson at a Glance

Chapter 11 Lesson 1

Overview This lesson explains the difference between phrases and clauses and between dependent and independent clauses.

Objectives

- To distinguish between phrases and clauses.
- To distinguish between dependent and independent clauses.

Student Pages 276–278

Teacher's Resource Library 

- **Workbook Activity** 58
- **Activity** 58
- **Alternative Activity** 58

Vocabulary

phrase

Warm-Up Activity

Write *word, phrase,* and *clause* on the board. Ask students to suggest a definition, explanation, or example for each word. Remind them that they have learned about certain kinds of phrases, such as verb phrases and prepositional phrases. Have volunteers give examples. Also remind students that they have learned about independent clauses. After students have given their suggestions for each word, write a simple definition and an example for each, based on students' suggestions.

Teaching the Lesson

Have students tell the difference between a phrase and a clause and give examples of each. Then ask students to describe the difference between an independent and a dependent clause. Discuss why a dependent clause is not a sentence even though it has a subject and a predicate. Then write these examples on the board:

We climbed to the top of the hill (*independent*)
After we climbed (*dependent*)
They worked on the shed (*independent*)
Until it got dark (*dependent*)

Ask students to identify each example as an independent clause or a dependent clause.

Activity A

Do Activity A orally with the class. Discuss each answer, having students explain how they determined whether the group of words was a phrase or a clause.

Activity A Answers

1. phrase 2. clause 3. phrase 4. phrase 5. clause

Either a subordinating conjunction or a relative pronoun can introduce a dependent clause.

Remember that subordinating conjunctions are words such as *because, if, when,* and *since.* Relative pronouns are words such as *that, which, who, whoever,* and *what.*

EXAMPLE

Independent Clause	Felipe walked to school.
Dependent Clause	Because he missed his ride.

Activity B Write on your paper whether each group of words is a *dependent clause* or an *independent clause.*

1. Whom you asked.
2. That girl is in my class.
3. Until he knows all the answers.
4. The team exercised before practice.
5. Whoever finishes first.

Activity C Write each dependent clause on your paper. Circle the word that introduces the dependent clause in each sentence.

1. Because Shelly left school late, she missed the bus.
2. I will fix dinner if you are hungry.
3. Since he didn't try out for a part, he won't be in the play.
4. We will start the movie when Tony and Maria arrive.
5. If that coat goes on sale, I will buy it.
6. The band members celebrated because the band won first place.
7. Rick admires the man who coaches his team.
8. We will elect the candidate who knows the issues.
9. The witness told the police what she had seen.
10. Hank's Restaurant is closed while the owner looks for a new cook.

Activity B

Write these clauses on the board: *Whenever you are ready/The wind howled during the storm.* Ask the class to identify the dependent clause and the independent clause. Invite volunteers to explain in their own words why the first group of words is a dependent clause and the second group of words is an independent clause. Then have students complete Activity B on their own.

Activity B Answers

1. dependent clause **2.** independent clause **3.** dependent clause **4.** independent clause **5.** dependent clause

Activity C

Before having students work on Activity C, review subordinating conjunctions on pages 187–188 with them. Then do the first two items in Activity C as a class. Point out that the dependent clause can appear at the beginning or end of a sentence.

Activity C Answers

1. (Because) Shelly left school late **2.** (if) you are hungry **3.** (Since) he didn't try out for a part **4.** (when) Tony and Maria arrive **5.** (If) that coat goes on sale **6.** (because) the band won first place **7.** (who) coaches his team **8.** (who) knows the issues **9.** (what) she had seen **10.** (while) the owner looks for a new cook

Reinforce and Extend

GLOBAL CONNECTION

When people are traveling in a country where a different language is spoken, communicating a problem or emergency to authorities can be difficult. Encourage students to create a list of phrases in English that might be helpful for travelers to know in case of a problem or emergency. Divide students into pairs and have them select a country where the people speak a different language from their own. Ask them to research to find the translations of the helpful phrases. Suggest that students look in bilingual dictionaries, talk to language instructors, or interview people in the community who speak the language. Students can then come together to create their own "Traveler's Dictionary of Helpful Phrases."

Lesson 1 Review Answers

1. clause **2.** phrase **3.** phrase **4.** clause **5.** clause **6.** dependent clause—After **7.** dependent clause—who **8.** independent clause **9.** independent clause **10.** dependent clause—Because

Vocabulary Builder

Before presenting the feature, write this definition on the board: *a sweet, tasty topping for toast.* Ask students to suggest possible words that fit the definition. Write the words on the board. Point out that, while the words are related and all fit the general definition, the words themselves have specific meanings, which differ from one another. Have students offer definitions for the words to show how the words differ in meaning. Then ask why it is important for students to choose the correct word when writing something like a grocery list or a description. Help students realize that for a grocery list a specific item is required. In a description, the exact word helps the reader picture what is being written about.

Answers to Vocabulary Builder: 1. A **2.** B **3.** C Jam would most likely have seeds.

Learning Styles

Auditory/Verbal

Divide the class into pairs. Assign each pair a sentence from items 6–10 on page 278 or from Activity C on page 277. Have one partner in each pair read the first clause in the sentence. Ask the class to listen carefully to hear whether the clause is complete. For example, the words *After the party was over* leave one wondering what happened, so this clause is dependent. It depends on other words to be complete. Then have the second partner read the second clause. Ask the class to listen carefully to hear whether that clause is complete.

Lesson 1 REVIEW

Write on your paper whether each group of words in bold is a *phrase* or a *clause.*

1. We huddled in the cabin **as the snow fell.**
2. She won't be back **until tomorrow.**
3. Everyone has arrived **except Jody and Bill.**
4. I can't leave **until I finish my report.**
5. **When you know the answer,** raise your hand.

Write on your paper whether the clause in bold is an *independent clause* or a *dependent clause.* Remember, an independent clause can stand alone as a sentence. Then write the word that introduces each dependent clause.

6. **After the party was over,** we cleaned up and went to bed.
7. Please take this to the woman **who lives next door.**
8. **I am so glad** that you made the team.
9. **Ask the girl** who is standing by the fence.
10. **Because the store closed,** people lost their jobs.

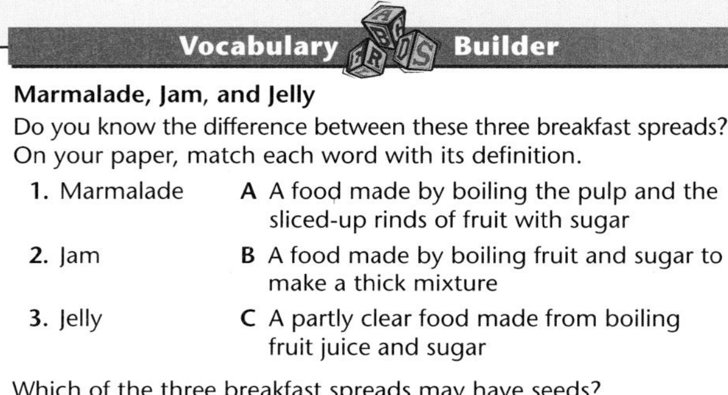

Vocabulary Builder

Marmalade, Jam, and Jelly

Do you know the difference between these three breakfast spreads? On your paper, match each word with its definition.

1. Marmalade — **A** A food made by boiling the pulp and the sliced-up rinds of fruit with sugar
2. Jam — **B** A food made by boiling fruit and sugar to make a thick mixture
3. Jelly — **C** A partly clear food made from boiling fruit juice and sugar

Which of the three breakfast spreads may have seeds?

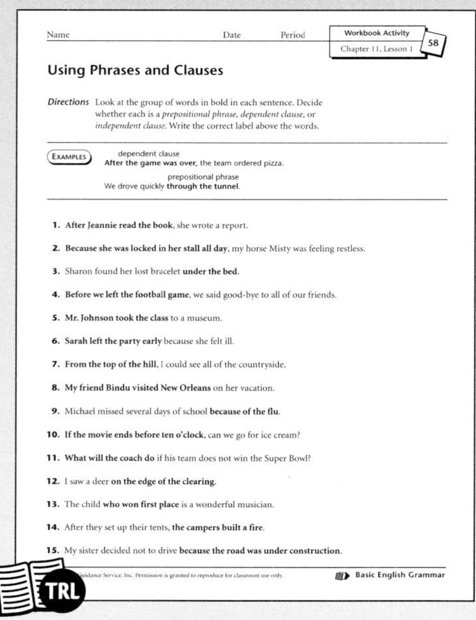

Name Date Period | Workbook Activity 58 | Chapter 11, Lesson 1

Using Phrases and Clauses

Directions Look at the group of words in bold in each sentence. Decide whether each is a *prepositional phrase, dependent clause,* or *independent clause.* Write the correct label above the words.

EXAMPLES
dependent clause
After the game was over, the team ordered pizza.
prepositional phrase
We drove quickly **through the tunnel**.

1. **After Jeannie read the book**, she wrote a report.
2. **Because she was locked in her stall all day**, my horse Misty was feeling restless.
3. Sharon found her lost bracelet **under the bed**.
4. **Before we left the football game**, we said good-bye to all of our friends.
5. **Mr. Johnson took the class** to a museum.
6. **Sarah left the party early** because she felt ill.
7. **From the top of the hill**, I could see all of the countryside.
8. **My friend Bindu visited New Orleans** on her vacation.
9. Michael missed several days of school **because of the flu**.
10. **If the movie ends before ten o'clock**, can we go for ice cream?
11. **What will the coach do** if his team does not win the Super Bowl?
12. I saw a deer **on the edge of the clearing**.
13. The child **who won first place** is a wonderful musician.
14. After they set up their tents, **the campers built a fire**.
15. My sister decided not to drive **because the road was under construction**.

 Basic English Grammar

TRL

Workbook Activity 58

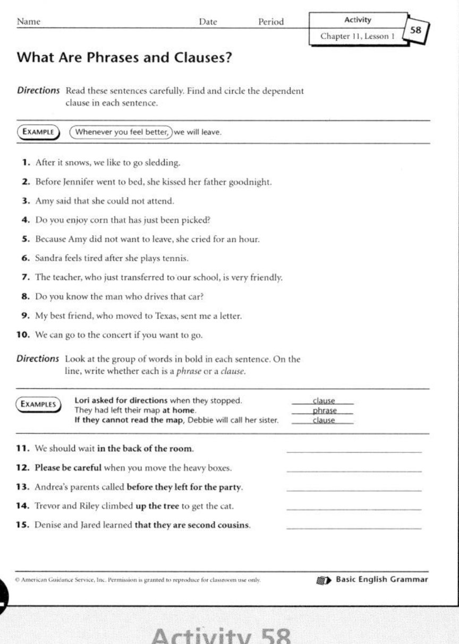

Name Date Period | Activity 58 | Chapter 11, Lesson 1

What Are Phrases and Clauses?

Directions Read these sentences carefully. Find and circle the dependent clause in each sentence.

EXAMPLE (Whenever you feel better,) we will leave.

1. After it snows, we like to go sledding.
2. Before Jennifer went to bed, she kissed her father goodnight.
3. Amy said that she could not attend.
4. Do you enjoy corn that has just been picked?
5. Because Amy did not want to leave, she cried for an hour.
6. Sandra feels tired after she plays tennis.
7. The teacher, who just transferred to our school, is very friendly.
8. Do you know the man who drives that car?
9. My best friend, who moved to Texas, sent me a letter.
10. We can go to the concert if you want to go.

Directions Look at the group of words in bold in each sentence. On the line, write whether each is a *phrase* or a *clause*.

EXAMPLES
Lori asked for directions when they stopped. ___clause___
They had left their map **at home**. ___phrase___
If they cannot read the map, Debbie will call her sister. ___clause___

11. We should wait **in the back of the room.** ________
12. **Please be careful** when you move the heavy boxes. ________
13. Andrea's parents called **before they left for the party**. ________
14. Trevor and Riley climbed **up the tree** to get the cat. ________
15. Denise and Jared learned **that they are second cousins**. ________

 Basic English Grammar

TRL

Activity 58

278 *Chapter 11* *Complex Sentences*

Lesson 2 The Adverb Clause

Adverb clause

A dependent clause that works like an adverb in a sentence

An **adverb clause** is a dependent clause that works like an adverb in a sentence. It answers questions about the verb.

EXAMPLE

Adverb	Carli went home early.
Adverb Phrase	Carli went home after practice.
Adverb Clause	Carli went home when practice was over.

Activity A Write on your paper whether the words in bold are *adverbs*, an *adverb phrase*, or an *adverb clause.*

1. Amy writes **well** and **often.**
2. Mom always knows exactly **where I put my things.**
3. **Except for you,** I haven't told anyone the news.
4. **Until you find your pen,** you can borrow mine.
5. I can hardly wait **until my birthday.**

Like adverbs, an adverb clause answers the questions *where, when, why, how much, how often,* and *how soon.*

EXAMPLE

Where?	Kim smiled wherever she went.
When?	When Dale was a boy, he lived in Haiti.
Why?	Joy joined the club because she likes art.
How Much?	Alex tried as hard as he could.
How Often?	Jo practices the piano whenever she can.
How Soon?	When practice is over, Paul will go home.

Activity B On your paper, write the adverb clause in each sentence.

1. Enrique runs whenever he has time.
2. If he gets up early, he runs in the morning.
3. He runs because he enjoys it.
4. Unless it is raining hard, Enrique runs every day.
5. Because I injured my knee, I walk for exercise.

Activity A

Before students complete Activity A on their own, have the class identify the adverb, adverb phrase, or adverb clause in each sentence.

Activity A Answers

1. adverbs **2.** adverb clause **3.** adverb phrase **4.** adverb clause **5.** adverb phrase

Activity B

Read through all the items in Activity B with students, helping them identify the two clauses in each sentence. Then have students complete Activity B on their own.

Activity B Answers

1. whenever he has time **2.** If he gets up early **3.** because he enjoys it **4.** Unless it is raining hard **5.** Because I injured my knee

Lesson at a Glance

Chapter 11 Lesson 2

Overview This lesson presents adverb clauses.

Objectives

- To distinguish between adverb phrases and clauses.
- To identify adverb clauses.
- To write sentences with adverb clauses.

Student Pages 279–281

Teacher's Resource Library 

Workbook Activity 59

Activity 59

Alternative Activity 59

Vocabulary

adverb clause

1 Warm-Up Activity

Write these partial sentences on the board as headings: *My bike skidded ____. I was not hurt ____. In the future, I will ride ____.* Ask students to complete each sentence by using words that answer one of these questions: *where, when, how.* Write students' responses that are adverbs, adverb phrases, and adverb clauses under the blank for the appropriate sentence beginning.

Ask what kind of word, phrase, or clause answers questions about a verb. Help students recall that adverbs serve this purpose and that the words they suggested to complete each sentence represent adverbs, adverb phrases, and adverb clauses.

2 Teaching the Lesson

Focus on the first set of examples. Discuss with students the difference between adverb phrases and adverb clauses. Ask volunteers to change the second example so that the sentence contains an adverb clause. Finally remind students that adverbs, adverb phrases, and adverb clauses can appear at the beginning or the end of a sentence.

Activity C

Write these sentences on the board: *That girl sings louder than everyone else in the group. She was not as excited as I.* Help students identify the adverb clause in each sentence. Ask them to tell what words are missing from the adverb clause in the second sentence. Then have them complete Activity C on their own.

Activity C Answers

1. than any other dog on our street (barks) **2.** than anyone else (practices) **3.** than Beth (is tall) **4.** than the others ran **5.** as happy as she can be

3 Reinforce and Extend

Teacher Alert

You may wish to point out to students that in comparisons such as *She was not as excited as I,* the words *as . . . as* are correlative conjunctions.

Learning Styles

Logical/Mathematical

Divide the class into groups of three. On the board, write the following patterns:

1. subject/predicate/adverb
2. subject/predicate/adverbial prepositional phrase
3. subject/predicate/adverbial dependent clause.

Invite each group to write a sentence for each pattern. Ask volunteers to read aloud one of their group's sentences. Call on other volunteers to go to the board and check the pattern each sentence represents. Next, call out possible predicates—action words—and ask volunteers to use these to create sentences for the three patterns.

An adverb clause can answer questions about another adverb. These adverb clauses can act like adverbs of degree. They answer questions such as *how much* or *how far.*

Example

S V DO Adv. S V
Devon hits the ball farther than anyone else can hit it.
(How much farther can Devon hit the ball? He can hit it farther *than anyone else can hit it.*)

An adverb clause can answer questions about an adjective. These adverb clauses also can act like adverbs of degree.

Example

S V Adj. S V
Sean is taller than the other students are.
(How much taller is Sean? He is taller *than the other students.*)

> Remember, an adverb clause answers questions about a verb, an adverb, or an adjective.

Sometimes part of an adverb clause is missing. The missing part is understood.

Example Devon hits the ball farther than anyone else. (In the clause *than anyone else,* the words *can hit it* are understood.)
Sean is taller than the other students. (In the clause *than the other students,* the verb *are* is understood.)

Activity C Write the adverb clauses on your paper. Then write any words that are understood.

1. My dog barks louder than any other dog on our street.
2. Irene practices longer than anyone else.
3. Is Vicky taller than Beth?
4. Enrique ran farther than the others ran.
5. Charlotte is as happy as she can be!

Lesson 2 REVIEW

On your paper, write whether each group of words in bold is an *adverb phrase* or an *adverb clause.*

1. Sue has been deaf **since birth.**
2. **Because she and Lisa became friends,** Lisa learned sign language.
3. **If you wish to learn,** Sue will help you.
4. Lisa has never signed to anyone **but Sue.**
5. **After she has been signing for a while,** Lisa will be good at it.

On your paper, write the adverb clause in each sentence. Then write any words that are understood.

6. We will go to the beach when summer arrives.
7. Alexa bought a new bicycle because her old one fell apart.
8. You should get some rest if you are tired.
9. No one can run faster than Enrique.
10. That building is higher than any other city building.

Write these sentences on your paper. Add an adverb clause to each sentence.

11. Angie and her brother went to the baseball game.
12. Rain had been falling.
13. The field was wet.
14. The game began.
15. Angie cheered louder.

Using What You've Learned

On your paper, write a note to a friend explaining why you cannot attend a party or school activity. Use at least three dependent clauses. Join them to your independent clauses with words such as *because, since, if, when,* and *which.*

Lesson 2 Review Answers

1. adverb phrase **2.** adverb clause **3.** adverb clause **4.** adverb phrase **5.** adverb clause **6.** when summer arrives **7.** because her old one fell apart **8.** if you are tired **9.** than Enrique (can run) **10.** than any other city building (is high) **11–15.** Sentences will vary. Each sentence should include an adverb clause.

Using What You've Learned

Read the directions together; but before having students write, ask them why *because, since, if, when,* and *which* would be helpful in writing the kind of note described in the activity. Students should answer that they will be providing explanations and alternatives in their note and these words are useful for doing so. After students have written their notes, ask volunteers to read a sentence that contains one of the target words. Encourage classmates to identify the word used.

Answers to Using What You've Learned: Notes will vary. Each note should contain at least three dependent clauses joined to an independent clause by *because, since, if, when,* or *which.*

Learning Styles

Interpersonal/Group Learning

Divide the class into small groups. Ask each group to select a topic in the news and to work together to write a brief paragraph about the topic. If possible, each sentence in the paragraph should have at least one adverb clause. When students have finished, invite a group representative to read the paragraph to the class. Then have members of the class point out how adverb clauses enhanced the meaning and flow of the paragraph.

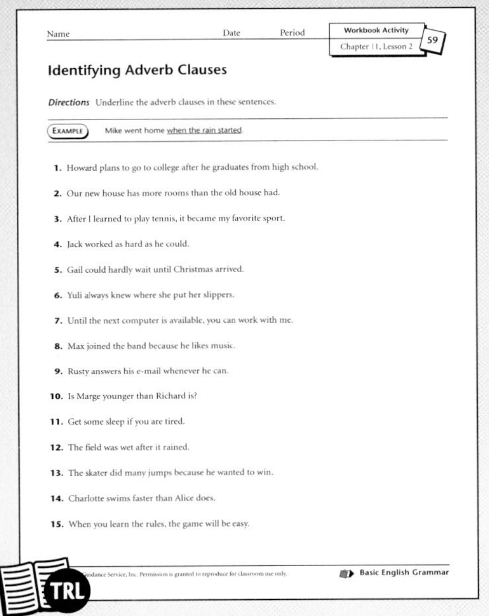

Name Date Period — Workbook Activity 59 — Chapter 11, Lesson 2

Identifying Adverb Clauses

Directions Underline the adverb clauses in these sentences.

EXAMPLE Mike went home when the rain started.

1. Howard plans to go to college after he graduates from high school.
2. Our new house has more rooms than the old house had.
3. After I learned to play tennis, it became my favorite sport.
4. Jack worked as hard as he could.
5. Gail could hardly wait until Christmas arrived.
6. Yuli always knew where she put her slippers.
7. Until the next computer is available, you can work with me.
8. Max joined the band because he likes music.
9. Rusty answers his e-mail whenever he can.
10. Is Marge younger than Richard is?
11. Get some sleep if you are tired.
12. The field was wet after it rained.
13. The skater did many jumps because he wanted to win.
14. Charlotte swims faster than Alice does.
15. When you learn the rules, the game will be easy.

 Basic English Grammar

TRL

Workbook Activity 59

Name Date Period — Activity 59 — Chapter 11, Lesson 2

Recognizing Adverb Clauses

Directions Decide whether the word or words in bold are an adverb, an adverb phrase, or an adverb clause. Write *adverb, adverb phrase,* or *adverb clause* on the line.

EXAMPLES My grandfather will arrive **in the morning.** adverb phrase
He will leave **when the family reunion is over.** adverb clause

1. Henry and Peter traveled **to their aunt's ranch** last summer. ________
2. She picked them up at the airport **when their flight arrived.** ________
3. Aunt Rachel gave them each a cowboy hat **after they arrived** at the ranch. ________
4. Frank, the ranch foreman, met them **at the corral.** ________
5. The boys slept in the bunkhouse **where the cowhands usually sleep.** ________
6. Peter learned horseback riding **quickly.** ________
7. Aunt Rachel said they would have to work hard **during the cattle drive.** ________
8. Henry built a campfire **while Peter set up the tent.** ________
9. The fire burned **brightly.** ________
10. Both boys were nervous **because they had seen a rattlesnake.** ________
11. They crawled **into their sleeping bags** in the tent. ________
12. **In the morning,** their aunt showed them how to rope cattle. ________
13. She had learned **when she was only six years old.** ________
14. **When they reached the trailhead,** Frank picked them up. ________
15. Their aunt made them a huge lunch **on the last day** of their visit. ________
16. **Under an old oak tree,** Aunt Rachel spread a picnic blanket. ________
17. Henry asked **politely** for some more biscuits. ________
18. He found an arrowhead **while they were exploring.** ________
19. They said good-bye **sadly.** ________
20. Peter and Henry said they would come again **when they had a chance.** ________

 Basic English Grammar

TRL

Activity 59

Complex Sentences *Chapter 11* 281

Lesson at a Glance

Chapter 11 Lesson 3

Overview This lesson introduces noun clauses.

Objective

- To identify the function of noun clauses in sentences.

Student Pages 282–286

Teacher's Resource Library 

Workbook Activity 60

Activity 60

Alternative Activity 60

Vocabulary

appositive
noun clause

Warm-Up Activity

Write these incomplete sentences on the board: *I know where* ___. *This is why* ___. *She believes that* ___. Ask students to complete each sentence with a clause. Write their suggestions under the blank line for each incomplete sentence. Help students locate and underline the subject and predicate in each clause. Then discuss how each clause works in the sentence. Circle those clauses that function as nouns. (Most responses will.) Point out that in the last lesson, they learned that some clauses work as adverbs. In this lesson, they will learn about clauses that work as nouns.

2 Teaching the Lesson

Read the definition of a noun clause on page 282. Then work through each item in the first example box. Help students recognize that a noun clause follows one of six patterns. Then go through the examples again, this time asking volunteers to read an example, omitting the noun clause. Help students recognize that noun clauses are needed in the sentences in which they appear. Omitting the noun clause either changes the meaning of the sentence or causes the sentence to not make sense.

Lesson 3 The Noun Clause

Noun clause
A dependent clause that works like a noun in a sentence

A **noun clause** is a group of words with a subject and a verb. A noun clause is a dependent clause that works like a noun in a sentence. A noun clause may follow any of the six sentence patterns.

EXAMPLE

Subject	S LV PA What you did was wonderful.
Predicate Noun	S LV PN That paper is what I need.
Direct Object	S V DO I remember what you said.
Indirect Object	S V IO DO I gave whoever wanted some a piece of my pretzel.
Object Complement	S V DO OC She can name the kitten whatever she wants.
Object of the Preposition	S V DO Obj. Prep. We made dinner for whoever was hungry.

Activity A On your paper, write whether the noun clause in bold is a *subject,* a *predicate noun,* a *direct object,* an *indirect object,* an *object complement,* or the *object of the preposition.*

1. The teacher said **that my answer was wrong.**
2. **Who will get the lead in the play** has not been decided.
3. They argued about **who should go first.**
4. This is **what I want.**
5. She offered **whoever was still around** a ride home.

Activity A

Before they complete Activity A on their own, ask students to identify the complete subject in each item.

Activity A Answers

1. direct object 2. subject 3. object of the preposition 4. predicate noun 5. indirect object

Reinforce and Extend

TEACHER ALERT

You might mention to students that one way to identify noun clauses is to replace them with the pronoun *it* or *somebody.* Because adjective and adverb clauses do not play the role of nouns, they cannot be replaced by pronouns. The pronouns *it* and *somebody* can replace noun clauses, because noun clauses are always singular.

A relative pronoun introduces a noun clause in a sentence.

Common Relative Pronouns	
that	who (subject)
what	whom (object)
whatever	whoever (subject)
whichever	whomever (object)
	whose (possessive)

The pronouns *that* and *what* each have only one form. They do not change, regardless of whether they are subjects or objects. The pronoun *who* does change, however.

- Use *who* when the relative pronoun is the subject of the noun clause.
- Use *whom* when the relative pronoun is the direct object or the object of the preposition in the noun clause.
- Use *who* when the relative pronoun is the predicate noun in the noun clause.

Example

S V DO
I remember who called me.

DO S V
I remember whom you called.

PN S LV
I remember who you are.

Activity B On your paper, complete these sentences with *who* or *whom.*

1. I know ______ called you.
2. I know ______ you are.
3. I know ______ you saw.
4. I know ______ you invited.
5. I know to ______ you wrote.

Activity B

Help students review the common relative pronouns and read the bulleted rules for using these pronouns. Then write these sentences on the board: *I saw to ___ you pointed. I saw ___ did that. I saw ___ they met at the mall.* Work with students to label the parts of the noun clause in each sentence to determine whether *who* or *whom* should be used. Then have students complete Activity B on their own.

Activity B Answers

1. who **2.** who **3.** whom **4.** whom **5.** whom

Teacher Alert

Point out to students that *whom* has virtually disappeared from spoken language. As a result, students who write by ear may have little awareness of how to use *whom* appropriately. Point out that a good way to test for the correct use of *who* or *whom* in noun clauses is to turn the clause into a separate sentence and substitute a personal pronoun for *who* or *whom.* For example, *The mayor, (who/whom) our teacher knows, will speak* when changed becomes *The mayor will speak. Our teacher knows her.* In the second sentence, *her* is an object pronoun and so is *whom.* The correct choice in the original sentence is *whom.*

Learning Styles

Visual/Spatial

List these sentence parts on the board: *subject, direct object, object of a preposition, predicate noun, object complement.* Have students work with partners to write a sentence in which *who* or *whom* is used in a noun clause for each of the purposes listed on the board. Tell partners to label each sentence with the purpose of the noun clause. Then have students share the sentences they wrote with the class.

Activity C

Invite volunteers to write on the board sentences with noun clauses. Have the class identify each noun clause and the word that introduces it. Then have students complete Activity C on their own.

Activity C Answers

1. Do you know (who) found my book? 2. I remember (that) the book is on sale. 3. (What) I really need are my notes! 4. I am offering a reward to (whoever) finds them. 5. Do you think (that) Raina found my notes, too?

Activity D

Read the directions and study the example together. Then ask volunteers to choose a sentence in Activity D, identify the noun clause, and tell how it is used. Finally have students complete Activity D independently.

Activity D Answers

1. whoever wants some—object of the preposition 2. that I would be late—direct object 3. what I need right now—predicate noun 4. What you see—subject, what you get—predicate noun 5. whoever was in the store—indirect object

Learning Styles

Auditory/Verbal

After discussing the Technology Note on page 284 with them, have students familiar with computers tell about other drives a computer may have and the purpose of each.

The relative pronoun *that* often introduces a noun clause. Sometimes it is left out of the sentence because it is understood. Either way is correct.

Do you think that he is nice?
Do you think he is nice?

The other relative pronouns cannot be left out.

Incorrect Did you hear I said?
Correct Did you hear what I said?

Activity C Write each sentence on your paper. Underline the noun clause. Circle the relative pronoun.

1. Do you know who found my book?
2. I remember that the book is on sale.
3. What I really need are my notes!
4. I am offering a reward to whoever finds them.
5. Do you think that Raina found my notes, too?

Technology Note

Many computers have a CD-ROM drive in addition to a disk drive. CD-ROM stands for "Compact Disk-Read Only Memory." This special drive can "read" the music, information, and computer software stored on a CD-ROM.

Activity D On your paper, write the noun clauses in these sentences. Then write whether each one acts as the *subject, predicate noun, direct object, indirect object, object complements,* or *object of the preposition.*

Example What I said was not important.
What I said—subject

1. I made supper for whoever wants some.
2. I knew that I would be late.
3. Some hot soup is what I need right now.
4. What you see is what you get!
5. The salesperson gave whoever was in the store a free CD.

In the Community

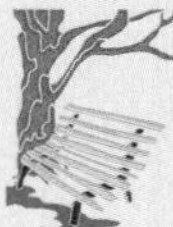

Engage students in a discussion of how their city or town could be improved. For example, students might feel that more after-school activities for teenagers are needed or that the public transportation system should be improved. Encourage students to choose an issue and write a persuasive speech about what the problem is, why it should be changed, and how this change will benefit the entire community. Remind students that dependent clauses add information to sentences and make ideas more complete. Also, a variety of sentence structures will help make their speeches more lively and interesting. Then have a "Community Issues Day." Invite government officials, parents, and other members of the community to hear students' speeches.

Appositive

A noun, a noun phrase, or a noun clause placed next to a noun to rename or explain it

An **appositive** renames or explains another noun in the same sentence. An appositive may be a noun, a noun phrase, or a noun clause. Look at the example. The appositive is in color. The noun the appositive renames or explains is in italics.

EXAMPLE

My *cousin* Helena has a bird.
Chiquita, a parakeet, belongs to her.
Chiquita's favorite *thing,* a small brass bell, is in its cage.
I have a secret *wish*—that I will someday be captain.

Writing Tip

Always use dashes to set apart an appositive that contains commas. For example:
Carla bought supplies—cups, plates, and streamers—for the surprise party.

Activity E On your paper, write the appositive in each sentence. Next to each appositive, write the noun or nouns the appositive renames or explains.

1. Do you know who wrote this line: "All the world's a stage"?
2. The committee members—Carlos, Jill, and Alma—met in the student lounge.
3. People laughed at Columbus's idea—the thought that the world was round.
4. Galileo's invention, the telescope, changed scientific method.
5. Friends since kindergarten, Rita and Marianne still enjoy each other's company.

Astronomy, the study of heavenly bodies, is fascinating.

Activity E

You may wish to read through all the items with students at least once. Then do one item together as a class, before asking students to complete Activity E on their own.

Activity E Answers

1. "All the world's a stage"—line 2. Carlos, Jill, and Alma—members 3. the thought that the world was round—idea 4. the telescope—invention 5. Friends since kindergarten—Rita and Marianne

LEARNING STYLES

LEP/ESL

Ask English language learners to choose a sentence from Activity E on page 285 and to print it on the board. Then have the students translate the sentence into their primary language. Ask them to circle the appositive and to underline the noun or nouns that the appositive renames or explains. Use these sentences to discover if the pattern and punctuation in other languages are similar to the English pattern and punctuation for appositives.

Lesson 3 Review Answers

1. We went shopping for whatever we needed.—object of the preposition 2. That love conquers all is a lofty idea.—subject 3. Mrs. Li gave whoever asked for it more time for the test.—indirect object 4. She said (that) she's tired.—direct object 5. When the paper is due is not clear.—subject 6. He will go on an errand for whoever asks him.—object of the preposition 7. Members of the same team, Carl and George go to practice together.—appositive 8. Is this what the dog brought home?—predicate noun 9. Seth forgot whom he invited.—direct object 10. You can name the dog whatever you choose.—object complement

Spelling Builder

Tell students that you are going to read two sentences. They are to listen for a word that sounds the same in both sentences. Then read these sentences: *It's time for Spelling. This subject has its own rules.* When students identify the words *It's* and *its* as the words that sound alike, write them on the board. Ask students if they are the same word. Help students recognize that *it's* is a contraction for *it is* and *its* is a possessive pronoun. Then review with students the lists of pronouns and contractions in the feature.

Answers to Spelling Builder: 1. its 2. your 3. They're 4. theirs 5. Who's

Spelling Practice

Refer to the list of pronouns and contractions. Point out that in oral language the words sound alike; but in writing, the context provides the clue as to what word and what spelling is needed. Let students suggest ways to avoid using the wrong word. They might mention that the writer could simply read the sentence aloud saying the words the contraction represents. This will often tell the writer if the contraction is correct or if a pronoun is needed instead. Let volunteers give oral sentences using the pronouns and contractions listed in the Spelling Builder on page 286. Have students write the sentences and check their spelling using the process described.

Lesson 3 REVIEW

Write these sentences on your paper. Underline the noun clause. Then identify each noun clause as a *subject*, a *predicate noun*, a *direct object*, an *indirect object*, an *object complement*, an *object of the preposition*, or an *appositive*. Circle the relative pronoun. If the relative pronoun *that* is understood, write it in and circle it.

1. We went shopping for whatever we needed.
2. That love conquers all is a lofty idea.
3. Mrs. Li gave whoever asked for it more time for the test.
4. She said she's tired.
5. When the paper is due is not clear.
6. He will go on an errand for whoever asks him.
7. Members of the same team, Carl and George go to practice together.
8. Is this what the dog brought home?
9. Seth forgot whom he invited.
10. You can name the dog whatever you choose.

Spelling Builder

Contractions vs. Possessive Pronouns

Some possessive pronouns and contractions are homonyms. The relative possessive pronoun *whose* sometimes is confused with the contraction *who's*. *Who's* stands for *who is* and is not possessive. Here are other possessive pronouns that can be confused with contractions:

Pronouns	Contractions
your	you're
its	it's
their	they're
theirs	there's

On your paper, write the correct pronoun or contraction for each sentence.

1. Look at (it's, its) cover to find the author's name.
2. Are (your, you're) gloves in the bag?
3. (They're, Their) going sledding.
4. This one is mine, but that one is (theirs, there's).
5. (Who's, Whose) coming with us?

Name Date Period Workbook Activity 60 Chapter 11, Lesson 3

Using Noun Clauses

Directions Find and circle the noun clauses in these sentences. On the line, write whether the noun clause is a *subject, direct object, indirect object, object of the preposition, predicate noun,* or *object complement.*

EXAMPLES The new computer is just what I needed. predicate noun
Please tell me what you want. direct object

1. The blue sweater is exactly what I wanted. _____
2. Name the puppy whatever you like. _____
3. That computer is what I want. _____
4. Show whoever you want my photographs. _____
5. Does anyone know what those people are doing? _____
6. Whoever finishes first wins the race. _____
7. We gave whoever wanted one a ride on the go-cart. _____
8. Whoever is hungry should come and eat. _____
9. The teacher said that my poster had won the contest. _____
10. Everyone asked who would be at the party. _____
11. Whatever you decide is fine. _____
12. Did Alison hear what you said? _____
13. You should let me know what you want. _____
14. What you said is very important. _____
15. The teachers brought pencils for whoever needed one. _____

 Basic English Grammar

TRL

Workbook Activity 60

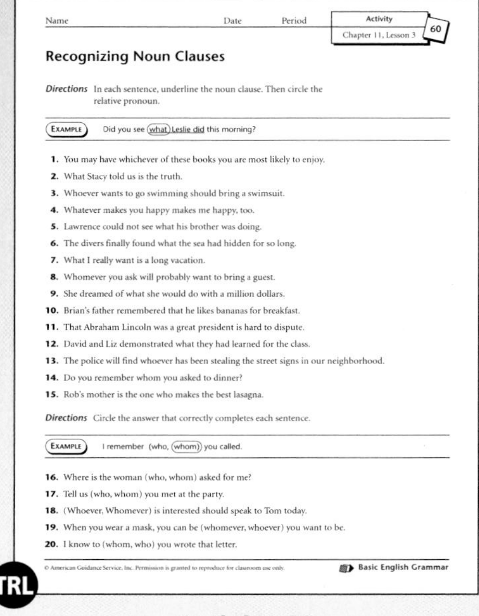
Name Date Period Activity 60 Chapter 11, Lesson 3

Recognizing Noun Clauses

Directions In each sentence, underline the noun clause. Then circle the relative pronoun.

EXAMPLE Did you see (what) Leslie did this morning?

1. You may have whichever of these books you are most likely to enjoy.
2. What Stacy told us is the truth.
3. Whoever wants to go swimming should bring a swimsuit.
4. Whatever makes you happy makes me happy, too.
5. Lawrence could not see what his brother was doing.
6. The divers finally found what the sea had hidden for so long.
7. What I really want is a long vacation.
8. Whomever you ask will probably want to bring a guest.
9. She dreamed of what she would do with a million dollars.
10. Brian's father remembered that he likes bananas for breakfast.
11. That Abraham Lincoln was a great president is hard to dispute.
12. David and Liz demonstrated what they had learned for the class.
13. The police will find whoever has been stealing the street signs in our neighborhood.
14. Do you remember whom you asked to dinner?
15. Rob's mother is the one who makes the best lasagna.

Directions Circle the answer that correctly completes each sentence.

EXAMPLE I remember (who, (whom)) you called.

16. Where is the woman (who, whom) asked for me?
17. Tell us (who, whom) you met at the party.
18. (Whoever, Whomever) is interested should speak to Tom today.
19. When you wear a mask, you can be (whomever, whoever) you want to be.
20. I know to (whom, who) you wrote that letter.

 Basic English Grammar

TRL

Activity 60

Lesson 4 The Adjective Clause

Adjective clause
A dependent clause that describes a noun or pronoun

An adjective describes a noun or pronoun. We use an **adjective clause** like an adjective in a sentence. An adjective clause is a dependent clause that describes a noun or pronoun.

EXAMPLE

Adjective	The middle boy is Ted.
Adjective Phrase	The boy in the middle is Ted.
Adjective Clause	The boy who is in the middle is Ted.

Activity A On your paper, write whether the words in bold are *adjectives*, an *adjective phrase*, or an *adjective clause*.

1. Terry is the player **who scores the most.**
2. The **best** and **most popular** player on our team is Terry.
3. The player **with the most points** on our team is Terry.
4. Pam, **who has played soccer all her life,** is the coach.
5. The team **that I enjoy watching the most** is Terry's.

Like an adjective phrase, an adjective clause follows the noun or pronoun it describes.

EXAMPLE The present that I gave him was expensive. (What present was expensive? *The present that I gave him* was expensive.)

Activity B On your paper, write the adjective clause in each sentence. Next to each clause, write the noun it describes.

1. A girl whom I know won first prize in a contest.
2. The present that Gayle gave Aron was for his birthday.
3. The package that she sent was heavy.
4. The boy who sits in the first seat has been absent all week.
5. We bought a new refrigerator that has an ice maker.

Lesson at a Glance

Chapter 11 Lesson 4

Overview This lesson introduces adjective clauses.

Objective

- To identify adjective clauses and the words they describe.

Student Pages 287–289

Teacher's Resource Library 

Workbook Activity 61

Activity 61

Alternative Activity 61

Vocabulary

adjective clause

1 Warm-Up Activity

Write these questions on the board: *What is an adjective? What is an adjective phrase? What is an adjective clause?* Have students offer their ideas. Then read these sentences orally, and ask volunteers to identify whether an adjective, adjective phrase, or adjective clause is used in each: *The tall plant grew quickly.* (adjective) *The plant with the red flowers grew tall.* (adjective phrase) *The plant that is tall and red grew quickly.* (adjective clause) Then ask students to write similar sentences by completing this sentence: *The students* ____.

2 Teaching the Lesson

Write this sentence on the board: *The woman who volunteers at the library is my neighbor.* Circle the relative pronoun *who* and ask who the word *who* tells about. (*woman*) Point out that an adjective phrase or clause follows the noun or pronoun it describes. Read the example in the second box on page 287 and ask a volunteer to identify the adjective clause and the noun or pronoun it describes.

Activity A

Write on the board: *That is a song.* Ask volunteers to read the sentence aloud, adding an adjective to describe song. Repeat this activity, having students add an adjective phrase next and an adjective clause after that. Then have students complete Activity A on their own.

Activity A Answers

1. adjective clause 2. adjectives 3. adjective phrase 4. adjective clause 5. adjective clause

Activity B

Do the first item in Activity B with students. Then have them complete Activity B on their own.

Activity B Answers

1. whom I know—girl 2. that Gayle gave Aron—present 3. that she sent—package 4. who sits in the first seat—boy 5. that has an ice maker—refrigerator

Activity C

Write these sentences on the board: *The band member whom I admire most is Karen. This is the room where the band practices.* Help students find the adjective clause in each sentence. Invite a volunteer to come to the board and circle the relative pronoun that introduces each clause. Then have students complete Activity C independently.

Activity C Answers

1. where a contest took place **2.** which is for high school bands **3.** whose name is Mr. Smith **4.** which had never won before **5.** where the weather is usually warm

Activity D

Have students take turns orally adding an adjective clause to item 1. Then have students do Activity D.

Activity D Answers

Sentences will vary. Possible sentences follow: **1.** The bus took the band to Florida, which is 400 miles from the band's hometown. **2.** Pedro, who plays trumpet, and Chris had a wonderful trip. **3.** They stayed in a hotel that was close to a theme park. **4.** Everyone who made the trip enjoyed the warm weather. **5.** The contest, which was held at the theme park, was exciting.

Speaking Practice

After students have completed Activity D, ask volunteers to read one or more of their sentences to the class. After a sentence is read, have other volunteers identify the adjective clause, the relative pronoun, and the noun or pronoun the adjective clause describes.

A relative pronoun can introduce an adjective clause. Some common relative pronouns are *who, whom, whose, which, what,* and *that.* We can also use the words *where* and *when* to introduce an adjective clause.

EXAMPLE The store where I bought my jacket has closed.

Activity C On your paper, write the adjective clause in each sentence. Underline the relative pronoun.

1. The band went to Florida, where a contest took place.
2. The contest, which is for high school bands, is an annual event.
3. The band director, whose name is Mr. Smith, was happy.
4. The band, which had never won before, performed well.
5. We took our swimsuits to Florida where the weather is usually warm.

Activity D Write these sentences on your paper. Add an adjective clause that describes the noun or pronoun in bold.

1. The bus took the band to **Florida.**
2. **Pedro** and Chris had a wonderful trip.
3. They stayed in a **hotel.**
4. **Everyone** enjoyed the warm weather.
5. The **contest** was exciting.

Everyone recognized the song that the band played.

288 *Chapter 11 Complex Sentences*

3 Reinforce and Extend

LEARNING STYLES

Logical/Mathematical

Divide the class into groups of three. On the board, print the following patterns:

1. adjective/subject/predicate
2. subject/adjective phrase/predicate
3. subject/dependent adjective clause/predicate

Invite each group to write a sentence for each pattern. Ask volunteer groups to read aloud one sentence they have written. Call on other volunteers to go to the board and check the pattern each sentence represents. Next call out possible subjects—people, places, things—and ask volunteers to use these to construct oral sentences for the three patterns.

REVIEW

Write these sentences on your paper. Underline each adjective clause once. Underline each relative pronoun twice.

1. Please get the bread that is baked at the grocery store.
2. Did you know the people who gave the party?
3. Mike is the one who plays right field.
4. The man whose brother drives our bus is very nice.
5. The outfit that Jenna wore to the party was new.

On your paper, write the adjective clause in each sentence. Next to each clause, write the noun it describes.

6. The girl who was in line behind me bought the last tickets.
7. The man who lived next door moved to Florida.
8. We rented a new apartment that had three bedrooms.
9. Nori showed me the notes that she had taken for the test.
10. I am the person whose book you found.

Where To Find It

Book of Quotations

Where would you look to find some words spoken by Winston Churchill, Eleanor Roosevelt, or Mohandas Gandhi? A book of quotations is a collection of words spoken by real people. The quotations may appear by topic or in alphabetical order by the last name of the speaker. You can use the book's index and table of contents to help you locate a speaker's name or a topic.

1. Choose a book of quotations from the library or your classroom.
2. Select a person or topic that interests you.
3. Find and write on your paper a quotation by that person or about that topic.
4. Pair up with a classmate. Read aloud the quotations to each other. Read as though you were the speaker.

Lesson 4 Review Answers

1. Please get the bread <u>that</u> is baked at the grocery store. 2. Did you know the people who gave the party? 3. Mike is the one who plays right field. 4. The man whose brother drives our bus is very nice. 5. The outfit that Jenna wore to the party was new. 6. who was in line behind me—girl 7. who lived next door—man 8. that had three bedrooms—apartment 9. that she had taken for the test—notes 10. whose book you found—person

Where To Find It

Begin by asking students to think of writing situations in which they might want to use the words of a famous person. After the discussion, show students some books of quotations such as *Bartlett's Familiar Quotations.* Discuss with students how to locate a quotation—either by topic or by the name of the person—by using the index and table of contents. Remind students that when using any reference book, they should look under the last name of the person they are interested in finding out about. Then have students use the reference materials to locate a quotation about a particular topic or by a specific individual.

Answers to Where To Find It: Students' quotations will vary. The quotations should be correctly written.

Writing Practice

Give each student a piece of tagboard or a large sheet of construction paper. Ask them to use a book of quotations to find a quote they find inspiring or meaningful. Have them write the quotation and the name of the person quoted on the tagboard or construction paper. Ask students to write a paragraph explaining why they chose the quotation. Together create a display of quotations.

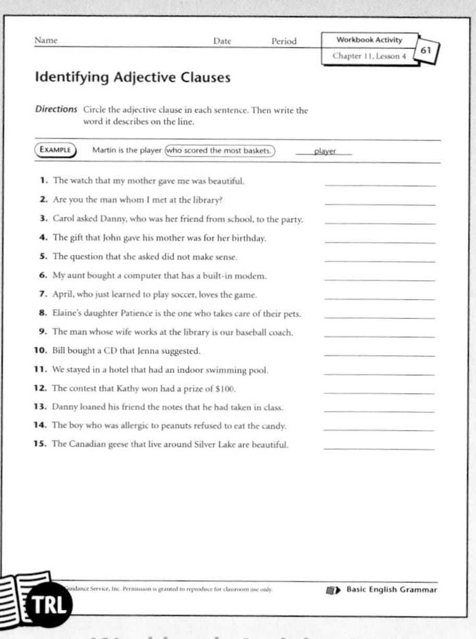

Name Date Period | Workbook Activity 61 | Chapter 11, Lesson 4

Identifying Adjective Clauses

Directions Circle the adjective clause in each sentence. Then write the word it describes on the line.

EXAMPLE Martin is the player (who scored the most baskets.) player

1. The watch that my mother gave me was beautiful. ________
2. Are you the man whom I met at the library? ________
3. Carol asked Danny, who was her friend from school, to the party. ________
4. The gift that John gave his mother was for her birthday. ________
5. The question that she asked did not make sense. ________
6. My aunt bought a computer that has a built-in modem. ________
7. April, who just learned to play soccer, loves the game. ________
8. Elaine's daughter Patience is the one who takes care of their pets. ________
9. The man whose wife works at the library is our baseball coach. ________
10. Bill bought a CD that Jenna suggested. ________
11. We stayed in a hotel that had an indoor swimming pool. ________
12. The contest that Kathy won had a prize of $100. ________
13. Danny loaned his friend the notes that he had taken in class. ________
14. The boy who was allergic to peanuts refused to eat the candy. ________
15. The Canadian geese that live around Silver Lake are beautiful. ________

 Basic English Grammar

TRL

Workbook Activity 61

Name Date Period | Activity 61 | Chapter 11, Lesson 4

The Adjective Clause

Directions Find and circle the adjective clauses in these sentences. Draw an arrow to the noun or pronoun that the adjective clause describes.

EXAMPLE The cake (that Terry baked) is delicious.

1. Greg is the person who collected the most donations.
2. Kelly and Charles cleaned the room where the children had been playing.
3. The novel that you are reading has some scary parts.
4. Chris lost the tennis match that was against her arch rival.
5. We saw a dog that we did not recognize.
6. Did Amanda read the note that Daniel wrote?
7. Don't use the bike that has a broken seat.
8. Jody is the woman who is wearing the green sweater.
9. I want to see the movie that is playing at our theater.
10. Ben works in the restaurant that my uncle owns.
11. Kendra is the horse that no one can ride.
12. Trent and Libby saw the show that Dave had recommended.
13. The job that I applied for has already been filled.
14. The box that Denise is carrying contains her father's birthday present.
15. Will you make the soup that everyone loves?

 Basic English Grammar

TRL

Activity 61

Lesson at a Glance

Chapter 11 Lesson 5

Overview This lesson explains complex and compound-complex sentences.

Objective

- To distinguish among simple, compound, complex, and compound-complex sentences.

Student Pages 290–295

Teacher's Resource Library TRL

Workbook Activity 62

Activity 62

Alternative Activity 62

Vocabulary

complex sentence
compound-complex sentence

1 Warm-Up Activity

Write the terms *simple sentences* and *compound sentences* on the board and ask students to explain each term and give examples of each kind of sentence. Then write *complex* on the board and ask for a general definition. (*complicated, many parts*) If necessary, remind students that a simple sentence has one independent clause and a compound sentence has two or more independent clauses. Ask what a complex sentence and a compound-complex sentence might be. Explain to students that sentences with dependent clauses are complex sentences and sentences with both two or more independent clauses and a dependent clause are compound-complex sentences. Ask volunteers to give examples of complex sentences and compound-complex sentences.

2 Teaching the Lesson

Refer students to page 276 and review what an independent clause, a dependent clause, and a phrase are. Ask students to give examples of each. Then discuss with students why it is important to know the difference between an independent clause, a dependent clause, and a phrase when talking about the structure of a sentence. Help students understand that to identify sentence structure, they need to differentiate phrases and types of clauses.

Activity A

Discuss the example given for Activity A. Ask students how they know that this is a complex sentence and not, for example, a simple sentence or a compound sentence. Then have students complete Activity A on their own.

Activity A Answers

1. S—team, V—practices; simple 2. S—practice, V—is, S—players, V—are; complex 3. S—team, V— begins; simple 4. S—players, V—do warm, S—injuries, V—are; complex 5. S—teams, V—do play; simple

---

Lesson 5 Complex and Compound-Complex Sentences

> **Complex sentence**
> *A sentence with one independent clause and one or more dependent clauses*

One way to group sentences is according to purpose (statement, question, command, or exclamation). We can also group them according to structure. A sentence may be *simple, compound, complex,* or *compound-complex.*

Remember that a simple sentence has one independent clause.

EXAMPLE S V
I will drive to work.

A **complex sentence** has one independent clause and one or more dependent clauses.

EXAMPLE S V S V PA
I will drive if you are tired.

Activity A Write these sentences on your paper. Label the subject and the verb of each clause as shown. Then write whether the sentence is *simple* or *complex.*

Example S V S V
The team was behind until Tim kicked a goal.—complex

1. Every afternoon the baseball team practices.
2. When practice is over, the players are tired.
3. The team begins with warm-up exercises.
4. If players don't warm up well, injuries are likely.
5. Baseball teams do not usually play during thunderstorms.

A complex sentence can have more than one dependent clause.

EXAMPLE

Adj. Clause
Toni Morrison, who was born in Ohio, studied at Howard
Adv. Clause
University before she became the author of *Beloved*.

To find an independent clause in a complex sentence:

- Identify the dependent clause or clauses in the sentence.
- Read all the words that are not in the dependent clause or clauses. These words make up the independent, or main, clause of the sentence.

When typed, the titles of books, magazines, and movies always appear in italics. Underline these titles when writing them by hand. The titles of short stories, songs, and articles appear in quotation marks.

Activity B Answer these questions about the following sentence. Write the answers on your paper.

Toni Morrison, who was born in Ohio, studied at Howard University before she became the author of Beloved.

1. What is the independent clause in the sentence?
2. What is the subject of the independent clause?
3. What is the verb of the independent clause?
4. Is the verb transitive or intransitive?
5. What are the parts of speech of the words in the phrase *at Howard University*?
6. What noun does the adjective clause describe?
7. What question does the adverb clause answer?
8. What are the subject and the verb of the adjective clause?
9. What are the subject and the verb of the adverb clause?
10. Which verb (or verb phrase) is a linking verb? What word completes the idea in that clause?

Activity B

Read the directions and the sentence under the directions with students. Be sure students understand what they are to do. Then divide the class into small groups and have each group complete Activity B. When they have finished, read each activity question aloud and ask a representative from each group to give the group's response. If all responses are the same and are correct, move on to the next item. If responses differ or are incorrect, discuss the answers given and help students identify the correct one.

Activity B Answers

1. Toni Morrison studied at Howard University **2.** Toni Morrison **3.** studied **4.** intransitive **5.** *at*—preposition, *Howard University*—proper noun **6.** Toni Morrison **7.** When did Toni Morrison study at Howard University? **8.** who—subject, was born—verb **9.** she—subject, became—verb **10.** became—linking verb, author—predicate noun

3 Reinforce and Extend

LEARNING STYLES

Auditory/Verbal

Have students write a simple sentence with at least one phrase and a complex sentence. Then divide the class into two teams. Have them stand facing one another. Ask the first student on Team 1 to read a sentence. Challenge the first student on Team 2 to tell whether the sentence is simple or complex and to identify the independent clause. The team scores one point for each correct answer. Continue until all players on both teams have had a turn reading and answering.

LEARNING STYLES

LEP/ESL

Ask students proficient in English and students learning English to work in pairs. Tell each person to select two sentences from something he or she has written recently. Ask the students to work together to revise the sentences so one is a compound sentence and one is a complex sentence. Then have them get together with another pair of students. Have each student read each original sentence and the revised sentence. Encourage the pairs to discuss the results of the changes.

Complex Sentences Chapter 11 291

Career Connection

The step-by-step approach of analyzing a compound-complex sentence by breaking it into smaller parts makes it easier for students to understand the construction and meaning of the sentence. Point out to students that the ability to analyze any complex project by breaking it into small, simple steps can mean the difference between completing a task and being overwhelmed by it. Workers who can break complicated tasks into manageable steps are an asset to any organization. Suggest that students interview people in different careers and different levels of management about how they deal with difficult or complex problems. Students should ask for examples of times when complicated tasks were made less difficult through a step-by-step approach.

Learning Styles

Body/Kinesthetic

Divide the class into small groups. Give several sheets of construction paper of varying colors to each group. Ask each group to write and analyze a compound-complex sentence. Then tell students to write each part of the sentence on a different color of construction paper. For example, each independent clause would be written on a separate sheet of construction paper but of the same color, red, for example. The conjunction would be on another color paper. Each dependent clause would be on a different color paper. When groups are ready, have them form a human sentence by having members of the group hold up the sheets of construction paper in the correct sentence order. Classmates could then identify the different parts of the sentence, using the colors as clues.

Compound-complex sentence

A sentence that has two or more independent clauses and one or more dependent clauses

A compound sentence has two independent clauses.

Example

S V S V PA
I would drive, **but** I am too tired.

A **compound-complex sentence** has two or more independent clauses and one or more dependent clauses.

Example

S V S V PA S V PN
I will drive if you are too tired, **but** it is your decision.

When you want to understand the construction of a sentence, analyze it. To analyze means to break something down into its parts. You can analyze a sentence to find out whether it is compound, complex, or compound-complex. Look at the following sentence:

Brady knows that college is important, but if he doesn't get a scholarship, he must wait until he saves money.

Here are the steps to analyze a sentence.

How to Analyze a Sentence

1. Identify the independent clauses in the sentence. In the example, the independent clauses are *Brady knows* and *he must wait.* They are joined by the conjunction *but.*
2. Identify the dependent clauses in the sentence. In the example, the noun clause *that college is important* is the direct object of the first independent clause. *If he doesn't get a scholarship* and *until he saves money* are adverb clauses that tell about the verb *must wait.*
3. The example sentence has two independent clauses and three dependent clauses. It is a compound-complex sentence.
4. These are the sentence patterns of each clause:

   S V Conj.
Brady knows (that college is important), but

   S V DO S V S
if he doesn't get a scholarship, he must wait until he

   V DO
saves money.

292 Chapter 11 Complex Sentences

Activity C Write each of these sentences on your paper. Find the independent clauses and the dependent clauses. Next to each sentence, write whether it is *complex* or *compound-complex.*

1. Mr. and Mrs. Johnson play golf when the weather is warm.
2. What I would like is a vacation.
3. Alicia works at the daycare center that is located next to the high school, and her sister works there, too.
4. Wildfires, which can start suddenly, may destroy trees and plants, but they also can create regrowth.
5. Both of us know that we must study hard, or we will not get into good colleges.

Direct and indirect quotations within sentences are noun clauses.

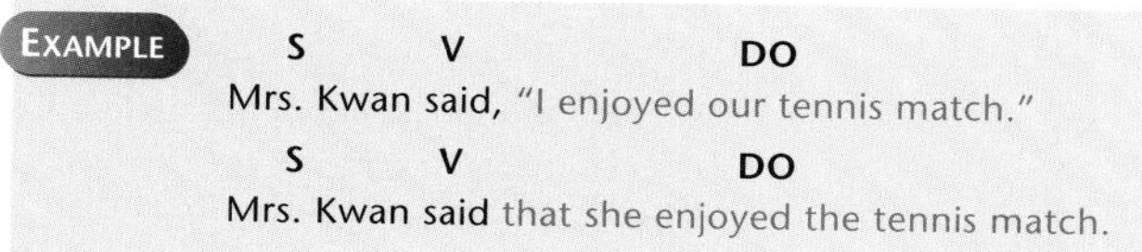
EXAMPLE

S V DO
Mrs. Kwan said, "I enjoyed our tennis match."

S V DO
Mrs. Kwan said that she enjoyed the tennis match.

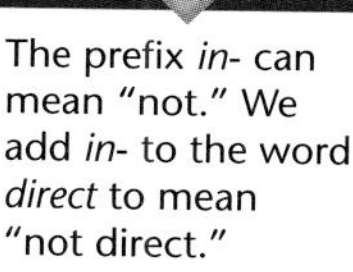
The prefix *in-* can mean "not." We add *in-* to the word *direct* to mean "not direct."

Activity D On your paper, change each of these indirect quotations to direct quotations. Use proper punctuation. Then circle each noun clause.

1. Mr. Kwan said that he wants a new tennis racket.
2. I told my boss that I could not come to work today.
3. Anita said that her mother was going back to college.
4. My brother Elvin whispered that he had a surprise for me.
5. Tina told me that she had found my book in her desk.

Activity C

Have students do Activity C on their own. Suggest that they follow steps similar to the ones shown on page 292 to tell whether a sentence is complex or compound-complex.

Activity C Answers

1. complex **2.** complex **3.** compound-complex **4.** compound-complex **5.** compound-complex

Activity D

Review the conventions for punctuating quotations. Then do item 1 on the board, having students tell you how to punctuate the sentence and what words to circle for the noun clause.

Activity D Answers

1. Mr. Kwan said, "I want a new tennis racket." **2.** I told my boss, "I cannot come to work today." **3.** Anita said, "My mother is going back to college." **4.** My brother Elvin whispered, "I have a surprise for you." **5.** Tina told me, "I found your book in my desk."

ONLINE CONNECTION

Suggest that students visit the Web site **www.lsilver.net** to review simple, compound, and complex sentences. At the site, students should click on first Table of Contents, then How Are Sentences Created?, and then a specific sentence type. The site provides explanations of each type of sentence, lists of conjunctions, and examples of simple, compound, and complex sentences.

Activity E

Do Activity E orally as a class. After the questions have been answered correctly, challenge students to make up additional questions about the construction of the sentences. Invite students to ask their questions for the class to answer.

Activity E Answers

1. the compound-complex sentence **2.** Rafael also writes poems. **3.** adjective clause **4.** two **5.** adjective clause

Activity F

Ask students to take turns giving examples of simple, compound, complex, and compound-complex sentences. The class should listen carefully to be sure students have provided accurate examples. Then have students complete Activity F independently.

Activity F Answers

1. After school gets out, Emily hopes that she can find a job.—complex **2.** She asked Vic's uncle about a job, but he was not hiring.—compound **3.** She became discouraged about her job search.—simple **4.** Emily kept looking because she needed money for college, and she knew there was a job for her somewhere.—compound-complex **5.** A person like Emily, who doesn't give up easily, will look until she finds a job.—complex

The same idea may be expressed in different kinds of sentences.

EXAMPLE

Simple	Rafael writes stories and poems.
Compound	Rafael writes stories, but he also writes poems.
Complex	Rafael, who writes stories, also writes poems.
Compound–Complex	Rafael writes stories, but he also has written poems that have been published.

Activity E Answer the following questions about the examples above. Write the answers on your paper.

1. Which sentence provides the most information?
2. What is the independent clause in the complex sentence example?
3. What kind of dependent clause is *who writes stories* in the complex example? Is it a noun clause, an adjective clause, or an adverb clause?
4. How many independent clauses are in the compound-complex example?
5. What kind of dependent clause is *that have been published*?

Activity F Write these sentences on your paper. Underline each independent clause once and each dependent clause twice. Then write whether each sentence is *simple, compound, complex,* or *compound-complex.*

1. After school gets out, Emily hopes that she can find a job.
2. She asked Vic's uncle about a job, but he was not hiring.
3. She became discouraged about her job search.
4. Emily kept looking because she needed money for college, and she knew there was a job for her somewhere.
5. A person like Emily, who doesn't give up easily, will look until she finds a job.

At Home

Encourage students to review personal letters and other writing projects to check for a variety of sentence structures. Suggest that they add adverb, noun, and adjective clauses to sentences to convey additional information and to make their writing more interesting.

Learning Styles

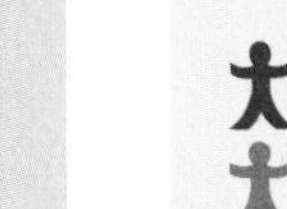

Visual/Spatial

On the board write the following sentence patterns:

1. simple
2. compound
3. complex
4. compound-complex

Give pairs of students magazine pictures to use in constructing sentences that represent the four sentence patterns listed on the board. Suggest that the partners do the following to help them write the sentences: find the nouns—people, places, things—in the pictures; consider the actions these nouns could do; look for relationships among the nouns and actions; write the four sentences. When sentences have been written, invite volunteers to read one or more of their sentences. Encourage the class to name the pattern each sentence represents.

Analyze each of these sentences. Find the independent clauses and the dependent clauses. Write on your paper whether the sentence is *simple, compound, complex,* or *compound-complex.*

1. Mrs. Huang planned a party for Kim because Kim was graduating from high school.
2. She invited Kim's friends to the party, and all of them came.
3. "It could be fun," Elena told the others.
4. Kim wanted a new watch for a graduation gift.
5. Kim went to the store with her friend Angie, and together they shopped for a waterproof watch that was not too expensive.

On your paper, write an example of each sentence structure—*simple, compound, complex,* and *compound-complex.* Then underline each independent clause once and each dependent clause twice.

Writing Project

Writing Complex Sentences

Imagine yourself 10 or 20 years from now. On your paper, write a paragraph describing your typical day. Be as specific as possible. Use these questions to help you:

- Where will you be?
- What will you be doing?
- What will you be like?

Use dependent clauses in your sentences. Include at least one adverb clause, one adjective clause, and one noun clause. When you are finished, underline and identify each dependent clause. Then read your paragraph to the class.

Lesson 5 Review Answers

1. complex 2. compound 3. complex 4. simple 5. compound-complex

Students should write an example of each of the four types of sentence structures—simple, compound, complex, and compound-complex. Sentences will vary. Check to see that students have underlined independent clauses once and dependent clauses twice.

Writing Project

Remind students that each kind of sentence—simple, compound, complex, and compound-complex—is needed in writing. Too many simple sentences make the writing sound choppy and dull. Long, complicated sentences aren't always the answer either. A variety of well-crafted sentences make writing interesting and lively. Have students orally respond to each question in the activity. Let volunteers expand the responses into a complex sentence in which the original response becomes part of a dependent or independent clause. Then have students complete the activity on their own.

Answers to Writing Project: Paragraphs will vary. Each paragraph should include an adverb clause, an adjective clause, and a noun clause. Each dependent clause should be underlined and identified as to type. Invite students to share their paragraphs with the class.

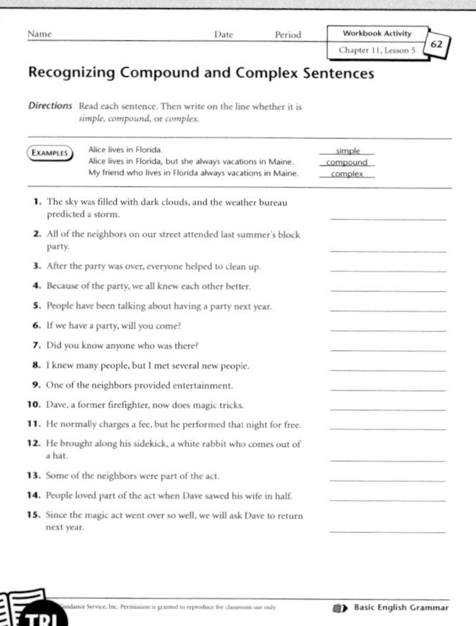

Name Date Period | Workbook Activity 62 | Chapter 11, Lesson 5

Recognizing Compound and Complex Sentences

Directions Read each sentence. Then write on the line whether it is *simple, compound,* or *complex.*

EXAMPLES
Alice lives in Florida. simple
Alice lives in Florida, but she always vacations in Maine. compound
My friend who lives in Florida always vacations in Maine. complex

1. The sky was filled with dark clouds, and the weather bureau predicted a storm. ________
2. All of the neighbors on our street attended last summer's block party. ________
3. After the party was over, everyone helped to clean up. ________
4. Because of the party, we all knew each other better. ________
5. People have been talking about having a party next year. ________
6. If we have a party, will you come? ________
7. Did you know anyone who was there? ________
8. I knew many people, but I met several new people. ________
9. One of the neighbors provided entertainment. ________
10. Dave, a former firefighter, now does magic tricks. ________
11. He normally charges a fee, but he performed that night for free. ________
12. He brought along his sidekick, a white rabbit who comes out of a hat. ________
13. Some of the neighbors were part of the act. ________
14. People loved part of the act when Dave sawed his wife in half. ________
15. Since the magic act went over so well, we will ask Dave to return next year. ________

 Basic English Grammar

TRL

Workbook Activity 62

Name Date Period | Activity 62 | Chapter 11, Lesson 5

Dependent Clauses in Complex and Compound-Complex Sentences

Directions Read each sentence. Underline the independent clause(s) once and the dependent clause(s) twice.

EXAMPLE If he doesn't remember to bring an umbrella, he will be soaked.

1. Her grandfather was fishing at the lake when she called, so she had to call again after he returned home.
2. The first time that they met was a bad experience, but they became friends after they got to know each other better.
3. The book that I want has colorful photographs in it.
4. My cousin, who is an airline pilot, has flown all over the world, but she has never visited Washington, D.C.
5. The families will go home when the fireworks display is finished.
6. Last summer, when I broke my arm and had to wear a cast, was miserably hot.
7. The plants that she is raising will be sold at the garden show, and the proceeds will benefit a local children's hospital.
8. Greg and Rebecca will open their own restaurant when they have saved enough money.
9. Cory's dream, which she has had for many years, is to learn to sail, but she must wait until another sailing class begins.
10. This computer screen flickers when anyone bumps the desk, so I must take it to the computer store for repairs.
11. Believe me when I tell you that horses cannot fly.
12. If Sarah needs to take a break, Caleb can drive for a while.
13. The tacos, which Lena made, are too spicy for me, but Sam will enjoy them because he likes spicy food.
14. The lake that is on the edge of my grandparents farm is full of fish, and I often fish there when I have a day off.
15. The painting that Beth contributed to the art show will hang where many people can enjoy it.

 Basic English Grammar

TRL

Activity 62

Chapter 11 Review

Use the Chapter Review to prepare students for tests and to reteach content from the chapter.

Chapter 11 Mastery Test TRL

The Teacher's Resource Library includes two parallel forms of the Chapter 11 Mastery Test. The difficulty level of the two forms is equivalent. You may wish to use one form as a pretest and the other form as a posttest.

Review Answers

Part A

1. noun clause 2. adverb clause 3. appositive 4. complex sentence 5. phrase 6. compound-complex sentence 7. adjective clause

Part B

8. clause 9. phrase 10. phrase 11. clause 12. clause 13. phrase

Part C

14. dependent clause—Before
15. independent clause
16. dependent clause—which
17. independent clause

Chapter 11 REVIEW

Word Bank
adjective clause
adverb clause
appositive
complex sentence
compound-complex sentence
noun clause
phrase

Part A On a sheet of paper, write the correct word or words from the Word Bank to complete each sentence.

1. A ________ is a dependent clause that works like a noun in a sentence.

2. An ________ is a dependent clause that works like an adverb in a sentence.

3. An ________ is a noun, phrase, or clause that is placed next to a noun to rename or explain it.

4. A ________ has one independent clause and one or more dependent clauses.

5. A ________ is a group of words that does not contain a subject and predicate, such as a prepositional phrase or a verb phrase.

6. A ________ has two or more independent clauses and one or more dependent clauses.

7. An ________ is a dependent clause that describes a noun or pronoun.

Part B On your paper, write whether each group of words is a *phrase* or a *clause.*

8. who planned the party
9. to the party
10. for Kim and her friends
11. that everyone will enjoy
12. because Kim is graduating
13. during her senior year

Part C Write on your paper whether the clause in bold is an *independent clause* or a *dependent clause.* Then write the word that introduces each dependent clause.

14. **Before his senior year was over,** Leigh applied to college.
15. If you are tired, **you should go to bed.**
16. My aunt gave me a sweater, **which she knitted.**
17. **Tell the clerk** that we need help.

Name ________ Date ________ Period ________ Mastery Test A, Page 1 Chapter 11

Chapter 11 Mastery Test A

Part A Write whether each group of words is a *phrase* or a *clause.*

1. He is my friend. ________
2. Unless it rains. ________
3. Having a picnic is fun. ________
4. Which her daughter gave her. ________
5. On top of the world. ________
6. Jackie planned a party. ________
7. For her mother. ________
8. Who was having a birthday. ________
9. The person in the middle. ________
10. Whoever plans the menu. ________

Part B Underline the independent clause once and the dependent clause(s) twice.

11. Deanne will bring plates and napkins when she gets off work.
12. The cake that was shaped like a football was a big hit.
13. If Jim decides to buy my car, I will give him a good deal.
14. Whoever wants to go to college must study hard.
15. We cannot play on the side of the pool where the lap swimmers work out.
16. Amber and Ben have been best friends since they were in first grade.
17. Because the temperature was dropping, the children went inside.
18. The recipe that I used to make this dessert is surprisingly simple.
19. Chad and Jonathan ride the train when they go to their grandmother's house.
20. Did she know what they were planning to do?

 Basic English Grammar

TRL

Name ________ Date ________ Period ________ Mastery Test A, Page 2 Chapter 11

Chapter 11 Mastery Test A, continued

Part C Write whether the bold words are an *adjective clause*, an *adverb clause*, or a *noun clause.*

21. Hal knew **what his father would say**. ________
22. We got the best seats **because we arrived early**. ________
23. Shelly bought a computer **that has a lot of memory**. ________
24. We disagree about **who should be the next president**. ________
25. They go surfing **whenever they have a chance**. ________
26. **After school is out,** Janice is going on vacation. ________
27. I travel **wherever I want to go**. ________
28. **Whoever wants to go swimming** can join us. ________
29. The person **who opened the door for me** was very kind. ________
30. The dog **that wandered into our yard** looked lost. ________

Part D Identify each kind of sentence as *simple, compound, complex,* or *compound-complex.* Circle the correct answer.

31. The forecast was for snow, and it was correct.
A simple **B** compound **C** complex **D** compound-complex

32. Perry attends junior college, and he has a part-time job, which helps him pay for school.
A simple **B** compound **C** complex **D** compound-complex

33. Kelly, who is quite tall, hopes to play basketball.
A simple **B** compound **C** complex **D** compound-complex

34. The United States has many national parks.
A simple **B** compound **C** complex **D** compound-complex

35. Mary drove for several miles, and then Josh, who doesn't like driving as well, took over.
A simple **B** compound **C** complex **D** compound-complex

 Basic English Grammar

TRL

Chapter 11 Mastery Test A

Part D Write on your paper whether each clause in bold is an *adjective clause,* an *adverb clause,* or a *noun clause.* If the noun clause is an appositive, write the appositive on your paper. Then write each relative pronoun.

18. Alex, **who has already graduated,** has gotten Kim a present **that he purchased in Bermuda.**

19. Mrs. Huang, **Kim's mother,** has planned a surprise for the person **who arrives first.**

20. **Whoever it is** will be surprised.

21. **Because the party is for Kim,** the guests will not expect a gift.

Part E On your paper, write the letter that tells the type of sentence structure—*simple, compound, complex,* or *compound-complex*—of each sentence.

22. Gordon made a present, but he also bought a book that Kim would like.

A simple **B** compound **C** complex **D** compound-complex

23. We had a wonderful time at the party.

A simple **B** compound **C** complex **D** compound-complex

24. Who won the CD that Mrs. Huang bought?

A simple **B** compound **C** complex **D** compound-complex

25. Carrie and Mark drove together, and they arrived first.

A simple **B** compound **C** complex **D** compound-complex

If you don't know the answer to a question, put a check next to it and go on. Then when you are finished, go back to any checked questions and try to answer them.

Review Answers

Part D

18. adjective clause—who, adjective clause—that **19.** appositive—Kim's mother, adjective clause—who **20.** noun clause—Whoever **21.** adverb clause

Part E

22. D **23.** A **24.** C **25.** B

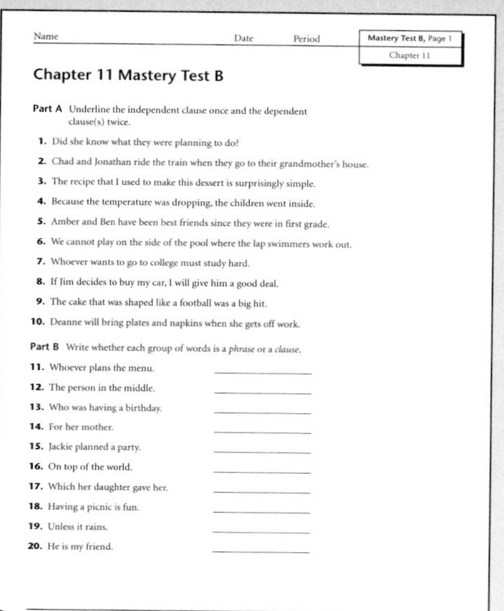

Name Date Period | Mastery Test B, Page 1 | Chapter 11

Chapter 11 Mastery Test B

Part A Underline the independent clause once and the dependent clause(s) twice.

1. Did she know what they were planning to do?
2. Chad and Jonathan ride the train when they go to their grandmother's house.
3. The recipe that I used to make this dessert is surprisingly simple.
4. Because the temperature was dropping, the children went inside.
5. Amber and Ben have been best friends since they were in first grade.
6. We cannot play on the side of the pool where the lap swimmers work out.
7. Whoever wants to go to college must study hard.
8. If Jim decides to buy my car, I will give him a good deal.
9. The cake that was shaped like a football was a big hit.
10. Deanne will bring plates and napkins when she gets off work.

Part B Write whether each group of words is a *phrase* or a *clause.*

11. Whoever plans the menu. ________
12. The person in the middle. ________
13. Who was having a birthday. ________
14. For her mother. ________
15. Jackie planned a party. ________
16. On top of the world. ________
17. Which her daughter gave her. ________
18. Having a picnic is fun. ________
19. Unless it rains. ________
20. He is my friend. ________

 Basic English Grammar

TRL

Name Date Period | Mastery Test B, Page 2 | Chapter 11

Chapter 11 Mastery Test B, continued

Part C Identify each kind of sentence as *simple, compound, complex,* or *compound-complex.* Circle the correct answer.

21. Mary drove for several miles, and then Josh, who doesn't like driving as well, took over.
A simple **B** compound **C** complex **D** compound-complex

22. The United States has many national parks.
A simple **B** compound **C** complex **D** compound-complex

23. Kelly, who is quite tall, hopes to play basketball.
A simple **B** compound **C** complex **D** compound-complex

24. Perry attends junior college, and he has a part-time job, which helps him pay for school.
A simple **B** compound **C** complex **D** compound-complex

25. The forecast was for snow, and it was correct.
A simple **B** compound **C** complex **D** compound-complex

Part D Write whether the bold words are an *adjective clause,* an *adverb clause,* or a *noun clause.*

26. The dog **that wandered into our yard** looked lost. ________
27. The person **who opened the door for me** was very kind. ________
28. **Whoever wants to go swimming** can join us. ________
29. I travel **wherever I want to go.** ________
30. **After school is out,** Janice is going on vacation. ________
31. They go surfing **whenever they have a chance.** ________
32. We disagree about **who should be the next president.** ________
33. Shelly bought a computer **that has a lot of memory.** ________
34. We got the best seats **because we arrived early.** ________
35. Hal knew **what his father would say.** ________

 Basic English Grammar

TRL

Chapter 11 Mastery Test B

Planning Guide

The Verbal and the Verbal Phrase

	Student Text Lesson				Language Skills		
	Student Pages	Vocabulary	Practice Exercises	Lesson Review	Identification Skills	Writing Skills	Punctuation Skills
Lesson 1 What Is a Verbal?	300–301	✔	✔	✔	✔	✔	✔
Lesson 2 Infinitives and Infinitive Phrases	302–307	✔	✔	✔	✔	✔	✔
Lesson 3 Gerunds and Gerund Phrases	308–311	✔	✔	✔	✔	✔	✔
Lesson 4 Participles and Participle Phrases	312–315	✔	✔	✔	✔	✔	✔

Chapter Activities

Teacher's Resource Library

Community Connection 12: Verbals in Reference Materials

Media and Literature Connection 12: Finding Verbals in Poetry

Assessment Options

Student Text

Chapter 12 Review

Teacher's Resource Library

Chapter 12 Mastery Tests A and B

Student Text Features						Teaching Strategies						Learning Styles						Teacher's Resource Library			
Spelling Builder	Vocabulary Builder	Where To Find It	Writing Project	Using What You've Learned	Writing Tips/Notes/Technology Notes	Teacher Alert	Online Connection	Applications (Home, Career, Community, Global)	Speaking Practice	Spelling Practice	Writing Practice	Auditory/Verbal	Body/Kinesthetic	Interpersonal/Group Learning	Logical/Mathematical	Visual/Spatial	LEP/ESL	Workbook Activities	Activities	Alternative Activities	Self-Study Guide
													301					63	63	63	✔
307					✔	305		303, 304		307	304	306		305				64	64	64	✔
	311			309	✔			310								310		65	65	65	✔
		314	315		✔	313	313	314, 315	314						313		312	66	66	66	✔

Pronunciation Key

a	hat	e	let	ī	ice	ô	order	ů	put	sh	she	ə { a	in about
ā	age	ē	equal	o	hot	oi	oil	ü	rule	th	thin	e	in taken
ä	far	ėr	term	ō	open	ou	out	ch	child	ŦH	then	i	in pencil
â	care	i	it	ȯ	saw	u	cup	ng	long	zh	measure	o	in lemon
												u	in circus

Alternative Activities

The Teacher's Resource Library (TRL) contains a set of lower-level worksheets called Alternative Activities. These worksheets cover the same content as the regular Activities but are written at a second-grade reading level.

Skill Track Software

Use the Skill Track Software for Basic English Grammar for additional reinforcement of this chapter. The software program allows students using AGS textbooks to be assessed for mastery of each chapter and lesson of the textbook. Students access the software on an individual basis and are assessed with multiple-choice items.

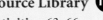

Chapter at a Glance

Chapter 12: The Verbal and the Verbal Phrase
pages 298–317

Skill Track Software for Basic English Grammar

Teacher's Resource Library TRL

Workbook Activities 63–66

Activities 63–66

Alternative Activities 63–66

Community Connection 12

Media and Literature Connection 12

Chapter 12 Self-Study Guide

Chapter 12 Mastery Tests A and B

(Answer Keys for the Teacher's Resource Library begin on page 340 of this Teacher's Edition.)

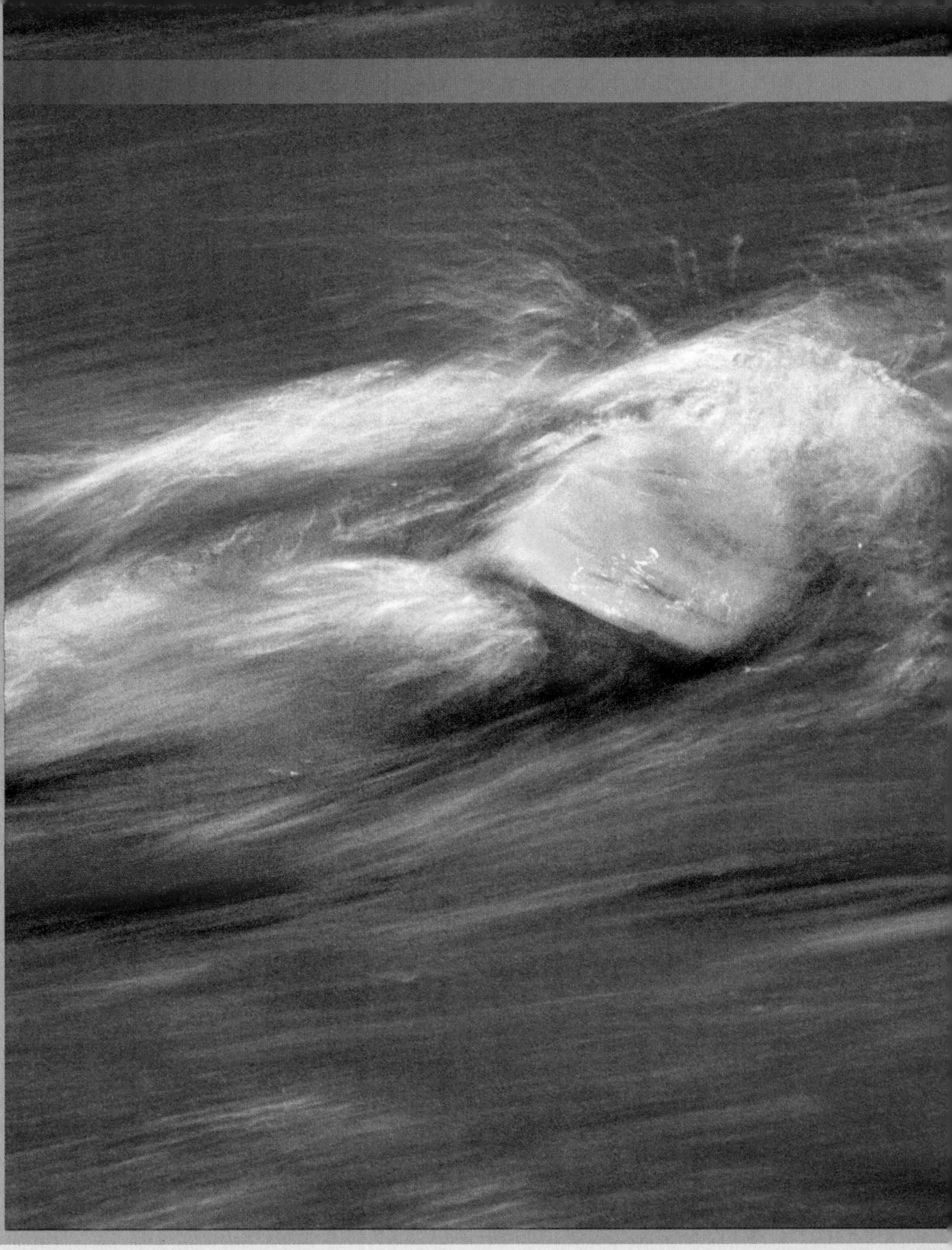

Name Date Period — Community Connection 12, Chapter 12

Verbals in Reference Materials

An **infinitive** is the word *to* plus a verb. An **infinitive phrase** is an infinitive plus any adverb, adjective, or complement it may have.

EXAMPLE Debbie wants to be a doctor.
(*to be*—infinitive *to be a doctor*—infinitive phrase)

A **gerund** is a verb form ending in *-ing*. A **gerund phrase** is a gerund plus any adjective, adverb, prepositional phrase, or complement it may have.

EXAMPLE Mr. Lopez likes driving in the mountains.
(*driving*—gerund *driving in the mountains*—gerund phrase)

A **participle** is a verb form used in a sentence as an adjective. A **participle phrase** is a participle plus an adverb or an adverb phrase.

EXAMPLE Measuring with a ruler, the clerk cut the fabric.
(*Measuring*—participle *Measuring with a ruler*—participle phrase)

We use reference books to find information. Dictionaries and encyclopedias are two kinds of reference books. These are found in the reference section of the library. Use reference books to practice finding infinitives, gerunds, and participles.

Step 1 Find a reference book at the library. Be sure to find one that uses complete sentences.

Step 2 Look for complete sentences with infinitives, gerunds, and participles. Find two of each kind. Write each sentence on the back of this page. Circle the infinitive, gerund, or participle. Underline any infinitive, gerund, or participle phrases.

Step 3 Write *infinitive*, *gerund*, or *participle* after each sentence.

EXAMPLE They enjoy walking in the woods. gerund

Basic English Grammar

Community Connection 12

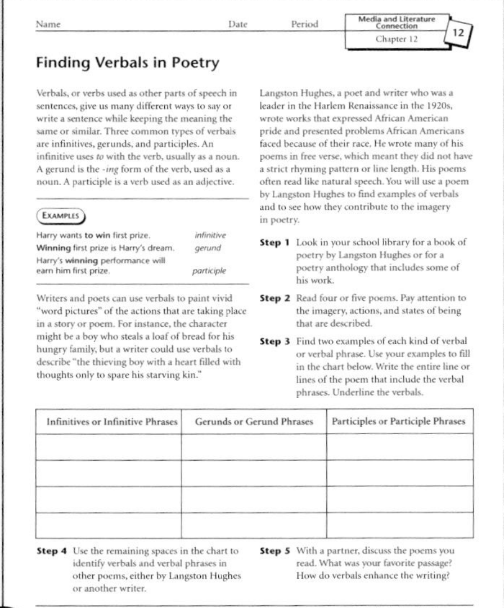

Name Date Period — Media and Literature Connection 12, Chapter 12

Finding Verbals in Poetry

Verbals, or verbs used as other parts of speech in sentences, give us many different ways to say or write a sentence while keeping the meaning the same or similar. Three common types of verbals are infinitives, gerunds, and participles. An infinitive uses *to* with the verb, usually as a noun. A gerund is the *-ing* form of the verb, used as a noun. A participle is a verb used as an adjective.

EXAMPLES

Harry wants **to win** first prize. *infinitive*
Winning first prize is Harry's dream. *gerund*
Harry's **winning** performance will earn him first prize. *participle*

Writers and poets can use verbals to paint vivid "word pictures" of the actions that are taking place in a story or poem. For instance, the character might be a boy who steals a loaf of bread for his hungry family, but a writer could use verbals to describe "the thieving boy with a heart filled with thoughts only to spare his starving kin."

Langston Hughes, a poet and writer who was a leader in the Harlem Renaissance in the 1920s, wrote works that expressed African American pride and presented problems African Americans faced because of their race. He wrote many of his poems in free verse, which meant they did not have a strict rhyming pattern or line length. His poems often read like natural speech. You will use a poem by Langston Hughes to find examples of verbals and to see how they contribute to the imagery in poetry.

Step 1 Look in your school library for a book of poetry by Langston Hughes or for a poetry anthology that includes some of his work.

Step 2 Read four or five poems. Pay attention to the imagery, actions, and states of being that are described.

Step 3 Find two examples of each kind of verbal or verbal phrase. Use your examples to fill in the chart below. Write the entire line or lines of the poem that include the verbal phrases. Underline the verbals.

Infinitives or Infinitive Phrases	Gerunds or Gerund Phrases	Participles or Participle Phrases

Step 4 Use the remaining spaces in the chart to identify verbals and verbal phrases in other poems, either by Langston Hughes or another writer.

Step 5 With a partner, discuss the poems you read. What was your favorite passage? How do verbals enhance the writing?

Basic English Grammar

Media and Literature Connection 12

Chapter

The Verbal and the Verbal Phrase

What does this photograph make you think of? Don't you think *moving* through the water at top speed would be fun? Does it remind you how much you like *to swim*? *Excited* fans make *swimming* a great sport *to watch.*

Each of the words in italic type is a verb form. But these words do not act as verbs in these sentences. Instead they act as nouns, adjectives, or adverbs. Verbs that we use as different parts of speech are called verbals. The three kinds of verbals are *infinitives, gerunds,* and *participles.*

In Chapter 12, you will learn about verbals and how to use them in sentences.

Goals for Learning

- ◆ To identify and use infinitives and infinitive phrases in sentences
- ◆ To identify and use gerunds and gerund phrases in sentences
- ◆ To identify and use participles and participle phrases in sentences

Introducing the Chapter

Have students examine and describe the photograph on page 298. Encourage them to use action verbs, such as *swim* and *splash,* to describe the activity in the photograph. Then ask questions about what students like to do in the water. Use a questioning strategy that encourages them to use verbals in their responses. Questions might include *What do you like to do in the water? What is your favorite water activity?* (Examples of responses: *I like to float on a raft in the water. Water skiing is my favorite water activity.*)

Write the responses on the board and underline the verbals. Point out to students that verbals are verbs used as different parts of speech. Then explain that Chapter 12 introduces the three types of verbals—infinitives, gerunds, and participles.

Writing Tips, Notes, and Technology Notes

Ask volunteers to read the tips and notes that appear in the margins throughout the chapter. Then discuss them with the class.

Teacher's Resource

The AGS Teaching Strategies in English Transparencies may be used with this chapter. The transparencies add an interactive dimension to expand and enhance the *Basic English Grammar* program content.

Career Interest Inventory

The AGS Harrington-O'Shea Career Decision-Making System–Revised (CDM) may be used with this chapter. Students can use the CDM to explore their interests and identify careers. The CDM defines career areas that are indicated by students' responses on the inventory.

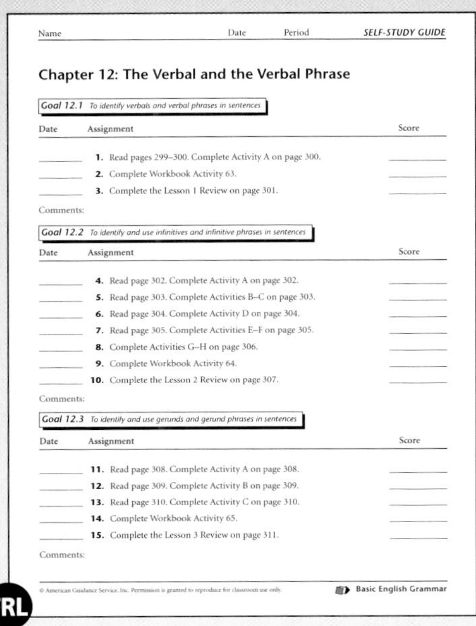

Name Date Period *SELF-STUDY GUIDE*

Chapter 12: The Verbal and the Verbal Phrase

Goal 12.1 *To identify verbals and verbal phrases in sentences*

Date	Assignment	Score
______	**1.** Read pages 299–300. Complete Activity A on page 300.	______
______	**2.** Complete Workbook Activity 63.	______
______	**3.** Complete the Lesson 1 Review on page 301.	______

Comments:

Goal 12.2 *To identify and use infinitives and infinitive phrases in sentences*

Date	Assignment	Score
______	**4.** Read page 302. Complete Activity A on page 302.	______
______	**5.** Read page 303. Complete Activities B–C on page 303.	______
______	**6.** Read page 304. Complete Activity D on page 304.	______
______	**7.** Read page 305. Complete Activities E–F on page 305.	______
______	**8.** Complete Activities G–H on page 306.	______
______	**9.** Complete Workbook Activity 64.	______
______	**10.** Complete the Lesson 2 Review on page 307.	______

Comments:

Goal 12.3 *To identify and use gerunds and gerund phrases in sentences*

Date	Assignment	Score
______	**11.** Read page 308. Complete Activity A on page 308.	______
______	**12.** Read page 309. Complete Activity B on page 309.	______
______	**13.** Read page 310. Complete Activity C on page 310.	______
______	**14.** Complete Workbook Activity 65.	______
______	**15.** Complete the Lesson 3 Review on page 311.	______

Comments:

 Basic English Grammar

TRL

Name Date Period *SELF-STUDY GUIDE*

Chapter 12: The Verbal and the Verbal Phrase, continued

Goal 12.4 *To identify and use participles and participle phrases in sentences*

Date	Assignment	Score
______	**16.** Read page 312. Complete Activity A on page 312.	______
______	**17.** Read page 313. Complete Activities B–C on page 313.	______
______	**18.** Read page 314. Complete Activity D on page 314.	______
______	**19.** Complete Workbook Activity 66.	______
______	**20.** Complete the Lesson 4 Review on page 315.	______
______	**21.** Complete the Chapter 12 Review on pages 316–317.	______

Comments:

Student's Signature ______________________ Date ______

Instructor's Signature ______________________ Date ______

 Basic English Grammar

TRL

Chapter 12 Self-Study Guide, Pages 1–2

Lesson at a Glance

Chapter 12 Lesson 1

Overview This lesson introduces the three types of verbals—infinitive, gerund, and participle.

Objective

- To identify verbals in sentences.

Student Pages 300–301

Teacher's Resource Library 

Workbook Activity 63

Activity 63

Alternative Activity 63

Vocabulary

verbal

1 Warm-Up Activity

Write on the board the following sentences: *I win all my races and I like to win.* Circle the word *win* in the first sentence, and ask students what part of speech it is. Elicit that *win* is a verb. Then circle *to win* and ask the same question. Lead students to understand that in the second sentence, *to win* serves as the direct object of the verb *like.* If students fail to understand this concept, write *I like pizza* on the board, identifying *pizza* as the direct object. Point out that *to win* has the same part in the sentence as does *pizza.* Explain to students that *to win* is one type of verbal, a verb that we use as another part of speech.

Teaching the Lesson

Have students read the definitions and examples of verbals on this page. Point out that the infinitive and the past participle forms are not easily confused with each other. Then write *laughing* on the board, and ask students if it is a gerund or a present participle. Explain that the only way to tell a gerund from a present participle is to identify its use in a sentence. Write *Laughing is good for you* and *The laughing boy played on the see-saw.* Help students identify *laughing* as a noun in the first example and as an adjective in the second. Write a selection of *-ing* words on the board and encourage students to use them as adjectives and nouns.

Activity A

Write examples of each type of verbal on the board. Then ask volunteers to identify verbals in the first two items of Activity A. Students should complete the remaining sentences on their own.

Activity A Answers

1. fishing 2. to fish 3. stocked 4. Boating 5. rowing 6. Being 7. thinking 8. to drive 9. packing 10. packed

Lesson 1 What Is a Verbal?

> ***Verbal***
> *A verb that we use as another part of speech*

A **verbal** is a verb that we use as another part of speech. The three kinds of verbals are infinitives, gerunds, and participles.

An infinitive is *to* + a verb. Usually we use an infinitive as a noun, but it may also be an adverb or an adjective.

EXAMPLE		
	Noun	I like to swim.
	Adverb	He practices to win.
	Adjective	We had lots of food to eat.

A gerund is a verb that ends in *-ing* that we use as a noun. A gerund can be any part of a sentence that a noun can be.

EXAMPLE		
	Subject	Swimming is good exercise.
	Direct Object	We enjoy swimming.

A participle is a verb form that we use as an adjective. There are present and past participles.

EXAMPLE		
	Past Participle	The cat seems lost.
		The lost cat returned.
	Present Participle	The barking dog scared me.

Activity A On your paper, write the verbals in these sentences.

1. Alex enjoys fishing.
2. This summer he hopes to fish at a national park.
3. The stocked lake is always full of bass.
4. Boating is also possible.
5. Alex thinks about rowing to the middle of the lake.
6. Being outdoors is enjoyable.
7. Just thinking about the trip makes Alex happy.
8. He plans to drive there.
9. He considers packing a lunch.
10. The packed lunch would save him time and money.

Lesson 1 REVIEW

On your paper, write the verbals in these sentences. Next to each one, write whether it is an *infinitive,* a *gerund,* or a *participle.*

1. Driving to the park will take an hour.
2. Alex has a map to follow.
3. He will not get lost.
4. The shimmering lake was a lovely sight.
5. Quickly Alex started to fish.
6. Casting was something that Alex enjoyed.
7. Patience is important in fishing.
8. The chirping birds provided background noise.
9. Alex cast out his baited hook.
10. He could hardly wait to catch a large bass.

Use each verbal in a sentence. Identify the part of the sentence. Do not use these verbals as part of a verb phrase.

11. barking
12. to write
13. laughing
14. playing
15. to recognize

Lesson 1 Review Answers

1. Driving—gerund **2.** to follow—infinitive **3.** lost—participle **4.** shimmering—participle **5.** to fish—infinitive **6.** Casting—gerund **7.** fishing—gerund **8.** chirping—participle **9.** baited—participle **10.** to catch—infinitive **11–15.** Sentences will vary. Example sentences follow. **11.** The barking dog frightened me. **12.** I have a report to write for history class. **13.** Some people say that laughing is good medicine. **14.** The children spend much of their time playing outside. **15.** I was unable to recognize you until you turned around.

3 Reinforce and Extend

Learning Styles

Body/Kinesthetic

Write a number of common verbs spaced out along the top of the board. Then have students form teams of three or four. Tell the class that you are going to call out the name of a verbal—gerund, infinitive, past or present participle. As soon as teams hear the word, they should go directly to a verb on the board and write a sentence that uses the verb in the form you specified. When each team has written a sentence, have them leave the board and prepare for another round. Tell the teams that they may not use the same verb twice in a row. Review their sentences after several rounds.

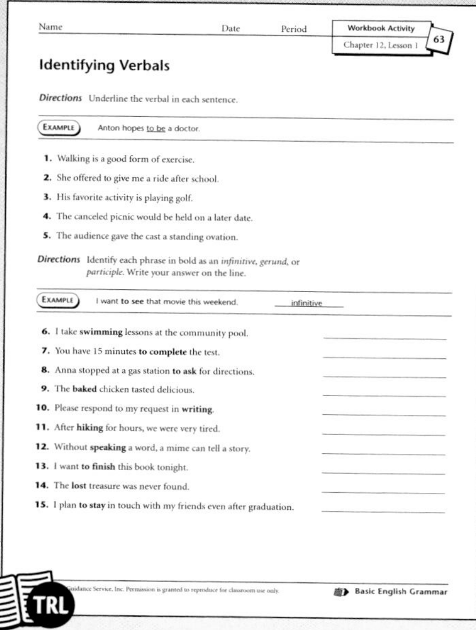

Name Date Period — Workbook Activity 63, Chapter 12, Lesson 1

Identifying Verbals

Directions Underline the verbal in each sentence.

EXAMPLE Anton hopes to be a doctor.

1. Walking is a good form of exercise.
2. She offered to give me a ride after school.
3. His favorite activity is playing golf.
4. The canceled picnic would be held on a later date.
5. The audience gave the cast a standing ovation.

Directions Identify each phrase in bold as an *infinitive, gerund,* or *participle.* Write your answer on the line.

EXAMPLE I want **to see** that movie this weekend. infinitive

6. I take **swimming** lessons at the community pool. ______
7. You have 15 minutes **to complete** the test. ______
8. Anna stopped at a gas station **to ask** for directions. ______
9. The **baked** chicken tasted delicious. ______
10. Please respond to my request in **writing**. ______
11. After **hiking** for hours, we were very tired. ______
12. Without **speaking** a word, a mime can tell a story. ______
13. I want **to finish** this book tonight. ______
14. The **lost** treasure was never found. ______
15. I plan **to stay** in touch with my friends even after graduation. ______

 Basic English Grammar

TRL

Workbook Activity 63

Name Date Period — Activity 63, Chapter 12, Lesson 1

Identifying Types of Verbals

Directions For each sentence, identify whether the word or words in bold are an *infinitive,* a *gerund,* or a *participle.* Write your answer on the line.

EXAMPLES
Tom and Jennifer decided **to plant** tulips in their garden. infinitive
Flying in a hot-air balloon looks like fun. gerund
The **rescued** swimmer is resting in the lifeguard station. participle

1. Scott asked Karen **to remind** him about the meeting. ______
2. Jenny dreams about **becoming** an actress. ______
3. **Soaring** above the clouds, the eagle is free. ______
4. **Dancing** is good exercise. ______
5. The company's goal was **to create** the best shoes on the market. ______
6. **Writing** a novel requires dedication as well as imagination. ______
7. The **parched** ground soaked up the rain. ______
8. Their plans were **to settle** on a farm in the West. ______
9. Jason did not eat any sweets while he was in **training** for the Olympics. ______
10. Leonardo da Vinci was an **accomplished** inventor and painter. ______
11. **Providing** care for the elderly is meaningful work. ______
12. My teacher encourages us **to be** the best that we can be. ______
13. **To write** well is a fine ambition. ______
14. The **crying** child missed his mother. ______
15. Josie is an alto **singing** in the school's chorus. ______

 Basic English Grammar

TRL

Activity 63

Lesson at a Glance

Chapter 12 Lesson 2

Overview This lesson introduces infinitives and infinitive phrases.

Objective

- To identify infinitives and infinitive phrases in sentences.

Student Pages 302–307

Teacher's Resource Library 

Workbook Activity 64

Activity 64

Alternative Activity 64

Vocabulary

infinitive phrase

Warm-Up Activity

Remind students of the definition of a verbal. Then write the following sentences on the board: *The place to eat is Jack's. I go there to eat. To eat at Jack's is an experience.* Ask students to identify the verbal that these sentences have in common. Point out that *to eat* is an infinitive that most of us use every day, but we don't always use it in the same way. Explain to students that infinitives can take the place of nouns, adverbs, or adjectives in a sentence. The three sentences on the board include an example of each type. Ask students to identify the role played by *to eat* in the model sentences (*adjective, adverb, noun*). Invite students to use infinitives in sentences of their own.

Teaching the Lesson

Help students distinguish an infinitive from a prepositional phrase by suggesting that they take the word immediately following *to* and put the word *will* in front of it. If they can use this *will*-phrase in a sentence, then the original *to*-phrase is an infinitive. If not, it is a prepositional phrase. Put this proof to the test with the phrases *to sit* and *to my house.*

Lesson 2 Infinitives and Infinitive Phrases

An infinitive is a verb form made up of *to* plus a verb. It is usually a noun, but it may be an adjective or adverb.

EXAMPLE

Noun	I like to dance.
Adverb	He practices to improve.
Adjective	There was plenty of time to eat.

An infinitive is usually in the present tense. It can also be in the present perfect tense (*to* + *have* + a verb).

EXAMPLE

Present	Alex and Scott decided to go to Springvale Lake.
Present Perfect	They hoped to have caught five trout by noon.

Activity A Write the infinitives in these sentences on your paper.

1. Alex and Scott really like to fish.
2. They hoped to catch enough trout for lunch.
3. Alex agreed to clean the trout.
4. Scott said he would like to cook the trout in a large skillet.
5. Alex and Scott were on Springvale Lake by six o'clock, ready to make their first cast.

An infinitive is not a part of the main verb or verb phrase. However, it may be part of the predicate. Remember that the predicate is the verb and all the words that answer questions about that verb.

EXAMPLE

Demonstrate for students how an infinitive phrase can take many forms, depending on its modifiers. Start off with the sentence *I like to eat* and invite students to add objects, adjectives, adverbs, or prepositional phrases to the infinitive. (Example: *I like to eat breakfast every day in that funny snack bar by the beach.*)

Activity A

Write these sentences on the board: *He is learning to drive. I'd like to read your story.* Help students identify the subject and the verb in each sentence. Then ask them to find the infinitive. After this activity, have students complete Activity A on their own.

Activity A Answers

1. to fish 2. to catch 3. to clean 4. to cook 5. to make

Activity B Write the predicate part of each sentence. Underline the verb or verb phrase. Circle the infinitive.

1. Tamika appeared to be happy.
2. Our family likes to go during the summer.
3. Greg seems to be taller than Reggie.
4. Elizabeth hoped to get the lead in the play.
5. Do you want to use the laptop?

Do not confuse infinitives with prepositional phrases. An infinitive is *to* + a verb. A prepositional phrase is *to* + a noun or pronoun.

EXAMPLE

Infinitive	They want to leave. (*Leave* is a verb.)
Prepositional Phrase	Let's go to the park. (*Park* is a noun and the object of the preposition *to*.)

Activity C On your paper, write the words in bold. Next to each group of words, write whether it is an *infinitive* or a *prepositional phrase*.

Example They wanted **to leave** early.
to leave—infinitive

1. When Alex and Scott got **to the lake,** they saw other people ready **to fish.**
2. They carried their equipment **to the boat.**
3. Soon they were ready **to begin.**
4. Scott always wanted **to be** the one **to catch** the first fish.
5. "I hope **to beat** the champion," Alex said **to Scott.**

Activity B

Do the first item in Activity B on the board. Ask volunteers to underline the main verb and circle the infinitive. Do the rest of the activity as a class or ask students to work on their own.

Activity B Answers

1. appeared (to be) happy 2. likes (to go) during the summer 3. seems (to be) taller than Reggie 4. hoped (to get) the lead in the play 5. Do want (to use) the laptop

Activity C

Write these phrases on the board: *to the office, to laugh, to enjoy, to the movie, to school, to play, to Mexico, to vote.* Have students list the infinitives on the left side of their paper and the prepositional phrases on the right. Then have students read their lists aloud to check their answers. Students can complete Activity C independently.

Activity C Answers

1. to the lake—prepositional phrase, to fish—infinitive 2. to the boat—prepositional phrase 3. to begin—infinitive 4. to be—infinitive, to catch—infinitive 5. to beat—infinitive, to Scott—prepositional phrase

3 Reinforce and Extend

AT HOME

Suggest that students create a "To Do" list of things they can do at home for themselves and for other members of the family. Students may wish to talk to their parents and other family members to determine what kinds of things they can do to benefit themselves and the family as a whole. Suggest that students use an infinitive to begin every item on their list. Provide the following as a model.

This week I plan
- to clean my room
- to visit my grandmother
- to help my sister learn to ride a two-wheeler

IN THE COMMUNITY

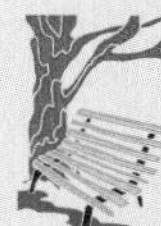

Encourage students to become familiar with community events—and with the use of the infinitive—by giving them each an article from a local newspaper. Have students read their articles, highlighting the word *to* each time it appears in an infinitive or a prepositional phrase. Invite volunteers to present brief oral reports about their articles and to copy on the board examples of the infinitives and prepositional phrases they encountered in their reading.

Activity D

Before they complete Activity D, suggest that students work with partners to list the kinds of questions they could ask to identify nouns, adjectives, and adverbs in sentences. If necessary, have students refer back to Chapters 1, 3, and 6 in their text. Then have partners complete Activity D together.

Activity D Answers

1. To catch—noun 2. to land—adjective 3. to move—noun 4. to find—noun 5. to catch—adverb

Writing Practice

Point out that the infinitive often serves as the direct object in a sentence. Give students the following prompts—*I like, I hope, I try, I want*—and ask them to use an infinitive phrase to complete these starters about themselves. Have students read their sentences aloud. Invite volunteers to write examples on the board.

Global Connection

Point out that the infinitive has no tense or number. This is the "pure" form of verbs that dictionaries use for definitions. Have students list some common infinitive verbs under the heading *English.* Then ask those familiar with other languages to translate these words and list them in separate columns. Encourage students to construct an international poster of infinitive forms of verbs for display in the classroom.

Infinitive phrase
An infinitive, its complements, and any adjectives or adverbs

The word *fish* can be a noun or a verb. As a noun, it has two plural forms—*fish* and *fishes.* Use *fishes* when you are describing more than one kind of fish: *I enjoy eating all kinds of fishes, but mackerel and sea bass are my favorite.*

Although an infinitive is a verb form, it can be used in a sentence as a noun, an adverb, or an adjective.

Study each sentence pattern to figure out how to use an infinitive in a sentence. Ask yourself the same kinds of questions you ask to identify parts of speech and sentence parts.

Noun	Alex wants to catch a big trout. (What does Alex want?)
Adverb	He will need a big fire to cook his trout. (Why does he need a big fire?)
Adjective	The best fishing rod to use is made of aluminum. (What kind of fishing rod?)

Activity D Write the infinitives in bold on your paper. Next to each infinitive, write whether it is used as a *noun,* an *adverb,* or an *adjective.* Remember that subjects, predicate nouns, and direct objects are nouns.

1. **To catch** a big fish was Alex's ambition.
2. He said, "My time **to land** a big fish has come."
3. After an hour, they decided **to move** to another spot.
4. They hoped **to find** a place with some fish.
5. The fish were hard **to catch.**

An **infinitive phrase** is an infinitive, its complements, and any adjectives or adverbs.

An infinitive may have an adverb or an adverb phrase to answer questions about its action.

Example

Inf. Adv. Adv. Phrase
To leave early for Springvale Lake was their idea. (The entire infinitive phrase is *to leave early for Springvale Lake. Early* is an adverb that answers the question *when.* The adverb phrase *for Springvale Lake* tells about *early.* It answers the question *where.*)

An infinitive may also have a complement such as a direct object, a predicate noun, or a predicate adjective.

EXAMPLE

Inf. DO
He wanted to buy a sailboat.
(*Sailboat* is the direct object of the infinitive *to buy.*)

Inf. PN
She wants to be the mayor.
(*Mayor* is the predicate noun. It follows the linking verb *to be.*)

Inf. PA
They wanted the trout to taste delicious.
(*Delicious* is a predicate adjective that follows the linking verb *to taste.* The infinitive *to taste* also acts as an object complement that tells about the direct object *trout.*)

Activity E On your paper, write the infinitive phrase in each sentence.

1. Scott began to reel the fish into the boat.
2. The fish started to fight hard.
3. Scott's fish struggled to win the battle.
4. Alex got a net to help Scott.
5. To land that fish was their goal.

Sometimes the preposition *to* is missing from the infinitive.

EXAMPLE

"Don't make me (to) laugh," shouted Alex.
Help me (to) reel it in.

Activity F On your paper, write the infinitive in each sentence.

1. Will you let me help you?
2. They heard the other boaters cheer for Scott.
3. "Let us see the size of that fish," they all said.
4. They watched Scott hold his fish high in the air.
5. Their attention made Scott feel proud.

TEACHER ALERT

Use the examples that precede Activity F to point out that adding the missing *to* to identify an infinitive may make a sentence sound odd. Students shouldn't rely on the sound of the sentence to identify an infinitive.

Activity E

Invite volunteers to read aloud the examples on pages 304–305. Make sure students understand that an infinitive phrase includes the infinitive and any accompanying words that describe or complement it.

Activity E Answers

1. to reel the fish into the boat 2. to fight hard 3. to win the battle 4. to help Scott 5. To land that fish

Activity F

Write these sentences on the board: *Let us go immediately. Will you help me fix my bike?* Help students locate the infinitive in each sentence. Then ask students to complete Activity F on their own.

Activity F Answers

1. (to) help 2. (to) cheer 3. (to) see 4. (to) hold 5. (to) feel

LEARNING STYLES

Interpersonal/Group Learning

Write these incomplete sentences on the board: *Lyn offered ____. Seth hopes ____. They expected the play ____. ____ is not a good idea.* Have student partners take turns filling in the blanks with infinitive phrases. Encourage students to vary the kinds of complements in each phrase. Suggest that they use the example sentences that precede Activity E as models. Invite students to share their sentence completions with the class.

Activity G

Discuss the example, helping students to recognize that *to catch some trout* follows the linking verb *was* and refers back to *goal.* Then, depending on the ability of your class, do Activity G together or have students work independently.

Activity G Answers

1. to go home—adjective **2.** to pack up their gear—direct object **3.** to set—direct object **4.** to see anything—adverb **5.** To be on the road before dark—subject

Activity H

Before having students do Activity H on their own, have them take turns making up sentences for item 1.

Activity H Answers

Answers will vary. Sample answers for items 1–5 follow. **1.** Brian asked us not to laugh during his presentation. **2.** Is it going to rain today? **3.** Micha wants to be home before 11 o'clock. **4.** Are you going to watch the special on dolphins tonight? **5.** The toddler has learned to count to 10.

Learning Styles

Auditory/Verbal

Play for the class a brief excerpt from a radio or television news broadcast or talk show. As they listen, have students write down any infinitives they hear. Afterwards, compile a list of their findings on the board. (If necessary, distinguish between infinitives and prepositional phrases.) Help students understand how the infinitives are used in the original sentences.

Activity G On your paper, write the infinitive phrase in each sentence. After each infinitive phrase, write how it is used in the sentence.

Example Their goal was to catch some trout.
to catch some trout—predicate noun

1. It was time to go home.
2. They began to pack up their gear.
3. The sun was beginning to set.
4. Soon, it would be too dark to see anything.
5. To be on the road before dark was their plan.

Activity H On your paper, write a sentence for each of these infinitives. Underline the infinitive phrase in each sentence.

1. to laugh	**6.** to fish
2. to rain	**7.** to see
3. to be	**8.** to catch
4. to watch	**9.** to go
5. to count	**10.** to eat

Alex and Scott fished until the sun began to set.

On your paper, write the infinitive phrase in each sentence. Underline the infinitive in each infinitive phrase. Then write how the infinitive phrase is used. (Remember that we use an infinitive as a *noun,* an *adverb,* or an *adjective.*)

1. Scott and Alex wanted to be home by dark.
2. They decided to stop at six o'clock.
3. Scott began to count the fish.
4. They had hoped to catch many fish.
5. To catch enough fish for dinner had been their goal.

On your paper, write the words in bold. Next to each group of words, write whether it is an *infinitive* or a *prepositional phrase.*

6. Jerod wants **to work** at the hardware store this summer.
7. He will go **to the store** three days a week.
8. Melanie and I are going **to the library** after school.
9. We need **to finish** our project.
10. "Look who is here," Melanie said, pointing **to Adam** at another table.

Spelling Builder

Practice with Possessive Nouns

Many of the sentences in this lesson refer to Scott and Alex. Suppose you want to tell someone about the fish they caught or the dinner Scott prepared. You would use apostrophes to form possessive nouns. Here are some simple rules:

- To form the possessive of most singular nouns, including those that end in *-s,* add *-'s:* school's, Wes's, Charles's.
- To form the possessive of a plural noun that ends in *-s,* add only the apostrophe: *boys', cities', coaches'.*
- To form the possessive of a plural noun that does not end in *-s,* add *-'s: women's, children's.*

Make each noun possessive. Write the possessive nouns on your paper.

1. James
2. class
3. player
4. movies
5. men

Lesson 2 Review Answers

1. to be home by dark—noun 2. to stop at six o'clock—noun 3. to count the fish—noun 4. to catch many fish—noun 5. To catch enough fish for dinner—noun 6. to work—infinitive 7. to the store—prepositional phrase 8. to the library—prepositional phrase 9. to finish—infinitive 10. to Adam—prepositional phrase

Spelling Builder

Say to the class, "The boy's toys are on the floor." Then invite a volunteer to write *boy's* on the board. Lead the class to understand that a possessive must have an apostrophe, but that it is not always possible to tell by sound whether the possessive noun is singular or plural. Remind students that word clues often help. Add "where they left them" to the end of the sample sentence above. Point out that this suggests the spelling *boys'.*

Answers to Spelling Builder: 1. James's **2.** class's **3.** player's **4.** movies' **5.** men's

Spelling Practice

Write *Sean and Amy's kittens,* then *Sean's and Amy's kittens* on the board. Ask students who owns the kittens in each sentence. Explain that when two or more people possess something jointly, we use the apostrophe for the last person named. When people possess things individually, each name is in the possessive form. Quiz students on the meaning of the following: *Tina's and Juan's cars, Hannah and Andrew's children, Peg's and Raf's cooking.*

Name Date Period | Workbook Activity 64 | Chapter 12, Lesson 2

Identifying Infinitives and Infinitive Phrases

Directions Identify each phrase in bold as an *infinitive* or a *prepositional phrase.* Write your answer on the line.

EXAMPLES Carrie likes **to jog**. infinitive
She went **to the park**. prepositional phrase

1. Susan has been **to many horse shows**.
2. Susan wants **to join** the equestrian team.
3. She likes **to jump** her horse over fences.
4. The challenge is **to ride** smoothly.
5. If you want to be the best, you have **to practice** every day.

Directions Underline the infinitive phrase in each sentence.

EXAMPLE John hoped to win a gold medal in the Olympics.

6. Melissa loves to eat scrambled eggs with ketchup.
7. My grandmother wants everyone in her family to be happy.
8. Suki wants to see the polar bears at the zoo.
9. Kurt chooses to collect old toy cars.
10. To run for office, you must be in touch with the issues.
11. Jared doesn't like to dust his house.
12. Lilly wants to learn how to cook low-fat meals.
13. I like to go skiing in Colorado.
14. Candice likes to sleep late on Saturdays.
15. Karen doesn't know wether she wants to read or watch television.

 Basic English Grammar

TRL

Workbook Activity 64

Name Date Period | Activity 64 | Chapter 12, Lesson 2

Infinitives and Infinitive Phrases

Directions Find and circle the infinitive phrase in each sentence.

EXAMPLES Lynn wanted (to join the circus.)
John hoped (to win a gold medal in the Olympics.)

1. In the winter, I like to go skiing in the Alps.
2. I don't know whether I want to be an engineer or a scientist.
3. Dan always wants to see the dolphins.
4. To be or not to be, that is the question.
5. Sam never wants to clean his room.
6. Sarah loves to eat steak with corn and potatoes.
7. No one wants to be alone.
8. Everyone's goal in life is to be happy.
9. John likes to fish for catfish.
10. To invest in the company, you must first be employed there.

Directions Identify each phrase in bold as an *infinitive* or a *prepositional phrase.* Write your answer on the line provided.

EXAMPLES Carrie likes **to jog**. infinitive
She went **to the park**. prepositional phrase

11. Susan went **to the stables**.
12. She wanted **to ride for an hour**.
13. She also wanted **to clean the stables**.
14. While she was there, she hoped **to see her friend Jim**.
15. Jim usually likes **to go there in the afternoon**.

 Basic English Grammar

TRL

Activity 64

Lesson at a Glance

Chapter 12 Lesson 3

Overview This lesson presents gerunds and gerund phrases.

Objective

- To identify gerunds and gerund phrases in sentences.

Student Pages 308–311

Teacher's Resource Library TRL

Workbook Activity 65

Activity 65

Alternative Activity 65

Vocabulary

gerund
gerund phrase

1 Warm-Up Activity

Write *I like to cook* on the board to remind students how an infinitive can be used as a noun. Now erase *to cook* and ask students to find another form of the same verb that can replace the infinitive. Elicit that *cooking* can also serve as a direct object in this sentence. Explain that when a verb ending in *-ing* is used as a noun, it is called a gerund. Demonstrate how the gerund *cooking* can serve several functions by writing *Cooking is fun* and *She supports herself by cooking* on the board. Then write *swim* and *paint* on the board. Invite students to form gerunds from these verbs and to use them in sentences.

2 Teaching the Lesson

Give students practice using gerunds in different parts of a sentence. Brainstorm with the class a list of common gerunds and write them on the board. Encourage students to get started by asking a leading question, such as *Which of these actions do you like the most?* Elicit answers such as *I like playing.* Encourage students to create gerund phrases by having them add modifiers or complements to their gerunds. (*I like playing baseball in the spring,* for example.)

Lesson 3 Gerunds and Gerund Phrases

Gerund
A verb form that ends in -ing; a gerund is always a noun

A **gerund** is a verb form that ends in *-ing*. In sentences, gerunds act like nouns.

Writing Tip

Gerunds add variety to your writing. They give readers a clear picture of what people are doing. Before you start writing, make a list of gerunds that identify people's actions. This will help you write exciting sentences.

EXAMPLE

Subject	Rock climbing is Mitsu's favorite activity.
Direct Object	Scott enjoys fishing.
Predicate Noun	My favorite exercise is hiking.
Object of the Preposition	The hiker got in trouble for climbing the steep cliff alone.
Appositives	Jennifer enjoys two things: dancing and skiing.
	You might try the following activities: walking, swimming, or skating.
	Her special talents—writing and speaking—helped her get the job.

Activity A Write the gerunds in these sentences on your paper.

1. Riding a bicycle on back roads is great exercise.
2. I like running better.
3. My favorite activity is playing my trumpet.
4. Getting to school on time is difficult.
5. Finding her way through the strange city was a challenge.
6. They were sent to the office for walking in the halls without a pass.
7. His greatest goal was catching a big fish.
8. Talking to my parents can be difficult sometimes.
9. Jerod thinks fishing is dull.
10. Reggie enjoys reading and going to the movies.

Activity A

Write these sentences on the board: *Helping you paint is my pleasure. Sam gets paid for walking his neighbors' dogs.* Help students identify the gerunds in each sentence. As a challenge, ask students to tell how the gerund functions in each sentence. Then ask students to complete Activity A on their own.

Activity A Answers

1. Riding 2. running 3. playing 4. Getting 5. Finding 6. walking 7. catching 8. Talking 9. fishing 10. reading, going

Gerund phrase
A gerund and any adjective, adverb, prepositional phrase, or complement the gerund may have

A **gerund phrase** is a gerund and any adjective, adverb, prepositional phrase, or complement the gerund may have.

Because a gerund acts like a noun in a sentence, it may have an adjective that describes it.

Adj. **Gerund**
Meg asked for expert training in weight lifting. (Meg asked for what kind of *training*? She asked for *expert* training. The gerund phrase is the object of the preposition *for*.)

Using What You've Learned

Find information on the Boston Marathon in an encyclopedia or on the Internet at www.bostonmarathon.com. Write a short paragraph on what you learn. Use at least three gerunds or gerund phrases in your paragraph. Underline the gerunds when you are finished.

A gerund phrase may also include an adverb or adverb phrase.

Gerund **Adv. Phrase**
Damon likes swimming after school. (When does Damon like *swimming*? Damon likes swimming *after school*. *After school* is a prepositional phrase used as an adverb. The entire gerund phrase is the direct object of the action verb *likes*.)

Because a gerund is a verb form, it may have complements.

Gerund **DO**
Rowing a boat is fun. (*Boat* is the direct object of the gerund *rowing*. The gerund phrase is the subject of the verb *is*.)

Activity B On your paper, write the gerund phrase in each sentence. Next to the gerund, write whether it acts as a *subject*, a *direct object*, a *predicate noun*, an *object of the preposition*, or an *appositive* in the sentence.

Example Making friends in a new school can be difficult.
Making friends in a new school—subject

1. Kaitlin watched the running of the Boston Marathon.
2. One of her dreams was winning that race.
3. She began thinking about entering a marathon some day.
4. Practicing for the race took a lot of time.
5. Kaitlin enjoys two things: running and winning!

Activity B

Discuss the example provided for Activity B. Help students understand that they can tell that the gerund phrase in the example is the subject because it answers the question "What can be difficult?" *Making friends in a new school can.* You may also wish to review how to identify direct objects, predicate nouns, objects of prepositions, and appositives in sentences. Then, depending on the needs of your class, do Activity B orally as a class or have students work with partners to complete the activity.

Activity B Answers

1. the running of the Boston Marathon—direct object **2.** winning that race—predicate noun **3.** thinking—direct object, entering a marathon some day—object of the preposition **4.** Practicing for the race—subject **5.** running and winning—appositive

Using What You've Learned

Before students begin their Internet research, brainstorm with them a list of gerunds that they might use in their paragraphs. (Examples: *running, training, sweating, winning, cheering, finishing*) Invite volunteers to use a selection of these gerunds in sentences. Remind students that gerunds serve as nouns. If there are helping words such as *is, will be* or *has been* in front of a word ending in *-ing*, it is a verb phrase, not a gerund.

Activity C

Invite volunteers to take turns providing oral sentences for items 1 and 2 and 6 and 7. Have the class listen carefully to check that students have used the verb phrases and the gerunds correctly. Then ask students to complete Activity C on their own.

Activity C Answers

Answers will vary. Check that students use verb forms and gerunds correctly. Five possible answers follow. **1.** The coach will be starting practice soon. **2.** It is beginning to rain. **5.** Tony and Jennifer are planning to go to the play this weekend. **7.** Finding a place to park downtown is always a challenge. **10.** I enjoy singing in the shower.

3 Reinforce and Extend

Career Connection

Job applicants are often asked to explain, in writing, their work experience and their career goals. The use of gerunds and gerund phrases can be especially helpful in accomplishing this task. For example, to explain past work experience, someone might write: *In my last position, I was responsible for answering the telephone, making appointments, and filing patient records.* Encourage students to write a brief paragraph describing their past work experience (at home, as a volunteer, or in a paid position) and a short paragraph describing their career goals. Encourage them to use as many gerunds and gerund phrases as possible in their paragraphs. Invite students to share their completed paragraphs with the class.

Progressive verb forms and gerunds both end in *-ing*. Do not confuse progressive verb forms with gerunds. When the *ing* form is the main verb in a verb phrase, it is not a gerund.

Example		
	Verb Phrase	Kaitlin has been running every morning.
	Gerund	Kaitlin likes running every morning.

Activity C Write sentences on your paper for each of these verb phrases and gerunds.

Verb Phrases	Gerunds
1. will be starting	**6.** being
2. is beginning	**7.** finding
3. were going	**8.** running
4. has been trying	**9.** wishing
5. are planning	**10.** singing

Running track is a popular school sport.

Learning Styles

Visual/Spatial

Have students bring to school photographs of people performing actions—at work or play. Mount these pictures on the board and invite pairs of students to write captions beneath them, describing the action with gerund phrases. (Example: *She loves lying on the beach in the sun.*) Make sure that students understand the difference between verb phrases and gerunds. When each picture has a caption, challenge students to write a second caption, using the same gerund as a different part of the sentence.

Lesson 3 REVIEW

Write the gerund phrases in these sentences on your paper. Underline the gerund or gerunds in each gerund phrase. Then write whether the gerund phrase acts as a *subject*, a *direct object*, a *predicate noun*, an *object of the preposition*, or an *appositive* in the sentence.

1. Flying an airplane must be a thrill.
2. My favorite activity, reading books, is a way to relax.
3. We enjoyed swimming in the lake.
4. An architect earns a salary by designing buildings.
5. Dana's favorite hobby is reading.

Write the word or words in bold on your paper. Next to each word or group of words, write whether it is a *gerund* or part of a *verb phrase*.

6. Kaitlin enjoys **going** to the art museum.
7. Jamal will be **attending** the play next week.
8. Some students earn extra credit by **remaining** after school.
9. **Buying** a car is an important decision.
10. Julie has been **taking** a yoga class in the evening.

Vocabulary Builder

Idioms

An idiom is a phrase or expression that does not follow the usual patterns of a language. For example, we say "It is raining." Usually, a pronoun must have an antecedent. In this sentence, the noun that *it* replaces is not clear. We don't say, "The sky is raining" or "The clouds are raining." We understand idioms because we are familiar with them.

Write the meanings of these idioms on your paper.

1. He caught my eye.
2. The puppy went missing.
3. It is raining cats and dogs.
4. Sarah put up a good fight.
5. She means well.

Lesson 3 Review Answers

1. Flying an airplane—subject **2.** reading books—appositive **3.** swimming in the lake—direct object **4.** designing buildings—object of the preposition **5.** reading—predicate noun **6.** going—gerund **7.** will be attending—verb phrase **8.** remaining—gerund **9.** Buying—gerund **10.** has been taking—verb phrase

Vocabulary Builder

Write the following animal idioms on the board and ask students to describe situations when they might use them.

Cat's got your tongue?

You're barking up the wrong tree.

What an eager beaver!

Don't go ape.

Hold your horses.

Encourage students to go online and search for idioms using the keywords *English idioms.* Ask them to bring to class one familiar and one unfamiliar idiom to share with their classmates.

Answers to Vocabulary Builder:
Answers will vary. Possible answers follow. **1.** He got my attention. **2.** The puppy got lost. **3.** It is raining heavily. **4.** Sarah struggled hard. **5.** She wants to do the right thing.

Name Date Period | Workbook Activity 65 | Chapter 12, Lesson 3

Recognizing Gerunds and Gerund Phrases

Directions Underline the gerund phrase in each sentence. Then write on the line whether it is used as a *subject*, a *direct object*, an *object of the preposition*, or a *predicate noun*.

EXAMPLE The family enjoys camping at national parks. direct object

1. Kate wrote a report on exploring the oceans.
2. Chasing tornadoes is a dangerous occupation.
3. Jefferson's contribution was writing the Declaration of Independence.
4. Rita often imagined becoming an opera singer.
5. The counselor talked about applying to colleges.
6. Shoveling snow is hard work.
7. The puppy enjoyed tearing up newspaper.
8. Traveling across the United States was something Ed wanted to do.
9. Mark's favorite exercise is bike riding.
10. Marleen won a prize for painting a picture.
11. Seeing the mountains inspired me to write a poem.
12. Her job includes reporting on high school sports.
13. By volunteering at the center, you help your community.
14. Caring for pets is a big responsibility.
15. After planning our trip, we made flight reservations.

 Basic English Grammar

TRL

Workbook Activity 65

Name Date Period | Activity 65 | Chapter 12, Lesson 3

Gerunds and Gerund Phrases

Directions Circle the gerund and underline the gerund phrase in each sentence. On the line, write whether the gerund phrase acts as a *subject*, a *direct object*, the *object of the preposition*, or a *predicate noun*.

EXAMPLE Barking gets Buddy into trouble. subject

1. I enjoy writing to my pen pal in New Zealand.
2. Finding the right house was difficult.
3. Her favorite summer activity is swimming.
4. Camping is popular in the United States.
5. You cannot go far without finishing school.
6. Hitting a tennis ball is a lot of fun.
7. Listening to my new stereo is enjoyable.
8. Relaxing after a busy day is important.
9. Jason's first chore every morning is taking out the garbage.
10. Many people like singing in a chorus.
11. We can keep the environment cleaner by recycling.
12. My aunt does not remember cooking that for us.
13. A pilot earns his living by flying an airplane.
14. Many people prefer eating fresh vegetables.
15. Designing our own clothes was an interesting experience.

 Basic English Grammar

TRL

Activity 65

Lesson 4 Participles and Participle Phrases

Participle
A verb form that is used as an adjective

A **participle** is a verb form. We use participles as adjectives in sentences. A participle may be in the present tense or in the past tense.

EXAMPLE		
	Present Tense	The sleeping baby was peaceful.
	Past Tense	The room looks smaller painted dark green.

Activity A Write the participles in these sentences on your paper.

1. The setting sun turned the sky red and purple.
2. Those cooked carrots are mushy.
3. The girl reading that book is my sister.
4. Will you help that lost child find her mother?
5. My rumbling stomach told me I was hungry.
6. The cracked glass hid the details of the painting.
7. Steamed vegetables are good for you.
8. The hikers climbed over the fallen log.
9. What a frightening movie that was!
10. Fish jumped in the bubbling brook.

Do not confuse a participle used as an adjective with a participle that is part of a verb phrase.

EXAMPLE		
	Participle	The stew simmering on the stove smelled delicious.
	Verb Phrase	The stew was simmering on the stove.

Lesson at a Glance

Chapter 12 Lesson 4

Overview This lesson presents participles and participle phrases.

Objective

- To identify participles and participle phrases in sentences.

Student Pages 312–315

Teacher's Resource Library 

- Workbook Activity 66
- Activity 66
- Alternative Activity 66

Vocabulary

participle
participle phrase

1 Warm-Up Activity

Write on the board *Help, I'm falling! and Falling is no fun.* Elicit that in the first sentence *falling* is part of the verb phrase *am falling;* in the second it is a gerund acting as the subject of the sentence. Now write *Look out for falling rocks.* Ask students how this use of *falling* differs from the previous two. Lead them to understand that *falling* here serves as an adjective. Explain that this is a participle, a verb form that is often used as an adjective. Finally write *Look out for fallen rocks.* Point out that here is another form of the verb *fall* acting as an adjective, only this time it is in the past tense. Explain that present and past participles can both take the place of adjectives in sentences.

2 Teaching the Lesson

Point out that while present participles always end in *-ing,* past participles may take a variety of forms. Have students turn back to page 92 and 93 to review irregular verbs. Make a list of some common irregular past participles and have students practice using them as adjectives in sentences.

To help students distinguish between a participle used as an adjective and a participle that is part of a verb phrase, write *He is playing marching songs* on the board. Have students identify the subject and verb. (*He / is playing*). The participle *marching* is used here as an adjective.

Activity A

Do the first two items in Activity A with the class. To avoid having students confuse the main verb with the participle in each sentence, help students first identify the main verb or verb phrase in each sentence.

Activity A Answers

1. setting 2. cooked 3. reading 4. lost 5. rumbling 6. cracked 7. Steamed 8. fallen 9. frightening 10. bubbling

3 Reinforce and Extend

Learning Styles

LEP/ESL

Give small groups of English language learners and students fluent in English a short passage from a magazine or textbook to read. While some students read aloud, the others should note the participles they hear, including any helping verbs. Invite English language learners to share examples of participles used as adjectives and those that are part of verb phrases.

Participle phrase
A participle and an adverb or adverb phrase

Activity B Write on your paper whether each word in bold is a participle used as an *adjective* or is part of a *verb phrase.*

Examples The **laughing** clown amused the baby. adjective
The clown was **laughing** at the baby. verb phrase

1. We will be **catching** the train.
2. The newly **painted** room was bright and cheery.
3. The wind was **howling** all night.
4. The **laughing** students enjoyed the amusing story.
5. Everyone avoids **annoying** people.

In British English, the word *howling* sometimes means "crying." Jill was *howling* with sadness.

A **participle phrase** is a participle and an adverb or adverb phrase. A participle comes right before or right after the noun or pronoun it describes.

EXAMPLE Running at full speed, she caught the taxi. (The participle phrase *Running at full speed* describes *she.*)

Activity C Write these sentences on your paper. Underline each participle phrase. Draw an arrow to the noun or pronoun it describes.

Example Fruit is the only dessert needed for our dinner.

1. Howling wildly, the wind frightened the child.
2. Dana lent her book to the girl sitting in the first row.
3. Expecting the worst, Julian was pleasantly surprised with his grade.
4. The keys locked inside the car were of little use.
5. Concentrating on her notes, Mrs. Agnello did not hear Julian enter the room.

Activity B

Write these sentences on the board: *The mirror was broken by the mover. She cut her hand on the broken glass.* Help students identify the past participle in each sentence. Ask students to identify the sentence in which the participle is used as an adjective and the one in which it is used as part of a verb phrase. Then have students do Activity B on their own.

Activity B Answers

1. verb phrase **2.** adjective **3.** verb phrase **4.** adjective **5.** adjective

Activity C

Write item 1 in Activity C on the board. Help students locate the participle phrase and the noun it describes. Then invite a volunteer to underline the participle phrase and draw an arrow to the noun it describes.

Activity C Answers

1. Howling wildly—wind **2.** sitting in the first row—girl **3.** Expecting the worst—Julian **4.** locked inside the car—keys **5.** Concentrating on her notes—Mrs. Agnello

LEARNING STYLES

Logical/Mathematical

Give each pair of students a different magazine article. Students should take turns reading aloud, making note of all infinitives, gerunds, and participles that they read. When they have finished reading, have pairs add up the total for each type of verbal that they found. Ask students to put these numbers in a chart on the board. Compare the individual statistics from each pair, add up the totals, and draw conclusions about the relative frequency of the verbals.

ONLINE CONNECTION

Suggest that students search the Internet for information about dangling participles (or dangling modifiers as they are often called). One useful Web site is Owl, Purdue University's Online Writing Lab. Students can find it at **owl.english.purdue.edu.** Once at the site, they should type *dangling modifiers* in the *search for* box for information about dangling participles.

TEACHER ALERT

Draw students' attention to the importance of locating a participle phrase next to the noun or pronoun it describes. Point out that sometimes people mistakenly omit the noun or pronoun entirely. Write the following sentence on the board: *Peering out of the window, the mountain came into view.* Ask students who or what is peering out of the window. Explain that a mistake of this kind is known as a dangling participle. Suggest that the sentence be rewritten as *Peering out of the window, I saw the mountain come into view.*

Activity D

Discuss the examples given for Activity D with the class. Then do item 1 on the board, having students identify the participle phrase and the word it describes. After they have completed Activity D independently, ask students to share their answers with the class.

Activity D Answers

1. Walking to school—we 2. Speaking in front of the class—Bobby 3. missing—items 4. Swimming at the beach—we 5. sunken—treasure 6. sleeping—kittens 7. chuckling softly to herself—her 8. broken—glass 9. pounding—drums 10. frozen—lake

Where To Find It

Point out that because almanacs are yearly publications, they are the place to go for up-to-date information. Supply groups of students with recent almanacs and ask them to find the latest statistics on a variety of subjects: state populations, Olympic medal winners, record temperatures, baseball batting averages. Have them share their information with the class.

Speaking Practice

Have students choose a passage that interests them from the almanac they used in the Where To Find It activity. Ask students to read their selection to the class. Point out that the writing in almanacs is factual and may sound dull if read in a low or monotonous tone of voice. Encourage speakers to communicate their interest by reading with expression.

On your computer, type a paragraph about a person you admire. Use the thesaurus in your word processing program to make your paragraph clear and more interesting. Select ordinary words and replace them with words that are more unusual.

Activity D Find the participle and participle phrase in each sentence. Write each participle phrase on your paper, and underline the participle. Then write the word that the participle or participle phrase describes.

Examples Running at full speed, the man caught the train.
Running at full speed—man

The crowd cheered the returning astronauts.
returning—astronauts

1. Walking to school, we passed a new apartment building.
2. Speaking in front of the class, Bobby got nervous.
3. Snacks are the only missing items in our backpacks.
4. Swimming at the beach, we saw a shark.
5. The book told a story about a sunken treasure.
6. The sleeping kittens looked adorable.
7. I heard her chuckling softly to herself.
8. Elena swept up the pieces of broken glass.
9. Carol enjoyed the pounding drums.
10. The skaters glided across the frozen lake.

Where To Find It

Almanac

Suppose you want to learn more about a topic. One place to look is an almanac. Almanacs contain all kinds of lists and facts on topics from weather to the types of jobs people have. Usually almanacs arrange information by topic. You can use the table of contents or the index to search for your topic.

If you want to know all about your state, look up your state name in the index. If you want to know about baseball teams, look for the section on sports or baseball.

Turn to the page numbers given for all kinds of lists related to your topic. Some almanacs contain only information about specific topics, such as presidents or sports.

1. Choose an almanac from your classroom, home, or library. Write its name and tell whether it covers only one topic or many topics.
2. Choose a topic that interests you. Look up some part of that topic in the almanac. List the kinds of information the almanac contains about that topic.

Global Connection

Every culture has familiar sayings that are meant to remind people to be practical, hardworking, moral, and so on. These sayings often include a verbal of some kind, as in the following examples: *Early to bed and early to rise, makes a man healthy, wealthy, and wise. To err is human, to forgive divine. Let sleeping dogs lie.* Discuss these examples. Then invite students to share their favorite sayings. Encourage bilingual students to provide sayings in another language and their translations. Have students note the sayings that contain a verbal of some kind.

Lesson 4 REVIEW

On your paper, write the participle or the participle phrase in each sentence. Then write the word that the participle or participle phrase describes.

1. We could see the boy running around the track.
2. Arriving early, we were first in line for tickets.
3. I wondered who the girl walking by the restaurant was.
4. Totally lost, Susan still would not stop to ask directions.
5. Waving its tail happily, the dog stood and waited for its dinner.

Write on your paper whether each word in bold is a participle used as an *adjective* or is part of the *verb phrase.* Then decide whether the participles are present tense or past tense.

6. The dog was **barking** at every car.
7. The children cheered for the **marching** band.
8. The flowers in the centerpiece had **wilted.**
9. The lawyer wanted a **signed** contract.
10. Yesterday John raked all of the **fallen** leaves.

Writing Project

Using Verbals to Tell a Story

Many people enjoy making up and telling scary stories. Write down a scary story you have heard, or make up a new story.

1. Tell the scary story in two or three paragraphs. Think it through before you start writing.
2. Include verbals—infinitives, gerunds, and participles—in your sentences.
3. Look at this example. You may use it to start your story.

   Walking through the woods I heard a growling sound. I stopped to see where the noise was coming from.
4. When you are finished, underline all the verbals.
5. Tell your scary story to a classmate, friend, or family member.

Lesson 4 Review Answers

1. running around the track—boy **2.** Arriving early—we **3.** walking by the restaurant—girl **4.** Totally lost—Susan **5.** Waving its tail happily—dog **6.** verb phrase—present tense **7.** adjective—present tense **8.** verb phrase—past tense **9.** adjective—past tense **10.** adjective—past tense

Writing Project

Before students begin to write, brainstorm with the class a list of verbs that they might use in their horror stories. (Examples: *shake, scream, moan, bleed, howl, haunt, run*) Then invite volunteers to write on the board the verbal forms of these words. Have students compose sentences using a selection of the verbals. Copy some of their sentences on the board for students to refer to as they write.

IN THE COMMUNITY

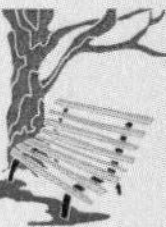

Encourage students to investigate places in the community where signs are needed for the protection and safety of the people or for the preservation of the environment. Then suggest that students design signs for these places. Each sign should have a gerund, an infinitive, or a participle. For example, students might write a sign with the words *Writing on public property is forbidden* for a place where graffiti often appears. Signs can also have illustrations and graphics. Have students prepare a booklet with their sign designs and suggestions for where to place them. If they wish, they can present a copy of their booklet to city or town officials.

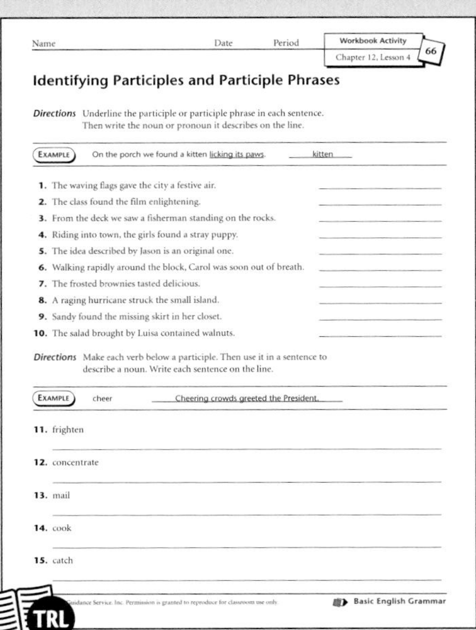

Name Date Period — Workbook Activity 66, Chapter 12, Lesson 4

Identifying Participles and Participle Phrases

Directions Underline the participle or participle phrase in each sentence. Then write the noun or pronoun it describes on the line.

EXAMPLE On the porch we found a kitten licking its paws. kitten

1. The waving flags gave the city a festive air. ________
2. The class found the film enlightening. ________
3. From the deck we saw a fisherman standing on the rocks. ________
4. Riding into town, the girls found a stray puppy. ________
5. The idea described by Jason is an original one. ________
6. Walking rapidly around the block, Carol was soon out of breath. ________
7. The frosted brownies tasted delicious. ________
8. A raging hurricane struck the small island. ________
9. Sandy found the missing skirt in her closet. ________
10. The salad brought by Luisa contained walnuts. ________

Directions Make each verb below a participle. Then use it in a sentence to describe a noun. Write each sentence on the line.

EXAMPLE cheer Cheering crowds greeted the President.

11. frighten ________
12. concentrate ________
13. mail ________
14. cook ________
15. catch ________

 Basic English Grammar

TRL

Workbook Activity 66

Name Date Period — Activity 66, Chapter 12, Lesson 4

Find the Verbals

Directions Find and circle the verbals in the following sentences. Identify each one as either an *infinitive*, a *gerund*, or a *participle*. Write each answer on the line provided.

EXAMPLES
Jack's (singing) thrilled the crowd. gerund
Do you like (to go skiing?) infinitive
The (singing) boy was very talented. participle

1. Vanessa likes to jog at least four times a week. ________
2. Alan goes to see a movie once a week. ________
3. Remember that reading can be fun. ________
4. Watching television is not always healthy for young children. ________
5. Patrice wanted to go to the prom. ________
6. Eating carrots is good for your eyes. ________
7. It is not hard to make pasta salad. ________
8. Growing children should drink plenty of milk. ________
9. Study hard to get good grades. ________
10. Listening to the radio at lunchtime is enjoyable. ________
11. The girl's dancing impressed everyone. ________
12. Marla loves to stay out late on the weekends. ________
13. Relaxing after a long day is essential. ________
14. Weight lifting is a difficult sport. ________
15. Many people attended the pie eating contest. ________
16. Megan's painting was well received. ________
17. Saving money for college was Alicia's goal. ________
18. Her winning smile was the first thing I noticed. ________
19. Pavel decided to start his own company. ________
20. I find collecting stamps a pleasant hobby. ________

 Basic English Grammar

TRL

Activity 66

Chapter 12 Review

Use the Chapter Review to prepare students for tests and to reteach content from the chapter.

Chapter 12 Mastery Test TRL

The Teacher's Resource Library includes two parallel forms of the Chapter 12 Mastery Test. The difficulty level of the two forms is equivalent. You may wish to use one form as a pretest and the other form as a posttest.

Review Answers

Part A

1. participle 2. participle phrase 3. infinitive phrase 4. gerund 5. gerund phrase 6. verbal

Part B

7. traveling 8. to leave 9. Visiting

Part C

10. Did you know that Sam wants to go to California this summer?—noun 11. "To travel to Italy is my dream," Val said.—noun 12. Let's get together in 10 years to talk about our accomplishments.—adverb

Part D

13. playing charades at a party—predicate noun 14. graduating from high school—subject 15. congratulating each other—object of the preposition

Chapter 12 REVIEW

Word Bank
gerund
gerund phrase
infinitive phrase
participle
participle phrase
verbal

Part A On a sheet of paper, write the correct word or words from the Word Bank to complete each sentence.

1. A ________ is a verb form that is used like an adjective.

2. A ________ includes a participle and an adverb or adverb phrase.

3. An ________ includes an infinitive, its complements, and any adjectives or adverbs.

4. A ________ is a verb form that ends in *-ing*.

5. A ________ includes a gerund and any adjective, adverb, prepositional phrase, or complement the gerund may have.

6. A ________ is a verb that we use as another part of speech.

Part B On your paper, write the verbals in these sentences.

7. Tina enjoys traveling.

8. She plans to leave for the summer.

9. Visiting Spain has been her dream.

Part C Write these sentences on your paper. Underline each infinitive, and tell whether it acts as a *noun,* an *adverb,* or an *adjective.*

10. Did you know that Sam wants to go to California this summer?

11. "To travel to Italy is my dream," Val said.

12. Let's get together in 10 years to talk about our accomplishments.

Part D Write the gerund phrase in each sentence on your paper. Next to it, write whether the gerund phrase acts as a *subject,* a *direct object,* a *predicate noun,* an *object of the preposition,* or an *appositive* in the sentence.

13. "My favorite activity is playing charades at a party," Ella said.

14. For Elena, graduating from high school was a wonderful event.

15. After congratulating each other, Al and Billy looked for their parents.

Name Date Period | Mastery Test A, Page 1 | Chapter 12

Chapter 12 Mastery Test A

Part A Identify the word or words in bold in each sentence as an *infinitive,* a *gerund,* or a *participle.*

1. Kathy likes **to swim.** ____________

2. The mother tried to calm the **crying** child. ____________

3. **Playing** the piano well takes practice. ____________

4. Dana wanted **to be** president of the club. ____________

5. They like **swimming,** so they go to the pool. ____________

6. The outfit was very **becoming** on Tasha. ____________

7. **Walking** to the store is good exercise. ____________

8. We ran **to get** to our gate in time. ____________

9. The **flowing** water looked clear and clean. ____________

10. Hugh's greatest pleasure is **skiing**. ____________

Part B Write whether each phrase in bold is an infinitive phrase (*IP*), a gerund phrase (*GP*), or a participle phrase (*PP*).

11. **Riding a motorcycle** is something Pedro likes to do. ____________

12. Martha agreed **to write the letter**. ____________

13. **The barking dog** kept everyone awake. ____________

14. The plan is **to leave late**. ____________

15. **Working at full speed,** we finished our chores early. ____________

16. **Building houses** is my dad's job. ____________

17. Jamal hoped **to win a scholarship**. ____________

18. **Getting ready for the party** took several hours. ____________

19. **Reeling the fish into the boat** was a struggle. ____________

20. **The chirping bird** awakens me each morning. ____________

 Basic English Grammar

TRL

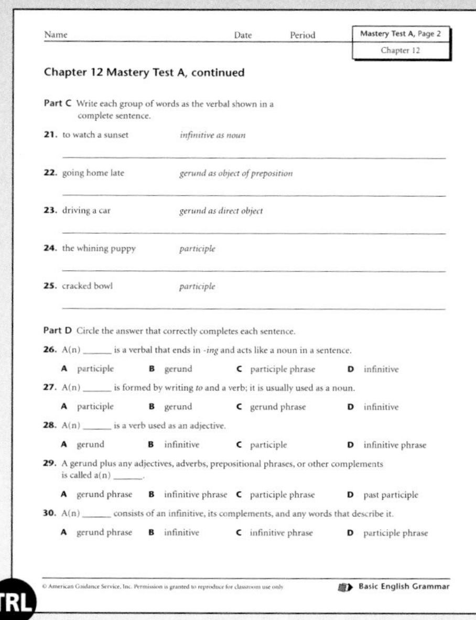

Name Date Period | Mastery Test A, Page 2 | Chapter 12

Chapter 12 Mastery Test A, continued

Part C Write each group of words as the verbal shown in a complete sentence.

21. to watch a sunset *infinitive as noun*

____

22. going home late *gerund as object of preposition*

____

23. driving a car *gerund as direct object*

____

24. the whining puppy *participle*

____

25. cracked bowl *participle*

____

Part D Circle the answer that correctly completes each sentence.

26. A(n) ______ is a verbal that ends in *-ing* and acts like a noun in a sentence.

A participle **B** gerund **C** participle phrase **D** infinitive

27. A(n) ______ is formed by writing *to* and a verb; it is usually used as a noun.

A participle **B** gerund **C** gerund phrase **D** infinitive

28. A(n) ______ is a verb used as an adjective.

A gerund **B** infinitive **C** participle **D** infinitive phrase

29. A gerund plus any adjectives, adverbs, prepositional phrases, or other complements is called a(n) ______.

A gerund phrase **B** infinitive phrase **C** participle phrase **D** past participle

30. A(n) ______ consists of an infinitive, its complements, and any words that describe it.

A gerund phrase **B** infinitive **C** infinitive phrase **D** participle phrase

 Basic English Grammar

TRL

Chapter 12 Mastery Test A

Part E On your paper, write the participle or participle phrase in each sentence. Then write the word the participle or participle phrase describes.

16. Sue received her well-earned diploma.

17. With trembling voices, the graduates said good-bye to one another.

Part F Identify each underlined phrase as an *infinitive phrase,* a *gerund phrase,* a *participle phrase,* or a *prepositional phrase.* Write the letter of the correct answer on your paper.

18. Standing in front of the school, the girls had tears in their eyes.
- **A** infinitive phrase
- **B** gerund phrase
- **C** participle phrase
- **D** prepositional phrase

19. Sue turned to take one last look at her school.
- **A** infinitive phrase
- **B** gerund phrase
- **C** participle phrase
- **D** prepositional phrase

20. Leaving school was not easy for her.
- **A** infinitive phrase
- **B** gerund phrase
- **C** participle phrase
- **D** prepositional phrase

Always read test directions more than once. Underline the words that tell you how many examples you are to give. Check the directions again after you have finished the test.

Review Answers

Part E

16. well-earned—diploma
17. trembling—voices

Part F

18. C 19. A 20. B

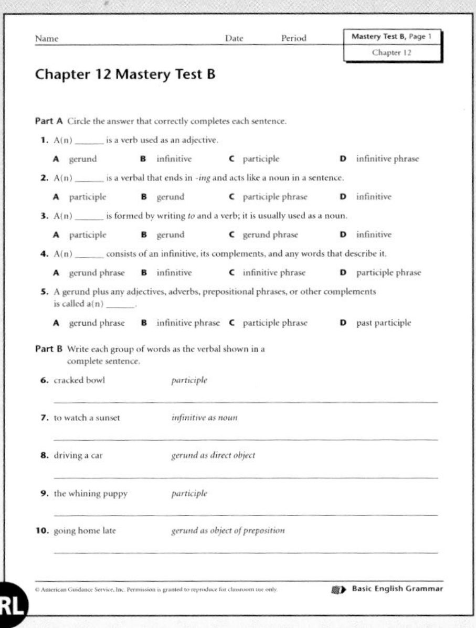

Name Date Period | Mastery Test B, Page 1 | Chapter 12

Chapter 12 Mastery Test B

Part A Circle the answer that correctly completes each sentence.

1. A(n) ______ is a verb used as an adjective.
A gerund **B** infinitive **C** participle **D** infinitive phrase

2. A(n) ______ is a verbal that ends in *-ing* and acts like a noun in a sentence.
A participle **B** gerund **C** participle phrase **D** infinitive

3. A(n) ______ is formed by writing *to* and a verb; it is usually used as a noun.
A participle **B** gerund **C** gerund phrase **D** infinitive

4. A(n) ______ consists of an infinitive, its complements, and any words that describe it.
A gerund phrase **B** infinitive **C** infinitive phrase **D** participle phrase

5. A gerund plus any adjectives, adverbs, prepositional phrases, or other complements is called a(n) ______.
A gerund phrase **B** infinitive phrase **C** participle phrase **D** past participle

Part B Write each group of words as the verbal shown in a complete sentence.

6. cracked bowl *participle*

7. to watch a sunset *infinitive as noun*

8. driving a car *gerund as direct object*

9. the whining puppy *participle*

10. going home late *gerund as object of preposition*

 Basic English Grammar

TRL

Name Date Period | Mastery Test B, Page 2 | Chapter 12

Chapter 12 Mastery Test B, continued

Part C Write whether each phrase in bold is an infinitive phrase (*IP*), a gerund phrase (*GP*), or a participle phrase (*PP*).

11. **Getting ready for the party** took several hours. ______
12. **Riding a motorcycle** is something Pedro likes to do. ______
13. The plan is **to leave late**. ______
14. **Building houses** is my dad's job. ______
15. **Working at full speed,** we finished our chores early. ______
16. Jamal hoped **to win a scholarship**. ______
17. **The barking dog** kept everyone awake. ______
18. **Reeling the fish into the boat** was a struggle. ______
19. Martha agreed **to write the letter**. ______
20. **The chirping bird** awakens me each morning. ______

Part D Identify the word or words in bold in each sentence as an *infinitive,* a *gerund,* or a *participle.*

21. The **flowing** water looked clear and clean. ______
22. Kathy likes **to swim.** ______
23. The mother tried to calm the **crying** child. ______
24. Dana wanted **to be** president of the club. ______
25. **Playing** the piano well takes practice. ______
26. **Walking** to the store is good exercise. ______
27. They like **swimming**, so they go to the pool. ______
28. We ran **to get** to our gate in time. ______
29. Hugh's greatest pleasure is **skiing**. ______
30. The outfit was very **becoming** on Tasha. ______

 Basic English Grammar

TRL

Chapter 12 Mastery Test B

Appendix A

The Writing Process

Overview This section may be used to review the steps of the writing process and to reinforce writing strategies.

Objectives

- To identify stages in the writing process.
- To use the writing process when writing.

Student Pages 318–324

Teacher's Resource Library 

Preparing for Writing Tests 1–4

Prewriting

Have students read the first paragraph on page 318. Encourage them to think about the strategies they use when they write. Help them make a list.

Read the Prewriting section on pages 318–320. Draw a two-column chart on the board or a transparency. Label one column "Choose a topic" and the other "Develop the topic." Have students list in the appropriate columns procedures that will enable them to complete the prewriting procedure.

Writing for Tests

Today many tests are designed to assess students' ability to communicate in writing. The writing process can be adapted to help students organize and write in testing situations.

Point out to students that writing tests provide writing prompts that may ask students to entertain, to inform, to persuade, to tell a story, or to describe. Emphasize that these are the purposes for writing. Knowing the purpose for writing will enable students to focus their writing. The prompt may also ask students to write to a particular format, such as letter, journal entry, paragraph, and poem.

Distribute copies of Preparing for Writing Tests 1. Ask students to read the prompts and identify what their writing purpose is. Also have them identify the format they are being asked to use.

The word *process* makes writing sound as if it is a simple set of steps every writer follows. In fact, every writer follows his or her own set of steps. But every writer must answer the same questions: *What do I write about? How do I organize my ideas? What do I leave in? What do I take out? How can I make my writing better?* Answering these questions is part of every writer's writing process. The process discussed below gives you guidelines to follow when you write.

Prewriting

Choosing a Topic

Some writers think this is the hardest part of writing. Certainly it is a very important part. Without a good topic, you have nowhere to go with your writing. Here are some ways to look for a topic:

- Think about people you know, places you have seen, and activities you enjoy.
- Think about memories or experiences from your past.
- Read newspapers and magazines. Listen to the radio. Watch TV.
- Write down anything that comes to mind. You may find an idea as you freewrite. When you freewrite, you write topics as you think of them. This is also called *brainstorming.*
- Talk to other people about your ideas. They may offer suggestions.
- Ask questions about a subject. A question can be a good topic to investigate.

Name Date Period **Preparing for Writing Tests 1**

Writing Prompts

When you take a writing test, you are given a writing prompt. The prompt will indicate the purpose for writing, suggest a topic, and sometimes identify the writing format to use. Identifying the purpose and format will help you focus your writing.

Directions Read each prompt. Circle the purpose for writing identified in the prompt. Then circle the format for writing. When a prompt does not include a format for writing, you may write paragraphs.

1. You want to spend most of next summer visiting a relative. Write a letter to your relative asking whether you may stay with him or her and offering reasons to convince him or her to let you stay.

   Purpose: to entertain to persuade to describe to inform

   Format: paragraphs letter poem list

2. Choose one of the following school events. Write a description of the event.

   concert track meet basketball game dance

   Purpose: to entertain to persuade to describe to inform

   Format: paragraphs letter poem list

3. You and a friend from school are working on a project together. You are meeting at your house on Saturday. You need to give directions to your friend to tell her how to get to your house. Write the directions in a numbered series of steps.

   Purpose: to entertain to persuade to describe to inform

   Format: paragraphs letter poem list

4. Think about something amusing that happened to you, a family member, or a friend. Write a story about the event that people will enjoy.

   Purpose: to entertain to persuade to describe to inform

   Format: paragraphs letter poem list

5. The school board is holding a special meeting to discuss increasing the school day by one hour. Decide how you feel about the issue. Write a letter to the board stating your position and trying to persuade the school board to support it.

   Purpose: to entertain to persuade to describe to inform

   Format: paragraphs letter poem list

 Basic English Grammar

TRL

Writing Tests 1

- Choose a topic that you feel strongly about. It may be something you like. It may be something you dislike.
- Use a graphic organizer such as a map, diagram, chart, or web. The details in a graphic organizer may provide a good topic. Here is an example of a graphic organizer you can use as you prewrite.

Four-Column Chart

Main Topic

Subtopic	Subtopic	Subtopic	Subtopic
details about the main topic	details about the main topic	details about the main topic	details about the main topic

You can use a four-column chart to organize your thoughts before you begin writing. It will help you see the relationship among ideas. Write your main topic as the title of the chart. Then write a subtopic at the top of each column. Use the columns beneath each subtopic to record details that you can use to support your main topic.

Once students have chosen a topic, they must develop ideas that support the topic. Using a four-column chart will enable them to list subtopics and details to support that topic. Draw a four-column chart on the board. Ask students to choose a topic that they might like to write about; then demonstrate how to use the chart to identify subtopics and supporting details for that topic.

Remind students of the variety of reference sources available for research. Display encyclopedia volumes, almanacs, atlases, dictionaries, thesauruses, and other resources that students can use to research information. Have students identify the type of information each resource provides.

Be sure to suggest the Internet as a reference source. Remind students that electronic versions of standard resources such as encyclopedias and almanacs are available on the Internet as well as numerous other sources.

Developing a Topic

Once you have chosen your topic, you need to find information about it. There are several kinds of details:

- Facts
- Reasons
- Examples
- Sensory images
- Stories or events

Where do you get these details? First, look back at anything you wrote when you were thinking about topics—notes, charts, webs, maps, and so on. To find more details, you might do the following:

- Research
- Interview
- Observe
- Remember
- Imagine

Before you begin to write your first draft, you need to answer two more questions:

- What is my reason for writing?
- Who is my audience?

Your reason for writing may be to entertain, to inform, to persuade, or a combination of these purposes. Your audience may be your classmates, your friends, or any other group of people. Knowing your reason for writing helps you focus. Knowing your audience helps you choose the information to include.

320 Appendix A Basic English Grammar

Drafting

Now it is time to write your first draft. In a first draft, you put down all your ideas on paper. Some writers make an outline or a plan first and follow it as they write. Other writers write their ideas in no particular order and then rearrange them later. Use whatever method works best for you.

Try to write the whole draft at once. Do not stop to rearrange or change anything. You can do that after you have finished the draft. Remember, a first draft will be rough.

How can you arrange your details? Here are some suggestions:

- Main idea and supporting details
- Chronological, or time, order
- Order of importance
- Comparison and contrast

How can you begin and end your writing? A good introduction should tell readers what they will be reading about. It should also catch their attention. You might begin with:

- A story
- A fact
- A question
- A quotation

A good conclusion tells readers that the writing is coming to a close. Generally, it makes a statement about what you have written. You might end with:

- A summary
- A suggestion
- The last event in a sequence

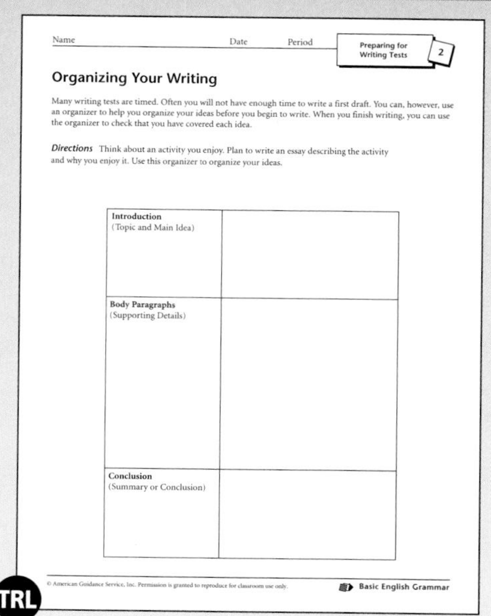

Name Date Period

Preparing for Writing Tests 2

Organizing Your Writing

Many writing tests are timed. Often you will not have enough time to write a first draft. You can, however, use an organizer to help you organize your ideas before you begin to write. When you finish writing, you can use the organizer to check that you have covered each idea.

Directions Think about an activity you enjoy. Plan to write an essay describing the activity and why you enjoy it. Use this organizer to organize your ideas.

Introduction (Topic and Main Idea)	
Body Paragraphs (Supporting Details)	
Conclusion (Summary or Conclusion)	

Basic English Grammar

TRL

Writing Tests 2

Drafting

Ask students to read the Drafting section on page 321. Explain that the first draft is an opportunity to jot down all their ideas. Remind them that when writing a first draft they need not worry about writing a polished written work. They can rework, reorganize, and edit in later drafts. The goal of the first draft is to record ideas.

Writing for Tests

Many writing tests are timed. Students may not have the opportunity to produce a complete first draft. However, they may have time to use a graphic organizer to help them organize ideas for the introductory paragraph, supporting paragraphs, and summary or concluding paragraph.

Distribute Preparing for Writing Tests 2. Show students how to complete the chart by developing ideas for a topic such as "what we are studying in social studies this week."

Suggest that students use graphic organizers to briefly outline their ideas when they are writing for tests.

Revising

Read the Revising section on page 322 with students. Discuss the suggestions for reviewing their writing to identify what needs to be revised.

Have students use samples of their writing from their writing portfolios. Ask them to implement one or more suggestions given in the Revising section to review and then revise their written work.

Proofreading

Read the Proofreading section on pages 322 and 323 with students. Explain to them the importance of carefully proofreading their work. Errors in usage, spelling, capitalization, and punctuation can confuse readers or make a written work harder to understand. Remind students that effective written communication conveys the writer's ideas to the readers. Errors in organization and mechanics can interfere with the message and thus make writing less effective.

Revising

Now it is time to revise your draft. When you revise, you try to improve what you have written. You decide what you like and do not like. You decide what you want to change and how you will change it. You might add or take out words. You might rearrange sentences or paragraphs. Here are some tips for revising:

- Set your draft aside for a while. Then read it. This will help you see your writing in a new way.
- Read your draft aloud. This will help you hear awkward sentences and see places where information is missing.
- Ask someone else to read your draft. Encourage the reader to tell you what you have done well and what needs work.
- Ask yourself (and your reader) questions about your draft. For example:
  —Is my main idea clear?
  —Have I arranged my ideas in a way that makes sense?
  —Is there any information that I should include?
  —Is there any information that I should leave out?

Now, using your comments and your reader's comments, rewrite your draft. Then read your second draft and revise it. You may have to write several drafts before you have one that you like.

Proofreading

Once you have a draft you like, proofread it. When you proofread, you look for and correct mistakes in spelling, grammar, punctuation, and capitalization. These kinds of mistakes distract your reader. Remember, you want your reader to notice your ideas, not your mistakes. Here are some suggestions to help you proofread:

- Make a checklist of things to look for. For example:
  —Did I spell words correctly?
  —Did I write complete sentences?
  —Did I vary my sentences?
  —Did I use vivid verbs and specific details?
  —Do my subjects and verbs agree?
  —Did I use correct capitalization?
  —Did I use correct end punctuation?

- Use a computer spell checker, but remember, it cannot catch some spelling errors.
- Ask someone else to proofread your work.
- Proofread more than once. Look for a different kind of mistake each time.
- Read your work aloud. You may hear mistakes.
- Set your writing aside. Proofread it later. You may see mistakes more clearly.
- Keep a thesaurus nearby. It will help you replace words that you have used too frequently.
- Keep a dictionary and a grammar reference book nearby. You may have questions that they can help answer.

To make your proofreading faster and easier to follow, use proofreaders' marks. Draw the mark at the place where you want to make the correction. Here are some common proofreaders' marks.

Proofreaders' Marks

Mark	Meaning	Mark	Meaning
ℊ	Delete or take out	⋎	Insert an apostrophe
(sp)	Spell out	⋎ (quotation)	Insert quotation marks
^	Insert	lc	Change to lowercase
#	Insert space	≡	Change to capital letter
⊙	Insert a period	⌒	Close up; take out space
^ (comma)	Insert a comma	¶	Begin a paragraph
^ (semicolon)	Insert a semicolon	tr	Transpose letter or words

Together with students, review the proofreaders' marks. Then have students use these marks to proofread newspaper columns or magazine articles. After proofing the pages, they can share with the class any errors they found.

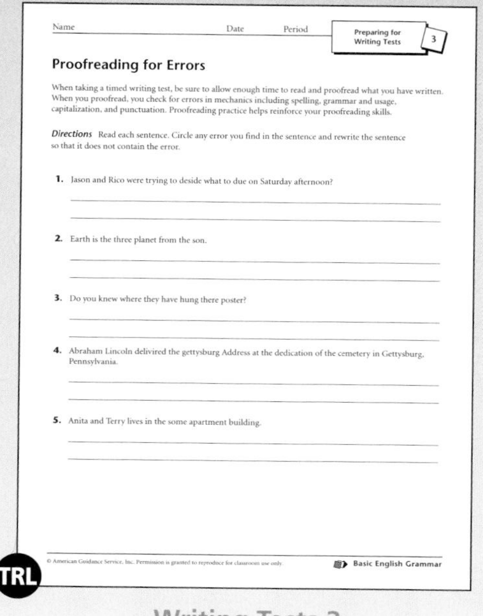

Name Date Period

Preparing for Writing Tests 3

Proofreading for Errors

When taking a timed writing test, be sure to allow enough time to read and proofread what you have written. When you proofread, you check for errors in mechanics including spelling, grammar and usage, capitalization, and punctuation. Proofreading practice helps reinforce your proofreading skills.

Directions Read each sentence. Circle any error you find in the sentence and rewrite the sentence so that it does not contain the error.

1. Jason and Rico were trying to deside what to due on Saturday afternoon?
2. Earth is the three planet from the son.
3. Do you knew where they have hung there poster?
4. Abraham Lincoln delivired the gettysburg Address at the dedication of the cemetery in Gettysburg, Pennsylvania.
5. Anita and Terry lives in the some apartment building.

Basic English Grammar

TRL

Writing Tests 3

Writing for Tests

When taking a writing test, students will want to review and proofread their writing carefully, yet quickly. They may wish to read their paper silently twice.

Suggest that they first read paragraphs for sense, making sure each paragraph contains the information or ideas essential to convey the intended message. Students can then reread each paragraph for mechanical corrections. Ask them to study each sentence separately, checking for correct spelling and usage, sentence structure, punctuation, and capitalization.

To help students practice their proofreading skills, have them complete Preparing for Writing Tests 3. Explain that they should look for spelling, punctuation, grammar and usage, and capitalization errors in each sentence.

Publishing

Read the Publishing section on page 324. Discuss the publishing ideas identified in the text. Then ask students to brainstorm additional ways they can publish their writing. List their ideas on the board.

Suggest that students select favorite written pieces from their portfolios. Encourage them to publish their work using one of the publishing methods identified.

Writing for Tests

The more students write, the better writers they will become and the better prepared they will be to write effectively on tests.

Distribute Preparing for Writing Tests 4. You can use this resource to simulate a writing test experience. You may wish to make this a timed test. Suggest ways that students can allocate their time. For example, if the test time is 20 minutes, they might spend 5 minutes in the prewriting and drafting phase, 10 minutes writing, and 5 minutes proofing and correcting their written work.

Publishing

Think of publishing as presenting and sharing your writing with others. Many writers get their writing published in a newspaper or magazine or as a book. However, there are other ways to publish your writing:

- Get together with other writers. Take turns reading your work aloud and discussing it.
- Send your writing to a school or community newspaper or magazine.
- Give copies of your work to anyone who is interested in reading it, including family members and friends.
- Post your work on the classroom bulletin board.
- Make a classroom newspaper or magazine several times a year. Use the newspaper or magazine to present things that you and your classmates write.

Each time you write, think about the writing process you used. Ask yourself the following questions: *What would I do the same next time? What would I do differently? What parts of the process do I need to work on?* Use the answers to these questions to help you the next time you write.

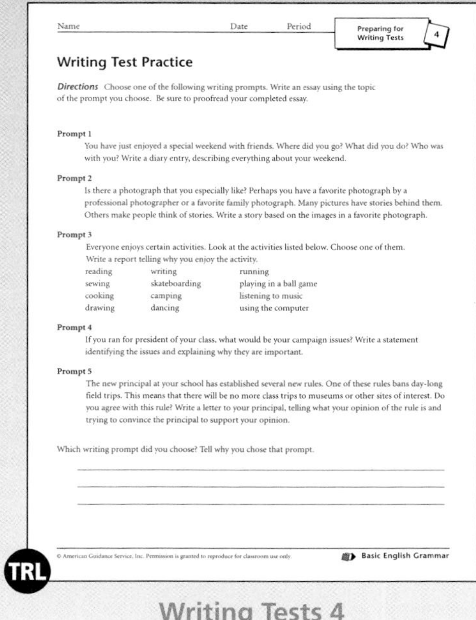

Name ________ Date ____ Period ____ Preparing for Writing Tests 4

Writing Test Practice

Directions Choose one of the following writing prompts. Write an essay using the topic of the prompt you choose. Be sure to proofread your completed essay.

Prompt 1

You have just enjoyed a special weekend with friends. Where did you go? What did you do? Who was with you? Write a diary entry, describing everything about your weekend.

Prompt 2

Is there a photograph that you especially like? Perhaps you have a favorite photograph by a professional photographer or a favorite family photograph. Many pictures have stories behind them. Others make people think of stories. Write a story based on the images in a favorite photograph.

Prompt 3

Everyone enjoys certain activities. Look at the activities listed below. Choose one of them. Write a report telling why you enjoy the activity.

reading	writing	running
sewing	skateboarding	playing in a ball game
cooking	camping	listening to music
drawing	dancing	using the computer

Prompt 4

If you ran for president of your class, what would be your campaign issues? Write a statement identifying the issues and explaining why they are important.

Prompt 5

The new principal at your school has established several new rules. One of these rules bans day-long field trips. This means that there will be no more class trips to museums or other sites of interest. Do you agree with this rule? Write a letter to your principal, telling what your opinion of the rule is and trying to convince the principal to support your opinion.

Which writing prompt did you choose? Tell why you chose that prompt.

____

____

____

Basic English Grammar

TRL

Writing Tests 4

Glossary

A

Abbreviation—(ə brē´ vē ā´ shən) A short form of a word (p. 8)

Abstract noun—(ab´ strakt noun) A word that names an idea that you cannot see or touch (p. 12)

Action verb—(ak´ shən vėrb) A word that tells what someone or something (subject) does, did, or will do (p. 82)

Active verb—(ak´ tiv vėrb) A verb form that we use when the subject is doing the action (p. 113)

Adjective—(aj´ ik tiv) A word that describes a noun or pronoun (p. 56)

Adjective clause—(aj´ ik tiv klȯz) A dependent clause that describes a noun or pronoun (p. 287)

Adjective phrase—(aj´ ik tiv frāz) A prepositional phrase that answers the question *which one, what kind,* or *how many* about the noun or pronoun in a sentence (p. 170)

Adverb—(ad´ vėrb) A word that answers questions about a verb, an adjective, or another adverb (p. 138)

Adverb clause—(ad´ vėrb klȯz) A dependent clause that works like an adverb in a sentence (p. 279)

Adverb of negation—(ad´ vėrb ov ni gā´ shən) The adverbs *never* and *not,* which tell that an action in a sentence will not happen or that a state of being is not present (p. 146)

Adverb phrase—(ad´ vėrb frāz) A prepositional phrase that answers the question *how, when, where, how much,* or *how long* about the verb in a sentence (p. 173)

Antecedent—(an tə sēd´ nt) The noun that the pronoun replaces (p. 28)

Apostrophe—(ə pos´ trə fē) A punctuation mark that indicates a noun is possessive (p. 20)

Appositive—(ə poz´ ə tiv) A noun, a noun phrase, or a noun clause placed next to a noun to rename or explain it (p. 285)

C

Capital letter—(kap´ ə təl let´ ər) The uppercase form of a letter such as *A, B, C* (p. 204)

Clause—(klȯz) A group of words with a subject and a verb (p. 182)

Collective noun—(kə lek´ tiv noun) The name of a group of people, places, or things (p. 3)

Comma—(kom´ ə) A punctuation mark (,) used to separate words, phrases, or clauses in a series (p. 183)

Common noun—(kom´ ən noun) The name of a general type of person, place, thing, or idea (p. 6)

Comparative form—(kəm par´ ə tiv fôrm) The form of an adjective used to compare two people or things (p. 74); the form of an adverb used to compare two people or things (p. 152)

Complement—(kom´ plə mənt) A word that completes the meaning of the verb (p. 250)

Complete subject—(kəm plēt´ sub´ jikt) All the words in the subject (p. 207)

Complex sentence—(kəm pleks´ sen´ təns) A sentence with one independent clause and one or more dependent clauses (p. 290)

Compound-complex sentence—(kom´ pound kəm pleks´ sen´ təns) A sentence that has two or more independent clauses and one or more dependent clauses (p. 292)

Compound noun—(kom´ pound noun) Two words joined together to form one new noun (p. 3)

Compound object—(kom´ pound ob´ jikt) Two or more objects connected by a conjunction (p. 163)

Pronunciation Key

a hat	e let	ī ice	ô order	ů put	sh she	ə { a in about
ā age	ē equal	o hot	oi oil	ü rule	th thin	e in taken
ä far	ėr term	ō open	ou out	ch child	ŦH then	i in pencil
â care	i it	ȯ saw	u cup	ng long	zh measure	o in lemon
						u in circus

Basic English Grammar Glossary **325**

Compound personal pronoun—(kom´ pound pėr´ sə nəl prō´ noun) A pronoun formed by combining a singular personal pronoun and *-self* or a plural personal pronoun and *-selves* (p. 33)

Compound predicate—(kom´ pound pred´ ə kit) Two or more predicates connected by a conjunction (p. 214)

Compound preposition—(kom´ pound prep´ ə zish´ ən) A preposition made up of more than one word (p. 164)

Compound relative pronoun—(kom´ pound rel´ ə tiv prō´ noun) A pronoun such as *whoever, whomever, whichever,* and *whatever* (p. 36)

Compound sentence—(kom´ pound sen´ təns) Two independent clauses joined by a conjunction such as *and, but,* or *or* (p. 219)

Compound subject—(kom´ pound sub´ jikt) Two or more subjects connected by a conjunction (p. 210)

Compound verb—(kom´ pound vėrb) Two or more verbs or verb phrases connected by a conjunction (p. 214)

Concrete noun—(kon´ krēt noun) A word that names something you can see or touch (p. 12)

Conditional verb—(kən dish´ ə nəl vėrb) A helping verb that puts a condition, or requirement, on an action (p. 109)

Conjunction—(kən jungk´ shən) A word (such as *and, or,* and *but*) that connects parts of a sentence (p. 182)

Contraction—(kən trak´ shən) Two words made into one by replacing one or more letters with an apostrophe (p. 50)

Coordinating conjunction—(kō ôrd´ n āt ing kən jungk´ shən) A word that connects two or more equal parts of a sentence (p. 182)

Correlative conjunctions—(kə rel´ ə tiv kən jungk´ shənz) A pair of conjunctions that connects words or groups of words (p. 192)

D

Definite article—(def´ ə nit är´ tə kəl) The word *the,* which is used to talk about a particular person or thing (p. 59)

Demonstrative adjective—(di mon´ strə tiv aj´ ik tiv) The word *this, that, these,* or *those* used as an adjective (p. 72)

Demonstrative pronoun—(di mon´ strə tiv prō´ noun) A pronoun that points out a particular person or thing: *this, these, that,* and *those* (p. 43)

Dependent clause—(di pen´ dənt klȯz) A clause that does not express a complete thought (p. 187)

Direct object—(də rekt´ ob´ jikt) The noun or pronoun that receives the action from a transitive verb (p. 233)

E

End punctuation—(end pungk chü ā´ shən) A mark at the end of a sentence that tells the reader where a sentence ends: a period (.), a question mark (?), or an exclamation mark (!) (p. 204)

F

First-person pronoun—(fėrst pėr´ sən prō´ noun) A pronoun that refers to the person who is speaking (p. 30)

Future perfect—(fyü´ chər pėr´ fikt) Shows an action that will be completed before a certain time in the future (p. 87)

G

Gerund—(jer´ ənd) A verb form that ends in *-ing;* it is always a noun (p. 308)

Gerund phrase—(jer´ ənd frāz) A phrase that includes the gerund and any adjective, adverb, prepositional phrase, or complement the gerund may have (p. 309)

H

Helping verb—(hel´ ping vėrb) A verb that combines with a main verb to form a verb phrase (p. 84)

Hyphen—(hī´ fən) A short dash between parts of a word (p. 4)

I

Indefinite article—(in def´ ə nit är´ tə kəl) The word *a* or *an,* which is used to talk about a general group of people or things (p. 59)

Indefinite pronoun—(in def´ ə nit prō´ noun) A pronoun that does not refer to a specific person or thing (p. 46)

326 *Glossary* *Basic English Grammar*

Independent clause—(in di pen′ dənt klòz) A clause that expresses a complete thought (p. 187)

Indirect object—(in də rekt′ ob′ jikt) A noun or pronoun that tells who receives the direct object of a verb (p. 242)

Infinitive—(in fin′ ə tiv) *To* plus the present tense of a verb (p. 86)

Infinitive phrase—(in fin′ ə tiv frāz) A phrase that includes the infinitive, its complements, and any adjectives or adverbs (p. 304)

Interjection—(in′ tər jek′ shən) A word or phrase that shows strong feeling (p. 195)

Interrogative pronoun—(in tə rog′ ə tiv prō′ noun) A pronoun that asks a question: *who, whom, which, what,* and *whose* (p. 39)

Intransitive verb—(in tran′ sə tiv vėrb) A verb that does not transfer action from the subject to an object (p. 226)

Irregular verb—(i reg′ yə lər vėrb) A verb that does not form its past tense and past participle by adding *-ed* or *-d* (p. 91)

L

Linking verb—(lingk′ ing vėrb) A verb that joins the subject with a noun, pronoun, or adjective in the predicate; it is always a state-of-being verb (p. 256)

M

Main verb—(mān vėrb) The last verb in a verb phrase (p. 84)

N

Noun—(noun) A word that names a person, a place, a thing, or an idea (p. 2)

Noun clause—(noun klòz) A dependent clause that works like a noun in a sentence (p. 282)

O

Object complement—(ob′ jikt kom′ plə mənt) A noun or an adjective that follows the verb and refers to a direct object (p. 250)

Object of the preposition—(ob′ jikt ov ŦHə prep ə zish′ ən) The noun or pronoun that follows the preposition in a prepositional phrase (p. 162)

P

Participle—(pär′ tə sip əl) A verb form that is used as an adjective (p. 312)

Participle phrase—(pär′ tə sip əl frāz) A phrase that includes the participle and an adverb or adverb phrase (p. 313)

Passive verb—(pas′ iv vėrb) A verb form that we use when the action happens to the subject (p. 113)

Past participle—(past pär′ tə sip əl) The verb form used to form the perfect tenses (p. 91)

Past perfect—(past pėr′ fikt) Shows one action completed before another action began (p. 87)

Personal pronoun—(pėr′ sə nəl prō′ noun) A pronoun that refers to a person or a thing (p. 30)

Phrase—(frāz) A group of words that does not contain a subject and predicate, such as a prepositional phrase or a verb phrase (p. 276)

Plural noun—(plůr′ əl noun) The name of more than one person, place, thing, or idea (p. 15)

Positive form—(poz′ ə tiv fôrm) The form of an adjective used to describe one person or thing (p. 74); the form of an adverb used to describe one person or thing (p. 152)

Possessive noun—(pə zes′ iv noun) A word that shows ownership or a relationship between two words (p. 20)

Predicate—(pred′ ə kit) The part of a sentence that tells something about the subject; it always contains a verb (p. 212)

Predicate adjective—(pred′ ə kit aj′ ik tiv) An adjective that follows a linking verb and tells about the subject (p. 264)

Predicate noun—(pred′ ə kit noun) A noun or pronoun that follows a linking verb and renames the subject (p. 256)

Pronunciation Key

a hat	e let	ī ice	ô order	ů put	sh she	ə { a in about
ā age	ē equal	o hot	oi oil	ü rule	th thin	e in taken
ä far	ėr term	ō open	ou out	ch child	ŦH then	i in pencil
â care	i it	ò saw	u cup	ng long	zh measure	o in lemon
						u in circus

Basic English Grammar   Glossary   **327**

Preposition—(prep ə zish′ ən) A word that shows a relationship between a noun or pronoun and other words in a sentence (p. 162)

Prepositional phrase—(prep ə zish′ ə nəl frāz) A group of words made up of a preposition, an object, and adjectives and adverbs that describe the object (p. 162)

Present participle—(prez′ nt pär′ tə sip əl) A verb form that shows continuing action (p. 96)

Present perfect—(prez′ nt pėr′ fikt) Shows an action started in the past and continuing to the present (p. 87)

Progressive form—(prə gres′ iv fôrm) The form of a verb that ends in *-ing* and shows continuing action (p. 96)

Pronoun—(prō′ noun) A word that replaces a noun (p. 28)

Proper adjective—(prop′ ər aj′ ik tiv) A proper noun used as an adjective, or the adjective form of a proper noun (p. 62)

Proper noun—(prop′ ər noun) The name of a particular person, place, thing, or idea (p. 6)

R

Regular verb—(reg′ yə lər vėrb) A verb that forms its past tense and past participle by adding *-ed* or *-d* (p. 91)

Relative pronoun—(rel′ ə tiv prō′ noun) A pronoun such as *who, whom, whose, which, that,* and *what* (p. 35)

S

Second-person pronoun—(sek′ ənd pėr′ sən prō′ noun) A pronoun that refers to the person who is being spoken to (p. 30)

Sentence—(sen′ təns) A group of words that expresses a complete thought (p. 204)

Series—(sir′ ēz) A group of three or more words, phrases, or clauses (p. 183)

Simple predicate—(sim′ pəl pred′ ə kit) The verb or verb phrase (p. 230)

Simple sentence—(sim′ pəl sen′ təns) A sentence with one subject and one predicate; an independent clause (p. 219)

Simple subject—(sim′ pəl sub′ jikt) The noun or pronoun that the sentence is about (p. 207)

Simple tenses—(sim′ pəl tens′ ez) Present, past, and future (p. 86)

Singular noun—(sing′ gyə lər noun) The name of one person, place, thing, or idea (p. 15)

State-of-being verb—(stāt ov bē′ ing vėrb) A verb that tells something about the condition of the subject of a sentence (p. 120)

Subject—(sub′ jikt) The part of a sentence that tells who or what the sentence is about (p. 82)

Subordinating conjunction—(sə bôrd′ n āt ing kən jungk′ shən) A word that connects a dependent clause to an independent clause in a sentence (p. 187)

Superlative form—(sə pėr′ lə tiv fôrm) The form of an adjective used to compare more than two people or things (p. 74); the form of an adverb used to compare more than two people or things (p. 152)

T

Tense—(tens) The time when an action takes place (p. 86)

Third-person pronoun—(thėrd pėr′ sən prō′ noun) A pronoun that refers to the person or thing that is being talked about (p. 30)

Transitive verb—(tran′ sə tiv vėrb) A verb that shows action passed from the subject of the sentence toward another person or thing (p. 233)

V

Verb—(vėrb) A word that expresses action or state of being (p. 82)

Verb phrase—(vėrb frāz) A main verb and one or more helping verbs (p. 84)

Verbal—(vėr′ bəl) A verb that we use as another part of speech (p. 300)

328 *Glossary Basic English Grammar*

Index

A

B

C

Basic English Grammar *Index* **329**

D

E

330 *Index Basic English Grammar*

Basic English Grammar *Index* **331**

O

P

332 *Index Basic English Grammar*

Q

R

Basic English Grammar *Index* **333**

S

T

334 *Index Basic English Grammar*

U

V

W

Basic English Grammar Index **335**

Photo Credits

Cover photos: background and back cover–© Boden/Ledingham/Masterfile; inset–© Joel Benard/Masterfile; p. xiv–© James Jackson/Stone; p. xvi–© J.P. Fruchet/FPG International; pp. 13, 217–© Michael Newman/PhotoEdit; p. 18–© Richard Hutchings Photo/Photo Researchers; p. 26–© Eyewire Collection; pp. 37, 153, 189–© David Young Wolff/PhotoEdit; p. 48–© Rudi Von Briel/PhotoEdit; p. 54–© Steve Satushek/Image Bank; p. 57–© Jim Steinberg/Photo Researchers; p.70–© Frederick Ayer/Photo Researchers; p. 80–© Manoj Shah/Image Bank; p. 83–© Mark C. Burnett/Photo Researchers; p. 99–© Ellen B. Senisi/Photo Researchers; p. 118–© Dann Coffey/Image Bank; p. 128–© Corbis/PictureQuest; pp. 130, 306–© SuperStock; p. 136–© Paul & Lindamarie Ambrose/FPG International; p. 139–© International Stock; p.160–David Fleetham/FPG International; pp. 164, 245–© David Kelly Crow/PhotoEdit; p. 167–© Visuals Unlimited; p. 180–© Todd Powell/Index Stock Imagery; p. 196–© Myrleen Ferguson Cate/PhotoEdit; p. 200–© Mark Segal/Stone; p. 202–© Ken Reid/FPG International; p. 205–© Elena Rooraid/PhotoEdit; p. 224–© Larry Grant/FPG International; p. 258–© Tom McCarthy/Unicorn Stock Photos; p. 274–© Japack Photo Library/Corbis; pp. 285, 288–© Tony Freeman/PhotoEdit; p. 298–© Ted Grant/Masterfile; p. 310–© Mark Romesser/Unicorn Stock Photos

336 *Index* *Basic English Grammar*

Midterm Mastery Test

Name Date Period | Midterm Mastery Test Page 1

Midterm Mastery Test, Chapters 1–6

Part A Identify the part of speech for each bold word. Write *noun, pronoun, adjective, action verb, state-of-being verb,* or *adverb.*

1. After the cold winter, spring **finally** arrived. ______
2. Labrador retrievers are known to be **friendly** dogs. ______
3. Damian and **I** often play cards. ______
4. She **dropped** her glasses on the floor. ______
5. Please make me a peanut butter **sandwich**. ______
6. The dinner **smells** good. ______
7. **Tanya** tried out for the cross-country team. ______
8. Every state **elects** two senators. ______
9. New York and Boston **are** both east coast cities. ______
10. We are having lunch together **tomorrow**. ______
11. *Fences* **was written** by August Wilson. ______
12. Have you answered these questions **correctly**? ______
13. **She** was at the library when we left. ______
14. The cat **pounded** on the catnip mouse. ______
15. We sat around the **hot** fire and warmed our toes. ______
16. They **are** late. ______
17. Enoch answered the question **loudly**. ______
18. **Those** are the books we've been looking for. ______
19. Have **you** heard the new CDs? ______
20. Could you please move **this** chair? ______

 Basic English Grammar

Midterm Mastery Test Page 1

Name Date Period | Midterm Mastery Test Page 2

Midterm Mastery Test, Chapters 1–6, continued

Part B Rewrite these sentences on the blank line. Capitalize the proper nouns and adjectives.

21. valerie has a french poodle named mimi.
______
22. Does tim like to eat swiss cheese?
______
23. We studied the native american tribes of new mexico.
______
24. My friend hanna is learning spanish with her computer.
______
25. karl enjoys his english and basic computer II classes.
______
26. samantha is reading *sense and sensibility*.
______
27. We plan to see a play on friday, april 21.
______
28. loren had an african family visit him over summer vacation.
______
29. Would you like italian dressing with your salad.
______
30. On vacation, tracy went to the rocky mountains in colorado.
______

 Basic English Grammar

Midterm Mastery Test Page 2

Name Date Period | Midterm Mastery Test Page 3

Midterm Mastery Test, Chapters 1–6, continued

Part C Choose the word in parentheses that correctly completes each sentence. Write the word on the line.

31. Either milk or water ______ fine with me. (is, are)
32. Neither Kathy nor her friends ______ in the band. (is, are)
33. We ______ going to sing at the concert. (was, were)
34. Edwin chased the ______ back into the pen. (gooses, geese)
35. The ______ tracks led under the woodpile. (mices, mice's)
36. Both of the ______ books were lost. (girl's, girls')
37. The store sold only ______ clothes. (ladies', ladys')
38. Henry VIII had six ______. (wifes, wives)
39. Have you ______ dinner yet? (eaten, ate)
40. Everyone has already ______ home. (gone, went)
41. ______ brother goes to our school. (Moe's, Moes')
42. The girls were early for ______ lesson. (their, them)
43. ______ of these CDs should I buy? (Which, What)
44. Each girl brought ______ own bat and ball. (their, her)
45. My uncle is ______ than my brother. (tall, taller, tallest)
46. This test is very ______. (tricky, trickier, trickiest)
47. Bo got the ______ news of anyone in the class. (good, better, best)
48. Jennifer was ______ her breakfast. (eat, ate, eaten, eating)
49. Alex has ______ math for four years. (take, took, taken, taking)
50. Which of you two sings ______? (well, better, best)

 Basic English Grammar

Midterm Mastery Test Page 3

Name Date Period | Midterm Mastery Test Page 4

Midterm Mastery Test, Chapters 1–6, continued

Part D Circle the correct answer to the question.

51. Which of these words is a concrete noun?
A love **B** hotdog **C** humor **D** honor
52. Which of these words is an abstract noun?
A field **B** freedom **C** menu **D** sandwich
53. Which of these words is a compound noun?
A classroom **B** tree **C** comedy **D** light
54. Which of these pronouns is in the first person?
A you **B** they **C** I **D** she
55. Which of these pronouns is in the second person?
A you **B** they **C** I **D** she
56. Which of these pronouns is in the third person?
A we **B** they **C** I **D** our
57. Which of these is a contraction?
A his **B** Jim's **C** can't **D** she
58. Which of these is a possessive pronoun?
A he **B** Jim's **C** I **D** her
59. Which of these adjectives is in the positive form?
A sweet **B** sweeter **C** sweetest **D** more sweetest
60. Which of these adjectives is in the comparative form?
A sweet **B** sweeter **C** sweetest **D** most sweetest
61. Which of these adjectives is in the superlative form?
A good **B** goodest **C** best **D** better
62. Which of these verbs is in the infinitive?
A leaving **B** to leave **C** left **D** had left
63. Which form of *be* is in the past tense?
A she is **B** I was **C** they are **D** it is
64. Which form of *be* is singular?
A we were **B** she was **C** they are **D** they were
65. Which form of *be* is in the third person?
A he was **B** you are **C** we were **D** I am

 Basic English Grammar

Midterm Mastery Test Page 4

Final Mastery Test

Name Date Period

Final Mastery Test
Page 1

Final Mastery Test

Part A Label the parts of each sentence. Use these abbreviations:
S Subject DO Direct Object PN Predicate Noun
V Verb IO Indirect Object

1. Amanda went to Howard University.

2. Jimmy won a scholarship.

3. He would play baseball for his school.

4. The college gave Jimmy a uniform.

5. Jimmy is a good athlete.

Part B Circle the correct answer to each question.

6. Which of these words is an abstract noun?
A globe **B** stationery **C** trust **D** apple

7. What type of pronoun is the underlined word in the following sentence?
Allie met the actor who is in that movie.
A personal **B** demonstrative **C** relative **D** interrogative

8. What kind of adjective is the word *Asian*?
A possessive **B** article **C** demonstrative **D** proper

9. Which of these verbs is in the present perfect tense?
A walk **B** will walk **C** have walked **D** had walked

10. Which of the following is the correct comparative form of the adverb.
A more quietly **B** most quiet **C** quieter **D** most quietly

11. Which prepositional phrase completes the following sentence? Jesse went to the movies ________ .
A with we **B** with them **C** with my **D** with your

12. Which of the following words is a subordinating conjunction?
A but **B** both **C** who **D** if

13. What is the purpose of the following sentence? Hand me that book please.
A statement **B** exclamation **C** command **D** question

14. In the following sentence, which word is the object complement?
The students elected Marietta president of the student council.
A students **B** Marietta **C** president **D** council

15. What kind of sentence is the following sentence? Although they are sisters, Su Li and Mai Lin have very different interests.
A simple **B** compound **C** complex **D** compound-complex

Final Mastery Test Page 1

Name Date Period

Final Mastery Test
Page 2

Final Mastery Test, continued

Part C Identify the part of speech for each word in bold. Write *noun, pronoun, adjective, action verb, state-of-being verb, adverb, preposition, conjunction,* or *interjection.*

16. Calico cats are **beautiful** animals. ____________

17. Trudy and **I** like to dance. ____________

18. We **chose** the blue balloons for the party. ____________

19. Alex **and** Jordan are shooting baskets. ____________

20. Please bring me a **pencil**. ____________

21. The food **tastes** delicious. ____________

22. The dog is barking **at** the door. ____________

23. Portland and Los Angeles **are** west coast cities. ____________

24. Some friends are coming over **today**. ____________

25. **Whew!** That feels better. ____________

Part D Write these sentences on your paper. Capitalize the proper nouns and proper adjectives.

26. ahmad has a cat named may.

27. julia likes dutch chocolate.

28. frank is taking spanish and computer I.

29. sherry read *a raisin in the sun* on her trip to arizona.

30. chuck is taking monday, august 15, off.

Final Mastery Test Page 2

Name Date Period

Final Mastery Test
Page 3

Final Mastery Test, continued

Part E Identify each kind of sentence. Write *simple, compound, complex,* or *compound-complex.*

31. Randy, David, and Alex had enjoyed high school. ____________

32. They knew their lives would be different now, but they looked forward to it. ____________

33. They could write letters, and they also could leave messages for each other on e-mail. ____________

34. David got a scholarship to Washington State University, which was his first choice. ____________

35. He will major in physical education, and because of what he has been told, he knows WSU is a good school for PE majors. ____________

Part F Write whether each group of words is a phrase (*P*), a dependent clause (*DC*), or an independent clause (*IC*).

36. When you finish the job. ________

37. They ate supper. ________

38. Seeing you is fun. ________

39. Using the computer. ________

40. Before we move. ________

41. Unless it snows. ________

Part G Identify the purpose of each sentence. Write *statement, question, command/request,* or *exclamation.*

42. Who knows how to use this software? ____________

43. Bring in the newspaper. ____________

44. I am so excited! ____________

45. The Yankees play the Twins next week. ____________

46. Tell me about your new apartment. ____________

Final Mastery Test Page 3

Name Date Period

Final Mastery Test
Page 4

Final Mastery Test, continued

Part H Write whether the verb in bold is transitive (*T*) or intransitive (*I*).

47. Glen **reads** short stories. ____________

48. Birds **fly**. ____________

49. She **found** the number in the telephone book. ____________

50. Toni Morrison **writes** poems. ____________

51. Jim Thorpe **lived** in Oklahoma. ____________

Part I Identify the pattern of each sentence. Circle the correct answer.

52. The plane will take off on time.
A Pattern 1 **B** Pattern 2 **C** Pattern 3 **D** Pattern 4

53. Give the agent your ticket.
A Pattern 1 **B** Pattern 2 **C** Pattern 3 **D** Pattern 5

54. Jennifer had the highest score on the math test.
A Pattern 2 **B** Pattern 3 **C** Pattern 4 **D** Pattern 6

55. She appeared happy with her accomplishment.
A Pattern 2 **B** Pattern 4 **C** Pattern 5 **D** Pattern 6

Part J Circle the verbal in each sentence. Write whether it is an *infinitive, gerund,* or *participle.*

56. Ms. Jones was at home watching television. ____________

57. She enjoys relaxing after a busy day. ____________

58. Tanya had gone to her room to study. ____________

59. They heard someone knocking at the door. ____________

60. Kirby had come to tell Tanya about his job. ____________

61. Smiling brightly, Tanya greeted her guest. ____________

62. Wondering what Tanya would like to do, Kirby asked her about her plans. ____________

63. Tanya thought she might get a job painting. ____________

64. Mr. Lee wanted Tanya to paint his house. ____________

65. Tanya wanted to paint his picture! ____________

Final Mastery Test Page 4

Final Mastery Test

Name Date Period

Final Mastery Test
Page 5

Final Mastery Test, continued

Part K Write whether the word or words in bold are a *predicate adjective*, a *predicate noun*, or a *predicate pronoun*.

66. That boy is my **brother**. ____________

67. Cardinals are **red**. ____________

68. Who is **she**? ____________

69. Kally will be **vice president**. ____________

70. Brothers all are **we**. ____________

71. Is he **frightened** or **unsure**? ____________

72. Her workshop is usually **messy** but **clean**. ____________

73. Before two months pass, he will be **president**. ____________

74. Mrs. Ruiz is **teacher** of the year. ____________

75. Gareth felt **calm** and **sure** about his test scores. ____________

Part L Write whether the words in bold are an *adjective clause*, an *adverb clause*, or a *noun clause*.

76. **After the sun sets**, the temperature drops. ____________

77. She does **whatever pleases her**. ____________

78. **Whenever you are ready** will be a good time to go. ____________

79. The person **who lost the kitten** was upset. ____________

80. The tree **that fell on the roof** was huge. ____________

81. Gina knew **what the plans were**. ____________

82. We got in the back door **because we knew the owner**. ____________

83. Drew bought a laptop computer **that he travels with**. ____________

84. He disagrees about **what we should do**. ____________

85. She goes biking **whenever she has time**. ____________

Basic English Grammar

Final Mastery Test Page 5

Name Date Period

Final Mastery Test
Page 6

Final Mastery Test, continued

Part M Write these sentences on your paper. Add the necessary punctuation.

86. Because Elsas mother is working Elsa watches her sister Kim

____

87. Len bought ten dollars worth of gas but he still did not fill the tank

____

88. Hello Is anybody home

____

89. Monica made supper however her father brought Chinese food

____

90. Shira left the back door open therefore she had to catch the bird that flew inside

____

Part N Choose the word in parentheses that correctly completes each sentence. Write the word on the line.

91. Neither Larry nor his friends ____________ in the play. (is, are)

92. Chris wants to leave, ____________ her car is stalled. (and, but)

93. The restaurant has a ____________ menu. (children's, childrens')

94. Husbands and ____________ can attend the meeting. (wifes, wives)

95. Have you ____________ your breakfast yet? (eaten, ate)

96. I had ____________ by the time they got there. (gone, went)

97. ____________ sister is in our class. (Zoe's, Zoes')

98. The boys were on time for ____________ game. (their, them)

99. Each girl brought ____________ own baseball glove. (their, her)

100. My aunt is ____________ than my mother. (tall, taller, tallest)

Basic English Grammar

Final Mastery Test Page 6

Teacher's Resource Library Answer Key

Activities

Activity 1—Identifying Nouns

1–10. Answers will vary. Possible answers are given. **1.** trust **2.** sidewalk **3.** race **4.** color **5.** ounce **6.** pencil **7.** minute **8.** courage **9.** cousin **10.** rally **11–20.** The collective nouns are (12) team, (13) flock, (15) herd, (16) bunch, (18) collection, and (19) assortment.

Activity 2—Common and Proper Nouns and Capitalization

1–20. The proper nouns are (2) Statue of Liberty, (3) Mexico, (5) May, (6) Steven Spielberg, (8) Colorado River, (10) United States Postal Service, (11) Engine Company #4, (12) New Year's Eve, (13) Sleeping Beauty, (16) Dr. Pascal, and (18) Helen Keller. **21.** birthdays, natalie, frances **22.** mother, *goodnight moon*, james **23.** tomorrow, falcons, tigers, springdale high school **24.** texas, alaska, united states, america **25.** halloween, howard, superman's **26.** anna, jennifer lopez **27.** greenes, washington, march, cherry blossom festival **28.** maui, hawaii, pacific ocean **29.** *daily herald* **30.** george washington

Activity 3—Concrete and Abstract Nouns

1. Stacy—C, loneliness—A, school—C **2.** mayor—C, expense—A **3.** blister—C, foot—C, pain—A **4.** job—C, time—A **5.** Jesse—C, confidence—A, idea—A, class—C **6.** exercise—C, health—A **7.** show—C, success—A **8.** Freedom—A, speech—A, right—A **9.** role—C, play—C, energy—A **10.** Friendship—A, source—A, happiness—A **11.** independence—A, July—A **12.** excitement—A, Frank—C, coat—C, house—C **13.** grandfather—C, courage—A, pioneers—C **14.** Louis—C, emotions—A, poem—C **15.** campaign—C, interest—A, politics—A

Activity 4—Spelling Singular and Plural Nouns

1. museum **2.** spies **3.** geese **4.** church **5.** knives **6.** navy **7.** skies **8.** plate **9.** buses **10.** leaves **11.** women **12.** puppies **13.** library **14.** pears **15.** kitty **16.** deer **17.** roofs **18.** injuries **19.** coins **20.** uncle **21.** feet **22.** wishes **23.** Mice **24.** peaches **25.** children, computers **26.** streets **27.** parties **28.** turkeys **29.** women **30.** beaches

Activity 5—Possessive Nouns

1. school's—S **2.** salesmen's—P **3.** walrus's—S **4.** buses'—P **5.** Harry's—S **6.** ladies'—P **7.** New York's—S **8.** libraries'—P **9.** bridge's—S **10.** fleet's—S **11.** hamburgers' **12.** James's **13.** Jane's **14.** school's **15.** seconds' **16.** love's **17.** radio's **18.** teachers' **19.** child's **20.** pencils'

Activity 6—Pronouns and Their Antecedents

1. Julie and Robert **2.** Mollie **3.** Selena **4.** friend **5.** boys and girls **6.** squirrel **7.** game **8.** Honesty **9.** doughnuts **10.** father **11.** her, her **12.** she, her **13.** this, him **14.** its **15.** it **16.** they **17.** We, that, our, them **18.** her, her **19.** they **20.** We, I, them

Activity 7—Singular and Plural Personal Pronouns

1. you or she **2.** their **3.** its **4.** We **5.** They, them **6.** Our—P **7.** her—S **8.** We—P **9.** we—P **10.** their—P, us—P **11.** We—P **12.** we—P, their—P, we—P, them—P **13.** them—P **14.** Their—P **15.** My—S, their—P

Activity 8—Working with Relative Pronouns

1. who **2.** that **3.** that **4.** Who **5.** Whose **6.** who **7.** What **8.** Which **9.** whom **10.** who **11.** Whoever **12.** whomever **13.** whatever **14.** whichever **15.** whatever **16.** whomever **17.** Whichever **18.** Whatever **19.** whomever **20.** whatever

Activity 9—Asking Questions with Pronouns

1. What **2.** Which **3.** What **4.** Whose **5.** Whom **6.** Who **7.** Which **8.** Whose **9.** What **10.** What **11.** What—D **12.** Which—D **13.** Who—D **14.** which—I **15.** who—I **16.** whose—D **17.** What—D **18.** which—I **19.** which—I **20.** What—D

Activity 10—Using Demonstrative Pronouns

1. boys—P **2.** proof—S **3.** stamps—P **4.** homework—S **5.** building—S **6.** sandwiches—P **7.** boxes—P **8.** fork—S **9.** park—S **10.** tracks—P **11.** story—S **12.** friend—S **13.** toys—P **14.** cookies—P **15.** keys—P **16.** These *or* Those—F **17.** this—N **18.** this *or* these—N **19.** this—N **20.** That—F

Activity 11—Indefinite Pronouns with Verbs

1. another **2.** Nothing **3.** something **4.** each **5.** another **6.** No one, anything **7.** everyone **8.** one, everyone **9.** Both **10.** several **11.** Either **12.** Anything **13.** much **14.** each **15.** everything **16.** Some—were **17.** Everyone—is **18.** Neither—wants **19.** others—have **20.** anyone—Is

Activity 12—Creating Contractions

1. What's **2.** they've **3.** Let's **4.** she's **5.** Who's **6.** We've **7.** It's **8.** we're **9.** We'd **10.** I'm **11.** you'll **12.** I'll **13.** That's **14.** we'll **15.** I'd **16.** it's **17.** He's **18.** they'd **19.** they're **20.** You're

Activity 13—Locating Adjectives in Sentences

1–10. Answers will vary. Possible answers are given. **1.** four, striped **2.** weekend, sightseeing **3.** small, green **4.** long, black **5.** fastest, wooden **6.** playful, adorable **7.** difficult, final **8.** challenging, important **9.** strong, spicy **10.** warm, breezy **11.** energetic **12.** chilly **13.** shining **14.** round **15.** favorite

Activity 14—Definite and Indefinite Articles

1. a **2.** the **3.** the, a *or* the **4.** a **5.** the **6.** an, a **7.** an **8.** the **9.** The **10.** a **11.** **The** prizes—P; **a** table—S **12.** **an** hour—S **13.** **The** hours—P **14.** **The** boys—P, **the** girl—S **15.** **an** honest opinion—S

Activity 15—Recognizing Proper Adjectives

1. American—flag **2.** French—dressing, Italian—dressing **3.** Irish—team **4.** French—government **5.** Revolutionary War—heroes **6.** African—continent **7.** Polish—heritage **8.** Italian—bicycle **9.** Native American—drums **10.** Chinese—children, Russian—children, American—hamburgers. **11.** St. Leonard—team **12.** Portuguese—language **13.** Mexican—grandparents **14.** French Canadian—citizens **15.** Library Association—conference **16.** Taft High School—gymnasium **17.** Russian—winters **18.** Japanese—calligraphy **19.** Swiss Army—knife **20.** Scottish—capital

Activity 16—Recognizing Nouns Used as Adjectives

1. highway—exit **2.** bell—bottoms **3.** chicken—sandwich **4.** forest—path **5.** fun—house **6.** oyster—pearl **7.** dress—shoes **8.** baseball—cap **9.** railroad—station **10.** corner—store **11.** war—memorial **12.** obedience—school **13.** telephone—number **14.** monkey—house **15.** water—fountain **16.** basketball—game **17.** lunch—meeting **18.** rope—trick, dude—ranch **19.** library—books **20.** raffle—ticket

Activity 17—Possessive Adjectives

1. her **2.** his **3.** our **4.** Their **5.** his **6.** their **7.** Your **8.** its **9.** your, my **10.** their **11.** my—coat **12.** her—spirit **13.** His—brother's, brother's—hair, my—sister's, sister's—hair **14.** His—mother's, mother's—job **15.** our—teacher's, teacher's—chair **16.** Their—painting **17.** my—sink's, sink's—drain **18.** her—cat **19.** Laura and Mike's—aunt, their—school **20.** your—sister's, sister's—boyfriend

Activity 18—Using Indefinite Pronouns and Numbers as Adjectives

I reminded myself several times, but I still forgot to bring the two dollars I needed for the bus. After some time passed, I decided to walk to the ballpark. It was three miles, but I knew my team needed all the players. A team needs nine players to start the game, and several members had been sick recently. Each person counted. No one wanted to lose the game, because our team had a one-game lead. Could I make it in twenty minutes? Before long there were only a few blocks to go. I ran most of the way. Everyone cheered when I showed up.

1. everyone [P], twenty [A] **2.** several [A], many [A] **3.** No one [P], three [A] **4.** All [A], thirty [A] **5.** anyone [P] **6.** Some [P], ten [A], many [A] **7.** Several [A], four [A] **8.** someone [P], one [A] **9.** A few [A], two [A] **10.** any [A]

Activity 19—Demonstrative Adjectives

1. this concert **2.** those tickets **3.** this rain **4.** this Tuesday **5.** these tickets **6.** *none* **7.** this crowd **8.** *none* **9.** these people **10.** This wait **11.** *none* **12.** that wait **13.** this concert **14.** those bands **15.** that night **16.** those people **17.** *none* **18.** these bands **19.** this rain **20.** those tickets

Activity 20—Creating Comparative Adjectives

1. sweet, sweetest **2.** better, best **3.** heavy, heavier **4.** colorful, more colorful **5.** old, oldest **6.** more graceful, most graceful **7.** careful, least careful **8.** smarter, smartest **9.** amazing, more amazing **10.** bad, worst **11.** pinker, pinkest **12.** sad, sadder **13.** terrible, most terrible **14.** happier, happiest **15.** funny, funnier **16.** awkward, least awkward **17.** loveable, more loveable **18.** sharp, sharpest **19.** tinier, tiniest **20.** tiring, less tiring

Activity 21—Recognizing Action Verbs

1. dances—Sonia **2.** will go—Terrence **3.** Can fly—you **4.** tasted—Kelly **5.** examined—jeweler **6.** had taken—Dr. Haller **7.** drive—Whos **8.** will bake—I **9.** ski—You **10.** raced—Randy **11.** littered—balls **12.** had steered—gladiator **13.** decorated—Drawings **14.** poured, spilled—Marcus **15.** had written—Lulu **16.** Will be going—Hilda **17.** nested—dove **18.** will eat—Andy **19.** had melted—tray **20.** Would like—you

Activity 22—Verbs Express Tense

1. present perfect **2.** past perfect **3.** past **4.** present **5.** future perfect **6.** present perfect **7.** future **8.** past **9.** future perfect **10.** past perfect **11.** present **12.** present **13.** present perfect **14.** past **15.** past **16.** past **17.** future **18.** past **19.** present perfect **20.** present perfect

Activity 23—Irregular Verb Forms

1. seen **2.** giving **3.** chose **4.** go **5.** eaten **6.** chosen **7.** broke **8.** doing **9.** taught **10.** began **11.** done **12.** gave **13.** sung **14.** teaching **15.** known **16.** swum **17.** wore **18.** written **19.** breaking **20.** forgot

Activity 24—Recognizing the Progressive Form

1. have been **2.** was **3.** were **4.** will have been **5.** has been **6.** is **7.** had been **8.** will be **9.** was **10.** has been **11.** had been **12.** is **13.** was **14.** will be **15.** was **16.** shall be **17.** were **18.** had been **19.** shall have been **20.** have been

Activity 25—Subject and Verb Agreement

1. eat **2.** sinks **3.** cry **4.** swims **5.** fly **6.** goes **7.** find **8.** jumps **9.** attend **10.** dives **11.** know **12.** finishes **13.** stay **14.** needs **15.** were

Activity 26—Learning to Work with *Do*

1. did **2.** doing **3.** did **4.** Does **5.** do **6.** had done **7.** done **8.** doing **9.** does **10.** have done **11.** Did **12.** do **13.** do **14.** doing **15.** done **16.** helping **17.** main **18.** helping **19.** main **20.** helping

Activity 27—Conditional and *Do* Verbs

1. must have gone **2.** might have gone **3.** should have exercised **4.** Did know **5.** might win **6.** must leave **7.** can sing **8.** might come **9.** Do like **10.** must rake **11.** Did finish **12.** did trim **13.** must trim **14.** Would help **15.** shall find **16.** might see **17.** might have helped **18.** must sleep **19.** might prefer **20.** Did attend

Activity 28—Using Passive and Active Verbs

1. Tendel and Margie funded the production. 2. Steve ran a race. 3. An engineer operated the machine. 4. Audley Technical challenged Sidney High School. 5. A courier delivered the package. 6. Mr. Feinbrow cancelled the Saturday class. 7. My mother kneaded the bread dough. 8. Firefighters extinguished the fire. 9. My little sisters messed up my bedroom. 10. Sarah cleaned up the mess.

Activity 29—Verbs That Express a State of Being

1. am *or* am being 2. has been 3. was 4. were being 5. are *or* were 6. will be 7. had been 8. is 9. was 10. were 11. are 12. were 13. am 14. will be 15. were 16. will have been 17. was 18. will have been 19. was 20. has been

Activity 30—Identifying Action or State-of-Being Verbs

1. A, B 2. B, A 3. B, A 4. B, A 5. B, A 6. A, B 7. A, B 8. B, A 9. B, A 10. B, A 11. B, A 12. A, B 13. A, B 14. A, B 15. A, B

Activity 31—State-of Being Verbs Express Tense

1. Will turn—future tense 2. is becoming—present progressive tense 3. looks—present tense 4. felt —past tense 5. is—present tense 6. Have looked—present perfect tense 7. will have been—future perfect tense 8. has been—present perfect tense 9. will be—future tense 10. became—past tense 11. keeps—present tense 12. seem—present tense 13. Will be—future tense 14. will be—future tense 15. was—past tense 16. will be—future tense 17. had looked—past perfect tense 18. will be—future tense 19. felt—past tense 20. Is—present tense

Activity 32—Adverbs Answer Questions About Verbs

Answers will vary. Possible answers are given. 1. expertly 2. gracefully 3. willingly 4. softly 5. loudly 6. quickly 7. regularly 8. neatly 9. well 10. carefully 11. swiftly 12. Silently 13. fearlessly 14. slowly 15. gently 16. independently 17. nicely 18. professionally 19. happily 20. Quietly

Activity 33—Adverbs of Degree

1. so 2. rather 3. very 4. extremely 5. too 6. too 7. extremely 8. exceedingly 9. unusually 10. extraordinarily 11. quite 12. very 13. much 14. very 15. sometime

Activity 34—Recognizing Adverbs of Negation

1. not (can't) 2. never 3. not 4. never 5. not (can't) 6. not (Haven't) 7. not 8. not (didn't) 9. never 10. not (Can't) 11. has been skiing 12. had played 13. could find 14. is 15. will return 16. ate 17. Will (Won't) say 18. left 19. could catch 20. is

Activity 35—Identifying Adjectives and Adverbs

Adjectives and adverbs used to complete the sentences will vary. Possible answers are given. 1. tall—adjective 2. quietly—adverb 3. sweetly—adverb 4. hungry—adjective 5. Merrily—adverb 6. greedily—adverb 7. beautiful—adjective 8. together—adverb 9. express—adjective 10. low—adjective 11. loudly—adverb 12. cloudy–adjective 13. happily—adverb 14. difficult—adjective 15. here—adverb 16. early—adverb 17. intelligent—adjective 18. dedicated—adjective 19. continually—adverb 20. Sadly—adverb

Activity 36—Comparing with Adverbs

1. harder 2. loudly 3. most maturely 4. slowest 5. more kindly 6. brightly 7. more quickly 8. better 9. most fondly 10. more comfortably 11. skillfully, more skillfully, most skillfully 12. wisely, more wisely, most wisely 13. well, better, best 14. politely, more politely, most politely 15. cruelly, more cruelly, most cruelly

Activity 37—Using Adverbs Correctly

1. will go 2. will tell 3. find 4. have taken 5. will show 6. will sing 7. will go 8. went 9. drove 10. traveled 11. beautiful—beautifully 12. slow—slowly 13. peaceful—peacefully 14. rapid—rapidly 15. gentle—gently 16. hearty—heartily 17. eager—eagerly 18. nice—nicely 19. soft—softly 20. loud—loudly

Activity 38—Recognizing Prepositional Phrases

1. in the closet 2. At the end, of the rainbow 3. during the lecture 4. Over the river, through the woods, to grandmother's house 5. with my breakfast 6. to freedom 7. before the Civil War 8. around the closed road, across the bridge 9. for you 10. to the party, on Saturday 11. **went** to a class 12. **looked** through her notebook 13. **open** to page 72 14. **reading** from the chapter 15. **question** about the material 16. **went** to her room 17. **went** to her sister's recital 18. **talked** with the children 19. **talked** to Katie 20. **teacher** of young children

Activity 39—Prepositions and Their Objects

1. I 2. P 3. I 4. P 5. P 6. I 7. P 8. I 9. P 10. P 11. he—him 12. she—her 13. I—me 14. they—them 15. she—her

Activity 40—Using Prepositional Phrases as Adjectives

1. ladies 2. sailor, girl 3. sock, hole 4. nightmare 5. birds, there 6. chairs 7. box, table 8. song, group 9. apples 10. Many, theater 11–20. Answers will vary. Possible answers are given. 11. of my friends 12. near the stairs 13. from working 14. from Seattle 15. under the sink 16. about the wizard 17. on the table 18. of gloves, of the drawer 19. above the trees 20. of California

Activity 41—Identifying Adverb and Adjective Phrases

1. in the parade—adverb 2. in the parade—adjective 3. through the woods—adverb 4. over the bridge—adverb 5. over the bridge—adjective 6. for the concert—adjective 7. from Iowa—adjective 8. from Iowa—adverb 9. at the supermarket—adverb 10. on the left side—adjective 11. on the left side—adverb 12. During the storm—adverb 13. in the fast lane—adverb 14. in the fast lane—adjective 15. to Boise—adjective 16. After dinner—adverb 17. after dinner—adjective 18. across the bed—adverb 19. in the microwave oven—adverb 20. in the microwave oven—adjective

Activity 42—Adverb or Preposition?

1. preposition—door 2. adverb 3. adverb 4. preposition—board 5. adverb 6. preposition—park 7. adverb 8. preposition—river 9. adverb 10. preposition—hallway 11. adverb 12. preposition—car 13. preposition—gate 14. adverb 15. preposition—race 16. adverb 17. adverb 18. preposition—bridge 19. preposition—line 20. adverb

Activity 43—Punctuating Compounds

1. Katie needs to hurry; otherwise, she will be late to school. **2.** After lunch Mary went shopping, Becky cleaned the house, and Rob worked in the yard. **3.** I thought about playing tennis today; however, it rained. **4.** Carlos like iced tea; therefore, the family chose to serve it often. **5.** Tom practiced all afternoon; nevertheless, he was not ready for his performance. **6.** The cat prefers fish; nevertheless, it just gets cat food. **7.** This year we planted a vegetable garden with tomatoes, cucumbers, and peppers, but no radishes. **8.** Tulips, daffodils, and crocuses all grow from bulbs. **9.** Cola drinks, chocolate, coffee, and tea all contain caffeine. **10.** To eat properly, avoid foods with fat as well as foods with sugar. **11.** *Hamlet, Romeo and Juliet,* and *Macbeth* are all plays written by William Shakespeare. **12.** Apples, peaches, plums, and pears are all fruits that grow on trees. **13.** Janet, Katie, and Laura are all living in the same neighborhood. **14.** Paula liked the movie, but she said the book was better. **15.** The book was very long; moreover, it was dull. **16.** Ask Jay to make it, for no one else has the recipe. **17.** Mike's family did not fly to California; instead, they took the train. **18.** I would rather have the red one; besides, green is Jesse's favorite color. **19.** Heather is not here yet, so Nancy will have to go first. **20.** Brittany studied very hard; therefore, she made an A on the exam.

Activity 44—Dependent Clauses

1. **Because** margarine and butter are mostly fat **2.** **until** I finish **3.** **When** Keesha arrives **4.** **Since** the party was over **5.** **In order that** everyone might have a chance to speak **6.** **Whenever** I am sad **7.** **Although** it was raining **8.** **while** they watched the movie **9.** **If** Jacob is late again **10.** **Because** an education leads to a better job **11.** **In order that** the workers look the same **12.** **Unless** you save your money **13.** **While** my brother is in the Navy **14.** **Wherever** Ramona goes **15.** **After** the rain come

Activity 45—Finding Conjunctions

1. Unless—subordinating **2.** Either . . . or—correlative **3.** however—subordinating **4.** when—subordinating **5.** since—subordinating **6.** whether . . . or—correlative **7.** and—coordinating **8.** Both . . . and—correlative **9.** Whenever—subordinating **10.** but—coordinating **11.** Because—subordinating **12.** but—coordinating **13.** and—coordinating **14.** or—coordinating **15.** Neither . . . nor—correlative **16.** Either . . . or—correlative **17.** and—coordinating **18.** not only . . . but also—correlative **19.** whether . . . or—correlative **20.** nevertheless—subordinating

Activity 46—Recognizing Interjections

1. Wow **2.** Hush **3.** really **4.** Hurry! **5.** Well; Oh **6.** Hmm; Now **7.** What a loss! **8.** Ouch! **9.** Brr **10.** Stop! **11–15.** Sentences and interjections will vary.

Activity 47—Making Sentences

Sentences will vary. Possible sentences are given. **1.** The wind then blew down the tower. **2.** The tree had low branches and big leaves. **3.** That green fruit seemed like strange food to be eating. **4.** George found the missing playing card. **5.** Use the wooden bowl, ceramic cup, and metal spoon. **6.** They were aware that I knew where it was. **7.** We heard about Jill's trip over the ocean. **8.** Alice took responsibility the last time this happened. **9.** Dana was confused and upset about Hector's absence. **10.** Dorothy clicked the ruby slippers together to go home.

Activity 48—Finding Subjects

The simple subjects are in bold. **1.** **People** **2.** The **beach** **3.** **He** **4.** **Several** of my friends **5.** **Teachers** **6.** **One** of the students **7.** **It** **8.** The black **cat** under the table **9.** **All** of us **10.** This **restaurant** **11.** The **principal** **12.** Young **children** **13.** My **sister** **14.** **You** **15.** **we** **16.** The heavy dark **clouds** **17.** **Karen, Chad,** and **Ben** **18.** **They** **19.** My bank **account** **20.** His **skills** in the kitchen

Activity 49—A Sentence Has Two Parts

1. The teacher opened the package. **2.** Where is my homework? **3.** Everyone on the trip was ready for lunch. **4.** The mailbox was entirely full of letters. **5.** (You) Stop that right now! **6.** Both Heather and I were late for class. **7.** My exam for English is scheduled to be at one o'clock. **8.** The bus driver missed our bus stop today. **9.** Two candy bars were left. **10.** Ice cream will melt fast in warm weather. **11.** The award committee's final decisions were made. **12.** I am very excited about college. **13.** We should go out to dinner tonight. **14.** Did one of you see that movie? **15.** They ran off in a hurry. **16.** The program had ended. **17.** The whole dozen eggs fell to the floor. **18.** Europe, Asia, and Africa are connected by land. **19.** The shuttle flight crew repaired the solar panels. **20.** (You) Please find my slippers.

Activity 50—Interrogative Sentences

1. Is this your book? **2.** Who can help me? **3.** Have you seen that show? **4.** Why are you so concerned? **5.** Will you be home for dinner? **6.** Has anyone finished the project? **7.** Do you feel tired? **8.** When is the game going to be over? **9.** Where did everyone go? **10.** Is your car still in the garage? **11.** Do you have a game today? **12.** Does anyone know the answer? **13.** How are we doing? **14.** What time is it? **15.** Are you going? **16.** Where are the decorations for the party? **17.** Who is traveling to Dallas with you? **18.** Why would anyone want to buy that? **19.** Do you want chicken or fish? **20.** Will Carlos arrive in time for dinner?

Activity 51—Using Compound Sentences

Independent clauses will vary. Sentences using possible independent clauses are given. **1.** We asked them several times, but Pilar and Kurt won't help us. **2.** Alex found two extra bottles, so he brought one to the picnic. **3.** Some people thought Mr. Snuffles was a toy, but I knew it was a valuable puppet. **4.** Hattie liked summer, but Ronnie liked winter's snow and ice. **5.** I haven't been to Rome, but I would like to go someday. **6.** Her friends like Celine Dion, but my sister still listens to Nirvana. **7.** The restaurant was known for its good food, but I never liked it. **8.** Superman can fly, and Spiderman can climb up buildings. **9.** Joyce has wonderful rhythm, but I like dancing more than she does. **10.** Movies sometimes make me cry, so I always take a handkerchief with me. **11.** I wanted to play the violin, but my mother made me play the tuba instead. **12.** Nathan was fast, but Webster beat him to the finish line. **13.** Dr. Zimmerman performed tests on the blood, but he could not determine a diagnosis. **14.** I feel full, but I haven't had lunch yet. **15.** There are two boats to the island; however, both are sold out today. **16.** Lee prefers to stay at home on vacation, but Stephen wants to travel. **17.** When the house is messy, Mom is not happy, so we try to keep it neat. **18.** She started out in Kansas, and she drove all the way to Virginia. **19.** Bonnie loves yellow, but pink is my favorite color. **20.** The assignment seemed long, and I didn't want to do it.

Activity 52—Recognizing Pattern 1 Sentences

1. Mike—S, will arrive—V, tomorrow—Adv. **2.** Your—Adj., sisters—S, have learned—V, quickly—Adv. **3.** last—Adj., bus—S, will leave—V, soon—Adv. **4.** sun—S, set—V **5.** Marla and Greg—S, are traveling—V, next—Adj. **6.** Is coming—V, Jenny—S, early—Adv. **7.** Rob—S, yelled—V, loudly—Adv. **8.** Sheila—S, draws—V, paints—V, beautifully—Adv. **9.** temperature—S, has dropped—V, this—Adj. **10.** Nayda's—Adj., younger—Adj., sister—S, laughed—V, played—V **11.** Who—S, runs—V, fastest—Adv. **12.** patient—S, coughs—V, frequently—Adv. **13.** old—Adj., brown—Adj., sat—V, lazily—Adv. **14.** My—Adj, grandmother's—Adj., rocking—Adj., chair—S, squeaks—V, loudly—Adv. **15.** Toni and Andrea—S, drove—V

Activity 53—Transitive Verbs and Direct Objects in Pattern 2 Sentences

1. exercises **2.** problem **3.** ball **4.** lesson **5.** column **6.** car **7.** thousands **8.** machine **9.** spaghetti or pizza **10.** sale **11.** ground **12.** movie **13.** softball **14.** pie **15.** keys **16.** jokes **17.** music **18.** salad **19.** sounds **20.** instruments

Activity 54—Finding Direct and Indirect Objects in Pattern 3 Sentences

1. direct object **2.** indirect object **3.** indirect object **4.** direct object **5.** indirect object **6.** direct object **7.** indirect object **8.** indirect object **9.** direct object **10.** indirect object **11.** us **12.** him **13.** me **14.** her **15.** them

Activity 55—Finding Object Complements in Pattern 4 Sentences

The direct objects are in bold.

The weather made the **day** perfect for a long walk. Jennifer had long considered **walking** one of the best kinds of exercise. She found **it** energizing and refreshing. The trees that lined the street kept the **sidewalk** shady. Nevertheless, as time passed, the walking made **her** thirstier and thirstier. The sun was also making the **air** warmer. She considered a **rest** necessary, and she found the neighborhood **park** an inviting place to stop for a while. As she sat under a tree, she considered **herself** lucky to have the time to be outside that day. As the sun was setting, a mild breeze turned the **air** cooler. Jennifer headed for home, and she declared the **day** very enjoyable.

1–10. Object complements will vary. Possible sentences using object complements are given. **1.** Lena called Marcus an ambitious student. **2.** Do you consider Shakespeare entertaining? **3.** The judges declared her performance flawless. **4.** The wind turned the air cooler. **5.** The blazing campfire made us sleepy. **6.** The large window made the room airy. **7.** My sister painted her bedroom light blue. **8.** He nicknamed his car the Blue Bomber. **9.** On a hot day, I find ice cream refreshing. **10.** The mayor named Mr. Rodriguez Volunteer of the Year.

Activity 56—Object or Predicate Noun?

1. predicate noun **2.** direct object **3.** predicate noun **4.** predicate noun **5.** direct object **6.** predicate noun **7.** direct object **8.** predicate noun **9.** predicate noun **10.** predicate noun **11.** predicate noun **12.** direct object **13.** predicate noun **14.** predicate noun **15.** direct object

Activity 57—Identifying Parts of Pattern 6 Sentences

1. We, were, tall **2.** dinner, was, difficult **3.** doctor, was, nice **4.** Yolanda, Is, friendly **5.** movie, is, long, boring **6.** children, Were, polite, quiet **7.** days, are, longer **8.** Nina, is, outgoing, talkative **9.** Lauren, seems, tired **10.** weather, Will be, warmer **11.** soup, is, delicious; desserts, are, better **12.** Summer, is, hot, humid **13.** story, Was, believable **14.** flowers, should stay, fresh **15.** teacher, looked, angry

Activity 58—What Are Phrases and Clauses?

1. After it snows **2.** Before Jennifer went to bed **3.** that she could not attend **4.** that has just been picked **5.** Because Amy did not want to leave **6.** after she plays tennis **7.** who just transferred to our school **8.** who drives that car **9.** who moved to Texas **10.** if you want to go **11.** phrase **12.** clause **13.** clause **14.** phrase **15.** clause

Activity 59—Recognizing Adverb Clauses

1. adverb phrase **2.** adverb clause **3.** adverb clause **4.** adverb phrase **5.** adverb clause **6.** adverb **7.** adverb phrase **8.** adverb clause **9.** adverb **10.** adverb clause **11.** adverb phrase **12.** adverb phrase **13.** adverb clause **14.** adverb clause **15.** adverb phrase **16.** adverb phrase **17.** adverb **18.** adverb clause **19.** adverb **20.** adverb clause

Activity 60—Recognizing Noun Clauses

The relative pronouns are in bold. **1.** **whichever** of these books you are most likely to enjoy **2.** **What** Stacy told us **3.** **Whoever** wants to go swimming **4.** **Whatever** makes you happy **5.** **what** his brother was doing **6.** **what** the sea had hidden for so long **7.** **What** I really want **8.** **Whomever** you ask **9.** **what** she would do with a million dollars **10.** **that** he likes bananas for breakfast **11.** **That** Abraham Lincoln was a great president **12.** **what** they had learned for the class **13.** **whoever** has been stealing the street signs in our neighborhood **14.** **whom** you asked to dinner **15.** **who** makes the best lasagna **16.** who **17.** whom **18.** Whoever **19.** whoever **20.** whom

Activity 61—The Adjective Clause

1. who collected the most donations—person **2.** where the children had been playing—room **3.** that you are reading—novel **4.** that was against her arch rival—match **5.** that we did not recognize—dog **6.** that Daniel wrote—note **7.** that has a broken seat—bike **8.** who is wearing the green sweater—woman **9.** that is playing at our theater—movie **10.** that my uncle owns—restaurant **11.** that no one can ride—horse **12.** that Dave had recommended—show **13.** that I applied for—job **14.** that Denise is carrying—box **15.** that everyone loves—soup

Activity 62—Dependent Clauses in Complex and Compound-Complex Sentences

1. Her grandfather was fishing at the lake when she called, so she had to call again after he returned home. **2.** The first time that they met was a bad experience, but they became friends after they got to know each other better. **3.** The book that I want has colorful photographs in it. **4.** My cousin, who is an airline pilot, has flown all over the world, but she has never visited Washington, D.C. **5.** The families will go home when the fireworks display is finished. **6.** Last summer, when I broke my arm and had to wear a cast, was miserably hot. **7.** The plants that she is raising will be sold at the garden show, and the proceeds will benefit a local children's hospital. **8.** Greg and Rebecca will open their own restaurant when they have saved enough money. **9.** Cory's dream, which she has had for many years, is to learn to sail, but she must wait until another sailing class begins. **10.** This computer screen flickers when anyone bumps the desk, so I must take it to the computer store for repairs. **11.** Believe me when I tell you that horses cannot fly. **12.** If Sarah needs to take a break, Caleb can drive for a while. **13.** The tacos, which Lena made, are too spicy for me, but Sam will enjoy them because he likes spicy food. **14.** The lake that is on the edge of my grandparents' farm is full of fish, and I often fish there when I have a day off. **15.** The painting that Beth contributed to the art show will hang where many people can enjoy it.

Activity 63—Identifying Types of Verbals

1. infinitive **2.** gerund **3.** participle **4.** gerund **5.** infinitive **6.** gerund **7.** participle **8.** infinitive **9.** gerund **10.** participle **11.** gerund **12.** infinitive **13.** infinitive **14.** participle **15.** participle

Activity 64—Infinitives and Infinitive Phrases

1. to go skiing in the Alps **2.** to be an engineer or a scientist **3.** to see the dolphins **4.** To be or not to be **5.** to clean his room **6.** to eat steak with corn and potatoes **7.** to be alone **8.** to be happy **9.** to fish for catfish **10.** To invest in the company **11.** prepositional phrase **12.** infinitive **13.** infinitive **14.** infinitive **15.** infinitive

Activity 65—Gerunds and Gerund Phrases

The gerunds and gerund phrases are in bold. **1.** **writing** to my pen pal in New Zealand—direct object **2.** **Finding** the right house—subject **3.** **swimming**—predicate noun **4.** **Camping**—subject **5.** **finishing** school—object of the preposition **6.** **Hitting** a tennis ball—subject **7.** **Listening** to my new stereo—subject **8.** **Relaxing** after a busy day—subject **9.** **taking** out the garbage—predicate noun **10.** **singing** in a chorus—direct object **11.** **recycling**—object of the preposition **12.** **cooking** that for us—direct object **13.** his **living**—direct object, **flying** an airplane—object of the preposition **14.** **eating** fresh vegetables—direct object **15.** **Designing** our own clothes—subject

Activity 66—Finding the Verbals

1. to jog—infinitive **2.** to see—infinitive **3.** reading—gerund **4.** Watching—gerund **5.** to go—infinitive **6.** Eating—gerund **7.** to make—infinitive **8.** Growing—participle **9.** to get—infinitive **10.** Listening—gerund **11.** dancing—gerund **12.** to stay—infinitive **13.** Relaxing—gerund **14.** Weight lifting—gerund **15.** pie eating—participle **16.** painting—gerund **17.** Saving—gerund **18.** winning—participle **19.** to start—infinitive **20.** collecting—gerund

Alternative Activities

Alternative Activity 1—Identifying Nouns

1–10. Answers will vary. Possible answers are given. **1.** store **2.** liter **3.** kite **4.** hour **5.** doctor **6.** freedom **7.** kindness **8.** election **9.** drive **10.** color **11–15.** The collective nouns are (11) team, (14) herd, and (15) bunch.

Alternative Activity 2—Common and Proper Nouns and Capitalization

1–20. The proper nouns are (2) Erie Canal, (3) Canada, (4) April, (9) Mississippi River, (10) National Museum of Art, (11) District Police Station, (14) Cinderella, (15) Benjamin Franklin, (16) Mrs. Kwan, (18) Big Ben, and (20) Justice of the Supreme Court.
21. halloween, sam's **22.** randall, *treasure island* **23.** hinsville high school **24.** rhode island, east coast, united states **25.** president washington

Alternative Activity 3—Concrete and Abstract Nouns

1. blister—C, foot—C, pain—A **2.** smile—C, face—C, happiness—A **3.** Miguel—C, friendship—A, Stephen—C **4.** exercise—C, health—A **5.** First Amendment—C, rights—A **6.** Florida—C, June—A **7.** backpack—C, pounds—A **8.** mother—C, decision—A, roses—C, garden—C **9.** Chad—C, aunt—C, weeks—A, summer—A **10.** Erin—C, courage—A, body—C

Alternative Activity 4—Spelling Singular and Plural Nouns

1. museum **2.** geese **3.** church **4.** knives **5.** skies **6.** buses **7.** women **8.** puppies **9.** library **10.** pears **11.** kitty **12.** deer **13.** roofs **14.** injuries **15.** uncle **16.** feet **17.** wishes **18.** Mice **19.** peaches **20.** children **21.** inches **22.** parties **23.** turkeys **24.** women **25.** beaches

Alternative Activity 5—Possessive Nouns

1. school's—S **2.** salesmen's—P **3.** walrus's—S **4.** buses'—P **5.** Harry's—S **6.** school's **7.** seconds' **8.** love's **9.** radio's **10.** hamburgers' **11.** James's **12.** Jane's **13.** child's **14.** pencils' **15.** teachers'

Alternative Activity 6—Pronouns and Their Antecedents

1. Julie and Robert **2.** Mollie **3.** Selena **4.** friend **5.** boys and girls **6.** squirrel **7.** team **8.** Honesty **9.** doughnuts **10.** father **11.** she, her **12.** this, him **13.** its **14.** it **15.** they

Alternative Activity 7—Singular and Plural Personal Pronouns

1. you *or* she **2.** their **3.** its **4.** We **5.** They, them **6.** Our—P **7.** her—S **8.** We—P **9.** we—P **10.** their—P, us—P

Alternative Activity 8—Working with Relative Pronouns

1. that **2.** Who **3.** Which **4.** whom **5.** who **6.** who **7.** What **8.** who **9.** that **10.** Whose **11.** Whoever **12.** whomever **13.** whatever **14.** whichever **15.** whatever

Alternative Activity 9—Asking Questions with Pronouns

1. Which **2.** Whose **3.** Which **4.** Whose **5.** What **6.** whose—D **7.** What—D **8.** which—I **9.** which—I **10.** What—D **11.** What—D **12.** Which—D **13.** Who—D **14.** which—I **15.** who—I

Alternative Activity 10—Using Demonstrative Pronouns

1. boys—P **2.** stamps—P **3.** house—S **4.** sandwiches—P **5.** boxes—P **6.** gift—S **7.** tracks—P **8.** friend—S **9.** toys—P **10.** keys—P **11.** These *or* Those—F **12.** this—N **13.** this *or* these—N **14.** this—N **15.** That—F

Alternative Activity 11—Indefinite Pronouns with Verbs

1. another **2.** Nothing **3.** something **4.** each **5.** another **6.** No one, anything **7.** everyone **8.** Both **9.** much **10.** each **11.** Some—were **12.** Everyone—is **13.** Neither—wants **14.** others—have **15.** anyone—Is

Alternative Activity 12—Creating Contractions

1. What's **2.** they've **3.** she's **4.** Who's **5.** We've **6.** It's **7.** we're **8.** We'd **9.** I'm **10.** it's **11.** That's **12.** we'll **13.** I'd **14.** He's **15.** You're

Alternative Activity 13—Locating Adjectives in Sentences

1–5. Answers will vary. Possible answers are given. **1.** small, green **2.** challenging, important **3.** warm, breezy **4.** playful, adorable **5.** loud, rock **6.** friendly **7.** chilly **8.** shining **9.** round **10.** favorite

Alternative Activity 14—Definite and Indefinite Articles

1. the **2.** a **3.** an, a **4.** the **5.** a **6.** **The** flowers—P, **a** table—S **7.** **an** hour—S **8.** **The** hours—P **9.** **The** boys—P, **the** trail—S **10.** **an** opinion—S

Alternative Activity 15—Recognizing Proper Adjectives

1. American—flag **2.** French—dressing, Italian—dressing **3.** Irish—team **4.** French—government **5.** Revolutionary War—heroes **6.** Asian—continent **7.** Italian—bicycle **8.** Native American—drums **9.** Portuguese—language **10.** Mexican—grandparents **11.** French Canadian—citizens **12.** Russian—winters **13.** Japanese—cartoons **14.** Swiss Army—knife **15.** Nigerian—capital

Alternative Activity 16—Recognizing Nouns Used as Adjectives

1. chicken—sandwich **2.** forest—path **3.** water—pitcher **4.** railroad—station **5.** corner—store **6.** obedience—school **7.** student—council **8.** baseball—games **9.** war—memorial **10.** telephone—number **11.** rope—trick, dude—ranch **12.** library—books **13.** monkey—house **14.** basketball—game **15.** raffle—ticket

Alternative Activity 17—Possessive Adjectives

1. their **2.** his **3.** our **4.** Their **5.** its **6.** their **7.** Her **8.** his **9.** your, my **10.** her **11.** her—teacher's, teacher's—desk **12.** His—brother's, brother's—hair, her—sister's, sister's—hair **13.** my—coat **14.** your—friends **15.** her—cat

Alternative Activity 18—Using Indefinite Pronouns and Numbers as Adjectives

I forgot to bring the <u>two</u> dollars I needed for the bus. After <u>some</u> time passed, I decided to walk to the ballpark. It was only <u>three</u> miles. A team needs <u>nine</u> players to start the game, and <u>several</u> members had been sick recently. No one wanted to lose the game. Could I make it in <u>twenty</u> minutes? I ran most of the way. Everyone cheered when I showed up.

1. Everyone—P, twenty—A **2.** several—A, many—A **3.** Some—P, four—A **4.** All—A, thirty—A **5.** anyone—P

Alternative Activity 19—Demonstrative Adjectives

1. this—concert **2.** those—tickets **3.** this—rain **4.** this—Tuesday **5.** these—tickets **6.** none **7.** this—crowd **8.** none **9.** these—people **10.** This—wait **11.** these—tickets **12.** that—wait **13.** this—concert **14.** those—bands **15.** that—night

Alternative Activity 20—Creating Comparative Adjectives

1. sweet, sweetest **2.** better, best **3.** heavy, heavier **4.** colorful, more colorful **5.** older, oldest **6.** more graceful, most graceful **7.** careful, least careful **8.** smart, smartest **9.** amazing, more amazing **10.** bad, worst **11.** pinker, pinkest **12.** sad, sadder **13.** terrible, most terrible **14.** happier, happiest **15.** funny, funnier

Alternative Activity 21—Recognizing Action Verbs

1. <u>smelled</u>—Louis **2.** <u>examined</u>—jeweler **3.** <u>had taken</u>—Dr. Haller **4.** <u>raced</u>—Randy **5.** <u>live</u>—trolls **6.** <u>had steered</u>—driver **7.** <u>drive</u>—Whos **8.** <u>will bake</u>—I **9.** <u>Will dance</u>—you **10.** <u>poured</u>, <u>spilled</u>—Marcus **11.** <u>had written</u>—Lulu **12.** <u>Will be going</u>—Hilda **13.** <u>runs</u>—Sonia **14.** <u>will go</u>—Terrence **15.** <u>Can fly</u>—you

Alternative Activity 22—Verbs Express Tense

1. past perfect **2.** future **3.** present **4.** future perfect **5.** future perfect **6.** present perfect **7.** future **8.** present perfect **9.** past perfect **10.** past **11.** present perfect **12.** present **13.** present **14.** past **15.** past

Alternative Activity 23—Irregular Verb Forms

1. eaten **2.** chosen **3.** broke **4.** teaching **5.** doing **6.** taught **7.** known **8.** began **9.** forgot **10.** swum **11.** seen **12.** giving **13.** done **14.** chose **15.** go

Alternative Activity 24—Recognizing the Progressive Form

1. will be **2.** was **3.** has been **4.** had been **5.** is **6.** will be **7.** shall be **8.** were **9.** had been **10.** have been **11.** have been **12.** was **13.** will have been **14.** has been **15.** is

Alternative Activity 25—Subject and Verb Agreement

1. swims **2.** go **3.** fly **4.** sinks **5.** cry **6.** eat **7.** jumps **8.** were **9.** needs **10.** dives

Alternative Activity 26—Learning to Work with *Do*

1. do **2.** do **3.** doing **4.** done **5.** does **6.** do **7.** had done **8.** done **9.** did **10.** have done **11.** main **12.** helping **13.** helping **14.** main **15.** helping

Alternative Activity 27—Conditional and *Do* Verbs

1. might have gone **2.** should have arrived **3.** Did learn **4.** must have gone **5.** must leave **6.** can take **7.** might come **8.** might win **9.** might buy **10.** must sleep **11.** might prefer **12.** Do like **13.** must rake **14.** Would help **15.** Did finish

Alternative Activity 28—Using Passive and Active Verbs

1. Mr. Feinbrow cancelled the Saturday class. **2.** Dana decorated the birthday cake. **3.** Firefighters helped the children. **4.** My little sisters invaded my bedroom. **5.** Drew cleaned up the mess. **6.** Louis and Margie funded the show. **7.** Steve ran a race. **8.** My father opened the window. **9.** Audley Technical defeated Sidney High School. **10.** Her best friend sent the package.

Alternative Activity 29—Verbs That Express a State of Being

1. am **2.** was **3.** has been **4.** was **5.** were being **6.** will have been **7.** is **8.** am *or* am being **9.** will look **10.** had been **11.** was being **12.** had been **13.** will be **14.** had been **15.** was

Alternative Activity 30— Identifying Action and State-of-Being Verbs

1. A, B **2.** B, A **3.** B, A **4.** B, A **5.** A, B **6.** B, A **7.** B, A **8.** B, A **9.** B, A **10.** B, A

Alternative Activity 31—State-of-Being Verbs Express Tense

1. will be—future **2.** looks—present **3.** became—past **4.** Will be—future **5.** keeps—present **6.** seem—present **7.** will be—future **8.** Have looked—present perfect **9.** felt—past **10.** felt—past **11.** is becoming—present progressive **12.** will be—future **13.** Is—present **14.** had looked—past perfect **15.** has been—present perfect

Alternative Activity 32—Adverbs Answer Questions About Verbs

Answers will vary. Possible answers are given. **1.** neatly **2.** loudly **3.** quickly **4.** expertly **5.** Silently **6.** fearlessly **7.** hungrily **8.** majestically **9.** safely **10.** gracefully **11.** willingly **12.** sweetly **13.** well **14.** quickly **15.** enthusiastically

Alternative Activity 33—Adverbs of Degree

1. rather **2.** very **3.** so **4.** especially **5.** too **6.** quite **7.** rather **8.** much **9.** very **10.** too

Alternative Activity 34—Recognizing Adverbs of Negation

1. not (Have<u>n't</u>) **2.** not **3.** not (did<u>n't</u>) **4.** never **5.** not (Ca<u>n't</u>) **6.** not (ca<u>n't</u>) **7.** never **8.** not **9.** never **10.** not (ca<u>n't</u>) **11.** would catch **12.** is **13.** ate **14.** Will (<u>Wo</u>n't) stay **15.** left

Alternative Activity 35—Identifying Adjectives and Adverbs

Adjectives and adverbs used to complete the sentences will vary. Possible answers are given. **1.** together—adverb **2.** express—adjective **3.** loudly—adverb **4.** cold—adjective **5.** playfully—adverb **6.** difficult—adjective **7.** here—adverb **8.** skillfully—adverb **9.** happy—adjective **10.** Later—adverb **11.** tall—adjective **12.** quickly—adverb **13.** Now—adverb **14.** quietly—adverb **15.** beautiful—adjective

Alternative Activity 36—Comparing with Adverbs

1. more quickly **2.** most slowly **3.** well **4.** more comfortably **5.** fastest **6.** softly, more softly, most softly **7.** politely, more politely, most politely **8.** unwisely, more unwisely, most unwisely **9.** well, better, best **10.** skillfully, more skillfully, most skillfully

Alternative Activity 37—Using Adverbs Correctly

1. have taken **2.** will show **3.** will sing **4.** will go **5.** went **6.** drove **7.** traveled **8.** will try **9.** will tell **10.** will find **11.** gentle—gently **12.** loud—loudly **13.** magical—magically **14.** slow—slowly **15.** peaceful—peacefully

Alternative Activity 38—Recognizing Prepositional Phrases

1. with my breakfast **2.** to freedom **3.** before dawn **4.** around the closed road, across the bridge **5.** for you **6.** to the party, on Saturday **7.** in the closet **8.** through the rain **9.** during the lecture **10.** Over the river, through the woods, to grandmother's house **11. went** to a class **12. looked** through her notebook **13. Look** at the outline, **outline** on the board **14. reading** from the chapter **15. question** about the material

Alternative Activity 39—Prepositions and Their Objects

1. I **2.** P **3.** I **4.** P **5.** P **6.** they—them **7.** she—her **8.** he—him **9.** she—her **10.** I—me

Alternative Activity 40—Using Prepositional Phrases as Adjectives

1. sock, hole **2.** film **3.** Many, theater **4.** ladies **5.** sailor, girl **6–15.** Answers will vary. Possible answers are given. **6.** on the table **7.** of tires, of the garage **8.** near the bushes **9.** of Scotland **10.** of my friends **11.** near the corner **12.** for lunch **13.** about Jim **14.** under the sink **15.** about your family

Alternative Activity 41—Identifying Adverb and Adjective Phrases

1. After dinner—adverb **2.** after dinner—adjective **3.** in the microwave oven—adjective **4.** in the microwave oven—adverb **5.** at the supermarket—adverb **6.** from Utah—adjective **7.** from Utah—adverb **8.** to Miami—adjective **9.** over the bridge—adjective **10.** over the bridge—adverb **11.** for the concert—adjective **12.** on the left side—adjective **13.** on the left side—adverb **14.** During the storm—adverb **15.** through the woods—adverb

Alternative Activity 42—Adverb or Preposition?

1. adverb **2.** preposition—park **3.** preposition—river **4.** adverb **5.** adverb **6.** preposition—hallway **7.** preposition—car **8.** adverb **9.** preposition—door **10.** adverb **11.** adverb **12.** preposition—board **13.** preposition—race **14.** adverb **15.** preposition—gate

Alternative Activity 43— Punctuating Compounds

1. The food was not very good; nevertheless, we enjoyed the party. **2.** This year we planted a vegetable garden with tomatoes, cucumbers, and peppers, but no radishes. **3.** Paula liked the movie, but she said the book was better. **4.** Heather is not here yet, so Nancy will have to go first. **5.** Tulips, daffodils, and crocuses all grow from bulbs. **6.** Cola drinks, chocolate, coffee, and tea all contain caffeine. **7.** To eat properly, avoid foods with fat as well as foods with sugar. **8.** Apples, peaches, plums, and pears are all fruits that grow on trees. **9.** Mike's family did not fly to California; instead, they took the train. **10.** Katie needs to hurry; otherwise, she will be late to school. **11.** After lunch Mary went shopping, Becky cleaned the house, and Rob worked in the yard. **12.** As Jay to make it, for no one else has the recipe. **13.** The track meet was scheduled for today; however, it has rained all week. **14.** Carlos likes iced tea; therefore, the family chose to serve it often. **15.** Tom practiced all afternoon; nevertheless, he was not ready for his performance.

Alternative Activity 44—Dependent Clauses

The subordinating conjunctions are in bold. **1. Whenever** I am sad **2. Although** we were dressed very warmly **3. while** they watched the movie **4. If** Jacob is late again **5. Because** an education leads to a better job **6. Because** margarine and butter are mostly fat **7. until** I finish **8. When** we finish our work **9. Since** the party was over **10. In order that** everyone might have a chance to speak

Alternative Activity 45—Finding Conjunctions

1. Neither . . . nor—correlative **2.** but—coordinating **3.** since—subordinating **4.** whether . . . or—correlative **5.** and—coordinating **6.** not only . . . but also—correlative **7.** Whenever—subordinating **8.** but—coordinating **9.** whenever—subordinating **10.** Unless—subordinating **11.** Either . . . or—correlative **12.** however—subordinating **13.** when—subordinating **14.** and—coordinating **15.** Both . . . and—correlative

Alternative Activity 46—Recognizing Interjections

1. Ouch! **2.** Oh, boy **3.** Wow **4.** Hush **5.** really **6–10.** Sentences and interjections will vary.

Alternative Activity 47—Making Sentences

Sentences will vary. Possible sentences are given. **1.** They said that I knew where the treasure was. **2.** Jill's trip over the ocean sounded thrilling. **3.** We play our arch rivals next Tuesday. **4.** Alice was confused and upset about her score. **5.** Dorothy clicked the ruby slippers together. **6.** Justin came for dinner. **7.** The tree had low branches and big leaves. **8.** The green fruit seemed like strange food to be eating. **9.** Heather found the missing playing card. **10.** Carry the bowl, cup, and spoon to the sink.

Alternative Activity 48—Finding Subjects

The simple subjects are in bold. **1.** His **skill** as a writer **2. People** **3.** The **principal** **4.** The **beach** **5.** The strong **currents** in the river **6. He** **7.** My **sister** **8. Several** of my friends **9. You** **10. Teachers** **11.** The black **cat** under the table **12. All** of us **13.** This **restaurant** **14. One** of the students **15. It**

Alternative Activity 49—A Sentence Has Two Parts

1. (You) Stop that right now! **2.** Both Heather and I were late for class. **3.** My exam for English is scheduled to be at one o'clock. **4.** The bus driver missed our bus stop today. **5.** Two candy bars were left. **6.** The teacher told us to read the chapter. **7.** Where is my homework? **8.** Everyone on the trip was ready for lunch. **9.** The page in my notebook was completely covered with writing. **10.** We should go out to dinner tonight. **11.** Did one of you see that movie? **12.** They ran off in a hurry. **13.** Ice cream will melt fast in warm weather. **14.** The award committee's final decisions were made. **15.** Aunt Teresa will be very happy to see you.

Alternative Activity 50—Interrogative Sentences

1. Has anyone finished the project? **2.** Do you feel tired? **3.** When is the game going to be over? **4.** Where did the children hide my book? **5.** Is your car still in the garage? **6.** Do you want chicken or fish? **7.** Will Carlos and his sister be arriving soon? **8.** What time is it? **9.** Are you going? **10.** Do elephants eat much? **11.** Is this your book? **12.** Who can help me? **13.** Have you seen that show? **14.** Why are you so concerned? **15.** Will you be home for dinner?

Alternative Activity 51—Using Compound Sentences

Independent clauses will vary. Sentences using possible independent clauses are given. **1.** She is tired, but Laura will perform anyway. **2.** The restaurant was known for its good food, but I never liked it. **3.** Superman can fly, and Spiderman can climb up buildings. **4.** Grace has wonderful rhythm, but I like dancing more than she does. **5.** Movies sometimes make me cry, so I always take a handkerchief with me. **6.** I wanted to play the violin, but my father bought me a cello. **7.** Jerry is fast, but Webster beat him to the finish line. **8.** Dr. Zimmerman performed tests on the blood, but the results were not clear. **9.** I feel full, but I haven't had lunch yet. **10.** There are two boats to the island, and both are sold out. **11.** We asked them several times, but Pilar and Kurt won't help us. **12.** Alex found two extra bottles, so he gave one to me. **13.** My brother thought the party would be dull, but it turned out to be fun. **14.** Christine loved summer, but Ronnie liked winter's snow and ice. **15.** I haven't been to Rome, but I hope to go someday.

Alternative Activity 52—Recognizing Pattern 1 Sentences

1. Your—Adj., sisters—S, have learned—V, quickly—Adv. **2.** Mike—S, will arrive—V, tomorrow—Adv. **3.** Is coming—V, Jenny—S **4.** sun—S, will rise—V, early—Adv. **5.** temperature—S, has dropped—V, this—Adj. **6.** Rob—S, yelled—V, loudly—Adv. **7.** old—Adj., brown—Adj., dog—S, sat—V, lazily—Adv. **8.** Nayda's—Adj., younger—Adj., sisters—S, laughed—V, played—V **9.** Toni and Andrea—S, drove—V **10.** My—Adj., grandmother's—Adj., rocking—Adj., chair—S, squeaks—V, loudly—Adv.

Alternative Activity 53—Transitive Verbs and Direct Objects in Pattern 2 Sentences

1. problem **2.** lesson **3.** spaghetti or pizza **4.** exercises **5.** ball **6.** poem **7.** machine **8.** instruments **9.** music **10.** softball **11.** car **12.** show **13.** sale **14.** jokes **15.** salad

Alternative Activity 54—Finding Direct and Indirect Objects in Pattern 3 Sentences

1. indirect object **2.** direct object **3.** indirect object **4.** indirect object **5.** direct object **6.** them **7.** us **8.** me **9.** him **10.** her

Alternative Activity 55—Finding Object Complements in Pattern 4 Sentences

The direct objects are in bold.

The weather made the **day** perfect for a long walk. Jennifer had long considered **walking** one of the best kinds of exercise. She found **it** energizing and refreshing. The trees that lined the street kept the **sidewalk** shady. Nevertheless, as time passed, the walking made **her** thirstier and thirstier. The sun was also making the **air** warmer. She considered a **rest** necessary, and she found the neighborhood **park** an inviting place to stop for a while. As she sat under a tree, she considered **herself** lucky to have the time to be outside that day. As the sun was setting, a mild breeze turned the **air** cooler. Jennifer headed for home, and she declared the **day** very enjoyable.

1–5. Object complements will vary. Possible sentences using object complements are given. **1.** The wind turned the air cool. **2.** The blazing campfire made us sleepy. **3.** My mother painted the porch sage green. **4.** He nicknamed his car the Blue Bomber. **5.** On a hot day, I find ice cream refreshing.

Alternative Activity 56—Object or Predicate Noun?

1. direct object **2.** predicate noun **3.** direct object **4.** predicate noun **5.** predicate noun **6.** predicate noun **7.** direct object **8.** direct object **9.** direct object **10.** predicate noun

Alternative Activity 57—Identifying Parts of Pattern 6 Sentences

The subjects are in bold. **1. Nina**, is, outgoing, talkative **2. soup**, is, delicious; **desserts**, are, better **3. Summer**, is, hot, humid **4. story**, Was, believable **5. flowers**, should stay, fresh **6. We**, were, tall **7. doctor**, was, nice **8. movie**, is, long, boring **9. children**, Were, polite, quiet **10. days**, are, longer

Alternative Activity 58—What Are Phrases and Clauses?

1. who is laughing at us **2.** who goes to a college in California **3.** if you want to go **4.** that has just been picked **5.** Because Amy did not want to leave **6.** clause **7.** clause **8.** phrase **9.** clause **10.** phrase

Alternative Activity 59—Recognizing Adverb Clauses

1. adverb phrase **2.** adverb clause **3.** adverb phrase **4.** adverb clause **5.** adverb phrase **6.** adverb clause **7.** adverb **8.** adverb clause **9.** adverb clause **10.** adverb **11.** adverb clause **12.** adverb phrase **13.** adverb phrase **14.** adverb **15.** adverb clause

Alternative Activity 60—Recognizing Noun Clauses

The relative pronouns are in bold. **1. what** she would do with a million dollars **2. That** Abraham Lincoln was a great president **3. what** they had learned for the class **4. whom** you asked to dinner **5. who** knows best **6. What** Stacy told us **7. Whoever** wants to go fishing **8. what** his brother was doing **9. what** the sea had hidden for so long **10. What** I really want **11.** Whoever **12.** whom **13.** who **14.** whom **15.** whoever

Alternative Activity 61—The Adjective Clause

1. that Dave had suggested—show **2.** that I applied for—job **3.** that everyone loves—soup **4.** where the children had been playing—room **5.** that you told—story **6.** that we did not recognize—dog **7.** that Daniel wrote—note **8.** that has a broken seat—bike **9.** that his father owns—store **10.** that no one can ride—horse

Alternative Activity 62—Dependent Clauses in Complex and Compound-Complex Sentences

1. The plants that she is raising will be sold at the garden show, and the proceeds will benefit a local children's hospital. **2.** Greg and Rebecca will open their own restaurant when they have saved enough money. **3.** This computer screen flickers when anyone bumps the desk, so I must take it to the computer store for repairs. **4.** If Sarah needs to take a break, Caleb can drive for a while. **5.** The tacos, which Lena made, are too spicy for me, but Sam will enjoy them because he likes spicy food. **6.** The painting that Beth contributed to the art show will hang where many people can enjoy it. **7.** The first time that they met was uncomfortable, but they became friends after they got to know each other better. **8.** My cousin, who is an airline pilot, has flown all over the world, but she has never visited Washington, D.C. **9.** The families will go home when the fireworks display is finished. **10.** Last summer, when I broke my arm and had to wear a cast, was miserably hot.

Alternative Activity 63—Identifying Types of Verbals

1. infinitive **2.** gerund **3.** gerund **4.** gerund **5.** gerund **6.** participle **7.** infinitive **8.** infinitive **9.** infinitive **10.** participle

Alternative Activity 64—Infinitives and Infinitive Phrases

1. to be an engineer or a scientist **2.** to see the dolphins **3.** to eat steak with corn and potatoes **4.** to be alone **5.** to fish for catfish **6.** prepositional phrase **7.** infinitive **8.** infinitive **9.** infinitive **10.** infinitive

Alternative Activity 65—Gerunds and Gerund Phrases

The gerunds are in bold. **1.** **skiing**—predicate noun **2.** **Camping**—subject **3.** **finishing** school—object of the preposition **4.** **Hitting** a tennis ball—subject **5.** **Listening** to my new stereo—subject **6.** **Relaxing** after a busy day—subject **7.** **taking** out the garbage—predicate noun **8.** **singing** in a chorus—direct object **9.** **recycling**—object of the preposition **10.** **cooking** that for us—direct object

Alternative Activity 66—Finding the Verbals

1. collecting—gerund **2.** Saving—gerund **3.** pie eating—participle **4.** to make—infinitive **5.** Growing—participle **6.** to get—infinitive **7.** dancing—gerund **8.** to stay—infinitive **9.** Relaxing—gerund **10.** Weight lifting—gerund **11.** reading—gerund **12.** painting—gerund **13.** to see—infinitive **14.** to start—infinitive **15.** to jog—infinitive

Workbook Activities

Workbook Activity 1—Finding the Nouns

1. Yoshi, mother, mall **2.** tourists, Niagara Falls **3.** Richard, note, door **4.** Mrs. Parham, George, politeness **5.** Cindy, family, Kansas **6.** Jose, wallet, couch **7.** audience, violinist **8.** Lucy, price, pair, shoes **9.** Walter, knowledge, football **10.** waters, Walden Pond, sunlight **11.** John Adams, president **12.** Lisa, dream, test **13.** Andre, ring, stone **14.** work, Chad, race **15.** Julio, friends, party **16.** Serena, atlas, shelf **17.** Red Knight, group **18.** soldier, medal, bravery **19.** horse, fence **20.** crowd, game, excitement

Workbook Activity 2—Finding Common and Proper Nouns

Answers will vary. Possible answers are given. **1.** Byland Supermarket **2.** Halle Berry **3.** Winter Olympics **4.** *Survivor* **5.** Springfield **6.** Nile **7.** Corvette **8.** Dr. Kessman **9.** Russian **10.** Thanksgiving **11.** "America the Beautiful" **12.** Lincoln Memorial **13.** Central Park **14.** Felice **15.** Lisa Simpson **16.** The Beatles **17.** Max **18.** Kobe Bryant **19.** Mercury **20.** Aunt Bette **21.** game **22.** city **23.** singer **24.** TV show **25.** automobile **26.** geyser **27.** state **28.** day **29.** motel **30.** state **31.** building **32.** school **33.** dog **34.** holiday **35.** ocean **36.** store **37.** baseball player **38.** magazine **39.** president **40.** country

Workbook Activity 3—Identifying Concrete and Abstract Nouns

Answers will vary. Possible answers are given. **1.** drive, ride, race **2.** loyalty, bravery, honesty **3.** amount, pound, ton **4.** minute, week, year **5.** happiness, joy, fear **6.** hot chocolate, milk shake, water **7.** elm, maple, oak **8.** silk, corduroy, cotton **9.** dog, rabbit, tiger **10.** screwdriver, drill, wrench **11.** library, warehouse, store **12.** friend, parent, teacher **13.** desk, couch, table **14.** circle, rectangle, diamond **15.** computer, photocopier, keyboard

Workbook Activity 4—Using Singular and Plural Nouns

1. sheep **2.** pennies **3.** monkeys **4.** houses **5.** geese **6.** children **7.** keys **8.** knives **9.** tomatoes **10.** shoes **11.** babies **12.** taxes **13.** leaves **14.** benches **15.** lives

Workbook Activity 5—Possessive or Plural Nouns?

1. band's **2.** children's **3.** mouse's **4.** hikers **5.** men's **6.** snake's **7.** Jean's **8.** coach's **9.** tree's **10.** team's **11.** plant's **12.** cat's **13.** books **14.** friend's **15.** fire's

Workbook Activity 6—Using Pronouns

The pronouns are in bold. **1. I**—Joe, **you**—Bob **2. she**—Mrs. Brandt **3. It**—game **4. they**—boys **5. she**—Lucy, **it**—pin **6. his**—Lee **7. his**—Mr. Wardrop **8. We**—Meg and Sally **9. their**—students **10. she**—Ellen **11. it**—vase **12. she**—Pam **13. his**—Pedro **14. it**—day **15. his**— Marat, **it**—suitcase **16. he**—Tony **17. she**—Tina **18. their**—Terry and Paul **19. me**—Sue **20. I**—Mrs. Parsons

Workbook Activity 7—Using Personal Pronouns

1. Ben likes animals and he wants to be a vet. **2.** I found a notebook and asked Corine, "Is this yours?" **3.** Kevin painted the room himself. **4.** Jamal asked us to go to the concert. **5.** Armando is very proud of his cooking skills. **6.** When the Harrisons moved to Phoenix, they bought a house. **7.** Coach Kim said to Leslie, "You can win this race!" **8.** They cooked dinner themselves. **9.** Alex worked hard on his project. **10.** Jack and I will be there at noon.

Workbook Activity 8—Finding Relative Pronouns

1. who—sister **2.** which—glasses **3.** that—party **4.** that—family **5.** who—girl **6.** that—shoes **7.** which—porch **8.** that—flowers **9.** who—people **10.** that—movies **11.** that—scarf **12.** who—student **13.** that— tools **14.** that—CD **15.** who—girl

Workbook Activity 9—Using Pronouns That Ask Questions

1. Who **2.** What **3.** What **4.** Whose **5.** What **6.** What or Which **7.** whom **8.** what **9.** Who **10.** Which **11.** What **12.** Which **13.** Who **14.** Whose **15.** What

Workbook Activity 10—Identifying Demonstrative Pronouns

1. that—singular **2.** that—singular **3.** these—plural **4.** This—singular **5.** Those—plural **6.** that **7.** that **8.** this **9.** These **10.** This **11.** These **12.** This **13.** That **14.** those **15.** that

Workbook Activity 11—Using Indefinite Pronouns

A	N	O	T	H	I	N	G	M	G	H	I
N	A	O	B	C	D	A	E	U	F	N	J
Y	Q	P	B	O	N	N	M	C	L	O	K
B	R	S	S	O	M	E	T	H	I	N	G
O	T	V	T	W	D	X	F	Y	Z	E	A
D	D	H	E	N	O	Y	R	E	V	E	B
Y	E	C	E	I	K	N	A	L	W	K	E
R	F	G	H	J	B	A	L	B	L	B	R
W	E	I	N	N	O	M	G	W	K	B	W

Sentences will vary. Each should include one of these words. **1.** anybody [example given] **2.** nothing **3.** much **4.** none **5.** something **6.** nobody **7.** few **8.** everyone **9.** many **10.** another

Workbook Activity 12—Recognizing Contractions

1. Who's—Who is **2.** he's—he is **3.** What's—What is **4.** I've—I have **5.** They're—They are **6.** We've—We have **7.** That's—That is **8.** We're—We are **9.** He's—He is **10.** It's—It is **11.** I'd—I would **12.** I'm—I am **13.** I'll—I will **14.** You'll—You will **15.** We're—We are

Workbook Activity 13—Identifying Adjectives

The adjectives are in bold. **1.** **thick**—woods **2.** **Young**—children, **wild**—birds, **cold**—weather **3.** **my**—pie, **pumpkin**—pie, **hot**—pie, **spicy**—pie **4.** **cat's**—fur, **soft**—fur **5.** **cold**—water, **refreshing**—water **6.** **lovely**—Laura, **sweet-tempered**—Laura, **popular**—girl **7.** **that**—box, **large**—box, **heavy**—box **8.** **cool**—Dina, **relaxed**—Dina **9.** **this**—cake, **delicious**—cake **10.** **bushy**—squirrel, **brown**—squirrel, **tall**—tree, **oak**—tree **11.** **funny**—Alex, **polite**—Alex, **cheerful**—Alex **12.** **tired**—Julio, **grumpy**—Julio **13.** **her**—puppy, **sweet**—puppy **14.** **freezing**—weather, **hot**—cocoa **15.** **tasty**—ice cream, **cold**—ice cream, **long**—walk

Workbook Activity 14—Identifying and Using Articles

1. An, the **2.** The, a, the **3.** a, the **4.** The, a **5.** a, a, an, the **6.** an **7.** the **8.** the **9.** a **10.** the **11.** an **12.** an **13.** the **14.** A **15.** an

Workbook Activity 15—Using Proper Adjectives

1. Chinese **2.** Spanish **3.** Swiss **4.** German **5.** European **6–10.** Students will use the following proper adjectives in sentences. **6.** Democratic **7.** Swiss **8.** African **9.** Shakespearean **10.** Japanese

Workbook Activity 16—Using Nouns as Adjectives

1. class **2.** map **3.** cereal **4.** road **5.** supplies **6.** adjective **7.** noun **8.** noun **9.** adjective **10.** noun **11.** adjective **12.** adjective **13.** noun **14.** noun **15.** adjective

Workbook Activity 17—Using Possessive Nouns and Pronouns as Adjectives

1–10. Students rewrite sentences, using the correct possessive noun form. **1.** students' **2.** Mike's **3.** Luke's **4.** companies' **5.** bus's **6.** lake's **7.** choir's **8.** mother's **9.** children's **10.** Michael's **11.** its **12.** it's **13.** its **14.** It's **15.** it's

Workbook Activity 18—Using Numbers as Adjectives

1–10. Answers will vary for sentences. Possible answers are given. **1.** two **2.** three **3.** four **4.** three **5.** four **6.** 150 **7.** three **8.** six **9.** five **10.** 10,000 **11.** cups **12.** presidents **13.** star **14.** dollars **15.** members

Workbook Activity 19—Using Demonstratives as Adjectives

1. that **2.** these **3.** This **4.** Those **5.** that **6.** That—hat **7.** that—camera **8.** this—shelf; those—shelves **9.** none **10.** this—skirt **11.** that—mechanic **12.** this—resort **13.** those—colors **14.** That—porch; this—porch **15.** these—characters

Workbook Activity 20—Using Adjectives to Make Comparisons

1. positive **2.** superlative **3.** comparative **4.** comparative **5.** superlative **6.** superlative **7.** comparative **8.** comparative **9.** positive **10.** superlative **11.** comparative **12.** comparative **13.** positive **14.** positive **15.** comparative **16.** positive **17.** positive **18.** superlative **19.** superlative **20.** comparative

Workbook Activity 21—Using Action Verbs

Answers will vary. Possible answers are given. **1.** searched **2.** glided **3.** glimmered **4.** lost **5.** fell, accumulated **6.** soared **7.** swerved **8.** adored **9.** relaxed, walked **10.** shopped **11.** tossed **12.** autograph **13.** appeared **14.** leaped **15.** devoured Students' sentences will vary.

Workbook Activity 22—Verb Tense

Sentences will vary. Possible sentences are given. **1.** danced—Henri danced for an international ballet company. **2.** had screamed—I had screamed so much at the movie that my throat was sore. **3.** will discover—The college professor will discover which students are serious about their studies. **4.** will have planned—Ed will have planned the entire party before the invitations are mailed. **5.** has/have framed—We have framed many of our vacation photographs. **6.** had cooked—Tom had cooked the main course and set the table by the time Ellen came home. **7.** drained—After finishing the dishes, Ana drained the water out of the sink. **8.** has/have joined—We have joined our friends for Thanksgiving dinner for the last five years. **9.** had measured—Ray had measured the wood carefully before he began cutting it. **10.** decorate/decorates—She decorates her house every holiday.

Workbook Activity 23—Identifying Irregular Verbs

1–5. Sentences will vary. Possible sentences are given. **1.** began—The movie began at eight o'clock. **2.** has (have) broken—This old camera has broken before. **3.** knew—Ed knew the answer to every question on the test. **4.** had given—Allie had given her speech before she received the award. **5.** have (has) chosen—We have chosen a new team mascot. **6.** Jim said he knew the answer. **7.** Kurt has gone to the grocery store twice this week **8.** Dorothy has eaten too much pizza tonight. **9.** The dam burst, and water flooded the valley. **10.** Marcus saw a bear while he was camping.

Workbook Activity 24—Using Progressive Forms

1–5. Answers will vary. Possible answers are given. **1.** has been increasing **2.** are making **3.** will have been standing **4.** had been running **5.** will be registering **6.** is washing—present progressive **7.** was fishing—past progressive **8.** will be leaving—future progressive **9.** Has been doing—present perfect progressive **10.** had been thinking—past perfect progressive **11.** is flying—present progressive **12.** will have been living—future perfect progressive **13.** were whispering—past progressive **14.** will have been waiting—future perfect progressive **15.** is beginning—present progressive

Workbook Activity 25—Making Subjects and Verbs Agree

1. hurry **2.** hopes **3.** catch **4.** hurries **5.** seems **6.** covers **7.** catches **8.** hope **9.** seem **10.** cover **11.** are **12.** is **13.** was **14.** goes **15.** enjoys **16.** paint **17.** is **18.** goes **19.** taste **20.** were

Workbook Activity 26—Using the Verb *Do*

1. do enjoy—helping verb **2.** does have—helping verb **3.** does—main verb **4.** did—main verb **5.** does—main verb **6.** Did write—helping verb **7.** had done—main verb **8.** will do—main verb **9.** Do agree—helping verb **10.** will have done—main verb **11.** does remember—helping verb **12.** does—main verb **13.** Did remind—helping verb **14.** do like—helping verb **15.** do—main verb

Workbook Activity 27—Using Conditional Verbs

1. should have **2.** May **3.** might have **4.** could **5.** should have **6.** could **7.** would have **8.** must have **9.** would have **10.** Can **11–15.** Answers will vary. Possible answers are given. **11.** Meg might have returned the book to the library. **12.** I should be leaving the house at six o'clock. **13.** Kim will have answered all your questions via e-mail. **14.** We shall pretend we are space explorers. **15.** The voters must have believed the candidate's explanations.

Workbook Activity 28—Identifying Active and Passive Verbs

1. Active **2.** Passive **3.** Passive **4.** Passive **5.** Active **6.** Passive **7.** Active **8.** Active **9.** Passive **10.** Passive **11.** Passive **12.** Passive **13.** Active **14.** Active **15.** Active **16.** Active **17.** Passive **18.** Passive **19.** Active **20.** Passive

Workbook Activity 29—Identifying State-of-Being Verbs

1. are **2.** are **3.** taste **4.** look **5.** tasted **6.** had become **7.** seemed **8.** appeared **9.** Have become **10.** have grown **11.** felt **12.** should look **13.** is **14.** could be **15.** remained **16.** tasted **17.** get **18.** look **19.** feel **20.** are

Workbook Activity 30—Identify Action and State-of-Being Verbs

1. ACTION **2.** BEING **3.** BEING **4.** ACTION **5.** ACTION **6.** ACTION **7.** BEING **8.** ACTION **9.** BEING **10.** ACTION **11.** BEING **12.** ACTION **13.** BEING **14.** ACTION **15.** BEING **16.** BEING **17.** ACTION **18.** BEING **19.** BEING **20.** ACTION

Workbook Activity 31—Using State-of-Being Verbs

1. be **2.** is **3.** was **4.** is **5.** been **6.** be **7.** be **8.** been **9.** been **10.** been **11.** is **12.** been **13.** been **14.** was **15.** been

Workbook Activity 32—Identifying Adverbs

1. softly **2.** easily **3.** quietly **4.** often **5.** well **6.** here **7.** promptly **8.** Finally **9.** loudly **10.** happily **11.** gracefully **12.** lightly **13.** Suddenly **14.** breathlessly **15.** carefully **16.** crossly **17.** quickly **18.** gleefully **19.** next **20.** quickly

Workbook Activity 33—Finding Adverbs of Degree

1. <u>so</u>, blue—adjective **2.** <u>extremely</u>, angry—adjective **3.** <u>only</u>, occasionally— adverb **4.** <u>very</u>, rarely—adverb **5.** <u>completely</u>, sure—adjective **6.** <u>just</u>, barely—adverb **7.** <u>especially</u>, tired—adjective **8.** <u>Only</u>, two—adjective **9.** <u>nearly</u>, always—adverb **10.** <u>Very</u>, little—adjective **11–15.** Answers will vary. Possible answers are given. **11.** An extremely quiet woman sat down beside me. **12.** Donald and his brother ride that bus rather frequently. **13.** The weather became unusually cool. **14.** The divers come to the surface very rapidly. **15.** Laura's painting seemed somewhat old-fashioned.

Workbook Activity 34—Identifying Adverbs of Negation

The adverbs of negation are in bold.

Jeremy had thought he could **never** enjoy painting. However, his mother did**n't** give him a choice. He could **not** talk her out of it. Jeremy had **never** tried anything creative. When he started painting, though, he did**n't** want to stop. His art teacher said she had **never** taught such a talented student. She entered one of Jeremy's paintings in a citywide art contest, although he did **not** believe his work was good enough. He did **not** believe her when she told him he had won first prize. Jeremy was happy. He would**n't** have succeeded if his mother and his teacher had **not** encouraged him.

1. n't (could**n't**) **2.** never **3.** never **4.** n't (wo**n't**) **5.** n't (did**n't**) **6.** never **7.** n't (would**n't**) **8.** n't (ca**n't**) **9.** n't (could**n't**) **10.** not

Workbook Activity 35—Recognizing Adverbs

1. adverb **2.** adjective **3.** adverb **4.** adverb **5.** adjective **6.** adverb **7.** adverb **8.** adjective **9.** adjective **10.** adverb **11.** adverb **12.** adjective **13.** adjective **14.** adverb **15.** adjective **16.** adjective **17.** adjective **18.** adverb **19.** adjective **20.** adjective

Workbook Activity 36—Using Adverbs to Compare

1. brilliantly—positive **2.** least clumsily—superlative **3.** generously—positive **4.** speedily—positive **5.** more energetically—comparative **6.** best—superlative **7.** better—comparative **8.** earlier—comparative **9.** farther—comparative **10.** more slowly—comparative **11–15.** Sentences using the following adverbs will vary. Possible sentences are given. **11.** loudly—Don played his music so loudly that the neighbors complained. **12.** brightly—The North Star twinkled brightly in the sky. **13.** gladly—Tina gladly accepted help with her science project. **14.** kindly—The teacher spoke kindly to her students. **15.** sadly—The president of the company sadly announced his resignation.

Workbook Activity 37—Choosing Adverbs

1. Heather presented her project <u>proudly</u>. **2.** Charlotte sings very <u>sweetly</u>. **3.** The apple tastes <u>bad</u>. **4.** The scout troop worked <u>steadily</u> all day. **5.** Yoshi sang <u>well</u> in the talent show. **6.** I understand this language as <u>well</u> as you do. **7.** Len <u>gradually</u> added the milk to the pancake batter. **8.** Gina felt <u>terrible</u> about making them wait for her. **9.** The wind howled <u>loudly</u>. **10.** Does Michael feel <u>good</u> about the decision?

Workbook Activity 38—Identifying Prepositions

Answers will vary. Possible answers are given. **1.** on **2.** with **3.** from **4.** on **5.** of **6.** of **7.** beside **8.** on **9.** on **10.** near

Workbook Activity 39—Recognizing the Object of the Preposition

The objects are in bold. **1.** with our **friends**, at a **restaurant** **2.** for **Rick** **3.** at the amusement **park** **4.** in a small **town**, in the southern **part**, of **Ohio** **5.** down the **path**, into the **field** **6.** from **Luke** **7.** Above the **fireplace**, of our **family** **8.** off your **coat** **9.** In 10 **minutes** **10.** to **children**, at the **carnival** **11.** over the **highway**, into the **woods** **12.** behind the **door**, for your **umbrella** **13.** into the **sky** **14.** over a large **river** **15.** about folk **music** **16.** from the **library**, under the **sofa** **17.** in the meeting **room**, during the **break** **18.** near a large **lake** **19.** on the window **sill**, in the living **room** **20.** to **Bob**, for his **birthday**

Workbook Activity 40—Recognizing Adjective Phrases

1. in England—tournament **2.** of the world's best players—Most **3.** of the matches—All; in the tournament—matches **4.** by Pete Sampras—play **5.** of his serves—Many **6.** with their grass surfaces—courts **7.** with powerful serves—Men **8.** in the world—player **9.** of a tennis magazine—publisher **10.** in America—tournament

Workbook Activity 41—Adding Adverb Phrases

Sentences will vary. Possible sentences are given. **1.** The lady bought a new bike at the store. **2.** Everyone joined the exercise class after lunch. **3.** For hours the snow was falling lightly. **4.** The puppy barked excitedly at the door. **5.** The store opens early in the morning. **6.** Before you arrive, Sally will be there. **7.** Because of the alarm, Bully, the St. Bernard puppy, barked loudly. **8.** Bake us a chocolate cake for the party. **9.** After finishing dinner, Carla wrote a short story. **10.** The teacher asked the class a question on the trip.

Workbook Activity 42—Identifying Prepositions and Adverbs

1. preposition **2.** adverb **3.** adverb **4.** preposition **5.** adverb **6.** preposition **7.** adverb **8.** preposition **9.** adverb **10.** preposition **11.** preposition **12.** adverb **13.** preposition **14.** adverb **15.** preposition

Workbook Activity 43—Using Coordinating Conjunctions

1. Plain water is sugar-free and caffeine-free. **2.** My older brother, Casey, and my little brother, Jimmy, play soccer. **3.** My favorite baseball players are Derek Jeter and Roger Clements. **4.** Toni Morrison wrote *Beloved* and *Tar Baby*. **5.** I have poodles named Velvet and Buffy. **6.** Velvet is black, but Buffy is white. **7.** My garden has roses, ivy, and herbs. **8.** My friend Mary enjoys sewing and reading. **9.** For the picnic, we bought potato salad and hot dogs. **10.** Betty likes hot dogs but doesn't like hamburgers.

Workbook Activity 44—Recognizing Subordinating Conjunctions

1. so that **2.** wherever **3.** if **4.** when **5.** When **6.** Even though **7.** Because **8.** as **9.** before **10.** Although **11.** Sara baby-sat for three hours **so that she can earn enough money to buy a CD.** **12. Although the movie began at 7:00 P.M.,** we didn't arrive at the theater until 7:10 P.M. **13.** I met José at the library **so that we could study together.** **14.** The President gave a speech **after he took the oath of office.** **15.** The groundhog saw its shadow **when it came out of its hole on February 2.**

Workbook Activity 45—Using Correlative Conjunctions

1. both . . . and **2.** either . . . or **3.** Neither . . . nor **4.** both . . . and **5.** either . . . or **6.** not only . . . but also **7.** Both . . . and **8.** either . . . or **9.** Whether . . . or **10.** not only . . . but also **11.A** Neither the gym nor the cafeteria is open now. **12.A** Not only Luke but also his younger sisters take violin lessons. **13.B** Neither the Senate nor the House of Representatives meets today. **14.A** Both Stephen and Maria tutor younger students. **15.B** Either Liza or Scott lives in that house.

Workbook Activity 46—Using Interjections

1. Oh, no! I forgot to turn off the oven. **2.** Oh! That waterfall is breathtaking. **3.** Hello! Is anyone there? **4.** Alas, they are tearing that beautiful old house down. **5.** My goodness, I am sleepy. **6.** Well, maybe I can finish this project by then. **7.** Wow! What a great gift! It's just what I wanted. **8.** Ummm, that stew smells wonderful. **9.** Hurry! We are going to be late again. **10.** Nonsense! You don't really think I would believe that. **11.** Hey, where do you think you're going? **12.** Oh, woe is me! I am so sad today. **13.** So what? Who cares if you're mad? **14.** Slow down! You are driving too fast. **15.** Brr, I'm freezing.

Workbook Activity 47—Recognizing Sentences

Students should circle items 1, 2, 5, 6, 9, 11, and 13 as fragments and underline items 3, 4, 7, 8, 10, 12, 14, and 15, which are complete sentences.

Workbook Activity 48—Finding the Subject of a Sentence

1. Soap operas **2.** People **3.** Many of the sponsors **4.** Daytime dramas **5.** One famous soap opera **6.** Your grandmother **7.** Another popular program in the 1940s **8.** My grandfather's favorite program **9.** "One Man's Family" **10.** It **11.** That program **12.** people **13.** You **14.** Soap opera stars **15.** People

Workbook Activity 49—Adding the Predicate

Sentence endings will vary. Possible endings are given. **1.** The car with the flat tire was on the side of the road. **2.** The entire class boarded the bus. **3.** The mayor of our town isn't running for reelection. **4.** The test on Monday will include an essay question. **5.** My favorite TV program is on tonight. **6.** My best friend and I are going camping. **7.** The students in this class organized the recycling drive. **8.** Our school basketball team has lost only three games. **9.** Thanksgiving dinner will be at three o'clock. **10.** The small town in Idaho where I grew up is near Boise.

Workbook Activity 50—Identifying the Purposes of Sentences

1. (?)—question **2.** (.)—statement **3.** (.)—statement **4.** (.)—command **5.** (?)—question **6.** Hey, (.) or (!)—command **7.** (.)—statement **8.** (?)—question **9.** (.)—statement **10.** (!)—exclamation **11.** (.)—statement **12.** (?)—question **13.** (!)—exclamation **14.** (.)—command **15.** (.)—statement

Workbook Activity 51—Identifying Simple and Compound Sentences

1. S **2.** S **3.** S **4.** C **5.** C **6.** C **7.** C **8.** S **9.** S **10.** C **11.** S **12.** C **13.** C **14.** S **15.** S

Workbook Activity 52—Using Pattern 1 Sentences

1. speech, will be televised **2.** birds, chirped **3.** friend, will study **4.** Who, can work **5.** We, will walk **6.** Plates, glasses; crashed **7.** team, Did practice **8.** George Washington, lived **9.** doctors, worked **10.** teacher, has performed

Workbook Activity 53—Using Pattern 2 Sentences

1. baked—cookies **2.** reads—books **3.** played—piece **4.** produces—computers **5.** made—skirt, wore—it **6.** will harvest—wheat **7.** collected—donations **8.** push—them **9.** met—Janice, sister **10.** Did bring—lunch **11.** me **12.** her **13.** we **14.** her **15.** them

Workbook Activity 54—Using Pattern 3 Sentences

The direct objects are in bold. **1.** **flowers**, mother **2.** **chills**, you **3.** **project**; Kurt, me **4.** **story**, friends **5.** **poem**, her **6.** **idea**, us **7.** **curveball**, batter **8.** **letter**, cousin **9.** **books**, them **10.** **ball**, Jason **11–15.** Indirect objects will vary. Possible answers follow. **11.** John sold Dennis his old computer. **12.** That university offered Ernesto a scholarship. **13.** The store issued the shopper a refund. **14.** Please lend them your support. **15.** Mr. Giles built the twins a swing set.

Workbook Activity 55—Using Pattern 4 Sentences

The direct objects are in bold. **1.** **hands**, orange **2.** **game**, tie **3.** **David**, dependable **4.** **Great Expectations**, book **5.** **Garrett**, assistant **6.** **chili**, spicy **7.** **drivers**, nervous **8.** **computers**, essential **9.** **job**; difficult, fulfilling **10.** **twin**, Kelly; **other**, Casey **11–20.** Complements will vary. Possible answers follow. **11.** mayor **12.** funny **13.** tasty **14.** a success **15.** dangerous **16.** lively, interesting **17.** positive, negative **18.** unfortunate **19.** the worst **20.** clean

Workbook Activity 56—Using Pattern 5 Sentences

The linking verbs are in bold. **1.** **will be**, Lisa **2.** **remains**, book **3.** **have been**, success **4.** **remains**, symbol **5.** **is**, novel **6.** **is**, musical **7.** **will become**, attorney **8.** **has been**, quilter **9.** **are**, role models **10.** **was**, prime minister **11–15.** Predicate nouns will vary. Possible answers follow. **11.** talented skater **12.** ice hockey **13.** the Lincoln Memorial **14.** Rosa Parks **15.** the computer

Workbook Activity 57—Using Pattern 6 Sentences

The linking verbs are in bold. **1.** **was**—long, boring **2.** **became**—dangerous **3.** **was**—visible **4.** **may be**—valuable **5.** **Was**—convenient **6.** **looked**—shaken **7.** **became**—hoarse **8.** **seemed**—real **9.** **were**—precise **10.** **was**—quiet, enjoyable **11.** **was**—fun, lively **12.** **felt**—damp, chilly **13.** **looks**—ragged, comfortable **14.** **feels**—energetic **15.** **were**—bare

Workbook Activity 58—Using Phrases and Clauses

1. dependent clause **2.** dependent clause **3.** prepositional phrase **4.** dependent clause **5.** independent clause **6.** independent clause **7.** prepositional phrase **8.** independent clause **9.** dependent clause **10.** dependent clause **11.** independent clause **12.** prepositional phrase **13.** dependent clause **14.** independent clause **15.** dependent clause

Workbook Activity 59—Identifying Adverb Clauses

1. after he graduates from high school **2.** than the old house had **3.** After I learned to play tennis **4.** as hard as he could **5.** until the holidays arrived **6.** where she put her slippers **7.** Until the next computer is available **8.** because he likes music **9.** whenever he can **10.** than Richard is **11.** if you are tired **12.** after it rained **13.** because he wanted to win **14.** than Alice does **15.** When you learn the rules

Workbook Activity 60—Using Noun Clauses

1. what I wanted—predicate noun **2.** whatever you like—object complement **3.** what I want—predicate noun **4.** whoever you want—indirect object **5.** what those people are doing—direct object **6.** Whoever finishes first—subject **7.** whoever wanted one—indirect object **8.** Whoever is hungry—subject **9.** that my poster had won the contest—direct object **10.** who would be at the party—direct object **11.** Whatever you decide—subject **12.** what you said—direct object **13.** what you want—direct object **14.** What you said—subject **15.** whoever needed one—object of the preposition

Workbook Activity 61—Identifying Adjective Clauses

The adjective clauses are in bold. **1.** **that my mother gave me**—watch **2.** **whom I met at the library**—man **3.** **who was her friend from school**—Danny **4.** **that John gave his mother**—gift **5.** **that she asked**—question **6.** **that has a built-in modem**—computer **7.** **who just learned to play soccer**—April **8.** **who takes care of their pets**—one **9.** **whose wife works at the library**—man **10.** **that Jenna suggested**—CD **11.** **that had an indoor swimming pool**—hotel **12.** **that Kathy won**—contest **13.** **that he had taken in class**—notes **14.** **who was allergic to peanuts**—boy **15.** **that live around Silver Lake**—geese

Workbook Activity 62—Recognizing Compound and Complex Sentences

1. compound **2.** simple **3.** complex **4.** simple **5.** simple **6.** complex **7.** complex **8.** compound **9.** simple **10.** simple **11.** compound **12.** complex **13.** simple **14.** complex **15.** complex

Workbook Activity 63—Identifying Verbals

1. Walking **2.** to give **3.** playing **4.** canceled **5.** standing **6.** participle **7.** infinitive **8.** infinitive **9.** participle **10.** gerund **11.** gerund **12.** gerund **13.** infinitive **14.** participle **15.** infinitive

Workbook Activity 64—Identifying Infinitives and Infinitive Phrases

1. prepositional phrase **2.** infinitive **3.** infinitive **4.** infinitive **5.** infinitive **6.** to eat scrambled eggs with ketchup **7.** to be happy **8.** to see the polar bears at the zoo **9.** to collect old toy cars **10.** To run for office **11.** to dust his house **12.** to learn how to cook low-fat meals **13.** to go skiing in Colorado **14.** to sleep late on Saturdays **15.** to read or watch television

Workbook Activity 65—Recognizing Gerunds and Gerund Phrases

1. exploring the oceans—object of the preposition **2.** Chasing tornadoes—subject **3.** writing the Declaration of Independence—predicate noun **4.** becoming an opera singer—direct object **5.** applying to colleges—object of the preposition **6.** Shoveling snow—subject **7.** tearing up newspaper—direct object **8.** Traveling across the United States—subject **9.** bike riding—predicate noun **10.** painting a picture—object of the preposition **11.** Seeing the mountains—subject **12.** reporting on high school sports—direct object **13.** volunteering at the center—object of the preposition **14.** Caring for pets—subject **15.** planning our trip—object of the preposition

Workbook Activity 66—Identifying Participles and Participle Phrases

1. waving—flags **2.** enlightening—film **3.** standing on the rocks—fisherman **4.** crying beside the road—puppy **5.** described by Jason—idea **6.** Walking rapidly around the block—Carol **7.** frosted—brownies **8.** raging—hurricane **9.** missing—skirt **10.** brought by Luisa—salad **11–15.** Answers will vary. Possible answers are given. **11.** The frightened rabbit hid in the bushes. **12.** She made drinks from concentrated fruit juice. **13.** Mailed yesterday, the letter arrived today. **14.** The cooking pot was on the stove. **15.** That surfer catching the wave now is my cousin Anton.

Diagramming Activities

Diagramming Activity 1—Diagramming Pattern 1 Sentences

1. They | swam

2.
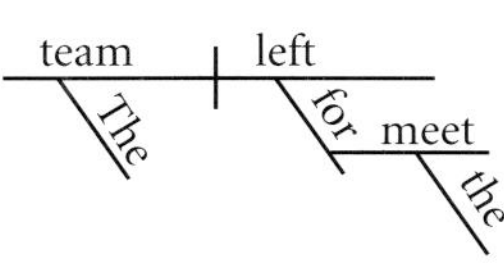

3.
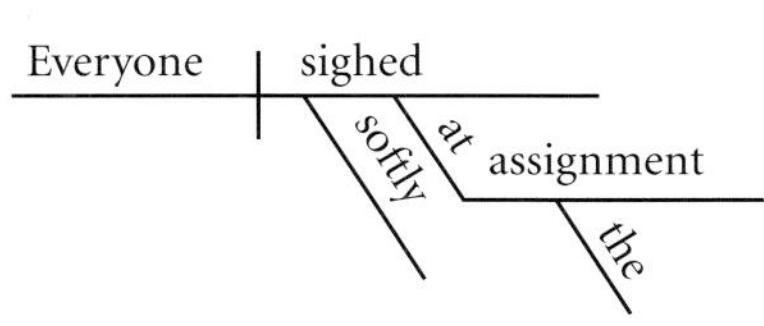

4.
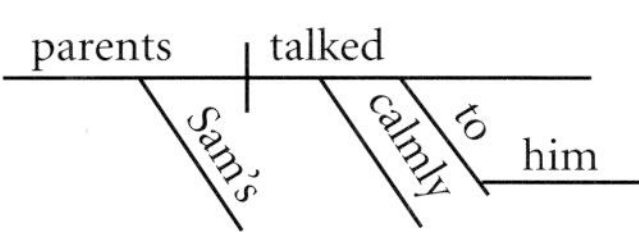

5.
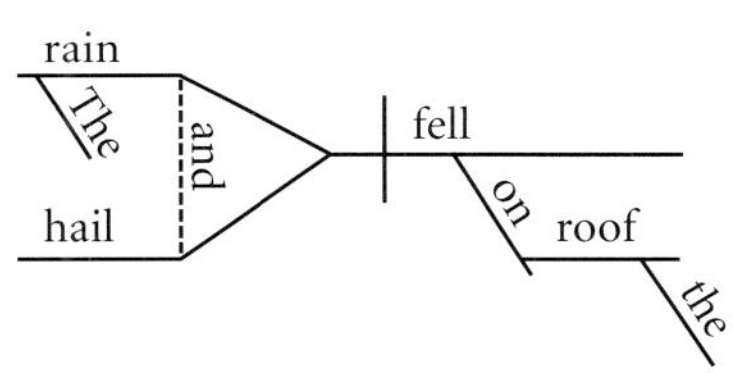

6.
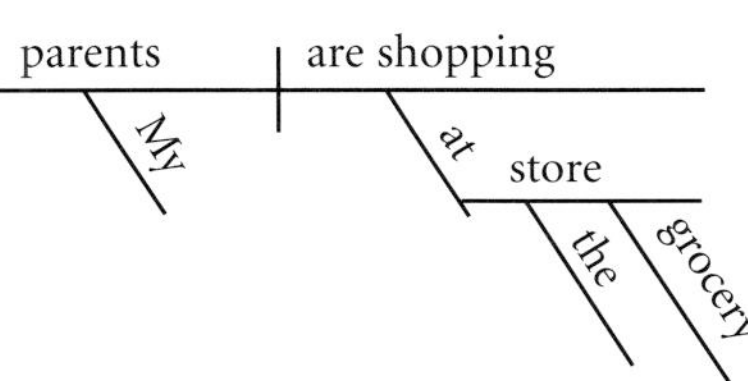

7.
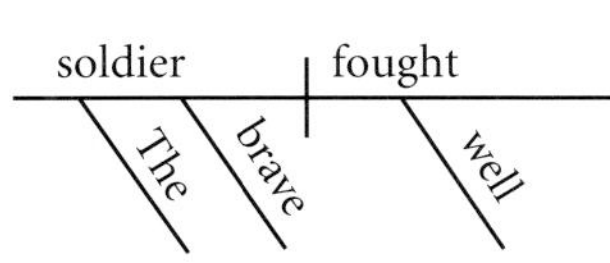

8.
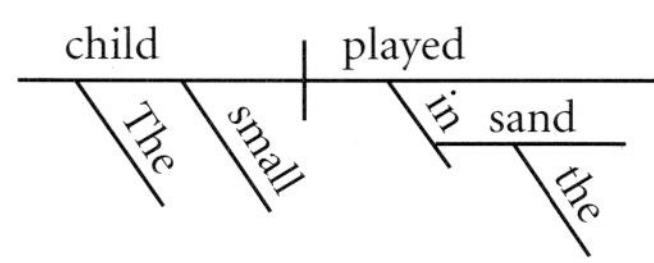

9.
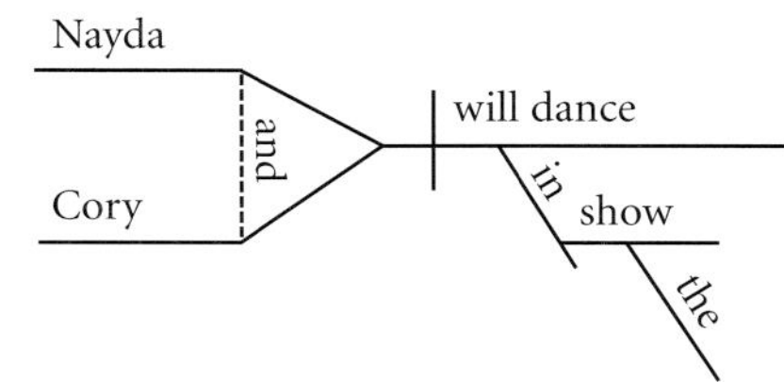

10.
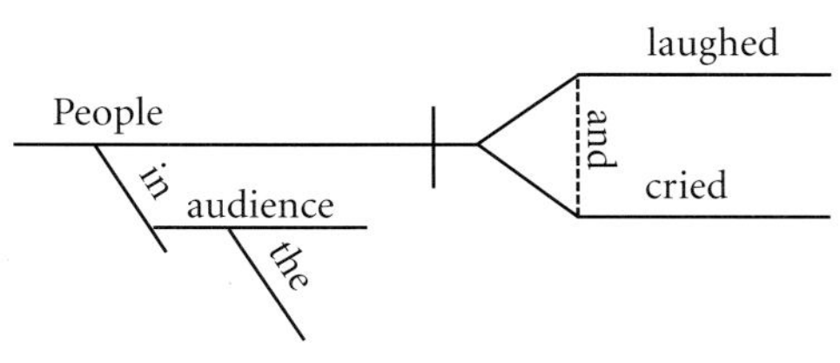

Diagramming Activity 2—Diagramming Pattern 2 Sentences (Direct Objects)

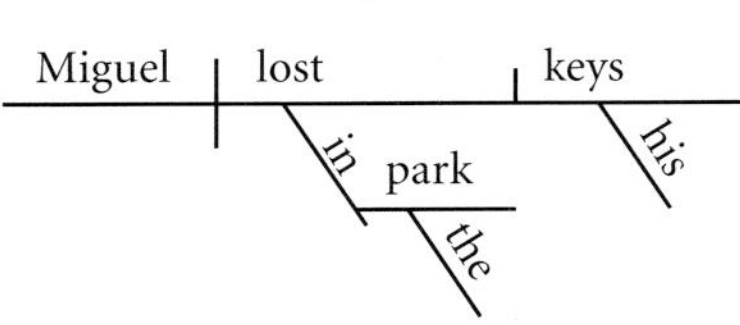

2.

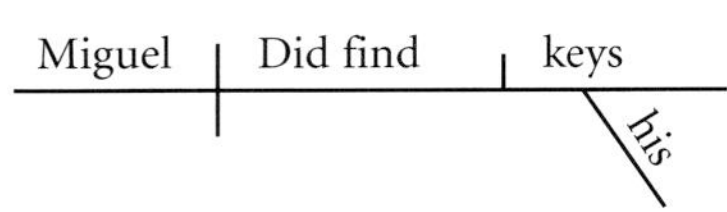

3.

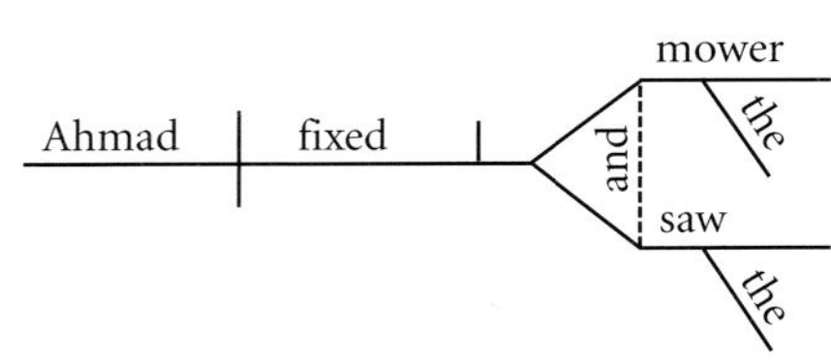

4.

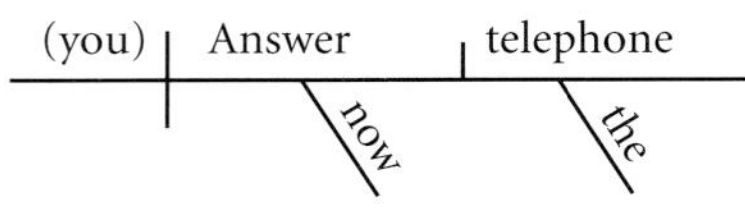

5.

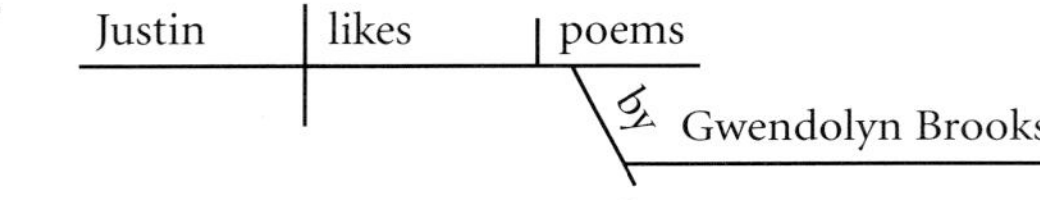

6.

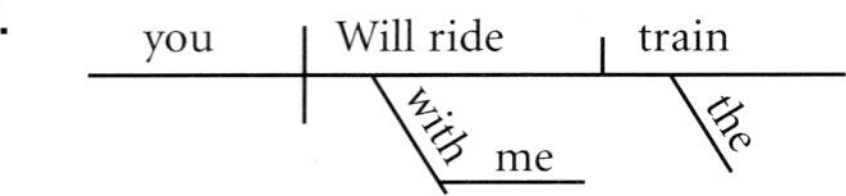

7.

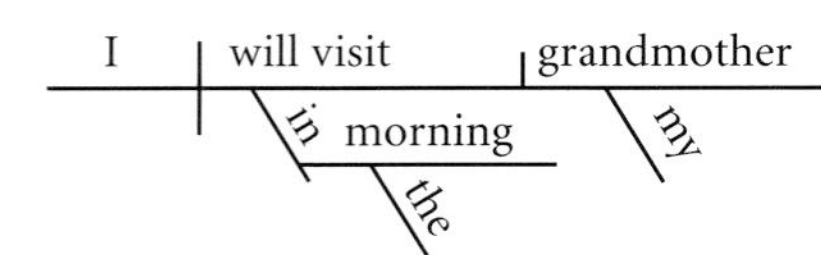

8.

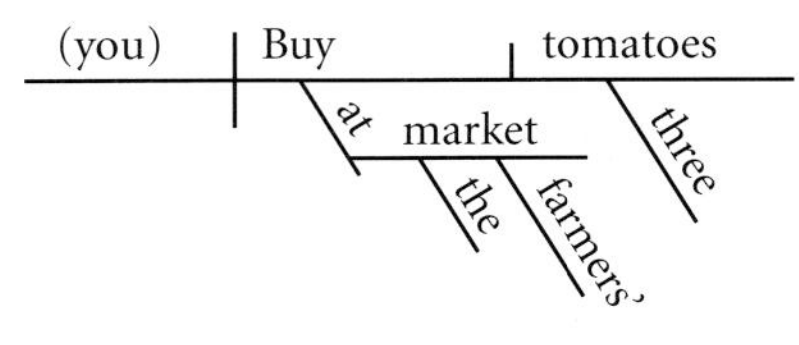

9.

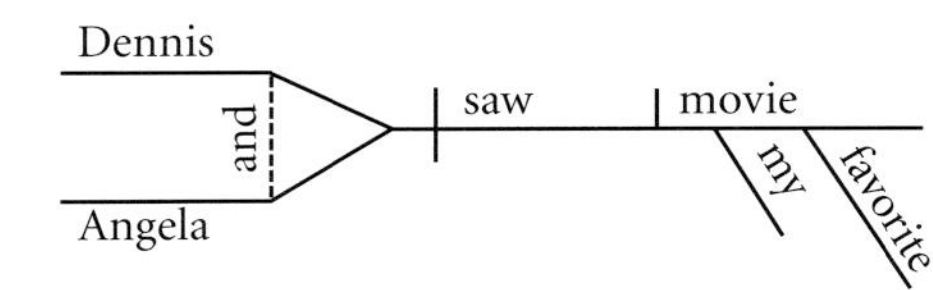

10.

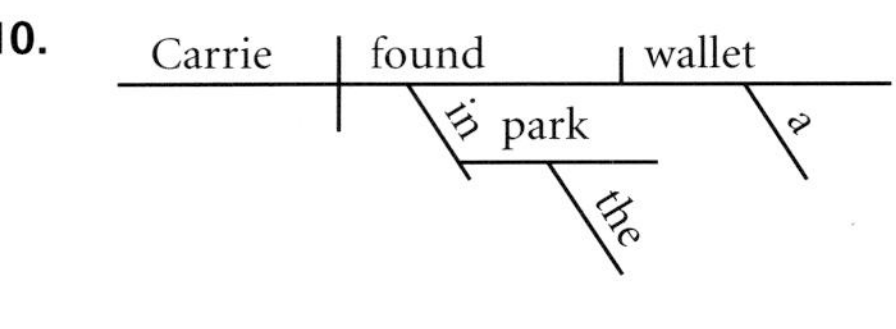

Diagramming Activity 3—Diagramming Pattern 3 Sentences (Indirect Objects)

1.

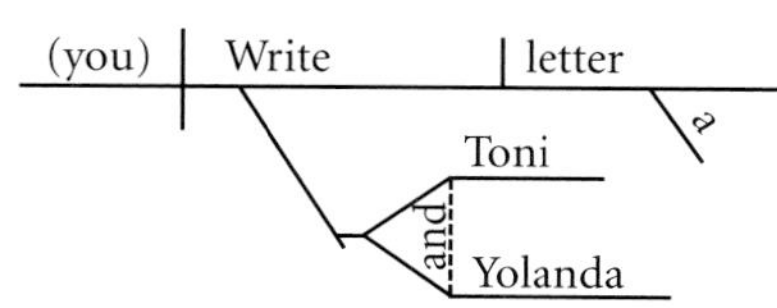

2.

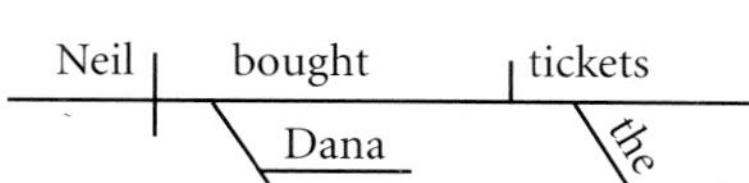

3.

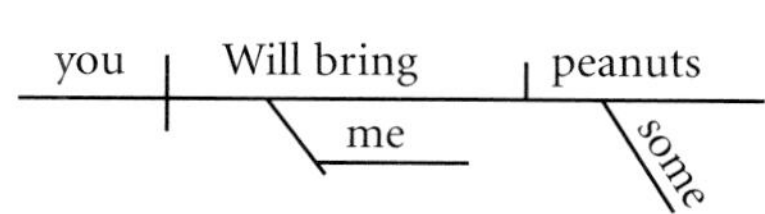

4.

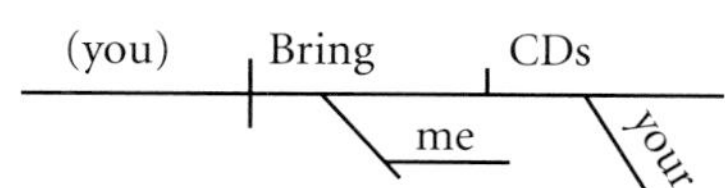

5.

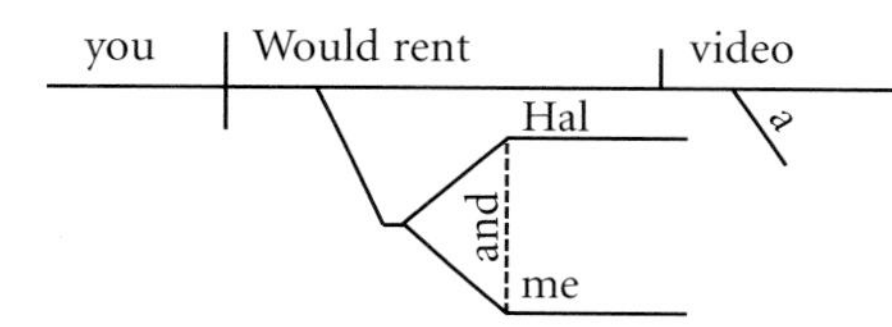

6.

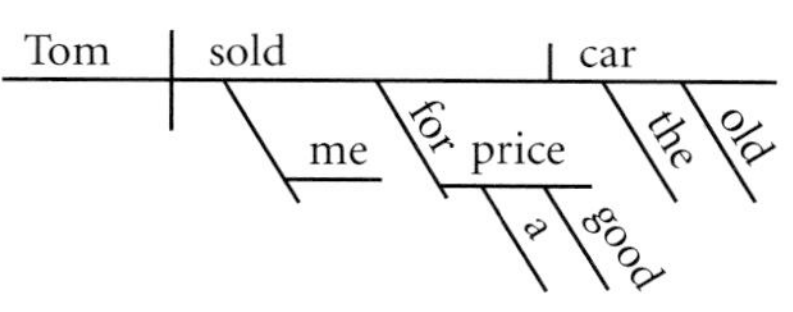

7.

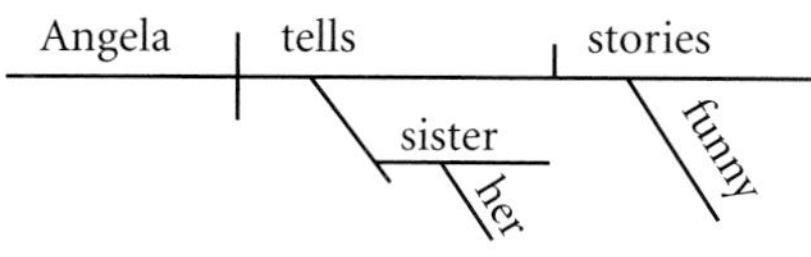

8.

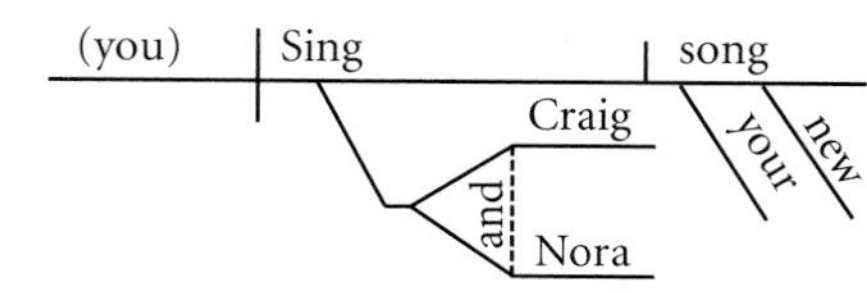

9.

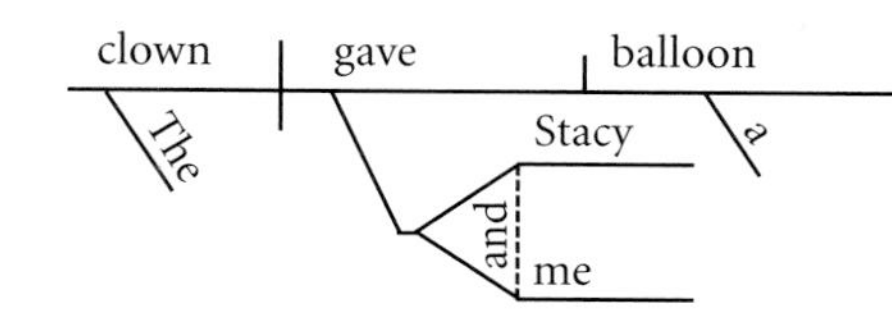

10.

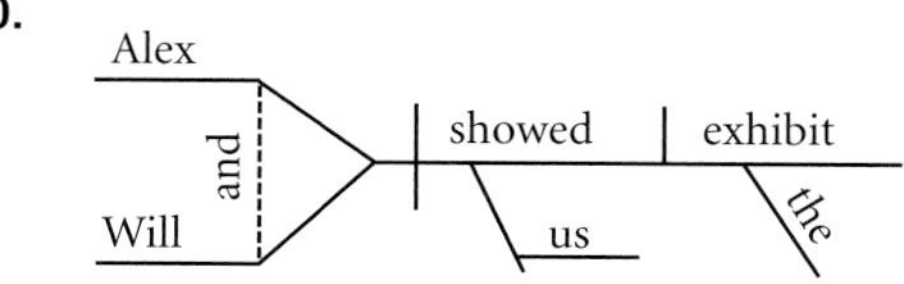

Diagramming Activity 4—Diagramming Pattern 4 Sentences (Object Complements)

1.

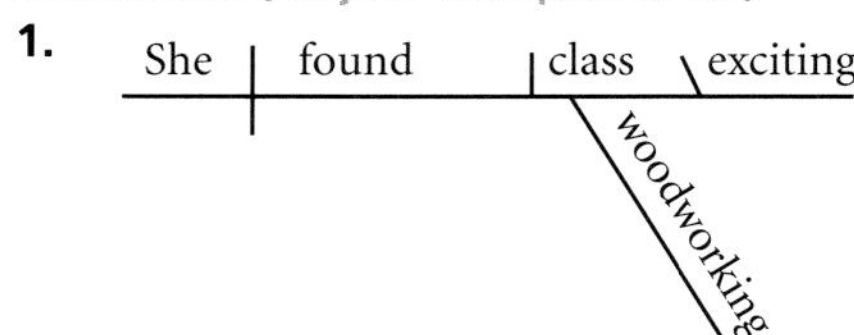

2.

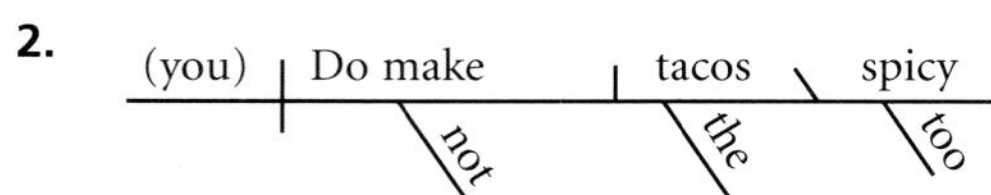

3.

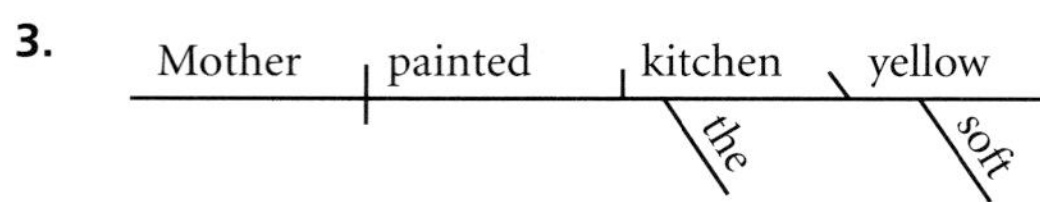

4.

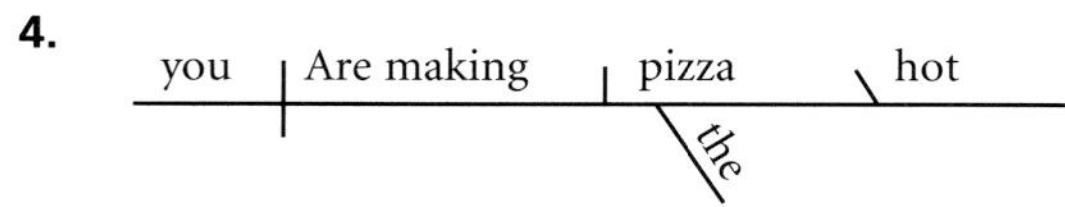

5.

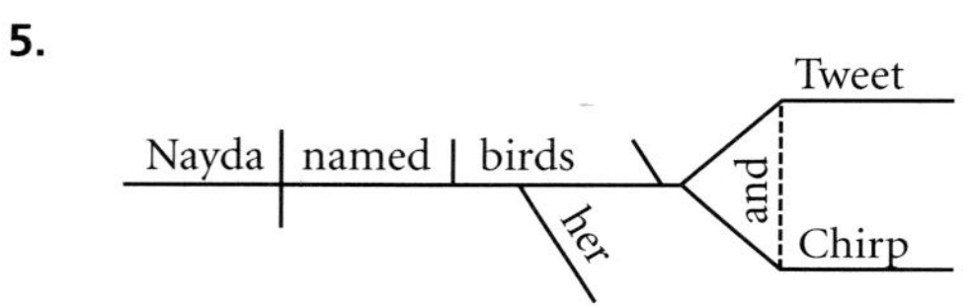

6.

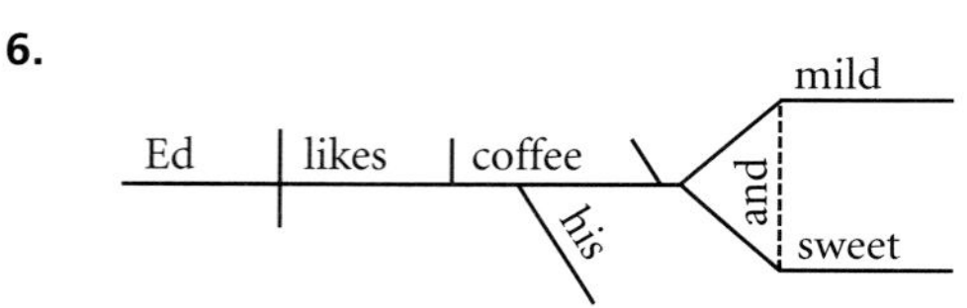

7.

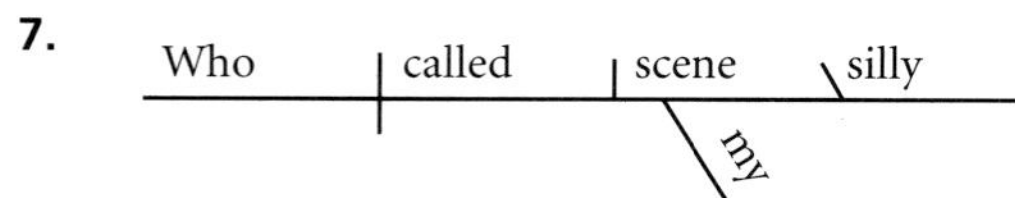

8.

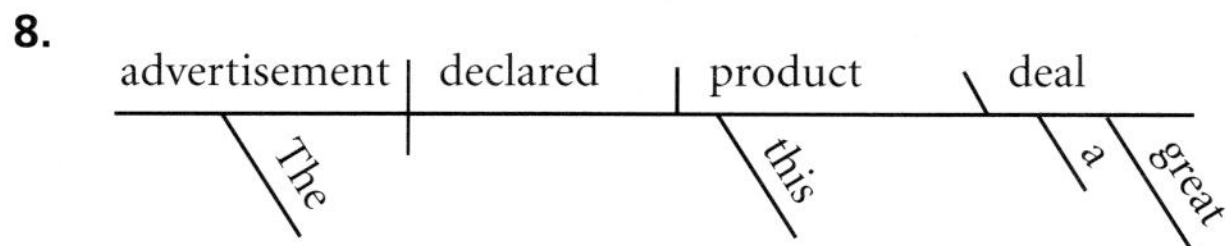

9.

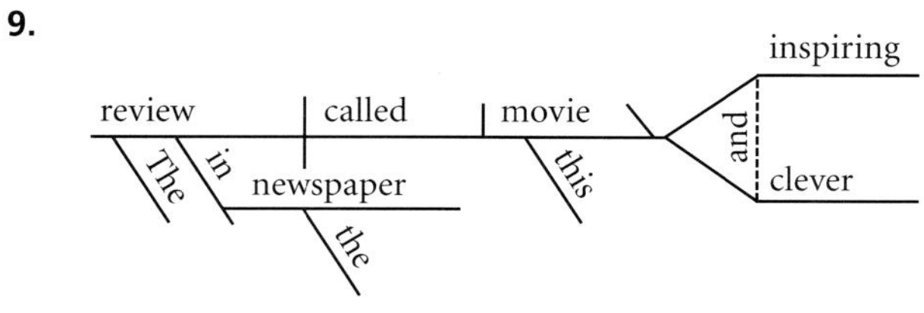

10.

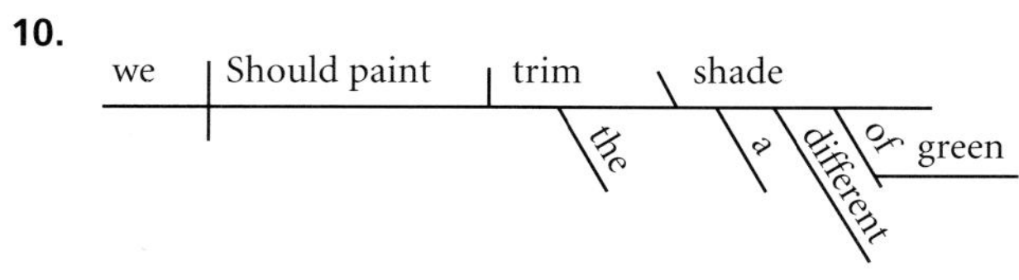

Diagramming Activity 5—Diagramming Pattern 5 Sentences (Predicate Nouns)

1.

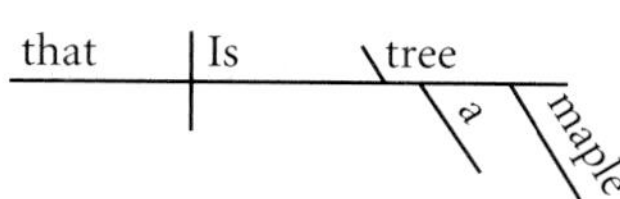

2.

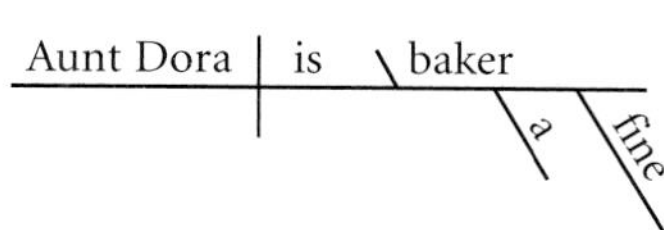

3.

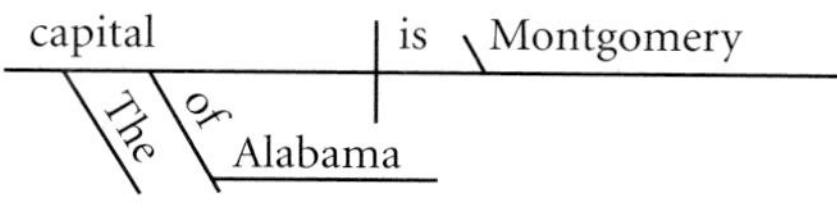

4.

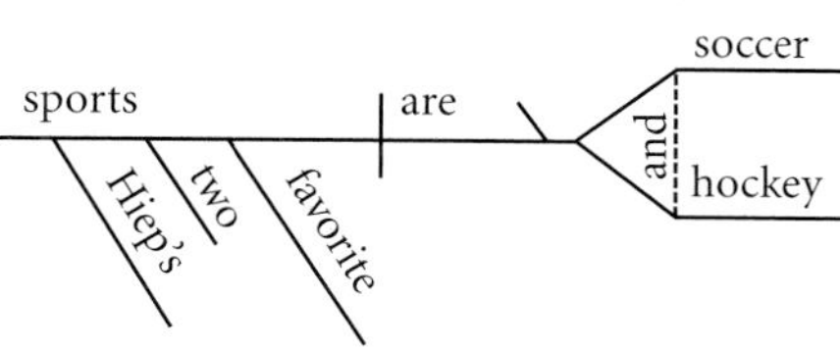

5.

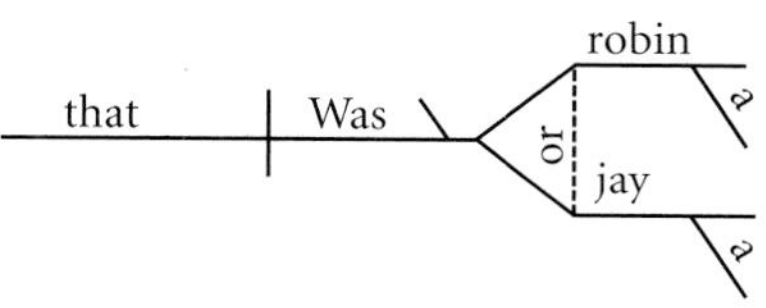

6.

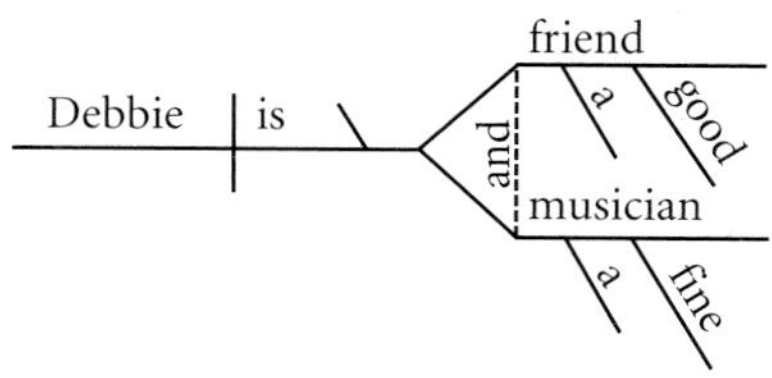

7.

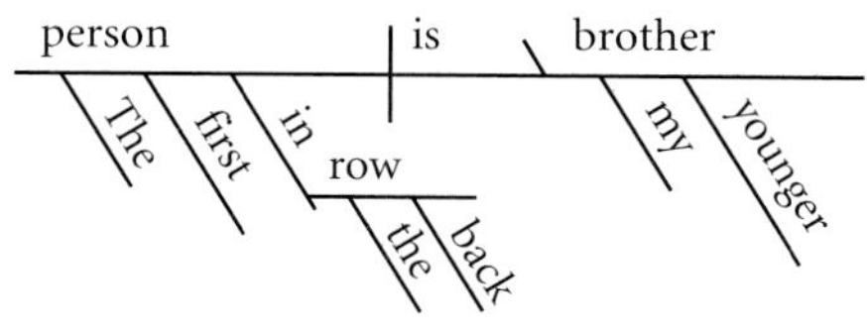

8.

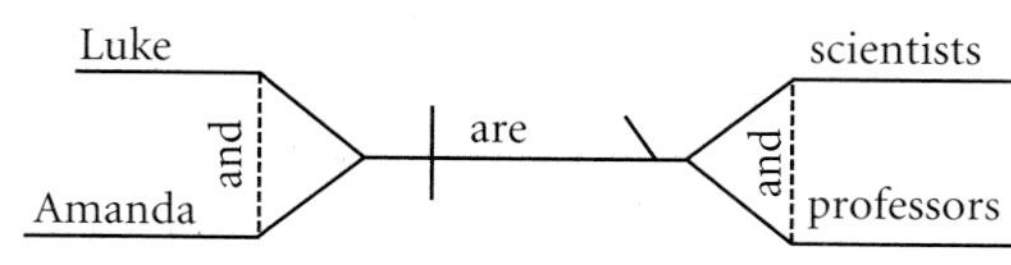

9.

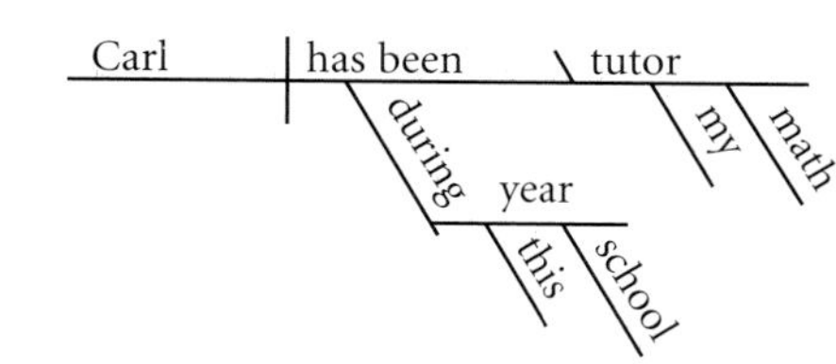

10.

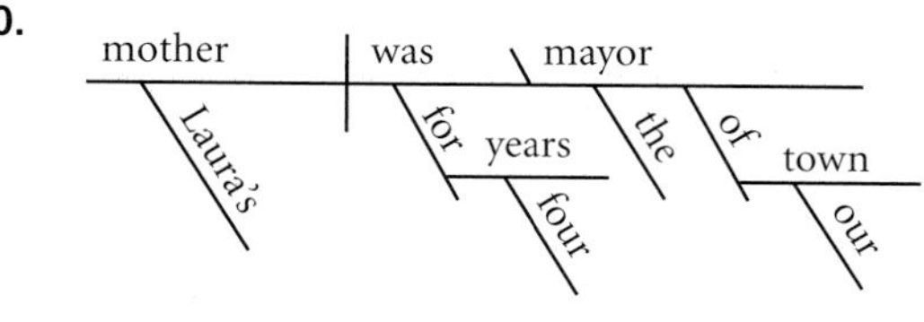

Diagramming Activity 6—Diagramming Pattern 6 Sentences (Predicate Adjectives)

1.

(you) | Keep \ still

2.

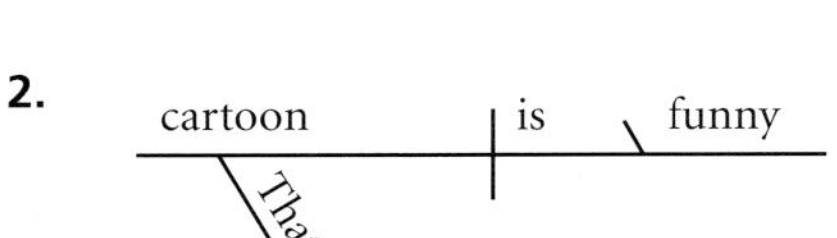

3.

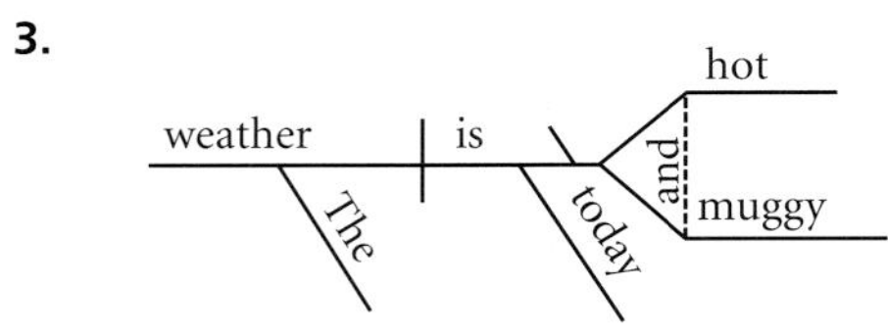

4.

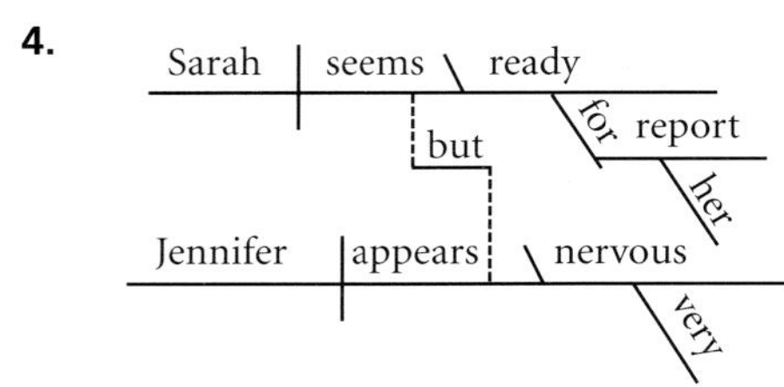

5.

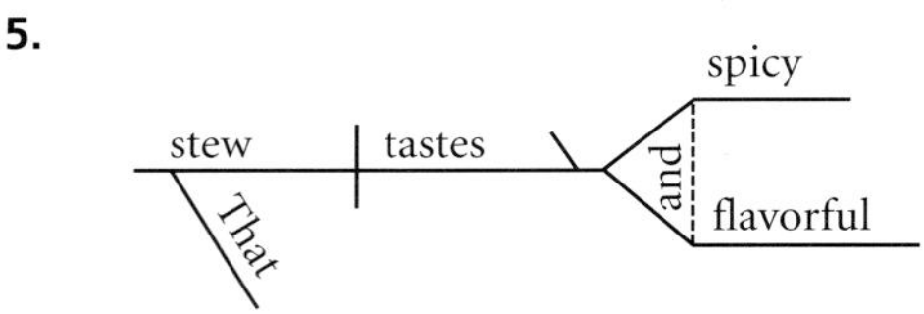

6.

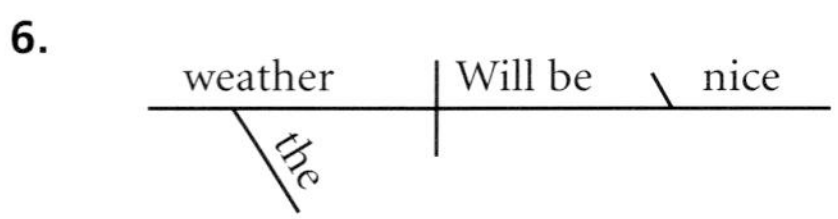

7.

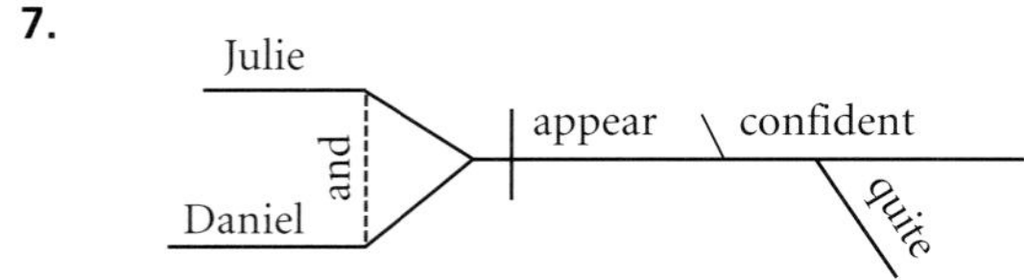

8.

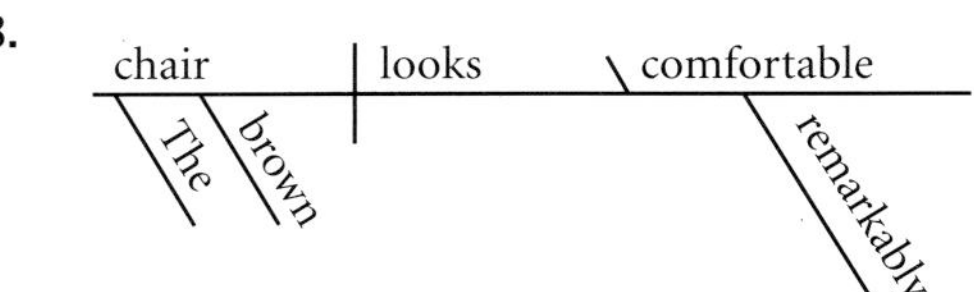

9.

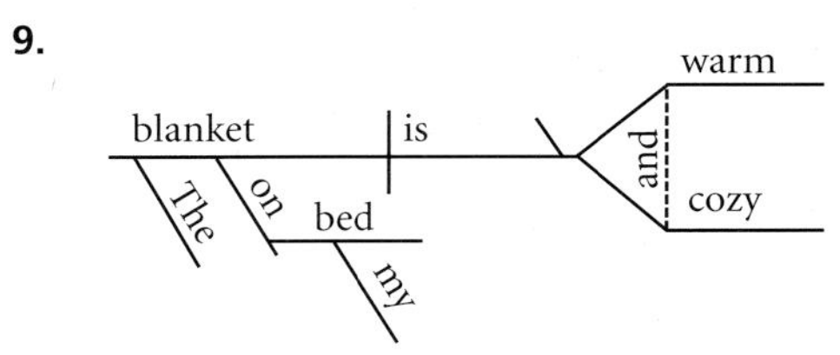

10.

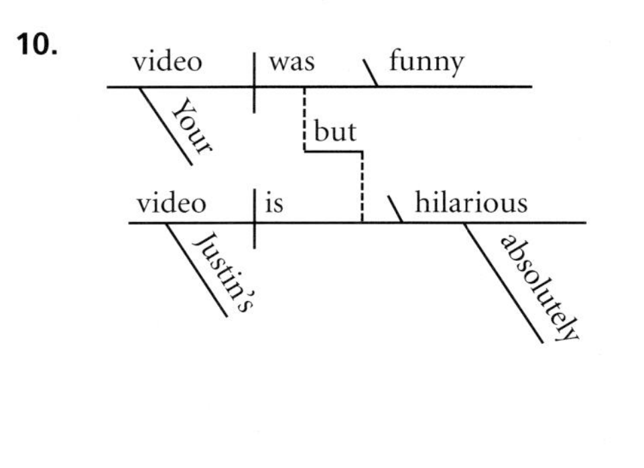

Community Connection

Completed activities will vary for each student. Community Connections activities are real-life activities that students complete outside of the classroom. These activities give students practical learning and practice of the skills taught in *Basic English Grammar*. Check completed activities to see that students have followed directions, completed each step, filled in all charts and blanks, provided reasonable answers to questions, written legibly, and used proper grammar and punctuation.

Media and Literature Connection

Completed activities will vary for each student. Media and Literature Connections are activities that students complete outside of the classroom. These activities give students practical learning and practice of the skills taught in *Basic English Grammar* through the use of various types of texts. Check completed activities to see that students have followed directions, completed each step, filled in all charts and blanks, provided reasonable answers to questions, written legibly, and used proper grammar and punctuation.

Self-Study Guides

Self-Study Guides outline suggested sections from the text and workbook. These assignment guides provide flexibility for individualized instruction or independent study.

Preparing for Writing Tests

Test 1–Writing Prompts

1. Purpose: to persuade Format: letter
2. Purpose: to describe Format: paragraphs
3. Purpose: to inform Format: list
4. Purpose: to entertain Format: paragraphs
5. Purpose: to persuade Format: letter

Test 2–Organizing Your Writing

Information in organizers will vary.

Test 3–Proofreading for Errors

1. Jason and Rico were trying to **decide** what to **do** on Saturday afternoon. **2.** Earth is the **third** planet from the **sun**. **3.** Do you **know** where they have hung **their** poster? **4.** Abraham Lincoln **delivered** the **Gettysburg** Address at the dedication of the cemetery in Gettysburg, Pennsylvania. **5.** Anita and Terry **live** in the **same** apartment building.

Test 4–Writing Test Practice

Essays and answers will vary.

Mastery Tests

Chapter 1 Mastery Test A

Part A

1. Cy Young, games, pitcher, baseball **2.** record, wins, person **3.** Old Hoss Radbourn **4.** Old Hoss, games, career **5.** year, pitcher, baseball, award

Part B

6. We saw Cal Ripken play baseball at Camden Yards in Baltimore. **7.** Next year Henry plans to take Spanish and Algebra I. **8.** Jackie visited the Midwest last August. **9.** In June Robert has an appointment with Dr. Welsey. **10.** For many years "60 Minutes" has been a popular news program.

Part C

11. bunches **12.** cities **13.** foxes **14.** spies **15.** keys **16.** knives **17.** reports **18.** feet **19.** women **20.** mice

Part D

21. book's **22.** dollars' **23.** children's **24.** churches' **25.** dish's

Part E

26. B **27.** B **28.** A **29.** B **30.** D

Chapter 1 Mastery Test B

Part A

1. We saw Cal Ripken play baseball at Camden Yards in Baltimore. **2.** Next year Henry plans to take Spanish and Algebra I. **3.** Jackie visited the Midwest last August. **4.** In June Robert has an appointment with Dr. Welsey. **5.** For many years "60 Minutes" has been a popular news program.

Part B

6. book's **7.** dollars' **8.** children's **9.** churches' **10.** dish's

Part C

11. Cy Young, games, pitcher, baseball **12.** record, wins, person **13.** Old Hoss Radbourn **14.** Old Hoss, games, career **15.** year, pitcher, baseball, award

Part D

16. B **17.** B **18.** A **19.** B **20.** D

Part E

21. bunches **22.** cities **23.** foxes **24.** spies **25.** keys **26.** knives **27.** reports **28.** feet **29.** women **30.** mice

Chapter 2 Mastery Test A

Part A

1. her **2.** I **3.** their **4.** his **5.** that **6.** himself **7.** We **8.** Which **9.** himself or herself **10.** who

Part B

11. personal **12.** indefinite **13.** demonstrative **14.** personal **15.** relative

Part C

16. friend **17.** Marie **18.** Kimberly **19.** man **20.** Jason, Todd

Part D

21. C **22.** D **23.** A **24.** B **25.** D

Part E

26. You, whatever, you **27.** Who, your **28.** This, we, that **29.** You, that, she, me **30.** We, ourselves, this **31.** They, someone, who **32.** She, her **33.** We, whose, that **34.** What, you **35.** anybody, these

Chapter 2 Mastery Test B

Part A

1. A **2.** B **3.** D **4.** C **5.** D

Part B

6. This, we , that **7.** you, that, she, me **8.** We, ourselves, this **9.** They, someone, who **10.** She, her **11.** We, whose, that **12.** Who, your **13.** You, whatever, you **14.** anybody, these **15.** What, you

Part C

16. personal **17.** indefinite **18.** demonstrative **19.** personal **20.** relative

Part D

21. Kimberly **22.** Marie **23.** friend **24.** Jason, Todd **25.** man

Part E

26. himself or herself **27.** who **28.** her **29.** I **30.** himself **31.** We **32.** Which **33.** their **34.** his **35.** that

Chapter 3 Mastery Test A

Part A

The adjectives are in bold. **1. a, large, hot**—breakfast; **a, cold**—morning **2. Clare's**—mother; **a, hearty**—breakfast **3. her**—mother; **a, tall**—glass; **fresh, orange**—juice **4. six, fluffy**—waffles; **four**—pieces; **French**—toast **5. Those, tasty**—waffles; **that, French, tasty**—toast

Part B

6. French, English **7.** Indian **8.** Vietnamese **9.** Latin **10.** African

Part C

11. proper **12.** possessive **13.** demonstrative **14.** article **15.** number **16.** article **17.** number **18.** proper **19.** demonstrative **20.** possessive

Part D

21. shorter **22.** best **23.** more careful **24.** strong **25.** wonderful **26.** heaviest **27.** easy **28.** larger **29.** most successful **30.** faster

Part E

31. B **32.** D **33.** C **34.** D **35.** B

Chapter 3 Mastery Test B

Part A

1. possessive **2.** demonstrative **3.** article **4.** number **5.** proper **6.** possessive **7.** demonstrative **8.** proper **9.** article **10.** number

Part B

The adjectives are in bold. **11. a, large, hot**—breakfast; **a, cold**—morning **12. Clare's**—mother; **a, hearty**—breakfast **13. her**—mother; **a, tall**—glass; **fresh, orange**—juice **14. six, fluffy**—waffles; **four**—pieces; **French**—toast **15. Those, tasty**—waffles; **that, French, tasty**—toast

Part C

16. Vietnamese **17.** Latin **18.** African **19.** French, English **20.** Indian

Part D

21. D **22.** D **23.** B **24.** B **25.** C

Part E

26. faster **27.** most successful **28.** larger **29.** shorter **30.** best **31.** more careful **32.** easy **33.** heaviest **34.** wonderful **35.** strong

Chapter 4 Mastery Test A

Part A

1. rides **2.** pass **3.** doing **4.** sanded **5.** studied **6.** broke **7.** purchased **8.** finished **9.** eating **10.** been

Part B

11. would like **12.** may come **13.** must plant **14.** Do know **15.** plays

Part C

16. passive **17.** active **18.** passive **19.** active **20.** passive

Part D

21. answered **22.** will have begun **23.** has gone **24.** had called **25.** were planning **26.** will close **27.** was practicing **28.** will have been lasting **29.** will be buying **30.** rakes *or* rake

Part E

31. B **32.** C **33.** D **34.** A **35.** B

Chapter 4 Mastery Test B

Part A

1. must plant **2.** Do know **3.** plays **4.** would like **5.** may come

Part B

6. had called **7.** were planning **8.** will close **9.** was practicing **10.** answered **11.** will have begun **12.** has gone **13.** rakes *or* rake **14.** will be buying **15.** will have been lasting

Part C

16. active **17.** passive **18.** passive **19.** active **20.** passive

Part D

21. D **22.** C **23.** B **24.** B **25.** A

Part E

26. finished **27.** eating **28.** been **29.** sanded **30.** studied **31.** broke **32.** purchased **33.** rides **34.** pass **35.** doing

Chapter 5 Mastery Test A

Part A

1. had felt—past perfect **2.** is—present **3.** appeared—past **4.** will have been—future perfect **5.** has become—present perfect **6.** is—present **7.** keep—present **8.** will be—future **9.** felt—past **10.** grew—past **11.** Are—present **12.** was—past **13.** seems—present **14.** will taste—future **15.** had become—past perfect

Part B

16. be **17.** is **18.** was **19.** are **20.** is

Part C

21. state of being **22.** action **23.** action **24.** state of being **25.** state of being **26.** action **27.** action **28.** state of being **29.** state of being **30.** action

Part D

31. C **32.** A **33.** D **34.** C **35.** A

Chapter 5 Mastery Test B

Part A

1. is **2.** be **3.** are **4.** is **5.** was

Part B

6. is—present **7.** keep—present **8.** will be—future **9.** had felt—past perfect **10.** is—present **11.** appeared—past **12.** seems—present **13.** will taste—future **14.** had become—past perfect **15.** will have been—future perfect **16.** has become—present perfect **17.** felt—past **18.** grew—past **19.** Are—present **20.** was—past

Part C

21. C **22.** A **23.** C **24.** A **25.** D

Part D

26. action **27.** state of being **28.** action **29.** state of being **30.** state of being **31.** action **32.** state of being **33.** action **34.** action **35.** state of being

Chapter 6 Mastery Test A

Part A

1. dances **2.** climbed **3.** shone **4.** picked **5.** easy **6.** fast **7.** finished **8.** will go **9.** walked **10.** flew

Part B

11. better **12.** most quickly **13.** slowly **14.** well *or* better **15.** more/less brightly **16.** more swiftly **17.** gladly **18.** more/less clearly **19.** most/least rapidly **20.** noisily

Part C

21. never, again, angrily **22.** loudly **23.** immediately **24.** Please, now **25.** up, down, almost, constantly **26.** never, too **27.** very **28.** forward, quickly **29.** higher, nearly **30.** here, cheerfully

Part D

31. C **32.** D **33.** C **34.** B **35.** D

Chapter 6 Mastery Test B

Part A

1. never, too **2.** very **3.** forward, quickly **4.** higher, nearly **5.** here, cheerfully **6.** never, again, angrily **7.** loudly **8.** immediately **9.** Please, now **10.** up, down, almost, constantly

Part B

11. most quickly **12.** better **13.** noisily **14.** most/least rapidly **15.** more/less clearly **16.** gladly **17.** more swiftly **18.** more/less brightly **19.** well *or* better **20.** slowly

Part C

21. C **22.** B **23.** D **24.** C **25.** D

Part D

26. will go **27.** walked **28.** flew **29.** picked **30.** easy **31.** fast **32.** finished **33.** dances **34.** climbed **35.** shone

Chapter 7 Mastery Test A

Part A

1. In, into, over **2.** off, around, of **3.** for, from **4.** about, of **5.** at, behind **6.** to, through, near **7.** of, across, under **8.** with, on, of **9.** beside, during **10.** beneath

Part B

11. adjective **12.** adverb **13.** adverb **14.** adjective **15.** adjective **16.** adjective **17.** adjective **18.** adverb **19.** adverb **20.** adverb

Part C

21. me **22.** him **23.** her **24.** them **25.** us

Part D

26. D **27.** A **28.** B **29.** C **30.** C

Chapter 7 Mastery Test B

Part A

1. B **2.** C **3.** C **4.** D **5.** A

Part B

6. them **7.** us **8.** me **9.** him **10.** her

Part C

11. In, into, over **12.** off, around, of **13.** for, from **14.** of, across, under **15.** with, on, of **16.** beside, during **17.** beneath **18.** about, of **19.** at, behind **20.** to, through, near

Part D

21. adjective **22.** adjective **23.** adjective **24.** adverb **25.** adverb **26.** adverb **27.** adjective **28.** adverb **29.** adverb **30.** adjective

Chapter 8 Mastery Test A

Part A

1. or **2.** nor **3.** Neither **4.** but also **5.** and

Part B

6. B **7.** D **8.** C **9.** A **10.** B

Part C

11. or **12.** but **13.** and **14.** but **15.** but

Part D

Answers will vary. Possible answers follow.

16. Because my mom is working, I have to watch my little sister.
17. After Greg flew on an airplane, he lost his fear of flying.
18. Although the sky was cloudy, the temperature was warm and comfortable. **19.** Since Sue and Harry will clean this week, we will clean next week. **20.** Rita went to the store because she needed groceries.

Part E

Answers will vary. Possible answers follow.

21. Goodness, **22.** Ouch! **23.** My, **24.** Gosh, **25.** Yippee! **26.** Boy, **27.** Gee, **28.** Grr! **29.** Say, **30.** Gee,

Chapter 8 Mastery Test B

Part A

1. and **2.** but **3.** but **4.** or **5.** but

Part B

Answers will vary. Possible answers follow.

6. After Greg flew on an airplane, he lost his fear of flying.
7. Although the sky was cloudy, the temperature was warm and comfortable. **8.** Since Sue and Harry will clean this week, we will clean next week. **9.** Rita went to the store because she needed groceries. **10.** Because my mom is working, I have to watch my little sister.

Part C

11. Neither **12.** but also **13.** and **14.** or **15.** nor

Part D

16. B **17.** A **18.** C **19.** D **20.** B

Part E

Answers will vary. Possible answers follow.

21. Gosh, **22.** Gee, **23.** Grr! **24.** Say, **25.** Gee, **26.** My, **27.** Ouch! **28.** Goodness, **29.** Boy, **30.** Yippee!

Chapter 9 Mastery Test A

Part A

1. N **2.** S **3.** S **4.** N **5.** N **6.** S **7.** N **8.** S **9.** S **10.** N

Part B

The nouns and pronouns in the subjects are in bold. **11. Irene** and **I** **12.** Neither the **television** nor the **radio** **13. Grandfather** and the entire **family** **14.** Our **friends Howard** and **Heidi** **15. Everything** in the **freezer**

Part C

16. C **17.** D **18.** A **19.** B **20.** D

Part D

The verbs and verb phrases are in bold. **21. had knocked** out the electrical power **22. had** electricity or telephones for three days **23. fly casts** in summer and **ice fishes** in winter **24. are working** day and night to plow the roads **25. have been married** for years

Part E

26. question **27.** command/request **28.** statement **29.** exclamation **30.** question

Part F

31. C: Jo / plays the drums; her mother/plays the banjo **32.** S: The very small child / sang sweetly **33.** C: A motorcycle / is not as expensive as a car; it / is trusty transportation **34.** C: We / stopped at the mall; we / came home after that **35.** S: Liza and her brother / play soccer **36.** S: Dennis / read six books last month **37.** C: Donna / has not had any piano lessons; she / plays very well **38.** C: Frank / is coming for dinner; he / is bringing a salad **39.** C: We / hiked to the lake; we / spent the whole afternoon there **40.** S: Matt / assembled his new computer in the den

Chapter 9 Mastery Test B

Part A

1. C: We / stopped at the mall; we / came home after that
2. C: Donna / has not had any piano lessons; she / plays very well
3. S: Dennis / read six books last month **4.** C: We / hiked to the lake; we / spent the whole afternoon there **5.** S: Liza and her brother / play soccer **6.** S: Matt / assembled his new computer in the den
7. C: Frank / is coming for dinner; he / is bringing a salad
8. C: Jo / plays the drums; her mother/plays the banjo
9. S: The very small child / sang sweetly **10.** C: A motorcycle / is not as expensive as a car; it / is trusty transportation

Part B

11. statement **12.** exclamation **13.** question **14.** question **15.** command/request

Part C

The verbs and verb phrases are in bold. **16. are working** day and night to plow the roads **17. have been married** for years **18. had knocked** out the electrical power **19. had** electricity or telephones for three days **20. fly casts** in summer and **ice fishes** in winter

Part D

21. C **22.** B **23.** A **24.** D **25.** D

Part E

The nouns and pronouns in the subjects are in bold. **26. Everything** in the **freezer** **27.** Our **friends Howard** and **Heidi** **28. Grandfather** and the entire **family** **29.** Neither the **television** nor the **radio** **30. Irene** and **I**

Part F

31. S **32.** N **33.** S **34.** S **35.** N **36.** N **37.** S **38.** S **39.** N **40.** N

Chapter 10 Mastery Test A

Part A

1. I **2.** T **3.** I **4.** I **5.** T

Part B

6. The loud man behind me is cheering enthusiastically for his favorite team. **7.** Many of the participants did not wear comfortable shoes. **8.** Will Damon and Janice sing at your sister's wedding? **9.** The brave old soldier in the faded uniform marched into camp slowly. **10.** A beautiful performance of the national anthem opened the evening's event, and a display of fireworks was the finale.

Part C

11. D **12.** A **13.** B **14.** D **15.** C

Part D

16. S—Ian, V—asked, IO—Mr. Collins, DO—question **17.** S—Everyone, V—calls, DO—her, OC—actress **18.** S—Anne, V—named, DO—cat, OC—Possum **19.** S—Louis, V—wrote , IO—coworkers, DO—memo **20.** S—boss, V—gave, IO—him, DO—reward **21.** S—hills, V—are, PA—alive **22.** S—All, V—must take, DO—exams **23.** S—Andrea, Gerald; V—are; PN—friends **24.** S—(you), V—Be, PA—quiet **25.** V—Can buy; S—you; IO—me; DO—loaves, pound

Part E

26.

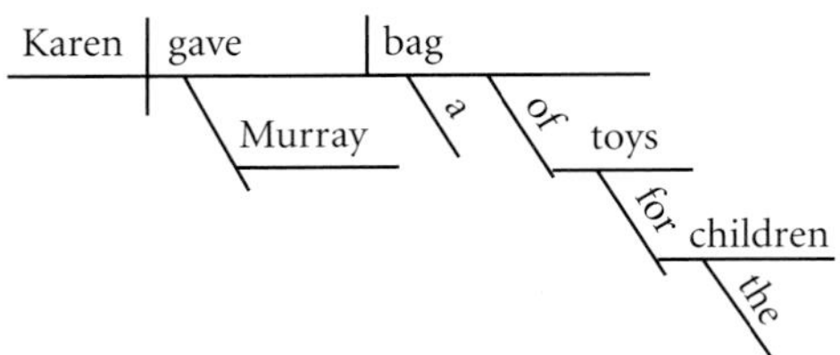

27.

boys | raced
The
to
park
the

28.

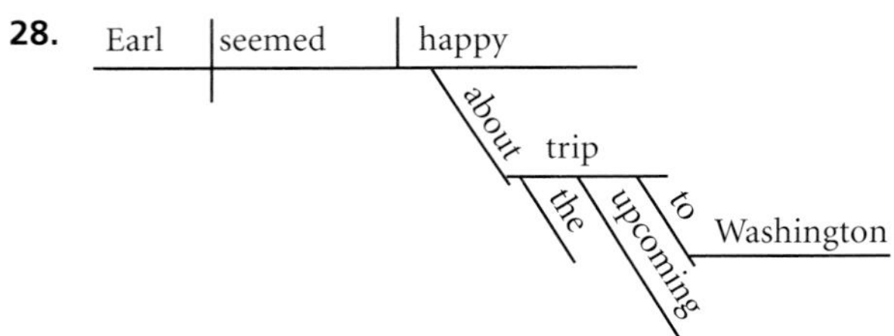

29.

trees | leafed
The
out
and
flowers | burst
the
into
bloom

30.

sister | will become
My
older
after
graduation
engineer
an
or
researcher
a
and
she | will be
good
very
at
work
her

Part A

1. S—All, V—must take, DO—exams **2.** S—hills, V—are, PA—alive **3.** S—Louis, V—wrote , IO—coworkers, DO—memo **4.** S—Anne, V—named , DO—cat, OC—Possum **5.** V—Can buy; S—you; IO—me; DO—loaves, pound **6.** S—(you), V—Be, PA—quiet **7.** S—Andrea, Gerald; V—are; PN—friends **8.** S—boss, V—gave, IO—him, DO—reward **9.** S—Everyone, V—calls, DO—her, OC—actress **10.** S—Ian, V—asked, IO—Mr. Collins, DO—question

Part B

11. I **12.** I **13.** T **14.** I **15.** T

Part C

16. B **17.** D **18.** C **19.** D **20.** A

Part D

21. A beautiful performance of the national anthem opened the evening's event, and a display of fireworks was the finale. **22.** The brave old soldier in the faded uniform marched into camp slowly. **23.** Will Damon and Janice sing at your sister's wedding? **24.** Many of the participants did not wear comfortable shoes. **25.** The loud man behind me is cheering enthusiastically for his favorite team.

Part E

26.

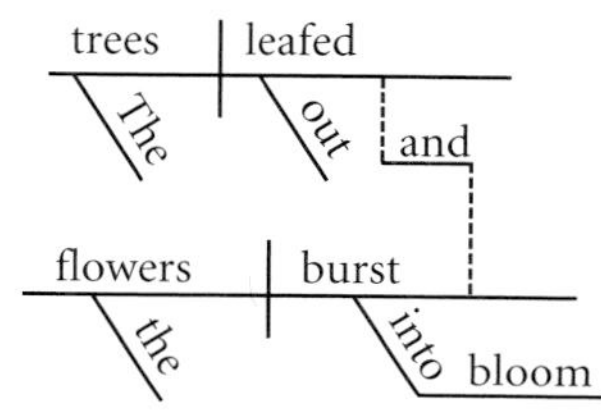

27.

Earl | seemed | happy
about
trip
the
upcoming
to
Washington

28.

boys | raced
The
to
park
the

29.

Karen | gave | bag
Murray
a
of
toys
for
children
the

30.

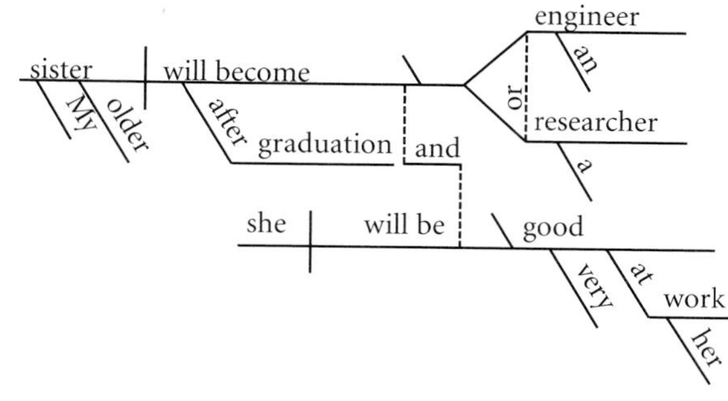

Chapter 11 Mastery Test A

Part A

1. clause **2.** clause **3.** clause **4.** clause **5.** phrase **6.** clause **7.** phrase **8.** clause **9.** phrase **10.** clause

Part B

11. Deanne will bring plates and napkins when she gets off work. **12.** The cake that was shaped like a football was a big hit. **13.** If Jim decides to buy my car, I will give him a good deal. **14.** Whoever wants to go to college must study hard. **15.** We cannot play on the side of the pool where the lap swimmers work out. **16.** Amber and Ben have been best friends since they were in first grade. **17.** Because the temperature was dropping, the children went inside. **18.** The recipe that I used to make this dessert is surprisingly simple. **19.** Chad and Jonathan ride the train when they go to their grandmother's house. **20.** Did she know what they were planning to do?

Part C

21. noun clause **22.** adverb clause **23.** adjective clause **24.** noun clause **25.** adverb clause **26.** adverb clause **27.** adverb clause **28.** noun clause **29.** adjective clause **30.** adjective clause

Part D

31. B **32.** D **33.** C **34.** A **35.** D

Chapter 11 Mastery Test B

Part A

1. Did she know what they were planning to do? **2.** Chad and Jonathan ride the train when they go to their grandmother's house. **3.** The recipe that I used to make this dessert is surprisingly simple. **4.** Because the temperature was dropping, the children went inside. **5.** Amber and Ben have been best friends since they were in first grade. **6.** We cannot play on the side of the pool where the lap swimmers work out. **7.** Whoever wants to go to college must study hard. **8.** If Jim decides to buy my car, I will give him a good deal. **9.** The cake that was shaped like a football was a big hit. **10.** Deanne will bring plates and napkins when she gets off work.

Part B

11. clause **12.** phrase **13.** clause **14.** phrase **15.** clause **16.** phrase **17.** clause **18.** clause **19.** clause **20.** clause

Part C

21. D **22.** A **23.** C **24.** D **25.** B

Part D

26. adjective clause **27.** adjective clause **28.** noun clause **29.** adverb clause **30.** adverb clause **31.** adverb clause **32.** noun clause **33.** adjective clause **34.** adverb clause **35.** noun clause

Chapter 12 Mastery Test A

Part A

1. infinitive **2.** participle **3.** gerund **4.** infinitive **5.** gerund **6.** participle **7.** gerund **8.** infinitive **9.** participle **10.** gerund

Part B

11. GP **12.** IP **13.** PP **14.** IP **15.** PP **16.** GP **17.** IP **18.** GP **19.** GP **20.** PP

Part C

Answers will vary. Possible answers follow.

21. To watch a sunset is a great way to end the day. **22.** Bill avoided most of the traffic by going home late. **23.** Most teens enjoy driving a car. **24.** The whining puppy kept me awake all night. **25.** Don't use that cracked bowl.

Part D

26. B **27.** D **28.** C **29.** A **30.** C

Chapter 12 Mastery Test B

Part A

1. C **2.** B **3.** D **4.** C **5.** A

Part B

Answers will vary. Possible answers follow.

6. Don't use that cracked bowl. **7.** To watch a sunset is a great way to end the day. **8.** Most teens enjoy driving a car. **9.** The whining puppy kept me awake all night. **10.** Bill avoided most of the traffic by going home late.

Part C

11. GP **12.** GP **13.** IP **14.** GP **15.** PP **16.** IP **17.** PP **18.** GP **19.** IP **20.** PP

Part D

21. participle **22.** infinitive **23.** participle **24.** infinitive **25.** gerund **26.** gerund **27.** gerund **28.** infinitive **29.** gerund **30.** participle

Midterm Mastery Test

Part A

1. adverb **2.** adjective **3.** pronoun **4.** action verb **5.** noun **6.** state-of-being verb **7.** noun **8.** action verb **9.** state-of-being verb **10.** adverb **11.** action verb **12.** adverb **13.** pronoun **14.** action verb **15.** adjective **16.** state-of-being verb **17.** adverb **18.** pronoun **19.** pronoun **20.** adjective

Part B

21. Valerie, French, Mimi **22.** Tim, Swiss **23.** Native American, New Mexico **24.** Hanna, Spanish **25.** Karl, English, Basic Computer II **26.** Samantha, Sense and Sensibility **27.** Friday, April **28.** Loren, African **29.** Italian **30.** Tracy, Rocky Mountains, Colorado

Part C

31. is **32.** are **33.** were **34.** geese **35.** mice's **36.** girls' **37.** ladies' **38.** wives **39.** eaten **40.** gone **41.** Moe's **42.** their **43.** Which **44.** her **45.** taller **46.** tricky **47.** best **48.** eating **49.** taken **50.** better

Part D

51. B **52.** B **53.** A **54.** C **55.** A **56.** B **57.** C **58.** D **59.** A **60.** B **61.** C **62.** B **63.** B **64.** B **65.** A

Final Mastery Test

Part A

1. S—Amanda, V—went **2.** S—Jimmy, V—won, DO—scholarship **3.** S—He, V—would play, DO—baseball **4.** S—College, V—gave, IO—Jimmy, DO—uniform **5.** S—Jimmy, V—is, PN—athlete

Part B

6. C **7.** C **8.** D **9.** C **10.** A **11.** B **12.** D **13.** C **14.** C **15.** C

Part C

16. adjective **17.** pronoun **18.** action verb **19.** conjunction **20.** noun **21.** state-of-being verb **22.** preposition **23.** state-of-being verb **24.** adverb **25.** interjection

Part D

26. Ahmad, May **27.** Julia, Dutch **28.** Frank, Spanish, Computer I **29.** Sherry, *A Raisin in the Sun*, Arizona **30.** Chuck, Monday, August

Part E

31. simple **32.** compound **33.** compound **34.** complex **35.** compound-complex

Part F

36. DC **37.** IC **38.** IC **39.** P **40.** DC **41.** DC

Part G

42. question **43.** command/request **44.** exclamation **45.** statement **46.** command/request

Part H

47. T **48.** I **49.** T **50.** T **51.** I

Part I

52. A **53.** C **54.** A **55.** D

Part J

56. watching–participle **57.** relaxing–gerund **58.** to study–infinitive **59.** knocking–gerund **60.** to tell–infinitive **61.** Smiling–participle **62.** Wondering–participle **63.** painting–gerund **64.** to paint–infinitive **65.** to paint–infinitive

Part K

66. predicate noun **67.** predicate adjective **68.** predicate pronoun **69.** predicate noun **70.** predicate pronoun **71.** predicate adjective **72.** predicate adjective **73.** predicate noun **74.** predicate noun **75.** predicate adjective

Part L

76. adverb clause **77.** noun clause **78.** noun clause **79.** adjective clause **80.** adjective clause **81.** noun clause **82.** adverb clause **83.** adjective clause **84.** noun clause **85.** adverb clause

Part M

86. Because Elsa's mother is working, Elsa watches her sister, Kim. **87.** Len bought ten dollars' worth of gas, but he still did not fill the tank. **88.** Hello! Is anybody home? **89.** Monica made supper; however, her father brought Chinese food. **90.** Shira left the back door open; therefore, she had to catch the bird that flew inside.

Part N

91. are **92.** but **93.** children's **94.** wives **95.** eaten **96.** gone **97.** Zoe's **98.** their **99.** her **100.** taller

AGS Teacher Questionnaire

Attention Teachers! As publishers of *Basic English Grammar,* we would like your help in making this textbook more valuable to you. Please take a few minutes to fill out this survey. Your feedback will help us to better serve you and your students.

1. What is your position and major area of responsibility? ______________________

____

____

2. Briefly describe your setting:

____ regular education ____ special education ____ adult basic education

____ community college ____ university ____ other ______________________

3. The enrollment in your classroom includes students with the following (check all that apply):

____ at-risk for failure ____ low reading ability ____ behavior problems

____ learning disabilities ____ ESL ____ other ______________________

4. Grade level of your students: ______________________

5. Racial/ethnic groups represented in your classes (check all that apply):

____ African-American ____ Asian ____ Caucasian ____ Hispanic

____ Native American ____ Other

6. School location:

____ urban ____ suburban ____ rural ____ other ______________________

7. What reaction did your students have to the materials? (Include comments about the cover design, lesson format, illustrations, etc.)

____

____

____

8. What features in the student text helped your students the most?

____

____

____

OVER ➤

9. What features in the student text helped your students the least? Please include suggestions for changing these to make the text more relevant.

____

____

10. How did you use the Teacher's Edition and support materials, and what features did you find to be the most helpful?

____

____

11. What activity from the program did your students benefit from the most? Please briefly explain.

____

____

____

12. Optional: Share an activity that you used to teach the materials in your classroom that enhanced the learning and motivation of your students.

____

____

____

Several activities will be selected to be included in future editions. Please include your name, address, and phone number so we may contact you for permission and possible payment to use the material.

Thank you!

▼ fold in thirds and tape shut at the top ▼

Name: ____________________

School: ____________________

Address: ____________________

City/State/ZIP: ____________________

Phone: ____________________

NO POSTAGE
NECESSARY
IF MAILED
IN THE
UNITED STATES

BUSINESS REPLY MAIL

FIRST-CLASS MAIL PERMIT NO.12 CIRCLE PINES MN

POSTAGE WILL BE PAID BY ADDRESSEE

AGS ATTN MARKETING SUPPORT
4201 WOODLAND ROAD
PO BOX 99
CIRCLE PINES MN 55014-9923